THE RECORDS OF THE FEDERAL CONVENTION OF 1787

VOLUME I

TO

JOHN FRANKLIN JAMESON

THE RECORDS

OF THE

FEDERAL CONVENTION

OF 1787

EDITED BY

MAX FARRAND

REVISED EDITION IN FOUR VOLUMES

VOLUME I

New Haven and London · Yale University Press

Published with assistance from
the John Ben Snow Memorial Trust.

Printed in the United States of America by
The Murray Printing Co., Westford, Mass.

International standard book numbers: 0–300–00447–8 (cloth)
0–300–00080–4 (pbk.)
Library of Congress catalog card number: 86–50311

12   11   10   9   8   7   6   5   4

PUBLISHER'S NOTE

The continuing demand by scholars, students, and the legal profession for Max Farrand's *Records of the Federal Convention* has prompted the publishers to reprint this edition, known as the Revised Edition since its preparation by Mr. Farrand in 1937. Meanwhile, the publishers have commissioned an entirely new edition of the *Records* which, however, will require several years to complete. Abundant material not readily available to Farrand will be included, but his sound principles of editing will be strictly adhered to.

When this work first appeared in the original, three-volume edition in 1911, Frederick Jackson Turner wrote to his friend Max Farrand as follows: "No one knows better than I do that such work as yours will permanently associate your name with the records of one of the enduring documents in the world's political history, and that my interpretations will become airy nothings as time goes on, and what I have seen discerningly becomes a commonplace, and what I thought I saw and didn't really see, becomes happily lost in the ruck. . . . A long line of scholars will be your debtors for this collection of sources and I'd envy you your monument if I didn't feel a sort of partnership in it by reason of our friendship."

It is suggested that authors citing from the *Records* refer when possible to the date of the document as well as to the volume and page, particularly when citing Madison's journal and the notes kept by delegates. With this information, the future reader will be enabled to locate the citation in the forthcoming edition instead of having to find a copy of the superseded edition.

CONTENTS

VOLUME I

VOLUME II

VOLUME III

CONTENTS

VOLUME IV

ILLUSTRATIONS

PREFACE

THE available sources of our information for studying the work of the convention that framed the present Constitution of the United States are scattered through various printed volumes; and some material has never been published. The present work was undertaken with the primary purpose of gathering all available records into a single work of two or three volumes, but it was also intended that these records should be in trustworthy form. The latter aspect has subsequently developed into the more important feature of this edition.

It has been found that most printed texts of the more important records cannot be accepted implicitly because of the liberties that have been taken with the manuscripts in preparing them for publication. Furthermore, in the case of the most important record of all, Madison's Debates, it is easily proved that, over thirty years after the Convention, the author revised the manuscript and made many changes upon insufficient data, which seriously impaired the value of his notes. This is also true of other records. It has accordingly become the first purpose of the editor in this work to present the records of the Federal Convention in the most trustworthy form possible. Mistakes and inaccuracies are unavoidable, but no effort has been spared to reduce these to a minimum.

The other purpose of this work, to gather all of the available records into a convenient and serviceable edition, has not, however, been neglected. From the editor's own experience and from that of others in studying and teaching the subject of the formation of our Constitution, certain needs have presented themselves in quite definite form, and the attempt has been made to meet those needs in the present edition. The extent and variety of the material has made the task a difficult one to accomplish, and the results are by no means satisfactory. Other methods of arrangement have been tried, but in every case insuperable objections presented themselves, and it finally seemed best to adopt the plan of gathering together all the records of each day's session, and of allowing each record for that day to remain complete by itself. This method has made it impossible to place subject headings at the top of each page, and the editor has endeavored partially to supply this lack by giving cross references to some of the more important subjects in foot-notes, and by making the general index as nearly exhaustive as is possible. A special index has been added, giving such references for every clause in the Constitution finally adopted as will enable any one to trace the origin and development of that particular clause, and to find every item in the present work that bears upon it.

While carrying on his investigations the editor has been fairly overwhelmed by the courtesies extended to him. In the examination of manuscripts, every possible facility has been afforded him. He was placed at a disadvantage by working most of the time at a great distance from the depositories of all the documents he required, and his work would have been prolonged indefinitely, — it would, perhaps, have been impossible — had it not been for the assistance rendered him whenever asked: documents have been examined, copied, and even photographed for his special use; every request has been cheerfully complied with, and no trouble seems to have been too great. Where the material was in printed form, permission to reprint has been readily granted in every instance. Assuredly, the "gospel of service" is a fundamental article in the creed of American historical scholarship.

In publicly acknowledging his indebtedness to so many who have been of service to him, the editor desires to express his obligations in particular: to Mr. John A. Tonner, Chief of the Bureau of Rolls and Library of the Department of State, to his predecessors, Mr. William McNeir and Mr. Andrew H. Allen, and to their obliging assistants, in whose care are most of the manuscripts from which the texts of this edition have been taken; to the late Edward King, of New York City, for permission to use the Rufus King manuscripts, to the New York Historical Society and its Librarian, Mr. Robert H. Kelby, the custodians of these manuscripts; to the Historical Society of Pennsylvania and its Librarian, Mr. John

W. Jordan, for the privilege of examining and copying the Wilson manuscripts; to Mr. Herbert Putnam and his able staff in the Library of Congress for their many courtesies, especially to Mr. Worthington C. Ford, the former Chief of the Division of Manuscripts and to the present Chief, Mr. Gaillard Hunt, who have been unfailing in their kindliness and assistance; to Mr. William Harden, Librarian of the Georgia Historical Society, for his scholarly description of the annotations on Baldwin's copy of the printed draft of September 12; to the Department of Foreign Affairs of the French Government for the privilege of examining and copying from its Archives; to the Editors of the *American Historical Review* for permission to reprint documents from that journal; to Miss Kate Mason Rowland for permission to use extracts from her *Life of George Mason;* to Mr. William M. Meigs for the privilege of reprinting the draft of the Committee of Detail, published in photograph facsimile in his *Growth of the Constitution;* to Messrs. G. P. Putnam's Sons for permission to reprint freely from their series of "Writings of the Fathers of the Republic" — Jefferson, King, Madison, Randolph and Washington; and to the Macmillan Company for permission to reprint extracts from A. H. Smyth, *Writings of Benjamin Franklin.*

The editor has repeatedly called upon his friends for advice and assistance, which have always been cheerfully given. Without holding them in any way responsible for its shortcomings, he wishes to express his appreciation of the fact that this work would not have taken its present form had it not been for their suggestions, nor would the editor have endured to the end but for their kindly encouragement. He is especially grateful to President Lowell of Harvard; to Mr. Frederick J. Turner, of Wisconsin; to Mr. Charles H. Hull, of Cornell; to the late Edward G. Bourne, of Yale; and to Mr. Roger Foster, of New York. He feels still more indebted to two others who have been his constant advisers and have rendered him every assistance ungrudgingly — Mr. Andrew C. McLaughlin, of Chicago, and Mr. J. Franklin Jameson, Director of the Department of Historical Research of the Carnegie Institution of Washington. To the latter this work has been dedicated in recognition of his great services to the cause of American historical scholarship.

Finally, the editor would express his appreciation of the consideration shown him by President David Starr Jordan and the authorities of Leland Stanford Junior University; their liberal policy, while he was a member of the faculty of that institution, made it possible for him to carry on and complete this work.

MAX FARRAND.

NEW HAVEN, CONNECTICUT
February 1, 1910

PREFACE TO 1937 EDITION

Volumes I, II, and III are being reprinted substantially as they were but with many corrections. In the Preface to Volume IV will be found an explanation of what has been attempted in this new edition.

M. F.

SAN MARINO, CALIFORNIA
April 10, 1937

INTRODUCTION

The official authorization of the Federal Convention was a resolution of the Congress of the Confederation, adopted February 21, 1787:

"Resolved, That in the opinion of Congress, it is expedient, that on the second Monday in May next, a convention of delegates, who shall have been appointed by the several states, be held at Philadelphia, . . ." [1]

The second Monday in May, 1787, fell on the fourteenth, and on that day delegates from several of the states gathered in the "long room" of the State House in Philadelphia.[2] It was not until the twenty-fifth, however, that a sufficient number of delegates appeared to constitute a representation of a majority of the states. On May 25, the Convention organized and remained in continuous session until September 17, with the exception of one adjournment of two days over the Fourth of July and another of ten days, from July 26 to August 6, to allow the Committee of Detail to prepare its report.

THE JOURNAL

The sessions of the Convention were secret; before the final adjournment the secretary was directed to deposit "the Journals and other papers of the Convention in the hands of the President", and in answer to an inquiry of Washington's, the Convention resolved "that he retain the Journal and other papers subject to the order of Congress, if ever formed under the Constitution." Accordingly the secretary, William Jackson, after destroying "all the loose scraps of paper", which he evidently thought unimportant, formally delivered the papers to the president.[3] Washington in turn deposited these papers with the Department of State in 1796,[4] where they remained untouched until Congress by a joint resolution in 1818 ordered

---

[1] Appendix A, I. [2] Appendix A, LXII.
[3] *Records* of September 17, and Appendix A, CX, CXI, CCCXX.
[4] Appendix A, CCLXXIII.

them to be printed.[5] They are still in the keeping of the Bureau of Rolls and Library of that department.

President Monroe requested the Secretary of State, John Quincy Adams, to take charge of the publication of the Journal. The task proved to be a difficult one. The papers were, according to Adams, "no better than the daily minutes from which the regular journal ought to have been, but never was, made out."[6] Adams reports that at his request William Jackson, the secretary of the Convention, called upon him and "looked over the papers, but he had no recollection of them which could remove the difficulties arising from their disorderly state, nor any papers to supply the deficiency of the missing papers." With the expenditure of considerable time and labor, and with the exercise of no little ingenuity, Adams was finally able to collate the whole to his satisfaction. General Bloomfield supplied him with several important documents from the papers of David Brearley; Charles Pinckney sent him a copy of the plan he "believed" to be one he presented to the Convention; Madison furnished the means of completing the records of the last four days; and Adams felt that "with all these papers suitably arranged, a correct and tolerably clear view of the proceedings of the Convention may be presented".[7]

The results of his labor were printed at Boston in 1819 in an octavo volume of some 500 pages, entitled, *Journal, Acts and Proceedings of the Convention, . . . which formed the Constitution of the United States*.[8] As Adams had nothing whatever to guide him in his work of compilation and editing, mistakes were inevitable, and not a few of these were important.

---

[5] Appendix A, CCCXXIII.

[6] From certain letters that have been preserved (Appendix A, VI, VIa, XVI, XXI, LXXIV), it would seem that Jackson may have owed his appointment as Secretary rather to influence than to any special fitness for the position. It would seem also that he had taken notes of the debates (Appendix A, CCCXXV, CCCLX) in addition to his formal minutes, and it is possible that he somewhat neglected his official duties in order to make his private records more complete.

[7] Appendix A, CCCXXIV–CCCXXVI, CCCXXVIII–CCCXXX.

[8] The *Journal* was reprinted in 1830 as volume IV of the first edition of Jonathan Elliot, *Debates in the Several State Conventions on the Adoption of the Federal Constitution*. In the second edition, 1836, and in all subsequent editions, it appears as volume I.

The Bureau of Rolls and Library of the Department of State, in 1894, reprinted with scrupulous accuracy as volume I of the *Documentary History of the Constitution*

In the present edition the secretary's minutes are printed exactly as he left them, except that the scattered notes are brought together for each day. They are grouped under the heading of JOURNAL. Where occasion requires, Adams' edition is cited as *Journal* (in italics), while the secretary's minutes are referred to as "the Journal".

The secretary's minutes consist of the formal journal of the Convention, the journal of the Committee of the Whole House and, partly on loose sheets and partly in a bound blank book, a table giving the detail of ayes and noes on the various questions. The detail of ayes and noes offers the greatest difficulty, for no dates are given and to about one tenth of the votes no questions are attached. The photograph of the first loose sheet of this table⁹ reveals the difficulties at a glance; the later pages are not as bad as the first, for the secretary evidently profited by experience, but uncertainty and confusion are by no means eliminated. For convenience of reference, in the present edition a number in square brackets is prefixed to each vote, and the editor has taken the liberty of dividing the detail of ayes and noes into what are, according to his best judgment, the sections for each day's records. The sections are retained intact, and a summary of each vote in square brackets is appended to that question in the Journal to which, in the light of all the evidence, it seems to belong.

This method seems to promise the greatest usefulness combined with a presentation that permits of another interpretation if any one so desires. In the judgment of the editor, however, a word of warning seems necessary. With notes so carelessly kept, as were evidently those of the secretary, the Journal cannot be relied upon absolutely. The statement of questions is probably accurate in most cases, but the

the papers which Adams had used in preparing the *Journal*. Volume I originally appeared in two installments as appendices to *Bulletins* 1 and 3 of the Bureau of Rolls and Library. Only 750 copies were printed. The *Report of the Public Printer* for the year ending June 30, 1900, Cong. Docs., 4029; 19, p. 161, shows 250 copies printed upon requisition of the Department of State. In 1901 Congress ordered to be printed 7,000 copies of volumes I–III of the *Documentary History*. In this Congressional edition there are some minor changes in type, spacing, etc., and Charles Pinckney's letter of December 30, 1818, to John Quincy Adams, is inserted in volume I, pp. 309-311, changing the page numbering of the pages following.

⁹ See *Records* of May 30.

determination of those questions and in particular the votes upon them should be accepted somewhat tentatively.

YATES

When the seal of secrecy had been broken by the publication of the *Journal*, there was printed in Albany shortly afterward (1821): *Secret Proceedings and Debates of the Convention Assembled at Philadelphia, in the year 1787, for the purpose of forming the Constitution of the United States of America. From Notes taken by the late Robert Yates, Esq. Chief Justice of New York, and copied by John Lansing, Jun, Esq.* etc,[10] J. C. Hamilton stated that Edmond C. Genet, former minister from France, was responsible for this publication.[11] This is borne out by the fact that in 1808 Genet published *A Letter to the Electors of President and Vice-President of the United States*,[12] which was an attack upon Madison, then a candidate for the presidency. The "Letter" consisted almost entirely of an abstract or extracts from the notes of Yates, mainly direct quotations, but cleverly pieced together in such a way as to represent Madison as the leader of the national party in the Federal Convention and working for the annihilation of the state governments.

As Yates and his colleague Lansing left the Convention early — because they felt that their instructions did not warrant them in countenancing, even by their presence, the action which the Convention was taking — Yates's notes cease with the fifth of July. For the earlier days of the Convention the notes of proceedings are quite brief; and while the reports are somewhat fuller after the presentation of the New Jersey plan on June 15, it was evident that they did not give at all a complete picture of the proceedings, though they threw a great deal of light upon what had taken place and in particular upon the attitude of individuals in the debates.[13]

---

[10] Reprinted in Elliot's *Debates* (in volume IV of the first edition and in volume I of all subsequent editions), and in separate editions in Washington, Richmond, Cincinnati, and Louisville, 1836–1844, and as Senate Document 728 of the 60th Congress, second session. Luther Martin's *Genuine Information* (Appendix A, CLVIII) was always printed with the *Secret Proceedings*.

[11] *Life of Alexander Hamilton*, II, 466, note.   [12] Appendix A, CCCX.

[13] For Madison's opinion of Yates's notes, see Appendix A, CCCXXXIX, CCCLXXXVIII, CCCXCI.

A careful search has failed to reveal the existence of the original manuscript, so that in the present work the editor has been compelled to reprint the *Secret Proceedings* from the first edition. As they are next in importance they have been placed immediately after Madison's notes in the records of each day.

MADISON

It was well known that James Madison had taken full and careful notes of the proceedings in the Convention, and he had often been urged to publish them. He had, however, decided that a posthumous publication was advisable.[14] Madison died in 1836. His manuscripts were purchased by Congress, and shortly afterwards, in 1840, under the editorship of H. D. Gilpin, *The Papers of James Madison* were published in three volumes.[15] More than half of this work was given over to his notes of the debates in the Federal Convention,[16] and at once all other records paled into insignificance.

---

[14] Appendix A, CCLXXV, CCLXXXIV, CCCXI, CCCXII, CCCXIV CCCXVI, CCCXXIV, CCCXXVI, CCCXL, CCCXLI, CCCLVIII, CCCLXVII.

[15] Washington: Langtree and O'Sullivan. Other issues of this edition with change of date were published in New York, Mobile, and Boston. (P. L. Ford, *Bibliography of the Constitution*, 1896.)

[16] The Debates entire and some of the other material from Gilpin were published in a revised form as volume V of Elliot's *Debates* in 1845. Albert, Scott and Company (Chicago, 1893) reprinted, both in a two-volume and a one-volume edition, the Gilpin text of the Debates, but inexcusably entitled the work *The Journal of the Federal Convention*. In 1900 the Bureau of Rolls and Library of the Department of State reprinted Madison's Debates with great care as volume III of the *Documentary History of the Constitution*, and in such a way as to show the corrections and changes Madison made in his manuscript. This appeared originally as an appendix to *Bulletin* no. 9 of the Bureau of Rolls and Library. For subsequent editions, see above, note 8. The Congressional edition of 1901 inserts (pp. 796a–796o) Madison's introduction to his Debates, of which only a partial version had appeared on pp. 1–7 of the previous edition. The preparation of the material for this volume of the *Documentary History* was more difficult than for the *Journal*, and the work was not done as accurately nor as satisfactorily. The present editor has noticed a considerable number of mistakes in the reading of the manuscript — some of which are important — and, as is shown below (note 23), the person who did the work was frequently misled in the endeavor to indicate corrections in the manuscript. Gaillard Hunt includes the Debates in volumes III and IV of his edition of *The Writings of James Madison* (New York, Putnam's, 1900), again unfortunately entitling them the "*Journal*". Mr. Hunt states in the preface to volume III that the "original manuscript has been followed with rigid accuracy," which is apparently true, but with one important limitation — the original manuscript was not copied, but the Gilpin text was corrected from the manuscript; accordingly a large number of errors (minor ones, in general) to be found in

In a preface to the Debates, written before his death, Madison had explained with what care the material was gathered and written up: [17]

"I chose a seat in front of the presiding member, with the other members, on my right and left hand. In this favorable position for hearing all that passed I noted in terms legible and in abbreviations and marks intelligible to myself what was read from the Chair or spoken by the members; and losing not a moment unnecessarily between the adjournment and reassembling of the Convention I was enabled to write out my daily notes during the session or within a few finishing days after its close."

Indeed Madison was evidently regarded by his fellow-delegates to the Convention as a semi-official reporter of their proceedings, for several of them took pains to see that he was supplied with copies of their speeches and motions. [18] And from the day of their publication until the present, Madison's notes of the Debates have remained the standard authority for the proceedings of the Convention.

Madison's correspondence and the manuscript itself reveal the fact that Madison went over his notes after the publication of the *Journal* in 1819. [19] He not only noted differences between his own record and that of the *Journal*, but also in many cases corrected his own notes from the *Journal*. In the wording of motions, this is not to be wondered at, for Madison, during the sessions of the Convention, in his haste to note what the speaker was saying could do no more than take down the substance of motions and resolutions, while these would be copied into the journal in full. Nor is it surprising, when we remember that Madison accepted the printed *Journal* as authoritative, to find him in not a few cases copying from it proceedings of which he had no record. But the importance of this fact is evident at once, for these items have been accepted upon the double record of the *Journal* and Madison,

---

Gilpin will be found in the Hunt text also. Hunt's text is not quite as accurate as that of the *Documentary History*. [17] Appendix A, CCCCI.

[18] Notice for example Franklin's speeches (June 2, June 11 and September 17), Randolph's opening address (May 29), and Charles Pinckney's effort on June 25; see also speeches by Hamilton, June 18, and Gouverneur Morris, July 2.

[19] See references under note 14 above.

whereas they are in reality to be stated upon the authority of the *Journal* alone.

But Madison went even one step farther and actually changed his records of votes in the Convention in order to bring them into conformity with the *Journal*. This might involve the change of the vote of a single state, or of several states, or even reverse his record of the decision of the Convention. On what basis or for what reasons Madison felt justified in changing his records of votes is not to be ascertained conclusively. Sometimes it seems to have been done because the records of *Journal* and Yates were in accord in their disagreement with him; sometimes he probably saw that subsequent action in the Convention proved the record of *Journal* to be correct, and his own to be wrong; sometimes it was done because the vote of a state as recorded in *Journal* harmonized better with the sentiments of the delegates from that state as expressed in their speeches; and sometimes there is no apparent reason.

The matter might be merely of antiquarian interest, were it not for the fact that the printed *Journal* is itself unreliable, and that there are not a few cases in which Madison has made corrections from the *Journal* that are undoubtedly mistaken: Votes ascribed in the *Journal* to the wrong questions were used, in several cases, to change records that were probably correct as first made. Questions and votes were copied into his manuscript from the printed *Journal* without observing that these same questions and votes were recorded in other places, sometimes even on the same day; an examination of the original records shows that in most of these cases the questions were not to be found in the body of the Journal, but were incorporated into the text by John Quincy Adams; they are only to be found in the Detail of Ayes and Noes, and their relative position in the proceedings could only be inferred from the order in which the votes happened to be recorded.

It is not surprising, indeed, to find that Madison was thus misled by the mistakes in the printed *Journal*, for if his own records were correct, these would be the very points in which the discrepancies would occur. It is only necessary then to recognize Madison's evident acceptance of the *Journal* as authoritative, to expect him to incorporate these mistakes in his Debates.[20]

Another extensive set of corrections is to be found in the speeches made in debate. These are generally in the form of additions to Madison's original record. Because of misquotations of his own remarks, Madison condemned Yates's notes severely, as being a "very erroneous edition of the matter".[21] It is more than surprising, then, to discover that these additions were taken from Yates. Such proves to have been the case, however, and in over fifty instances. There were a number of speeches or remarks, including several of his own, that Madison failed to note in any form, but later thought worthy of inclusion. And there were also new ideas or shades of thought which Yates had noticed but which Madison failed to catch.

The fact of these changes being made does not rest merely upon the wording of the text and Madison's statement in 1821 that he was intending to prepare his notes for posthumous publication. The manuscript[22] shows that most of the changes thus made are easily recognizable. The ink which was used at the later date has faded quite differently from that of the original notes, so that most of the later revisions stand out from the page almost as clearly as if they had been written in red ink.[23]

---

[20] It should be noted that Madison was at least seventy years old when these revisions of his manuscript were made, and it is not to be wondered at that he did not always show the accuracy and discrimination for which the work of his earlier years has given him a reputation. And if it be true, as suggested below, note 23, that Madison made these revisions at two different times, it would be quite natural for him to make more radical changes in the second revision, when he had accustomed himself to the idea of changes being necessary, or when he had forgotten the criteria of his earlier revision.   [21] References under note 13 above.

[22] In the keeping of the Bureau of Rolls and Library, Department of State, Washington, D. C.

[23] This is not always the case, for the original manuscript has faded differently in different parts, perhaps because of different exposure or the use of more than one kind of ink. There also seem to have been at least two distinct sets of later corrections, probably made at different times. It is, therefore, sometimes difficult and sometimes impossible to determine whether or not the correction is a later one. A reference to the "printed Journal" must of course be of a later date than 1819, and the ink and writing of these words will frequently make clear all of the corrections of that date. It is also very helpful to know that it was Madison's invariable practise in his original notes to refer to himself as "M" or "Mr. M." In the revision of his manuscript he filled out his own name, so that the ink and writing of "adison" often furnish the necessary clue.

In the present edition such changes — except in trivial instances — are indicated by enclosing them within angle brackets ⟨ ⟩, and in foot-notes the original readings are given, wherever they have any significance, and the editor expresses his opinion as to the probable source of the change, wherever it is possible to trace it.[24]

In view of the fact that the *Journal* is so imperfect and not altogether reliable, and that Madison made so many changes in his manuscript, all other records of the Convention take on a new importance. Formerly they have been regarded only in so far as they might supplement our information; now it is seen that they may be of service also in determining what the action really was in doubtful cases.

KING

Without question, the next most important notes to those which have been considered are the notes of Rufus King, that have not received the attention they deserve, because of the form in which they were first printed. The original notes are, in the main, memoranda taken at the time in the Convention on odds and ends of paper.[25] Each sheet or scrap of paper is dated and most of them are endorsed with date and

---

A note at the end of the Debates, formally signed by Madison, "The few alterations and corrections made in these debates which are not in my handwriting, were dictated by me and made in my presence by John C. Payne" (*Records* of September 17), undoubtedly refers to this revision. Hunt, *Writings of Madison*, IV, 456, states that a slight correction on September 14 is the only one in Payne's handwriting, but the present editor is unwilling to accept this, although unable to make any other positive determination for himself. The editor of the *Documentary History* confesses his inability to distinguish between the two handwritings (III, 771, marginal note).

In publishing Madison's notes in volume III of the *Documentary History*, the attempt was made to show all corrections of the manuscript by the use of small type, but this includes every correction whether made at the time of first writing or later. It is also misleading in that small type is used where Madison was forced to write in a cramped hand at the end of a line or the bottom of a page, and many places are overlooked where there happened to be sufficient space in the manuscript to enable Madison to make the correction in his natural handwriting.

[24] It perhaps should be noted as a matter of record that Madison had copies of Pierce's notes which appeared in the *Savannah Georgian* in 1828 (Appendix A, CCCLXXIII), and that he doubtless knew of King's notes, and may have seen them.

[25] The King MSS. are deposited in the library of the New York Historical Society, and the privilege of using them freely was extended to the editor through the courtesy of the late Edward King, of New York, and the kindness of the librarian, Mr. R. H. Kelby.

XX

substance of the contents, so that in only one or two cases can
there be any doubt as to the place and order of the notes.

It is altogether probable that Rufus King was induced by
the printing of the *Journal* and Yates, *Secret Proceedings*, to
prepare his notes for publication. At any rate, many years
after the Convention was over, he attempted to put his notes
into better form.[26] In doing this work, although in most
cases he did not venture to change the substance of his earlier
records, he did drop out the dates in a number of instances;
he sometimes omitted important items or notes, either unin-
tentionally or because he could not understand them; and in
a few cases, at least one or two of which are important, he
modified his original notes. It was this revised copy that was
printed (1894) as an appendix to volume I of the *Life and
Correspondence of Rufus King*. The editor, Doctor Charles
R. King, grandson of Rufus King, attempted to insert some
of the omitted items, but as he evidently was not familiar
with the other records of the Convention his well-meant efforts
only added to the confusion. The original notes are reprinted
in the present edition.

Within the last few years there have been brought to light
the notes and memoranda of proceedings in the Convention
found among the papers of some of the delegates. The greater
part of this material has been printed in the *American Historical Review*, and in the present edition the texts as there
printed have been used, although in most cases they have been
compared with the original documents. The care shown in
preparing these documents for publication, and the accuracy
of printing these texts in the *Review*, have made necessary
almost no changes, and those but minor ones.

McHenry

Quite the best of these are the notes of James McHenry, of
Maryland.[27] McHenry started out with the evident intention
of taking somewhat extensive notes, and he adds not a little
to our information of Randolph's speech in presenting the

[26] The paper bears the watermark of 1818.
[27] *American Historical Review*, April, 1906, XI, 595–624.

Virginia Resolutions on May 29. On account of his brother's illness, he left Philadelphia on June 1, and remained away during June and July, but in August he returned to the Convention and to his note-taking with all the enthusiasm of the beginner. The records became more and more brief as time passed, but they are valuable because they are, for the latter part of the Convention's work, almost the only material we have besides the *Journal* and Madison's Debates.

PIERCE

The notes of William Pierce of Georgia, which were first printed in the *Savannah Georgian* in 1828,[28] add somewhat to our information of the proceedings of the first few days of the sessions. The character sketches of his fellow-members in Convention, which accompany these notes,[29] are not only interesting, but are also helpful in portraying the delegates as they appeared to a contemporary.

PATERSON

The notes of William Paterson, of New Jersey,[30] were evidently taken solely for his own use. While they are of little help in studying the general proceedings of the Convention, they are of great assistance in following Paterson's own line of reasoning, and in particular in studying the development of the resolutions Paterson presented on June 15, commonly called the New Jersey Plan. This is here given in its various stages of construction.[31]

HAMILTON

Alexander Hamilton's notes were found among the Hamilton Papers in the Library of Congress.[32] They are little more than brief memoranda and, like those of Paterson, are of importance not so much in determining what others thought or said as in tracing the development of the writer's own reasoning.

---

[28] Reprinted from the original MSS. in the *American Historical Review*, January 1898, III, 310–334. [29] Appendix A, CXIX.

[30] *American Historical Review*, January, 1904, IX, 310–340.

[31] Appendix E.

[32] Edited by Worthington C. Ford and first printed in the *Proceedings* of the Massachusetts Historical Society for June, 1904. Carefully revised for reprinting in the *American Historical Review* for October, 1904, X, 97–109.

PINCKNEY

The plan of government which Pinckney presented to the Convention on May 29 is not among the papers of the Convention, nor has any copy of it ever been found. Among the Wilson manuscripts in the library of the Historical Society of Pennsylvania, however, are an outline of the plan and extracts from the same.[33] These documents confirm and supplement another method of working, and make it possible to present a fairly complete restoration of the original text.[34]

MASON

A few notes and memoranda relating to the Federal Convention were found among the papers of George Mason, and were printed in 1892 by Miss K. M. Rowland in her *Life of George Mason*. They are not of much importance, except in so far as they throw a little further light upon Mason's position in the Convention.

COMMITTEE OF DETAIL

For the first two months of its sessions the Convention had devoted itself mainly to the discussion of general principles, modifying and developing the resolutions Randolph had presented on behalf of the Virginia delegation. Late in July, the conclusions that had been reached were turned over to a committee of five, known as the Committee of Detail, of which Rutledge was chairman and Wilson an important member. On July 26, the Convention adjourned for ten days to permit this committee to prepare a draft of a constitution. Among the Wilson papers in the Library of the Historical Society of Pennsylvania are various documents revealing the work of the Committee of Detail in different stages of its progress.[35] These documents, taken with an

---

[33] Printed in the *American Historical Review*, April, 1903, VIII, 509–511, and July, 1904, IX, 735–747. The identification of the extracts by Professor Jameson (*Studies in the History of the Federal Convention of 1787*, 128–132), without seeing the manuscripts themselves, is an interesting and suggestive piece of historical criticism.

[34] Appendix D.

[35] Through the courtesy of the librarian, Mr. John W. Jordan, the editor was permitted to examine and copy freely such parts of these papers as he desired.

important document found among the Mason papers,[36] present clearly the work of the committee in preparing the draft of the constitution presented to the Convention on August 6.

In the present edition, all of these documents are brought together and placed in the *Records* between July 26 and August 6.

PRINTED DRAFTS

The draft of August 6 was printed for the use of the delegates and was the subject of their discussions for over a month. The proceedings were then referred to a committee of five, known as the Committee of Style and Revision, of which William Samuel Johnson was chairman and Gouverneur Morris the most important member. The Committee of Style made its report on September 12, which was also printed for the delegates' use.

Several copies of the drafts of August 6 and September 12, belonging to various delegates, are extant, and most of them have emendations and marginal notes indicating the action taken upon particular clauses and sections, and sometimes revealing the writer's attitude or preference.

These documents are hardly worthy of being reprinted, for the marginal notes are in general only confirmatory of other records, but where the comments give any additional information of proceedings in the Convention, they have been embodied in foot-notes.

It is possible, indeed probable, that other records of the Convention will be brought to light. Charles Pinckney stated explicitly that he had taken careful notes of the proceedings;[37] William Jackson, secretary of the Convention, kept minutes of the debates;[38] in a communication to the Massachusetts convention, Elbridge Gerry "subjoined a state of facts, founded on documents";[39] Gouverneur Morris referred to "some gentlemen" writing up their notes between sessions;[40] and James Wilson in the Pennsylvania convention

---

[36] An early, perhaps the first, draft of the committee's work in Randolph's handwriting with extensive emendations in Rutledge's hand.

[37] Appendix A, CCCXXVI. Hunt, *Writings of Madison*, III, 25, note (with correction in IV, p. vii), states that none of the notes are extant. *Cf.* Jameson, *Studies*, p. 131, note *a*.   [38] See above note 6.   [39] Appendix A, CLXXXI.

[40] Appendix A, CCCXIV.

on December 4, 1787, stated that within a week he had "spoken with a gentleman, who had not only his memory, but full notes that he had taken in that body".[41] Whatever may be the accuracy or the value of these various statements, at least they indicate that there once existed material of which we have no present knowledge, but which may at any time be found. It is not probable, however, that any such new material would modify to any great extent our conceptions of the Convention's work, and it has, therefore, seemed worth while to gather in the present edition the existing records of the Federal Convention.

Supplementary Material

Although the sessions of the Convention were secret, and it was understood that the delegates would regard the proceedings as confidential, when the question of the adoption of the Constitution was before the country, and in later years when the interpretation of the Constitution was discussed, many of the delegates referred to and explained the action or the intention of the Convention upon particular subjects. Such statements are to be found in the private correspondence of the delegates, in contributions to the press, in public orations, in the debates in state legislatures and conventions, and in the debates in Congress. The farther away from the Convention one gets, the less reliable these reports become, owing to the deforming influence of memory. But taken as a whole, this supplementary material throws not a little light upon the work of the Convention, and in particular upon the parts taken by individual delegates, and upon opinions and personalities.

In the present edition, all of this supplementary material that could be found has been collected and reprinted in Appendix A; but a few words of explanation are necessary. In the first place, this collection could not be made exhaustive without covering practically all of the material, printed and unprinted, on American history since 1787; the editor has accordingly confined his efforts to the more obvious and accessible sources. In the second place, a distinction has been made

---

[41] Appendix A, CXLIX.

between notes taken as a part of, or in connection with, the
work of the Convention, and information supplied to others;
accordingly, letters written while the Convention was in
session, and such items as Charles Pinckney's *Observations*
and Luther Martin's *Genuine Information* have been classed
as supplementary material. In the next place, the editor has
tried to discriminate carefully between statements of proceedings in the Convention and theoretical interpretations
of clauses in the Constitution; only the former are included.
And finally, to render this material serviceable, in foot-notes
to the main text of the *Records*, references have been made to
this supplementary material wherever it seems to throw any
light on the proceedings.[42]

In the present edition, the original manuscripts have been
reprinted exactly, except that in abbreviations superior letters
have not been used, and in the few cases where it occurs the
tilde has been resolved into the corresponding "m" or "n".
In the case of Yates's *Secret Proceedings*, Mason's notes, and
the supplementary material in Appendix A, the most reliable
printed texts have been followed. Footnotes in the originals
are marked by "*" and "†" while the editor's notes are *numbered* consecutively for each day. Because Madison's records
have proven to be the best and most reliable source of information, the editor's notes and references have been attached,
in most cases, to Madison's Debates.

[42] Attention should be called to two items in Appendix A — CXLVI*a* and CXLVI*b*
— the original records of McHenry's and Martin's reports to the Maryland House
of Delegates, which were obtained too late to permit a complete series of cross-refer-
ences to be made.

THE RECORDS OF THE FEDERAL
CONVENTION OF 1787

JOURNAL

In fœderal-Convention.

On Monday the 14th of May. A.D. 1787. and in the eleventh year of the independence of the United States of America, at the State-House in the city of Philadelphia — in virtue of appointments from their respective States, sundry Deputies to the fœderal-Convention appeared — but, a majority of the States not being represented, the Members present adjourned from day to day until friday the 25th of the said month, when, in virtue of the said appointments appeared from the States of

Massachusetts . . . . The honorable Rufus King Esquire.

New-York . . . . The honorable Robert Yates, and Alexander Hamilton Esquires.

New-Jersey . . . . The honorable David Brearly, William Churchill Houston, and William Patterson Esquires.

Pennsylvania . . . . The honorable Robert Morris, Thomas Fitz Simmons, James Wilson, and Gouverneur Morris Esquires.

Delaware . . . . The honorable George Read, Richard Basset, and Jacob Broom Esquires.

Virginia . . . . His Excellency George Washington, Esquire, His Excellency Edmund Randolph Esquire The honorable John Blair, James Madison, George Mason, George Wythe, and James McClurg Esquires.

North-Carolina . . . . . . The honorable Alexander Martin, William Richardson Davie, Richard Dobbs Spaight, and Hugh Williamson Esquires.

South-Carolina ...... The honorable John Rutledge, Charles Cotesworth Pinckney, Charles Pinckney, and Pierce Butler Esquires.

Georgia .... The honorable   Few Esquire.

In fœderal-Convention Friday May 25. 1787.

It was moved by the honorable Robert Morris Esquire, One of the Deputies from Pennsylvania, that a President be elected by ballot, which was agreed to — and thereupon he nominated, on the part of the said State,

His Excellency George Washington Esquire

The Members then proceeded to ballot on behalf of their respective States — and, the ballots being taken, it appeared that the said George Washington was unanimously elected — and he was conducted to the chair by

The honorable Robert Morris, and John Rutledge Esquires. The President then proposed to the House that they should proceed to the election of a Secretary — and, the ballots being taken, it appeared that

William Jackson Esquire was elected.

The following credentials were produced and read — (here insert the Credentials).

The House then appointed Nicholas Weaver Messenger, and Joseph Fry Door-Keeper.

On motion of Mr C. Pinckney — ordered that a Committee be appointed to draw up rules to be observed as the standing Orders of the Convention — and to report the same to the House. — a Committee by ballot was appointed of

Mr Wythe, Mr Hamilton, and Mr C. Pinckney. And then the House adjourned 'till monday next at 10 o'clock A.M.[1]

---

[1] It seems to have been the practise of the Convention at the close of the day's session to adjourn until the next morning at ten o'clock. Apparently the hours were somewhat irregular, and on August 18, it was agreed to meet precisely at 10 A.M., and no motion to adjourn was to be in order until 4 P.M. On August 24, the hour of adjournment was fixed at 3 P.M. See further August 18 note 9, and Appendix A, LXXXIIIa, XCIVa, CX, CXX.

MADISON

Monday May 14th 1787 was the day fixed for the meeting of the deputies in Convention for revising the federal[2] system of Government. On that day a small number only had assembled   Seven States were not convened till,[3]

Friday 25 of May,

⟨when the following members appeared to wit:
viz. From *Massachusetts* Rufus King. *N. York* Robert Yates, Alexr. Hamilton. *N. Jersey*, David Brearley, William Churchill Houston, William Patterson. *Pennsylvania*, Robert Morris, Thomas Fitzsimmons, James Wilson, Gouverneur Morris. *Delaware*, George Read, Richard Basset, Jacob Broom. *Virginia*, George Washington, Edmund Randolph, John Blair, James Madison, George Mason, George Wythe, James McClurg. *N. Carolina*, Alexander Martin, William Richardson Davie, Richard Dobbs Spaight, Hugh Williamson. *S. Carolina*, John Rutledge, Charles Cotesworth Pinckney, Charles Pinckney, Pierce Butler. *Georgia*, William Few.⟩[4]

Mr Robert Morris informed the members assembled that by the instruction & in behalf, of the deputation of Pena. he proposed George Washington Esqr. late Commander in chief for president of the Convention. Mr. Jno. Rutledge seconded the motion; expressing his confidence that the choice would be unanimous, and observing that the presence of Genl Washington forbade any observations on the occasion which might otherwise be proper.

General ⟨Washington⟩[5] was accordingly unanimously elected by ballot,[6] and conducted to the chair by Mr. R. Morris and Mr. Rutlidge; from which in a very emphatic manner he thanked the Convention for the honor they had conferred on him, reminded them of the novelty of the scene

---

[2] Crossed out "Constitution".

[3] For further information regarding the Convention, May 14–25, see Appendix A, VIII–XXVI, XXIX, CCLXXXV.   [5] Originally "The General".

[4] Copied from *Journal*.   [6] See Appendix A, XX *et seq.*

of business in which he was to act, lamented his want of ⟨better qualifications⟩,[7] and claimed the indulgence of the House towards the involuntary errors which his inexperience might occasion.

(The nomination came with particular grace from Penna, as Docr. Franklin alone could have been thought of ⟨as a competitor⟩.[8] The Docr. was himself to have made the nomination ⟨of General Washington, but the state of the weather and of his health confined him to his house.⟩[9])

Mr. Wilson moved that a Secretary be appointed, and nominated Mr. Temple Franklin.

Col. Hamilton nominated Major Jackson.

On the ballot Majr. Jackson had 5 votes & Mr. Franklin 2 votes.[10]

On[11] reading the Credentials of the deputies it was noticed that those from Delaware were prohibited from changing the Article in the Confederation establishing an equality of votes among the States.[12]

The appointment of a Committee, consisting of Messrs. Wythe, Hamilton & C. Pinckney, on the motion of Mr. C. Pinckney, to prepare standing rules & orders was the only remaining step taken on this day

---

May 14, 1787 [13] — appointed for the meeting of ye Convention on the 7 States met

May 25. —— (page 1 to 4) list of members assembled — G. Washington unanimously elected prest. notes of J. M. Major Jackson elected Secy — credentials of deputies read. Commee appd to prepare rules.

---

[7] Crossed out "the requisites for it ".

[8] Crossed out "for the President ".

[9] Crossed out "of the Genl. but the season of the rain did not permit him to venture to the Convention chamber."

[10] On the election of Jackson as secretary see Introduction, note 6.

[11] This paragraph may be a later insertion suggested by Yates.

[12] See below *Records*, May 30, and Appendix A, XXIII, CLVIII (3), Appendix B, note 6.

[13] Memoranda by Madison, preserved with his Debates. Evidently a summary of his notes.

YATES

Friday, May 25, 1787.

Attended the convention of the states, at the state house in Philadelphia, when the following states were represented:

New-York,	Alexander Hamilton,
	Robert Yates.
New-Jersey,	David Brearly,
	William Churchill Houston,
	William Patterson.
Pennsylvania,	Robert Morris,
	Thomas Fitzsimons,
	James Wilson,
	Gouverneur Morris.
Delaware,	George Read,
	Richard Bassett,
	Jacob Broom.
Virginia,	George Washington,
	Edmund Randolph,
	George Wythe,
	George Mason,
	James Madison,
	John Blair,
	James M'Clurg.
North-Carolina,	Alexander Martin,
	William Richardson Davie,
	Richard Dobbs Spaight,
	Hugh Williamson.
South-Carolina,	John Rutledge,
	Charles Cotesworth Pinckney,
	Charles Pinckney,
	Pierce Butler.

A motion by R. Morris, and seconded, that General Washington take the chair — unanimously agreed to.

When seated, he (Gen. Washington) declared, that as he never had been in such a situation, he felt himself embarrassed;

that he hoped his errors, as they would be unintentional, would be excused.

Mr. Hamilton, in behalf of the state of New-York, moved that Major Jackson be appointed secretary; the delegates for Pennsylvania, moved for Temple Franklin: by a majority Mr. Jackson carried it — called in and took his seat.

After which, the respective credentials of the seven states were read.   N. B. That of Delaware restrained its delegates from assenting to an abolition of the fifth article of the confederation, by which it is declared that each state shall have one vote.

Door keeper and messengers being appointed, the house adjourned to Monday the 28th day of May, at ten o'clock.

MONDAY, MAY 28, 1787.

JOURNAL

Monday May 28. 1787.

The Convention met agreeably to adjournment —
The honorable Nathaniel Gorham, and Caleb Strong Esquires,
Deputies from the State of Massachusetts, The honorable
Oliver Elsworth Esq, a deputy from the State of Connecticut
— The honble Gunning Bedford Esq. a Deputy from the State
of Delaware and The honorable James McHenry Esquire, a
Deputy from the State of Maryland, attended and took their
seats.

The following Credentials were produced and read.

(here insert the credentials of the Deputies from the States
of Massachusetts, and Connecticut, and the credentials of
James McHenry Esquire from the State of Maryland)[1] His
Excellency Benjamin Franklin Esquire, and of The honorable
George Clymer, Thomas Mifflin and Jared Ingersol Esquires
four of the Deputies of the State of Pennsylvania attended and
took their seats

Mr Wythe reported from the Committee, (to whom the
drawing up rules, proper in their opinion, to be observed by
the Convention in their proceedings, as standing Orders, was
referred) that the Committee had drawn up the rules accordingly, and had directed him to report them to the House —
and he read the report in his place, and afterwards delivered
it in at the Secretary's table; where the said rules were once
read throughout, and then a second time one by one; and upon
the question severally put thereupon two of them were disagreed to; and the rest with amendments to some of them were

---

[1] See Appendix B.

agreed to by the House, which rules, so agreed to, are as follow:

Rules to be observed as the standing Orders of the Convention.

A House, to do business, shall consist of the Deputies of not less than seven States; and all questions shall be decided by the greater number of these which shall be fully represented; but a less number than seven may adjourn from day to day.

Immediately after the President shall have taken the Chair, and the members their seats, the minutes of the preceding day shall be read by the Secretary.

Every member, rising to speak, shall address the President; and, whilst he shall be speaking, none shall pass between them, or hold discourse with another, or read a book, pamphlet, or paper, printed or manuscript — and of two members, rising at the same time, the President shall name him who shall be first heard.

A member shall not speak oftner than twice, without special leave, upon the same question; and not the second time, before every other, who had been silent, shall have been heard, if he choose to speak, upon the subject.

A motion made and seconded, shall be repeated and, if written, as it shall be when any member shall so require, read aloud, by the Secretary, before it shall be debated; and may be withdrawn at any time before the vote upon it shall have been declared.

Orders of the day shall be read next after the minutes, and either discussed or postponed before any other business shall be introduced.

When a debate shall arise upon a question, no motion, other than to amend the question, to commit it, or to postpone the debate shall be received.

A question, which is complicated, shall, at the request of any member, be divided, and put separately upon the propositions, of which it is compounded.

The determination of a question, although fully debated, shall be postponed, if the Deputies of any State desire it, until the next day.

A Writing, which contains any matter brought on to be considered, shall be read once throughout, for information, then by paragraphs, to be debated, and again, with the amendments, if any, made on the second reading; and afterwards the question shall be put upon the whole, amended, or approved in it's original form, as the case shall be.

That Committees shall be appointed by ballot; and that the members who have the greatest number of ballots, although not a majority of the votes present, be the Committee. When two or more Members have an equal number of votes, the Member standing first on the list in the order of taking down the ballots shall be preferred.

A member may be called to order by any other Member, as well as by the President, and may be allowed to explain his conduct or expressions, supposed to be reprehensible — And all questions of order shall be decided by the President without appeal or debate.

Upon a question to adjourn, for the day, which may be made at any time, if it be seconded, the question shall be put without a debate.

When the House shall adjourn every Member shall stand in his place until the President pass him.

Resolved that the said rules be observed as standing Orders of the House.

a letter from sundry Persons of the State of Rhode Island addressed to the honorable the Chairman of the General Convention was presented to the Chair by Mr G. Morris[2] — and, being read, ordered that the said letter do lye upon the table for farther consideration.

A motion was made by Mr Butler, one of the Deputies of South Carolina, that the House provide against interruption of business by absence of members, and against licentious publication of their proceedings: also

A motion was made by Mr Spaight, one of the Deputies of North-Carolina, to provide, that, on the one hand, the house, may not be precluded, by a vote upon any question,

---

[2] For this letter see Appendix A, VII.

from revising the subject matter of it, when they see cause, nor, on the other hand, be led too hastily to rescind a decision, which was the result of mature discussion.

Ordered that the said motions be referred to the consideration of the Committee appointed on friday last, to draw up rules to be observed as the standing orders of the Convention; and that they do examine the matters thereof, and report thereupon to the House.

adjourned till to-morrow at 10 o'clock A. M

MADISON

Monday May 28. —

⟨From Masst's Nat: Gorham & Caleb Strong. From Connecticut Oliver Elseworth. From Delaware Gunning Bedford. From Maryland James McHenry. From Penna. B. Franklin, George Clymer, Ths. Mifflin & Jared Ingersol took their seats.⟩[3]

Mr. Wythe from the Committee for preparing rules made a report which employed the deliberations of this day.

Mr. King objected to one of the rules in the Report authorising any member to call for the yeas & nays and have them entered on the minutes. He urged that as the acts of the Convention were not to bind the Constituents it was unnecessary to exhibit this evidence of the votes; and improper as changes of opinion would be frequent in the course of the business & would fill the minutes with contradictions.

Col. Mason seconded the objection; adding that such a record of the opinions of members would be an obstacle to a change of them on conviction; and in case of its being hereafter promulged must furnish handles to the adversaries of the Result of the Meeting.

The proposed rule was rejected nem. contradicente.

⟨The standing rules * agreed to were as follow:[4]

* Previous to the arrival of a majority of the States, the rule by which they ought to vote in the Convention had been made a subject of conversation among the mem-

---

[3] Copied from *Journal.*

[4] Originally Madison had recorded:

"The Rule restraining members from communicating the proceedings of the

viz, A House to do business shall consist of the Deputies of not less than seven States; and all questions shall be decided by the greater number of these which shall be fully represented: but a less number than seven may adjourn from day to day.

Immediately after the President shall have taken the chair, and the members their seats, the minutes of the preceding day shall be read by the Secretary.

Every member, rising to speak, shall address the President; and whilst he shall be speaking, none shall pass between them, or hold discourse with another, or read a book, pamphlet or paper, printed or manuscript — and of two members rising at the same time, the President shall name him who shall be first heard.

A member shall not speak oftener than twice, without special leave, upon the same question; and not the second time, before every other, who had been silent, shall have been heard, if he choose to speak upon the subject.

A motion made and seconded, shall be repeated, and if written, as it shall be when any member shall so require, read aloud by the Secretary, before it shall be debated; and may be withdrawn at any time, before the vote upon it shall have been declared.

Orders of the day shall be read next after the minutes,

bers present. It was pressed by Gouverneur Morris and favored by Robert Morris and others from Pennsylvania, that the large States should unite in firmly refusing to the small States an equal vote, as unreasonable, and as enabling the small States to negative every good system of Government, which must in the nature of things, be founded on a violation of that equality. The members from Virginia, conceiving that such an attempt might beget fatal altercations between the large & small States, and that it would be easier to prevail on the latter, in the course of the deliberations, to give up their equality for the sake of an effective Government, than on taking the field of discussion, to disarm themselves of the right & thereby throw themselves on the mercy of the large States, discountenanced & stifled the project.

Convention &c. was agreed to nem. con. for reasons similar to those above mentioned.

One Another of the Rules being disagreed to, the sett was agreed to understand as follows. See note B."

This was later struck out and there was substituted, "see the Journal & copy here the printed rules." The rules as given in the text were copied from the *Journal* and pasted over the original record.

and either discussed or postponed, before any other business shall be introduced.

When a debate shall arise upon a question, no motion, other than to amend the question, to commit it, or to postpone the debate shall be received.

A question[5] which is complicated, shall, at the request of any member, be divided, and put separately on the propositions. of which it is compounded.

The determination of a question, altho' fully debated, shall be postponed, if the deputies of any State desire it until the next day.

A writing which contains any matter brought on to be considered, shall be read once throughout for information, then by paragraphs to be debated, and again, with the amendments if any, made on the second reading; and afterwards, the question shall be put on the whole, amended, or approved in its original form, as the case shall be.

Committees shall be appointed by ballot; and the members who have the greatest number of ballots, altho' not a majority of the votes present, shall be the Committee — When two or more members have an equal number of votes, the member standing first on the list in the order of taking down the ballots, shall be preferred.

A member may be called to order by any other member, as well as by the President; and may be allowed to explain his conduct or expressions supposed to be reprehensible. — and all questions of order shall be decided by the President without appeal or debate.

Upon a question to adjourn for the day, which may be made at any time, if it be seconded, the question shall be put without a debate.

When the House shall adjourn, every member shall stand in his place, until the President pass him.⟩

⟨A letter[6] from sundry persons of the State of Rho. Island

---

[5] From this point to the end of the rules a line is drawn across the page of the MS, but not apparently to strike it out, as the rules were actually adopted by the Convention.

[6] The remainder of this day's records were copied from *Journal.*

addressed to the Honorable The Chairman of the General Convention was presented to the chair by Mr. Govr. Morris, and being read, was ordered to lie on the table for further consideration. (For the letter see Note in the appendix).[7]

Mr Butler moved that the house provide agst. interruption of business by absence of members, and against licentious publications of their procedings — to which was added by — Mr. Spaight — a motion to provide that on the one hand the House might not be precluded by a vote upon any question, from revising the subject matter of it, When they see cause, nor, on the other hand, be led too hastily to rescind a decision, which was the result of mature discussion. — Whereupon it was ordered that these motions be referred to the consideration of the Committee appointed to draw up the standing rules and that the Committee make report thereon.

Adjd till to morrow 10. OClock)[8]

[May] 28.[9] (pa. 4 to 10). Other members attended — Mr. Wythe from Commee reports rules — one of them rejected others adopted — note of J. M. on rule of voting. a letter from R. I. presented by G. Morris.

YATES

Monday, May 28, 1787

Met pursuant to adjournment.

A committee of three members, (whose appointment I omitted in the entry of the proceedings of Friday last,) reported a set of rules for the order of the convention; which being considered by articles, were agreed to, and additional ones proposed and referred to the same committee. The representation was this day increased to nine states — Massachusetts and Connecticut becoming represented. Adjourned to next day.

---

[7] See Appendix A, VII, XLV, CII.
[8] See further Appendix A, XXV, XXVI.
[9] Memoranda by Madison, see May 25 note 13.

McHENRY

PHILADELPHIA 14 May 1787.[10]
Convention.

On the 25th seven states being represented viz. New-York New Jersey, Pennsylvania, Delaware, Virginia, North Carolina and South Carolina George Washington was elected (unanimously) president of the convention.

The convention appoint a committee to prepare and report rules for conducting business which were reported, debated, and in general agreed to on the 28th.

---

[10] According to the Journal, McHenry first attended on May 28; his notes are therefore assigned to this date.

TUESDAY, MAY 29, 1787.

JOURNAL

Tuesday May 29, 1787.

Mr Wythe reported, from the Committee to whom the motions made by Mr Butler and Mr Spaight were referred, that the Committee had examined the matters of the said motions, and had come to the following resolution thereupon,

resolved that it is the opinion of this Committee that provision be made for the purposes mentioned in the said motions — and to that end.

The Committee beg leave to propose that the rules written under their resolution be added to the standing orders of the House.

And the said rules were once read throughout and then a second time, one by one; and, on the question severally put thereupon, were, with amendments to some of them, agreed to by the House which rules so agreed to are as follow.

rules.

That no member be absent from the House so as to interrupt the representation of the State without leave.

That Committees do not sit whilst the House shall be, or ought to be, sitting.

That no copy be taken of any entry on the journal during the sitting of the House without the leave of the House.[1]

That members only be permitted to inspect the journal.

That nothing spoken in the House be printed, or otherwise published, or communicated without leave.[2]

---

[1] See Appendix A, CXC.

[2] On secrecy of Convention proceedings see Appendix A, XXIII–CXVIII *passim*, CLVIII (3), CCLXX, CCCLXVII. That this was not always strictly observed, see Appendix A, XLVI, LVI, LXXVI, CVI.

That a motion to reconsider a matter, which had been determined by a majority, may be made, with leave unanimously given,-on-the same day in which the vote passed, but otherwise, not without one days previous notice; in which last case, if the House agree to the reconsideration some future day shall be assigned for that purpose.

Resolved that the said rules be added to the standing orders of the House.

The honorable John Dickinson Esq a Deputy of the State of Delaware — and the honorable Elbridge Gerry Esquire, a Deputy from the State of Massachusetts, attended and took their seats.

Mr Randolph, one of the Deputies of Virginia, laid before the House, for their consideration, sundry propositions, in writing, concerning the american confederation, and the establishment of a national government [3]

Resolved that the House will to-morrow resolve itself into a Committee of the whole House to consider of the state of the American Union.

Ordered that the propositions this day laid before the House, for their consideration, by Mr Randolph be referred to the said Committee.

Mr Charles Pinckney, one of the Deputies of South Carolina, laid before the House for their consideration, the draught of a fœderal government to be agreed upon between the free and independent States of America.[4]

Ordered that the said draught be referred to the Committee of the whole House appointed to consider of the state of the american Union

And then the House adjourned till to-morrow morning at 10 o'clock

---

[3] The papers of Secretary Jackson do not include a copy of the Randolph Resolutions. That which was printed in the *Journal* was taken from the papers of David Brearley. See Appendix A, CCCXXV, CCCXXVI, CCCXXVIII.

[4] For the Pinckney Plan, see Appendix D.

MADISON

Tuesday May 29

⟨John Dickenson, and Elbridge Gerry, the former from Delaware, the latter from Massts. took their seats,[5]
The following rules were added, on the report of Mr. Wythe, from the Committee

Additional rules.[5]

That no member be absent from the House, so as to interrupt the representation of the State, without leave.

That Committees do not sit whilst the House shall be or ought to be, sitting.

That no copy be taken of any entry on the journal during the sitting of the House without leave of the House.

That members only be permitted to inspect the journal.

That nothing spoken in the House be printed, or otherwise published or communicated without leave.

That a motion to reconsider a matter which had been determined by a majority, may be made, with leave unanimously given, on the same day on which the vote passed, but otherwise not without one day's previous notice: in which last case, if the House agree to the reconsideration, some future day shall be assigned for the purpose.⟩

Mr. C. Pinckney moved that a Committee be appointed to superintend the minutes.

Mr. Govr. Morris objected to it. The entry of the proceedings of the Convention belonged to the Secretary as their impartial officer. A committee might have an interest & bias in moulding the entry according to their opinions and wishes

The motion was negatived 5 noes 4 ays.[6]

---

[5] Copied from *Journal*.

[6] Madison tried two other ways of expressing the result of this vote. This uncertainty as to the best form of expression may indicate that it was the first vote recorded. See below *Records* of May 30, note 6.

Upon the method of voting in the Convention, see Appendix A, CCXCV, CCCXXVIII, CCCLXXVI.

Mr. Randolph ⟨then⟩ opened the main business [7]
He expressed his regret, that it should fall to him, rather than those, who were of longer standing in life and political experience, to open the great subject of their mission. But, as the convention had originated from Virginia, and his colleagues supposed, that some proposition was expected from them, they had imposed this task on him.[8]

He then commented on the difficulty of the crisis, and the necessity of preventing the fulfilment of the prophecies of the American downfal.

He observed that in revising the fœderal system we ought to inquire 1. into the properties, which such a government ought to possess, 2. the defects of the confederation, 3. the danger of our situation &. 4. the remedy.

1. The character of such a governme[nt] ought to secure 1. against foreign invasion: 2. against dissentions between members of the Union, or seditions in particular states: 3. to p[ro]cure to the several States various blessings, of which an isolated situation was i[n]capable: 4. to be able to defend itself against incroachment: & 5. to be paramount to the state constitutions.

2. In speaking of the defects of the confederation he professed a high respect for its authors, and considered, them as having done all that patriots could do, in the then infancy of the science, of constitutions, & of confederacies, — when the inefficiency of requisitions was unknown — no commercial discord had arisen among any states — no rebellion had appeared as in Massts. — foreign debts had not become urgent — the havoc of paper money had not been foreseen — treaties

---

[7] Madison originally had written: "in a long speech in which he pointed out the various defects of the federal system, the necessity of transforming it into a national efficient Government, and the extreme danger of delaying this great work, concluding with sundry propositions as the outlines of a proper form." This was struck out, and there is written: "(here insert his speech including his resolutions.)"

The speech which follows is in Randolph's hand, see Madison's note at the end of the speech, and Appendix A, CCXLVII. There are slight mutilations in the MS.

[8] Upon the formation of the Virginia Plan and the choice of Randolph to present it, see Appendix A, XV, XVI, XXXII, CCCVIII, CCCLVI, CCCLXXXVIII, CCCXCII, CCCXCIII, CCCXCVII, CCCCI.

had not been violated — and perhaps nothing better could be obtained from the jealousy of the states with regard to their sovereignty.

He then proceeded to enumerate the defects: 1. that the confederation produced no security agai[nst] foreign invasion; congress not being permitted to prevent a war nor to support it by th[eir] own authority — Of this he cited many examples; most of whi[ch] tended to shew, that they could not cause infractions of treaties or of the law of nations, to be punished: that particular states might by their conduct provoke war without controul; and that neither militia nor draughts being fit for defence on such occasions, enlistments only could be successful, and these could not be executed without money.

2. that the fœderal government could not check the quarrals between states, nor a rebellion in any not having constitutional power Nor means to interpose according to the exigency:

3. that there were many advantages, which the U. S. might acquire, which were not attainable under the confederation — such as a productive impost — counteraction of the commercial regulations of other nations — pushing of commerce ad libitum — &c &c.

4. that the fœderal government could not defend itself against the incroachments from the states:

5. that it was not even paramount to the state constitutions, ratified as it was in may of the states.

3. He next reviewed the danger of our situation appealed to the sense of the best friends of the U. S. — the prospect of anarchy from the laxity of government every where; and to other considerations.

4. He then proceeded to the remedy; the basis of which he said, must be the republican principle

He proposed as conformable to his ideas the following resolutions,[9] which he explained one by one.

---

[9] See Appendix A, CCV, CCXCII.

Resolutions [10] proposed by Mr Randolph in Convention.

May 29. 1787.

1. Resolved that the articles of Confederation ought to be so corrected & enlarged as to accomplish the objects proposed by their institution; namely. "common defence, security of liberty and general welfare." [11]

2. Resd. therefore that the rights of suffrage in the National [12] Legislature ought to be proportioned to the Quotas of contribution, or to the number of free inhabitants, as the one or the other rule may seem best in different cases.

3. Resd. that the National Legislature ought to consist of two branches.

4. Resd. that the members of the first branch of the National Legislature ought to be elected by the people of the several States every   for the term of   ; to be of the age of   years at least, to receive liberal stipends by which they may be compensated for the devotion of their time to public service; to be ineligible to any office established by a particular State, or under the authority of the United States, except those beculiarly belonging to the functions of the first branch, during the term of service, and for the space of   after its expiration; to be incapable of re-election for the space of   after the expiration of their term of service, and to be subject to recall.

5. Resold. that the members of the second branch of the National Legislature ought to be elected by those of the first, out of a proper number of persons nominated by the individual Legislatures, to be of the age of   years at least; to hold their offices for a term sufficient to ensure their independency, to receive liberal stipends, by which they may be compensated for the devotion of their time to public service;

[10] For a discussion of the correct text of the Randolph Resolutions or the Virginia Plan, see Appendix C.

[11] On terms "common defence . . . and general welfare," see Appendix A, CCCLXXII.

[12] On the term "National" see Appendix A, CCCLVI, CCCLVII, CCCLXXXVIII, CCCXCII, also debates of June 19–20.

and to be ineligible to any office established by a particular State, or under the authority of the United States, except those peculiarly belonging to the functions of the second branch, during the term of service, and for the space of after the expiration thereof.

6. Resolved that each branch ought to possess the right of originating Acts; that the National Legislature ought to be impowered to enjoy the Legislative Rights vested in Congress by the Confederation & moreover to legislate in all cases to which the separate States are incompetent, or in which the harmony of the United States may be interrupted by the exercise of individual Legislation; to negative all laws passed by the several States, contravening in the opinion of the National Legislature the articles of Union; and to call forth the force of the Union agst. any member of the Union failing to fulfill its duty under the articles thereof.

7. Resd. that a National Executive be instituted; to be chosen by the National Legislature for the term of years, to receive punctually at stated times, a fixed compensation for the services rendered, in which no increase or diminution shall be made so as to affect the Magistracy, existing at the time of increase or diminution, and to be ineligible a second time; and that besides a general authority to execute the National laws, it ought to enjoy the Executive rights vested in Congress by the Confederation.

8. Resd. that the Executive and a convenient number of the National Judiciary, ought to compose a council of revision with authority to examine every act of the National Legislature before it shall operate, & every act of a particular Legislature before a Negative thereon shall be final; and that the dissent of the said Council shall amount to a rejection, unless the Act of the National Legislature be again passed, or that of a particular Legislature be again negatived by of the members of each branch.

9. Resd. that a National Judiciary be established to consist of one or more supreme tribunals, and of inferior tribunals to be chosen by the National Legislature, to hold their offices during good behaviour; and to receive punctually at stated

times fixed compensation for their services, in which no increase or diminution shall be made so as to affect the persons actually in office at the time of such increase or diminution. that the jurisdiction of the inferior tribunals shall be to hear & determine in the first instance, and of the supreme tribunal to hear and determine in the dernier resort, all piracies & felonies on the high seas, captures from an enemy; cases in which foreigners or citizens of other States applying to such jurisdictions may be interested, or which respect the collection of the National revenue; impeachments of any National officers, and questions which may involve the national peace and harmony.

10. Resolvd. that provision ought to be made for the admission of States lawfully arising within the limits of the United States, whether from a voluntary junction of Government & Territory or otherwise, with the consent of a number of voices in the National legislature less than the whole.

11. Resd. that a Republican Government & the territory of each State, except in the instance of a voluntary junction of Government & territory, ought to be guaranteed by the United States to each State

12. Resd. that provision ought to be made for the continuance of Congress and their authorities and privileges, until a given day after the reform of the articles of Union shall be adopted, and for the completion of all their engagements.

13. Resd. that provision ought to be made for the amendment of the Articles of Union whensoever it shall seem necessary, and that the assent of the National Legislature ought not to be required thereto.

14. Resd. that the Legislative Executive & Judiciary powers within the several States ought to be bound by oath to support the articles of Union

15. Resd. that the amendments which shall be offered to the Confederation, by the Convention ought at a proper time, or times, after the approbation of Congress to be submitted to an assembly or assemblies of Representatives, recommended by the several Legislatures to be expressly chosen by the people, to consider & decide thereon.

He concluded with an exhortation, not to suffer the present opportunity of establishing general peace, harmony, happiness and liberty in the U. S. to pass away unimproved.*

⟨It[13] was then Resolved &c — &c — That the House will to-morrow resolve itself into a Committee of the whole House to consider of the State of the American Union, — and that the propositions moved by Mr. Randolph be referred to the said Committee.

Mr. Charles Pinkney laid before the house the draught of a federal Government which he had prepared to be agreed upon between the free and independent States of America.[14]— Mr. P. plan ordered that the same be referred to the Committee of the whole appointed to consider the State of the American Union.   adjourned.⟩[15]

* This abstract of the Speech was furnished to J. M. by Mr. Randolph and is in his hand writing. As a report of it from him, had been relied, on, it was omitted by J. M.[16]

———————

[May][17] 29. — (pages 10 to 38.)   two additional members take their seats — other rules added on report of Mr W.   Mr Randolph on the part of the Virginia delegation opened the main business, enumerating defects of the confederation & proposed his resolutions which were referred to a Comee of the whole—copy of C. Pinkneys resolutions (journal) & note &co on them by J. M.— resolutions referred to same Comee

YATES

Tuesday, May 29th, 1787.

The additional rules agreed to.

His excellency Governor Randolph, a member from Virginia, got up, and in a long and elaborate speech, shewed the defects in the system of the present federal government as

———————

[13] The remainder of Madison's records for this day were copied from *Journal*.
[14] For the Pinckney Plan see Appendix D.
[15] See further Appendix A, XXVII–XXIX.
[16] The resolutions are in Madison's handwriting.
[17] Memoranda by Madison, see May 25, note 13.

totally inadequate to the peace, safety and security of the confederation, and the absolute necessity of a more energetic government.

He closed these remarks with a set of resolutions, fifteen in number, which he proposed to the convention for their adoption, and as leading principles whereon to form a new government— He candidly confessed that they were not intended for a federal government — he meant a strong *consolidated* union, in which the idea of states should be nearly annihilated.   (I have taken a copy of these resolutions, which are hereunto annexed.) [18]

He then moved that they should be taken up in committee of the whole house.

Mr. C. Pinkney, a member from South-Carolina, then added, that he had reduced his ideas of a new government to a system, which he read, and confessed that it was grounded on the same principle as of the above resolutions.

The house then resolved, that they would the next day form themselves into a committee of the whole, to take into consideration *the state of the union.*

Adjourned to next day.

McHENRY

29.

Governor Randolph opened the business of the convention.[18a]   He observed that the confederation fulfilled *none* of the objects for which it was framed.   1st. It does not provide against foreign invasions.   2dly. It does not secure harmony to the States.   3d. It is incapable of producing certain blessings to the States.   4 It cannot defend itself against encroachments.   5th. It is not superior to State constitutions.

1st *It does not provide against foreign invasion.*   If a State acts against a foreign power contrary to the laws of nations or violates a treaty, it cannot punish that State, or compel

---

[18] "The several papers referred to did not accompany his notes."   See *Records* of July 5, note 18.

[18a] See Appendix A, CXLVI *a.*

its obedience to the treaty. It can only leave the offending State to the operations of the offended power. It therefore cannot prevent a war. If the rights of an ambassador be invaded by any citizen it is only in a few States that any laws exist to punish the offender. A State may encroach on foreign possessions in its neighbourhood and Congress cannot prevent it. Disputes that respect naturalization cannot be adjusted. None of the judges in the several States under the obligation of an oath to support the confederation, in which view this writing will be made to yield to State constitutions.

Imbecility of the Confederation equally conspicuous when called upon to support a war. The journals of Congress a history of expedients. The States in arrears to the federal treasury from the
            to the
What reason to expect that the treasury will be better filled in future, or that money can be obtained under the present powers of Congress to support a war. *Volunteers* not to be depended on for such a purpose. *Militia* difficult to be collected and almost impossible to be kept in the field. *Draughts* stretch the strings of government too violently to be adopted. Nothing short of a regular military force will answer the end of war, and this only to be created and supported by money.

2. *It does not secure harmony to the States.*

It cannot preserve the particular States against seditions within themselves or combinations against each other. What laws in the confederation authorise Congress to intrude troops into a State. What authority to determine which of the citizens of a State is in the right, The supporters or the opposers of the government, Those who wish to change it, or they who wish to preserve it.

No provision to prevent the States breaking out into war. One State may as it were underbid another by duties, and thus keep up a State of war.

3 *Incapable to produce certain blessings.*

The benefits of which we are *singly incapable* cannot be produced by the union. The 5 per cent impost not agreed; a blessing congress ought to be enabled to obtain.

Congress ought to possess a power to prevent emissions of bills of credit.

Under this head may be considered the establishment of great national works — the improvement of inland navigation — agriculture — manufactures — a freer intercourse among the citizens.

4 *It cannot defend itself against incroachments.* Not an animated existence which has not the powers of defence. Not a political existence which ought not to possess it. In every Congress there has been a party opposed to federal measures? In every State assembly there has been a party opposed to federal measures. The States have been therefore delinquent. To What expedient can congress resort, to compel delinquent States to do what is right. If force, this force must be drawn from the States, and the States may or may not furnish it.

5 *Inferior to State constitutions.*

State constitutions formed at an early period of the war, and by persons *elected by the people* for that purpose. These in general with one or two exceptions established about 1786. The *confederation* was formed long after this, and had its ratification not by any *special appointment* from the people, but from the several assemblies. No judge will say that the *confederation* is paramount to a State constition.

Thus we see that the confederation is incompetent to any *one* object for which it was instituted. The framers of it wise and great men; but human rights were the chief knowlege of the times when it was framed so far as they applied to oppose Great Britain. Requisitions for men and money had never offered their form to our assemblies. None of those vices that have since discovered themselves were apprehended. Its defects therefore no reflextion on its contrivers.

Having pointed out its defects, let us not be affraid to view with a steady eye the perils with which we are surrounded. Look at the public countenance from New Hampshire to Georgia. Are we not on the eve of war, which is only prevented by the hopes from this convention.

Our chief danger arises from the democratic parts of our constitutions. It is a maxim which I hold incontrovertible, that the powers of government exercised by the people swallows up the other branches.   None of the constitutions have provided sufficient checks against the democracy.   The feeble Senate of Virginia is a phantom.   Maryland has a more powerful senate, but the late distractions in that State, have discovered that it is not powerful enough.   The check established in the constutution of New York and Massachusetts is yet a stronger barrier against democracy, but they all seem insufficient.

He then submitted the following propositions which he read and commented upon seriatim. . . .[19]

The convention resolved that on to-morrow, the convention resolve itself into a committee of the whole.

to take into consideration the state of the american union.

It was observed by Mr. Hamilton before adjourning that it struck him as a necessary and preliminary inquiry to the propositions from Virginia whether the united States were susceptible of one government, or réquired a separate existence connected only by leagues offensive and defensive and treaties of commerce.

PATERSON

Govr. Randolph —

Propositions founded upon republican Principles.[20]

1. The Articles of the Confdn. should be so enlarged and corrected as to answer the Purposes of the Instn.

2. That the Rights of Suffrage shall be ascertained by the Quantum of Property or Number of Souls — This the Basis upon which the larger States can assent to any Reform.

Objn. — Sovereignty is an integral Thing — We ought to be one Nation —

3. That the national Legr. should consist of two Branches—

4. That the Members of the first Branch should be elected

---

[19] In all essential particulars McHenry's copy of the Virginia Plan is identical with that of Madison.   It is accordingly omitted here.   For further discussion of the correct text of the Virginia Plan, see Appendix C.

[20] Among the Paterson MSS. there is a copy of the Virginia Plan, which does not differ from the Madison copy sufficiently to warrant reprinting here, see Appendix C.

by the People, etc.   This the democratick Branch — Perhaps, if inconvenient, may be elected by the several Legrs. —

5. Members of the 2d. Branch to be elected out of the first — to continue for a certain Length of Time, etc.   To be elected by Electors appointed for that Purpose —

6. The Powers to be vested in the national Legr. — A negative upon particular acts, etc. contravening the Articles of the Union — Force —

7. A national Executive to be elected by the national Legr.

Checks upon the Legv. and Ex. Powers —

1. A Council of Revision to be selected out of the ex. and judy. Departments, etc.

2. A natl Judiciary to be elected by the natl. Legr. — To consist of an inferior and superior Tribunal — To determine Piracies, Captures, Disputes between Foreigners and Citizens, and the Citizen of one State and that of another, Revenue-matters, national Officers —

1. Provision for future States —

2. A Guary. by the United States to each State of its Territory, etc.

3. Continuation of Congress till a given Day.

4. Provision, that the Articles of national Union should be amended —

5. That the leg. ex. and judy. Officers should be bound by Oath to observe the Union.

6. That Members be elected by the People of the several States to ratify the Articles of national Union —

WEDNESDAY, MAY 30, 1787.

JOURNAL

Wednesday May 30. 1787.

The honorable Roger Sherman Esquire a Deputy of the State of Connecticut attended and took his seat.

The order of the day being read

The House resolved itself into a Committee of the whole House to consider of the state of the American union

Mr President left the chair.

Mr Gorham, chosen by ballot,[1] took the chair of the Committee.

Mr President resumed the chair

Mr Gorham reported from the Committee, that the Committee had made a progress in the matter to them referred; and had directed him to move that they may have leave to sit again

Resolved that this House will to-morrow again resolve itself into a Committee of the whole House to consider of the state of the American union

And then the House adjourned till to-morrow at 10 o'clock A.M.

In a Committee of the Whole House.

Wednesday May 30. 1787.

Agreeably to the order of the day the House resolved itself

---

[1] On the back of the first loose page of the Detail of Ayes and Noes is

    "Mr. Gorham | | | | | | |

      Mr. Rutledge |."

This is undoubtedly the vote for chairman of the committee of the whole. John Quincy Adams notes: "The vote for Rutledge was probably Gorham's." See Appendix A, CCCXXVIII.

into a Committee of the whole House to consider of the State of the American union. — Mr Gorham in the Chair:

The propositions offered yesterday to the consideration of the House by Mr Randolph were read — and on motion of Mr Randolph, seconded by Mr G. Morris

That the consideration of the first resolution contained in the said propositions be postponed.

it passed in the affirmative.

It was then moved by Mr Randolph and seconded by Mr G Morris to substitute the following resolution in the place of the first resolution

Resolved that an union of the States, merely fœderal, will not accomplish the objects proposed by the articles of confederation, namely "common defence, security of liberty, and general welfare.

It was moved by Mr Butler seconded by Mr Randolph to postpone the consideration of the said resolution in order to take up the following resolution submitted by Mr Randolph namely

Resolved that a national government ought to be established consisting of a supreme legislative, judiciary and executive.

It was moved by Mr Read seconded by Mr C. C. Pinckney to postpone the consideration of the last resolution in order to take up the following

Resolved That in order to carry into execution the design of the States in forming this convention and to accomplish the objects proposed by the confederation "a more effective government consisting of a Legislative, Judiciary, and Executive ought to be established"

On the question to postpone, in order to take up the last resolution, the question was lost.

On motion to agree to the said resolution moved by Mr Butler it passed in the affirmative [ayes — 6; noes — 1; divided — 1.] [2] — and the resolution, as agreed to, is as follows.

Resolved that it is the opinion of this Committee that a

---

[2] Vote 2, Detail of Ayes and Noes, see below note 6.

national government ought to be established consisting of a supreme Legislative, Judiciary, and Executive

The following resolution was then moved by Mr Randolph,

Resolved that the rights of suffrage in the national legislature ought to be proportioned to the quotas of contribution, or to the number of free inhabitants, as the one or the other rule may seem best in different cases.

It was moved by Mr Hamilton seconded by Mr Spaight that the resolution be altered so as to read

Resolved that the rights of suffrage in the national legislature ought to be proportioned to the number of free inhabitants

It was moved and seconded that the resolution be postponed — and on the question to postpone it passed in the affirmative

The following resolution was moved by Mr Randolph seconded by Mr Madison

Resolved that the rights of suffrage in the national legislature ought to be proportioned — it was moved and seconded to add the words "and not according to the present system" — On the question to agree to the amendment it passed in the affirmative. [Ayes — 7; noes — 0.] [3]

It was then moved and seconded so to alter the resolution that it should read

Resolved that the rights of suffrage in the national legislature ought not to be according

It was then moved and seconded to postpone the consideration of the last resolution — And, on the question to postpone, it passed in the affirmative

The following resolution was then moved by Mr Madison seconded by Mr G. Morris.

Resolved that the equality of suffrage established by the articles of confederation ought not to prevail in the national legislature and that an equitable ratio of representation ought to be substituted

---

[3] Vote 3, Detail of Ayes and Noes. This is, however, by no means certain, see below note 6.

It was moved and seconded to postpone the consideration of the last resolution

And on the question to postpone it passed in the affirmative. [Ayes — 7; noes — 1.] [4]

It was moved and seconded that the Committee do now rise.

---

[4] Vote 4, Detail of Ayes and Noes.   This is quite uncertain, see below note 6.

[5] This photograph reveals the carelessness with which the Secretary, William Jackson, kept certain of the records of the Convention (see INTRODUCTION, note 6). Subsequent pages were better arranged and are more serviceable, but as no dates are given, the assignment of votes is always more or less uncertain.   In the present edition the original is produced as closely as possible by typographic devices.   The votes have been assigned to the various days according to the editor's best judgment in the light of all evidence obtainable.   The numbers in brackets are prefixed to each vote by the editor for convenience of reference.

DETAIL OF AYES AND NOES [6]

[Loose Sheet]

	I N. H.	2 Massa:	3 C:	4 R. I.	5 N. Y.	6 N. J:	7 P:	8 D:	9 Mary:	10 V:	11 N.C.	12 S.C.	13. G.
[1]		aye	aye		no		no	aye		no	no	aye	
[2]		aye	no		divid.		aye	aye		aye	aye	aye	
[3]		aye	aye		aye		aye			aye	aye	aye	
[4]		aye	aye		aye		no	aye		aye	aye	aye	

[6] Vote 2 is readily identified by the records of Madison, Yates and McHenry. *Journal* ascribed vote 1 to the question immediately preceding, and Madison revised his record accordingly.   This is probably a mistake.   It is doubtful that a first tie vote would have been declared in the negative without comment or discussion (*cf.* last vote, *Records* of June 1).   It would seem more probable that vote 1 corresponds to the first vote recorded by Madison on May 29 (see *Records*, May 29 note 6).

Votes 3 and 4 evidently belong to this day's records as only eight votes were cast; on the following day, May 31, ten states were present and voted.   The only clue to the identifiction of vote 3 is the failure or refusal of Delaware to vote, which might point to any of the resolutions in favor of proportional suffrage.   *Journal* ascribes this vote to the question to postpone the resolution offered by Randolph and Madison, but it would seem to apply better to an earlier amendment of that resolution, to the effect that the rights of suffrage were to be "not according to the present system ".

Journal ascribes vote 4 to the first question on the following day, May 31.   But as above explained, it probably belongs to May 30.   It might be ascribed to the last question of the day, viz. Read's motion to postpone — Gouverneur Morris's opposition would account for Pennsylvania's negative vote.

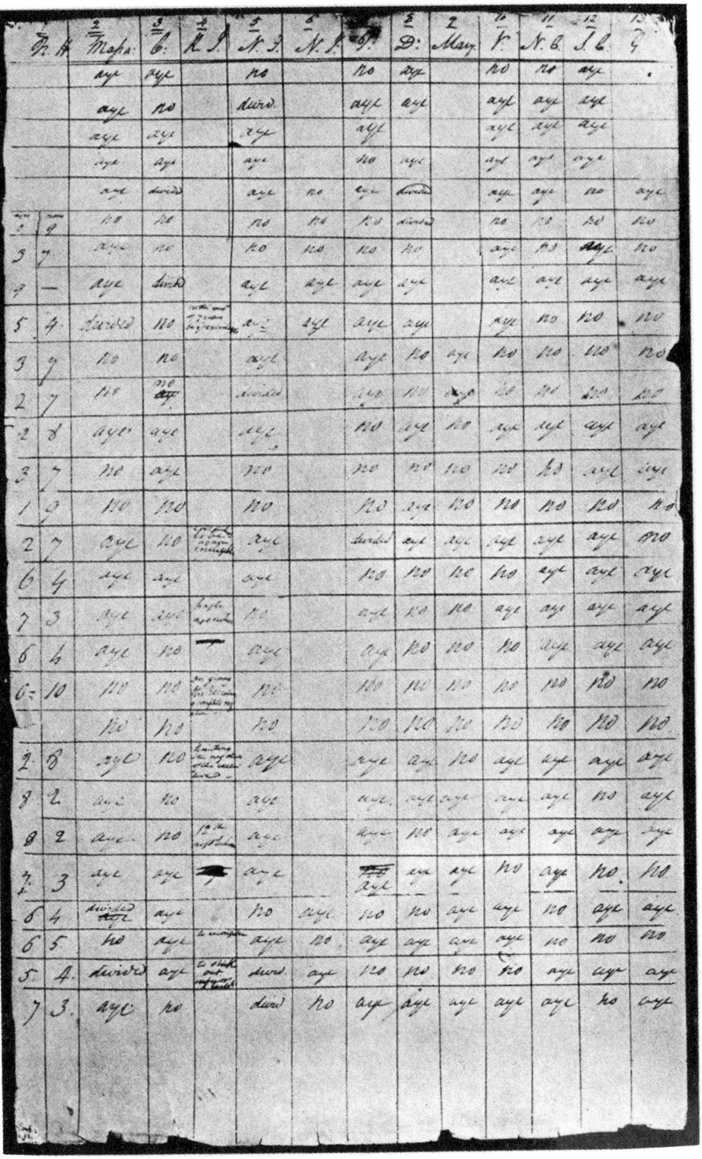

PHOTOGRAPH OF FIRST PAGE OF SECRETARY'S RECORD OF VOTES [5]

MADISON

Wednesday May 30.

⟨Roger Sherman (from Connecticut) took his seat.⟩[7]

The House went into Committee of the Whole on the State of the Union. Mr. Gorham was elected to the Chair by Ballot.

The propositions of Mr. Randolph which had been referred to the Committee being taken up. He moved on the suggestion of Mr G. Morris

that the first of his propositions to wit ⟨"Resolved[8] that the articles of Confederation ought to be so corrected & enlarged, as to accomplish the objects proposed by their institution; namely, common defence, security of liberty & general welfare⟩ ....

should be postponed in order to consider the 3 following.

1. that a Union of the States merely federal ⟨will not accomplish the objects proposed by the articles of Condeferation, namely common defence, security of liberty, & genl. welfare.⟩[9]

2. that no treaty or treaties among the whole or part of the States, as individual sovereignties, would be sufficient.

3 that a *national* Government ⟨ought to be established⟩ consisting of a *supreme* Legislative, Executive & Judiciary.

The motion for postponing was seconded by Mr. Govr. Morris and unanimously agreed to.

Some verbal criticisms were raised agst. the first proposition, and it was agreed ⟨on motion of Mr Butler seconded by Mr. Randolph,⟩[7] to pass on to the third, which underwent a discussion. less however on its general merits than on the force and extent of the particular terms *national*[10] & *supreme.*

Mr. Charles Pinkney wished to know of Mr. Randolph

---

[7] Taken from *Journal*, see also Appendix A, XXXV.

[8] Copied from *Journal*, — a blank space had been left in the original record.

[9] Copied from *Journal;* crossed out "was insufficient for the purpose of securing the liberty and happiness &c." See Appendix A, CCCLXXII.

[10] On the use of the term "national", see above May 29 note 12.

whether he meant to abolish the State Governts. altogether. Mr. R. replied that he meant by these general propositions merely to introduce the particular ones which explained the outlines of the system he had in view.

Mr. Butler said he had not made up his mind on the subject, and was open to the light which discussion might throw on it. ⟨After some general observations he concluded with saying that he had⟩[11] opposed the grant of powers to Congs. heretofore, because the whole power was vested in one body. The proposed distribution of the powers into different bodies changed the case, and would induce him to go great lengths.

Genl. Pinkney expressed a doubt whether the act of Congs. recommending the Convention,[12] or the Commissions of the deputies to it,[13] could authorize a discussion of a System founded on different principles from the federal Constitution.

Mr. Gerry seemed to entertain the same doubt.

Mr. Govr. Morris explained the distinction between a *federal* and *national, supreme,* Govt.; the former being a mere compact resting on the good faith of the parties; the latter having a compleat and *compulsive* operation. He contended that in all communities there must be one supreme power, and one only.

Mr. Mason observed that the present confederation was not only deficient in not providing for coercion & punishment agst. delinquent States; but argued very cogently that punishment could not ⟨in the nature of things be executed on⟩ the States collectively, and therefore that such a Govt. was necessary as could directly operate on individuals, and would punish those only whose guilt required it.

Mr. Sherman who took his seat to day, admitted that the Confederation had not given sufficient power to Congs. and that additional powers were necessary; particularly that of raising money which he said would involve many other powers. He admitted also that the General & particular jurisdictions

---

[11] Madison struck out his original note and two later revisions of it, all of which were attempts to phrase a sentence to the effect that Butler was "guarded" or "cautious" in these observations.

[12] See Appendix A, I.   [13] See Appendix B.

ought in no case to be concurrent. He seemed however not be disposed to Make too great inroads on the existing system; intimating as one reason, that it would be wrong to lose every amendment, by inserting such as would not be agreed to by the States

⟨It was moved by Mr. Read 2ded by Mr. Chas. Cotesworth Pinkney, to postpone the 3d. proposition last offered by Mr. Randolph viz that a national Government ought to be established consisting of a supreme legislative Executive and Judiciary," in order to take up the following — viz. "Resolved that in order to carry into execution the Design of the States in forming this Convention, and to accomplish the objects proposed by the Confederation a more effective Government consisting of a Legislative, Executive and Judiciary ought to be established." The motion to postpone for this purpose was lost:

Yeas Massachusetts, Connecticut. Delaware S. Carolina — 4 Nays N. Y. Pennsylvania, Virginia, North Carolina — 4⟩[14]

On the question ⟨as moved by Mr. Butler on the third proposition⟩[15] it was resolved in Committee of the whole that a national Governt. ought to be established consisting of a supreme Legislative Executive & Judiciary." Massts. being ay — Connect. no. N. York divided (Col. Hamilton ay Mr. Yates no) Pena. ay. Delaware ay. Virga. ay. N. C. ay. S. C. ay. [Ayes — 6; noes — 1; divided — 1.]

⟨The following Resolution being the 2d. of those proposed by Mr. Randolph was taken up. viz — "that the rights of suffrage in the National Legislature ought to be proportioned to the quotas of contribution, or to the number of free inhabitants, as the one or the other rule may seem best in different cases."⟩[16]

Mr. M⟨adison⟩ observing that the words ⟨"*or to the number*

---

[14] Taken from *Journal*. The vote probably should not be assigned to this question. See above note 6.

[15] Taken from *Journal*.

[16] Substance of this resolution was in the original, this wording was copied from *Journal*.

For further discussion of this subject of proportional representation, see *Records* of June 9, June 11, June 27–July 16. See also June 27 note 2.

of ⟩ *free inhabitants.*" might occasion debates which would divert the Committee from the general question whether the principle of representation should be changed, moved that they might be struck out.

Mr. King observed that the quotas of contribution which would alone remain as the measure of representation, would not answer; because waving every other view of the matter, the revenue might hereafter be so collected by the general Govt. that the sums respectively drawn from the States would ⟨not⟩ appear; and would besides be continually varying.

⟨Mr. Madison admitted the propriety of the observation, and that some better rule ought to be found.[17]

Col. Hamilton moved to alter the resolution so as to read "that the rights of suffrage in the national Legislature ought to be proportioned to the number of free inhabitants. Mr. Spaight 2ded. the motion.

It was then moved that the Resolution be postponed, which was agreed to.

Mr. Randolph and Mr. Madison then moved the following resolution — "that the rights of suffrage in the national Legislature ought to be proportioned"

It was moved and 2ded. to amend it by adding "and not according to the present system" — which was agreed to.

It was then moved and 2ded. to alter the resolution so as to read "that the rights of suffrage in the national Legislature ought not to be according to the present system."

It was then moved & 2ded. to postpone the Resolution moved by Mr. Randolph & Mr. Madison, which being agreed to;

Mr. Madison, moved, in order to get over the difficulties, the following resolution — "that the equality of suffrage established by the articles of Confederation ought not to prevail in the national Legislature, and that an equitable ratio of representation ought to be substituted" This was 2ded. by Mr. Govr. Morris, and being generally relished, would have been agreed to; when,⟩

---

[17] Of this and seven paragraphs following the original record contained only the first and last paragraphs (with slightly different wording). The record as it stands was taken from *Journal.*

Mr. Reed moved that the whole clause relating to the point of Representation be postponed; reminding the Come. that the deputies from Delaware were restrained by their commission from assenting to any change of the rule of suffrage, and in case such a change should be fixed on, it might become their duty to retire from the Convention.[18]

Mr. Govr. Morris observed that the valuable assistance of those members could not be lost without real concern, and that so early a proof of discord in the convention as a secession of a State, would add much to the regret; that the change proposed was however so fundamental an article in a national Govt. that it could not be dispensed with.

Mr. M⟨adison⟩ observed that whatever reason might have existed for the equality of suffrage when the Union was a federal one among sovereign States, it must cease when a national Governt. should be put into the place. In the former case, the acts of Congs. depended so much for their efficacy on the cooperation of the States, that these had a weight both within & without Congress, nearly in proportion to their extent and importance. In the latter case, as the acts of the Genl. Govt. would take effect without the intervention of the State legislatures, a vote from a small State wd. have the same efficacy & importance as ⟨a vote⟩ from a large one, and there was the same reason for ⟨different numbers⟩ of representatives from different States, as from Counties of different extents within particular States. He suggested as an expedient for at once taking the sense of the members on this point and saving the Delaware deputies from embarrassment, that the question should be taken in Committee, and the clause on report to the House ⟨be postponed without a question there⟩. This however did not appear to satisfy Mr. Read.

By several it was observed that no just construction of the Act of Delaware, could require or justify a secession of her deputies, even if the resolution were to be carried thro' the House as well as the Committee. It was finally agreed however that the clause should be postponed: it being understood

18 See *Records*, May 25, note 12.

that in the event the proposed change of representation would certainly be agreed to, no objection or difficulty being started from any other quarter ⟨than from Delaware.[19]

The motion of Mr. Read to postpone being agreed to

The Committee then rose. The Chairman reported progress, and the House having resolved to resume the subject in Committee tomorrow,[20]

Adjourned to 10 OClock⟩

[May][21] 30. — (pa. 38 to 47) Mr Sherman attended. In Comee of the whole — Mr Rs 1. res. was on his motion postponed. to consider three others introduced by him — the two first asserting the inefficiency of the federal & the 3d the necessity for a *national* & *supreme* govt. The latter after some discussion was resolved after debating the 2. res. on the right of suffrage it was postponed —

YATES

WEDNESDAY, MAY 30th, 1787.

Convention met pursuant to adjournment.

The convention, pursuant to order, resolved itself into a committee of the whole — Mr. Gorham (a member from Massachusetts) appointed chairman.

Mr. Randolph then moved his first resolve, to wit: "Re-"solved, that the articles of the confederation ought to be "so corrected and enlarged, as to accomplish the objects pro-"posed by their institution, namely, common defence, security "of liberty, and general welfare."

Mr. G. Morris observed, that it was an unnecesaary resolution, as the subsequent resolutions would not agree with it. It was then withdrawn by the proposer, and in lieu thereof the following were proposed, to wit:

---

[19] This and the remainder of Madison's records for this day were evidently based upon *Journal* and Yates.

[20] See further Appendix A, XXX.

[21] Memoranda by Madison, see May 25 note 13.

1. *Resolved,* That a union of the states, merely federal, will not accomplish the objects proposed by the articles of the confederation, namely, common defence, security of liberty, and general welfare.

2. *Resolved,* That no treaty or treaties among any of the states as sovereign, will accomplish or secure their common defence, liberty or welfare.

3. *Resolved,* That a national government ought to be established, consisting of a supreme judicial, legislative and executive.

In considering the question on the first resolve, various modifications were proposed, when Mr. Pinkney [22] observed, at last, that if the convention agreed to it, it appeared to him that their business was at an end; for as the powers of the house in general were to revise the present confederation, and to alter or amend it as the case might require; to determine its insufficiency or incapability of amendment or improvement, must end in the dissolution of the powers.

This remark had its weight, and in consequence of it, the 1st and 2d resolve was dropt, and the question agitated on the third.

This last resolve had also its difficulties; the term *supreme* required explanation — It was asked whether it was intended to annihilate state governments? It was answered, only so far as the powers intended to be granted to the new government should clash with the states, when the latter was to yield.

For the resolution — Massachusetts, Pennsylvania, Delaware, Virginia, North-Carolina, South-Corolina.

Against it — Connecticut, New-York divided, Jersey and the other states unrepresented.

The next question was on the following resolve:

In substance that the mode of the present representation was unjust — the suffrage ought to be in proportion to number or property.

---

[22] Madison and McHenry ascribe expressions similar to this to Gen. C. C. Pinckney. Yates does not always distinguish between General Charles Cotesworth Pinckney and Mr. Charles Pinckney.

To this Delaware objected, in consequence of the restrictions in their credentials, and moved to have the consideration thereof postponed, to which the house agreed.

Adjourned to to-morrow.

McHENRY

May 30.

Mr. Randolph wished the house to dissent from the first proposition on the paper delivered in to the convention in order to take up the following

1st. That a union of the States merely federal will not accomplish the object proposed by the articles of confederation, namely "common defence, security of liberty, and general welfare."

2. That no treaty or treaties between the whole or a less number of the States in their sovereign capacities will accomplish their common defence, liberty, or welfare.

3. That therefore a national government ought to be established consisting of a supreme legislature, judi[c]iary and executive.

On a question taken on the last proposition after various attempts to amend it, the same was agreed to. For it, Massachusets Pennsylv. Delaware, Virginia, N. Carolina, and S. Carolina — against it Connecticut. New York divided.

The Committee then proceeded to consider the 2 Resolution in Mr. Randolphs paper viz

That the rights of suffrage in the national legislature ought to be proportioned to the quotas of contribution or to the number of free inhabitants as the one or the other rule may seem best in different cases.

As this gave the large States the most absolute controul over the lesser ones it met with opposition which produced an adjournment without any determination.

The Committee of the whole to sit to-morrow.

May 30th [23]

1st resolution from Mr. Randol.

Mr. R. wishes to have that resol. dissented to.   The resol. postponed to take up the following:

1st. That a union of the States merely fœderal will not accomplish the object proposed by the articles of confederation, namely, "common defence, security of liberty, and general welfare".

Mr. C. Pinkney wishes to know whether the establishment of this Resolution is intended as a ground for a consolidation of the several States into one.

Mr. Randol has nothing further in contemplation than what the propositions he has submitted yesterday has expressed.

2. Resolved that no treaty or treaties between the whole or a less number of the States in their sovereign capacities will accomplish their common defence, liberty or welfare.

3. Resolved therefore that a national governmen ought to be established consisting of a supreme legislature, judiciary and executive.

Mr. Whythe presumes from the silence of the house that they gentn. are prepared to pass on the resolution and proposes its being put.

Mr. Butler — does not think the house prepared, that he is not.   Wishes Mr. Randolph to shew that the existence of the States cannot be preserved by any other mode than a national government.

Gen. Pinkney — Thinks agreeing to the resolve is declaring that the convention does not act under the authority of the recommendation of Congress.

The first resolution postponed to take up the 3d. viz — Resolved that a national government ought to be established consisting of a supreme legislature, judiciary and executive.

1787, 21 Febry.   Resolution of Congress.

Resolved that in the opinion of Congress it is expedient

---

[23] This is from a loose folio sheet, in Dr. McHenry's handwriting, which was found lying in the book containing the main body of his notes.

that on the 2d Monday of May next a convention of delegates who shall have been appointed by the several States
to be held at Philada. for the sole and expres purpose of *revising the articles of confederation,* and reporting to Congress and
the several legislatures, such alterations and provisions therein
as shall when agreeed to in Congress, and confirmed by the
States, render the *fœderal constitution,* adequate to the exigencies
of government and the preservation of the union."

Mr. Randolph explains the intention of the 3d Resolution.
Repeats the substance of his yesterdays observations. It is
only meant to give the national government a power to defend
and protect itself. To take therefore from the respective
legislatures or States, no more soverignty than is competent
to this end.

Mr. Dickinson. Under obligations to the gentlemen who
brought forward the systems laid before the house yesterday.
Yet differs from the mode of proceeding to which the resolutions or propositions before the Committee lead. Would propose a more simple mode. All agree that the confederation
is defective all agree that it ought to be amended. We are a
nation altho' consisting of parts or States — we are also confederated, and he hopes we shall always remain confederated.
The enquiry should be —

1. What are the legislative powers which we should vest
in Congress.

2. What judiciary powers.

3 What executive powers.

We may resolve therefore, in order to let us into the business.
That the confederation is defective; and then proceed to the
definition of such powers as may be thought adequate to the
objects for which it was instituted.

Mr. E. Gerry. Does not rise to speak to the *merits* of the
question before the Committee but to the *mode.*

A distinction has been made between a *federal* and *national*
government. We ought not to determine that there is this
distinction for if we do, it is questionable not only whether
this convention can propose an government totally different
or whether Congress itself would have a right to pass such a

resolution as that before the house. The commission from Massachusetts empowers the deputies to proceed agreeably to the recommendation of Congress. This the foundation of the convention. If we have a right to pass this resolution we have a right to annihilate the confederation.

Proposes — In the opinion of this convention, provision should be made for the establishment of a fœderal legislative, judiciary, and executive.

Governeur Morris. Not yet ripe for a decision, because men seem to have affixed different explanations to the terms before the house. 1. We are not now under a fœderal government. 2. There is no such thing. A fœderal government is that which has a right to compel every part to do its duty. The fœderal gov. has no such compelling capacities, whether considered in their legislative, judicial or Executive qualities.

The States in their appointments Congress in their recommendations point directly to the establishment of a *supreme* government capable of "the common defence, security of liberty and general welfare.

Cannot conceive of a government in which there can exist two *supremes*. A federal agreement which each party may violate at pleasure cannot answer the purpose. One government better calculated to prevent wars or render them less expensive or bloody than many.

We had better take a supreme government now, than a despot twenty years hence — for come he must.

Mr. Reed, Genl. Pky [Pinckney] 2dng. proposes — In order to carry into execution the design of the States in   this meeting and to accomplish the *objects* proposed by the confederation resolved that A more effective government consisting of a legislative judiciary and executive ought to be established.

In order to carry into execution

Mr. R. King — The object of the motion from Virginia, an establishment of a government that is to act upon the whole people of the U. S.

The object of the motion from Delaware seems to have

application merely to the strenghtening the confederation by some additional powers —

Mr. Maddison — The motion does go to bring out the sense of the house — whether the States shall be governed by one power.   If agreed to it will decide nothing.   The meaning of the States that the confed. is defect. and ought to be amended.   In agreeing to the . . .[24]

[24] End of paper.   Unfinished.

THURSDAY, MAY 31, 1787.

JOURNAL
Thursday May 31. 1787.

The honorable William Pierce Esquire, a Deputy of the State of Georgia attended and took his seat [1]

The following credentials were produced and read

(here insert the credentials of Mr Few and Mr Pierce) [2]

The order of the day being read,

The House resolved itself into a Committee of the whole House to consider of the State of the American Union

Mr President left the Chair

Mr Gorham took the Chair of the Committee

Mr President resumed the Chair

Mr Gorham reported from the Committee that the Committee had made a further progress in the matter to them referred; and had directed him to move that they may have leave to sit again.

Resolved that this House will to-morrow again resolve itself into a Committee of the whole House to consider of the state of the American union

And then the House adjourned till to-morrow at 10 o'clock A M.

In a Committee of the whole House

Thursday May 31. 1787.

Mr Gorham in the Chair.

It was moved & seconded that the Committee proceed to the consideration of the following resolution (submitted by Mr Randolph) namely

"Resolved that the national legislature ought to consist of two branches." —

---

[1] See Appendix A, XXXI.   [2] See Appendix B.

45

And on the question to agree to the said resolution it passed in the affirmative.[3]

It was then moved & seconded to proceed to the consideration of the following clause of the fourth resolution (submitted by Mr Randolph) namely

"Resolved that the members of the first branch of the national legislature ought to be elected by the people of the several States:"

and on the question to agree to the said clause of the fourth resolution

it passed in the affirmative [Ayes—6; noes — 2; divided—2.][4]

It was then moved and seconded to postpone the consideration of the remaining clauses of the said fourth resolution

and on the question to postpone the remaining clauses of the said fourth resolution

it passed in the affirmative

[Ayes — o; noes — 9; divided — 1.][5]

It was then moved and seconded to proceed to the consideration of the following resolution (being the fifth submitted by Mr Randolph)

Resolved that the members of the second branch of the national legislature ought to be elected by those of the first: out of — &ca

and on the question to agree to the said fifth resolution

it passed in the negative   [Ayes — 3; noes — 7.][6]

It was then moved and seconded to proceed to the consideration of the following resolution (being the sixth submitted by Mr Randolph)

Resolved "that each branch ought to possess the right of originating acts:"

---

[3] *Journal* ascribes to this question Detail of Ayes and Noes, Vote 4, which is probably a mistake. (See May 30, note 6.) Madison's original record made the vote unanimous, which is apparently confirmed by Yates and McHenry.

[4] Vote 5, Detail of Ayes and Noes.

[5] Question omitted, to which belongs Vote 6, Detail of Ayes and Noes, see Madison's note, below.

[6] Vote 7, Detail of Ayes and Noes. *Journal* mistakenly assigns Vote 6, this to question.

"That the national legislature ought to be empowered"
"to enjoy the legislative rights vested in Congress by the
confederation; and moreover

To legislate in all cases, to which the separate States are
incompetent: [Ayes — 9; noes — o; divided — 1.][7] or

in which the harmony of the united States may be interrupted by the exercise of individual legislation

To negative all laws, passed by the several States, contravening, in the opinion of the national legislature, the articles
of union: (the following words were added to this clause on
motion of Mr Franklin, "or any Treaties subsisting under the
authority of the union

Questions being taken separately on the foregoing clauses
of the sixth resolution they were agreed to.

It was then moved and seconded to postpone the consideration of the last clause of the sixth resolution, namely,

"to call forth the force of the union against any member
of the union, failing to fulfil it's duty under the articles thereof."

on the question to postpone the consideration of the said
clause   it passed in the affirmative

DETAIL OF AYES AND NOES

	1 N. H.		2 Massa:	3 C:	4 R. I.	5 N. Y.	6 N. J:	7 P:	8 D:	9 Mary:	10 V:	11 N. C.	12 S. C.	13. G.
[5]			aye	divided		aye	no	aye	divided		aye	aye	no	aye
	ayes	noes												
[6]	o	9	no	no		no	no	no	divided		no	no	no	no
[7]	3	7	aye	no		no	no	no	no		aye	no	aye	no
[8]	9	—	aye	divided		aye	aye	aye	aye		aye	aye	aye	aye

MADISON

Thursday May 31.

⟨William Pierce from Georgia took his seat.⟩[8]
In Committee of the whole on Mr. R.⟨andolph's⟩ propositions.

---

[7] Vote 8, Detail of Ayes and Noes.   Assigned here because Madison does so.
[8] Taken from *Journal*.

⟨The 3d. Resolution⟩ "that the national Legislature ought to consist of two branches" was agreed to without debate or dissent, ⟨except that of Pennsylvania, given probably from complaisance to Docr. Franklin who was understood to be partial to a single House of Legislation.⟩ [9]

⟨Resol: 4. first clause⟩ "that the ⟨members of the first branch of the National Legislature⟩ ought to be elected by the people of ⟨the several⟩ States" ⟨being taken up,⟩ [10]

Mr. Sherman opposed the election by the people, insisting that it ought to be by the ⟨State⟩ Legislatures. The people he said, ⟨immediately⟩ should have as little to do as may be about the Government. They want information and are constantly liable to be misled.

Mr. Gerry. The evils we experience flow from the excess of democracy. The people do not want virtue; but are the dupes of pretended patriots.[11] In Massts. it has been fully confirmed by experience that they are daily misled into the most baneful measures and opinions by the false reports circulated by designing men, and which no one on the spot can refute. One principal evil arises from the want of due provision for those employed in the administration of Governnt. It would seem to be a maxim of democracy to starve the public servants. He mentioned the popular clamour in Massts. for the reduction of salaries and the attack made on that of the Govr. though secured by the spirit of the Constitution itself. He had he said been too republican heretofore: he was still however republican, but had been taught by experience the danger of the levilling spirit.

Mr. Mason. argued strongly for an election of the larger branch by the people. It was to be the grand depository of the democratic principle of the Govt. It was, so to speak, to be our House of Commons — It ought to know & sympathise with every part of the community; and ought therefore to be

---

[9] Revised to conform with what is probably a mistake in *Journal*, see above, note 3. But note also Appendix A, XXXIV, CXCVII.

[10] Revised from *Journal*.

[11] Originally "demagogues"; "pretended patriots" may be a correction made at the time or later.

taken not only from different parts of the whole republic, but also from different districts of the larger members of it, which had in several instances particularly in Virga., different interests and views arising from difference of produce, of habits &c &. He admitted that we had been too democratic but was afraid we sd. incautiously run into the opposite extreme. We ought to attend to the rights of every class of the people. He had often wondered at the indifference of the superior classes of society to this dictate of humanity & policy, considering that however affluent their circumstances, or elevated their situations, might be, the course of a few years, not only might but certainly would, distribute their posterity throughout the lowest classes of Society. Every selfish motive therefore, every family attachment, ought to recommend such a system of policy as would provide no less carefully for the rights — and happiness of the lowest than of the highest orders of Citizens.

Mr. Wilson contended strenuously for drawing the most numerous branch of the Legislature immediately from the people. He was for raising the federal pyramid to a considerable altitude, and for that reason wished to give it as broad a basis as possible. No government could long subsist without the confidence of the people. In a republican Government this confidence was peculiarly essential. He also thought it wrong to increase the weight of the State Legislatures by making them the electors of the national Legislature. All interference [12] between the general and local Governmts. should be obviated as much as possible. On examination it would be found that the opposition of States to federal measures had proceded much more from the Officers of the States, than from the people at large.

Mr. Madison considered the popular election of one branch of the national Legislature as essential to every plan of free Government. He observed that in some of the States one branch of the Legislature was composed of men already removed from the people by an intervening body of electors.

---

[12] Crossed out "competition".

That if the first branch of the general legislature should be elected by the State Legislatures, the second branch elected by the first — the Executive by the second together with the first; and other appointments again made for subordinate purposes by the Executive, the people would be lost sight of altogether; and the necessary sympathy between them and their rulers and officers, too little felt. He was an advocate for the policy of refining the popular appointments by successive filtrations, but thought it might be pushed too far. He wished the expedient to be resorted to only in the appointment of the second branch of the Legislature, and in the Executive & judiciary branches of the Government. He thought too that the great fabric to be raised would be more stable and durable if it should rest on the solid foundation of the people themselves, than if it should stand merely on the pillars of the Legislatures.

Mr. Gerry did not like the election by the people. The maxims taken from the British constitution were often fallacious when applied to our situation which was extremely different. Experience he said had shewn that the State Legislatures drawn immediately from the people did not always possess their confidence. He had no objection however to an election by the people if it were so qualified that men of honor & character might not be unwilling to be joined in the appointments. He seemed to think the people might nominate a certain number out of which the State legislatures should be bound to choose.

Mr. Butler thought an election by the people an impracticable mode.

On the question for an election of the first branch of the national Legislature, by the people, Massts. ay. Connect. divd. N. York ay. N. Jersey no. Pena. ay. Delawe. divd. Va. ay. N. C. ay. S. C. no. Georga. ay. [Ayes — 6; noes — 2; divided — 2.]

The ⟨remaining⟩ Clauses ⟨of Resolution 4th.⟩[13] relating to the qualifications of members of the National Legislature

---

[13] Revised according to *Journal*.

⟨being⟩ postpd. nem. con. as entering too much into detail
for general propositions;

The ⟨Committee proceeded to Resolution 5,⟩ "that the
second, (or senatorial) branch of the National Legislature
⟨ought to⟩ be chosen by the first branch out of persons nominated by the State Legislatures." [13]

Mr. Spaight contended [14] that the 2d. branch ought to be
chosen by the State Legislatures and moved an amendment
to that effect.

Mr. Butler apprehended that the taking so many powers
out of the hands of the States as was proposed, tended to
destroy all that balance ⟨and security⟩ of interests among
the States which it was necessary to preserve; and called on
Mr. Randolph the mover of the propositions, to explain the
extent of his ideas, and particularly the number of members
he meant to assign to this second branch.

Mr. Randf. observed that he had at the time of offering
his propositions stated his ideas as far as the nature of general
propositions required; that details made no part of the plan,
and could not perhaps with propriety have been introduced.
If he was to give an opinion as to the number of the second
branch, he should say that it ought to be much smaller than
that of the first; so small as to be exempt from the passionate
proceedings to which numerous assemblies are liable. He
observed that the general object was to provide a cure for the
evils under which the U. S. laboured; that in tracing these
evils to their origin every man had found it in the turbulence
and follies of democracy: that some check therefore was to
be sought for agst. this tendency of our Governments: and
that a good Senate seemed most likely to answer the purpose.

Mr. King reminded the Committee that the choice of the
second branch as proposed (by Mr. Spaight) viz. by the State
Legislatures would be impracticable, unless it was to be very
numerous, or *the idea of proportion* among the States was to
be disregarded. According to this *idea*, there must be 80 or

---

[14] According to Pierce, all of the discussion following would seem to have taken
place before the determination of the question of the election of the first branch.

100 members to entitle Delaware to the choice of one of them.—
Mr. Spaight withdrew his motion.

Mr. Wilson opposed both a nomination by the State Legislatures, and an election by the first branch of the national
Legislature, because the second branch of the latter, ought to
be independent of both. He thought both branches of the
National Legislature ought to be chosen by the people, but
was not prepared with a specific proposition. He suggested
the mode of chusing the Senate of N. York. to wit of uniting
several election districts, for one branch, in chusing members
for the other branch, as a good model.

Mr. Madison observed that such a mode would destroy
the influence of the smaller States associated with larger ones
in the same district; as the latter would [15] chuse from within
themselves, altho' better men might be found in the former.
The election of Senators in Virga. where large & small counties
were often formed into one district for the purpose, had illustrated this consequence Local partiality, would often prefer
a resident within the County or State, to a candidate of superior merit residing out of it. Less merit also in a resident
would be more known throughout his own State.

Mr. Sherman favored an election of one member by each
of the State Legislatures,

Mr. Pinkney moved to strike out the "nomination by the
State Legislatures." On this question.

* Massts. no. Cont. no. N. Y. no. N. J. no. Pena. no. Del.
divd. Va. no. N. C. no. S. C. no Georg no. [Ayes — 0; noes
— 9; divided — 1.]

On the whole question for electing by the first branch out of
nominations by the State Legislatures, Mass. ay. Cont. no.
N. Y. no. N. Jersey. no. Pena. no. Del. no. Virga. ay. N. C.
no. S. C. ay. Ga. no. [Ayes — 3; noes — 7.]

So the clause was disagreed to & a chasm left in this part
of the plan.

The ⟨sixth Resolution⟩ stating the cases in which the

* ⟨this question omitted in the printed Journal; & the votes applied to the
succeeding one, instead of the votes as here stated.⟩ [16]

---

[15] Crossed out "be sure to ".   [16] McHenry confirms Madison on this point.

national Legislature ought to legislate was next taken into discussion. On the question whether each branch shd. originate laws, there was an unanimous affirmative without debate. On the question for transferring all the Legislative powers of the ⟨existing⟩ Congs. to this Assembly,[17] there was also a silent affirmative nem. con.

On the proposition for giving "Legislative power in all cases to which the State Legislatures were individually incompetent".

Mr. Pinkney, & Mr. Rutledge objected to the vagueness of the term *incompetent*, and said they could not well decide how to vote until they should see an exact enumeration of the powers comprehended by this definition.[18]

Mr. Butler repeated his fears that we were running into an extreme in taking away the powers of the States, and called on Mr. Randolp for the extent of his meaning.

Mr. Randolph disclaimed any intention to give indefinite powers to the national Legislature, declaring that he was entirely opposed to such an inroad on the State jurisdictions, and that he did not think any considerations whatever could ever change his determination. His opinion was fixed on this point.

Mr. Madison said that he had brought with him into the Convention a strong bias in favor of an enemeration and definition of the powers necessary to be exercised by the national Legislature; but had also brought doubts concerning its practicability. His wishes remained unaltered; but his doubts had become stronger. What his opinion might ultimately be he could not yet tell. But he should shrink from nothing which should be found essential to such a form of Govt. as would provide for the safety, liberty and happiness of the Community. This being the end of all our deliberations, all the necessary means for attaining it must, however reluctantly, be submitted to.

On the question for giving powers, in cases to which the States are not competent,

---

[17] See Appendix A, CLXXXIII.
[18] Pierce adds quite a little to this discussion.

Massts. ay. Cont. divd. (Sharman no Elseworth ay) N. Y. ay. N. J. ay. Pa. ay. Del. ay. Va. ay. N. C. ay, S. Carolina ay. Georga. ay. [Ayes — 9; noes — o; divided — 1.]

The other clauses giving powers necessary to preserve harmony among the States ⟨to negative all State laws contravening in the opinion of the Nat Leg the articles of Union down to the last clause, (the words "or any treaties subsisting under the authority of the Union", being added after the words "contravening &c. the articles of the Union"; on motion of Dr. Franklin)⟩[19] were agreed to witht. debate or dissent.

The ⟨last⟩ clause ⟨of Resolution 6. authorizing⟩ an exertion of the force of the whole agst. a delinquent State came next into consideration.

Mr. ⟨Madison⟩, observed that the more he reflected on the use of force, the more he doubted the practicability, the justice and the efficacy of it when applied to people collectively and not individually. — , A Union of the States ⟨containing such an ingredient⟩ seemed to provide for its own destruction. The use of force agst. a State, would look more like a declaration of war, than an infliction of punishment, and would probably be considered by the party attacked as a dissolution of all previous compacts by which it might be bound. He hoped that such a system would be framed as might render this recourse unnecessary, and moved that the clause be postponed.[20] This motion was agreed to nem. con.

⟨The Committee then rose & the House
Adjourned⟩[21]

[May] 31.[22]. — Mr Pierce attended.

The 3. res. dividing the Nat. Leg. into 2 branches agreed to without debate.

The 1st clause of 4th res. referring the election of the first branch to the people debated and carried. 6 ays. 2 noes —

---

[19] Taken from *Journal*.
[20] Madison struck out after postponed "till the contrary should be found on trial to be the case ".
[21] See further Appendix A, XXXI.
[22] Memoranda by Madison, see May 25 note 13.

2 divided.   The other clauses postponed.   The 5. Res. for
electing the 2d branch by the first from nominations of State
Legislatures, & after debate proposed amendment to leave out
the nomination, negatived.

YATES

THURSDAY, MAY 31st, 1787.

Met pursuant to adjournment.

This day the state of Jersey was represented, so that there
were now ten states in convention.

The house went again into committee of the whole, Mr.
Gorham in the chair.

The 3d resolve, to wit, "That the national legislature
"ought to consist of two branches," was taken into consideration, and without any debate agreed to. (N. B. As a previous
resolution had already been agreed to, to have a supreme legislature, I could not see any objection to its being in two branches.)

The 4th resolve, "That the members of the first branch
"of the national legislature ought to be elected by the people
"of the several states," was opposed; and strange to tell, by
Massachusetts and Connecticut, who supposed they ought
to be chosen by the legislatures; and Virginia supported the
resolve, alledging that this ought to be the democratic branch
of government, and as such, immediately vested in the people.

This question was carried, but the remaining part of the
resolve detailing the powers, was postponed.

The 5th resolve, That the members of the second branch
of the national legislature ought to be elected by those of the
first out of a proper number of persons nominated by the individual legislatures, and the detail of the mode of election and
duration of office, was postponed.[23]

The 6th resolve is taken in detail: "That each branch
ought to possess the right of originating acts."   Agreed to.

"That the national legislature ought to be empowered

---

[23] Journal, Madison, and McHenry all agree that this resolution was negatived,
not postponed.

to enjoy the legislative rights vested in congress by the confederation." — Agreed to.

"And, moreover, to legislate in all cases to which the separate states are incompetent." — Agreed to.

KING

Thursday 31 May

The first br. to be elected by ye. People.

Ger. opposed to the measure, & prefers appointments by the state Legis — because the people are not imformed —

Mason. in favor, because the first Br. is to represent the people, we must not go too far, we must preserve a portion of Democ. our own Children will in a short time be among the genl. mass —

Wilson — agrees wt. Mason. we ought to adopt the measure to secure the popular Confidence and to destroy the rivalry between the State & Genl. Govts — They will in this way both proceed immediately from the people &c —

Madison — agrees with Wilson — this mode immediately introduces the people, and naturally inspires that affection for the Genl. Govt. wh. takes place towards our own offspring — The alternative of a Legislative appt. removes the Genl. Govt. too far from the People — in Maryland the Senate is two removes from the People, a Depy. appointed by ym. will be three, the first Br. having power to appt. the 2d. Br. they will be four, the Genl. Legis. appts. the Executive which will be five removes from the People — if the Election is made by the Peop. in large Districts there will be no Danger of Demagogues —

Carried thus "that the first Br. be elected by the people of the sevl. States.

Mass. NYk. Penn. Virg. N. Car. & Georg. Ay
Cont. & Delr. divd.
N Jersey & S. Caro. no —[24]

---

[24] [Endorsed:] *31 May*, | Representatives to be chosen by the People & not State Legislrs | Mass. NYk. Pen. Virg. N Car. Geor aye | Con & Del. divided — | N Jersey & So. Car. no —

P I E R C E [25]

On the 30th May Govr. Randolph brought forward the principles of a federal Government. The idea suggested was, a national Government to consist of three branches. Agreed. The Legislature to consist of two branches.[26]

Resolved that the first branch of the Legislature ought to be elected by the People of the several States.

A debate arose on this point.

Mr. Sherman thought the State Legislatures were better qualified to elect the Members than the people were.

Mr. Gerry was of the same opinion.

Mr. Mason was of the opinion that the appointment of the Legislature coming from the people would make the representation actual, but if it came from the State Legislatures it will be only virtual.

Mr. Wilson thought that one branch of the Legislature ought to be drawn from the people, because on the great foundation of the people all Government ought to rest. He would wish to see the new Constitution established on a broad basis, and rise like a pyramid to a respectable point.

Mr. Maddison was of the opinion that the appointment of the Members to the first branch of the national Legislature ought to be made by the people for two reasons, — one was that it would inspire confidence, and the other that it would induce the Government to sympathize with the people.

Mr. Gerry was of opinion that the representation would not be equally good if the people chose them, as if the appointment was made by the State Legislatures. He also touched on the principles of liberal support, and reprobated that idea of œconomy in the different States that has been so injuriously practised.

---

[25] There are no dates given in Pierce's notes and they are assigned to the records of different days in this edition upon internal evidence alone.

[26] According to the Journal, Pierce attended the Convention May 31, for the first time. In beginning his notes he summed up in a few words what had already taken place. It was on the 29th and not the 30th that Randolph presented the resolutions in question. But it was the 30th when it was agreed that the government should consist "of a supreme legislative, executive, and judiciary."

Mr. Strong would agree to the principle, provided it would undergo a certain modification, but pointed out nothing.

Mr. Butler was opposed to the appointment by the people, because the State Legislatures he thought better calculated to make choice of such Members as would best answer the purpose.

Mr. Spaight thought it necessary previous to the decision on this point that the mode of appointing the Senate should be pointed out. He therefore moved that the second branch of the Legislature should be appointed by the State Legislatures.[27]

Mr. King observed that the Question called for was premature, and out of order, — that unless we go on regularly from one principle to the other we shall draw out our proceedings to an endless length.

Mr. Butler called on Govr. Randolph to point out the number of Men necessary for the Senate, for on a knowledge of that will depend his opinion of the style and manner of appointing the first branch.

Mr. Randolph said he could not then point out the exact number of Members for the Senate, but he would observe that they ought to be less than the House of Commons. He was for offering such a check as to keep up the balance, and to restrain, if possible, the fury of democracy. He thought it would be impossible for the State Legislatures to appoint the Senators, because it would not produce the check intended. The first branch of the fœderal Legislature should have the appointment of the Senators, and then the check would be compleat.

Butler said that until the number of the Senate could be known it would be impossible for him to give a vote on it.

Mr. Wilson was of opinion that the appointment of the 2d branch ought to be made by the people provided the mode of election is as he would have it, and that is to divide the union into districts from which the Senators should be chosen. He

---

[27] According to Madison all of this discussion was after the 5th resolution was formally before the Committee, but as Pierce reports the debate it seems clearly to have preceded.

hopes that a fœderal Government may be established that will insure freedom and yet be vigorous.

Mr. Maddison thinks the mode pointed out in the original propositions the best.

Mr. Butler moved to have the proposition relating to the first branch postponed, in order to take up another, — which was that the second branch of the Legislature consist of blank.

Mr. King objected to the postponement for the reasons which he had offered before.

Mr. Sherman was of opinion that if the Senate was to be appointed by the first branch and out of that Body that it would make them too dependent, and thereby destroy the end for which the Senate ought to be appointed.

Mr. Mason was of opinion that it would be highly improper to draw the Senate out of the first branch; that it would occasion vacancies which would cost much time, trouble, and expence to have filled up, — besides which it would make the Members too dependent on the first branch.

Mr. Chs. Pinckney said he meant to propose to divide the Continent into four Divisions, out of which a certain number of persons shd. be nominated, and out of that nomination to appoint a Senate.

I was myself of opinion that it would be right first to know how the Senate should be appointed, because it would determine many Gentlemen how to vote for the choice of Members for the first branch, — it appeared clear to me that unless we established a Government that should carry at least some of its principles into the mass of the people, we might as well depend upon the present confederation. If the influence of the States is not lost in some part of the new Government we never shall have any thing like a national institution. But in my opinion it will be right to shew the sovereignty of the State in one branch of the Legislature, and that should be in the Senate.

On the proposition in the words following — "to legislate in all cases where the different States shall prove incompetent."

Mr. Sherman was of opinion that it would be too indifinitely expressed, — and yet it would be hard to define all the powers by detail. It appeared to him that it would be improper for the national Legislature to negative all the Laws that were connected with the States themselves.

Mr. Maddison said it was necessary to adopt some general principles on which we should act, — that we were wandering from one thing to another without seeming to be settled in any one principle.

Mr. Wythe observed that it would be right to establish general principles before we go into detail, or very shortly Gentlemen would find themselves in confusion, and would be obliged to have recurrence to the point from whence they sat out.

Mr. King was of opinion that the principles ought first to be established before we proceed to the framing of the Act. He apprehends that the principles only go so far as to embrace all the power that is given up by the people to the Legislature, and to the fœderal Government, but no farther.

Mr. Randolph was of opinion that it would be impossible to define the powers and the length to which the federal Legislature ought to extend just at this time.

Mr. Wilson observed that it would be impossible to enumerate the powers which the federal Legislature ought to have.

Mr. Maddison said he had brought with him a strong prepossession for the defining of the limits and powers of the federal Legislature, but he brought with him some doubts about the practicability of doing it: — at present he was convinced it could not be done.

McHENRY

31 May

Mr. Randolph motioned to take into consideration, vz. That the national legislature ought to consist of two branches.
agreed to.

Part of the 4 resolution moved. vz. That the members of the first branch ought to be elected by the people of the several States.
6 States aff. 2 neg. 2 divided.

5 Reso. so far as follows taken up vz. That the members
of the second branch of the national legislature ought to be
elected by those of the first out of a proper number of persons nominated by the individual legislatures.

Neg. 7. affirm 3. aff. Mass. S. C. Virginia.

Motioned vz.

That each branch ought to possess the right of originating
acts.

agreed.

That the national legislature ought to be empowered to
enjoy the *legislative rights vested in Congress by the confedn.* and *moreover* to legislate in all cases to which the
seperate States are incompetent.

agreed.

or in which the harmony of the U. S. may be interrupted
by the exercise of individual legislation.

agreed.

To negative all laws passed by the several States contravening in the opinion of the national legislature the articles
of union, (or any treaty subsisting under the authority
of the union, added by Dr. Franklin).

agreed.

And to call forth the force of the union against any member
of the union failing to fulfil its duty under the articles
thereof.

postponed.

Mr. E. Gery thought this clause "ought to be expressed
so as the people might not understand it to prevent their
being alarmed".

This idea rejected on account of its *artifice*, and because the
system without such a declaration gave the government the
means to secure itself.

FRIDAY, JUNE 1, 1787.

JOURNAL

Friday June 1. 1787.

The honorable William Houstoun, Esq a Deputy of the State of Georgia, attended and took his seat.

The following credential was produced and read

(here insert Mr Houstoun's credential) [1]

The Order of the day being read,

The House resolved itself into a Committee of the whole House to consider of the State of the American Union — Mr President left the Chair.

Mr Gorham took the Chair of the Committee

Mr President resumed the Chair

Mr Gorham reported from the Committee that the Committee had made a further progress in the matter to them referred; and had directed him to move that they may have leave to sit again

Resolved that this House will to-morrow again resolve itself into a Committee of the whole House to consider of the State of the american union.

And then the House adjourned till to-morrow at 10 o'clock. A.M.

In a Committee of the whole House

Friday June 1. 1787.

Mr Gorham in the Chair

It was moved and seconded to proceed to the consideration of the 7th resolution submitted by Mr Randolph, namely

"Resolved that a national executive be instituted; to

---

[1] See Appendix B.

"be chosen by the national legislature; for the term of
"years

"to receive punctually at stated times a fixed compensa-
"tion for the services rendered; in which no encrease or dimi-
"nution shall be made so as to affect the magistracy existing
"at the time of such encrease or diminution; and

"to be ineligible a second time; and that besides a general
"authority to execute the national laws, it ought to enjoy the
"executive rights vested in Congress by the confederation."

On motion, by Mr Wilson seconded by Mr C. Pinckney,
to amend the first clause of the resolution by adding, after
the word instituted, the words "to consist of a single person" — so as to read

"resolved "that a national executive to consist of a single
person be instituted"

It was moved and seconded to to postpone the consideration of the amendment — and on the question to postpone
                it passed in the affirmative

It was then moved and seconded to agree to the first clause
of the resolution, namely

"Resolved that a national executive be instituted" and on
the question to agree to the said clause
                it passed in the affirmative

It was then moved, by Mr Madison, seconded by Mr Wilson,
after the word instituted to add the words

"with power to carry into execution the national laws, —
"to appoint to offices in cases not otherwise provided for; and
"to execute such powers, not legislative or judiciary in their
"nature, as may from time to time be delegated by the na-
"tional legislature"

and on a division of the amendment the following clauses
were agreed to — namely

"with power to carry into execution the national laws";
"to appoint to offices in cases not otherwise provided for" [2]

On the question to continue the last clause of the amendment namely

---

[2] *Journal* assigns to this question, Vote 8, Detail of Ayes and Noes. This is
doubtless a mistake, see *Records*, May 31, notes 5, 6, and 16

"and to execute such other powers, not legislative or
"judiciary in their nature, as may from time to time be dele-
"gated by the national legislature."
    it passed in the negative.[3]
It was then moved and seconded to fill up the blank with the
word "seven" — so as to read
    "for the term of seven years"
And on the question to fill up the blank with the word
"seven"
    it passed in the affirmative [Ayes — 5; noes — 4; divided — 1.][4]
    It was then moved and seconded to postpone the consid-
eration of the following words — namely
    "to be chosen by the national legislature"
    and on the question to postpone it passed in the affirmative.
    It was then moved and seconded that the Committee do
now rise — and report a further progress

DETAIL OF AYES AND NOES

	1 N. H.		*2* Massa:	*3* C:	*4* R. I.	*5* N. Y.	*6* N. J:	*7* P:	*8* D:	*9* Mary:	*10* V.	*11* N. C.	*12* S. C.	*13.* G.
	ayes	noes												
[9]	5	4	divided	no	on the questn of 7 years to ye executive	aye	aye	aye	aye		aye	no	no	no

MADISON

Friday June 1st. 1787.

⟨William Houston from Georgia took his seat⟩ [5]
    ⟨The⟩ Committee of the whole ⟨proceeded to Resolution 7.⟩
"that a national Executive be ⟨instituted, to be chosen⟩ by
the national Legislature —————— for the term of
years ⟨&c⟩ to be ineligible thereafter, to possess the executive
powers of Congress &c" — [6]
    Mr. Pinkney was for a vigorous Executive but was afraid

---

    [3] *Journal* mistakenly assigns to this question Vote 7, Detail of Ayes and Noes.
See above note 2, and below note 12.   [5] Taken from *Journal.*
    [4] Vote 9, Detail of Ayes and Noes.   [6] Revised from *Journal.*

the Executive powers of ⟨the existing⟩ Congress might extend to peace & war &c which would render the Executive a Monarchy, of the worst kind, towit an elective one.

Mr. Wilson moved that the Executive consist of a single person. Mr. C Pinkney seconded the motion, ⟨so as to read "that a national Ex. to consist of a single person, be instituted—⟩ [6]

A considerable pause ensuing and the Chairman asking if he should put the question, Docr. Franklin observed that it was a point of great importance and wished that the gentlemen would deliver their sentiments on it before the question was put.

Mr. Rutlidge animadverted on the shyness of gentlemen on this and other subjects. He said it looked as if they supposed themselves precluded by having frankly disclosed their opinions from afterwards changing them, which he did not take to be at all the case. He said he was for vesting the Executive power in a single person, tho' he was not for giving him the power of war and peace. A single man would feel the greatest responsibility and administer the public affairs best.

Mr. Sherman said he considered the Executive magistracy as nothing more than an institution for carrying the will of the Legislature into effect, that the person or persons ought to be appointed by and accountable to the Legislature only, which was the despositary of the supreme will of the Society. As they were the best judges of the business which ought to be done by the Executive department, and consequently of the number necessary from time to time for doing it, he wished the number might ⟨not⟩ be fixed, but [7] that the legislature should be at liberty to appoint one or more as experience might dictate.

Mr. Wilson preferred a single magistrate, as giving most energy dispatch and responsibility to the office. He did not consider the Prerogatives of the British Monarch as a proper guide in defining the Executive powers. Some of these prerogatives were of a Legislative nature. Among others that

---

[7] Crossed out "left to be determined by the Legislature from time to time ".

of war & peace &c. The only powers he conceived strictly Executive were those of executing the laws, and appointing officers, not ⟨appertaining to and⟩ appointed by the Legislature.

Mr. Gerry favored the policy of annexing a Council ⟨to the Executive⟩ in order to give weight & inspire confidence.

Mr. Randolph strenuously opposed a unity in the Executive magistracy.[8] He regarded it as the fœtus of monarchy. We had he said no motive to be governed by the British Governmt. as our prototype. He did not mean however to throw censure on that Excellent fabric. If we were in a situation to copy it he did not know that he should be opposed to it; but the fixt genius of the people of America required a different form of Government. He could not see why the great requisites for the Executive department, vigor, despatch & responsibility could not be found in three men, as well as in one man. The Executive ought to be independent. It ought therefore ⟨in order to support its independence⟩ to consist of more than one.[9]

Mr. Wilson said that Unity in the Executive instead of being the fetus of Monarchy would be the best safeguard against tyranny. He repeated that he was not governed by the British Model which was inapplicable to the situation of this Country; the extent of which was so great, and the manners so republican, that nothing but a great confederated Republic would do for it.

Mr. Wilson's motion for a single magistrate was postponed by common consent, the ⟨Committee⟩ seeming unprepared for any decision on it; ⟨and the first part of the clause agreed to, viz. "that a National Executive be instituted."⟩[10]

Mr. ⟨Madison⟩ — ⟨thought⟩ it would be proper, before a choice shd. be made between a unity and a plurality in the Executive, to fix the extent of the Executive authority; that

---

[8] See Appendix A, CXXXVII.

[9] Madison had added at the end of Randolph's remarks, but later struck out, "Three distinct from one wd. use it to his equal partialities: Three taken from so many divisions of the Union wd. inspire more confidence."

[10] Taken from *Journal*.

as certain powers were in their nature Executive, and must be given to that departmt. whether administered by one or more persons, a definition of their extent would assist the judgment in determining how far they might be safely entrusted to a single officer. He accordingly moved that so much of the clause before the Committee as related to the powers of the Executive shd. be struck out & that ⟨after the words⟩ "that a national Executive ought to be instituted" ⟨there be inserted the words following⟩ viz, "with power to carry into effect. the national laws. to appoint to offices in cases not otherwise provided for, and to execute such other powers ⟨"not Legislative nor Judiciary in their nature."⟩ as may from time to time be delegated by the national Legislature". The words ⟨"not legislative nor judiciary in their nature"⟩ were added to the proposed amendment in consequence of a suggestion by Genl Pinkney that improper powers might ⟨otherwise⟩ be delegated,[11]

⟨Mr. Wilson seconded this motion⟩ [10]

Mr. Pinkney moved to amend the amendment by striking out the last member of it; viz. "and to execute such other powers not Legislative nor Judiciary in their nature as may from time to time be delegated." He said they were unnecessary, the object of them being included in the "power to carry into effect the national laws".

Mr. Randolph seconded the motion.

Mr. Madison did not know that the words were absolutely necessary, or even the preceding words. "to appoint to offices &c. the whole being perhaps included in the first member of the proposition. He did not however see any inconveniency in retaining them, and cases might happen in which they might serve to prevent doubts and misconstructions.

⟨In consequence of the motion of Mr. Pinkney, the question on Mr. Madison's motion was divided; and the words objected to by Mr. Pinkney struck out; by the votes of Connecticut. N. Y. N. J. Pena. Del. N. C. & Geo: agst. Mass. Virga. & S. Carolina the preceding part of the motion being first agreed to: Connecticut divided, all the other States in the affirmative.

---

[11] Crossed out "as the motion first stood". The whole resolution revised from *Journal.*

The next clause in Resolution 7, relating to the mode of appointing, & the duration of, the Executive being under consideration,⟩ [12]

Mr. Wilson said he was almost unwilling to declare the mode which he wished to take place, being apprehensive that it might appear chimerical. He would say however at least that in theory he was for an election by the people; Experience, particularly in N. York & Massts, shewed that an election of the first magistrate by the people at large, was both a convenient & successful mode. The objects of choice in such cases must be persons whose merits have general notoriety.

Mr. Sherman was for the appointment by the Legislature, and for making him absolutely dependent on that body, as it was the will of that which was to be executed. An independence of the Executive on the supreme Legislative, was in his opinion the very essence of tyranny if there was any such thing.

Mr. Wilson moves that the blank for the term of duration should be filled with three years, observing at the same time that he preferred this short period, on the supposition that a re-eligibility would be provided for.

Mr. Pinkney moves for seven years.

Mr. Sherman was for three years, and agst. the doctrine of rotation as throwing out of office the men best qualified to execute its duties.

Mr. Mason was for seven years at least, and for probibiting a re-eligibility as the best expedient both for preventing the effect of a false complaisance on the side of the Legislature towards unfit characters; and a temptation on the side of the Executive to intrigue with the Legislature for a re-appointment.

Mr. Bedford was strongly opposed to so long a term as seven years. He begged the committee to consider what the

---

[12] Madison had originally written: "The motion was agreed to. as was the amendment of Mr.   thus amended by the motion." Later he added "(Note — this was done by a division of the Question, the first part of Mr — amendt. being agreed to — the last disagreed to in consequence of the Objection of Mr. P. & Mr. R.—)", but then substituted the form in the text above, taken from *Journal*, which is in error in assigning these votes to these questions. See May 31, note 16.

situation of the Country would be, in case the first magistrate should be saddled on it for such period and it should be found on trial that he did not possess the qualifications ascribed to him, or should lose them after his appointment. An impeachment he said would be no cure for this evil, as an impeachment would reach misfeasance only, not incapacity. He was for a triennial election, and for an ineligibility after a period of nine years.

On the question for seven years,

Massts. dividd. Cont. no. N. Y. ay. N. J. ay. Pena. ay. Del. ay. Virga. ay. N. C. no. S. C. no. Georg. no [Ayes — 5; noes — 4; divided — 1.]

There being 5. ays, 4 noes, 1 divd. a question was asked whether a majority had voted in the affirmative? The President decided that it was an affirmative vote.

The *mode of appointing* the Executive was the next question.

Mr. Wilson renewed his declarations in favor of an appointment by the people. He wished to derive not only both branches of the Legislature from the people, without the intervention of the State Legislatures ⟨but the Executive also;⟩ in order to make them as independent as possible of each other, as well as of the States;

Col. Mason favors the idea, but thinks it impracticable. He wishes however that Mr. W⟨ilson⟩ might have time to digest it into his own form.—⟨the clause "to be chosen by the National Legislature" — was accordingly postponed. —⟩ [13]

Mr. Rutledge suggests an election of the Executive by the second branch only of the national Legislature —

⟨The Committee then rose and the House ⟨adjourned.⟩ [14]

---

[13] Taken from *Journal*.   [14] See further Appendix A, XXXII.

YATES

FRIDAY, JUNE 1st, 1787.

Met pursuant to adjournment.

The 7th resolve, that a national executive be instituted. Agreed to.

To continue in office for seven years.   Agreed to.

A general authority to execute the laws.   Agreed to.

To appoint all officers not otherwise provided for.   Agreed to.

Adjourned to the next day.

KING

Comee. of the Whole

1 June.   Ex. power to be in one person

Friday 1 June

This amend. moved by Wilson & secd. by Cs. Pinck.

Rutledge in favor of it.   Sherman proposes to leave the number wth. the Legislature —

Wilson — an extive. ought to possess the powers of secresy, vigour & Dispatch — and to be so constituted as to be responsible — Extive. powers are designed for the execution of Laws, and appointing Officers not otherwise to be appointed — If appointments of Officers are made by a sing. Ex he is responsible for the propriety of the same.   not so where the Executive is numerous

Mad: agrees wth. Wilson in his difinition of executive powers — executive powers ex vi termini, do not include the Rights of war & peace &c. but the powers shd. be confined and defined — if large we shall have the Evils of elective Monarchies — probably the best plan will be a single Executive of long duration wth. a Council, with liberty to depart from their Opinion at his peril —

Gerry — I am in favr. of a council to advise the Ex — they will be the organs of information of the persons proper for

offices—their opinions may be recorded—they may be called
to acct. for yr. Opinions. & impeached — if so their Responsibility will be certain, and in Case of misconduct their punishment certain —

Randolph — Danger of Monarchy, or Tyranny, if the ex.
consists of three persons they may execute yr. Functions
without Danger — if one he can not be impeached until the
expiration of his Office, or he will be dependent on the Legislature — such an Unity wd. be agt. the fixed Genius of America
&c &c —

Wilson

We must consider two points of Importance existing in our
Country — the extent & manners of the United States — the
former seems to require the vigour of Monarchy, the manners
are agt. a King and are purely republican — Montesquieu
is in favor of confederated Republicks — I am for such a
confedn. if we can take for its basis liberty, and can ensure
a vigourous execution of the Laws.

A single ex. will not so soon introduce a Mony. or Despotism, as a complex one.

The people of Amer. did not oppose the British King but
the parliament — the opposition was not agt. an Unity but
a corrupt multitude —

Wmson — There is no true difference between a complex
executive, formed by a single person with a Council, or by
three or more persons as the executive —

The Question of the unity or plurality of the Exve. postponed — and the Come. proceeded to examine the powers —
these points being discussed — the Come took into consideration the Duration of the Office of the Ex —

Wilson for 3 Yrs and no exclusion or rotation —
Mad. 7 years and an exclusion for ever after — or during
good behavior —

Mason—in Favor of 7 years. and an exclusion afterwards—
thereby he is made independent of the Legislature, who are
proposed as his Electors — if he is capable of reelection by
the Leg: the Ex. will be complaisant, & reelect — the Execu-

tive will be subservient and court a reelection — on the Quest
to fill the Blank for seven yrs

Mass. divd.	Con	no	NY.	ay	
Gor. & K. ay ⎱ NC.		no	NJ.	ay	
Ger. & Sg. no ⎰ SC.		no	Pen.	ay	filled [15]
	G.	no	Del.	ay	
			Vir	ay	

HAMILTON

1 — The way to prevent a majority from having
an interest to oppress the minority is to
enlarge the sphere.

Madison 2 — Elective Monarchies turbulent and unhappy —
Men unwilling to admit so decided a superiority of merit in an individual as to accede
to his appointment to so preeminent a station —

If several are admitted as there will be many
competitors of equal merit they may be all
included — contention   prevented — &   the
republican genius consulted —

Randolph — I   Situation of this Country peculiar —

II — Taught the people an aversion to Monarchy

III   All their constitutions opposed to it —

IV — Fixed character of the people opposed to it —

V — If proposed 'twill prevent a fair discussion of
the plan.

VI — Why cannot three execute?

View of ⎱__ — Great exertions only requisite on particular
America ⎰   occasions

---

[15] [Endorsed: June 1 — | Number power and duration of Ex. | Duration 7 yrs
and no reelection | Mass. dived | Con N Car S Car Geor No. | N Y N J Pen
Del Virg Aye | Madison 7 yrs or good Behaviour

Safety to liberty the great object —
- Legislature may appoint a dictator when necessary —
- Seeds of destruction — Slaves might be easily enlisted —
- May appoint men devoted to them — & even bribe the legislature by offices —
- Chief Magistrate must be free from impeachment

Wilson — extent — manners —

Confederated republic unites advantages & banishes disadvantages of other kinds of governments —

————— rendering the executive ineligible an infringement of the right of election —

Bedford — peculiar talents requisite for *executive*, therefore ought to be opportunity of ascertaining his talents — therefore frequent change —

Princ 1 The further men are from the ultimate point of importance the readier they will be concur in a change —

2 Civilization approximates the different species of governments —

3 — Vigour is the result of several principles — Activity wisdom — confidence —

4 — Extent of limits will occasion the non attendance of remote members & tend to throw the government into the hands of the Country near the seat of government — a reason for strengthening the upper branch & multiplying the Inducements to attendance —

PIERCE

On the Executive Power

Mr. Wilson said the great qualities in the several parts of the Executive are vigor and dispatch. Making peace and war are generally determined by Writers on the Laws of Nations to be legislative powers.

Mr. Maddison was of opinion that an Executive formed of one Man would answer the purpose when aided by a Council, who should have the right to advise and record their proceedings, but not to control his authority.

Mr. Gerry was of opinion that a Council ought to be the medium through which the feelings of the people ought to be communicated to the Executive.

Mr. Randolph advanced a variety of arguments opposed to a unity of the Executive, and doubted whether even a Council would be sufficient to check the improper views of an ambitious Man. A unity of the Executive he observed would savor too much of a monarchy.

Mr. Wilson said that in his opinion so far from a unity of the Executive tending to progress towards a monarchy it would be the circumstance to prevent it. A plurality in the Executive of Government would probably produce a tyranny as bad as the thirty Tyrants of Athens, or as the Decemvirs of Rome.

A confederated republic joins the happiest kind of Government with the most certain security to liberty.

(A CONSIDERATION.)

Every Government has certain moral and physical qualities engrafted in their very nature, — one operates on the sentiments of men, the other on their fears.

Mr. Dickinson was of opinion that the powers of the Executive ought to be defined before we say in whom the power shall vest.

Mr. Bedford said he was for appointing the Executive Officer for three years, and that he should be eligible for nine years only.

Mr. Maddison observed [16] that to prevent a Man from holding an Office longer than he ought, he may for malpractice be impeached and removed; — he is not for any ineligibility.

---

[16] This speech of Madison's may belong to the records of June 2. See June 2 note 25.

McHENRY

June 1st.

Recd an express from home that my brother lay danger-ously sick in consequence of which I set out immediately for Baltimore.

SATURDAY, JUNE 2, 1787.

JOURNAL
Saturday June 2nd 1787.

The honorable William Samuel Johnson Esquire, a Deputy of the State of Connecticut, and the honorable Daniel of St Thomas Jenifer, a Deputy of the State of Maryland,[1] and the honorable John Lansing junior a Deputy of the State of New-York attended and took their seats.

The following credentials were produced and read.
(here insert the credentials of the Deputies of the State of Maryland)[2]

The Order of the day being read,

The House resolved itself into a Committee of the whole House to consider of the State of the American union.

Mr President left the Chair

Mr. Gorham took the Chair of the Committee.

Mr President resumed the Chair

Mr Gorham reported from the Committee that the Committee had made a further progress in the matter to them referred; and had directed him to move that they may have leave to sit again

Resolved that this House will on Monday again resolve itself into a Committee of the whole House to consider of the State of the american union.

And then the House adjourned till Monday next at 11 o'clock A.M.

In a Committee of the whole House

Saturday June 2nd 1787.

Mr Gorham in the Chair.

It was moved and seconded to postpone the farther con-

---

[1] See Appendix A, XXXIII.   [2] See Appendix B.

sideration of the resolution, submitted by Mr Randolph, which respects the Executive — in order to take up the consideration of the resolution respecting the second branch of the Legislature.

And on the question to postpone

it passed in the negative [3]

it was then moved and seconded to postpone the consideration of these words namely

"to be chosen by the Natl. Lege"

in order to take up the following resolution submitted by Mr Wilson. namely.

"Resolved that the Executive Magistracy shall be elected "in manner following.

"That the States be divided into   Districts — and "that the persons, qualified to vote in each District, elect "   Members for their respective Districts to be elec-"tors of the Executive Magistracy

"That the electors of the Executive Magistracy meet and "they or any   of them shall elect by ballot, but not out "of their own Body,   Person in whom the Execu-"tive authority of the national government shall be vested." "and on the question to postpone

it passed in the negative   [Ayes—2; noes—7; divided—1.][4]
It was then moved and seconded to agree to the words in the resolution, submitted by Mr. Randolph, so as to read

" To be chosen by the national legislature for the term of seven years"

And on the question to agree to these words.

it passed in the affirmative.   [Ayes — 8; noes — 2][5]

It was then moved and seconded to postpone the consideration of that part of the resolution, as submitted by Mr Randolph, which respects the stipend of the Executive, in Order to introduce the following motion made by Dr Franklin namely

---

[3] *Journal* ascribes to this question Vote 10, Detail of Ayes and Noes.

[4] Vote 11, Detail of Ayes and Noes. Madison makes New York's vote "no" instead of "divided ".

[5] Vote 12, Detail of Ayes and Noes, which is evidently mistaken in giving the summary of the vote.

"whose necessary expences shall be defrayed, but who "shall receive no salary, stipend, Fee or reward whatsoever "for their services."

and on the question to postpone
        it passed in the affirmative.

It was then moved and seconded to postpone the consideration of the said motion offered by Dr Franklin.

and on the question to postpone
        it passed in the affirmative.

It was then moved by Mr Dickinson seconded by Mr Bedford to amend the resolution, before the Committee, by adding after the words "to be chosen by the national legislature for the term of seven years" the following words

"to be removable by the national legislature upon re-"quest by a majority of the legislatures of the individual "States"

it was moved and seconded to strike out the words "upon request by a majority of the legislatures of the individual States"

On the question to strike out
        it passed in the negative [6]

The question being taken to agree to the amendment, offered by Mr Dickinson
        it passed in the negative. [Ayes — 1; noes — 9.][7]

The question being then taken on the words contained in the resolution submitted by Mr Randolph, namely "to be ineligible a second time"

it passed in the affirmative. [Ayes — 7; noes — 2; divided — 1.][8]

It was then moved by Mr. Williamson seconded by Mr Davie to add the following words to the last clause of the resolution respecting the executive namely "and to be removable on impeachment and conviction of mal-practice or neglect of duty"

---

[6] *Journal* ascribes to this question Vote 13, Detail of Ayes and Noes.

[7] Vote 14, Detail of Ayes and Noes.

[8] Vote 15, Detail of Ayes and Noes, which is evidently mistaken in giving the summary of the vote.

On the question to add the words
    it passed in the affirmative.[9]
It was then moved by Mr Rutledge seconded by Mr C
Pinckney to fill up the blank after the words "executive to
consist of — with the words "One person."
It was then moved and seconded to postpone the consider-
eration of the last motion.
    and on the question to postpone.
        it passed in the affirmative.[9]
It was then moved and seconded that the Committee do now
rise, report a further progress, and request leave to sit again
the Committee then rose.

DETAILS OF AYES AND NOES

	1 N. H.		*2* Massa:	*3* C:	*4* R. I.	*5* N. Y	*6* N.J:	*7* P:	*8* D:	*9* Mary:	*10* V.	*11* N. C.	*12* S. C.	*13.* G.
	ayes	noes												
[10]	3	7	no	no		aye		aye	no	aye	no	no	no	no
[11]	2	7	no	no		divided		aye	no	aye	no	no	no	no
[12]	2	8	aye	aye		aye		no	aye	no	aye	aye	aye	aye
[13]	3	7	no	aye		no		no	no	no	no	no	aye	aye
[14]	1	9	no	no		no		no	aye	no	no	no	no	no
[15]	2	7	aye	no	Executive to be again ineligible	aye		divided	aye	aye	aye	aye	aye	no
[16]	6	4	aye	aye		aye		no	no	no	no	aye	ay	aye

MADISON

Saturday June 2d.   In Committee of whole.

⟨William Saml. Johnson, from Connecticut, Daniel of St.
Thomas Jennifer, from Maryld — & John Lansing Jr. from
N. York, took their seats —⟩[10]

⟨It was movd. & 2ded. to postpone ye Resol: of Mr.
Randolph respecting the Executive in order to take up the
2d. branch of the Legislature; which being negatived by Mas:
Con: Del: Virg: N. C. S. C. Geo: agst. N. Y. Pena. Maryd⟩[10]

---

[9] Vote 16, Detail of Ayes and Noes, might be assigned to either of these last two
questions.   [10] Taken from *Journal.*

⟨The⟩ mode of appointg ye Executive ⟨was⟩ resumed.

Mr. Wilson made the following motion, ⟨to be substituted for the mode proposed by Mr. Randolph's resolution.⟩

"that the Executive Magistracy shall be ⟨elected⟩ in the following manner: ⟨That⟩ the States be divided into districts: ⟨& that⟩ the persons qualified ⟨to vote in each⟩ district for members of the first branch of the national Legislature elect   members for their respective districts to be electors of the Executive magistracy.   that the said Electors of the Executive magistracy meet at   and they or any of them so met shall proceed to elect by ballot, but not out of their own body   person   in whom the Executive authority of the national Government shall be vested." [11]

Mr. Wilson repeated his arguments in favor of an election without the intervention of the States. He supposed too that this mode would produce more confidence among the people in the first magistrate, than an election by the national Legislature.

Mr. Gerry, opposed the election by the national legislature. There would be a constant intrigue kept up for the appointment. The Legislature & the candidates wd. bargain & play into one another's hands. votes would be given by the former under promises or expectations from the latter, of recompensing them by services to members of the Legislature or to their friends. He liked the principle of Mr. Wilson's motion, but fears it would alarm & give a handle to the State partizans, as tending to supersede altogether the State authorities. He thought the Community not yet ripe for stripping the States of their powers, even such ⟨as⟩ might ⟨not⟩ be requisite for local purposes. He ⟨was⟩ for waiting till people ⟨should⟩ feel more the necessity of it. He seemed to prefer the taking the suffrages of the States instead of Electors, or letting the Legislatures nominate, and the electors appoint. ⟨He was⟩ not clear that the people ought to act directly even in ⟨the⟩ choice of electors, being too little informed of personal characters in large districts, and liable to deceptions.

---

[11] Revised from *Journal.*

Mr Williamson could see no advantage in the introduction of Electors chosen by the people who who would stand in the same relation to them as the State Legislatures, whilst the expedient would be attended with great trouble and expence. On the question for agreeing to Mr. Wilson's ⟨substitute, it was negatived:⟩ Massts. no. Cont. no. N. Y. no.* Pa. ay. Del. no. Mard. ay. Virga. no. N. C. no. S. C. no. Geoa. no. [Ayes — 2; noes — 8.]

On the question for electing the Executive by the national legislature, ⟨for the term of seven years,[12] it was agreed to⟩ [13] Massts. ay. Cont. ay. N. Y. ay. Pena. no. Del. ay. Maryd. no. Va. ay. N. C. ay. S. C. ay. Geo. ay. [ayes — 8; noes — 2.]

⟨Docr. Franklin [14] moved that what related to the compensation for the services of the Executive be postponed, in order to substitute — "whose necessary expences shall be defrayed, but who shall receive no salary, stipend fee or reward whatsoever for their services" — He said that being very sensible of the effect of age on his memory, he had been unwilling to trust to that for the observations which seemed to support his motion, and had reduced them to writing, that he might with the permission of the Committee, read instead of speaking them. Mr. Wilson made an offer to read the paper, which was accepted —⟩ [15]

⟨The following is a literal copy of the paper.⟩ [16]
Sir.

It is with reluctance that I rise to express a disapprobation of any one article of the plan for which we are so much obliged to the honorable gentleman who laid it before us. From its first reading I have borne a good will to it, and in general

*⟨N. Y. in the printed Journal — 'divided'.⟩

[12] For further discussion of this subject see references under September 6 note 23.
[13] Taken from *Journal.*
[14] Madison's original record was very similar to this revised form.
[15] See Appendix A, CCCLXVII.
[16] Among the Franklin Papers is the original, or at least an earlier draft, of this paper. Madison's copy differs only in the omission of the frequent capital letters affected by Franklin.

wished it success.   In this particular of salaries to the Executive branch I happen to differ; and as my opinion may appear new and chimerical, it is only from a persuasion that it is right, and from a sense of duty that I hazard it.   The Committee will judge of my reasons when they have heard them, and their judgment may possibly change mine. — I think I see inconveniences in the appointment of salaries; I see none in refusing them, but on the contrary, great advantages.

Sir, there are two passions which have a powerful influence on the affairs of men.   These are ambition and avarice; the love of power, and the love of money.   Separately each of these has great force in prompting men to action; but when united in view of the same object, they have in many minds the most violent effects.   place before the eyes of such men a post of *honour* that shall at the same time be a place of *profit*, and they will move heaven and earth to obtain it. The vast number of such places it is that renders the British Government so tempestuous.   The struggles for them are the true sources of all those factions which are perpetually dividing the Nation, distracting its councils, hurrying sometimes into fruitless & mischievous wars, and often compelling a submission to dishonorable terms of peace.

And of what kind are the men that will strive for this profitable pre-eminence, through all the bustle of cabal, the heat of contention, the infinite mutual abuse of parties, tearing to pieces the best of characters?   It will not be the wise and moderate, the lovers of peace and good order, the men fittest for the trust.   It will be the bold and the violent, the men of strong passions and indefatigable activity in their selfish pursuits.   These will thrust themselves into your Government and be your rulers.   And these too will be mistaken in the expected happiness of their situation: For their vanquished competitors of the same spirit, and from the same motives will perpetually be endeavouring to distress their administration, thwart their measures, and render them odious to the people.

Besides these evils, Sir, tho' we may set out in the beginning with moderate salaries, we shall find that such will not be of long continuance. Reasons will never be wanting for proposed augmentations. And there will always be a party for giving more to the rulers, that the rulers may be able in return to give more to them.—Hence as all history informs us, there has been in every State & Kingdom a constant kind of warfare between the Governing & Governed: the one striving to obtain more for its support, and the other to pay less. And this has alone occasioned great convulsions, actual civil wars, ending either in dethroning of the Princes or enslaving of the people. Generally indeed the ruling power carries its point, the revenues of princes constantly increasing, and we see that they are never satisfied, but always in want of more. The more the people are discontented with the oppression of taxes; the greater need the prince has of money to distribute among his partizans and pay the troops that are to suppress all resistance, and enable him to plunder at pleasure. There is scarce a king in a hundred who would not, if he could, follow the example of Pharoah, get first all the peoples money, then all their lands, and then make them and their children servants forever. It will be said, that we don't propose to establish Kings. I know it. But there is a natural inclination in mankind to Kingly Government. It sometimes relieves them from Aristocratic domination. They had rather have one tyrant than five hundred. It gives more of the appearance of equality among Citizens, and that they like. I am apprehensive therefore, perhaps too apprehensive, that the Government of these States, may in future times, end in a Monarchy. But this Catastrophe I think may be long delayed, if in our proposed system we do not sow the seeds of contention, faction & tumult, by making our posts of honor, places of profit. If we do, I fear that tho' we do employ at first a number, and not a single person, the number will in time be set aside, it will only nourish the fœtus of a King, as the honorable gentleman from Virginia very aptly expressed it, and a King will the sooner be set over us.

It may be imagined by some that this is an Utopian Idea, and that we can never find men to serve us in the Executive department, without paying them well for their services. I

conceive this to be a mistake.   Some existing facts present
themselves to me, which incline me to a contrary opinion.
The high Sheriff of a County in England is an honorable
office, but it is not a profitable one.   It is rather expensive
and therefore not sought for.   But yet, it is executed and
well executed, and usually by some of the principal Gentlemen of the County.   In France the office of Counsellor or
Member of their Judiciary Parliaments is more honorable.   It
is therefore purchased at a high price: There are indeed fees
on the law proceedings, which are divided among them, but
these fees do not amount to more than three per Cent on the
sum paid for the place.   Therefore as legal interest is there
at five per Ct. they in fact pay two per Ct. for being allowed to
do the Judiciary business of the Nation, which is at the same
time entirely exempt from the burden of paying them any
salaries for their services.   I do not however mean to recommend this as an eligible mode for our Judiciary department.
I only bring the instance to shew that the pleasure of doing
good & serving their Country and the respect such conduct
entitles them to, are sufficient motives with some minds to
give up a great portion of their time to the Public, without
the mean inducement of pecuniary satisfaction.

Another instance is that of a respectable Society who have
made the experiment, and practiced it with success more than
an hundred years.   I mean the Quakers.   It is an established
rule with them, that they are not to go to law; but in their
controversies they must apply to their monthly, quarterly and
yearly meetings.   Committees of these sit with patience to
hear the parties, and spend much time in composing their differences.   In doing this they are supported by a sense of
duty, and the respect paid to usefulness.   It is honorable to
be so employed, but it was never made profitable by salaries,
fees, or perquisites.   And indeed in all cases of public service
the less the profit the greater the honor.

To bring the matter nearer home, have we not seen the
great and most important of our officers, that of General of
our armies executed for eight years together without the
smallest salary, by a Patriot whom I will not now offend by

any other praise; and this through fatigues and distresses in common with the other brave men his military friends & companions, and the constant anxieties peculiar to his station? And shall we doubt finding three or four men in all the U. States, with public spirit enough to bear sitting in peaceful Council for perhaps an equal term, merely to preside over our civil concerns, and see that our laws are duly executed. Sir, I have a better opinion of our country. I think we shall never be without a sufficient number of wise and good men to undertake and execute well and faithfully the Office in question.

Sir, The saving of the salaries that may at first be proposed is not an object with me. The subsequent mischiefs of proposing them are what I apprehend. And therefore it is that I move the amendment. If it is not seconded or accepted I must be contented with the satisfaction of having delivered my opinion frankly and done my duty.

The motion was seconded by Col. Hamilton with the view he said merely of bringing so respectable a proposition before the Committee, and which was besides enforced by arguments that had a certain degree of weight. No debate ensued, and the proposition was postponed for the consideration of the members. It was treated with great respect, but rather for the author of it, than from any apparent conviction of its expediency or practicability.

Mr. Dickenson moved "that the Executive be made removeable by the National Legislature on the request of a majority of the Legislatures of individual States". It was necessary he said to place the power of removing somewhere. He did not like the plan of impeaching the Great Officers of State. He did not know how provision could be made for removal of them in a better mode than that which he had proposed. He had no idea of abolishing the State Governments as some gentlemen seemed inclined to do. The happiness of this Country in his opinion required considerable powers to be left in the hands of the States.

Mr. Bedford seconded the motion.

Mr. Sherman contended that the National Legislature should have power to remove the Executive at pleasure.

Mr. Mason. Some mode of displacing an unfit magistrate is rendered indispensable by the fallibility of those who choose, as well as by the corruptibility of the man chosen. He opposed decidedly the making the Executive the mere creature of the Legislature as a violation of the fundamental principle of good Government.

Mr. ⟨Madison⟩ & Mr. Wilson observed that it would leave an equality of agency in the small with the great States; that it would enable a minority of the people to prevent ye removal of an officer who had rendered himself justly criminal in the eyes of a majority; that it would open a door for intrigues agst. him in States where his administration tho' just might be unpopular, and might tempt him to pay court to particular States whose leading partizans he might fear, or wish to engage as his partizens. They both thought it bad policy ⟨to introduce such a mixture⟩ of the State authorities, when their agency could be otherwise supplied.

Mr. Dickenson considered the business as so important that no man ought to be silent or reserved. He went into a discourse of some length, the sum of which was, that the Legislative, Executive, & Judiciary departments ought to be made as independt. as possible; but that such an Executive as some seemed to have in contemplation was not consistant with a republic; that a firm Executive could only exist in a limited monarchy. In the British Govt. itself the weight of the Executive arises from the attachments which the Crown draws to itself, & not merely from the force of its prerogatives. In place of these attachments we must look out for something else. One source of stability is the double branch of the Legislature. The division of the Country into distinct States formed the other principal source of stability. This division ought therefore to be maintained, and considerable powers to be left with the States. This was the ground of his consolation for the future fate of his Country. Without this, and in case of a consolidation of the States into one great Republic[17] we might read its fate in the history of smaller ones. A limited Mon-

---

[17] Crossed out "nation".

archy he considered as *one* of the best Governments in the world. It was not *certain* that the same blessings were derivable from any other form. It was certain that equal blessings had never yet been derived from any of the republican form. A limited monarchy however was out of the question. The spirit of the times — the state of our affairs, forbade the experiment, if it were desireable. Was it possible moreover in the nature of things to introduce it even if these obstacles were less insuperable. A House of Nobles was essential to such a Govt. Could these be created by a breath, or by a a stroke of the pen? No. They were the growth of ages, and could only arise under a complication of circumstances none of which existed in this Country. But though a form the most perfect *perhaps* in itself be unattainable. we must not despair. If antient republics have been found to flourish for a moment only & then vanish forever, it only proves that they were badly constituted; and that we ought to seek for every remedy for their diseases. One of these remedies he conceived to be the accidental lucky division of this country into distinct States; a division which some seemed desirous to abolish altogether.

As to the point of representation in the national legislature as it might affect States of different sizes, he said it must probably end in mutual concession. He hoped that each State would retain an equal voice at least in one branch of the National Legislature, and supposed the sums paid within each state would form a better ratio for the other branch than either the number of inhabitants or the quantum of property.

⟨A motion, being made to strike out "on request by a majority of the Legislatures of the individual States" and rejected, Connecticut. S. Carol: & Geo. being ay. the rest no: the question was taken —⟩[18]

On Mr. Dickenson's motion for making Executive removeable by Natl. Legislature at request of majority of State Legislatures ⟨was also rejected⟩ all the States ⟨being in the negative⟩ except Delaware which ⟨gave an⟩ affirmative vote.

---

[18] Taken from *Journal.*

The Question for making ye. Executive ineligible after seven years, ⟨was next next taken, and agreed to:⟩

Massts. ay. Cont. no. N Y — ay Pa. divd. Del. ay. Maryd. ay. Va. ay. N. C. ay. S. C. ay. Geo. no: * [Ayes — 7; noes — 2; divided — 1.]

⟨Mr. Williamson 2ded. by Mr. Davie moved to add to the last Clause, the words — "and to be removeable on impeachment & conviction of mal-practice or neglect of duty" — which was agreed to.⟩[18]

⟨Mr. Rutlidge &⟩[18] Mr. C. Pinkney moved that the blank for the no. of persons in the Executive be filled with the words "one person". He supposed the reasons to be so obvious & conclusive in favor of one that no member would oppose the motion.

Mr. Randolph opposed it with great earnestness, declaring that he should not do justice to the Country which sent him if he were silently to suffer the establishmt. of a Unity in the Executive department. He felt an opposition to it which he believed he should continue to feel as long as he lived. He urged 1. that the permanent temper of the people was adverse to the very semblance of Monarchy. 2. that a unity was unnecessary a plurality being equally competent to all the objects of the department. 3. that the necessary confidence would never be reposed in a single Magistrate. 4. that the appointments would generally be in favor of some inhabitant near the center of the Community, and consequently the remote parts would not be on an equal footing. ⟨He was in favor of three members of the Executive to be drawn from different portions of the Country.⟩[20]

Mr. Butler contended strongly for a single magistrate as most likely to answer the purpose of the remote parts. If one man should be appointed he would be responsible to the whole, and would be impartial to its interests. If three or

* ⟨In printed Journal Geo: ay.⟩[19]

---

[18] Taken from *Journal*.

[19] Simply a copyist's mistake in *Journal*. Detail of Ayes and Noes, Vote 15, gives Georgia's vote as "no".

[20] Probably taken from Yates, possibly from Pierce.

more should be taken from as many districts, there would be a constant struggle for local advantages. In Military matters this would be particularly mischievous. He said his opinion on this point had been formed under the opportunity he had had of seeing the manner in which a plurality of military heads distracted Holland when threatened with invasion by the imperial troops. One man was for directing the force to the defence of this part, another to that part of the Country, just as he happened to be swayed by prejudice or interest.

⟨The motion was then⟩ postpd. ⟨the Committee rose⟩ & the House Adjd.[21]

YATES

SATURDAY, JUNE 2d, 1787.

Met pursuant to adjournment. Present 11 states.

Mr. Pinkney called for the order of the day.

The convention went into committee of the whole.

Mr. Wilson moved that the states should be divided into districts, consisting of one or more states, and each district to elect a number of senators to form the second branch of the national legislature — The senators to be elected, and a certain proportion to be annually dismissed — avowedly on the plan of the New-York senate.[22]—Question put—rejected.

In the 7th resolve, the words *to be chosen by the national legislature*, were agreed to.

President Franklin moved, that the consideration of that part of the 7th resolve, which had in object the making provision for a compensation for the service of the executive, be postponed for the purpose of considering a motion, *that the executive should receive no salary, stipend or emolument for the devotion of his time to the public services, but that his expenses should be paid.*

Postponed.

Mr. Dickinson moved that in the seventh resolution, the

---

[21] See further Appendix A, XXXIV.

[22] Yates evidently misunderstood Wilson's proposal, which was a plan for the election of the executive and not for the composition of the senate.

words, *and removable on impeachment and conviction for mal-conduct or neglect in the execution of his office,* should be inserted after the words *ineligible a second time.* Agreed to. The remainder postponed.

Mr. Butler moved to fill the number of which the executive should consist.

Mr. Randolph. — The sentiments of the people ought to be consulted — they will not hear of the semblance of monarchy — He preferred three divisions of the states, and an executive to be taken from each. If a single executive, those remote from him would be neglected — local views would be attributed to him, frequently well founded, often without reason. This would excite disaffection. He was therefore for an executive of three.[23]

Mr. Butler. — Delays, divisions and dissentions arise from an executive consisting of many. Instanced Holland's distracted state, occasioned by her many counsellors. Further consideration postponed.

Mr. C. Pinkney gave notice for the re-consideration of the mode of election of the first branch.

Adjourned till Monday next.

KING

Saturday

2 June

Dickinson

A vigs. executive with checks &c can not be republican, it is peculiar to monarchy —

The monarchl. Ex is vigour — not alone from power but attachment or respect —

The Repub. plan may have an equivalent to the attachmt. that is the 3d Br. of the Legis:

We cannot have a limited monarchy instanter — our situation will not allow it — Repubs. are for a while industrious but finally destroy ymselves — they were badly constituted — I dread a Consolidation of the States

---

[23] Compare Genet's version of this in Appendix A, CCCX.

I hope for a good national Govt. from the present Division
of the State —
With a feeble executive — We are to have a Legis: of 2 Br.
or 2 Legislatures the Sovereign of the nation.   This will bring
a Change unless you have the Judicial to aid and correct the
Executive — The first Br: will be on another plan, but the
2d. may be on the present plan — 1st. Br. to be formed by
the Quotas pd. into ye. Genl Treasury — 2d B.

The Ex to be removed on the, petition of 7. Sts by the national Legislature — [24]

PIERCE

Mr. Charles Pinckney [25] was of opinion that the election
of the Executive ought to be by the national Legislature,
that then respect will be paid to that character best qualified
to fill the Executive department of Government.

Mr. Wilson proposed that the U. States should be divided
into districts, each of which should elect a certain number of
persons, who should have the appointment of the Executive.

Mr. Gerry observed that if the appointment of the Executive should be made by the national Legislature, it would
be done in such a way as to prevent intrigue.   If the States
are divided into districts, there will be too much inconvenience
in nominating the Electors.

Mr. Wm'son observed that if the Electors were to chuse
the Executive it would be attended with considerable expence
and trouble; whereas the appointment made by the Legislature would be easy, and in his opinion, the least liable to
objection.

On the subject of salary to the Executive Dr. Franklin
arose and produced a written Speech.   It was, on account of
his age, read by Mr. Wilson, in which was advanced an opinion
that no salaries should be allowed the public Officers, but that
their necessary expences should be defrayed.   This would
make Men, he said, more desirous of obtaining the Esteem of

[24] [Endorsed:] 2 June | Dickinson | Extive Power
[25] This speech of Pinckney's may belong to records of June 1.   See June 1 note 16.

their Countrymen, — than avaricious or eager, in the pursuit of wealth.

Mr. Dickinson moved that the Executive should be removed at the request of a majority of the State Legislatures.

No Government can produce such good consequences as a limited monarchy, especially such as the English Constitution.

The application of the several Legislatures brings with it no force to the national Legislature.

Mr. Maddison said it was far from being his wish that every executive Officer should remain in Office, without being amenable to some Body for his conduct.

Mr. Randolph was for appointing three Persons, from three districts of the Union, to compose the Executive. A single Person may be considered the foetus of a Monarchy.

Mr. Butler was of opinion that a unity of the Executive would be necessary in order to promote dispatch; — that a plurality of Persons would never do. When he was in Holland the States general were obliged to give up their power to a French Man to direct their military operations.

MONDAY, JUNE 4, 1787.

JOURNAL

Monday June 4th 1787.

The Order of the day being read

The House resolved itself into a Committee of the whole House to consider of the state of the american Union.

Mr President left the Chair

Mr Gorham took the Chair of the Committee.

Mr President resumed the Chair

Mr Gorham reported from the Committee that the Committee had made a further progress in the matter to them referred; and had directed him to move that they may have leave to sit again.

Resolved that this House will to-morrow again resolve itself into a Committee of the whole House to consider of the state of the american union.

And then the House adjourned till to-morrow at 11 o'clock a. m.

In a Committee of the whole House

Monday June 4. 1787.

Mr Gorham in the Chair

It was moved and seconded to proceed to the farther consider of the propositions submitted to the Committee by Mr Randolph — when

On motion of Mr C. Pinckney seconded by Mr Wilson to fill up the blank after the words "that a national executive be instituted to consist of" with the words "a single person"

On the question to fill up the blank with the words "a single person"

it passed in the affirmative. [Ayes — 7; noes — 3.][1]

It was then moved and seconded to take into consideration the first clause of the eighth resolution, submitted by Mr Randolph. namely

---

[1] Vote 17, Detail of Ayes and Noes.

"Resolved that the national executive and a convenient
"number of the national judiciary ought to compose a
"Council of revision"

It was then moved and seconded to postpone the consideration of the said clause in order to introduce the following
resolution submitted by Mr Gerry namely

"resolved that the national Executive shall have a right to
"negative any legislative act, which shall not be afterwards
"passed unless by   parts of each branch of the national
"legislature."

and on the question to postpone

it passed in the affirmative   [Ayes — 6; noes — 4.] [2]

It was then moved by Mr Wilson seconded by Mr Hamilton
to strike out the words

"shall not be afterwards passed but but by   parts of
"each branch of the national legislature."

and on the question to strike out the words

it passed unan: in the negative [3]

It was then moved by Mr Butler seconded by Dr Franklin
that the resolution be altered so as to read

"resolved that the national executive have a power to
suspend any legislative act for

and on the question to agree to the alteration

it passed unan: in the negative. [4]

A question was then taken on the resolution submitted
by Mr Gerry [5] namely

"resolved that the national executive shall have a right
"to negative any legislative act which shall not be afterwards
"passed unless by two third parts of each branch of the na-
"tional legislature"

And on the question to agree to the same

it passed in the affirmative [Ayes — 8; noes — 2.] [6]

It was then moved by Mr Wilson seconded by Mr Madison

---

[2] Vote 18, Detail of Ayes and Noes.
[3] Vote 19, Detail of Ayes and Noes.   [4] Vote 20, Detail of Ayes and Noes.
[5] A preliminary question is omitted, see Madison and Yates.
[6] Vote 21, Detail of Ayes and Noes, where there is an evident mistake in the
summary of the vote.

that the following amendment be made to the last resolution after the words "national Executive" to add the words "a convenient number of the national judiciary." —

An objection of order being taken by Mr Hamilton to the introduction of the last amendment at this time. — notice was given by Mr Wilson seconded by Mr Madison that the same would be moved to-morrow. — Wednesday assigned to reconsider

It was then moved and seconded to proceed to the consideration of the 9th resolution submitted by Mr Randolph

When on motion to agree to the first clause namely

"resolved that a national judiciary be established"

it passed in the affirmative

It was then moved and seconded to add these words to the first clause of the ninth resolution namely

"to consist of One supreme tribunal, and of one or more inferior tribunals.

and on the question to agree to the same.

it passed in the affirmative.

It was then moved and seconded that the Committee do now rise, report a further progress, and request leave to sit again

The Committee then rose.

DETAIL OF AYES AND NOES

1 N. H. (ayes | noes)		2 Massa:	3 C:	4 R. I.	5 N. Y.	6 N. J:	7 P:	8 D:	9 Mary:	10 V:	11 N. C.	12 S. C.	13. G.
[17] 7	3	aye	aye	single executive	no		aye	no	no	aye	aye	aye	aye
[18] 6	4	aye	no		aye		aye	no	no	no	aye	aye	aye
[19] 0	10	no	no	On giving the Executive a complete negative	no		no	no	no	no	no	no	no
[20]		no	no		no		no	no	no	no	no	no	no
[21] 2	8	aye	no	limiting the negative of the executive	aye		aye	aye	no	aye	aye	aye	aye

MADISON

Monday June 4.   In Committee of the whole

⟨The⟩ Question ⟨was⟩ resumed ⟨on motion of Mr. Pinkney 2ded. by Wilson⟩ "shall the blank for the number of the Executive be filled with ⟨"a single⟩ person"? [7]

Mr. Wilson was in favor of the motion. It had been opposed by the gentleman from Virga. (Mr. Randolph) but the arguments used had not convinced him. He observed that the objections of Mr. R. were levelled not so much agst. the measure itself, as agst. its unpopularity. If he could suppose that it would occasion a rejection of the plan of which it should form a part, though the part was an important one, yet he would give it up rather than lose the whole. On examination he could see no evidence of the alledged antipathy of the people. On the contrary he was persuaded that it does not exist. All know that a single magistrate is not a King.   one fact has great weight with him. All the 13 States tho' agreeing in scarce any other instance, agree in placing a single magistrate at the head of the Governmt. The idea of three heads has taken place in none. The degree of power is indeed different: but there are no co-ordinate heads. In addition to his former reasons for preferring a Unity, he would mention another. The *tranquility* not less than the vigor of the Govt. he thought would be favored by it. Among three equal members, he foresaw nothing but uncontrouled, continued, & violent animosities; which would not only interrupt the public administration; but diffuse their poison thro' the other branches of Govt., thro' the States, and at length thro' the people at large. If the members were to be unequal in power the principle of the opposition to the Unity was given up. If equal, the making them an odd number would not be a remedy. In Courts of Justice there are two sides only to a question. In the Legislative & Executive departmts. questions have commonly many sides. Each member therefore might espouse a separate one & no two agree.

---

[7] Revised from *Journal.*

Mr. Sherman. This matter is of great importance and ought to be well considered before it is determined. Mr. Wilson he said had observed that in each State a single magistrate was placed at the head of the Govt. It was so he admitted, and properly so, and he wished the same policy to prevail in the federal Govt. But then it should be also remarked that in a all the States there was a Council of advice, without which the first magistrate could not act. A Council he thought necessary to make the establishment acceptable to the people. Even in G. B. the King has a council; and though he appoints it himself, its advice has its weight with him, and attracts the Confidence of the people.

Mr. Williamson asks Mr. Wilson whether he means to annex a Council

Mr. Wilson means ⟨to have⟩ no Council, which oftener serves to cover, than prevent malpractices.

Mr Gerry. was at a loss to discover the policy of three members for the Executive. It wd. be extremely inconvenient in many instances, particularly in military matters, whether relating to the militia, an army, or a navy. It would be a general with three heads.[8]

On the question for a single Executive ⟨it was agreed to⟩ Massts. ay. Cont. ay. N. Y. no. Pena. ay. Del. no. Maryd. no. Virg. ay. (Mr. R & Mr. Blair no — Docr. Mc.Cg. Mr. M. & Gen W. ay. Col. Mason being no, but not in house, Mr. Wythe ay but gone home). N. C. ay. S. C. ay. Georga. ay. [Ayes — 7; noes — 3.]

⟨First⟩ Clause ⟨of Proposition 8th⟩ relating *to a Council of Revision* taken into consideration.

Mr. Gerry doubts whether the Judiciary ought to form a part of it, as they will have a sufficient check agst. encroachments on their own department by their exposition of the laws, which involved a power of deciding on their Constitutionality. In some States the Judges had ⟨actually⟩ set aside laws as being agst. the Constitution. This was done too with general approbation. It was quite foreign from the

---

[8] See further Appendix A, CCXXVII.

nature of ye. office to make them judges of the policy of public measures. ⟨He moves to postpone⟩ the clause ⟨in order⟩ to propose "that the National Executive ⟨shall⟩ have a right to negative any Legislative act ⟨which⟩ shall not be afterwards passed by   parts of each branch of the national Legislature.[9]

Mr. King seconds the motion, observing that the Judges ought to be able to expound the law as it should come before them, free from the bias of having participated in its formation.

Mr. Wilson thinks neither the original proposition nor the amendment go far enough. If the Legislative Exētiv & Judiciary ought to be distinct & independent, The Executive ought to have an absolute negative. Without such a Self-defence the Legislature can at any moment sink it into non-existence. He was for varying the proposition in such a manner as to give the Executive & Judiciary jointly an absolute negative

On the question to postpone in order to take Mr. Gerry's proposition into consideration ⟨it was agreed to⟩ Massts. ay. Cont. no. N. Y. ay. Pa. ay. Del. no. Maryd. no. Virga. no. N. C. ay. S. C. ay. Ga. ay. [Ayes — 6; noes — 4.]

Mr. Gerry's proposition being now before Committee, Mr. Wilson & Mr. Hamilton move that the last part of it ⟨⟨viz wch. sl. not be afterwds. passed" unless by   parts of each branch of the National legislature⟩⟩[10] be struck out, so as to give the Executive an absolute negative on the laws. ⟨There was no danger they thought of such a power being too much exercised. It was mentioned (by Col: Hamilton) that the King of G. B. had not exerted his negative since the Revolution.⟩[11]

Mr. Gerry sees no necessity for so great a controul over the legislature as the best men in the Community would be comprised in the two branches of it.

Docr. Franklin, said he was sorry to differ from his col-

[9] Revised from *Journal*.   [10] Taken from *Journal*.

[11] In place of "(by Col. Hamilton)" Madison first wrote "by one of them". The only source for this interpolation would seem to be King's notes which were probably known to Madison.

league for whom he had a very great respect, on any occasion, but he could not help it on this. He had had some experience of this check in the Executive on the Legislature, under the proprietary Government of Pena. The negative of the Governor was constantly made use of to extort money. No good law whatever could be passed without a private bargain with him. An increase of his salary, or some donation, was always made a condition; till at last it became the regular practice, to have orders in his favor on the Treasury, presented along with the bills to be signed, so that he might actually receive the former before he should sign the latter. When the Indians were scalping the western people, and notice of it arrived, the concurrence of the Governor in the means of self-defence could not be got, till it was agreed that his Estate should be exempted from taxation. so that the people were to fight for the security of his property, whilst he was to bear no share of the burden. This was a mischievous sort of check. If the Executive was to have a Council, such a power would be less objectionable. It was true the King of G. B. had not, As was said, exerted his negative since the Revolution: but that matter was easily explained. The bribes and emoluments now given to the members of parliament rendered it unnecessary, everything being done according to the will of the Ministers. He was afraid, if a negative should be given as proposed, that more power and money would be demanded, till at last eno' would be gotten to influence & bribe the Legislature into a compleat subjection to the will of the Executive.

Mr. Sherman was agst. enabling any one man to stop the will of the whole. No one man could be found so far above all the rest in wisdom. He thought we ought to avail ourselves of his wisdom in revising the laws, but not permit him to overrule the decided and cool opinions of the Legislature.

⟨Mr.⟩ M⟨adison⟩ supposed that if a proper proportion of each branch should be required to overrule the objections of the Executive, it would answer the same purpose as an absolute negative. It would rarely if ever happen that the Executive constituted as ours is proposed to be would, have firmness eno' to resist the Legislature, unless backed by a certain part of the body itself.[12] The King of G. B. with all his splendid attributes would not be able to withstand ye. unanimous and eager wishes of both houses of Parliament. To give such a prerogative would certainly be obnoxious to the ⟨temper of this country; its present temper at least.⟩

Mr. Wilson believed as others did that this power would seldom be used. The Legislature would know that such a power existed, and would refrain from such laws, as it would be sure to defeat. Its silent operation would therefore preserve harmony and prevent mischief. The case of Pena. formerly was very different from its present case. The Executive was not then as now to be appointed by the people. It will not in this case as in the one cited be supported by the head of a Great Empire, actuated by a different & sometimes opposite interest. The salary too is now proposed to be fixed by the Constitution, or if Dr. F's idea should be adopted all salary whatever interdicted. The requiring a large proportion of each House to overrule the Executive check might do in peaceable times; but there might be tempestuous moments in which animosties may run high between the Executive and Legislative branches, and in which the former ought to be able to defend itself.

Mr. Butler had been in favor of a single Executive Magistrate; but could he have entertained an idea that a compleat negative on the laws was to be given him he certainly should have acted very differently. It had been observed that in all countries the Executive power is in a constant course of increase. This was certainly the case in G. B. Gentlemen seemed to think that we had nothing to apprehend from an abuse of the Executive power. But why might not a Cataline or a Cromwell arise in this Country as well as in others.

Mr. Bedford was opposed to every check on the Legislative, even the Council of Revision first proposed. He thought it would be sufficient to mark out in the Constitution the boundaries to the Legislative Authority, which would give all the

---

[12] Crossed out "or actuated by some foreign support agst. his own Country."

requisite security to the rights of the other departments. The Representatives of the People were the best judges of what was for their interest, and ought to be under no external controul whatever. The two branches would produces a sufficient controul within ⟨the Legislature itself.⟩

Col. Mason[13] observed that a vote had already passed he found (he was out at the time) for vesting the executive powers in a single person. Among these powers was that of appointing to offices in certain cases. The probable abuses of a negative had been well explained by Dr. F as proved by experience, the best of all tests. Will not the same door be opened here. The Executive may refuse its assent to necessary measures till new appointments shall be referred to him; and having by degrees engrossed all these into his own hands, the American Executive, like the British, will by bribery & influence, save himself the trouble & odium of exerting his negative afterwards. We are Mr. Chairman going very far in this business. We are not indeed constituting a British Government, but a more dangerous monarchy, an elective one. We are introducing a new principle into our system, and not necessary as in the British Govt. where the Executive has greater rights to defend. Do gentlemen mean to pave the way to hereditary Monarchy? Do they flatter themselves that the people will ever consent to such an innovation? If they do I venture to tell them, they are mistaken. The people never will consent. And do gentlemen consider the danger of delay, and the still greater danger of a a rejection not for a moment but forever, of the plan which shall be proposed to them. Notwithstanding the oppressions & injustice experienced among us from democracy; the genius of the people is in favor of it, and the genius of the people must be consulted. He could not but consider the federal system as in effect dissolved by the appointment of this Convention to devise a better one. And do gentlemen look forward to the dangerous interval between the extinction of an old, and the establishment of a new Governmt. and to the scenes of confusion which may ensue. He

---

[13] For Mason's draft of a speech on this subject see below.

hoped that nothing like a monarchy would ever be attempted in this Country.   A hatred to its oppressions had carried the people through the late Revolution.   Will it not be eno' to enable the Executive to suspend offensive laws, till they shall be coolly revised, and the objections to them overruled by a greater majority than was required in the first instance.   He never could agree to give up all the rights of the people to a single Magistrate.   If more than one had been fixed on, greater powers might have been entrusted to the Executive.   He hoped this attempt to give such powers would have its weight hereafter ⟨as an argument⟩ for increasing the number of the Executive.

Docr. Franklin.[14]   A Gentleman from S. C. (Mr. Butler)

---

[14] The following is evidently Franklin's own draft of this speech:

The Steady Course of public Measures is most probably to be expected from a Number.

A single Person's Measures may be good.   The Successor, often differs in Opinion of those Measures, & adopts others.   Often is ambitious of distinguishing himself, by opposing them, and offering new Projects.   One is peaceably dispos'd.   Another may be food of War, &c: Hence foreign States can never have that Confidence, in the Treaties or Friendship of such a Governent as in that which is conducted by a Number.

The Single Head may be Sick.   Who is to conduct the Public Affairs in that Case?   When he dies, who are to conduct, till a new Election? — If a Council why not continue them? — Shall we not be harass'd with Factions for the Election of Successors? become like Poland, weak from our Dissensions?

Consider the present distracted Condition of Holland.   They had at first a Stadtholder, the Prince of Orange, a Man of undoubted and great Merit.   They found some Inconveniencies however in the Extent of Powers annex'd to that Office, and exercis'd by a single Person.   On his Death They resum'd and divided those Powers among the States and Cities.   But there has been a constant Struggle since between that Family & the Nation.   In the last Century the then Prince of Orange found Means to inflame the Populace against their Magistrates, excite a general Insurrection in which an excellent Minister, *Dewit*, was murdered, all the old Magistrates displac'd, and the Stadtholder re-invested with all the former Powers.   In this Century, the Father of the present Stadtholder, having married a British Princess, did, by exciting another Insurrection, force from the Nation a Decree that the Stadtholdership should be thenceforth hereditary in his Family.   And now his Son, being suspected of having favour'd England in the late War, and thereby lost the Confidence of the Nation, he is forming an internal Faction to support his Power, & reinstate his Favourite the Duke of Brunswick; and he holds up his Family Alliances with England and Prussia to terrify Opposition.   It was this Conduct of the Stadtholder which induc'd the States to recur to the Protection of France, and put their Troops under a French rather than the Stadtholder's German General the Duke of Brunswick. And this is the Source of all the present Disorders in Holland, which if the Stadtholder

a day or two ago called our attention to the case of the U. Netherlands. He wished the gentleman had been a little fuller, and had gone back to the original of that Govt. The people being under great obligations to the Prince of Orange whose wisdom and bravery had saved them, chose him for the Stadtholder. He did very well. Inconveniences however were felt from his powers; ⟨which growing more & more oppressive, they were at length set aside.⟩ Still however there was a party for the P. of Orange, which descended to his son who excited insurrections, spilt a great deal of blood, murdered the de Witts, and got the powers revested in the Stadtholder. Afterwards another Prince had power to excite insurrections & to make the Stadtholdership hereditary. And the present Stadthder. is ready to wade thro' a bloody civil war to the establishment of a monarchy. Col. Mason had mentioned the circumstance of appointing officers. He knew how that point would be managed. No new appointment would be suffered as heretofore in Pensa. unless it be referred to the Executive; so that all profitable offices will be at his disposal. The first man, put at the helm will be a good one. No body knows what sort may come afterwards. The Executive will be always increasing here, as elsewhere, till it ends in a monarchy

On the question for striking out so as to give Executive an absolute Negative —

Massts. no. Cont. no. N. Y. no. Pa. no. Dl. no. Md. no. Va. no. N. C. no. S. C. no. Georga. no. [Ayes — o; noes — 10.][15]

Mr. Butler moved that ⟨the Resoln. be altered so as to read — "Resolved that the National Executive have a power to suspend any legislative act for the term of   ."⟩[16]

Doctr. Franklin seconds the motion.

---

has Abilities equal to his Inclinations, will probably after a ruinous & bloody civil War, end in establishing an hereditary Monarchy in his Family.

[In Franklin's Works (Sparks edition, V, 142, Smyth edition, IX, 603-4) these notes are mistakenly attached to a proposal by Franklin on June 30.]

[15] *Cf.* King's record of this vote.
[16] Madison originally had this motion in substance, but revised it from *Journal.*

Mr. Gerry observed that a power of suspending might do all the mischief dreaded from the negative of useful laws; without answering the salutary purpose of checking unjust or unwise ones.

On question "for giving this suspending power". all the States, to wit Massts. Cont. N. Y. Pa. Del. Maryd. Virga. N. C. S. C. Georgia. were *no*.

On a question for enabling *two thirds* of each branch of the Legislature to overrule the revisionary check: it passed in the affirmative sub silentio; ⟨and was inserted in the blank of Mr. Gerry's motion.⟩[17]

On the question on Mr. Gerry's motion which gave the Executive alone without the Judiciary the revisionary controul on the laws ⟨unles overruled by ⅔ of each branch.⟩[18] Massts. ay. Cont. no. N. Y. ay. Pena. ay. Del. ay. Maryd. no. Va. ay N. C. ay. S. C. ay. Geo. ay. [Ayes — 8; noes — 2.] [19]

⟨It was moved by Mr. Wilson 2ded. by Mr. Madison — that the following amendment be made to the last resolution — after the words "National Ex." to add "& a convenient number of the National Judiciary."[20]

An Objection of order being taken by Mr. Hamilton to the introduction of the last amendment at this time, notice was given by Mr. W. &. Mr. M — that the same wd. be moved tomorrow. — whereupon Wednesday (the day after) was assigned to reconsider the amendment of Mr. Gerry.

It was then moved & 2ded. to proceed to the consideration of the 9th. resolution submitted by Mr. Randolph — when on motion to agree to the first clause namely "Resolved that a National Judiciary be established" It passed in the Affirmative nem. con.

It was then moved and 2ded. to add these words to the first clause of the ninth resolution namely — "to consist of one

---

[17] Probably based upon Yates.   [18] Corrected from *Journal*.
[19] See Appendix A, XLI, CXXXVII, CLVIII (47).
[20] Originally Madison had only recorded "Clause. — 'That a national Judiciary be established' passed nem. con." This was crossed out and the rest of this day's records copied from *Journal*. See below, note 25.

supreme tribunal, and of one or more inferior tribunals".
which passed in the affirmative —

The Comme. then rose and the House

Adjourned.)

YATES

Monday, June 4th, 1787.

Met pursuant to adjournment.

Mr. Pinkney moved that the blank in the 7th resolve *consisting of*   be filled up with an individual.

Mr. Wilson, in support of the motion, asserted, that it would not be obnoxious to the minds of the people, as they in their state governments were accustomed and reconciled to a single executive. Three executives might divide so that two could not agree in one proposition — the consequence would be anarchy and confusion.

Mr. Sherman thought there ought to be one executive, but that he ought to have a council. Even the king of Great Britain has his privy council.

Mr. Gerry was for one executive — if otherwise, it would be absurd to have it consist of three   Numbers equally in rank would oddly apply to a general or admiral.

Question put — 7 states for, and 3 against. New-York against it.

The 8th resolve, That the executive and a number of the judicial officers ought to compose a council of revision.

Mr. Gerry objects to the clause — moves its postponement in order to let in a motion — *that the right of revision should be in the executive only.*

Mr. Wilson contends that the executive and judicial ought to have a joint and full negative — they cannot otherwise preserve their importance against the legislature.

Mr. King was against the interference of the judicial — they may be biased in the interpretation — He is therefore to give the executive a complete *negative.*

Carried to be postponed, 6 states against 4 — New-York for it.

The next question, that the executive have a complete negative; and it was therefore moved to expunge the remaining part of the clause.

Dr. Franklin against the motion — the power dangerous, and would be abused so as to get money for passing bills.

Mr. Madison against it — because of the difficulty of an executive venturing on the exercise of this negative, and is therefore of opinion that the revisional authority is better.

Mr. Bedford is against the whole, either negative or revisional — the two branches are sufficient checks on each other — no danger of subverting the executive, because his powers may by the convention be so well defined that the legislature cannot overleap the bounds.

Mr. Mason against the negative power in the executive, because it will not accord with the genius of the people.

On this the question was put and carried, *nem. con.* against expunging part of the clause so as to establish a complete negative.

Mr. Butler then moved that all acts passed by the legislature be suspended for the space of   days by the executive.

Unanimously in the negative.

It was resolved and agreed, that the blank be filled up with the words *two thirds of the legislature*.   Agreed to.

The question was then put on the whole of the resolve as amended and filled up.   Carried, 8 states for — 2 against. New-York for it.

Mr. Wilson then moved for the addition *of a convenient number of the national judicial* to the executive as a council of revision.   Ordered to be taken into consideration to-morrow.

Adjourned until to-morrow.

KING

4 June Comee. of y Whole

On the Question of vesting the executive powers in one or more persons — it was carried for the former

Mas. Cont. NYk. Pen. Virg. NC. SC. Geor. Ay
N Jer. Del. Mar. No.[21]

Motion by Mr Gerry & Mr Kg to postpone the article for a
Council of Revision and adopt one vesting a qualified negative
in the Executive —
8 ays   2 no — Cont. & Mard.[22]

Wilson moves & Hamilton seconds him that the Executive
shd. have a complete and full negative — the former is in
favor because the natural operation of the Legislature will
be to swallow up the Executive — power divided is the object
of Contest — the strongest will finally acquire the whole —
Butler agt. it — it will terminate in a King — Franklin agt.
it — one former Govr. abused his power of negative and extorted Money from the Legislature before he wd. sign yr.
Acts. — in one instance of an indian Invasion, he wd. not
agree to an act for marching the Militia agt. the Indians unless
the Estate of the Proprietors was exempted from Taxes for
the support of the Militia —
We ought not to believe that one man Can possess more wisdom than both br's. of the Legislature — The Negative of
the King of G. B. has not been exercised since the Revolution — he effects that by Corruption wh. he might with hazard
accomplish by his negative —
Mad: I am opposed to the complete negative, because no man
will dare exercise it whn. the law was passed almost unanimously. I doubt whether the Kng of Eng. wd. have firmness
sufficient to do it.

Mason. opposed to the Complete negative, We have voted
that the Ex. powers be vested in one person, we now propose
to give that single person a negative in all Cases. You have
agreed that he shall appoint all Officers not otherwise to be
appointed — and those which he has not the sole right of
appointing, he has a power to negative — with these powers
the executive may soon currupt the Legislature & we shall

---

[21] Journal, Madison and Yates omit New Jersey and make New York's vote "no".
[22] Journal, Madison and Yates, all give this vote: Ayes — 6, Noes — 4.

have a monarchy & we must consult the Genius of our People
wh. is republican — this Genius will not receive a King —

Franklin
      The Pr. of Orange first had limited powers and for life —
his son raised a faction and caused himself to be elected by
force — in the present Century the Pr. of Orange caused himself to be declared hereditary & — we shall meet with the same
misfortune —

Wil ⎫
Ham ⎬ ay   Unanimous negative
Kg ⎭

Mad. The Judicial ought to be introduced in the business
of Legislation — they will protect their Department, and
uniting wh. the Executive render their Check or negative
more respectable — there is weight in the objections agt.
this measure— but a Check is necessary experience proves it,
and teaches us that what we once thought the Calumny of
the Enemies of Republican Govts. is undoubtedly true —
There is diversity of Interest in every Country the Rich &
poor, the Dr. & Cr. the followers of different Demagogues, the
diversity of religious Sects — The Effects of these parties
are obvious in the ant'. Govts. — the same causes will operate
with us —
We must introduce the Checks, which will destroy the measures
of an interested majority — in this view a negative in the Ex:
is not only necessary for its own safety, but for the safety of
a minority in Danger of oppression from an unjust and interested majority — The independent condition of the Ex. who
has the Eyes of all Nations on him will render him a just Judge
— add the Judiciary and you increase the respectability —
      Wilson moves the addition of the Judiciary — Madison
seconds —
Dickerson — agt. it — you must separate the Leg. Jud. &
Ex. — but you propose to give the Executive a share in Legislation — why not the Judicial —
There is a Difference — the Judges must interpret the Laws
they ought not to be legislators. The Executive is merely

ministerial — besides we have Experience in the British Constitution of the Executive's having a negative —
The motion was waved — [23]

PIERCE.

Mr. Wilson said that all the Constitutions of America from New Hampshire to Georgia have their Executive in a single Person. A single Person will produce vigor and activity. Suppose the Executive to be in the hands of a number they will probably be divided in opinion.

It was proposed that the Judicial should be joined with the Executive to revise the Laws.

Mr. King was of opinion that the Judicial ought not to join in the negative of a Law, because the Judges will have the expounding of those Laws when they come before them; and they will no doubt stop the operation of such as shall appear repugnant to the constitution.

Dr. Franklin thinks it would be improper to put it in the power of any Man to negative a Law passed by the Legislature because it would give him the controul of the Legislature; and mentioned the influence of the British King, and the influence which a Governor of Pennsylvania once had in arresting (for the consideration of an encrease of salary) the power out of the hands of the Legislature.

Mr. Maddison was of opinion that no Man would be so daring as to place a veto on a Law that had passed with the assent of the Legislature [24]

Mr. Butler observed that power was always encreasing on the part of the Executive. When he voted for a single Person to hold the Executive power he did it that Government be expeditiously executed, and not that it should be clogged.

Mr. Bedford was of opinion that no check was necessary on a Legislature composed as the national Legislature would be, with two branches, — an upper and a lower House.

Mr. Mason was of opinion that it would be so dangerous

---

[23] [Endorsed:] 4 June | Complete Neg. of the Extive | addn. of judiciary
[24] See Appendix A, CCCLXXIII.

for the Executive in a single Person to negative a Law that the People will not accept of it. He asked if Gentlemen had ever reflected on that awful period of time between the passing and final adoption of this constitution; — what alarm might possibly take place in the public mind.

Mr. Maddison in a very able and ingenious Speech,[25] ran through the whole Scheme of the Government,— pointed out all the beauties and defects of ancient Republics; compared their situation with ours wherever it appeared to bear any anology, and proved that the only way to make a Government answer all the end of its institution was to collect the wisdom of its several parts in aid of each other whenever it was necessary. Hence the propriety of incorporating the Judicial with the Executive in the revision of the Laws. He was of opinion that by joining the Judges with the Supreme Executive Magistrate would be strictly proper, and would by no means interfere with that indepence so much to be approved and distinguished in the several departments,

Mr. Dickinson could not agree with Gentlemen in blending the national Judicial with the Executive, because the one is the expounder, and the other the Executor of the Laws.

M A S O N [26]

It is not yet determined how the Executive is to be regulated, whether it is to act solely from its own judgment, or with the advice of others; whether there is, or is not to be a council annexed to it, and if a council how far their advice shall operate in controlling the judgment of the supreme magistracy. If there is no Council of State and the executive power be vested in a single person, what are the provisions for its

---

[25] Professor Jameson (*American Historical Review*, III, 323 note) ascribes this speech by Madison and the one following by Dickinson to June 6. But the text above shows that Madison's records at the close of this day's sessions were quite defective. It is possible that he inserted in his record of his remarks on June 6 a portion of his speech on June 4.

[26] This document in Mason's handwriting was found among the Mason papers. It is evidently the draft of a speech in the Convention and probably of this date. The copy in the text is taken from K. M. Rowland, *Life of George Mason*, II, 112–115.

proper operation, upon casual disability by sickness or otherwise. These are subjects which must come under our consideration, and perhaps some of the most important objections would be obviated by placing the executive power in the hands of three, instead of one person.

There is also to be a council of revision, invested, in a great measure, with a power of negative upon the laws; and an idea has been suggested, either within or without doors, that this council should be formed of the principal officers of the state, I presume of the members of the Treasury Board, the Board of War, the Navy Board, and the Department for Foreign Affairs. It is unnecessary, if not improper, to examine this part of the subject now, but I will venture to hazard an opinion, when it comes to be thoroughly investigated, that we can hardly find worse materials out of which to create a council of revision, or more improper or unsafe hands in which to place the power of a negative upon our laws. It is proposed, I think, sir, in the plan upon your table, that this council of revision shall be formed out of the members of the Judiciary departments joined with the Executive; and I am inclined to think, when the subject shall be taken up, it may be demonstrated, that this will be the wisest and safest mode of constituting this important council of revision. But the federal inferior courts of justice must, I presume, be fixed in the several respective States, and consequently most of them at a great distance from the seat of the federal government. The almost continual operation of the council of revision upon the acts of the national parliament, and upon their negative of the acts of the several State legislatures, will require that this council should be easily and speedily convened, and consequently, that only the judges of the Supreme Federal Court, fixed near the seat of government, can be members of it. Their number will be small. By placing the Executive in three persons, instead of one, we shall not only increase the number of the council of revision (which I have endeavored to show will want increasing), but by giving to each of the three a vote in the council of revision, we shall increase the strength of the Executive in that particular circumstance in which it will most want strength — in the power of defending itself against the encroachments of the legislature. These, I must acknowledge, are, with me, weighty considerations for vesting the Executive rather in three than in one person.

The chief advantages which have been urged in favor of unity in the Executive, are the secresy, the dispatch, the vigor and energy which the government will derive from it, especially in time of war. That these are great advantages, I shall most readily allow. They have been strongly insisted on by all monarchical writers; they have been acknowledged by the ablest and most candid defenders of republican government; and it cannot be denied that a monarchy possesses them in a much greater degree than a republic. Yet perhaps a little reflection may incline us to doubt whether these advantages are not greater in theory than in practice, or lead us to enquire whether there is not some pervading principle in republican government which sets at naught and tramples upon this boasted superiority, as hath been experienced to their cost, by most monarchies which have been imprudent enough to invade or attack their republican neighbors. This invincible principle is to be found in the love, the affection, the attachment of the citizens to their laws, to their freedom, and to their country. Every husbandman will be quickly converted into a soldier when he knows and feels that he is to fight not in defence of the rights of a particular family, or a prince, but for his own. This is the true construction of the *pro aris et focis* which has, in all ages, performed such wonders. It was this which in ancient times enabled the little cluster of Grecian republics to resist, and almost constantly to defeat, the Persian monarch. It was this which supported the States of Holland against a body of veteran troops through a thirty years' war with Spain, then the greatest monarchy in Europe, and finally rendered them victorious. It is this which preserves the freedom and independence of the Swiss Cantons in the midst of the most powerful nations. And who that reflects seriously upon the situation of America, in the beginning of the late war — without arms — without soldiers — without trade, money or credit, in a manner destitute of all resources, but must ascribe our success to this pervading, all-powerful principle?

We have not yet been able to define the powers of the Executive, and however moderately some gentlemen may talk or think upon the subject, I believe there is a general tendency to a strong Executive, and I am inclined to think a strong Executive necessary. If strong and extensive powers are vested in the Executive, and that executive consists only of one person, the government will of course degenerate (for I will call it degeneracy) into a monarchy — a government so contrary to the genius of the people that they will reject even the appearance of it. I consider the federal government as in some measure dissolved by the meeting of this Convention. Are there no dangers to be apprehended from procrastinating the time between the breaking up of this Assembly and the adoption of a new system of government? I dread the interval. If it should not be brought to an issue in the course of the first year the consequences may be fatal. Have not the different parts of this extensive government, the several States of which it is composed a right to expect an equal participation in the Executive, as the best means of securing an equal attention to their interests? Should an insurrection, a rebellion or invasion happen in New Hampshire when the single supreme magistrate is a citizen of Georgia, would not the people of New Hampshire naturally ascribe any delay in defending them to such a circumstance and *vice versa*? If the Executive is vested in three persons, one chosen from the Northern, one from the Middle, and one from the Southern States, will it not contribute to quiet the minds of the people and convince them that there will be proper attention paid to their respective concerns? Will not three men so chosen bring with them, into office, a more perfect and extensive knowledge of the real interests of this great Union? Will not such a mode of appointment be the most effectual means of preventing cabals and intrigues between the legislature and the candidates for this office, especially with those candidates who from their local situation, near the seat of the federal government, will have the greatest temptations and the greatest opportunities? Will it not be the most effectual means of checking and counteracting the aspiring views of dangerous and ambitious men, and consequently the best security for the stability and duration of our government upon the invaluable principles of liberty? These Sir, are some of my motives for preferring an Executive consisting of three persons rather than of one.[27]

---

[27] For a transcription of this document from the original manuscript, see Volume IV.

TUESDAY, JUNE 5, 1787.

JOURNAL
Tuesday June 5 1787.

The Order of the day being read

The House resolved itself into a Committee of the whole House to consider of the State of the American union.

His Excellency William Livingston Esquire, a Deputy of the State of New Jersey, attended and took his seat

Mr President left the chair

Mr Gorham took the Chair of the Committee

Mr President resumed the chair

Mr Gorham reported from the Committee that the Committee had made a further progress in the matter to them referred; and had directed him to move that they may have leave to sit again

Resolved that this House will to-morrow again resolve itself into a Committee of the whole House to consider of the State of the American union.

The following credentials were then produced and read.

(here insert the credentials of His Excellency William Livingston Esquire, and the honorable Abraham Clark Esquire) [1]

And then the House adjourned till to-morrow at 11 o'clock. A M.

In a Committee of the whole House
Tuesday June 5. 1787.
Mr Gorham in the Chair

It was moved and seconded to proceed to the further considn of the 9th resolution, submitted by Mr Randolph.

---

[1] See Appendix B.

It was then moved and seconded to amend the last clause by striking out the words "One or more" so as to read "and of inferior to tribunals"
> and on the question to strike out
>> it passed in the affirmative

It was then moved and seconded to strike out the words "the national legislature" so as to read
> to be appointed by.
> On the question to strike out
> it passed in the affirmative   [Ayes — 8;   noes — 2.] [2]

Notice was given by Mr. Wilson that he should at a future day move for a reconsideration of that clause which respects "inferior tribunals"
Mr C. Pinckney gave notice that when the clause which respects the appointment of the Judiciary came before the Committee he should move to restore the words
> "the national legislature"

It was then moved and seconded to agree to the following part of the 9th resolution namely.
> "To hold their offices during good behaviour and to re-
> "ceive punctually, at stated times, a fixed compensation for
> "their services, in which no encrease or diminution shall be
> "made, so as to affect the persons actually in office at the
> "time of such encrease or diminution"
>> and on the question to agree to the same
>>> it passed in the affirmative

It was then moved and seconded to postpone the remaining clause of the 9th resolution
> and on the question to postpone
>> it passed in the affirmative

On the question to agree to the 10th resolution, as submitted by Mr Randolph namely

---

[2] Vote 22, Detail of Ayes and Noes.   Madison includes New Jersey in the affirmative making eleven votes in all, but Yates gives only ten.

"resolved that provision ought to be made for the admis-
"sion of States lawfully arising within the limits of the
"United States, whether from a voluntary junction of gov-
"ernment and territory or otherwise, with the consent of a
"number of voices in the national legislature less than the
"whole"
      it passed in the affirmative

It was moved and seconded to postpone the consideration of
the 11th resolution submitted by Mr Randolph.
      and on the question to postpone
            it passed in the affirmative [3]

On the question to agree to the 12th resolution submitted by
Mr Randolph — namely
      "resolved that provision ought to be made for the contin-
"uance of a Congress and their authorities and privileges,
"until a given day, after the reform of the articles of union
"shall be adopted, and for the completion of all their engage-
"ments"
      it passed in the affirmative   [Ayes — 8; noes — 2.] [4]

It was then moved and seconded to postpone the consideration of the 13th resolution submitted by Mr Randolph
      and on the question to postpone
            it passed in the affirmative [5]
It was moved and seconded to postpone the considn of the
14th resolution submitted by Mr Randolph.
      and on the question to postpone
            it passed in the affirmative [6]

---

[3] *Journal* ascribes Vote 22, Detail of Ayes and Noes, to this question.   A mistake,
see above, and note 19 below.

[4] Vote 23, Detail of Ayes and Noes.   Madison includes New Jersey in the affirmative.

[5] *Journal* ascribes Vote 24, Detail of Ayes and Noes, to this question.   There is
no reason for assigning it here except that of the order in which it comes.   Probably
a mistake, see note 20, and *cf.* Yates.

[6] *Journal* ascribes to this question Vote 25, Detail of Ayes and Noes, but without
any apparent reason.

It was moved and seconded to postpone the considn of the 15th resolution submitted by Mr Randolph
  and on the question to postpone
      it passed in the affirmative

It was moved by Mr C Pinckney seconded by Mr Rutledge that to-morrow be assigned to reconsider that clause of the 4th resolution which respects the election of the first branch of the national legislature.
  And on the question to reconsider the same to-morrow
      it passed in the affirmative   [Ayes — 6; noes — 5.][7]
It was moved by Mr Rutledge seconded by Mr. Sherman
  To strike out the following words in the 9th resolution submitted by Mr Randolph namely
  "and of inferior tribunals"
  And on the question to strike out
it passed in the affirmative [Ayes — 5; noes — 4; divided — 2.][8]

It was then moved and seconded that the following clause be added to the 9th resolution namely
  "That the national legislature be empowered to appoint inferior Tribunals"
  And on the question to agree to the same
it passed in the affirmative [Ayes — 7; noes — 3; divided — 1.][9]

It was then moved and seconded that the Committee do now rise, report a further progress, and request leave to sit again.
  The Committee then rose

---

[7] Vote 26, Detail of Ayes and Noes.
[8] Vote 27, Detail of Ayes and Noes.
[9] Vote 28, Detail of Ayes and Noes.

DETAIL OF AYES AND NOES

1 N. H.		*2* Massa:	*3* C:	*4* R. I.	*5* N. Y.	*6* N. J:	*7* P:	*8* D:	*9* Mary:	*10* V:	*11* N. C.	*12* S. C.	*13.* G.
ayes	noes												
[22] 8	2	aye	no		aye		aye	aye	aye	aye	aye	no	aye
[23] 8	2	aye	no	12th resolu- tion	aye		aye	no	aye	aye	aye	aye	aye
[24] 7	3	aye	aye		aye		aye	aye	aye	no	aye	no	no
[25] 6	4	divided	aye		no	aye	no	no	aye	aye	no	aye	aye
[26] 6	5	no	aye	to reconsider	aye	no	aye	aye	aye	aye	no	no	no
[27] 5	4	divided	aye	to strike out inferior tribs	divid.	aye	no	no	no	no	aye	aye	aye
[28] 7	3	aye	no		.divid.	no	aye	aye	aye	aye	aye	no	aye

[End of first loose sheet]

MADISON

Teusday June 5.   In Committee of the Whole

⟨Governor Livingston from New Jersey took his seat.

The words, "one or more" were struck out before "inferior tribunals" as an amendment to the last clause of Resoln. 9th.⟩[10]   ⟨The⟩ Clause — "that the national Judiciary be ⟨chosen⟩[11] by the National Legislature ", ⟨being under consideration.⟩

Mr. Wilson opposed the appointmt ⟨of Judges by the⟩ national Legisl: Experience shewed the impropriety of such appointmts. by numerous bodies. Intrigue, partiality, and concealment were the necessary consequences. A principal reason for unity in the Executive was that officers might be appointed by a single, responsible person.[12]

Mr. Rutlidge was by no means disposed to grant so great a power to any single person. The people will think we are leaning too much towards Monarchy. He was against establishing any national tribunal except a single supreme one. The State Tribunals ⟨are most proper⟩ to decide in all cases in the first instance.

Docr. Franklin observed that two modes of chusing the

---

[10] Taken from *Journal*.   [11] Revised from *Journal*.
[12] Crossed out: "The examples in the States are in favor."

Judges had been mentioned, to wit, by the Legislature and by the Executive. He wished such other modes to be suggested as might occur to other gentlemen; it being a point of great moment. He would mention ⟨one which⟩ he had understood was practiced in Scotland. He then in a brief and entertaining manner related a Scotch mode, in which the nomination proceeded from the Lawyers, who always selected the ablest of the profession in order to get rid of him, and share his practice ⟨among themselves⟩. It was here he said the interest of the electors to make the best choice, which should always be made the case if possible.

Mr. Madison disliked the election of the Judges by the Legislature or any numerous body. Besides, the danger of intrigue and partiality, many of the members were not judges of the requisite qualifications. The Legislative talents which were very different from those of a Judge, commonly recommended men to the favor of Legislative Assemblies. It was known too that the accidental circumstances of presence and absence, of being a member or not a member,[13] had a very undue influence on the appointment. On the other hand He was not satisfied with referring the appointment to the Executive. He rather inclined to give it to the Senatorial branch, as numerous eno' to be confided in — as not so numerous as to be governed by the motives of the other branch; and as being sufficiently stable [14] and independent to follow their deliberate judgments. He hinted this only and moved that the *appointment by the Legislature* might be struck out, & and a blank left to be hereafter filled on maturer reflection. Mr. Wilson seconds it. On the question for striking out. Massts. ay. Cont. no. N. Y. ay. N. J. ay. Pena. ay. Del. ay. Md. ay. Va. ay. N. C. ay. S. C. no. Geo. ay. [Ayes — 9; noes — 2.] [15]

⟨Mr. Wilson gave notice that he should at a future day move for a reconsideration of that clause which respects "inferior tribunals" [16]

---

[13] Crossed out "of the body at the time of election".
[14] Crossed out "and cool ".   [15] See note 2.
[16] This and the four paragraphs following were taken from *Journal.*

Mr. Pinkney gave notice that when the clause respecting the appointment of the Judiciary should again come before the Committee, he should move to restore the "appointment by the national Legislature" [17]

The following clauses of Resol: 9. were agreed to viz "to hold their offices during good behaviour, and to receive punctually at stated times, a fixed compensation for their services, in which no increase or diminution shall be made so as to affect the persons actually in office at the time of such increase or diminution"

The remaining clause of Resolution 9. was postponed.

Resolution 10 was agreed to — viz — that provision ought to be made for the admission of States lawfully arising within the limits of the U. States, whether from a voluntary junction of Government & territory, or otherwise with the consent of a number of voices in the National Legislature less than the whole.⟩

⟨The 11. propos:⟩ *"for guarantying to States ⟨Republican Govt. & territory &c,"* being read,⟩ [18] Mr. Patterson wished the point of representation could be decided before this clause should be considered, and moved to postpone it: which was not. opposed, and agreed to: ⟨Connecticut & S. Carolina only voting agst. it.[19]

propos. 12⟩ *"for continuing Congs. till a given day, and for fulfilling their engagements."* ⟨produced⟩ no debate On the question Mass. ay. Cont. no. N. Y. ay. N. J.* ay. Pa. ay. Del. no. Md. ay. Va. ay. N C. ay. S. C. ay. G. ay. [Ayes — 9; noes — 2.]

⟨propos: 13.⟩ "that *provision ought to be made for* ⟨hereafter⟩ *amending the system now to be established, without requiring the assent of the Natl. Legislature."* ⟨being taken up.⟩

Mr. Pinkney doubted the propriety or necessity of it.

*⟨New Jersey omitted in the Printed Journal⟩

---

[17] See Appendix A, CCLXXXVII.   [18] Revised from *Journal.*
[19] Vote taken from *Journal.* A mistake, as Madison's original record shows the question was passed without opposition and this is the same vote recorded by Madison above. See above Vote 22, Detail of Ayes and Noes, and note 3.

Mr. Gerry favored it. The novelty & difficulty of the experiment requires periodical revision. The prospect of such a revision would also give intermediate stability to the Govt. Nothing had yet happened in the States where this provision existed to proves its impropriety. — The Proposition was postponed for further consideration: ⟨the votes being. Mas: Con. N. Y. Pa. Del. Ma. N. C. — ay

Virga. S. C. Geo: no⟩ [20]

propos. 14. *"requiring oath from the State officers to support national Govt."* was postponed after a short uninteresting conversation; ⟨the votes, Con. N. Jersey. Md. Virg: S. C. Geo. ay

N. Y. Pa. Del. N. C. . . . no

Massachusetts. . . . divided⟩ [21]

⟨propos. 15.⟩ for *"recommending conventions under appointment* ⟨of the people⟩ *to ratify the new Constitution &c."* ⟨being taken up.⟩

Mr. Sherman thought such a popular ratification unnecessary. the articles of Confederation providing for changes and alterations with the assent of Congs. and ratification of State Legislatures.

Mr. M⟨adison⟩ thought this provision essential. The articles of Confedn. themselves were defective in this respect, resting in many of the States on the Legislative sanction only. Hence in conflicts between acts of the States, and of Congs. especially where the former are of posterior date, and the decision is to be made by State Tribunals, an uncertainty must necessarily prevail, or rather perhaps a certain decision in favor of the State authority. He suggested also that as far as the articles of Union were to be considered as a Treaty only of a particular sort, among the Governments of Independent States, the doctrine might be set up that a breach of any one article, by any of the parties, absolved the other parties

---

[20] Madison originally recorded that this provision was "postponed nem. con.," but later substituted this vote from *Journal*. His original record was doubtless correct as there is no apparent reason for ascribing this vote to this question. See note 5 above.

[21] Vote taken from *Journal*, see note 6 above.

from ⟨the whole⟩ obligation. For these ⟨reasons as well as others⟩ he thought it indispensable that the new Constitution should be ratified in the most unexceptionable form, and by the supreme authority of the people themselves.

Mr. Gerry. Observed that in the Eastern States the Confedn. had been sanctioned by the people themselves. He seemed afraid of referring the new system to them. The people in that quarter have ⟨at this time⟩ the wildest ideas of Government in the world. They were for abolishing the Senate in Massts. and giving all the other powers of Govt. to the other branch of the Legislature.

Mr. King supposed the last article of ye Confedn. Rendered the legislature competent to the ratification. The people of the Southern States where the federal articles had been ratified by the Legislatures only, had since *impliedly* given their sanction to it. He thought notwithstanding that there might be policy in varying the mode. A Convention being a single house, the adoption may more easily be carried thro' it. than thro' the Legislatures where there are several branches. The Legislatures also being to lose power, will be most likely to raise objections. ⟨The people having already parted with the necessary powers it is immaterial to them, by which Government they are possessed, provided they be well employed.⟩

Mr. Wilson took this occasion to lead the Committee by a train of observations to the idea of not suffering a disposition in the plurality of States to confederate anew on better principles, to be defeated by the inconsiderate or selfish opposition of a few ⟨States⟩. He hoped the provision for ratifying would be put on such a footing as to admit of such a partial union, with a door open for the accession of the rest. —*

Mr. Pinkney hoped that in the case the experiment should not unanimously take place nine States might be authorized to unite under the same Governmt.

The ⟨propos. 15.⟩ was postponed nem. cont:[22]

* This hint was probably meant in terrorem to the smaller States of N. Jersey & Delaware. Nothing was said in reply to it.

[22] According to Yates, the vote was, Ayes — 7, Noes — 3.

⟨Mr. Pinkney & Mr. Rutlidge moved that tomorrow be assigned to reconsider that clause of Propos. 4: which respects the elections of the first branch of the National Legislature—which passed in affirmative: Con: N. Y. Pa. Del: Md. Va. ay — 6   Mas. N J. N. C. S. C. Geo. no. 5⟩ [23]

Mr. Rutlidge havg. obtained a rule for reconsideration of the clause for establishing *inferior* tribunals under the national authority, now moved that that part of the clause ⟨in propos. 9.⟩ should be expunged: arguing that the State Tribunals might and ought to be left in all cases to decide in the first instance the right of appeal to the supreme national tribunal being sufficient to secure the national rights & uniformity of Judgmts: that it was making an unnecessary encroachment on the jurisdiction ⟨of the States,⟩ and creating unnecessary obstacles to their adoption of the new system. — ⟨Mr. Sherman 2ded. the motion.⟩

Mr. ⟨Madison⟩ observed that unless inferior tribunals were dispersed throughout the Republic with *final* juridsiction in *many* cases, appeals would be multiplied to a most oppressive degree; that besides, an appeal would not in many cases be a remedy. What was to be done after improper Verdicts in State tribunals obtained under the biassed directions of a dependent Judge, or the local prejudices of an undirected jury? To remand the cause for a new trial would answer no purpose. To order a new trial at the supreme bar would oblige the parties to bring up their witnesses, tho' ever so distant from the seat of the Court. An effective Judiciary establishment commensurate to the legislative authority, was essential. A Government without a proper Executive & Judiciary would be the mere trunk of a body without arms or legs to act or move.

Mr. Wilson opposed the motion on like grounds. he said the admiralty jurisdiction ought to be given wholly to the national Government, as it related to cases not within the jurisdiction of particular states, & to a scene in which controversies with foreigners would be most likely to happen.

---

[23] Taken from *Journal*.

Mr. Sherman was in favor of the motion. He dwelt chiefly on the supposed expensiveness of having a new set of Courts, when the existing State Courts would answer the same purpose.

Mr. Dickinson contended strongly that if there was to be a National Legislature, there ought to be a national Judiciary, and that the former ought to have authority to institute the latter.

On the question for Mr. Rutlidge's motion to strike out "inferior tribunals"

Massts. divided, Cont. ay. N. Y. divd. N. J. ay. Pa. no. Del. no. Md. no. Va. no. N. C. ay. S. C. ay. Geo ay [Ayes — 5; noes — 4; divided — 2.]

Mr. Wilson & Mr. Madison then moved, in pursuance of the idea expressed above by Mr. Dickinson, to add to Resol: 9. the words following "that the National Legislature be empowered to institute inferior tribunals". They observed that there was a distinction between establishing such tribunals absolutely, and giving a discretion to the Legislature to establish or not establish them. They repeated the necessity of some such provision.

Mr. Butler. The people will not bear such innovations. The States will revolt at such encroachments. Supposing such an establishment to be useful, we must not venture on it. We must follow the example of Solon who gave the Athenians not the best Govt. he could devise; but the best they wd. receive.

Mr. King remarked as to the comparative expence that the establishment of inferior tribunals wd. cost infinitely less than the appeals that would be prevented by them.[24]

On this question as moved by Mr. W. and Mr. M.

Mass. ay. Ct. no. N. Y. divd. N. J.* ay. Pa. ay. Del. ay. Md. ay. Va. ay. N. C. ay. S. C. no. Geo. ay. [Ayes — 8; noes — 2; divided — 1.]

* ⟨In the printed Journal N. Jersey — no.⟩[25]

[24] See further Appendix A, CLVIII (50), CCXIV, CCLXXII, CCXC.

[25] Yates apparently confirms *Journal.*

The Committee then rose & the House adjourned to 11 OC. tomw.

YATES

TUESDAY, JUNE 5th, 1787.

Met pursuant to adjournment.

The 9th resolve, *That a national judicial be established to consist of one supreme tribunal, and of inferior tribunals, to hold their offices during good behaviour, and no augmentation or diminution in the stipends during the time of holding their offices.* Agreed to.

Mr. Wilson moved *that the judicial be appointed by the executive,* instead of *the national legislature.*

Mr Madison opposed the motion, and inclined to think that the executive ought by no means to make the appointments, but rather that branch of the legislature called the senatorial; and moves that the words, *of the appointment of the legislature,* be expunged.

Carried by 8 states — against it 2.

The remaining part of the resolve postponed.

The 10th resolve read and agreed to.

The 11th resolve agreed to be postponed.

The 12th resolve agreed to without debate.

The 13th and 14th resolves postponed.

The 15th or last resolve, *That the amendment which shall be offered to the confederation, ought at a proper time or times after the approbation of congress to be submitted to an assembly or assemblies of representatives, recommended by the several legislatures, to be expressly chosen by the people, to consider and decide thereon,* was taken into consideration.

Mr. Madison endeavored to enforce the necessity of this resolve — because the new national constitution ought to have the highest source of authority, at least paramount to the powers of the respective constitutions of the states — points out the mischiefs that have arisen in the old confederation, which depends upon no higher authority than the confirmation of an ordinary act of a legislature — Instances the law operation of treaties, when contravened by any antecedent acts of a particular state.

Mr. King supposes, that as the prople have tacitly agreed to a federal government, that therefore the legislature in every state have a right to confirm any alterations or amendments in it — a convention in each state to approve of a new government he supposes however the most eligible.[26]

Mr. Wilson is of opinion, that the people by a convention are the only power that can ratify the proposed system of the new government.

It is possible that not all the states, nay, that not even a majority, will immediately come into the measure; but such as do ratify it will be immediately bound by it, and others as they may from time to time accede to it.

Question put for postponement of this resolve. 7 states for postponment — 3 against it.

Question on the 9th resolve to strike out the words, *and of inferior tribunals.*

Carried by 5 states against 4 — 2 states divided, of which last number New-York was one.

Mr. Wilson then moved, *that the national legislature shall have the authority to appoint inferior tribunals*, be added to the resolve.

Carried by 7 states against 3. New-York divided. (N. B. Mr. Lansing from New-York was prevented by sickness from attending this day.)

Adjourned to to-morrow morning.

KING

5 June. Come. whole

How shall the Judiciary be appointed by the Legislative or Executive —
Wilson in favor of the latter because the Executive will be responsible —
Rutledge agt. it because the States in genl. appt. in yt. way

---

[26] Note Genet's comment in Appendix A, CCCX.

Franklin.   The 16 lords of Sessions in Scotland are the Judicial — they are appointed by the Barristers or Doctors.
They elect the most learned, Doctor, because he has the most
business wh. they may divide when he becomes a Judge —

Madison — I am for farther Diliberation perhaps it will be
best that the appointment shd. be by the Senate — *postponed.*
N. H. Mas. N Y. Pen. Mard. by ye. Executive
R I   by the people
Con. N Jer. Del. Virg. N C. S C. by the Leg.

Rutledge proposes to have a supreme Tribunal to be appointed
by the Genl. Govt. but no subordinate Tribunals — except
those already in the several States — Wilson agt. it —
Dickerson — agt. Wilson the State and Genl. Tribunals will
interfere — we want a National Judicial — let it be entire
and originate from the Genl. Govt.
Madison proposes to vest the Genl. Govt. with authority to
erect an Independent Judicial, coextensive wt. ye. Nation —
5 A.   4 No.   2 divd.[27]

PIERCE

Mr. Rutledge was of opinion that it would be right to
make the adjudications of the State Judges, appealable to the
national Judicial.

Mr. Madison was for appointing the Judges by the Senate.

Mr. Hamilton suggested the idea of the Executive's appointing or nominating the Judges to the Senate which should have
the right of rejecting or approving.

Mr. Butler was of opinion that the alteration of the confederation ought not to be confirmed by the different Legislatures because they have sworn to support the Government
under which they act, and therefore that Deputies should be
chosen by the People for the purpose of ratifying it.

Mr. King thought that the Convention would be under
the necessity of referring the amendments to the different

---

[27] [Endorsed:] 5 June | Judicial by wh. appointed

Legislatures, because one of the Articles of the confederation expressly made it necessary.

As the word perpetual in the Articles of confederation gave occasion for several Members to insist upon the main principles of the confederacy, i e that the several States should meet in the general Council on a footing of compleat equality each claiming the right of sovereignty, Mr. Butler observed that the word perpetual in the confederation meant only the constant existence of our Union, and not the particular words which compose the Articles of the union.

Some general discussions came on. —

WEDNESDAY, JUNE 6, 1787.

JOURNAL

Wednesday June 6. 1787.

The Order of the day being read.

The House resolved itself into a Committee of the whole House to consider of the State of the American Union

Mr President left the Chair.

Mr. Gorham took the Chair of the Committee

Mr President resumed the Chair

Mr Gorham reported from the Committee that the Committee had made a further progress in the matter to them referred; and had directed him to move that they may have leave to sit again.

Resolved that this House will to-morrow again resolve itself into a Committee of the whole House to consider of the State of the american union.

And then the House adjourned till to-morrow at 11 o'Clock A. M.

In a Committee of the whole House

Wednesday June 6. 1787.

Mr Gorham in the Chair

It was moved by Mr C. Pinckney seconded by Mr Rutledge to strike the word "people" out of the 4th resolution submitted by Mr Randolph, and to insert in it's place the word

"Legislatures" so as to read "resolved that the Members "of the first branch of the national legislature ought to be "elected by the Legislatures of the several states"

and On the question to strike out

it passed in the negative [Ayes — 3; noes — 8.] [1]

---

[1] Vote 29, Detail of Ayes and Noes.

On motion of Mr Wilson seconded by Mr Madison to amend the   resolution, which respects the negative to be vested in the national executive by adding after the words "national executive" the words

"with a convenient number of the national Judiciary" On the question to agree to the addition of these words
    it passed in the negative. [Ayes — 3; noes — 8.][2]

Mr C. Pinckney gave notice that to-morrow he should move for the reconsideration of that clause in the   resolution, adopted by the Committee, which vests a negative in the national legislatute on the laws of the several States. friday assigned to reconsider

It was then moved and seconded that the Committee do now rise, report a further progress, and request leave to sit again.

The Committee then rose.

DETAIL OF AYES AND NOES

[Beginning of second loose sheet]

	New Hampshire	Massachusetts	Rhode Island	Connecticut	New York	New Jersey	Pennsylvania	Delaware	Maryland	Virginia	North Carolina	South Carolina	Georgia	Questions	Ayes	Noes	Divided
[29]	no	aye	no	aye	no	no	no	no	no	aye	no			for striking out the words "people" in the first clause of the 4th resolution and inserting the words "Legislatures	3	8	
[30]	no	aye	aye	no	no	no	no	aye	no	no	no			for adding a convenient number of the national Judiciary to the Executive in the exercise of the negative	3	8	

[2] Vote 30, Detail of Ayes and Noes.

MADISON

Wednesday June 6th.   In Committee of the whole

Mr. Pinkney according to previous notice & rule obtained, moved "that the first branch of the national Legislature be elected by the State Legislatures, and not by the people". contending that the people were less fit Judges ⟨in such a case,⟩ and that the Legislatures would be less likely to promote the adoption of the new Government, if they were to be excluded from all share in it.[3]

Mr. Rutlidge 2ded. the motion.

Mr. Gerry.   Much depends on the mode of election.   In England, the people will probably lose their liberty from the smallness of the proportion having a right of suffrage.   Our danger arises from the opposite extreme: hence in Massts. the worst men get into the Legislature.   Several members of that Body had lately been convicted of infamous crimes.   Men of indigence, ignorance & baseness, spare no pains however dirty to carry their point agst. men who are superior to the artifices practiced.   He was not disposed to run into extremes. He was as much principled as ever agst. aristocracy and monarchy.   It was necessary on the one hand that the people should appoint one branch of the Govt. in order to inspire them with the necessary confidence.   But he wished the election on the other to be so modified as to secure more effectually a just preference of merit.   His idea was that the people should nominate certain persons in certain districts, out of whom the State Legislatures shd. make the appointment.

Mr. Wilson.   He wished for vigor in the Govt. but he wished that vigorous authority to flow immediately from the legitimate source of all authority.   The Govt. ought to possess not only 1st. the *force* but 2ndly. the *mind or sense* of the people at large.   The Legislature ought to be the most exact transcript of the whole Society.   Representation is made neces-

---

[3] See Appendix A, CCXXXVII, CCXXXVIII.

sary only because it is impossible for the people to act collectively. The opposition was to be expected he said from the *Governments*, not from the Citizens of the States. The latter had parted as was observed (by Mr. King) with all the necessary powers; and it was immaterial to them, by whom they were exercised, if well exercised. The State officers were to be losers of power. The people he supposed would be rather more attached to the national Govt. than to the State Govts. as being more important in itself, and more flattering to their pride. There is no danger of improper elections if made by *large* districts. Bad elections proceed from the smallness of the districts which give an opportunity to bad men to intrigue themselves into office.

Mr. Sherman. If it were in view to abolish the State Govts. the elections ought to be by the people. If the State Govts. are to be continued, it is necessary in order to preserve harmony between the national & State Govts. that the elections to the former shd. be made by the latter. The right of participating in the National Govt. would be sufficiently secured to the people by their election of the State Legislatures. The objects of the Union, he thought were few. 1. defence agst. foreign danger. 2. agst. internal disputes & a resort to force. 3. Treaties with foreign nations 4 regulating foreign commerce, & drawing revenue from it. These & perhaps a few lesser objects alone rendered a Confederation of the States necessary. All other matters civil & criminal would be much better in the hands of the States. The people are more happy in small than large States. States may indeed be too small as Rhode Island, & thereby be too subject to faction. Some others were perhaps too large, the powers of Govt not being able to pervade them. He was for giving the General Govt. power to legislate and execute within a defined province.

Col. Mason. Under the existing Confederacy, Congs. represent the *States* not the *people* of the States: their acts operate on the *States* not on the individuals. The case will be changed in the new plan of Govt. The people will be represented; they ought therefore to choose the Representatives. The requisites in actual representation are that the

Reps. should sympathize with their constituents; shd. think as they think, & feel as they feel; and that for these purposes shd. even be residents among them.   Much he sd. had been alledged agst. democratic elections.   He admitted that much might be said; but it was to be considered that no Govt. was free from imperfections & evils; and that improper elections in many instances, were inseparable from Republican Govts. But compare these with the advantage of this Form in favor of the rights of the people, in favor of human nature.   He was persuaded there was a better chance for proper elections by the people, if divided into large districts, than by the State Legislatures.   Paper money had been issued by the latter when the former were against it.   Was it to be supposed that the State Legislatures then wd. not send to the Natl. legislature patrons of such projects. if the choice depended on them.

Mr. Madison considered an election of one branch at least of the Legislature by the people immediately, as a clear principle of free Govt. and that this mode under proper regulations had the additional advantage of securing better representatives, as well as of avoiding too great an agency of the State Governments in the General one. — He differed from the member from Connecticut (Mr. Sherman) in thinking the objects mentioned to be all the principal ones that required a National Govt.   Those were certainly important and necessary objects; but he combined with them the necessity, of providing more effectually for the security of private rights, and the steady dispensation of Justice.   Interferences with these were evils which had more perhaps than any thing else, produced this convention.   Was it to be supposed that republican liberty could long exist under the abuses of it practiced in ⟨some of⟩ the States.   The gentleman (Mr. Sherman) had admitted that in a very small State, faction & oppression wd. prevail.   It was to be inferred then that wherever these prevailed the State was too small.   Had they not prevailed in the largest as well as the smallest tho' less than in the smallest; and were we not thence admonished to enlarge the sphere as far as the nature of the Govt. would admit.   This was the only defence agst. the inconveniences of democracy consistent with the democratic form of Govt. All civilized Societies would be divided into different Sects, Factions, & interests, as they happened to consist of rich & poor, debtors & creditors, the landed the manufacturing, the commercial interests, the inhabitants of this district, or that district, the followers of this political leader or that political leader, the disciples of this religious sect or that religious sect. In all cases where a majority are united by a common interest or passion, the rights of the minority are in danger. What motives are to restrain them? A prudent regard to the maxim that honesty is the best policy is found by experience to be as little regarded by bodies of men as by individuals. Respect for character is always diminished in proportion to the number among whom the blame or praise is to be divided. Conscience, the only remaining tie is known to be inadequate in individuals: In large numbers, little is to be expected from it. Besides, Religion itself may become a motive to persecution & oppression.—These observations are verified by the Histories of every Country antient & modern. In Greece & Rome the rich & poor, the creditors & debtors, as well as the patricians & plebeians alternately oppressed each other with equal unmercifulness. What a source of oppression was the relation between the parent Cities of Rome, Athens & Carthage, & their respective provinces: the former possessing the power & the latter being sufficiently distinguished to be separate objects of it? Why was America so justly apprehensive of Parliamentary injustice? Because G. Britain had a separate interest real or supposed, & if her authority had been admitted, could have pursued that interest at our expense. We have seen the mere distinction of colour made in the most enlightened period of time, a ground of the most oppressive dominion ever exercised by man over man. What has been the source of those unjust laws complained of among ourselves? Has it not been the real or supposed interest of the major number? Debtors have defrauded their creditors. The landed interest has borne hard on the mercantile interest. The Holders of one species of property have thrown a disproportion of taxes on the holders of another species.   The lesson we are to draw from the whole is that where a majority are united by a common sentiment and have an opportunity, the rights of the minor party become insecure.   In a Republican Govt. the Majority if united have always an opportunity.   The only remedy is to enlarge the sphere, & thereby divide the community into so great a number of interests & parties, that in the 1st. place a majority will not be likely at the same moment to have a common interest separate from that of the whole or of the minority; and in the 2d. place, that in case they shd. have such an interest, they may not be apt to unite in the pursuit of it.   It was incumbent on us then to try this remedy, and with that view to frame a republican system on such a scale & in such a form as will controul all the evils wch. have been experienced.[4]

Mr. Dickinson considered it as essential that one branch of the Legislature shd. be drawn immediately from the people; and as expedient that the other shd. be chosen by the Legislatures of the States.   This combination of the State Govts. with the National Govt. was as politic as it was unavoidable.   In the formation of the Senate we ought to carry it through such a refining process as will assimilate it as near as may be to the House of Lords in England.   He repeated his warm eulogiums on the British Constitution.   He was for a strong National Govt. but for leaving the States a considerable agency in the System.   The objection agst. making the former dependent on the latter might be obviated by giving to the Senate an authority permanent & irrevocable for three, five or seven years.   Being thus independent they will speak & decide with becoming freedom.

Mr. Read.   Too much attachment is betrayed to the State Govermts.   We must look beyond their continuance.   A national Govt. must soon of necessity swallow all of them up. They will soon be reduced to the mere office of electing the national Senate.   He was agst. patching up the old federal System: he hoped the idea wd. be dismissed.   It would be

---

[4] See June 4, note 25.

like putting new cloth on an old garment.   The confederation
was founded on temporary principles.   It cannot last: it
cannot be amended.   If we do not establish a good Govt. on
new principles, we must either go to ruin, or have the work
to do over again.   The people at large are wrongly suspected
of being averse to a Genl. Govt.   The aversion lies among
interested men who possess their confidence.

Mr. Pierce was for an election by the people as to the 1st.
branch & by the States as to the 2d. branch; by which means
the Citizens of the States wd. be represented both *individually*
& *collectively.*

General Pinkney wished to have a good national Govt. &
at the same time to leave a considerable share of power in the
States.   An election of either branch by the people scattered
as they are in many States, particularly in S. Carolina was
totally impracticable.   He differed from gentlemen who
thought that a choice by the people wd. be a better guard
agst. bad measures, than by the Legislatures.   A majority
of the people in S. Carolina were notoriously for paper money
as a legal tender; the Legislature had refused to make it a
legal tender.   The reason was that the latter had some sense
of character and were restrained by that consideration.   The
State Legislatures also he said would be more jealous, & more
ready to thwart the National Govt. if excluded from a participation in it.   The Idea of abolishing these Legislatures wd.
never go down.

Mr. Wilson, would not have spoken again, but for what had
fallen from Mr. Read; namely, that the idea of preserving the
State Govts. ought to be abandoned.   He saw no incompata-
bility between the national & State Govts. provided the latter
were restrained to certain local purposes; nor any probability
of their being devoured by the former.   In all confederated
systems antient & modern the reverse had happened; the
Generality being destroyed gradually by the usurpations of
the parts composing it.

On the question for electing the 1st. branch by the State
Legislatures as moved by Mr. Pinkney; ⟨it was negatived:⟩

Mass no. Ct. ay. N. Y. no. N. J. ay. Pa. no. Del. no. Md.

no. Va. no. N. C. no. S. C. ay. Geo. no. [Ayes — 3; noes — 8.]

Mr. Wilson moved to reconsider the vote excluding the Judiciary from a share in the revision of the laws, and to add after "National Executive" the words "with a convenient number of the national Judiciary"; remarking the expediency of reinforcing the Executive with the influence of that Department.

Mr. Madison 2ded. the motion. He observed that the great difficulty in rendering the Executive competent to its own defence arose from the nature of Republican Govt. which could not give to an individual citizen that settled pre-eminence in the eyes of the rest, that weight of property, that personal interest agst. betraying the National interest, which appertain to an hereditary magistrate. In a Republic personal merit alone could be the ground of political exaltation, but it would rarely happen that this merit would be so pre-eminent as to produce universal acquiescence. The Executive Magistrate would be envied & assailed by disappointed competitors: His firmness therefore wd. need support. He would not possess those great emoluments from his station, nor that permanent stake in the public interest which wd. place him out of the reach of foreign corruption: He would stand in need therefore of being controuled as well as supported. An association of the Judges in his revisionary function wd. both double the advantage and diminish the danger. It wd. also enable the Judiciary Department the better to defend itself agst. Legislative encroachments. Two objections had been made 1st. that the Judges ought not to be subject to the bias which a participation in the making of laws might give in the exposition of them. 2dly. that the Judiciary Departmt. ought to be separate & distinct from the other great Departments. The 1st. objection had some weight; but it was much diminished by reflecting that a small proportion of the laws coming in question before a Judge wd. be such wherein he had been consulted; that a small part of this proportion wd. be so ambiguous as to leave room for his prepossessions; and that but a few cases wd. probably arise in the life of a Judge under such ambiguous passages. How much good on the other hand wd. proceed from the perspicuity, the conciseness, and the systematic character wch. the Code of laws wd. receive from the Judiciary talents. As to the 2d. objection, it either had no weight, or it applied with equal weight to the Executive & to the Judiciary revision of the laws. The maxim on which the objection was founded required a separation of the Executive as well as of the Judiciary from the Legislature & from each other. There wd. in truth however be no improper mixture of these distinct powers in the present case. In England, whence the maxim itself had been drawn, the Executive had an absolute negative on the laws; and the supreme tribunal of Justice (the House of Lords) formed one of the other branches of the Legislature. In short, whether the object of the revisionary power was to restrain the Legislature from encroaching on the other co-ordinate Departments, or on the rights of the people at large; or from passing laws unwise in their principle, or incorrect in their form, the utility of annexing the wisdom and weight of the Judiciary to the Executive seemed incontestable.[5]

Mr. Gerry thought the Executive, whilst standing alone wd. be more impartial than when he cd. be covered by the sanction & seduced by the sophistry of the Judges

Mr. King. If the Unity of the Executive was preferred for the sake of responsibility, the policy of it is as applicable to the revisionary as to the Executive power.

Mr. Pinkney had been at first in favor of joining the heads of the principal departmts. the Secretary at War, of foreign affairs & — in the council of revision. He had however relinquished the idea from a consideration that these could be called on by the Executive Magistrate whenever he pleased to consult them. He was opposed to an introduction of the Judges into the business.

Col Mason was for giving all possible weight to the revisionary institution. The Executive power ought to be well secured agst. Legislative usurpations on it. The purse & the

---

[5] See June 4 note 25.

sword ought never to get into the same hands ⟨whether Legislative or Executive.⟩

Mr. Dickinson. Secrecy, vigor & despatch are not the principal properties reqd. in the Executive. Important as these are, that of responsibility is more so, which can only be preserved; by leaving it singly to discharge its functions. He thought too a junction of the Judiciary to it, involved an improper mixture of powers.

Mr Wilson remarked, that the responsibility required belonged to his Executive duties. The revisionary duty was an extraneous one, calculated for collateral purposes.

Mr. Williamson, was for substituting a clause requiring $\frac{2}{3}$ for every effective act of the Legislature, in place of the revisionary provision

On the question for joining the Judges to the Executive in the revisionary business Mass. no. Cont. ay. N. Y. ay. N. J. no. Pa. no. Del. no. Md. no. Va. ay. N. C. no. S. C. no. Geo. no. [Ayes — 3; noes — 8.]

⟨Mr. Pinkney gave notice [6] that to morrow he should move for the reconsideration of that clause in the sixth Resolution adopted by the Comme. which vests a negative in the National Legislature on the laws of the several States.

The Come rose & the House adjd. to 11 OC.⟩[7]

YATES

WEDNESDAY, JUNE 6th, 1787.

Met pursuant to adjournment.

Mr. Pinkney moved (pursuant to a standing order for re-consideration) that in the 4th resolve, the words _by the people_, be expunged, and the words _by the legislature_, be inserted.

Mr. Gerry. — If the national legislature are appointed by the state legislatures, demagogues and corrupt members will creep in.

---

[6] Taken from _Journal._

[7] See further Appendix A, XXXVI–XXXVIIIa.

Mr. Wilson is of opinion that the national legislative powers ought to flow immediately from the people, so as to contain all their understanding, and to be an exact transcript of their minds. He observed that the people had already *parted* with as much of their power as was necessary, to form on its basis a perfect government; and the particular states must part with such a portion of it as to make the present national government, adequate to their peace and the security of their liberties. He admitted that the state governments would probably be rivals and opposers of the national government.

Mr. Mason observed that the national legislature, as to one branch, ought to be elected by the people; because the objects of their legislation will not be on states, but on individual persons.

Mr. Dickinson is for combining the state and national legislatures in the same views and measures, and that this object can only be effected by the national legislature flowing from the state legislatures.

Mr. Read is of opinion, that the state governments must sooner or later be at an end, and that therefore we must make the present national government as perfect as possible.

Mr. Madison is of opinion, that when we agreed to the first resolve of having a national government, consisting of a supreme executive, judicial and legislative power, it was then intended to operate to the exclusion of a federal government, and the more extensive we made the basis, the greater probability of duration, happiness and good order.[8]

The question for the amendment was negatived, by 8 states against 3. New-York in the majority.

On the 8th resolve, Mr. Wilson moved (in consequence of a vote to re-consider the question on the revisional powers vested in the executive) that there be added these words, *with a convenient number of the national judicial.*

Upon debate, carried in the negative — 3 states for and 8 against. New-York for the addition.

Adjourned to to-morrow morning.

---

[8] Compare Genet's comment in Appendix A, CCCX.

KING

5 [6] June Com. wh.

Pinckney Cs. proposes that the Election of the members of the first Br. or Commons, shd. be by the State Legis: and not by the people —

Gerry — proposes that the people sd. choose double the Number required, & the Legislature shd. out of them elect the members to the first Br — he states yt. the people will be imposed on by corrupt & unworthy men &c

Wilson contra — they shd. be appointed by the people you will then come nearer to the will or sense of the majority — the protrait is excellent in proportion to its being a good likeness — if you leave the Election with the Legislature you leave it wt. the Rivals of the Genl. Govt. for the people have already parted with powers sufficient to form a vigourous Govt: it remains only to divide the granted powers between the Genl. & State Govts & the people will love and respect the Genl. Govt. if it is immediately founded in yr. consent — it will take rank over the State Governments —

Mason — at present the representation in congress are not representatives of the people, but of the States—now it is proposed to form a Govt for men & not for Societies of men or States, therefore you shd. draw the Representatives immediately from the people. it shd. be so much so, that even the Diseases of the people shd. be represented — if not, how are they to be cured —? but how will this be remedied by an appt. by the Legislature—suppose a majority of the Legislat. in favor of paper money or any other Bad measure, wd. they not consider the opinions of the candidates on these favorite measures?

Sherman — If the State Govts. are to remain it will be best to appoint by their Legislatures; if they are to be totally abolished then the people must elect — but the State Governments must continue — Few objects then will be before the Genl. Government — foreign War, Treaties of commerce &c — in short let the Genl. Government be a sort of collateral

Government which shall secure the States in particular difficulties such as foreign war, or a war between two or more
States — I am agt. a Genl. Govt. and in favor of the independence and confederation of the States, with powers to
regulate comerce & draw therefrom a revenue—

Dickson. We cannot form a national Govt. as is proposed
unless we draw a Br. from the people, & a Br. from the legislature — it is necessary in theory — And essential to the success of the project — The objections to an election by the
people arise from the nature of a Free Government and are
slight when compared with the excellence of the Government
— The 2d Br. must come from the State sovereignties or Legislature, they will be more respectable and they must for yr
respectability & duration be something like the British House
of peers —

But can one Br. be drawn from the Legislatures who are
and have been opposed to ye Genl. Govt. It can— the
appointment of the Legisture. of the States, to be in office
3-5 or 7. yrs; not subject to a recall and to depend on the
Genl. Govt. for yr. support —

Read — We must come to a consolidation — The State Govts
must be swept away — We had better speak out — the Idea
that the people will not approve perhaps is a mistake — The
State Magistrates may disagree but the people are with us —

Gnl. Pinckney — I think that an election by the people is
impracticable in So. Car. the Inhabitants are so sparse that
four or five thousand men can not be brought together to vote
— I am in favor of the appointment by the Legis: in S. Car.
they are agt. an issue of paper with a Tender; but I think
the majority of the people are in favor of yt. measure —

Wilson—I am in favor of a preservation of the State Govts
there is no apprehension of the State Govts being swallowed
up by the Genl. Govt. in every instance of a Confedn. of
States; the contrary has been the Case — the Amphictionic
Council — the   & Achaian Leagues were dissolved by
the encroachments of the constituent members —

Madison — The election may safely be made by the People
if you enlarge the Sphere of Election — Experience proves it

— if bad elections have taken place from the people, it will generally be found to have happened in small Distracts —

Butler — I am agt: determining the mode of election until the ratio of Representation is fixed — if that proceeds on a principle favorable to wealth as well as numbers of Free Inhabitants, I am content to unite wh. Delaware (Mr Read) in abolishing the State Legislatures, and becoming one Nation instead of a confedn. of Republics —

On the Question to agree to the amendmt. Cont. N Jersey & S Car Ay   the eight other states No.

Motion by Mr. Wilson secd. by Madison to reconsider the vote vesting the Executive with a partial negative, and vesting that power in him jointly wh a part of the Judicial —

Madison

A check is devised for three purposes — to prevent encroachments by the Legislature on the Executive, the Judicial, or on private Rights.   If on the executive, his negative will be corroberated by an union with the Judicial; and so in every other case — The Dificulty is this; the check will be too weak if in the Executive only — perhaps the British King wd not interpose his negative agt. the unanimous voice of both houses of Parliament —

Gerry — The motion unites orders wh. ought to be separate — it connects with the Executive numbers to divide the infamy of bad conduct.

Pinckney Cs. agt. the motion because the responsibility —

Mason.   The purse and sword must not be in the same hands, if this is true, and the Legislature are able to raise revenues and make & direct a war;   I shall agree to a restraining power of the Legislature either in the Executive or a council of Revision —

Dickerson — Secresy, vigour & Dispatch, are not the properties of Repubs — we cannot have them in that Form — but Responsibility is the great point — if you unite the Judicial the Executive will no longer be responsible — it is bad because it mingles separate Orders — and the Object may be acquired by the acquisition of the voluntary Opinions of wise and discreet men —

It will require as great Talents, Firmness, & Abilities, to discharge the proper Duties of the Executive, as to interpose their veto, or negative which shall require ⅔ of both Branches to remove —
but the Comee have not thought proper to introduce a plurality in the Executive in the former instance, why then in this — On the Question to agree to the reconsideration Con. NYk. Virg. Ay — 8 States No — [9]

H A M I L T O N [10]

Sent:

A free government to be preferred to an absolute monarchy not because of the occasional violations of *liberty* or *property* but because of the tendency of the Free Government to interest the passions of the community in its favour beget public spirit and public confidence —

Re:[11] When public mind is prepared to adopt the present plan they will outgo our proposition — They will never part with Sovereignty of the state till they are tired of the state governments —

Mr. Pinkney. If Legislatures do not partake in the appointment of they will be more jealous

Pinckney— Elections by the state legislatures will be better than those by the people —

Principle — Danger that the Executive by too frequent communication with the judicial may corrupt it — They may learn to enter into his passions —

Note — At the period which terminates the duration of the Executive there will be always an awful crisis — in the National situation.

---

[9] [Endorsed:] 5 June | Rep. to be chosen by State Legs. | Con Jers So Car aye | Other 8 States no | Negative. of Extive.

[10] Hamilton's notes being without date, it is impossible to assign them satisfactorily. The notes here given seem to refer to the debates of this day.

[11] "Re" may refer to Read.

Note — The arguments to prove that a negative would not be used would go so far as to prove that the revisionary power would not be exercised.

Mr. Mason — The purse & sword will be in the hands of the — legislature.[12]

    I   One great defect of our Governments are that they do not present objects sufficiently interesting to the human mind.

    I — A reason for leaving little or nothing to the state legislatures will be that as their objects are diminished they will be worse composed — Proper men will be less inclined to participate in them

Principles [13]

I — Human mind fond of Compromise —
Maddisons Theory —

Two principles upon which republics ought to be constructed —

I that they have such extent as to render combinations on the ground of interest difficult—

II By a process of election calculated to refine the representation of the People —

Answer — There is truth in both these principles but they do not conclude so strongly as he supposes —

— The Assembly when chosen will meet in one room if they are drawn from half the globe — & will be liable to all the passions of popular assemblies.

If more *minute links* are wanting others will supply then — Distinctions of Eastern middle and Southern states will come into view; between commercial and non commercial states — Imaginary lines will influence &c — Human mind prone to limit its view by near and local objects —

Paper money is capable of giving a general impulse. It

---

[12] "Executive" struck out and "legislature" substituted. *Cf.* Madison and King.

[13] These notes of Hamilton's are on a separate sheet from those preceding. They are included here because they seem to refer to Madison's speeches of this day.

is easy to conceive a popular sentiment pervading the E states —

Observ: { large districts less liable to be influenced by factious demagogues than small—

Note — This is in some degree true but not so generally as may be supposed — Frequently small portions of [mutilated] large districts carry elections — An influential demagogue will give an impulse to the whole — Demagogues are not always *inconsiderable* persons — Patricians were frequently demagogues — Characters are less known & a less active interest taken in them —

PIERCE

Mr. Charles Pinckney said he was for appointing the first branch of the Legislature by the State Legislatures, and that the rule for appointing it ought to be by the contributions made by the different States.

Mr. Wilson was of opinion that the Judicial, Legislative and Executive departments ought to be commensurate.

Mr. Cotesworth Pinckney was of opinion that the State Legislatures ought to appoint the 1st branch of the national Legislature; — that the election cannot be made from the People in South Carolina. If the people choose it will have a tendency to destroy the foundation of the State Governments.

Mr. Maddison observed that Gentlemen reasoned very clear on most points under discussion, but they drew different conclusions. What is the reason? Because they reason from different principles. The primary objects of civil society are the security of property and public safety.

THURSDAY, JUNE 7, 1787.

JOURNAL

Thursday June 7. 1787.

The Order of the day being read

The House resolved itself into a Committee of the whole House to consider of the state of the American Union

Mr President left the Chair

Mr Gorham took the Chair of the Committee.

Mr President resumed the Chair

Mr Gorham reported from the Committee that the Committee had made a further progress in the matter to them referred; and had directed him to move that they may have leave to sit again.

Resolved that the House will to-morrow again resolve itself into a Committee of the whole House to consider of the State of the american union

And then the House adjourned till to-morrow at 11 o'Clock A. M.

In a Committee of the whole House.

Thursday June 7. 1787.

Mr Gorham in the Chair

The following resolution was submitted by Mr Dickinson seconded by Mr Sherman. namely

Resolved that the members of the second branch of the national Legislature ought to be chosen by the individual Legislatures.

It was then moved and seconded to postpone the last resolution, in order to introduce the following — submitted by Mr Wilson seconded by Mr Morris, namely

Resolved that the second Branch of the national Legisla-

ture be elected by the people in Districts to be formed for that
purpose.

And on the question to postpone

      it passed in the negative   [Ayes — 1; noes— 10.][1]

A question was then taken on the resolution submitted by
Mr Dickinson namely

"Resolved that the members of the second branch of the
"national Legislature ought to be chosen by the individual
"Legislatures"

And on the question to agree to the same

      it passed unanimously in the affirmative [2]

Mr Gerry gave notice that he would to-morrow move for
the reconsideration of the resolution which respects the appointment of the national executive — when he should offer to
substitute the following mode of appointing the national
Executive namely

    by the Executives of the several States

The Committee then rose.   [Ayes — 11; noes — o.] [3]

DETAIL OF AYES AND NOES

	New Hampshire	Massachusetts	Rhode Island	Connecticut	New York	New Jersey	Pennsylvania	Delaware	Maryland	Virginia	North Carolina	South Carolina	Georgia	Questions	Ayes	Noes
[31]	no		no	no	no	aye	no	no	no	no	no	no	To postpone Mr Dickinson's motion for electing the second branch to take up Mr Wilson's	1	10
[32]	aye		aye	aye	aye	aye	aye	aye	aye	aye	aye	aye	That the second branch of the national legislature be elected by the individual legislatures	11	
[33]	aye		aye	aye	aye	aye	aye	aye	aye	aye	aye	aye	The Committee to rise	11	

[1] Vote 31, Detail of Ayes and Noes.
[2] Vote 32, Detail of Ayes and Noes.   Madison does not include New Jersey.
[3] Vote 33, Detail of Ayes and Noes.

MADISON

Thursday June 7th. 1787. ⟨In Committee of the whole.⟩

Mr. Pinkney ⟨according to notice⟩ moved to reconsider the clause respecting the negative on State laws which was agreed to and ⟨tomorrow⟩ fixed for the purpose.

The Clause providing for ye appointment of the 2d branch of the national Legislature, having lain blank since the last vote on the mode of electing it, to wit, by the 1st. branch, Mr. Dickenson now moved "that the members ⟨of the 2d. branch ought to be chosen⟩[4] by the individual Legislatures."

Mr. Sherman seconded the motion; observing that the particular States would thus become interested in supporting the National Governmt. and that a due harmony between the two Governments would be maintained. He admitted that the two ought to have separate and distinct jurisdictions, but that they ought to have a mutual interest in supporting each other.

Mr. Pinkney. If the small States should be allowed one Senator only, the number will be too great, there will be 80 at least.

Mr. Dickenson had two reasons for his motion. 1. because the sense of the States would be better collected through their Governments; than immediately from the people at large. 2. because he wished the Senate to consist of the most distinguished characters, distinguished for their rank in life and their weight of property, and bearing as strong a likeness to the British House of Lords as possible; and he thought such characters more likely to be selected by the State Legislatures, than in any other mode. The greatness of the number was no objection with him. He hoped there would be 80 and twice 80. of them. If their number should be small, the popular branch could not be [ba]lanced by them. The legislature of a numerous people ought to be a numerous body.

Mr. Williamson, preferred a small number of Senators, but wished that each State should have at least one. He sug-

---

[4] Revised from *Journal*.

gested 25 as a convenient number. The different modes of representation in the different branches, will serve as a mutual check.

Mr. Butler was anxious to know the ratio of representation before he gave any opinion.

Mr. Wilson. If we are to establish a national Government, that Government ought to flow from the people at large. If one branch of it should be chosen by the Legislatures, and the other by the people, the two branches will rest on different foundations, and dissentions will naturally arise between them. He wished the Senate to be elected by the people as well as the other branch, and the people might be divided into proper districts for the purpose & moved to postpone the motion of Mr. Dickenson, in order to take up one of that import.

Mr Morris 2ded. him.

Mr. Read proposed "that the Senate should be appointed by the Executive Magistrate out of a proper number of persons to be nominated by the individual legislatures." He said he thought it his duty, to speak his mind frankly. Gentlemen he hoped would not be alarmed at the idea. Nothing short of this approach towards a proper model of Government would answer the purpose, and he thought it best to come directly to the point at once. — His proposition was not seconded nor supported.

Mr. Madison, if the motion (of Mr. Dickenson) should be agreed to, we must either depart from the doctrine of proportional representation; or admit into the Senate a very large number of members. The first is inadmissable, being evidently unjust. The second is inexpedient. The use of the Senate is to consist in its proceeding with more coolness, with more system, & with more wisdom, than the popular branch. Enlarge their number and you communicate to them the vices which they are meant to correct. He differed from Mr. D. who thought that the additional number would give additional weight to the body. On the contrary it appeared to him that their weight would be in an inverse ratio to their number. The example of the Roman Tribunes was applicable. They lost their influence and power, in proportion as their number was augmented. The reason seemed to be obvious: They were appointed to take care of the popular interests & pretensions at Rome, because the people by reason of their numbers could not act in concert; were liable to fall into factions among themselves, and to become a prey to their aristocratic adversaries. The more the representatives of the people therefore were multiplied, the more they partook of the infirmaties of their constituents, the more liable they became to be divided among themselves either from their own indiscretions or the artifices of the opposite factions, and of course the less capable of fulfilling their trust. When the weight of a set of men depends merely on their personal characters; the greater the number the greater the weight. When it depends on the degree of political authority lodged in them the smaller the number the greater the weight. These considerations might perhaps be combined in the intended Senate; but the latter was the material one.

Mr. Gerry. 4 modes of appointing the Senate have been mentioned. 1. by the 1st. branch of the National Legislature. This would create a dependence contrary to the end proposed. 2. by the National Executive. This is a stride towards monarchy that few will think of. 3. by the people. the people have two great interests, the landed interest, and the commercial including the stockholders. To draw both branches from the people will leave no security to the latter interest; the people being chiefly composed of the landed interest, and erroneously, supposing, that the other interests are adverse to it. 4 by the Individual Legislatures. The elections being carried thro' this refinement, will be most likely to provide some check in favor of the commercial interest agst. the landed; without which oppression will take place, and no free Govt. can last long when that is the case. He was therefore in favor of this last.

Mr. Dickenson.* The preservation of the States in a cer-

---

* ⟨It will throw light on this discussion, to remark that an election by the State Legislatures involved a surrender of the principle insisted on by the large States & dreaded by the small ones, namely that of a proportional representation in the Senate.

tain degree of agency is indispensible. It will produce that collision between the different authorities which should be wished for in order to check each other. To attempt to abolish the States altogether, would degrade the Councils of our Country, would be impracticable, would be ruinous. He compared the proposed National System to the Solar System, in which the States were the planets, and ought to be left to move freely in their proper orbits. The Gentleman from Pa. (Mr. Wilson) wished he said to extinguish these planets. If the State Governments were excluded from all agency in the national one, and all power drawn from the people at large, the consequence would be that the national Govt. would move in the same direction as the State Govts. now do, and would run into all the same mischiefs. The reform would only unite the 13 small streams into one great current pursuing the same course without any opposition whatever. He adhered to the opinion that the Senate ought to be composed of a large number, and that their influence ⟨from family weight & other causes⟩ would be increased thereby. He did not admit that the Tribunes lost their ⟨weight⟩ in proportion as their no. was augmented and gave a historical sketch of this institution. If the reasoning of (Mr. ⟨Madison⟩) was good it would prove that the number of the Senate ought to be reduced below ten, the highest no. of the Tribunitial corps.

Mr. Wilson. The subject it must be owned is surrounded with doubts and difficulties. But we must surmount them. The British Governmt. cannot be our model. We have no materials for a similar one. Our manners, our laws, the abolition of entails and of primogeniture; the whole genius of the people, are opposed to it. He did not see the danger of the States being devoured by the Nationl. Govt. On the contrary, he wished to keep them from devouring the national Govt. He was not however for extinguishing these planets as was supposed by Mr. D. — neither did he on the other hand, believe that they would warm or enlighten the Sun. Within their proper orbits they must still be suffered to act for sub-

Such a rule wd make the body too numerous. As the smallest State must elect one member at least.⟩

ordinate purposes ⟨for which their existence is made essential by the great extent of our Country.⟩ He could not comprehend in what manner the landed interest wd. be rendered less predominant in the Senate, by an election through the medium of the Legislatures than by the people themselves. If the Legislatures, as was now complained, sacrificed the commercial to the landed interest, what reason was there to expect such a choice from them as would defeat their own views. He was for an election by the people in large districts which wd. be most likely to obtain men of intelligence & uprightness; subdividing the districts only for the accomodation of voters.

Mr. Madison could as little comprehend in what manner family weight, as desired by Mr. D. would be more certainly conveyed into the Senate through elections by the State Legislatures, than in some other modes. The true question was in what mode the best choice wd. be made? If an election by the people, or thro' any other channel than the State Legislatures promised as uncorrupt & impartial a preference of merit, there could surely be no necessity for an appointment by those Legislatures. Nor was it apparent that a more useful check would be derived thro' that channel than from the people thro' some other. The great evils complained of were that the State Legislatures run into schemes of paper money &c, whenever solicited by the people, & sometimes without even the sanction of the people. Their influence then, instead of checking a like propensity in the National Legislature, may be expected to promote it. Nothing can be more contradictory than to say that the Natl. Legislature witht. a proper check will follow the example of the State legislatures, & in the same breath, that the State Legislatures are the only proper check.

Mr. Sharman opposed elections by the people in districts, as not likely to produce such fit men as elections by the State Legislatures.

Mr. Gerry insisted that the commercial & monied interest wd. be more secure in the hands of the State Legislatures, than of the people at large. The former have more sense of character, and will be restrained by that from injustice. The people are for paper money when the Legislatures are agst. it. In Massts. the County Conventions had declared a wish for a *depreciating* paper that wd. sink itself. Besides, in some States there are two Branches in the Legislature, one of which is somewhat aristocratic. There wd. therefore be so far a better chance of refinement in the choice. There seemed, he thought to be three powerful objections agst. elections by districts   1. It is impracticable; the people can not be brought to one place for the purpose; and whether brought to the same place or not, numberless frauds wd. be unavoidable.   2. small States forming part of the same district with a large one, or large part of a large one, wd. have no chance of gaining an appointment for its citizens of merit.   3 a new source of discord wd. be opened between different parts of the same district.

Mr. Pinkney thought the 2d. branch ought to be permanent & independent, & that the members of it wd. be rendered more so by receiving their appointment from the State Legislatures. This mode wd. avoid the rivalships & discontents incident to the election by districts. He was for dividing the States into three classes according to their respective sizes, & for allowing to the 1st. class three members — to the 2d. two. & to the 3d. one.

On the question for postponing Mr. Dickinson's motion referring the appointment of the Senate to the State Legislatures, in order to consider Mr. Wilson's for referring it to the people.

Mass. no. Cont. no. N. Y. no. N. J. no. Pa. ay Del. no. Md. no. Va. no. N. C. no. S. C. no. Geo. no. [Ayes — 1; noes — 10.]

Col. Mason. whatever power may be necesary for the Natl. Govt. a certain portion must necessarily be left in the States. It is impossible for one power to pervade the extreme parts of the U. S. so as to carry equal justice to them. The State Legislatures also ought to have some means of defending themselves agst. encroachments of the Natl. Govt. In every other department we have studiously endeavored to provide for its self-defence. Shall we leave the States alone unprovided with the means for this purpose? And what better means can we provide than the giving them some share in, or rather to make them a constituent part of, the Natl. Establishment. There is danger on both sides no doubt; but we have only seen the evils arising on the side of the State Govts. Those on the other side remain to be displayed. The example of Cong: does not apply. Congs. had no power to carry their acts into execution as the Natl. Govt. will have.

On Mr. Dickinson's motion for an appointment of the Senate by the State-Legislatures.

Mass. ay. Ct. ay. N. Y. ay. Pa. ay Del. ay. Md. ay. Va. ay N. C. ay. S. C. ay. Geo. ay. [Ayes — 10; noes — 0.] [5]

Mr. Gerry gave notice that he wd. tomorrow move for a reconsideration of the mode of appointing the Natl. Executive in order to substitute an appointm. by the State Executives

The Committee rose & The House adjd.

YATES

THURSDAY, JUNE 7th, 1787.

Met pursuant to adjournment.

Mr. Rutledge moved to take into consideration the mode of electing the second branch of the national legislature.

Mr. Dickinson thereupon moved, *that the second branch of the national legislature be chosen by the legislatures of the individual states.* He observed, that this mode will more intimately connect the state governments with the national legislature — it will also draw forth the first characters either as to family or talent, and that it ought to consist of a considerable number.

Mr. Wilson against the motion, because the two branches thus constituted, cannot agree, they having different views and different sentiments.

Mr. Dickinson is of opinion that the mode by him proposed, like the British house of lords and commons, whose powers flow from different sources, are mutual checks on each

---

[5] Detail of Ayes and Noes, Vote 32, includes New Jersey.

other, and will thus promote the real happiness and security of the country — a government thus established would harmonize the whole, and like the planetary system, the national council like the sun, would illuminate the whole — the planets revolving round it in perfect order; or like the union of several small streams, would at last form a respectable river, gently flowing to the sea.

Mr. Wilson. The state governments ought to be preserved — the freedom of the people and their internal good police depends on their existence in full vigor — but such a government can only answer local purposes — That it is not possible a general government, as despotic as even that of the Roman emperors, could be adequate to the government of the whole without this distinction. He hoped that the national government would be independent of state governments, in order to make it vigorous, and therefore moved that the above resolution be postponed, and that the convention in its room adopt the following resolve: *That the second branch of the national legislature be chosen by districts, to be formed for that purpose.*[6]

Mr. Sherman supposes the election of the national legislature will be better vested in the state legislatures, than by the people, for by pursuing different objects, persons may be returned who have not one tenth of the votes.

Mr. Gerry observed, that the great mercantile interest and of stockholders, is not provided for in any mode of election — they will however be better represented if the state legislatures choose the second branch.

Question carried against the postponement — 10 states against 1.

Mr. Mason then spoke to the general question — observing on the propriety, that the second branch of the national legislature should flow from the legislature of each state, to prevent the encroachments on each other and to harmonize the whole.

The question put on the first motion, and carried unanimously. Adjourned to to-morrow morning.

---

[6] Compare Genet's interpretation of this speech in Appendix A, CCCX.

KING

7 June. Come. whole

The proposition before the comee. — that the Senate be appointed by the other Br. of the national legislature out of persons nominated by the State Legislatures being negatived—

Dickerson—proposed an amendment so that the appointment of the Senate shd. be by the Legislatures of the individual States — for two reasons, first, that the mind & body of the State as such shd. be represented in the national Legislature. Second, that the men of first Talents may be employed in the national Legislature; they first will have a chance in the Election of the people, failing there, wealth, family, or Talents may hold them up to the State Legislatures as fit characters for the Senate—let their numbers be more than 200; by inlarging their Numbers you increase their consequence & weight & by combining the families and wealth of the aristocracy, you establish a balance that will check the Democracy —

Wilson — If this amendment passes — we shall not have a national Govt: the Senate will be too numerous, and will not represent the property or numbers of the Nation, but they will represent the *States*, whose interests may oppose the Genl. Government — the consequence will be unfavorable to the Harmony of the Nation.

Madison — We are about to form a national Govt. and therefore must abandon Ideas founded alone in the plan of confedn. the Senate ought to come from, & represent, the Wealth of the nation, and this being the Rule, the amendment cannot be adopted — besides the numbers will be too large — the Proofs of History establish this position, that delegated power will have the most weight & consequence in the hands of a few — when the Roman Tribunes were few, they checked the Senate; when multiplied, they divided, were weak, ceased to be that Guard to the people which was expected in their institution —

Dickerson — The objection is that you attempt to unite distinct Interests — I do not consider this an objection, Safety may flow from this variety of Interests — there exists this Diversity in the constitution of G. Britain — We cannot abolish the States and consolidate them into one Govt — Indeed if we could I shd. be agt. it — Let our Govt. be like that of the solar System; let the Genl. Govt. be the Sun and the States the Planets repelled yet attracted, and the whole moving regularly and harmoniously in their respective Orbits — the Objection from Virgina. (Madison) that power delegated to a few will be a better & more weighty check to the Democy. & the Instance of the Roman Tribunes proves too much; *they* never exceeded ten in number; no Gentlemen has an Idea that the Senate shd. be so small as the number of Roman Tribunes at any Time, much less when their Numbers were only *three*—

Wilson — I am not in favor of an abolition of the States — I revere the theory of the Brit. Govt. but we can't adopt it — we have no laws in favor of primogeniture — no distinction of families — the partition of Estates destroys the influence of the Few — But I know that all confederations have been destroyed by the growth & ambition of some of *their members* — if the State Legisltures. appoint the Senate, the principle, which has formerly operated the ruin of antient Confederacies, will be received and cherished, in that we are abt. to establish —

I therefore propose that the Senate be elected by the people and that the Territory be thrown into convenient Districts—

Dickerson — opposed the substitute proposed by Wilson because the same is either impracticable or unfair — the Districts must be either parts of States, or entire States, or parts of distinct States united — if the first, how will you prevent fraudulent or corrupt Elections, if the second, how will you establish an intermediate body to elect from those who have the most votes and are not elected — if the third the small States will never have a member therefore it is unfair —

On the Question to agree to Wilson's substitute providing for an Election in Districts

Pen. ay — the 10. other States no —

Mason—It is true that the antient confederacies were dissolved by the overgrown power and unreasonable ambition

of some one of its members. but their situation was different
from that which is proposed for the U. S. — we have agreed
that the national Legislature shall have a negative on the State
Legislatures — the Danger is that the national, will swallow
up the State Legislatures — what will be a reasonable guard
agt. this Danger, and operate in favor of the State authorities
— The answer seems to me to be this, let the State Legislatures appoint the Senate —

On the Question whether the Senate shd. be appointed by the
State Legislatures the Question was carried unanimously in
the affirmative —[7]

HAMILTON

Dickinson II — He would have the state legislatures elect
senators, because he would bring into the
general government the sense of the state
Governments &

II — because the more respectable choices would
be made —

Note — Separate states may give stronger organs to their
governments & engage more the good will of
Ind: — while Genl Gov —

☞ Consider the Principle of Rivalship by excluding
the state Legislatures —

Mason ⎰ General government could not know how to make
laws for every part — such as respect *agriculture* &c

particular governments would have *no defensive*
power unless let into the constitution as a Constituent part — — —

MASON [8]

At a time when our government is approaching to dissolution, when some of its principles have been found utterly

---

[7] [Endorsed:] | 7 June | Senators to be chosen | by State Legislatures | *unani-
mous*

[8] This document in Mason's handwriting was found among the Mason Papers
and is printed in K. M. Rowland, *Life of George Mason*, II, 386–387. There are

inadequate to the purposes for which it was established, and it is evident that without some material alterations it can not much longer subsist, it must give real concern to every man who has his country's interest at heart to find such a difference of sentiment and opinion in an assembly of the most respectable and confidential characters in America, appointed for the special purpose of revising and amending the federal constitution, so as to obtain and preserve the important objects for which it was instituted — the protection, safety and happiness of the people. We all agree in the necessity of new regulations; but we differ widely in our opinions of what are the safest and most effectual. Perhaps this contrariety of sentiment arises from our not thoroughly considering the peculiar circumstances, situation, character and genius of the people of America, differing materially from that of any other nation. The history of other nations has been minutely investigated, examples have been drawn from and arguments founded on the practice of countries very dissimilar to ours. The treaties, leagues, and confederacies between different sovereign, independent powers have been urged as proofs in support of the propriety and justice of the single and equal representation of each individual State in the American Union; and thence conclusions have been drawn that the people of these United States would refuse to adopt a government founded more on an equal representation of the people themselves, than on the distinct representation of each separate, individual State. If the different States in our Union always had been as now substantially and in reality distinct, sovereign and independent, this kind of reasoning would have great force; but if the premises on which it is founded are mere assumptions not founded on facts, or at best upon facts to be found only upon a paper of yesterday, and even these contradictory to each other, no satisfactory conclusions can be drawn from them.

erasures and interlineations, and it would seem to represent a part of a speech in the first days of the Convention. It is assigned to this date because it corresponds more closely to the ideas reported of his speech on this day than on any other occasion.

FRIDAY, JUNE 8, 1787.

JOURNAL

Friday June 8. 1787

The Order of the day being read

The House resolved itself into a Committee of the whole House to consider of the State of the American union

Mr President left the Chair

Mr Gorham took the Chair of the Committee

Mr President resumed the Chair

Mr Gorham reported from the Committee that the Committee had made a further progress in the matter to them referred; and had directed Him to move that they may have leave to sit again.

Resolved that this House will to-morrow again resolve itself into a Committee of the whole House to consider of the State of the american union.

And then the House adjourned till to-morrow at 11 o'Clock A. M.

In a Committee of the whole House

Friday June 8. 1787.

Mr Gorham in the Chair

It was moved by Mr C Pinckney seconded by Mr Madison to strike out the following words in the 6th resolution adopted by the Committee namely

"to negative all laws passed by the several States contra-
"vening, in the opinion of the national legislature, the articles
"of union; or any treaties subsisting under the authority of
"the union."

—— and to insert the following words in their place namely
"to negative all laws which to them shall appear improper."

And on the question to strike out

it passed in the negative. [Ayes—3; noes—7; divided—1.][1]
It was moved by Mr Gerry seconded by Mr King to recon-
sider that clause of the seventh resolution, adopted by the
Committee, which respects the appointment of the national
Executive

On the question to reconsider

it passed in the affirmative [Ayes — 9; noes — 2.][2]

and to-morrow was assigned for the reconsideration

It was then moved by Mr C Pinckney seconded by Mr Rutledge that the following resolution be added after the 4th resolution adopted by the Committee namely.

Resolved That the States be divided into three Classes —
the first Class to have three members, the second two, and
the third One member each — that an estimate be taken of
the comparative importance of each State, at fixed periods,
so as to ascertain the number of members they may from time
to time be entitled to.

Before any debate was had, or determination taken on Mr
Pinckney's proposition—it was moved and seconded that the
Committee do now rise, report a further progress, and request
leave to sit again.

The Committee then rose.

DETAIL OF AYES AND NOES

	New Hampshire	Massachusetts	Rhode Island	Connecticut	New York	New Jersey	Pennsylvania	Delaware	Maryland	Virginia	North Carolina	South Carolina	Georgia	Questions	Ayes	Noes	Divided
[34]	aye		no	no	no	aye	dd	no	aye	no	no		no	for vesting the national legislature with a negative on all State laws which shall appear to them improper	3	7	1
[35]	aye		no	aye	aye	aye	aye	aye	aye	no	aye		aye	To reconsider the mode of appointing the executive	9	2	

[1] Vote 34, Detail of Ayes and Noes.   [2] Vote 35, Detail of Ayes and Noes.

MADISON

Friday June 8th. In Committee of the Whole.

On a reconsideration of the clause giving the Natl. Legislature a negative on such laws of the States as might be contrary to the articles of Union, or Treaties with foreign nations,[3]

Mr. Pinkney moved "that the National Legislature shd. have authority to negative all Laws which they shd. judge to be improper". He urged that such a universality of the power was indispensably necessary to render it effectual; that the States must be kept in due subordination to the nation; that if the States were left to act of themselves in any case, it wd. be impossible to defend the national prerogatives, however extensive they might be on paper; that the acts of Congress had been defeated by this means; nor had foreign treaties escaped repeated violations; that this universal negative was in fact the corner stone of an efficient national Govt.; that under the British Govt. the negative of the Crown had been found beneficial, and the *States* are more one nation now, than the *Colonies* were then.

Mr. ⟨Madison⟩ seconded the motion. He could not but regard an indefinite power to negative legislative acts of the States as absolutely necessary to a perfect system. Experience had evinced a constant tendency in the States to encroach on the federal authority; to violate national Treaties, to infringe the rights & interests of each other; to oppress the weaker party within their respective jurisdictions. A negative was the mildest expedient that could be devised for preventing these mischiefs. The existence of such a check would prevent attempts to commit them. Should no such precaution be engrafted, the only remedy wd. lie in an appeal to coercion. Was such a remedy elegible? was it practicable? Could the national resources, if exerted to the utmost enforce a national decree agst. Massts. abetted perhaps by several

---

[3] Upon this subject, see above May 31, below July 17, August 23, and Appendix A, XLI, LXXIV, CXXXVII, CCXCVI, CCCXXVI, CCCLXXXIII, CCCLXXXVIII, CCCXCI, CCCXCII, CCCCI.

of her neighbours? It wd. not be possible. A; small proportion of the Community in a compact situation, acting on the defensive, and at one of its extremities might at any time bid defiance to the National authority. Any Govt. for the U. States formed on the supposed practicability of using force agst. the ⟨unconstitutional proceedings⟩[4] of the States, wd. prove as visionary & fallacious as the Govt. of Congs. The negative wd. render the use of force unnecessary. The States cd. of themselves then pass no operative act, any more than one branch of a Legislature where there are two branches, can proceed without the other. But in order to give the negative this efficacy, it must extend to all cases. A discrimination wd. only be a fresh source of contention between the two authorities. In a word, to recur to the illustrations borrowed from the planetary System, This prerogative of the General Govt. is the great pervading principle that must controul the centrifugal tendency of the States; which, without it, will continually fly out of their proper orbits and destroy the order & harmony of the political system.

Mr. Williamson was agst. giving a power that might restrain the States from regulating their internal police.

Mr. Gerry cd. not see the extent of such a power, and was agst. every power that was not necessary. He thought a remonstrance agst. unreasonable acts of the States wd. reclaim them. If it shd. not force might be resorted to. He had no objection to authorize a negative to paper money and similar measures. When the confederation was depending before Congress, Massachusetts was then for inserting the power of emitting paper money amg. the exclusive powers of Congress. He observed that the proposed negative wd. extend to the regulations of the militia, a matter on which the existence of a State might depend. The Natl. Legislature with such a power may enslave the States. Such an idea as this will never be acceded to. It has never been suggested or conceived among the people. No speculative projector, and there are eno' of that character among us, in politics as well as in other things, has

---

[4] Originally "misdeeds".

in any pamphlet or newspaper thrown out the idea. The States too have different interests and are ignorant of each other's interests. The negative therefore will be abused, New States too having separate views from the old States will never come into the Union, They may even be under some foreign influence; are they in such case to participate in the negative on the will of the other States?

Mr. Sherman thought the cases in which the negative ought to be exercised, might be defined. He wished the point might not be decided till a trial at least shd. be made for that purpose

Mr. Wilson would not say what modifications of the proposed power might be practicable or expedient. But however novel it might appear the principal of it when viewed with a close & steady eye, is right. There is no instance in which the laws say that the individuals shd. be bound in one case, & at liberty to judge whether he will obey or disobey in another. The cases are parallel, Abuses of the power over the individual person may happen as well as over the individual States. Federal liberty is to States, what civil liberty, is to private individuals. And States are not more unwilling to purchase it, by the necessary concession of their political sovereignty, that the savage is to purchase Civil liberty by the surrender of the personal sovereignty. which he enjoys in a State of nature. A definition of the cases in which the Negative should be exercised, is impracticable. A discretion must be left on one side or the other? Will it not be most safely lodged on the side of the Natl. Govt.? — Among the first sentiments expressed in the first Congs. one was that Virga. is no more. That Massts. is no [more], that Pa. is no more &c. We are now one nation of brethren. We must bury all local interests & distinctions. This language continued for some time. The tables at length began to turn. No sooner were the State Govts. formed than their jealousy & ambition began to display themselves. Each endeavoured to cut a slice from the common loaf, to add to its own morsel, till at length the confederation became frittered down to the impotent condition in which it now stands. Review the progress of the articles of Confederation thro' Congress & compare the first & last draught of it. To correct its vices is the business of this convention. One of its vices is the want of an effectual controul in the whole over its parts. What danger is there that the whole will unnecessarily sacrifice a part? But reverse the case, and leave the whole at the mercy of each part, and will not the general interest be continually sacrificed to local interests?

Mr. Dickenson deemed it impossible to draw a line between the cases proper & improper for the exercise of the negative. We must take our choice of two things. We must either subject the States to the danger of being injured by the power of the Natl. Govt. or the latter to the danger of being injured by that of the States. He thought the danger greater from the States. To leave the power doubtful, would be opening another spring of discord, and he was for shutting as many of them as possible.

Mr. Bedford. In answer to his colleagues question, where wd. be the danger to the States from this power, would refer him to the smallness of his own State which may be injured at pleasure without redress. It was meant he found to strip the small States of their equal right of suffrage. In this case Delaware would have about $\frac{1}{90}$ ⟨for its⟩ share in the General Councils, whilst Pa. & Va. would possess $\frac{1}{3}$ of the whole. Is there no difference of interests, no rivalship of commerce, of manufactures? Will not these large States crush the small ones whenever they stand in the way of their ambitions or interested views. This shows the impossibility of adopting such a system as that on the table, or any other founded on a change in the prinple of representation. And after all, if a State does not obey the law of the new System, must not force be resorted to as the only ultimate remedy, in this as in any other system. It seems as if Pa. & Va. by the conduct of their deputies wished to provide a system in which they would have an enormous & monstrous influence. Besides, How can it be thought that the proposed negative can be exercised? are the laws of the States to be suspended in the most urgent cases until they can be sent seven or eight hundred miles, and undergo the deliberations of a body who may be incapable of

Judging of them? Is the National Legislature too to sit continually in order to revise the laws of the States?

⟨Mr.⟩⟨Madison⟩observed that the difficulties which had been started were worthy of attention and ought to be answered before the question was put. The case of laws of urgent necessity must be provided for by some emanation of the power from the Natl. Govt. into each State so far as to give a temporary assent at least. This was the practice in Royal Colonies before the Revolution and would not have been inconvenient; if the supreme power of negativing had been faithful to the American interest, and had possessed the necessary information. He supposed that the negative might be very properly lodged in the senate alone, and that the more numerous & expensive branch therefore might not be obliged to sit constantly. — He asked Mr. B. what would be the consequence to the small States of a dissolution of the Union wch. seemed likely to happen if no effectual substitute was made for the defective System existing, and he did not conceive any effectual system could be substituted on any other basis than that of a proportional suffrage? If the large States possessed the Avarice & ambition with which they were charged, would the small ones in their neighbourhood, be more secure when all controul of a Genl. Govt. was withdrawn.

Mr. Butler was vehement agst. the Negative in the proposed extent, as cutting off all hope of equal justice to the distant States. The people there would not he was sure give it a hearing.

On the question for extending the negative power to all cases as proposd. by (Mr. P. & Mr- M——) Mas. ay. Cont. no. N. Y. no. N. J. no. Pa. ay. Del. divd. Mr. Reed & Mr. Dickenson ay. Mr. Bedford & Mr. Basset no. Maryd. no. Va. ay. Mr. R. Mr. Mason no. Mr. Blair, Docr. Mc. Cg. Mr. M. ay. Genl. W. not consulted. N. C. no. S. C. no Geo. no. [Ayes — 3; noes — 7; divided — 1.]

⟨On motion of Mr. Gerry and Mr. King tomorrow was assigned for reconsidering the mode of appointing the National Executive: the reconsideration being voted for by all the States except Connecticut & N. Carolina.

Mr. Pinkney and Mr. Rutlidge moved to add to Resoln. 4. agreed to by the Come. the following, viz. "that the States be divided into three classes, the 1st. class to have 3 members, the 2d. two. & the 3d. one member each; that an estimate be taken of the comparative importance of each State at fixed periods, so as to ascertain the number of members they may from time to time be entitled to" The Committee then rose and the House adjourned.)[5]

YATES

FRIDAY, JUNE 8, 1787.

Met pursuant to adjournment — 11 states.

Mr. Pinkney moved, *That the national legislature shall have the power of negativing all laws to be passed by the state legislatures which they may judge improper,* in the room of the clause as it stood reported.

He grounds his motion on the necessity of one supreme controlling power, and he considers this as the *corner-stone* of the present system; and hence the necessity of retrenching the state authorities in order to preserve the good government of the national council.

Mr. Williamson against the motion. The national legislature ought to possess the power of negativing such laws only as will encroach on the national government.

Mr. Madison wished that the line of jurisprudence could be drawn — he would be for it — but upon reflection he finds it impossible, and therefore he is for the amendment. If the clause remains without the amendment it is inefficient — The judges of the state must give the state laws their operation, although the law abridges the rights of the national government — how is it to be repealed? By the power who made it? How shall you compel them? By force? To prevent this disagreeable expedient, the power of negativing is absolutely necessary — this is the only attractive principle which will retain its centrifugal force, and without this the planets will fly from their orbits.[6]

---

[5] Taken from *Journal.*

[6] Compare Genet's interpretation of this speech in Appendix A, CCCX.

Mr. Gerry supposes that this power ought to extend to all laws already made; but the preferable mode would be to designate the powers of the national legislature, to which the negative ought to apply — he has no objection to restrain the laws which may be made for issuing paper money. Upon the whole he does not choose on this important trust, *to take a leap in the dark.*[6]

Mr. Pinkney supposes that the proposed amendment had no retrospect to the state laws already made. The adoption of the new government must operate as a complete repeal of all the constitutions and state laws, as far as they are inconsistent with the new government.

Mr. Wilson supposes the surrender of the rights of a federal government to be a surrender of sovereignty. True, we may define some of the rights, but when we come near the line it cannot be found. One general excepting clause must therefore apply to the whole. In the beginning of our troubles, congress themselves were as one state — dissentions or state interests were not known — they gradually crept in after the formation of the constitution, and each took to himself a slice. The original draft of confederation was drawn on the first ideas, and the draft concluded on how different!

Mr. Bedford was against the motion, and states the proportion of the intended representation of the number 90: Delaware 1 — Pennsylvania and Virginia one third. On this computation where is the weight of the small states when the interest of the one is in competition with the other on trade, manufactures and agriculture? When he sees this mode of government so strongly advocated by the members of the great states, he must suppose it a question of *interest.*

Mr. Madison confesses it is not without its difficulties on many accounts—some may be removed, others modified, and some are unavoidable. May not this power be vested in the senatorial branch? they will probably be always sitting. Take the question on the other ground, who is to determine the line when drawn in doubtful cases? The state legislatures

---

[6] Compare Genet's interpretation of this speech in Appendix A, CCCX.

cannot, for they will be partial in support of their own powers — no tribunal can be found.   It is impossible that the articles of confederation can be amended — they are too tottering to be invigorated — nothing but the present system, or something like it, can restore the peace and harmony of the country.

The question put on Mr. Pinkney's motion — 7 states against it — Delaware divided — Virginia, Pennsylvania and Massachusetts for it.

Adjourned to to-morrow morning.

KING

8 June

Conee. of the whole — Mr. C. Pinckney moves to reconsider a former vote of the Comee. vesting the national Legislatr. with a negative on the State Laws in certain instances, for the purpose of vesting them with the power of a general Negative —

The interruption of the Laws and Treaties passed and entered into by Congress, by particular State laws have been sufficiently experienced, the Harmony of the Union makes this measure necessary, and the national independence must in a great Degree rest on its adoption —

Williamson — agt. the reconsideration because he thinks the State Legislatures ought to possess independent powers in cases purely local, and applying to their internal policy —

Madison — The amendment or a reconsideration for discussion seems necessary — I am of opinion that ye Genl. Govt. will not be able to compel the large and important State to rescind a popular law passed by their Legislature.   If this power does not rest in the national Legisl: there will be wanting a check to the centrifugal Force which constantly operates in the several states to force them off from a common Centre, or a national point —

Gerry — this power may enable the Genl. Govt. to depress a part for the benefit of another part — it may prevent the encouragements which particular States may be disposed to

give to particular manufactures, it may prevent the States from
traing. their militia, and thereby establish a military Force
& finally a Despotism —

Wilson — In the Establishment of society every man yields
his life, his liberty, property & Character to the society. there
is no reservation of this sort, that the individual shall be subject to one and exempt from another Law — Indeed we have
seen the Legislatures in our own Country deprive the citizen
of Life, of Liberty, & property we have seen Attainders, Ban-
ishment, & Confiscations.

If we mean to establish a national Govt. the States must
submit themselves as individuals — the lawful Government
must be supreme — either the Genl. or the State Government
must be supreme — We must remember the language with
wh. we began the Revolution, it was this, Virginia is no more,
Massachusetts is no more — we are one in name, let us be
one in Truth & Fact — Unless this power is vested in the Genl.
Govt. the States will be used by foreign powers as Engines agt
the Whole — New States will be soon formed, the Inhabitants may be foreigners and possess foreign affections, unless
the Genl. Govt. can check their State laws they may involve
the Nation in Tumult and Confusion.

Dickerson — There can be no line of separation dividing the
powers of legislation between the State & Genl. Govts.   The
consequence is inevitable that there must be a supreme &
august national Legislature — the objection that the States
may be prevented from training the Militia, is obviated by
the mode of appointing the Senate and the actual representation of the people —

Bedford — Agt. the amendment — Delaware now stands $\frac{1}{13}$th
of the whole — when the system of equal representation obtains Delaware will be $\frac{1}{90}$th — Virginia & Pensylvania will
stand $\frac{28}{90}$th — Suppose a rivalry in commerce or manufacture
between Delaware and these two States; what chance has
Delaware agt. them? Bounties may be given in Virgina. &
Pensylvania, and their influence in the Genl. Govt. or Legislature will prevent a negative, not so if the same measure
is attempted in Delaware —

The Committee having agreed to a reconsideration on the question to agree to the proposed amendment

Mass. Penn. & Virgin. Ay ⎫
Dela — divid — ⎬ lost[7]
Cont. NYk. NJ. Mar. N.C SC. & Geor. No ⎭

HAMILTON

Pinckey—For general Negative—

Gerry—Is for a negative on paper emissions—
>New states will arise which cannot be controuled —
>& may outweigh & controul —

Wilson — Foreign influence may infect certain corners of
>confederacy which ought to be restrained —
>Union basis of our oppos & Ind:

Bedford — ⎰ Arithmetical calculation of proportional influ-
>⎱ ence in General Government —
>⎰ *Pensyl.* & *Delaware* may have rivalship in com-
>⎱ merce — & influence of Pens — sacrifice *delaware*
>If there be a negative in G G — yet if a law can
>pass through all the forms of S - C. it will
>require force to abrogate it

Butler — Will a man throw afloat his property & confide it
>to a government a thousand miles *distant?*

---

[7] [Endorsed:] 8 June | Shall Congress have power to negative State Laws |
Mass. Pen. Virgin. aye | Del. divided | Con. NY. Jers. Mar. N. & S. Car and Geor no

SATURDAY, JUNE 9, 1787.

JOURNAL

Saturday June 9. 1787.

The honorable Luther Martin Esquire One of the Deputies of the State of Maryland attended and took his Seat.

The order of the day being read

The House resolved itself into a Committee of the whole House to consider of the State of the american union.

Mr President left the Chair

Mr Gorham took the Chair of the Committee.

Mr President resumed the Chair.

Mr Gorham reported from the Committee that the Committee had made a further progress in the matter to them referred; and had directed him to move that they may have leave to sit again

Resolved that this House will on Monday next again resolve itself into a Committee of the whole House to consider of the State of the American union

And then the House adjourned till Monday next at 11 o'Clock A. M.

In a Committee of the whole House

Saturday June 9. 1787.

Mr Gorham in the Chair.

A question being taken, on Mr Gerry's motion, to strike out the following words in that clause of the 7th resolution, adopted by the Committee, which respects the appointment of the national Executive

namely "to be chosen by the national legislature" and to insert

"to be chosen by the Executives of the individual States"

it passed in the negative. [Ayes—o; noes—10; divided—1.][1]
It was moved by Mr Patterson seconded by Mr Brearley to
enter on the consideration of the   resolution submitted by
Mr Randolph.

After some time passed in debate —

It was moved and seconded that the Committee do now
rise, report a further progress, and request leave to sit again.

The Committee then rose.

DETAIL OF AYES AND NOES

	New Hampshire	Massachusetts	Rhode Island	Connecticut	New York	New Jersey	Pennsylvania	Delaware	Maryland	Virginia	North Carolina	South Carolina	Georgia	Questions	Ayes	Noes	Divided
[36]	no		no	no	no	no	dd	no	no	no	no	no	no	To appoint the national Executive by the Executives of the sevl States		10	1

MADISON

Saturday June 9th. ⟨Mr. Luther Martin from Maryland
took his Seat⟩[2]   In committee of the whole

Mr. Gerry, according to previous notice given by him,
moved "that the National Executive should be elected by
the Executives of the States whose proportion of votes should
be the same with that allowed to the States in the election of
the Senate." If the appointmt. should be made by the Natl.
Legislature, it would lessen that independence ⟨of the Execu-
tive⟩ which ought to prevail, would give birth to intrigue and
corruption between the Executive & Legislature previous to
the election, and to partiality in the Executive afterwards
to the friends who promoted him. Some other mode therefore appeared to him necessary. He proposed that of appointing by the State Executives as most analogous to the principle observed in electing the other branches of the Natl.

---

[1] Vote 36. Detail of Ayes and Noes.   [2] Taken from *Journal.*

Govt.; the first branch being chosen by the *people* of the States, & the 2d. by the Legislatures of the States; he did not see any objection agst. letting the Executive be appointed by the Executives of the States. He supposed the Executives would be most likely to select the fittest men, and that it would be their interest to support the man of their own choice.

Mr. Randolph urged strongly the inexpediency of Mr. Gerry's mode of appointing the Natl. Executive. The confidence of the people would not be secured by it to the Natl. magistrate. The small States would lose all chance of an appointmt. from within themselves. Bad appointments would be made; the Executives of the States being little conversant with characters not within their own small spheres. The State Executives too notwithstanding their constitutional independence, being in fact dependent on the State Legislatures will generally be guided by the views of the latter, and prefer either favorites within the States, or such as it may be expected will be most partial to the interests of the State. A Natl. Executive thus chosen will not be likely to defend with becoming vigilance & firmness the national rights agst. State encroachments. Vacancies also must happen. How can these be filled? He could not suppose either that the Executives would feel the interest in supporting the Natl. Executive which had been imagined. They will not cherish the great Oak which is to reduce them to paltry shrubs.[3]

On the question for referring the appointment of the Natl. Executive to the State Executives as propd. by Mr. Gerry Massts. no. Cont. no. N. Y. no. N. J. no. Pa. no. Del. divd. Md. no. Va. no. S. C. no. Geo. no. [Ayes — 0; noes — 9; divided — 1.][4]

Mr. Patterson moves that the Committee resume the clause relating to the rule of suffrage in the Natl. Legislature.

Mr. Brearly seconds him. He was sorry he said that any question on this point was brought into view. It had been much agitated in Congs. at the time of forming the Confederation and was then rightly settled by allowing to each sovereign

---

[3] For further discussion of this subject, see references under September 6, note 23.
[4] Journal and Yates include North Carolina voting "no".

State an equal vote. Otherwise the smaller States must have been destroyed instead of being saved. The substitution of a ratio, he admitted carried fairness on the face of it; but on a deeper examination was unfair and unjust. Judging of the disparity of the States by the quota of Congs. Virga. would have 16 votes, and Georgia but one. A like proportion to the others will make the whole number ninity.[5] There will be 3. large states and 10 small ones. The large States by which he meant Massts. Pena. & Virga. will carry every thing before them. It had been admitted, and was known to him from facts within N. Jersey that where large and small counties were united into a district for electing representatives for the district, the large counties always carried their point, and Consequently that the large States would do so. Virga. with her sixteen votes will be a solid column indeed, a formidable phalanx. While Georgie with her Solitary vote, and the other little States will be obliged to throw themselves constantly into the scale of some large one, in order to have any weight at all. He had come to the convention with a view of being as useful as he could in giving energy and stability to the Federal Government. When the proposition for destroying the equality of votes came forward, he was astonished, he was alarmed. Is it fair then it will be asked that Georgia should have an equal vote with Virga.? He would not say it was. What remedy then? One only, that a map of the U. S. be spread out, that all the existing boundaries be erased, and that a new partition of the whole be made into 13 equal parts [6]

Mr. Patterson considered the proposition for a proportional representation as striking at the existence of the lesser States. He wd. premise however to an investigation of this question some remarks on the nature structure and powers of the Convention. The Convention he said was formed in pursuance of an Act of Congs. that this act was recited in several of the Commissions, particularly that of Massts. which he required to be read: That the amendment of the confederacy was the object of all the laws and commissions on the subject; that the articles

---

of the confederation were therefore the proper basis of all the proceedings of the Convention. We ought to keep within its limits, or we should be charged by our constituents with usurpation. that the people of America were sharpsighted and not to be deceived. But the Commissions under which we acted were not only the measure of our power. they denoted also the sentiments of the States on the subject of our deliberation. The idea of a national Govt. as contradistinguished from a federal one, never entered into the mind of any of them, and to the public mind we must accommodate ourselves. We have no power to go beyond the federal scheme, and if we had the people are not ripe for any other. We must follow the people; the people will not follow us. _The proposition_ could not be maintained whether considered in reference to us as a nation, or as a confederacy. A confederacy supposes sovereignty in the members composing it & sovereignty supposes equality. If we are to be considered as a nation, all State distinctions must be abolished, the whole must be thrown into hotchpot, and when an equal division is made, then there may be fairly an equality of representation. He held up Virga. Massts. & Pa. as the three large States, and the other ten as small ones; repeating the calculations of Mr. Brearly as to the disparity of votes which wd. take place, and affirming that the small States would never agree to it. He said there was no more reason that a great individual State contributing much, should have more votes than a small one contributing little, than that a rich individual citizen should have more votes than an indigent one. If the rateable property of A was to that of B as 40 to 1. ought A for that reason to have 40 times as many votes as B. Such a principle would never be admitted, and if it were admitted would put B entirely at the mercy of A. As A. has more to be protected than B so he ought to contribute more for the common protection. The same may be said of a large State wch. has more to be protected than a small one. Give the large States an influence in proportion to their magnitude, and what will be the consequence? Their ambition will be proportionally increased, and the small States will have every thing to fear. It was once proposed by Galloway & some others that America should be represented in the British Parlt. and then be bound by its laws. America could not have been entitled to more than $\frac{1}{3}$ of the no. of Representatives which would fall to the share of G. B. Would American rights & interests have been safe under an authority thus constituted? It has been said that if a Natl. Govt. is to be formed so as to operate on the people and not on the States, the representatives ought to be drawn from the people. But why so? May not a Legislature filled by the State Legislatures operate on the people who chuse the State Legislatures? or may not a practicable coercion be found. He admitted that there was none such in the existing System. He was attached strongly to the plan of the existing confederacy, in which the people chuse their Legislative representatives; and the Legislatures their federal representatives. No other amendments were wanting than to mark the orbits of the States with due precision, and provide for the use of coercion, which was the great point. He alluded to the hint thrown out heretofore by Mr. Wilson of the necessity to which the large States might be reduced of confederating among themselves, by a refusal of the others to concur. Let them unite if they please, but let them remember that they have no authority to compel the others to unite. N. Jersey will never confederate on the plan before the Committee. She would be swallowed up. He had rather submit to á monarch, to a despot, than to such a fate. He would not only oppose the plan here but on his return home do everything in his power to defeat it there

Mr. Wilson. hoped if the Confederacy should be dissolved, that a *majority*, that a *minority* of the States would unite for their safety. He entered elaborately into the defence of a proportional representation, stating for his first position that as all authority was derived from the people, equal numbers of people ought to have an equal no. of representatives, and different numbers of people different numbers of representatives. This principle had been improperly violated in the Confederation, owing to the urgent circumstances of the time. As to the case of A. & B, stated by Mr. Patterson, he observed that in districts as large as the States, the number of people was the best measure of their comparative wealth. Whether therefore wealth or numbers were to form the ratio it would be the same. Mr. P. admitted persons, not property to be the measure of suffrage. Are not the citizens of Pena. equal to those of N. Jersey? does it require 150 of the former to balance 50 of the latter? Representatives of different districts ought clearly to hold the same proportion to each other, as their respective constituents hold to each other. If the small States will not confederate on this plan, Pena. & he presumed some other States, would not confederate on any other. We have been told that each State being sovereign, all are equal. So each man is naturally a sovereign over himself, and all men are therefore naturally equal. Can he retain this equality when he becomes a member of civil Government? He can not. As little can a Sovereign State, when it becomes a member of a federal Governt. If N. J. will not part with her Sovereignty it is in vain to talk of Govt. A new partition of the States is desireable, but evidently & totally impracticable.

Mr. Williamson, illustrated the cases by a comparison of the different States, to Counties of different sizes within the same State; observing that proportional representation was admitted to be just in the latter case, and could not therefore be fairly contested in the former.

The question being about to be put Mr. Patterson hoped that as so much depended on it, it might be thought best to postpone the decision till tomorrow, which was done nem. con — [7]

⟨The Come. rose & the House adjourned.⟩[8]

YATES

SATURDAY, JUNE 9th, 1787.

Met pursuant to adjournment.

Motion by Mr. Gerry to reconsider the appointment of the national executive.

---

[7] For further discussion of proportional representation, see Records of May 30, June 11, June 27–July 16, with references under June 27 note 2.

[8] See further Appendix A, XXXIX–XLI.

That the national executive be appointed by the state executives.
He supposed that in the national legislature there will be a great number of bad men of various descriptions — these will make a wrong appointment. Besides, an executive thus appointed, will have his partiality in favor of those who appointed him — that this will not be the case by the effect of his motion, and the executive will by this means be independent of the national legislature, but the appointment by the state executives ought to be made by votes in proportion to their weight in the scale of the representation.

Mr. Randolph opposes the motion. The power vested by it is dangerous — confidence will be wanting — the large states will be masters of the election — an executive ought to have great experience, integrity and activity. The executives of the states cannot know the persons properly qualified as possessing these. An executive thus appointed will court the officers of his appointment, and will relax him in the duties of commander of the militia — Your single executive is already invested with negativing laws of the state. Will he duly exercise the power? Is there no danger in the combinations of states to appoint such an executive as may be too favorable to local state governments? Add to this the expense and difficulty of bringing the executives to one place to exercise their powers. Can you suppose they will ever cordially raise the great oak, when they must sit as shrubs under its shade?

Carried against the motion, 10 noes, and Delaware divided.

On motion of Mr. Patterson, the consideration of the 2d resolve was taken up, which is as follows: *Resolved, therefore, that the rights of suffrage in the national legislature ought to be apportioned to the quotas of contribution, or to the number of inhabitants, as the one or other rule may seem best in different cases.*

Judge Brearly. — The present question is an important one. On the principle that each state in the union was sovereign, congress, in the articles of confederation, determined that each state in the public councils had *one* vote. If the states still remain sovereign, the form of the present resolve is founded on principles of injustice. He then stated the comparative weight of each state — the number of votes 90. Georgia would be 1, Virginia 16, and so of the rest. This vote must defeat itself, or end in despotism. If we must have a national government, what is the remedy? Lay the map of the confederation on the table, and extinguish the present boundary lines of the respective state jurisdictions, and make a new division so that each state is equal — then a government on the present system will be just.

Mr. Patterson opposed the resolve. Let us consider with what powers are we sent here? (moved to have the credentials of Massachusetts read, which was done.) By this and the other credentials we see, that the basis of our present authority is founded on a revision of the articles of the present confederation, and to alter or amend them in such parts where they may appear defective. Can we on this ground form a national government? I fancy not. — Our commissions give a complexion to the business; and can we suppose that when we exceed the bounds of our duty, the people will approve our proceedings?

We are met here as the deputies of 13 independent, sovereign states, for federal purposes. Can we consolidate their sovereignty and form one nation, and annihilate the sovereignties of our states who have sent us here for other purposes?

What, pray, is intended by a proportional representation? Is property to be considered as part of it? Is a man, for example, possessing a property of £4000 to have 40 votes to one possessing only £100? This has been asserted on a former occasion. If state distinctions are still to be held up, shall I submit the welfare of the state of New-Jersey, with 5 votes in the national council, opposed to Virginia who has 16 votes? Suppose, as it was in agitation before the war, that America had been represented in the British parliament, and had sent 200 members; what would this number avail against 600? We would have been as much enslaved in that case as when unrepresented; and what is worse, without the prospect of redress. But it is said that this national government is to act on individuals and not on states; and cannot a federal government be so framed as to operate in the same way? It surely may. I therefore declare, that I will never consent to the present system, and I shall make all the interest against it in the state which I represent that I can. Myself or my state will never submit to tyranny or despotism.[9]

Upon the whole, every sovereign state according to a confederation must have an equal vote, or there is an end to liberty. As long therefore as state distinctions are held up, this rule must invariably apply; and if a consolidated national government must take place, then state distinctions must cease, or the states must be equalized.

Mr. Wilson was in favor of the resolve. He observed that a majority, nay even a minority, of the states have a right to confederate with each other, and the rest may do as they please. He considered numbers as the best criterion to determine representation. Every citizen of one state possesses the same rights with the citizen of another. Let us see how this rule will apply to the present question. Pennsylvania, from its numbers, has a right to 12 votes, when on the same principle New-Jersey is entitled to 5 votes. Shall New-Jersey have the same right or influence in the councils of the nation with Pennsylvania? I say no. It is unjust — I never will confederate on this plan. The gentleman from New-Jersey is candid in declaring his opinion — I commend him for it — I am equally so. I say again I never will confederate on his principles. If no state will part with any of its sovereignty, it is in vain to talk of a national government. The state who has five times the number of inhabitants ought, nay must have the same proportion of weight in the representation. If there was a probability of equalizing the states, he would be for it. But we have no such power. If however, we depart from the principle of representation in proportion to numbers, we will lose the object of our meeting.

The question postponed for farther consideration.

Adjourned to to-morrow morning.

---

[9] According to Madison and King this is the end of Paterson's speech. The paragraph following probably represents Yates's own ideas.

KING

9 June

Brearly. opposes the equality of Representation, alledges that although it is numerically equal, yet in its operation it will be unequal — illustrates by saying there will be two divisions in the States thus represented, the one made up of Mass. Penn. & Virgin. the other including the Ten other states — when Georga. sends one member, Virginia will send sixteen — These 16 members are united, the members of three or four small States although equal in number are not capable of combination, the influence of the 16 members of Virginia will be different, for these Reasons, from those from three or four small States — I agree that the Rule of confedn. is unequal — I shall be willing to take the map of the U S. and divide it into 13 equal parts — this being done there may fairly be an equality in the representation of the States —

Patterson. Our powers do not extend to the abolition of the State Governments, and the Erection of a national Govt. — They only authorise amendments in the present System, and have for yr. Basis the present Confederation which establishes the principle that each State has an equal vote in Congress — agrees wth. Brearly for an equal Division of the Territory of the US, and then the equality of Territory will be the parent or origin of an equality of Representation — But perhaps the inequality of the present system is not so obvious — the States are equals and they vote equal, in every state the individual Citizens have equal votes although their property is unequal — a man of 4000£ has one vote, and the man of 100£ has one vote, yet one has forty times as much property as the other — why shd. not this be the case in the several States —

Mr. Galloway who was early in Cong. proposed that america shd. be represented in the Brith. parl. perhaps they wd. have sent 200 members, and G. Britain 500 members; but it was clearly seen that this project wd. not secure the american Liberties — neither wd. the smaller States be secured in their Liberties — the project of an equality in Representation will never succeed — Admit that a majority of the States in Convention shd. agree in the Measure — they cannot give the assent of the other States — I never will agree to this project here, and I will use my influence agt. it in N Jersey — New Jersey never will agree to the Scheme —

Wilson — the Doctrine of Representation is this — first the representative ought to speak the Language of his Constituents, and secondly that his language or vote shd. have the same influence as though the Constituents gave it — apply this principle and it concludes in favor of an equality of Representation & agt. the present System — [10]

P A T E R S O N [11]

[A] [12]

1. The Plan.

2. The words national and federal.

3. Collection of Sentiment — Object, to take under Consideration the State of the American Union —

Consider the Nature and Construction of this Assembly. Formed under the act of Congress passed in Conformity with one of the Articles of the Confedn.

See the Comn. from Massts. [13]

Assumption of Power [13a] — The Comn. measures our Power — to revise the Confedn. to report to Congress and the several Legs. — must not go beyond our Powers —

Self-constituted and self-ordained Body.

The Coms. give the political Complexion of the several

---

[10] [Endorsed:] 9 June | Question | Representation according to census — *Debate* | Brearly and Patterson no | Wilson aye

[11] Reprinted from *American Historical Review* (IX, 320–324, 330).

[12] The notes numbered A–E probably represent Paterson's careful preparation for his speech of this date: A is a long and elaborate draft; B is the same in shorter form, but with some additional notes; C includes some notes for reference; D seems to consist of catch-words; and E is an elaboration of one or two points. These drafts contain notes of previous debates, but apparently only in so far as Paterson wished to use them for this speech. F seems to represent notes on the debate of this day, taken in a similar way for future use.

[13] See C below.

[13a] In MS. these first words were in the margin.

States — not ripe — we must follow the People; the People will not follow us — The Plan must be accommodated to the public Mind — consult the Genius, the Temper, the Habits, the Prejudices of the People.

A little practicable Virtue to be preferred to Theory.

Not to sport Opinions of my own — not to say wt. is the best Govt. or what ought to be done — but what can be done — wt. can we do consistently with our Powers; wt. can we do that will meet with the Approbation of the People — their Will must guide —

Insurrections — So there are in every Govt. — even in England — it may shew, that our particular Systems are wrong — that our Instns. are too pure — not sufficiently removed from a State of Nature to answer the Purposes of a State of Society — it will not militate agt. the democratick Principle when properly regulated and modified —

The democratick Spirit beats high —

Not half wrong enough to have a good Govt. —

2. The Plan proposed — The 1st. Propn. withdrawn [14] — it was incompatible with the 2d. The Principles were gradually unfolded —

Wt. Qy. of Land [14a] — The 1 Propn. accords with the Spirit of the Constn.

Each State is sovereign, free, and independt. etc. Sovereignty includes Equality —

If then the States in Union are as States still to continue in Union, they must be considered as Equals —

13 sovereign and independent States can never constitute one Nation, and at the same Time be States — they may by Treaty make one confederated Body —

Mr. Randolph — We ought to be one Nation — etc. The States as States must be cut up, and destroyed — This is the way to form us into a Nation — It has Equality — it will not break in upon the Rights of any Citizen — it will destroy State Politicks and Attachmts. Will it be acceded to, etc.

---

[14] Refers to action of May 30.
[14a] In MS. these first words were in the margin.

G. Morris — Every Citizen should enjoy a rateable Proportion of Sovereignty —

Fœtus of a Monarch —[15] An infant Hercules in his Cradle —[15a] The Mind of Man is fond of Power —

Enlarge his prospects, you increase his Desires — Proportion of Votes — State-Politicks, State-Attachments, State-Influence, State-Passions — Districts —

Great Britain and America — Suppose Representn. from the latter before the Revolutn. according to the Quantum of Property or Number of Souls — Wt. the Consequence —

3 Article —[16] Com. Defence, Security of Liberty, mutual and general Welfare.

A national Govt. to operate individually upon the People in the first Instance, and not upon the States — and therefore a Representation from the People at large and not from the States —

Will the Operation of the natl. Govt. depend upon the Mode of Representn. — No — it depends upon the Quantum of Power lodged in the leg. ex. and judy. Departments — it will operate individually in the one Case as well as in the other —

Why not operate upon the States — if they are coerced, they will in Turn coerce each individual —

Let the People elect the State-Legr. — The State-Legr. elect the federal Legr. — assign to the State Legr. its Duty — the same to the federal — they will be Checks upon each other, and the best Checks that can be formed — Cong. the Sun of out political System —[17]

Why a Representation from the People at large — to equalize Representn. Majr. Butler[18] — Representn. — Property — People —

Mr. Wilson — Majority of the States sufficient. This in Opposition to Mr. King —[19]

---

[15] Randolph's expression, see June 1 and June 2.
[15a] In MS. these first words were in the margin.
[16] Refers to Article III of Articles of Confederation.
[17] Dickinson's metaphor, see June 7.
[18] Butler, see June 6.   [19] Debate of June 5.

2 Views.   1. Under the Confedn. — 13th. Article — Rhode-Island.   2. As forming an original Combinn. or Confederacy — can bind the contracting Parties only —

The large States can agree upon a Reform only upon the Principle of an equal Representn.

11 Propn.[20]

If the lesser States form a Junction of Govt. and Territory, the Gy.[21] ceases to operate as to them — This will prevent a Consolidn. of Govt. and Territory —

The people will likewise prevent any new State from being taken from the old — Vermont — Kentucky — several in Embryo — Republicks — Monarchies — large Frontiers.

[B]

1. The Confederation — its leading Principle. unanimously assented to —

2. The Nature and Construction of this Assembly. Formed under the Confedn. Resn. of Congress — The Comn. measures our Power — it gives the political Complexion of each State — to revise the Confedn.

Must not go beyond our Powers — People not ripe —

A little practicable Virtue to be preferred to Theory.

What expected — Regulation of Commerce, Colln. of the Revenue, Negative, etc   this will draw after it such a Weight of Influence and Power as will answer the Purpose — they will call forth the dormant Powers —

3. The Plan proposed.   The 1 Propn. withdrawn — it was incompatible with the 2d.   Much Dispute about Distn. between federal and National Governments.   The Principle was gradually unfolded —

Wt Qy. of Land, etc they approach each other, etc. [21a] — The 1 Prop. accords with the Spirit of the Confedn.

Each State is sovereign, free, and independent etc.   The Idea of a Supreme, and the Maxim Imperium in Imperio —

---

[20] Refers to the 11th of the Randolph Resolutions or Virginia Plan.
[21] Guaranty.
[21a] In MS. these first words were in the margin.

If then the States in Union are as States still to continue in Union, they must be considered as Equals, etc.

13 sovereign and independant states can never constitute one Nation; they may by Treaty make one confederated Body —

Mr. Randolph — we ought to be one Nation — 2 Article — 5th. Article —[22]

G. Morris — Every Individual should enjoy a rateable Proportion of Sovereignty —

Districts —

3 Article — Common Defence, Security of Liberty, mutual and general Welfare — Proportion of Votes.

11 Propn.

If the lesser States form a Junction of Govt. and Territory, the Gy. ceases to operate as to them — This will prevent a Consoln. of Govt. and Territory —

The Propn. will likewise prevent any new States from being taken from the old — Vermont, Kentucky — Several in embryo — Republics — Monarchies — large Frontiers —

The large States can agree to a Reform only upon the Principle of an Equality of Representn.

In what we are all agreed —

[C]

Massts.

"for the sole and express Purpose of revising the Articles of Confdn. and reporting to Congress and the several Legs. such Alterations and Provisions therein as shall when agreed to in Congress and confirmed by the States render the federal Constn. adequate to the Exigencies of Government and the Preservn. of the Union." [23]

Connectt. as above —

Jersey, etc

Georgia,

---

[22] Refers to Articles of Condeferation.

[23] Quotation from Commission of Massachusetts delegates. Used by Paterson in his speech.

States.[24]	Quota of Tax.	Delegates.	
Virginia	512,974	16.	
Massachusetts	448,854	14.	
Pennsylvania	410,378	12.$\frac{3}{4}$.	42$\frac{3}{4}$
Maryland	283,034	8.$\frac{3}{4}$.	
Connecticut	264,182	8-	
New York	256,486	8-	
North Carolina	218,012	6$\frac{3}{4}$.	
South Carolina	192,366	6-	
New Jersey	166,716	5-	
New Hampshire	105,416	3$\frac{1}{4}$.	
Rhode Island	64,636	2-	
Delaware	44,886	1$\frac{1}{4}$.	
Georgia	32,060	1.	
		90-	

[D]

Ambition goads him on. The Impulse is progressive—
enlarge his Prospects, and you enlarge his Desires. As to
orders — as to Societies. Mithradates — Com. Defence —
Liberty.

Mr. Madison — Districts.

Mr. King.

Guarranty.

Nature of Govts.

So corrected and enlarged.

Regulation of Commerce,

the Collection of Revenue.

Negative in particular

Cases.

---

[24] Among the Wilson papers in the Library of the Historical Society of Pennsylvania, upon the first page of the copy of the resolutions used by the Committee of Detail, is a duplicate of this document except that: the names of states are abbreviated; New Jersey's quota is given as 166,316; and in the column of "Delegates", instead of a line after the number for Pennsylvania, lines are drawn after the numbers for New York and South Carolina and after the total of "90", "24" and "25$\frac{1}{4}$" have been crossed out, and then "12" written, showing that an estimate had been made of the total number of the delegates for the seven and five smaller states.

See a similar document from the Brearley Papers, below July 10.

To promote the general Welfare, to protect Liberty and Property.

Cr. Lands.

[E]

1 — Great Britain and America — Representn. from the latter before the Revolution according to the Number of Souls — Wt. the Consequence.

2. Representation from the People at large and not from the States —

3. National Governmt. to operate individually upon the People in the first Instance, and not upon the States — *Durability.*

[F]

Mr. Brearley.   unfair; because of the Combination of the Parts.

Districts —

Equalize the States —

Mr. Wilson — All Authority is derived from the People — the People entitled to exercise Authority in Person — Italy — Roman Citizens —

2 Things necessary — 1. That the Representatives express the Sentiments of the represented.   2. That the Sentiments thus expressed should have the same Operation as if expressed by the People themselves —

Numbers the best Estimate of Property.   One free Citizen ought to be of equal Importance with another.

One Mass — 13 — it will be given away $\frac{1}{3}$ of the Territory —

No Authority — it is besides impracticable.

He wishes the Distinction of States might be destroyed.

A Principle given up in the first Confedn.

Mr. Wm.son.   It does not appear to him, that the lesser States will be swallowed up.

A small County, and a large County; according to Numbers —

Mr. Maddison

MONDAY, JUNE 11, 1787.

JOURNAL

Monday June 11. 1787.

The Honorable Abraham Baldwin Esquire, one of the Deputies of the State of Georgia, attended and took his seat.

The Order of the day being read

The House resolved itself into a Committee of the whole House to consider of the State of the american union

Mr President left the chair

Mr Gorham took the Chair of the Committee

Mr President resumed the Chair

Mr Gorham reported from the Committee that the Committee had made a further progress in the matter to them referred: and had directed him to move that they may have leave to sit again.

Resolved that this House will to-morrow again resolve itself into a Committee of the whole House to consider of the State of the American union

And then the House adjourned till to-morrow at 11 o clock A. M

In a Committee of the whole House

Monday June 11. 1787.

Mr Gorham in the Chair.

It was moved by Mr King seconded by Mr Rutledge to agree to the following resolution namely

Resolved that the right of suffrage in the first branch of the national Legislature ought not to be according to the rule established in the articles of confederation; but according to some equitable ratio of representation

And on the question to agree to the same

it passed in the affirmative. [Ayes—7; noes—3; divided—1.][1]
It was then moved by Mr Rutledge seconded by Mr Butler to
add the following words to the last resolution

"namely, according to the quotas of contribution"
It was moved by Mr Wilson seconded by Mr C. Pinckney to
postpone the consideration of the last motion in order to
introduce the following words, after the words "equitable ratio
of representation" namely.

"in proportion to the whole number of white and other
"free Citizens and inhabitants of every age, sex and condi-
"tion, including those bound to servitude for a term of years,
"and three fifths of all other persons not comprehended in
"the foregoing description, except Indians, not paying taxes
"in each State"

On the question to postpone
      it passed in the affirmative. [Ayes — 10; noes — 1.]
On the question to agree to Mr Wilson's motion
      it passed in the affirmative [Ayes — 9; noes — 2.]
It was moved by Mr Sherman seconded by Mr Ellsworth

"That in the second branch of the National Legislature
each State have One vote"

On the question to agree to the same
      it passed in the negative. [Ayes — 5; noes — 6.]
It was then moved by Mr Wilson seconded by Mr Hamilton
to adopt the following resolution, namely,

"Resolved that the right of suffrage in the second branch
"of the national Legislature ought to be according to the rule
"established for the first"

On the question to agree to the same
      it passed in the affirmative [Ayes—6; noes 5.]

[To amend the 11th resolution submitted by Mr Randolph
by adding the words voluntary junction or partition. Ayes
— 7; noes — 4.

To amend the   resolution by adding the words "national
government" after the words   [Ayes — 7; noes —4.] [2]
It was moved and seconded to agree to the 11th resolution

---

[1] Vote 37, Detail of Ayes and Noes.
[2] Votes 42 and 43, Detail of Ayes and Noes.

submitted by Mr Randolph — and amended to read as follows —

"Resolved that a republican constitution, and it's existing "laws ought to be guaranteed to each State by the United "States."

And on the question to agree to the same
            it passed unanimously in the affirmative
It was then moved and seconded to agree to the following resolution

Resolved that provision ought to be made for the amendment of the articles of union whensoever it shall seem necessary.

On the question to agree to the same
            it passed in the affirmative
It was agreed to postpone the following clause in the 13th resolution submitted by Mr Randolph namely

"and that the assent of the national legislature ought not to be required thereto"
It was then moved and seconded to agree to the 14 resolution submitted by Mr Randolph namely

"Resolved that the legislative, executive, and judiciary "powers within the several States ought to be bound by oath "to support the articles of union"

It was then moved by Mr Martin seconded by   to strike out the words "within the several States"

and on the question to strike out.
            it passed in the negative   [Ayes — 4; noes — 7.]
It was then moved and seconded to agree to the 14th resolution as submitted by Mr. Randolph

And on the question to agree to the same.
            it passed in the affirmative   [Ayes — 6; noes — 5.]
It was then moved and seconded that the Committee do now rise, report a further progress, and request leave to sit again

The Committee then rose.

DETAIL OF AYES AND NOES

#	Questions	N.H.	Mass.	R.I.	Conn.	N.Y.	N.J.	Penn.	Del.	Md.	Va.	N.C.	S.C.	Geo.	Ayes	Noes	Divided
[37]	That the right of suffrage in the first branch of the N. L. ought not to be accordg to the rule established in the confedn but accordg to some equitable ratio of representation		aye		aye	no	no	aye	no	dd	aye	aye	aye	aye	7	3	1
[38]	To postpone Mr Rutledge's motion in order to take up Mr Wilson's, respecting the right of suffrage in the N. L.		aye		aye	aye	no	aye	aye	aye	aye	aye	aye	aye	10	1	
[39]	That the right of suffrage in the first branch be accordg to the whole number of white and three fifths of the other inhabitants		aye		aye	aye	no	aye	no	aye	aye	aye	aye	aye	9	2	
[40]	That in the second branch of the national Legislature each State have One vote		no		aye	aye	aye	no	aye	aye	no	no	no	no	5	6	
[41]	That the right of suffrage in the second branch ought to be accordg to the rule established for the first		aye		no	no	no	aye	no	no	aye	aye	aye	aye	6	5	
[42]	To amend the 11th resolution submitted by Mr Randolph by adding the words voluntary junction or partition		aye		no	no	no	aye	no	aye	aye	aye	aye	aye	7	4	
[43]	To amend the resolution by adding the words "national government" after the words		aye		aye	no	no	aye	no	no	aye	aye	aye	aye	7	4	
[44]	To strike these words out of the 14 resolution "within the sevl States"		no		aye	no	aye	no	aye	aye	no	no	no	no	4	7	
[45]	To agree to the 14 resolution as submitted by Mr Randolph		aye		no	no	no	aye	no	no	aye	aye	aye	aye	6	5	

MADISON

Monday, June 11th. ⟨Mr Abraham Baldwin from Georgia took His Seat.⟩[3] In Committee of the Whole.

The clause concerning the rule of suffrage in the natl. Legislature postponed ⟨on Saturday,⟩ was resumed.[4]

Mr. Sharman proposed that the proportion of suffrage in the 1st branch should be according to the respective numbers of free inhabitants; and that in the second branch or Senate, each State should have one vote and no more. He said as the States would remain possessed of certain individual rights, each State ought to be able to protect itself: otherwise a few large States will rule the rest. The House of Lords in England he observed had certain particular rights under the Constitution, and hence they have an equal vote with the House of Commons that they may be able to defend their rights.

Mr. Rutlidge proposed that the proportion of suffrage in the 1st branch should be according to the quotas of contribution. The justice of this rule he said could not be contested. Mr. Butler urged the same idea: ⟨adding that money was power; and that the States ought to have weight in the Govt. — in proportion to their wealth.⟩[5]

Mr. King & Mr. Wilson* ⟨in order to bring the question to a point ⟩[5] moved "that the right of suffrage in ⟨the first branch of ⟩[6] the national Legislature ought not to be according the rule established in the articles of Confederation, but according to some equitable ratio of representation". The clause so far as it related to suffrage in the first branch was postponed in order to consider this motion:

Mr. Dickenson contended for the *actual* contributions of the States as the rule of their representation & suffrage ⟨in the first branch⟩. By thus connecting the interest of the States with their duty, the latter would be sure to be performed.

* ⟨In the printed Journal Mr Rutlidge is named as the seconder of the motion.⟩

[3] Taken from *Journal.*
[4] See also Records of May 30, June 27–July 16, and references under June 27 note 2.   [5] Taken from Yates.   [6] Taken from *Journal.*

Mr. King remarked that it was uncertain what mode might be used in levying a national revenue; but that it was probable, imports would be one source of it. If the *actual* contributions were to be the rule the non-importing States, as Cont. & N. Jersey, wd. be in a bad situation indeed. It might so happen that they wd. have no representation. This situation of particular States had been always one powerful argument in favor of the 5 Per Ct. impost.

The question being abt. to be put Docr. Franklin sd. he had thrown his ideas of the matter on a paper wch. Mr. Wilson read to the Committee in the words following — [7]

Mr Chairman

It has given me a great pleasure to observe that till this point, the proportion of representation, came before us, our debates were carried on with great coolness & temper. If any thing of a contrary kind, has on this occasion appeared. I hope it will not be repeated; for we are sent here to *consult* not to *contend*, with each other; and declarations of a fixed opinion, and of determined resolution, never to change it, neither enlighten nor convince us. Positiveness and warmth on one side, naturally beget their like on the other; and tend to create and augment discord & division in a great concern, wherein harmony & Union are extremely necessary to give weight to our Councils, and render them effectual in promoting & securing the common good.

I must own that I was originally of opinion it would be better if every member of Congress, or our national Council, were to consider himself rather as a representative of the whole, than as an Agent for the interests of a particular State; in which case the proportion of members for each State would be of less consequence, & it would not be very material whether they voted by States or individually. But as I find this is not to be expected, I now think the number of Representatives should bear some proportion to the number of the Represented; and that the decisions shd. be by the majority of members,

---

[7] In the Franklin Papers in the Library of Congress is the first, or an earlier, draft of this speech which differs from Madison's copy only in the use of capitals (and in a few cases in spelling).

not by the majority of States. This is objected to from an apprehension that the greater States would then swallow up the smaller. I do not at present clearly see what advantage the greater States could propose to themselves by swallowing the smaller, and therefore do not apprehend they would attempt it. I recollect that in the beginning of this Century, when the Union was proposed of the two Kingdoms, England & Scotland, the Scotch Patriots were full of fears, that unless they had an equal number of Representatives in Parliament, they should be ruined by the superiority of the English. They finally agreed however that the different proportions of importance in the Union, of the two Nations should be attended to, whereby they were to have only forty members in the House of Commons, and only sixteen in the House of Lords; A very great inferiority of numbers! And yet to this day I do not recollect that any thing has been done in the Parliament of Great Britain to the prejudice of Scotland; and whoever looks over the lists of public officers, Civil & military of that nation will find I believe that the North Britons enjoy at least their full proportion of emolument.

But, Sir, in the present mode of voting by States, it is equally in the power of the lesser States to swallow up the greater; and this is mathematically demonstrable. Suppose for example, that 7 smaller States had each 3 members in the House, and the 6 larger to have one with another 6 members; and that upon a question, two members of each smaller State should be in affirmative and one in the Negative, they will make

Affirmatives .... 14.... Negatives   7
And that all the larger States should
      be unanimously
in   the   negative,   they   would
      make ....Negatives 36
                                    ____
                      In all ...   43

It is then apparent that the 14 carry the question against the 43. and the minority overpowers the majority, contrary to the common practice of Assemblies in all Countries and Ages.

The greater States Sir are naturally as unwilling to have their property left in the disposition of the smaller, as the smaller are to have theirs in the disposition of the greater. An honorable gentleman has, to avoid this difficulty, hinted a proposition of equalizing the States. It appears to me an equitable one, and I should, for my own part, not be against such a measure, if it might be found practicable. Formerly, indeed, when almost every province had a different Constitution, some with greater others with fewer privileges, it was of importance to the borderers when their boundaries were contested, whether by running the division lines, they were placed on one side or the other. At present when such differences are done away, it is less material. The Interest of a State is made up of the interests of its individual members. If they are not injured, the State is not injured. Small States are more easily well & happily governed than large ones. If therefore in such an equal division, it should be found necessary to diminish Pennsylvania, I should not be averse to the giving a part of it to N. Jersey, and another to Delaware. But as there would probably be considerable difficulties in adjusting such a division; and however equally made at first, it would be continually varying by the augumentation of inhabitants in some States, and their [more][8] fixed proportion in others; and thence frequent occasion for new divisions, I beg leave to propose for the consideration of the Committee another mode which appears to me to be as equitable, more easily carried into practice, and more permanent in its nature.

Let the weakest State say what proportion of money or force it is able and willing to furnish for the general purposes of the Union.

Let all the others oblige themselves to furnish each an equal proportion.

The whole of these joint supplies to be absolutely in the disposition of Congress.

The Congress in this case to be composed of an equal number of Delegates from each State:

---

[8] "more" in Franklin MS.

And their decisions to be by the majority of individual members voting.

If these joint and equal supplies should on particular occasions not be sufficient, Let Congress make requisitions on the richer and more powerful States for farther aids, to be voluntarily afforded, leaving to each State the right of considering the necessity and utility of the aid desired, and of giving more or less as it should be found proper.

This mode is not new, it was formerly practiced with success by the British Government with respect to Ireland and the Colonies. We sometimes gave even more than they expected, or thought just to accept; and in the last war carried on while we were united, they gave us back in five years a million Sterling. We should probably have continued such voluntary contributions, whenever the occasions appeared to require them for the common good of the Empire. It was not till they chose to force us, and to deprive us of the merit and pleasure of voluntary contributions that we refused & resisted. Those contributions however were to be disposed of at the pleasure of a Government in which we had no representative. I am therefore persuaded, that they will not be refused to one in which the Representation shall be equal

My learned colleague (Mr. Wilson) has already mentioned that the present method of voting by States, was submitted to originally by Congress, under a conviction of its impropriety, inequality, and injustice. This appears in the words of their Resolution. It is of Sep. 6. 1774. The words are

> "Resolved that in determining questions in this
> "Congs. each colony or province shall have one vote:
> "the Congs. not being possessed of or at present able
> "to procure materials for ascertaining the importance
> "of each Colony."

On the question for agreeing to Mr. Kings and Mr. Wilsons motion. ⟨it passed in the affirmative⟩ Massts. ay. Ct. ay. N. Y no. N. J. no. Pa. ay. Del. no. Md. divd. Va. ay. N. C. ay. S. C. ay. Geo. ay. [Ayes — 7; noes — 3; divided — 1.]

⟨It was then moved by Mr. Rutlidge 2ded. by Mr. Butler to add to the words "equitable ratio of representation" at the end of the motion just agreed to, the words "according to the quotas of Contribution.")[9] On motion of

Mr. Wilson seconded by Mr. C. *Pinckney*,[9] this was postponed; in order to add, after, after the words "equitable ratio of representation" the words following "in proportion to the whole number of white & other free Citizens & inhabitants of every age sex & condition including those bound to servitude for a term of years and three fifths of all other persons not comprehended in the foregoing description, except Indians not paying taxes, in each State."[10] this being the rule in the Act of Congress agreed to by eleven States, for apportioning quotas of revenue on the States.   and requiring a census only every 5 — 7, or 10 years.

Mr. Gerry thought property not the rule of representation. Why then shd. the blacks, who were property in the South, be in the rule of representation more than the cattle & horses of the North.[11]

On the question.

Mass: Con: N. Y. Pen: Maryd. Virga. N. C. S. C. and Geo: were in the affirmative: N. J. &. Del: in the negative. [Ayes — 9; noes — 2.])[12]

Mr. Sharman moved that a question be taken whether each State shall have ⟨one⟩ vote[13] in the 2d. branch.   Every thing he said depended on this.   The smaller States would never agree to the plan on any other principle ⟨than an equality of suffrage in this branch.   Mr. Elsworth[14] seconded the motion.⟩ On the question for allowing each State ⟨one⟩ vote in the 2d. branch.

Massts. no. Cont. ay. N. Y. ay. N. J. ay. Pa. no. Del. ay

---

[9] Taken from *Journal.*

[10] Madison originally had recorded the substance of this motion, but later revised it as given from *Journal.*

[11] Taken from Yates.   For further discussion of the "three fifths rule" see July 11, note 5.

[12] Madison originally had recorded this vote in his usual form, and confusing two votes in *Journal* had made a note that New Jersey was there recorded as voting "ay." Then, apparently seeing his mistake, this was all struck out and the vote rewritten. All of this portion of the records was twice revised by Madison.

[13] Madison originally had "an equal vote ".   Revised from *Journal.*

[14] Taken from *Journal.*

Md. ay. Va. no. N. C. no. S. C. no. Geo. no. [Ayes — 5; noes — 6.]

⟨Mr. Wilson & Mr. Hamilton moved that the right of suffrage in the 2d. branch ought to be according to the same rule as in the 1st. branch.⟩[14a]

On this question for making the ratio of representation the same in the 2d. as in the 1st. branch ⟨it passed in the affirmative:⟩ Massts. ay. Cont. no. N. Y. no. N. J. no. Pa. ay. Del. no. Md. no. Va. ay. N. C. ay. S. C. ay. Geo. ay. [Ayes — 6; noes — 5.][15]

⟨Resol: 11.⟩ for guarantying Republican Govt. & territory to each State ⟨being⟩ considered: ⟨the words "or partition" were, on motion of Mr. Madison added, after the words "voluntary junction": Mas. N. Y. P. Va. N. C. S. C. G. ay.

Con: N. J. Del. Md. - - - no.⟩[16]

Mr. Read disliked the idea of guarantying territory. It abetted the idea of distinct States wch. would be a perpetual source of discord. There can be ⟨no⟩ cure for this evil but in doing away States altogether and uniting them all into ⟨one⟩ great Society.

Alterations ⟨having been made in the Resolution, making it read "that a republican Constition & its existing laws ought to be guaranteed to each State by the U. States"⟩[17] the whole was agreed to nem. con.

⟨Resolution 13.⟩ for amending the national Constitution hereafter without consent of Natl. Legislature ⟨being⟩ considered, several members did not see the necessity of the ⟨Resolution⟩ at all, nor the propriety of making the consent of the Natl. Legisl. unnecessary.

Col. Mason urged the necessity of such a provision. The plan now to be formed will certainly be defective, as the Confederation has been found on trial to be. Amendments there-

---

[14a] Taken from *Journal*.

[15] Gerry voted in the affirmative, see Appendix A, CLXXXI.

[16] Taken from *Journal* and Yates.

[17] Madison originally wrote: "The Alterations made in clause (compare its original state with the Report of Comte. of Whole, June 14)" but struck this out and substituted from *Journal* the wording given.

fore will be necessary, and it will be better to provide for them, in an easy, regular and Constitutional way than to trust to chance and violence.   It would be improper to require the consent of the Natl. Legislature, because they may abuse their power, and refuse their consent on that very account. The opportunity for such an abuse, may be the fault of the Constitution calling for amendmt.

Mr. Randolph ⟨enforced⟩ these arguments.

The words, "without requiring the consent of the Natl. Legislature" were postponed.   The other provision in the clause passed nem. con.

⟨Resolution 14.⟩ requiring oaths from the ⟨members of the State Govts.⟩ to observe the Natl. Constitution ⟨& laws, being⟩ considered.

Mr. Sharman opposed it as unnecessarily intruding into the State jurisdictions.

Mr. Randolph considered ⟨it⟩ as necessary to prevent that competition between the National Constitution & laws & those of the particular States, which had already been felt. The officers of the States are already under oath to the States. To preserve a due impartiality they ought to be equally bound to the Natl. Govt.   The Natl. authority needs every support we can give it.   The Executive & Judiciary of the States, notwithstanding their nominal independence on the State Legislatures are in fact, so dependent on them, that unless they be brought under some tie ⟨to⟩ the Natl. system, they will always lean too much to the State systems, whenever a contest arises between the two.

Mr. Gerry did not like the clause.   He thought there was as much reason for requiring an oath of fidelity to the States, from Natl. officers, as vice. versa.

Mr. Luther Martin moved to strike out the ⟨words⟩ requiring such an oath from the State Officers ⟨viz "within the several States."⟩ observing that if the new oath should be contrary to that already taken ⟨by them⟩ it wou d be improper; if coincident the oaths already taken will be sufficient.[18]

---

[18] Revised from *Journal.*

On the question for striking out as proposed by Mr. L. Martin

Massts. no. Cont. ay. N. Y. no. N. J. ay. Pa. no. Del. ay. Md. ay. Va. no. N. C. no. S. C. no. Geo. no. [Ayes — 4; noes — 7.]

Question on whole ⟨Resolution as proposed by Mr. Randolph;⟩

Massts. ay. Cont. no. N. Y. no. N. J. no. Pa. ay. Del. no. Md. no. Va. ay. N. C. ay. S. C. ay. Geo. ay. [Ayes — 6; noes — 5.]

⟨Come. rose & House⟩ adjd.[19]

YATES

Monday, June 11th, 1787.

Met pursuant to adjournment. Present 11 states.

Mr. Sherman moved *that the first branch of the national legislature be chosen in proportion to the number of the whole inhabitants in each state.* He observed that as the people ought to have the election of one of the branches of the legislature, the legislature of each state ought to have the election of the second branch, in order to preserve the state sovereignty; and that each state ought in this branch to have one vote.

Gov. Rutledge moved as an amendment of the first proposition, *that the proportion of representation ought to be according to and in proportion to the contribution of each state.*

Mr. Butler supported the motion, by observing that money is strength; and every state ought to have its weight in the national council in proportion to the quantity it possesses. He further observed, that when a boy he read this as one of the remarks of Julius Cæsar, who declared if he had but money he would find soldiers, and every thing necessary to carry on a war.

Mr. King observed, that it would be better first to establish a principle (that is to say) whether we will depart from federal grounds in forming a national government; and there-

---

[19] See further Appendix A, XLII.

fore, to bring this point to view, he moved as a previous question, that the sense of the committee be taken on the following question:

That the right of suffrage in the first branch of the national legislature, ought not to be according to the rule in the articles of confederation, but according to some equitable ratio of representation.

Gov. Franklin's written remarks on this point were read by Mr. Wilson. In these Gov. Franklin observes, that representation ought to be in proportion to the importance of numbers or wealth in each state — that there can be no danger of undue influence of the the greater against the lesser states. This was the apprehension of Scotland when the union with England was proposed, when in parliament they were allowed only 16 peers and 45 commons; yet experience has proved that their liberties and influence were in no danger.

The question on Mr. King's motion was carried in the affirmative — 7 ayes — 3 noes, and Maryland divided. New-York, New-Jersey and Delaware in the negative.

Mr. Dickinson moved as an amendment, to add the words, *according to the taxes and contributions of each state actually collected and paid into the national treasury.*

Mr. Butler was of opinion that the national government will only have the right of making and collecting the taxes, but that the states individually must lay their own taxes.

Mr. Wilson was of opinion, and therefore moved, *that the mode of representation of each of the states ought to be from the number if its free inhabitants, and of every other description three fifths to one free inhabitant.* He supposed that the impost will not be the only revenue — the post office he supposes would be another substantial source of revenue. He observed further, that this mode had already received the approbation of eleven states in their acquiescence to the quota made by congress. He admitted that this resolve would require further restrictions, for where numbers determined the representation a census at different periods of 5, 7 or 10 years, ought to be taken.

Mr. Gerry. The idea of property ought not to be the

rule of representation. Blacks are property, and are used to the southward as horses and cattle to the northward; and why should their representation be increased to the southward on account of the number of slaves, than horses or oxen to the north? [20]

Mr. Madison was of opinion at present, to fix the standard of representation, and let the detail be the business of a sub-committee.

Mr. Rutledge's motion was postponed.

Mr. Wilson's motion was then put, and carried by 9 states against 2. New York in the majority.

Mr. Wilson then moved, as an amendment to Mr. Sherman's motion, *That the same proportion be observed in the election of the second branch as the first.*

The question however was first put on Mr. Sherman's motion, and lost — 6 states against, and 5 for it.

Then Mr. Wilson's motion was put and carried — 6 ayes, 5 noes.

The eleventh resolve was then taken into consideration. Mr. Madison moved to add after the word *junctions*, the words, *or separation.*

Mr. Read against the resolve *in toto.* We must put away state governments, and we will then remove all cause of jealousy. The guarantee will confirm the assumed rights of several states to lands which do belong to the confederation.

Mr. Madison moved an amendment, to add to or alter the resolution as follows: *The republican constitutions and the existing laws of each state, to be guaranteed by the United States.*

Mr. Randolph was for the present amendment, because a republican government must be the basis of our national union; and no state in it ought to have it in their power to change its government into a monarchy. — Agreed to

13th Resolve — the first part agreed to.

14th Resolve — taken into consideration.

---

[20] Luther Martin cites this comparison in his *Genuine Information.* See Appendix A, CLVIII (38).

Mr. Williamson.   This resolve will be unnecessary, as the union will become the law of the land.

Governor Randolph.   He supposes it to be absolutely necessary.   Not a state government, but its officers will infringe on the rights of the national government.   If the state judges are not sworn to the observance of the new government, will they not judicially determine in favor of their state laws?   We are erecting a supreme national government; ought it not to be supported, and can we give it too many sinews?

Mr. Gerry rather supposes that the national legislators ought to be sworn to preserve the state constitutions, as they will run the greatest risk to be annihilated — and therefore moved it.

For Mr. Gerry's amendment, 7 ayes, 4 noes.

Main question then put on the clause or resolve — 6 ayes, 5 noes.   New-York in the negative.

Adjourned to to-morrow morning.

PATERSON

Resolved, That the Rights of Suffrage in the first Branch of the national Legr. ought not to be according to the Article of Confedn., but according to some equitable Ratio of Representation —

Rutledge.   Not by the Number of free Inhabitants, but according to the Quotas of Contribution —

Dickinson — The Terms, "Quotas of Contribution," very indefinite—it ought to be according to the *actual Contribution* —

Wm.son.   Supposes, that there will not be any Assignment or Quotas to States; the Governmt. to operate individually, and not on States —

Dickinson   The Power to be in Proportion to actual Contribution —

King — Suppose an Impost — Connecticut and Jersey do not import — they will have no Representatives —

Butler.   This to be left to the State Legrs. — Sum to be proportioned —

Wilson.   Either Rule good — by Numbers best to ascertain the Right of Representn. this agreeably to the Sentiments of 11 States — Impost alone will not be sufficient to answer the national Exigencies — Revenues arising from Postage — The present Quota not a lasting Rule — People to be numbered at fixed Periods — A Rule arising from Property and Numbers —

Gerry.   Rule of Taxation not the Rule of Representation — 4 might then have more Voices than ten — Slaves not to be put upon the Footing of freemen — Freemen of Massts. not to be put upon a Footing with the Slaves of other States — Horses and Cattle ought to have the Right of Representn. Negroes — Mules —

The Taxes must be drawn by the natl. Governmt. immediately from the People; otherwise will never be collected —

Madison.   Leave the particular Rule for the present. A common Standard ought to be provided —

TUESDAY, JUNE 12, 1787.

JOURNAL

Tuesday June 12. 1787.

The Order of the day being read

The House resolved into a Committee of the whole House to consider of the state of the american union

Mr President left the Chair

Mr Gorham took the chair of the Committee

Mr President resumed the Chair

Mr Gorham reported from the Committee that the Committee had made a further progress in the matter to them referred; and had directed him to move that they may have leave to sit again

Resolved that this House will tomorrow again resolve itself into a Committee of the whole House to consider of the State of the american union

And then the House adjourned till to-morrow at 11 o'Clock A. M.

In a Committee of the whole House

Tuesday June 12. 1787

Mr Gorham in the Chair

[To agree to the 15 resolution submitted by Mr. Randolph
Ayes — 5; noes — 3; divided — 2.] [1]

It was moved and seconded to fill up the blank in the resolution respecting the term for which the members of the first branch of the national Legislature should be chosen with the words "three years"

On the question to fill up with three years
it passed in the affirmative. [Ayes — 7; noes — 4.]

---

[1] Vote 46, Detail of Ayes and Noes. The resolutions adopted by the Convention up to this point will be found below *Records*, June 13, Journal (document A).

It was moved and seconded to strike out the following words
in the   resolution namely
    to be of   years at least.
    And on the question to strike out
        it passed in the affirmative   [Ayes — 10; noes — 1.]
It was moved and seconded to add the words
    "and fixed" after the word "liberal" in that clause of
the   resolution which respects the stipend of the first
branch
                    passed in the affirmative   [Ayes — 8; noes — 3.]
It was then moved and seconded to add the words
    "to be paid out of the public Treasury"
                        agreed to   [Ayes — 8; noes — 3.]
    [To agree to the clause respectg the salary of the first
branch   Ayes — 8; noes — 3.] [2]
It was moved and seconded to strike out the words
    "by a particular State"
passed in the negative [Ayes — 4; noes — 5; divided — 2.]
    a question being taken on the clause which respects the
ineligibility of the members of the first branch
        it passed in the affirmative   [Ayes — 10; noes — 1.]
It was moved and seconded to amend the   resolution by
inserting the words
    "and under the national government for the space of three
years after it's expiration."
                    passed in the negative   [Ayes — 1; noes — 10.]
Moved and seconded to fill up the blank with
    "One year".
        passed in the affirmative [Ayes—8; noes—2; divided—1.]
it was moved and seconded to strike out the following words
namely
    "to be incapable of re-election for the space of   after
the expiration of their term of service and to be subject to
re-call.
    On the question to strike out
            passed in the affirmative

---

[2] Vote 51, Detail of Ayes and Noes.

It was moved and seconded to strike out the words to be of   years at least
  passed in the negative [Ayes—3; noes—6; divided—2.]
Moved to fill up the blank with
 "Thirty"
    passed in the affirmative   [Ayes — 7; noes — 4.]
Moved and seconded to fill up the blank after the words "sufficient to ensure their independency" with
 "seven years"
passed in the affirmative. [Ayes—8; noes—1; divided—2.]
It was moved by Mr Rutledge seconded by Mr Butler to strike out the clause which respects stipends to be allowed to the second branch
 On the question to strike out
  passed in the negative [Ayes—3; noes—7; divided—1.]
It was then moved and seconded that the clause which respects the stipends to be given to the second branch be the same as that of the first
  passed in the affirmative
It was moved and seconded that the ineligibility of the second branch to office be the same as the first.
   passed in the affirmative   [Ayes — 10; noes — 1.]
It was moved and seconded to alter the resolution submitted by Mr Randolph, so as to read as follows namely.
 "That the jurisdiction of the supreme Tribunal shall be "to hear and determine in the dernier resort all piracies, "felonies &ca"
 It was moved and seconded to postpone the whole of the last clause generally.
 It was then moved and seconded to strike out the words "all piracies and felonies on the high seas"
  passed in the affirmative
It was moved and seconded to strike out the words
 "all captures from an enemy"
  passed in the affirmative
It was moved and seconded to strike out the words "other States" and to insert the words "two distinct States in the union"
  passed in the affirmative

It was moved and seconded to postpone the consideration of the resolution which respects the Judiciary.

> passed in the affirmative

It was then moved and seconded that the Committee do now rise, report a further progress, and request leave to sit again

The Committee then rose

DETAIL OF AYES AND NOES

#	Questions	New Hampshire	Massachusetts	Rhode Island	Connecticut	New York	New Jersey	Pennsylvania	Delaware	Maryland	Virginia	North Carolina	South Carolina	Georgia	Ayes	Noes	Divided
[60]	To agree to the 15 resolution submitted by Mr Randolph		aye		no	aye	aye	aye	aye	aye	aye	aye	aye	aye	10	1	
[59]	To fill up the term of election for the first branch with three year		dd		no	no	dd	aye	no	aye	no	no	no	no	3	7	1
[58]	For striking out the words "to be of age at least.		dd		no	dd	no	aye	aye	aye	aye	aye	aye	dd	8	1	2
[57]	For adding the words "& fixed" after the words liberal stipend		aye		aye	no	aye	aye	aye	no	aye	aye	no	aye	7	4	
[56]	To add the words "to be paid out of the national Treasury"		no		aye	aye	aye	aye	aye	aye	aye	no	no	no	3	6	2
[55]	To agree to the clause respectg the salary of the first branch		aye		aye	aye	aye	aye	no	no	no	aye	aye	aye	8	2	1
[54]	To strike out the words "by a particular State or" in the clause		no		no	no	no	no	aye	no	no	no	no	no	1	10	
[53]	To agree to the clause respecting the ineligibility of the first branch of the resolution		aye		no	aye	no	aye	no	no	aye	aye	aye	aye	10	1	
[52]	To fill the blank of ineligibility to office after the term with three years to offices		dd		aye	no	aye	aye	no	no	no	no	dd	aye	4	5	2
[51]	To fill up the blank with One year		aye		no	aye	no	aye	aye	aye	aye	dd	aye	aye	8	3	
[50]	To strike out the words ", to be of years at least" in the resolution		aye		no	aye	aye	aye	aye	aye	aye	aye	aye	no	8	3	
[49]	To fill up the blank with "Thirty"		no		no	aye	aye	aye	aye	aye	aye	aye	aye	dd	8	3	
[48]	To fill up the blank in the election of the 2 branch with Seven years: respectg the second bran.		aye		aye	aye	no	aye	aye	aye	aye	aye	aye	aye	10	1	
[47]	To strike out the clause which respects stipends to be allowed to the second branch		no		no	no	aye	aye	no	dd	no	aye	aye	aye	5	4	2
[46]	That the ineligibility of the 2 branch to office be the same as the first		aye		no	no	aye	aye	dd	no	no	aye	aye	aye	2	7	2

MADISON

Teusday June 12th. in Committee of whole.

⟨The⟩ Question taken on ⟨Resolution 15⟩, to wit, referring the new system to the people of the States for ratification ⟨it passed in the affirmative⟩: Massts. ay. Cont. no. N. Y. no. N. J. no. Pa. ay * Del. divd. Md. divd. Va. ay. N. C. ay. S. C. ay. Geo. ay. [Ayes—6, noes—3; divided — 2.][3]

Mr. Sharman & Mr. Elseworth moved to fill the blank ⟨left in the 4th Resolution⟩[4] for the periods of electing the members of the first branch with the words "every year." Mr. Sharman observing that he did it in order to bring on some question.

Mr. Rutlidge proposed "every two years."

Mr. Jennifer propd. "every three years." observing that the too great frequency of elections rendered the people indifferent to them, and made the best men unwilling to engage in so precarious a service.

Mr. M⟨adison⟩ seconded the motion for three years. Instability is ⟨one of⟩ the great vices of our republics, to be remedied. Three years will be necessary, in a Government so extensive, for members to form any knowledge of the various interests of the States to which they do not belong, and of which they can know but little from the situation and affairs of their own. One year will be almost consumed in preparing for and traveling to & from the seat of national business.

Mr. Gerry. The people of New England will never give up the point of annual elections. they know of the transition made in England from triennial to Septennial elections, and will consider such an innovation here as the prelude to a like usurpation. He considered annual Elections as the only

* ⟨Pennsylvania omitted in the printed Journal. The vote is there entered as of June 11th.⟩ [5]

---

[3] The resolutions adopted by the Convention up to this point will be found below *Records*, June 13, Journal, (document A).

[4] Taken from *Journal*.

[5] Yates confirms Madison that this vote was taken on the 12th, but agrees with Journal that only ten votes were cast.

defence of the people agst. tyranny.   He was as much agst. a triennial House as agst. a hereditary Executive.

Mr. M⟨adison.⟩ observed that if the opinions of the people were to be our guide, it wd. be difficult to say what course we ought to take.   No member of the Convention could say what the opinions of his Constituents were at this time; much less could he say what they would think if possessed of the information & lights possessed by the members here; & still less what would be their way of thinking 6 or 12 months hence.   We ought to consider what was right & necessary in itself for the attainment of a proper Governmt.   A plan adjusted to this idea will recommend itself — The respectability of this convention will give weight to their recommendation of it.   Experience will be constantly urging the adoption of it. and all the most enlightened & respectable citizens will be its advocates.   Should we fall short of the necessary & proper point, this influential class of citizens will be turned against the plan, and little support in opposition to them can be gained to it from the unreflecting multitude.

Mr. Gerry repeated his opinion that it was necessary to consider what the people would approve.   This had been the policy of all Legislators.   If the reasoning of Mr. M⟨adison⟩ were just, and we supposed a limited Monarchy the best form in itself, we ought to recommend it, tho' the genius of the people was decidedly adverse to it, and having no hereditary distinctions among us, we were destitute of the essential materials for such an innovation.

On the question for triennial election of the 1st branch

Mass. no. (Mr King ay.) Mr. Ghorum wavering. Cont. no. N. Y. ay. N. J. .ay. Pa. ay. Del. ay. Md. ay. Va. ay. N. C. no. S. C. no. Geo. ay.   [Ayes — 7; noes — 4.]

The ⟨words⟩[6] requiring members of ye. 1st. branch to be of the age of   years were struck out ⟨Maryland alone, no⟩[7] ⟨The words⟩ "*liberal compensation for members*" ⟨being⟩ considd. Mr. M⟨adison⟩ moves to inset the words "*& fixt.*" He observed that it would be improper to leave the members

---

[6] Crossed out "section".   [7] Crossed out "10 ays, 1 no."

of the Natl. legislature to be provided for by the State Legisls: because it would create an improper dependence; and to leave them to regulate their own wages, was an indecent thing, and might in time prove a dangerous one. He thought wheat or some other article ⟨of which⟩ the average price throughout a reasonable period precedn'g might be settled in some convenient mode, would form a proper standard.

Col. Mason seconded the motion; adding that it would be improper for other reasons to leave the wages to be regulated by the States. 1. the different States would make different provision for their representatives, and an inequality would be felt among them, whereas he thought they ought to be in all respects equal. 2. the parsimony of the States might reduce the provision so low that as had already happened in choosing delegates to Congress, the question would be not who were most fit to be chosen, but who were most willing to serve.

On the question for inserting the words "and fixt."

Massts. no. Cont. no. N. Y. ay. N. J. ay. Pa. ay. Del. ay. Md. ay. Va. ay. N. C. ay. S. C. no. Geo. ay. [Ayes — 8; noes — 3.]

Doctr. Franklyn said he approved of the amendment just made for rendering the salaries as fixed as possible; but disliked the word "*liberal*". He would ⟨prefer⟩ the word moderate if it was necessary to substitute any other. He remarked the tendency of abuses in every case, to grow of themselves when once begun. and related very pleasantly the progression in ecclesiastical benefices, from the first departure from the gratuitous ⟨provision for⟩[8] the Apostles, to the establishment of the papal system. The word "liberal" was struck out nem. con.

On the motion of Mr. Pierce,[9] that the wages should be paid out of the National Treasury, Massts. ay. Ct. no. N. Y. no. N. J. ay. Pa. ay. Del. ay Md. ay. Va. ay. N. C. ay. S. C. no. G. ay. [Ayes — 8; noes — 3.] [10]

Question on the clause relating to term of service & compensation of 1st. branch

---

[8] Crossed out "practice of."   [9] Crossed out "words were inserted providing ".
[10] See further August 14, note 7.

Massts. ay. Ct. no. N. Y no. N. J. ay. Pa. ay. Del. ay. Md. ay. Va. ay. N. C. ay. S. C. no. Geo. ay.   [Ayes—8; noes—3.]

On a question for striking ⟨out⟩ the "*ineligibility* of members of Natl. Legis: to *State Offices*."

Massts. divd.[11] Cont. ay. N. Y. ay. N. J. no. Pa. no. Del. no. Md. divd. Va. no. N. C. ay. S. C. ay. Geo. no   [Ayes — 4; noes — 5; divided — 2.]

On the question for agreeing to the clause as amended.[12]

Massts. ay. Cont. no. N. Y. ay. N. J. ay. Pa. ay. Del. ay Md. ay. Va. ay. N. C. ay. S. C. ay. Geo. ay.   [Ayes — 10; noes — 1.]

On a question for making Members of Natl. legislature *ineligible* to any Office under the Natl. Govt. for the term of 3 years after ceasing to be members.

Massts. no. Cont. no. N. Y. no. N. J. no. Pa. no. Del. no. Md. ay. Va. no. N C. no. S. C. no. Geo. no.   [Ayes — 1; noes — 10.]

On the question for such ineligibility for one year.[13]

Massts. ay. Ct. ay. N. Y. no. N. J. ay. Pa. ay. Del. ay. Md. divd. Va. ay. N. C. ay. S. C. ay. Geo. no.   [Ayes — 8; noes—2; divided — 1.]

On question ⟨moved by Mr. Pinckney⟩[14] for striking out "incapable of re-election into 1st. branch of Natl. Legisl. for   years and subject to recall"   agd. to nem. con.

On question for striking out ⟨from Resol: 5⟩ the words requiring members of the Senatorial branch to be of the age of   years ⟨at least⟩[15]

Massts. no. Cont. ay. N. Y. no. N. J. ay. Pa. .ay. Del. no. Md. no. Va. no. N. C. divd. S. C. no. Geo. divd.   [Ayes — 3; noes — 6; divided — 2.]

On the question for filling the blank with 30 years as the qualification; it was agreed to.

---

[11] Madison first wrote "Massts. ay." and changed it to "Massts. divd." It is possible that this change may have been made at a later date in consequence of the records of *Journal* and Yates.

[12] The clause had not been amended. The statements of the question in Journal and Yates are to be preferred.

[13] For further references upon this whole subject, see under September 3 note 7.

[14] Taken from Yates.   [15] Revised from *Journal*.

Massts. ay Ct. no. N. Y. ay N. J. no Pa. ay Del. no Md. ay Va. ay N. C. ay S. C. ay Geo. no [Ayes — 7; noes — 4.]

Mr. Spaight moved to fill the blank for the duration of the appointmts. to the 2d branch of the National ⟨Legislature⟩ with the words "7 years.

Mr. Sherman thought 7 years too long. He grounded his opposition he said on the principle that if they did their duty well, they would be reelected. And if they acted amiss, an earlier opportunity should be allowed for getting rid of them. He preferred 5 years which wd. be between the terms of 1st branch & of the executive

Mr. Pierce proposed 3 years. 7 years would raise an alarm. Great mischiefs had arisen in England from their septennial act which was reprobated by most of their patriotic Statesmen.

Mr. Randolph was for the term of 7 years. The Democratic licentiousness of the State Legislatures proved the necessity of a firm Senate. The object of this 2d. branch is to controul the democratic branch of the Natl. Legislature. If it be not a firm body, the other branch being more numerous, and coming immediately from the people, will overwhelm it. The Senate of Maryland constituted on like principles had been scarcely able to stem the popular torrent. No mischief can be apprehended, as the concurrence of the other branch, and in some measure, of the Executive, will in all cases be necessary. A firmness & independence may be the more necessary also in this branch, as it ought to guard the Constitution agst. encroachments of the Executive who will be apt to form combinations with the demagogues of the popular branch.

⟨Mr. ⟩ M⟨adison⟩, considered 7 years as a term by no means too long. What we wished was to give to the Govt. that stability which was every where called for, and which the enemies of the Republican form alleged to be inconsistent with its nature. He was not afraid of giving too much stability by the term of seven years. His fear was that the popular branch would still be too great an overmatch for it. It was to be much lamented that we had so little direct experience to guide us. The Constitution of Maryland was the only one that bore any analogy to this part of the plan. In no instance had

the Senate of Maryd. created just suspicions of danger from
it.   In some instances perhaps it may have erred by yielding
to the H. of Delegates.   In every instance of their opposition
to the measures of the H. of. D. they had had with them the
suffrages of the most enlightened and impartial people of the
other States as well as of their own.   In the States where the
Senates were chosen in the same manner as the other branches,
of the Legislature, and held their seats for 4 years, the institution was found to be no check whatever agst. the ⟨insta-
bilities of the other branches.⟩   He conceived it to be of great
importance that a stable & firm Govt. organized in the republican form should be held out to the people.   If this be not done,
and the people be left to judge of this species of Govt. by ye.
operations of the defective systems under which they now
live, it is much to be feared the time is not distant when, in
universal disgust, they will renounce the blessing which they
have purchased at so dear a rate, and be ready for any change
that may be proposed to them.[16]
    On the question for "seven years", as the term for the
2d. branch
    Massts. divided. (Mr. King. Mr. Ghorum ay — Mr. Gerry,
Mr. Strong, no.) Cont. no. N. Y. divd. N. J. ay. Pa. ay Del.
ay. Md. ay. Va. ay. N. C. ay. S. C. ay. Geo. ay.   [Ayes — 8;
noes — 1; divided — 2.]
    Mr. Butler ⟨& Mr. Rutlidge⟩[17] proposed that the members
of the 2d. branch should be entitled to no salary or compensation for their services.   on the question
    Masts. divd. Cont. ay. N. Y. no. N. J. no. P. no. Del. ay.
Md. no Va. no. N. C. no. S. C. ay. Geo. no.*   [Ayes — 3; noes
—7; divided—1.]
    ⟨It was then moved[18] & agreed that the clauses respecting
the stipends & ineligibility of the 2d. branch be the same as,
of the 1st. branch: Con: disagreeing to the ineligibility.

    *⟨It is probable ye votes here turned chiefly on the idea that if the salaries
were not here provided for, the members would be paid by their respective States.⟩

---

[16] Crossed out "He was a friend to Republican".   [17] Taken from *Journal*.
[18] The remainder of this day's records taken from *Journal*.

It was moved & 2ded. to alter Resol: 9. so as to read "that the jurisdiction of the supreme tribunal shall be to hear & determine in the dernier resort, all piracies, felonies, &c"

It was moved & 2ded. to strike out "all piracies & felonies on the high seas," which was agreed to.

It was moved & agreed to strike out "all captures from an enemy".

It was moved & agreed to strike out "other States" and insert "two distinct States of the Union"

It was moved & agree to postpone the consideration of Resolution 9. relating to the Judiciary:

The Come. then rose & the House adjourned)[19]

YATES

TUESDAY, JUNE 12th, 1787.

Met pursuant to adjournment. Present 11 states.

The 15th or last resolve was taken into consideration. No debate arose on it, and the question was put and carried — 5 states for it, 3 against, and 2 divided. New-York in the negative.

Having thus gone through with the resolves, it was found necessary to take up such parts of the preceding resolves as had been postponed, or not agreed to.[20] The remaining part of the 4th resolve was taken into consideration.

Mr. Sherman moved that the blank of the duration of the first branch of the national legislature, be filled with *one year*. Mr. Rutledge with *two years*, and Mr. Jenifer with *three years*.

Mr. Madison was for the last amendment — observing that it will give it stability, and induce gentlemen of the first weight to engage in it.

Mr. Gerry is afraid the people will be alarmed, as savoring of despotism.

Mr. Madison. The people's opinions cannot be known,

---

[19] See further Appendix A, XLIII.

[20] The resolutions at this stage of the proceedings will be found below, *Records*, June 13, Journal (document A.)

as to the particular modifications which may be necessary in the new government — In general they believe there is something wrong in the present system that requires amendment; and he could wish to make the republican system the basis of the change — because if our amendments should fail of securing their happiness, they will despair it can be done in this way, and incline to monarchy.

Mr. Gerry could not be governed by the prejudices of the people — Their good sense will ever have its weight. Perhaps a limited monarchy would be the best government, if we could organize it by creating a house of peers; but that cannot be done.

The question was put on the three year's amendment and carried — 7 ayes — 4 noes. New-York in the affirmative.

On motion to expunge the clause of the qualification as to age, it was carried, 10 states against one.

On the question for fixed stipends, without augmentation or diminution, to this branch of the legislature, it was moved that the words, *to be paid by the national treasury*, be added — Carried, 8 states for — 3 against. New-York in the negative.

The question was then put on the clause as amended, and carried, 8 ayes — 3 noes. New-York in the negative.

On the clause respecting the ineligibility to any other office, it was moved that the words, *by any particular state*, be expunged. 4 states for — 5 against, and 2 divided. New-York affirmative.

The question was then put on the whole clause, and carried 10 ayes — 1 no.

The last blank was filled up with *one year*, and carried — 8 ayes — 2 noes, 1 divided.

Mr. Pinkney moved to expunge the clause. Agreed to, *nem. con.*

The question to fill up the blank with *30 years*. Agreed to — 7 states for — 4 against.

It was moved to fill the blank, as to the duration, with *seven years*.

Mr. Pierce moved to have it for three years — instanced the danger of too long a continuance, from the evils arising in the British parliaments from their septenual duration, and the clamors against it in that country by its real friends.

Mr. Sherman was against the 7 years, because if they are bad men it is too long, and if good they may be again elected.

Mr. Madison was for 7 years — Considers this branch as a check on the democracy—It cannot therefore be made too strong.

For the motion, 8 ayes — 1 no — 2 states divided. New-York one of the last.

Mr. Butler moved to expunge the clause of the stipends.

Lost — 7 against — 3 for — 1 divided.

Agreed that the second branch of the national legislature be paid in the same way as the first branch.

Upon the subject of ineligibility, it was agreed that the same rule should apply as to the first branch.

6th resolve agreed to be postponed, *sine die.*

9th resolve taken into consideration, but postponed to to-morrow. Then adjourned to to-morrow morning.

W.EDNESDAY, JUNE 13, 1787.

JOURNAL

Wednesday June 13. 1787.

The Order of the day being read

The House resolved itself into a Committee of the whole House to consider of the state of the american Union.

Mr President left the Chair

Mr Gorham took the Chair of the Committee

Mr President resumed the Chair

Mr Gorham reported from the Committee that the Committee having considered and gone through the propostions offered to the House by the honorable Mr Randolph, and to them referred, were prepared to report thereon — and had directed him to submit the report to the consideration of the House.

The report was then delivered in at the Secretary's table, and having been once read

It was moved by Mr. Randolph seconded by Mr Martin to postpone the farther consideration of the report till to-morrow

and on the question to postpone

it passed in the affirmative.

And then the House adjourned till to-morrow at 11 o'Clock A. M.

In a Committee of the whole House

Wednesday June 13. 1787.

Mr Gorham in the Chair

It was moved by Mr Randolph seconded by Mr Madison to adopt the following resolution respecting the national Judiciary namely

"That the jurisdiction of the national Judiciary shall

223

"extend to cases which respect the collection of the national
"revenue, impeachments of any national officers, and ques-
"tions which involve the national peace and harmony"
            passed in the affirmative
It was moved by Mr Pinckney seconded by Mr Sherman to
insert after the words "One supreme Tribunal" "the Judges
of which to be appointed by the second branch of the national
Legislature.[1]
            passed in the affirmative.
It was moved by Mr Gerry seconded by Mr Pinckney[2] to add
the following words to the fifth resolution adopted by the
Committee namely
    "excepting money bills, which shall originate in the first
"branch of the national Legislature"
            passed in the negative [Ayes — 3; noes — 8.][3]
It was then moved and seconded that the Committee do rise
and report their proceedings to the House.
    The Committee then rose

DETAIL OF AYES AND NOES

New Hampshire	Massachusetts	Rhode Island	Connecticut	New York	New Jersey	Pennsylvania	Delaware	Maryland	Virginia	North Carolina	South Carolina	Georgia	Questions	Ayes	Noes	Divided
[61] no			no	aye	no	no	aye	no	aye	no	no	no	That money biils should only originate in the first branch	3	8	

[A]

State of the resolutions submitted to the consideration of
the House by the honorable Mr Randolph, as agreed to in a
Committee of the whole House.[4]
    RESOLVED that it is the opinion of this Committee

---

[1] The Journal is probably wrong in its statement of this motion, see below note 12.
[2] It hardly seems as if Pinckney could have seconded this motion if the sentiments ascribed to him by Madison are correct.   [3] Vote 61, Detail of Ayes and Noes.
[4] This document was among the papers of the Convention turned over to the

that a national government ought to be established, consisting of

a Supreme Legislative, Judiciary, and Executive.

Resolved that the National Legislature ought to consist of two branches.

Resolved that the members of the first branch of the National Legislature ought to be elected by the people of the several States.

Resolved [5] that the members of the second branch of the national Legislature ought to be chosen by the individual Legislatures.

Resolved that each branch ought to possess the right of originating acts.

Resolved that the national Legislature ought to be empowered.
to enjoy the legislative rights vested in Congress by the confederation; and moreover.
to legislate in all cases to which the separate States are incompetent: or in which the harmony of the United States may be interrupted by the exercise of individual legislation.
to negative all laws passed by the several States contravening, in the opinion of the national legislature, the articles of union; or any treaties subsisting under the authority of the Union

Resolved that a national Executive be instituted to consist of

---

Secretary of State by President Washington in 1796. Its heading is misleading as it represents the work of the Convention only to the beginning of June 12, when, as Yates said, "it was found necessary to take up such parts of the preceeding resolves as had been postponed, or not agreed to." The document has a peculiar value in that it gives, with a few exceptions noted, the resolutions in the order of their adoption.

[5] If put in the order of its adoption this paragraph should come just before the paragraph on the "suffrage in the first branch".

a single person.[6]

with power

to carry into execution the national laws;

to appoint to offices in cases not otherwise provided for.

To be chosen by the national Legislature

for the term of seven years.

to be ineligible a second time; and; to be removable on impeachment and conviction of mal-practice, or neglect of duty.

Resolved that the national Executive shall have a right to negative any legislative act; which shall not be afterwards passed unless by two third parts of each branch of the national Legislature.

Resolved that a national Judiciary be established to consist of

One supreme tribunal

To hold their Offices during good behaviour; and to receive punctually, at stated times, a fixed compensation for their services; in which no encrease or diminution shall be made, so as to affect the persons actually in Office at the time of such encrease or diminution.

Resolved[7] that the national Legislature be empowered to appoint inferior Tribunals.

Resolved that provision ought to be made for the admission of States, lawfully arising within the limits of the United States, whether from a voluntary junction of government and territory, or otherwise, with the consent of a number of voices in the national Legislature, less than the whole.

---

[6] That the executive should "consist of a single person" was not adopted until later, and should come after the impeachment of the executive.

[7] In order of adoption should come after the second paragraph below, on the continuance of Congress.

Resolved that provision ought to be made for the continuance of a Congress, and their authorities and privileges, until a given day after the reform of the articles of Union shall be adopted; and for the completion of all their engagements.

Resolved that the right of suffrage in the first branch of the national Legislature ought not to be according to the rule established in the articles of confederation; but according to some equitable ratio of representation — namely in proportion to the whole number of white and other free citizens and inhabitants, of every age, sex and condition, including those bound to servitude for a term of years and three fifths of all other persons not comprehended in the foregoing description, except Indians, not paying taxes in each State.

Resolved that the right of suffrage in the second branch of the national Legislature ought to be according to the rule established for the first

Resolved that a republican constitution, and it's existing laws, ought to be guaranteed to each State by the United-States.

Resolved that provision ought to be made for the amendment of the articles of union whensoever it shall seem necessary.

Resolved that the Legislative, Executive, and judiciary powers within the several States ought to be bound by oath to support the articles of union

Resolved that the amendments which shall be offered to the confederation by the Convention, ought at a proper time or times, after the approbation of Congress, to be submitted to an assembly or assemblies of representatives, recommended by the several legislatures, to be expressly chosen by the people to consider and decide thereon

[B] [8]

State of the resolutions submitted to the consideration of the House by the honorable Mr Randolph, as altered, amended, and agreed to in a Committee of the whole House.

1. Resolved that it is the opinion of this Committee that a national government ought to be established consisting of a Supreme Legislative, Judiciary, and Executive.

2 Resolved. that the national Legislature ought to consist of Two Branches.

3 Resolved that the Members of the first branch of the national Legislature ought to be elected by

the People of the several States

for the term of Three years.

to receive fixed stipends, by which they may be compensated for the devotion of their time to public service

to be paid out of the National-Treasury.

to be ineligible to any Office established by a particular State or under the authority of the United-States (except those peculiarly belonging to the functions of the first branch) during the term of service, and under the national government for the space of one year after it's expiration.

4 Resolved. that the Members of the second Branch of the national Legislature ought to be chosen by

the individual Legislatures.

to be of the age of thirty years at least.

to hold their offices for a term sufficient to ensure their independency, namely

seven years.

---

[8] This document was among the papers of the Convention turned over to the Secretary of State by President Washington in 1796.

to receive fixed stipends, by which they may be compensated for the devotion of their time to public service — to be paid out of the National Treasury

to be ineligible to any Office established by a particular State, or under the authority of the United States (except those pecularily belonging to the functions of the second branch) during the term of service, and under the national government, for the space of One year after it's expiration.

5. Resolved that each branch ought to possess the right of originating acts

6. Resolved. that the national Legislature ought to be empowered

to enjoy the legislative rights vested in Congress by the confederation — and moreover

to legislate in all cases to which the separate States are incompetent: or in which the harmony of the United States may be interrupted by the exercise of individual legislation.

to negative all laws passed by the several States contravening, in the opinion of the national legislature, the articles of union, or any treaties subsisting under the authority of the union.

7. Resolved. that the right of suffrage in the first branch of the national Legislature ought not to be according to the rule established in the articles of confederation: but according to some equitable ratio of representation — namely.

in proportion to the whole number of white and other free citizens and inhabitants of every age, sex, and condition including those bound to servitude for a term of years, and three fifths of all other persons not comprehended in the foregoing description, except Indians, not paying taxes in each State.

8 Resolved. that the right of suffrage in the second branch
  of the national Legislature ought to be according to
  the rule established for the first

9 Resolved. that a national Executive be instituted to consist of
        a Single Person.
        to be chosen by the National Legislature.
        for the term of Seven years.
        with power to carry into execution the National
          Laws.
            to appoint to Offices in cases not otherwise
              provided for
            to be ineligible a second time, and
            to be removable on impeachment and convic-
              tion of mal practice or neglect of duty.
            to receive a fixed stipend, by which he may
              be compensated for the devotion of his time
              to public service [9]
            to be paid out of the national Treasury.[9]

10 Resolved. that the national executive shall have a right to
   negative any legislative act: which shall not be afterwards passed unless by two third parts of each branch
   of the national Legislature.

11 Resolved. that a national Judiciary be established to consist of
            One supreme Tribunal
    The Judges of which to be appointed by the second
      Branch of the National Legislature.
      to hold their offices during good behaviour
      to receive, punctually, at stated times, a fixed com-
        pensation for their services: in which no encrease
        or diminution shall be made so as to affect the per-

---

[9] There seems to be no record of any favorable action on this point. It was postponed on June 2; it does not appear in A; and there is no such action noticed on June 12.
It was perhaps voted on June 12, when similar action was taken for the legislature.

sons actually in office at the time of such encrease
or diminution

12 Resolved. That the national Legislature be empowered to
   appoint
                     inferior Tribunals.
13 Resolved. that the jurisdiction of the national Judiciary
   shall extend to cases which respect the collection of
   the national revenue: impeachments of any national
   Officers: and questions which involve the national
   peace and harmony.

14. Resolved. that provision ought to be made for the admis-
    sion of States, lawfully arising within the limits of the
    United States, whether from a voluntary junction of
    government and territory, or otherwise, with the con-
    sent of a number of voices in the national Legislature
    less than the whole.

15. Resolved. that provision ought to be made for the continu-
    ance of Congress[10] and their authorities until a given
    day after the reform of the articles of Union shall be
    adopted; and for the completion of all their engage-
    ments.

16. Resolved that a republican Constitution, and it's existing
    laws, ought to be guaranteed to each State by the
    United States.

17. Resolved. that provision ought to be made for the amend-
    ment of the articles of Union, whensoever it shall seem
    necessary.

18. Resolved. that the Legislative, Executive, and Judiciary
    powers within the several States ought to be bound
    by oath to support the articles of Union

---

[10] A reads "a Congress ".

19 Resolved. that the amendments which shall be offered to the confederation by the Convention, ought at a proper time or times, after the approbation of Congress to be submitted to an assembly or assemblies of representatives, recommended by the several Legislatures, to be expressly chosen by the People to consider and decide thereon.

MADISON

Wednesday June 13. in Committee of the whole

⟨Resol: 9. being resumed⟩ The latter parts of the clause relating to the jurisdiction of the Natl. tribunals, was struck out nem. con in order to leave full room for their organization.

⟨Mr. Randolph & Mr. Madison, then moved the following resolution respecting a National Judiciary, viz "that the jurisdiction of the national Judiciary shall extend to cases, which respect the collection of the National revenue, impeachments of any national officers, and questions which involve the national peace and harmony" which was agreed to.[11]

Mr. Pinkney & Mr. Sherman moved to insert after the words "one supreme tribunal" the words "the Judges of which to be appointed by the national Legislature" [12]⟩

⟨Mr.⟩ M⟨adison⟩, objected to an appt. by the whole Legislature. Many of them were incompetent Judges of the requisite qualifications. They were too much influenced by their partialities. The candidate who was present, who had displayed a talent for business in the legislative field, who had perhaps assisted ignorant members in business of their own, or of their Constituents, or used other winning means, would without any of the essential qualifications for an expositor of

---

[11] Taken from *Journal.*

[12] Originally Madison had recorded "Mr. Pinkney proposed that the National Judiciary should be appointed by the Natl. Legislature. Mr. Sherman seconds him." This was struck out, and the wording of the text, revised from *Journal*, was substituted. Note that Madison retains his own form of the motion, *i.e.*, appointment by the "Legislature", and not by the "second branch" as stated in the *Journal*. See above, note 1. Yates agrees with Madison, and they are undoubtedly right and the Journal wrong as the subsequent records show.

the laws prevail over a competitor not having these recommendations but possessed of every necessary accomplishment. He proposed that the appointment should be made by the Senate, which as a less numerous & more select body, would be more competent judges, and which was sufficiently numerous to justify such a confidence in them.

Mr. Sharman & Mr. Pinkney withdrew their motion, and the appt. by the Senate was agd. to nem. con.

Mr. Gerry. moved to restrain the Senatorial branch from originating money bills.[13] The other branch was more immediately the representatives of the people, and it was a maxim that the people ought to hold the purse-strings. If the Senate should be allowed to originate such bills, they wd. repeat the experiment, till chance should furnish a sett of representatives in the other branch who will fall into their snares.

Mr. Butler saw no reason for such a discrimination. We were always following the British Constitution when the reason of it did not apply. There was no analogy between the Ho of Lords and the body proposed to be established. If the Senate should be degraded by any such discriminations, the best men would be apt to decline serving in it in favor of the other branch. And it will lead the latter into the practice of tacking other clauses to money bills.

⟨Mr.⟩ M⟨adison⟩ observed that the Commentators on the Brit: Const: had not yet agreed on the reason of the restriction on the H. of L. in money bills. Certain it was there could be no similar reason in the case before us. The Senate would be the representatives of the people as well as the 1st. branch. If they sd. have any dangerous influence over it, they would easily prevail on some member of the latter to originate the bill they wished to be passed. As the Senate would be generally a more capable sett of men, it wd. be wrong to disable them from any preparation of the business, especially of that which was most important and in our republics, worse prepared than any other. The Gentleman in pursuance of

---

[13] Upon this subject, see *Records* of July 5–7, July 14, July 16, August 8, September 5, September 8, note 9, and Appendix A, XLI, CLVIII (43–46), CCXL.

his principle ought to carry the restraint to the *amendment;* as well as the originating of money bills. Since, an addition of a given sum wd. be equivalent to a ⟨distinct⟩ proposition of it.

Mr. King[14] differed from Mr. Gerry, and concurred in the objections to the proposition.

Mr. Read favored the proposition, but would not extend the restraint to the case of amendments.

Mr. Pinkney thinks the question premature. If the Senate shd. be formed on the *same* proportional representation as it stands at present, they sd have equal power; otherwise if a different principle sd. be introduced.

Mr. Sherman. As both branches must concur, there can be no danger whichever way the Senate be formed. We establish two branches in order to get more wisdom, which is particularly needed in the finance business — The Senate bear their share of the taxes, and are also the representatives of the people. What a man does by another, he does by himself is a maxim. In Cont. both branches can originate in all cases, and it has been found safe & convenient. Whatever might have been the reason of the rule as to The H. of Lords, it is clear that no good arises from it now even there.

Genl. Pinkney. This distinction prevails in S. C. & has been a source of pernicious disputes between ye. 2 branches. The constitution is now evaded, by informal schedules of amendments handed ⟨from ye. Senate to the other House.⟩

Mr. Williamson wishes for a question chiefly to prevent re-discussion. The restriction will have one advantage, it will oblige some member in lower branch to move, & people can then mark him

On the question for excepting money bills as propd. by Mr. Gerry. Mas. no. Cont. no. N. Y. ay. N. J. no. Del. ay. Md. no. Va. ay. N. C. no. S. C. no. Geo. no. [Ayes — 3; noes — 7.][15]

Committee rose[16] & Mr. Ghorum made report, which was

---

[14] Crossed out "Mr. King reinforced the arguts."
[15] Detail of Ayes and Noes, Vote 61, includes Pennsylvania in the negative.
[16] See Appendix A, CLVIII (8–9).

postponed till tomorrow, to give an opportunity for other plans to be proposed, the report was in the words following.

June 13

Report of the Committee of Whole on Mr. Randolphs propositions [17]

1. Resd. that it is the opinion of this Committee that a National Governmt. ought to be established, consisting of a supreme Legislative, Executive & Judiciary.

2. Resold. that the National Legislature ought to consist of two branches.

3. Resd. that the members of the first branch of the National Legislature ought to be elected by the people of the several States for the term of three years, to receive fixed Stipends by which they may be compensated for the devotion of their time to public service, to be paid out of the National Treasury: to be ineligible to any office established by a particular State, or under the authority of the U. States, (except those peculiarly belonging to the functions of the first branch), during the term of service, and under the national Government for the space of one year after its expiration.

4. Resd. that the members of the second branch of the Natl. Legislature ought to be chosen by the individual Legislatures, to be of the age of 30 years at least, to hold their offices for a term sufficient to ensure their independency, namely, seven years, to receive fixed stipends by which they may be compensated for the devotion of their time to public service to be paid out of the National Treasury; to be ineligible to any office established by a particular State, or under the authority of the U. States, (except those peculiarly belonging to the functions of the second branch) during the term of service, and under the Natl. Govt. for the space of one year after its expiration.

---

[17] The differences between the wording of this document and that of B above are too slight to be noticed, except in Resolution 19 where Madison omits the words "of representatives" after "Assemblies". Copies of this report are found among the papers of various delegates, but they are not sufficiently distinctive to warrant reprinting. *Cf.* Appendix A, CLVIII (6).

5. Resd. that each branch ought to possess the right of originating Acts

6. Resd. that the Natl. Legislature ought to be empowered to enjoy the Legislative rights vested in Congs. by the Confederation, and moreover to legislate in all cases to which the separate States are incompetent; or in which the harmony of the U. S. may be interrupted by the exercise of individual legislation; to negative all laws passed by the several States contravening in the opinion of the National Legislature the articles of Union, or any treaties subsisting under the authority of the Union.

7. Resd. that the rights of suffrage in the 1st. branch of the National Legislature, ought not to be according to the rule established in the articles of confederation but according to some equitable ratio of representation, namely, in proportion to the whole number of white & other free citizens & inhabitants, of every age sex and condition, including those bound to servitude for a term of years, & three fifths of all other persons, not comprehended in the foregoing description, except Indians not paying taxes in each State:

8. Resolved that the right of suffrage in the 2d. branch of the National Legislature ought to be according to the rule established for the first.

9. Resolved that a National Executive be instituted to consist of a single person, to be chosen by the Natl. Legislature for the term of seven years, with power to carry into execution the national laws, to appoint to offices in cases not otherwise provided for — to be ineligible a second time, & to be removeable on impeachment and conviction of malpractices or neglect of duty — to receive a fixed stipend by which he may be compensated for the devotion of his time to public service to be paid out of the national Treasury.

10. Resold. that the natl. Executive shall have a right to negative any Legislative Act, which shall not be afterwards passed unless by two thirds of each branch of the National Legislature

11. Resold. that a Natl. Judiciary be established, to consist of one supreme tribunal, the Judges of which to be ap-

pointed by the 2d. branch of the Natl. Legislature, to hold their offices during good behaviour, & to receive punctually at stated times a fixed compensation for their services, in which no increase or diminution shall be made, so as to affect the persons actually in office at the time of such increase or diminution.

12. Resold. that the Natl. Legislature be empowered to appoint inferior Tribunals.

13. Resd. that the jurisdiction of the Natl. Judiciary shall extend to all cases which respect the collection of the Natl. revenue,[18] impeachments of any Natl. Officers, and questions which involve the national peace & harmony.

14. Resd. that provision ought to be made for the admission of States lawfully arising within the limits of the U. States, whether from a voluntary junction of Government & territory or otherwise, with the consent of a number of voices in the Natl. Legislature less than the whole.

15. Resd. that provision ought to be made for the continuance of Congress and their authorities and privileges untill a given day after the reform of the articles of Union shall be adopted and for the completion of all their engagements.

16. Resd. that a Republican Constitution & its existing laws ought to be guaranteed to each State by the U. States.

17. Resd. that provision ought to be made for the amendment of the Articles of Union whensoever it shall seem necessary.

18. Resd. that the Legislative, Executive, & Judiciary powers within the several States ought to be bound by oath to support the articles of Union

19. Resd. that the amendments which shall be offered to the confederation by the convention ought at a proper time or times after the approbation of Congs. to be submitted to an Assembly or Assemblies [19] recommended by the several Legislatures to be expressly chosen by the people to consider and decide thereon.

---

[18] In Wilson's copy is a marginal note opposite this clause: - - "(or the national Regulations of Trade) N. B. the Judicial should be commensurate to the legislative and executive Authority ".   [19] See above, note 17.

YATES

WEDNESDAY, JUNE 13th, 1787.

Met pursuant to adjournment. Present 11 states.

Gov. Randolph observed the difficulty in establishing the powers of the judiciary — the object however at present is to establish this principle, to wit, the security of foreigners where treaties are in their favor, and to preserve the harmony of states and that of the citizens thereof. This being once established, it will be the business of a sub-committee to detail it; and therefore moved to obliterate such parts of the resolve so as only to establish the principle, to wit, *that the jurisdiction of the national judiciary shall extend to all cases of national revenue, impeachment of national officers, and questions which involve the national peace or harmony.* Agreed to unanimously.

It was further agreed, that the judiciary be paid out of the national treasury.

Mr. Pinkney moved that the judiciary be appointed by the national legislature.

Mr. Madison of is opinion that the second branch of the legislature ought to appoint the judiciary, which the convention agreed to.

Mr. Gerry moved that the first branch shall have the only right of originating bills to supply the treasury.

Mr. Butler against the motion. We are constantly running away with the idea of the excellence of the British parliament, and with or without reason copying from them; when in fact there is no similitude in our situations. With us both houses are appointed by the people, and both ought to be equally trusted.

Mr. Gerry. If we dislike the British government for the oppressive measures by them carried on against us, yet he hoped we would not be so far prejudiced as to make ours in every thing opposite to theirs.

Mr. Madison's question carried.

The committee having now gone through the whole of the propositions from Virginia — Resolved, That the committee do report to the convention their proceedings — This was accordingly done. (*See a copy of it hereunto annexed.*) [20]

The house resolved on the report being read, that the consideration thereof be postponed to to-morrow, and that members have leave to take copies thereof.

Adjourned to to-morrow morning.

---

[20] Not found, see *Records*, July 5, note 18.

THURSDAY, JUNE 14, 1787.

JOURNAL
Thursday June 14. 1787.

It was moved by Mr Patterson seconded by Mr Randolph that the farther consideration of the report from the Committee of the whole House be postponed till to-morrow.

and before the question for postponement was taken.

It was moved by Mr Randolph seconded by Mr Patterson that the House adjourn.

And then the House adjourned till to-morrow at 11 o'clock.

MADISON
Thursday June 14. ⟨In Convention⟩

Mr. Patterson, observed to the Convention that it was the wish of several deputations, particularly that of N. Jersey, that further time might be allowed them to contemplate the plan reported from the Committee of the Whole, and to digest one purely federal, and contradistinguished from the reported plan. He said they hoped to have such an one ready by tomorrow to be laid before the Convention: and the Convention adjourned that leisure might be given for the purpose.[1]

YATES
THURSDAY, JUNE 14TH, 1787.

Met pursuant to adjournment. Present 11 States.

Mr. Patterson moved that the further consideration of the report be postponed until to-morrow, as he intended to give in principles to form a federal system of government materially different from the system now under consideration. Postponement agreed to.

Adjourned until to-morrow morning.

---

[1] See further Appendix A, XLIV.

FRIDAY, JUNE 15, 1787.

JOURNAL
Friday June 15. 1787.

Mr. Patterson submitted several resolutions to the consideration of the House, which he read in his place, and afterwards delivered in at the Secretary's table —¹ They were then read — and

It was moved by Mr Madison seconded by Mr Sherman to refer the resolutions, offered by Mr Patterson, to a Committee of the whole House

which passed in the affirmative [Ayes — 11; noes — o.] ²

It was moved by Mr Rutledge seconded by Mr Hamilton to recommit the resolutions reported from a Committee of the whole House.

which passed in the affirmative.

Resolved that this House will to-morrow resolve itself into a Committee of the whole House to consider of the state of the american union.

And then the House adjourned till to-morrow at 11 o'clock. A. M.

DETAIL OF AYES AND NOES

New Hampshire	Massachusetts	Rhode Island	Connecticut	New York	New Jersey	Pennsylvania	Delaware	Maryland	Virginia	North Carolina	South Carolina	Georgia	Questions	Ayes	Noes	Divided
[62] aye	aye		aye	aye	aye	aye	aye	aye	aye	aye	aye	aye	To resolve the House into a Committee of the whole House	11		
[63]³ aye	aye					aye	aye	aye	aye	aye	aye	aye	The Electors to be paid out of the national Treasury			

[End of second loose sheet]

¹ A copy of these resolutions is not to be found among the papers of the Convention deposited by Washington with the Secretary of State in 1796.

² Vote 62, Detail of Ayes and Noes. But this vote might apply to any of the questions of this day, or to the first question on June 16, 18, or 19.

³ Vote 63 belongs to the Records of July 21.

MADISON

Friday June 15th. ⟨1787.⟩

Mr. Patterson, laid before the Convention the plan which he said several of the deputations wished to be substituted in place of that proposed by Mr. Randolp. After some little discussion of the most proper mode of giving it a fair deliberation it was agreed that it should be referred to a Committee of the Whole, and that in order to place the two plans in due comparison, the other should be recommitted. At the earnest desire of Mr. Lansing & some other gentlemen, it was also agreed that the Convention should not go into Committee of the whole on the subject till tomorrow, by which delay the friends of the plan proposed by Mr. Patterson wd. be better prepared to explain & support it, and all would have an opportuy of taking copies.* —

The propositions from N. Jersey moved by Mr. Patterson were in the words following.[5]

1. Resd. that the articles of Confederation ought to be so revised, corrected & enlarged, as to render the federal Constitution adequate to the exigences of Government, & the preservation of the Union.

---

* (this plan had been concerted among the deputations or members thereof, from Cont. N. Y. N. J. Del. and perhaps Mr Martin from Maryd. who made with them a common cause on different principles. Cont. and N. Y. were agst. a departure from the principle of the Confederation, wishing rather to add a few new powers to Congs. than to substitute, a National Govt. The States of N. J and Del. were opposed to a National Govt. because its patrons considered a proportional representation of the States as the basis of it. The eagourness displayed by the Members opposed to a Natl. Govt. from these different ⟨motives⟩ began now to produce serious anxiety for the result of the Convention. — Mr. Dickenson said to Mr. Madison you see the consequence of pushing things too far. Some of the members from the small States wish for two branches in the General Legislature, and are friends to a good National Government; but we would sooner submit to a foreign power, than submit to be deprived of an equality of suffrage, in both branches of the legislature, and thereby be thrown under the domination of the large States.)[4]

---

[4] See Appendix A, CLVIII (5) and (10), CCXXXIII, CCCLXXVI, and Appendix E.

[5] The various texts of the New Jersey Plan or Paterson Resolutions are discussed in Appendix E.

2. Resd. that in addition to the powers vested in the U. States in Congress, by the present existing articles of Confederation, they be authorized to pass acts for raising a revenue, by levying a duty or duties on all goods or merchandizes of foreign growth or manufacture, imported into any part of the U. States, by Stamps on paper, vellum or parchment, and by a postage on all letters or packages passing through the general post-Office, to be applied to such federal purposes as they shall deem proper & expedient; to make rules & regulations for the collection thereof; and the same from time to time, to alter & amend in such manner as they shall think proper: to pass Acts for the regulation of trade & commerce as well with foreign nations as with each other: provided that all punishments, fines, forfeitures & penalties to be incurred for contravening such acts rules and regulations shall be adjudged by the Common law Judiciarys of the State in which any offence contrary to the true intent & meaning of such Acts rules & regulations shall have been committed or perpetrated, with liberty of commencing in the first instance all suits & prosecutions for that purpose in the superior Common law Judiciary in such State, subject nevertheless, for the correction of all errors, both in law & fact in rendering judgment, to an appeal to the Judiciary of the U. States

3. Resd. that whenever requisitions shall be necessary, instead of the rule for making requisitions mentioned in the articles of Confederation, the United States in Congs. be authorized to make such requisitions in proportion to the whole number of white & other free citizens & inhabitants of every age sex and condition including those bound to servitude for a term of years & three fifths of all other persons not comprehended in the foregoing description, except Indians not paying taxes; that if such requisitions be not complied with, in the time specified therein, to direct the collection thereof in the non complying States & for that purpose to devise and pass acts directing & authorizing the same; provided that none of the powers hereby vested in the U. States in Congs. shall be exercised without the consent of at least

States, and in that proportion if the number of Confederated States should hereafter be increased or diminished.

4. Resd. that the U. States in Congs. be authorized to elect a federal Executive to consist of   persons, to continue in office for the term of   years, to receive punctually at stated times a fixed compensation for their services, in which no increase or diminution shall be made so as to affect the persons composing the Executive at the time of such increase or diminution, to be paid out of the federal treasury; to be incapable of holding any other office or appointment during their time of service and for   years thereafter; to be ineligible a second time, & removeable by Congs. on application by a majority of the Executives of the several States; that the Executives besides their general authority to execute the federal acts ought to appoint all federal officers not otherwise provided for, & to direct all military operations; provided that none of the persons composing the federal Executive shall on any occasion take command of any troops, so as personally to conduct any enterprise as General, or in other capacity.

5. Resd. that a federal Judiciary be established to consist of a supreme Tribunal the Judges of which to be appointed by the Executive, & to hold their offices during good behaviour, to receive punctually at stated times a fixed compensation for their services in which no increase or diminution shall be made, so as to affect the persons actually in office at the time of such increase or diminution; that the Judiciary so established shall have authority to hear & determine in the first instance on all impeachments of federal officers, & by way of appeal in the dernier resort in all cases touching the rights of Ambassadors, in all cases of captures from an enemy, in all cases of piracies & felonies on the high seas, in all cases in which foreigners may be interested, in the construction of any treaty or treaties, or which may arise on any of the Acts for regulation of trade, or the collection of the federal Revenue: that none of the Judiciary shall during the time they remain in Office be capable of receiving or holding any other office or appointment during their time of service, or for   thereafter.

6. Resd. that all Acts of the U. States in Congs. made by virtue & in pursuance of the powers hereby & by the articles of confederation vested in them, and all Treaties made & ratified under the authority of the U. States shall be the supreme law of the respective States so far forth as those Acts or Treaties shall relate to the said States or their Citizens, and that the Judiciary of the several States shall be bound thereby in their decisions, any thing in the respective laws of the Individual States to the contrary notwithstanding; and that if any State, or any body of men in any State shall oppose or prevent ye. carrying into execution such acts or treaties, the federal Executive shall be authorized to call forth ye power of the Confederated States, or so much thereof as may be necessary to enforce and compel an obedience to such Acts, or an Observance of such Treaties.

7. Resd. that provision be made for the admission of new States into the Union.

8. Resd. the rule for naturalization ought to be the same in every State

9. Resd. that a Citizen of one State committing an offence in another State of the Union, shall be deemed guilty of the same offence as if it had been committed by a Citizen of the State in which the Offence was committed.*

Adjourned

* ⟨This copy of Mr. Patterson's propositions varies in a few clauses from that in the printed Journal furnished from the papers of Mr. Brearley a Colleague of Mr. Patterson. A confidence is felt, notwithstanding, in its accuracy. That the copy in the Journal is not entirely correct is shewn by the ensuing speech of Mr. Wilson (June 16) in which he refers to the mode of removing the Executive by impeachment & conviction as a feature in the Virga. plan forming one of its contrasts to that of Mr. Patterson, which proposed a removal on the application of a majority of the Executives of the States. In the copy printed in the Journal, the two modes are combined in the same clause; whether through inadvertence, or as a contemplated amendment does not appear.⟩[6]

[6] See Appendix E.

YATES

FRIDAY, JUNE 15th, 1787.

Met pursuant to adjournment.   Present 11 states.

Mr. Patterson, pursuant to his intentions as mentioned yesterday, read a set of resolves as the basis of amendment to the confederation.   (*See those resolves annexed.*)[7]

He observed that no government could be energetic on paper only, which was no more than straw — that the remark applied to the one as well as to the other system, and is therefore of opinion that there must be a small standing force to give every government weight.

Mr. Madison moved for the report of the committee, and the question may then come on whether the convention will postpone it in order to take into consideration the system now offered.

Mr. Lansing is of opinion that the two systems are fairly contrasted.   The one now offered is on the basis of amending the federal government, and the other to be reported as a national government, on propositions which exclude the propriety of amendment.   Considering therefore its importance, and that justice may be done to its weighty consideration, he is for postponing it a day.

Col. Hamilton cannot say he is in sentiment with either plan — supposes both might again be considered as federal plans, and by this means they will be fairly in committee, and be contrasted so as to make a comparative estimate of the two.

Thereupon it was agreed, that the report be postponed, and that the house will resolve itself into a committee of the whole, to take into consideration both propositions to-morrow. Then the convention adjourned to to-morrow morning.

---

[7] Not found, see *Records*, July 5, note 18.

KING

1. To enlarge the powers of Confed. &c

2. To authorise Congress to receive an Imp. on the Imp. of For. Goods—stampt Art. & Postage of Letters—to pass acts regulating Foreign & Domest. Commerce, to pass regulations or ordinance relative to revennue & commerce, *provided* that the recovery of Fines Forfitures shd. be in the common law Judiciaries of the several States wh. appeal &c

3. The rule of apportioning Requis: on the States shall be the Whites ⅔ of all others — if the Req. is in arrear in any State, Congress shall have authority to divise & pass acts remedial in such case

4. Cong. to app —— persons as an Executive to be in Office — years wh. fixed Salary & ineligible a secd. Time, & removable by Cong. on appln. of a majory. of the Executives of the several States, but none of the Executive personally to command any military Expedn.

5. Sup. Judl. appd. by the Executive during good behaviour to try impeachmts. of fed. Officers, & appeals from the State Judicials in all cases where Foreigrs. are concernd. in the Construction of Treaties, or where the Acts of Trade & Revenue are contravened

6. The Acts Treaties &c &c to be paramount to State Laws and when any State or body of men oppose Treaties or general Laws, the Executive to call forth the force of the Union to enforce the Treaty or Law — 8 Naturalization to be the same in every State —

9 a Citizen offending in one state & belonging to another State, to be deemed Guilty of the same Offence as though the offence was committed by a Citizen of the State where the Offence was committed

---

[8] [Endorsed:] Plan of | Reform of Old Confedn | Quere if by N. Jersey

SATURDAY, JUNE 16, 1787.

JOURNAL

Saturday June 16. 1787.

The Order of the day being read

The House resolved itself into a Committee of the whole House to consider of the state of the american union

Mr. President left the Chair

Mr Gorham took the Chair of the Committee

Mr President resumed the Chair

Mr Gorham reported from the Committee that the Committee had made a progress in the matter to them referred; and had directed him to move that they may have leave to sit again.

Resolved that this House will on monday next again resolve itself into a Committee of the whole House to consider of the state of the American Union.

And then the House adjourned till Monday next at 11 o'Clock A. M.

In a Committee of the whole House

Saturday June 16. 1787.

Mr Gorham in the Chair.

After some time passed in debate on the propositions offered by the honorable Mr Paterson.

It was moved and seconded that the Committee do now rise, report a further progress, and request leave to sit again —

The Committee then rose.

MADISON

Saturday June 16.   In Committee of the whole on Resolutions proposd. by Mr. P. & Mr. R [1]

Mr. Lansing called for the reading of the 1st. resolution of each plan, which he considered as involving principles directly in contrast; that of Mr. Patterson says he sustains the sovereignty of the respective States, that of Mr. Randolph distroys it: the latter requires a negative on all the laws of the particular States; the former, only certain general powers for the general good. The plan of Mr. R. in short absorbs all power except what may be exercised in the little local matters of the States which are not objects worthy of the supreme cognizance. He grounded his preference of Mr. P'.s plan, chiefly on two objections agst that of Mr. R. 1. want of power in the Convention to discuss & propose it.[2] 2 the improbability of its being adopted. 1. He was decidedly of opinion that the power of the Convention was restrained to amendments of a federal nature, and having for their basis the Confederacy in being. The Act of Congress The tenor of the Acts of the States, the commissions produced by the several deputations all proved this. and this limitation of the power to an amendment of the Confederacy, marked the opinion of the States, that it was unnecessary & improper to go farther. He was sure that this was the case with his State. N. York would never have concurred in sending deputies to the convention, if she had supposed the deliberations were to turn on a consolidation of the States, and a National Government. 2. was it probable that the States would adopt & ratify a scheme, which they had never authorized us to propose? and which so far exceeded what they regarded as sufficient? We see by their several acts ⟨particularly in relation to the plan of revenue proposed by Congs. in 1783 not authorized by the articles of

---

[1] For this debate June 16–18, Martin's *Genuine Information* (Appendix A, CLVIII) is important.

[2] On this question, see debates of June 16–18, and Appendix A, CXLIII, CLXVII, CLXX, CLXXI, CLXXIV, CCXXX.

Confederation, what were)[3] the ideas they then entertained. Can so great a change be supposed to have already taken place. To rely on any change which is hereafter to take place in the sentiments of the people would be trusting to too great an uncertainty. We know only what their present sentiments are, and it is in vain to propose what will not accord with these. The States will never feel a sufficient confidence in a general Government to give it a negative on their laws. The Scheme is itself totally novel. There is ⟨no⟩ parallel to it to be found. The authority of Congress is familiar to the people, and an augmentation of the powers of Congress will be readily approved by them.

Mr. Patterson. said ⟨as⟩ he had on a former occasion given his sentiments on the plan proposed by Mr. R. he would now avoiding repetition as much as possible give his reasons in favor of that proposed by himself. He preferred it because it accorded 1. with the powers of the Convention.[4] 2 with the sentiments of the people. If the confederacy was radically wrong, let us return to our States, and obtain larger powers, not assume them of ourselves. I came here not to speak my own sentiments, but ⟨the sentiments of⟩ those who sent me. Our object is not such a Governmt. as may be best in itself, but such a one as our Constituents have authorized us to prepare, and as they will approve. If we argue the matter on the supposition that no Confederacy at present exists, it can not be denied that all the States stand on the footing of equal sovereignty. All therefore must concur before any can be bound. If a proportional representation be right, why do we not vote so here? If we argue on the fact[5] that a federal compact actually exists, and consult the articles of it we still find an equal Sovereignty to be the basis of it. He reads the 5th. art: of Confederation giving each State a vote — & the 13th. declaring that no alteration shall be made without unanimous consent. This is the nature of all treaties. What is unanimously done, must be unanimously undone. It was observed (by Mr. Wilson) that the larger State gave up the

---

[3] Taken from Yates.   [4] See above, note 2.   [5] Crossed out, "supposition".

point, not because it was right, but because the circumstances
of the moment urged the concession. Be it so. Are they for
that reason at liberty to take it back. Can the donor resume
his gift Without the consent of the donee. This doctrine may
be convenient, but it is a doctrine that will sacrifice the lesser
States. The large States acceded readily to the confederacy.
It was the small ones that came in reluctantly and slowly.
N. Jersey & Maryland were the two last, the former objecting
to the want of power in Congress over trade: both of them
to the want of power to appropriate the vacant territory to
the benefit of the whole. If the sovereignty of the States is
to be maintained, the Representatives must be drawn immediately from the States, not from the people: and we have no
power to vary the idea of equal sovereignty. The only expedient that will cure the difficulty, is that of throwing the States
into Hotchpot. To say that this is impracticable, will not
make it so. Let it be tried, and we shall see whether the
Citizens of Massts. Pena. & Va. accede to it. It will be
objected that Coercion will be impracticable. But will it be
more so in one plan than the other? Its efficacy will depend
on the quantum of power collected, not on its being drawn
from the States, or from the individuals; and according to his
plan it may be exerted on individuals as well as according that
of Mr. R. a distinct executive & Judiciary also were equally
provided by this plan. It is urged that two branches in the
Legislature are necessary. Why? for the purpose of a check.
But the reason of the precaution is not applicable to this case.
Within a particular State, when party heats prevail, such a
check may be necessary. In such a body as Congress it is
less necessary, and besides, the delegations of the different
States are checks on each other. Do the people at large complain of Congs.? No: what they wish is that Congs. may have
more power. If the power now proposed be not eno'. the people
hereafter will make additions to it. With proper powers
Congs. will act with more energy & wisdom than the proposed
Natl. Legislature; being fewer in number, and more secreted
& refined by the mode of election. The plan of Mr. R. will
also be enormously expensive. Allowing Georgia & Del. two

representatives each in the popular branch the aggregate number of that branch will be 180. Add to it half as many for the other branch and you have 270. members coming once at least a year from the most distant parts as well as the most central parts of the republic. In the present deranged State of our finances can so expensive a system be seriously thought of? By enlarging the powers of Congs. the greatest part of this expense will be saved, and all purposes will be answered. At least a trial ought to be made.

Mr. Wilson[6] entered into a contrast of the principal points of the two plans so far ⟨he said⟩ as there had been time to examine the one last proposed. These points were 1. in the Virga. plan there ⟨are⟩ 2 & in some degree 3 branches in the Legislature ÷ in the plan from N. J. there is to be a *single* legislature only — 2. Representation of the people at large is the basis of the one ÷ the State Legislatures the pillars of the other —— 3. proportional representation prevails in one ÷ equality of suffrage in the other — 4. a single Executive Magistrate is at the head of the one: — a plurality is held out in the other. — 5. in the one the majority of ⟨the people of⟩ [7] the U. S. must prevail: — in the other a minority may prevail. 6. the Natl. Legislature is to make laws in all cases to which the separate States are incompetent & —: — ⟨in place of this⟩ Congs. are to have additional power in a few cases only — 7. a negative on the laws of the States: — ⟨in place of this⟩ coertion to be substituted — 8. The Executive to be removeable on impeachment & conviction; — ⟨in one plan: in the other⟩ to be removeable at the instance of majority of the Executives of the States —— 9. Revision of the laws ⟨provided for in one:⟩ —— no such check ⟨in the other⟩ — 10. inferior national tribunals ⟨in one:⟩ — none such ⟨in the other⟩ — 11 ⟨In ye. one⟩ jurisdiction of Natl. tribunals to extend &c —; an appellate jurisdiction only ⟨allowed in the other⟩. 12. ⟨Here⟩ the jurisdiction is to extend to all cases affecting the Natl. peace & harmony: — ⟨there⟩ a few cases only ⟨are⟩ marked out.

---

[6] For Wilson's outline of this speech, see below, also Appendix A, CXLII.

[7] This modification would seem to have been made on the authority of King, whose notes Madison may have seen.

13. ⟨finally ye⟩ ratification ⟨is in this to be⟩ by the people themselves — ⟨in that⟩ by the legislative authorities according to the 13 art: of Confederation.

With regard to the *power of the Convention*,[8] he conceived himself authorized to *conclude nothing*, but to be at liberty to *propose any thing*. In this particular he felt himself perfectly indifferent to the two plans.

With *regard to the sentiments of the people*, he conceived it difficult to know precisely what they are. Those of the particular circle in which one moved, were commonly mistaken for the general voice. He could not persuade himself that the State Govts. & sovereignties were so much the idols of the people, nor a Natl. Govt. so obnoxious to them, as some supposed. Why sd. a Natl. Govt. be unpopular? Has it less dignity? will each Citizen enjoy under it less liberty or protection? Will a Citizen of *Delaware* be degraded by becoming a Citizen of the *United States*? Where do the people look at present for relief from the evils of which they complain? Is it from an internal reform of their Govt.? No. Sir, It is from the Natl. Councils that relief is expected. For these reasons he did not fear, that the people would not follow us into a national Govt. and it will be a further recommendation of Mr. R.'s plan that it is to be submitted to *them* and not to the *Legislatures*, for ratification.

proceeding now to the 1st. point on which he had contrasted the two plans, he observed that anxious as he was for some augmentation of the federal powers, it would be with extreme reluctance indeed that he could ever consent to give powers to Congs. he had two reasons either of wch. was sufficient. 1. Congs. as a Legislative body does not stand on the people.[9] 2. it is a *single* body. 1. He would not repeat the remarks he had formerly made on the principles of Representation. he would only ⟨say⟩ that an inequality in it, has ever been a poison contaminating every branch of Govt. In G. Britain where this poison has had a full operation, the security of private

---

[8] The italicized words in this and the following paragraph were underscored by Madison when he revised his notes.

[9] Crossed out: "Here then a fundamental principle of free Govt. is violated".

rights is owing entirely to the purity of her tribunals of Justice, the Judges of which are neither appointed nor paid by a venal Parliament. The political liberty of that Nation, owing to the inequality of representation is at the mercy of its rulers. He means not to insinuate that there is any parallel between the situation of that country & ours at present. But it is a lesson we ought not to disregard, that the smallest bodies in G. B. are notoriously the most corrupt. Every other source of influence must also be stronger in small than large bodies of men. When Lord Chesterfield had told us that one of the Dutch provinces had been seduced into the views of France, he ⟨need⟩ not have added, that it was not Holland, but one of the *smallest* of them. There are facts among ourselves which are known to all. Passing over others, he will only remark that the *Impost*, so anxiously wished for by the public was defeated not by any of the *larger* States in the Union. 2. *Congress is a single Legislature.* Despotism comes on mankind in different shapes. sometimes in an Executive, sometimes in a military, one. Is there no danger of a Legislative despotism? Theory & practice both proclaim it. If the Legislative authority be not restrained, there can be neither liberty nor stability; and it can only be restrained by dividing it within itself, into distinct and independent branches. In a single house there is no check, but the inadequate one, of the virtue & good sense of those who compose it.

On another great point, the contrast was equally favorable to the plan reported by the Committee of the Whole. It vested the Executive powers in a single Magistrate. The plan of N. Jersey, vested them in a plurality. In order to controul the Legislative authority, you must divide it. In order to controul the Executive you must unite it. One man will be more responsible than three. Three will contend among themselves till one becomes the master of his colleagues. In the triumvirates of Rome first Cæsar, then Augustus, are witnesses of this truth. The Kings of Sparta, & the Consuls of Rome prove also the factious consequences of dividing the Executive Magistracy. Having already taken up so much time he wd. not he sd. proceed to any of the other points. Those on which he had dwelt, are sufficient of themselves: and on a decision of them, the fate of the others will depend.

Mr. Pinkney, the whole comes to this, as he conceived. Give N. Jersey an equal vote, and she will dismiss her scruples, and concur in the Natil. system. He thought the Convention authorized to go any length in recommending, which they found necessary to remedy the evils which produced this Convention.

Mr. Elseworth proposed as a more distinctive form of collecting the mind of the Committee on the subject, "that the Legislative power of the U. S. should remain in Congs.". This was not seconded, though it seemed better calculated for the purpose than the 1st. proposition of Mr. Patterson in place of which Mr. E. wished to substitute it.

Mr. Randolph. was not scrupulous on the point of power.[10] When the salvation of the Republic was at stake, it would be treason to our trust, not to propose what we found necessary. He painted in strong colours, the imbecility of the existing confederacy, & the danger of delaying a substantial reform. In answer to the objection drawn from the sense of our Constituents as denoted by their acts relating to the Convention and the objects of their deliberation, he observed that as each State acted separately in the case, it would have been indecent for it to have charged the existing Constitution with all the vices which it might have perceived in it. The first State that set on foot this experiment would not have been justified in going so far, ignorant as it was of the opinion of others, and sensible as it must have been of the uncertainty of a successful issue to the experiment. There are certainly reasons of a peculiar nature where the ordinary cautions must be dispensed with; and this is certainly one of them. He wd. ⟨not⟩ as far as depended on him leave any thing that seemed necessary, undone. The present moment is favorable, and is probably the last that will offer.

The true question is whether we shall adhere to the federal plan, or introduce the national plan. The insufficiency of the

---

[10] See above note 2.

former has been fully displayed by the trial already made.
There are but two modes, by which the end of a Genl. Govt.
can be attained: the 1st. is by coercion as proposed by Mr. Ps.
plan. 2. by real legislation as propd. by the other plan.
Coercion he pronounced to be _impracticable, expensive, cruel
to individuals_. It tended also to habituate the instruments of
it to shed the blood & riot in the spoils of their fellow Citizens,
and consequently trained them up for the service of Ambition.
We must resort therefore to a national _Legislation over indi-
viduals_, for which Congs. are unfit. To vest such power in
them, would be blending the Legislative with the Executive,
contrary to the recd. maxim on this subject: If the Union of
these powers heretofore in Congs. has been safe, it has been
owing to the general impotency of that body. Congs. are
moreover not elected by the people, but by the Legislatures
who retain even a power of recall. They have therefore no
will of their own, they are a mere diplomatic body, and are
always obsequious to the views of the States, who are always
encroaching on the authority of the U. States. A provision
for harmony among the States, as in trade, naturalization &c.
— for crushing rebellion whenever it may rear its crest — and
for certain other general benefits, must be made. The powers
for these purposes, can never be given to a body, inadequate
as Congress are in point of representation, elected in the mode
in which they are, and possessing no more confidence than they
do: for notwithstanding what has been said to the contrary,
his own experience satisfied him that a rooted distrust of Congress pretty generally prevailed. A Natl. Govt. alone, properly constituted, will answer the purpose; and he begged it to
be considered that the present is the last moment for establishing one. After this select experiment, the people will yield to
despair.

The Committee rose & the House adjourned.

YATES

SATURDAY, JUNE 16, 1787.

Met pursuant to adjournment. Present 11 states.

Mr. Lansing moved to have the first article of the last plan of government read; which being done, he observed, that this system is fairly contrasted with the one ready to be reported—the one federal, and the other national. In the first, the powers are exercised as flowing from the respective state governments — The second, deriving its authority from the people of the respective states — which latter must ultimately destroy or annihilate the state governments. To determine the powers on these grand objects with which we are invested, let us recur to the credentials of the respective states, and see what the views were of those who sent us. The language is there expressive — it is, upon the revision of the present confederation, to alter and amend such parts as may appear defective, so as to give additional strength to the union. And he would venture to assert, that had the legislature of the state of New-York, apprehended that their powers would have been construed to extend to the formation of a national government, to the extinguishment of their independency, no delegates would have here appeared on the part of that state. This sentiment must have had its weight on a former occasion, even in this house; for when the second resolution of Virginia, which declared, in substance, that a federal government could not be amended for the good of the whole, the remark of an honorable member of South-Carolina, that by determining this question in the affirmative their deliberative powers were at an end, induced this house to wave the resolution. It is in vain to adopt a mode of government, which we have reason to believe the people gave us no power to recommend — as they will consider themselves on this ground authorized to reject it. See the danger of exceeding your powers by the example which the requisition of congress of 1783 afforded. They required an impost on all imported articles; to which, on federal grounds, they had no right unless voluntarily granted. What was the consequence? Some, who had least to give, granted it; and others, under various restrictions and modifications, so that it could not be systematized. If we form a government, let us do it on principles which are likely to meet the approbation of the states. Great changes can only be gradually introduced. The states will never sacrifice their essential rights to a national government. New plans, annihilating the rights of the states (unless upon evident necessity) can never be approved. I may venture to assert, that the prevalent opinion of America is, that granting additional powers to congress would answer their views; and every power recommended for their approbation exceeding this idea, will be fruitless.

Mr. Patterson. — As I had the honor of proposing a new system of government for the union, it will be expected that I should explain its principles.

1st. The plan accords with our own powers.

2d. It accords with the sentiments of the people.

But if the subsisting confederation is so radically defective as not to admit of amendment, let us say so and report its insufficiency, and wait for enlarged powers. We must, in the present case, pursue our powers, if we expect the approbation of the people. I am not here to pursue my own sentiments of government, but of those who have sent me; and I believe that a little practical virtue is to be preferred to the finest theoretical principles, which cannot be carried into effect. Can we, as representatives of independent states, annihilate the essential powers of independency? Are not the votes of this convention taken on every question under the idea of independency? Let us turn to the 5th article of confederation — in this it is mutually agreed, that each state should have one vote — It is a fundamental principle arising from confederated governments. The 13th article provides for amendments; but they must be agreed to by every state — the dissent of one renders every proposal null. The confederation is in the nature of a compact; and can any state, unless by the consent of the whole, either in politics or law, withdraw their powers? Let it be said by Pennsylvania, and the other large

states, that they, for the sake of peace, assented to the confederation; can she now resume her original right without
the consent of the donee?

And although it is now asserted that the larger states
reluctantly agreed to that part of the confederation which
secures an equal suffrage to each, yet let it be remembered,
that the smaller states were the last who approved the confederation.

On this ground, representation must be drawn from the
states to maintain their independency, and not from the
people composing those states.

The doctrine advanced by a learned gentleman from
Pennsylvania, that all power is derived from the people, and
that in proportion to their numbers they ought to participate equally in the benefits and rights of government, is right
in principle, but unfortunately for him, wrong in the application to the question now in debate.

When independent societies confederate for mutual defence,
they do so in their collective capacity; and then each state
for those purposes must be considered as *one* of the contracting parties. Destroy this balance of equality, and you
endanger the rights of the *lesser* societies by the danger of
usurpation in the greater.

Let us test the government intended to be made by the
Virginia plan on these principles. The representatives in
the national legislature are to be in proportion to the number
of inhabitants in each state. So far it is right upon the principles of equality, when state distinctions are done away;
but those to certain purposes still exist. Will the government
of Pennsylvania admit a participation of their common stock
of land to the citizens of New-Jersey? I fancy not. It therefore follows, that a national goverment, upon the present
plan, is unjust, and destructive of the common principles of
reciprocity. Much has been said that this government is to
operate on persons, not on states. This, upon examination,
will be found equally fallacious; for the fact is, it will, in the
quotas of revenue, be proportioned among the states, as
states; and in this business Georgia will have 1 vote, and

Virginia 16. The truth is both plans may be considered to compel individuals to a compliance with their requisitions, although the requisition is made on the states.

Much has been said in commendation of two branches in a legislature, and of the advantages resulting from their being checks to each other. This may be true when applied to state governments, but will not equally apply to a national legislature, whose legislative objects are few and simple.

Whatever may be said of congress, or their conduct on particular occasions, the people in general, are pleased with such a body, and in general wish an increase of their powers, for the good government of the union. Let us now see the plan of the national government on the score of expense. The least the second branch of the legislature can consist of is 90 members — The first branch of at least 270. How are they to be paid in our present impoverished situation? Let us therefore fairly try whether the confederation cannot be mended, and if it can, we shall do our duty, and I believe the people will be satisfied.

Mr. Wilson first stated the difference between the two plans.

Virginia plan proposes two branches in the legislature.

Jersey a single legislative body.

Virginia, the legislative powers derived from the people.

Jersey, from the states.

Virginia, a single executive.

Jersey, more than one.

Virginia, a majority of the legislature can act.

Jersey, a small minority can control.

Virginia, the legislature can legislate on all national concerns.

Jersey, only on limited objects.

Virginia, legislature to negative all state laws.

Jersey, giving power to the executive to compel obedience by force.

Virginia, to remove the executive by impeachment.

Jersey, on application of a majority of the states.

Virginia, for the establishment of inferior judiciary tribunals.

Jersey, no provision.

It is said and insisted on, that the Jersey plan accords with our powers. As for himself he considers his powers to extend to every thing or nothing; and therefore that he has a right and is at liberty to agree to either plan or none. The people expect relief from their present embarrassed situation, and look up for it to this national convention; and it follows that they expect a *national government*, and therefore the plan from Virginia has the preference to the other. I would (says he) with a reluctant hand add any powers to congress, because they are not a body chosen by the people, and consist only of one branch, and each state in it has one vote. Inequality in representation poisons every government. The English courts are hitherto pure, just and incorrupt, while their legislature are base and venal. The one arises from unjust representation, the other from their independency of the legislature. Lord Chesterfield remarks, that one of the States of the United Netherlands withheld its assent to a proposition until a major of their state was provided for. He needed not to have added (for the conclusion was self evident) that it was one of the lesser states. I mean no reflection, but I leave it to gentlemen to consider whether this has not also been the case in congress? The argument in favor of the Jersey plan goes too far, as it cannot be completed, unless Rhode-Island assents. A single legislature is very dangerous. — Despotism may present itself in various shapes. May there not be legislative despotism if in the exercise of their power they are unchecked or unrestrained by another branch? On the contrary an executive to be restrained must be an individual. The first triumvirate of Rome combined, without law, was fatal to its liberties; and the second, by the usurpation of Augustus, ended in despotism. — The two kings of Sparta and the consuls of Rome, by sharing the executive, distracted their governments.

Mr. C. C. Pinkney supposes that if New-Jersey was indulged with one vote out of 13, she would have no objection to a national government. He supposes that the convention have already determined, virtually, that the federal government cannot be made efficient. A national government being therefore the object, this plan must be pursued — as our business is not to conclude but to recommend.

Judge Elsworth is of opinion that the first question on the new plan will decide nothing materially on principle, and therefore moved the postponement thereof, in order to bring on the second.

Gov. Randolph. — The question now is which of the two plans is to be preferred. If the vote on the first resolve will determine it, and it is so generally understood, he has no objection that it be put. The resolutions from Virginia must have been adopted on the supposition that a federal government was impracticable — And it is said that power is wanting to institute such a government. — But when our all is at stake, I will consent to any mode that will preserve us. View our present deplorable situation — France, to whom we are indebted in every motive of gratitude and honor, is left unpaid the large sums she has supplied us with in the day of our necessity — Our officers and soldiers, who have successfully fought our battles — and the loaners of money to the public, look up to you for relief.

The bravery of our troops is degraded by the weakness of our government.

It has been contended that the 5th article of the confederation cannot be repealed under the powers to new modify the confederation by the 13th article. This surely is false reasoning, since the whole of the confederation upon revision is subject to _amendment and alteration;_ besides our business consists in recommending a system of government, not to make it. There are great seasons when persons with limited powers are justified in exceeding them, and a person would be contemptible not to risk it. Originally our confederation was founded on the weakness of each state to repel a foreign enemy; and we have found that the powers granted to congress are insufficient. The body of congress is ineffectual to carry the great objects of safety and protection into execution. What would their powers be over the commander of the military, but for the virtue of the commander? As the state assemblies are constantly encroaching on the powers of congress, the Jersey plan would rather encourage such encroachments than be a check to it; and from the nature of the institution, congress would ever be governed by cabal and intrigue — They are besides too numerous for an executive, nor can any additional powers be sufficient to enable them to protect us against foreign invasion. Amongst other things congress was intended to be a body to preserve peace among the states, and in the rebellion of Massachusetts it was found they were not authorized to use the troops of the confederation to quell it. Every one is impressed with the idea of a general regulation of trade and commerce. Can congress do this? when from the nature of their institution they are so subject to cabal and intrigue? And would it not be dangerous to entrust such a body with the power, when they are dreaded on these grounds? I am certain that a national government must be established, and this is the only moment when it can be done — And let me conclude by observing, that the best exercise of power is to exert it for the public good.

Then adjourned to Monday morning.

                              K I N G [11]
        Natl.   Fedl.
                            Lansing

One Br. to come from the   To come from the State Legis-
people in propn. to yr. num-   latures equally & to repre-
bers   sent the States

All acts of ind. States sub-   To possess enumerated powers
ject to a national Negative

Will absorb the State sovereignties & leave them mere
Corporations, & Electors of
the natl. Senate —

---

[11] King's notes of these proceedings are somewhat confused in their arrangement as they are now bound in his MSS. Internal evidence points clearly to the order in which they are here given, and there is nothing in their external form which would prevent this.

Remarks — The confedn. admits the sovereignties of the States — it speaks of an Union — but it never meant a consolidation — If this had been in view NYk never wd. have sent Delegates — we must attend to the Disposition of the People — They never will agree to a consolidation — the System of Imp: proved the Jealousies of the States — they introduced provisos &c &c — If the people are unfavorable at will it be prudent to form a plan for Futurity — I think not — Experience dont warnt. our forming a Natl. Govt. — Where we have no experience there can be no reliance on Reason [12]

Patterson

The plan from Jersey —
1. accd. wt. our powers —

2 in accord with the Sentiments of the People

If we are of opinion that the confedn. is incapable of amendment, let us tell them so & obtain larger powers —

I dont expect to deliver my own Sentiments — I aim at a delivery of the Opinions of my Constituents

I am willing to take it on the Plan of no confed — we are then all Equal — The confedn. was formed unanimously — it can be altered or disolved only by unanimous Consent —

Federal or national — It is sd. that to be national the Representation shd. be from & proportionable to, the people and operate on the people — the first part is unnecessary — if so a federal Govt. may operate on the people individually — It is proposed to have two Brs. because one will check the other — this is unnecessary because the Delegates in Cong. are a Check to each other — two Br. will be expensive and the plan will be burdensome in the extreme — they will be less segacious and able than Congress — because the latter will be few & the former numerous —

---

[12] This page of King's MS. is endorsed "Genl. Remarks on Natl. & fedl. Gov."

Wilson — contrasts the two —

Nat.	Fed.
1	
Legis. of 2 Brs.	A Congress or one Br.
2	
The People are the basis of Rep —	The Legislatures of the State
3	
A repn. according to Numbers or Wealth	The States are equal
4	
A single person as Ex.	More than one person
5	
A majority of the People are to govern	A minority
6	
The Nal. Legis. to legislate in national Cases	enumerated and partial Instances
7	
Nat. Leg. to negative State laws	The Right to call out the force of the Union
8	
Ex. removeable for Misbehavior by impeach of ye. Legis —	Majory. Executives of the States
to possess a qualified Neg.	
infr. Tribunls.	None but the States Courts to have cognizance in cases of Revenue

Relative to the powers of this convention — We have powers to conclude nothing — we have power to propose anything — we expect the Approbation of Cong. we hope for that of the Legis. of the several States perhaps it will not be inconsistent wth Revolution principles, to promise ourselves the Assent of the People provided a more regular establishment cannot be obtained &c &c

As to the Sentiments of the People
I don't think that State Governments and State Sovereignties is so much the Idol of the People, or that they are averse to receive a national Government—the latter is as precious as the former — a Citizen of N. Jersey will not conceive himself complimented by that epithet, and degraded by being called a citizen of the US — the people expect Relief from national & not from State measures — They therefore expect it from a national & not from State Governments —

It is said we may enlarge the powers of Congress — there are two Objections agt. this proposal
1st Congress as a legislative body dont stand on the principles of a Free Govt. the authority of the people
2d. They are a legislature of a single Br. when they ought to be devided [13] —
1st Where the principle of unequal Represtn. prevails there exists a poison wh. eventually will destroy it the Government — A measure has been prevented in the S Genl. until a particular person was made a majr. this was one of the small Gratifications of a small Province —
2d. The single Br — we dread a military despot — is there no danger of a Legislative Despotism there is it must therefore be limited — It cannot be limited or restrained when single — The restraint must be in its own formation, namely a Division —Although it is true that to restrain the powers of a Legislature you must divide them and make them independent; the contrary is true in the Executive — if divided the respon-

---

sibility of the Executive is destroyed; they will contend wh.
each other or combine for wicked purposes — this was the
case of the first triumvirs of Rome, and afterwards with the
Congress.

HAMILTON

Mr. Lansing — N S — proposes to draw representation from
            the whole body of people, without regard to
            S Sovereignties —

            Subs: proposes to preserve the state Sov-
            ereignties

          — Powers — ⎰ — Different Legislatures had a dif-
                            ferent object —
                      — Revise the Confederation —
                         Ind. States cannot be supposed
                         to be willing to annihilate the
                         States —
                         State of New York would not
                         have agreed to send members
                         on this ground —

          — In vain to devise systems however good which
            will not be adopted ————

            If convulsions happen nothing we can do will
            give them a direction —

            Legislatures cannot be expected to make such
            a sacrifice —

            The wisest men in forming a system from
            theory apt to be mistaken —

            The present national government has no pre-
            cedent or experience to support it —

            General opinion that certain additional powers
            ought to be given to Congress —

Mr. Patterson — 1 — plan accords with powers
               2   —— accords with sentiment of the
                 People —

            If Confederation radically defective we ought
            to return to our states and tell them so —

            Comes not here to sport sentiments of his

own but to speak the sense of his Con-
stitu[en]ts —

— States treat as equal —

— Present Compact gives one *Vote to* each
state.

alterations are to be made by Congress and
all the Legislatures —

All parties to a Contract must assent to its
dissolution —

— States collectively have advantages in which
the smaller states do not participate —
therefore individual rules do not apply.

— Force of government will not depend on proportion of representation — but on Quantity
of power —

— Check not necessary in a ge[ne]ral government
of communities — but

in an individual state spirit of faction is to
be checked —

— How have Congress hitherto conducted themselves?

The People approve of Congress but think
they have not powers enough —

— body constituted like Congress from the
fewness of their numbers more wisdom and
energy — than the complicated system of
Virginia

— Expence enormous —

180 — commons
90 — senators
———
270 —

Wilson — Points of Disagreement —

V — 1	2 or three branches...N J	one branch —
2	Derives authority from People	from states —
3	Proportion of suffrage ...	Equality —
4	Single Executive	Plural —
5 —	Majority to govern	Minority to govern—
6 —	Legislate in all matters of general Concern	partial objects —
7	Negative	None —
8	Removeable by impeach-ment	on application of majority of Executives

9 — Qualified Negative by Executive .... None

10 — Inf. tribunals .... None —

11 — Orig: Jurisdiction in all
  cases of Nat: Rev. .... None —

12. National Government to be   to be ratified by
  ratified by People ....   Legislatures —

— Empowered to propose every thing
  to conclude nothing —

— Does not think state governments the idols of the
 people —

 Thinks a competent national government will be a
  favourite of the people —

 Complaints from every part of United States
  that the purposes of government cannot be
  answered

— In constituting a government — not merely necessary to give proper powers — but to give them to
 proper hands —

 Two reasons against giving additional powers to
  Congress —

— First it does not stand on the authority of the
 people —

 Second — It is a single branch —

 Inequality — the poison of all governments —

— Lord Chesterfield speaks of a Commission to be
obtained for a member of a small province.

Pinkney —

Mr. Elseworth —

Mr. Randolp — Spirit of the People in favour of the Virginian
scheme —

We have powers; but if we had not we ought
not to scruple —

P A T E R S O N [14]

Lansing [14a]—Contrasts the Principles of the two Systems—
The national Plan proposes to draw Representn. from the
People.

The federal Plan proposes to draw Representn. from the
States.

The first will absorb the State-Governmts.

1. The Powers of the Convention.

2. The Probability as to the Adoption of either System —
Publick Acts — particularly the Act respecting the Impost.

Reasoning upon Systems unsupported by Experience generally erroneous —

Paterson. [15]

Wilson [14a] — The Plans do not agree in the following
Instances.

1. The Govt. consists of 2 Branches.

to connect them together as States. [14a]   2. The original
Authority of the People at Large is brought forward.

3. Representation to be according to the Number and
Importance of the Citizens.

4. A single Executive.

5. A Majority of the United States are to control.

6. The national Leg. can operate in all Cases in which
the State Leg. cannot.

---

[14] Taken from *American Historical Review*, IX, 331–334, 325–327.

[14a] In margin opposite words following.

[15] In margin.   For Paterson's outline of his own speech, see below.

7. The national Leg. will have a Right to negative all State-Acts contravening Treaties, etc.

8. Ex. Mag. removable on Conviction.

9. The Ex. to have a qualified Negative over Acts of the Legr. —

10. Provision is made for superior [16] Tribunals —

11. The Jurisdn. of the national Legr.[17] is to extend to all Cases of a national Nature.

12. National Peace, all Questions comprehending it, will be the Object of the national Judiciary —

13. Delegates [18] to come from the People.

The relative Merit of the two Plans.

1. Upon Principles

2. Upon Experience.

3. The joint Result of both.

He can conclude finally Nothing; and to propose every Thing — he may propose any Plan —

Sentiments of the People; those with whom we converse we naturally conclude to be the Sentiments of the People.

States Sovereignments and State Governmts. not so much an Idol as is apprehended — a national Government to protect Property and promote Happiness, the Wish of the People.

Will a Citizen of New Jersey think himself honoured when addressed as a Citzn. of that State, and degraded when addressed as a Citizen of the U. S.

The People expect Relief from the national Councils; it can be had only from a national Governmt. —

Equalization[14a] — A new Proposal thrown out for the Sentiments of the People.

Adl Powers ought not to be given to Congress. Objns. to that Body.

1. Congress as a legislative Body does not stand upon the Authority of the People.

---

[16] Superior" evident mistake for "inferior".

[17] "Legr" evident mistake for "Judiciary".

[18] "Delegates" evident mistake for "Ratification".

2. Congress consists of but one Branch.

An equal Representn. in Proportion to Numbers.

Answr. Citizens of the same State. [18a] — The Foundation, the Progress, and Principles of Representation — Look at England — Holland — the Vote of every Province necessary. Ld. Chesterfield —

Impost opposed and defeated not by one of the large States —

The Consent of Rhode-Island will be necessary on the Jersey-Plan —

A single Legr.

Despotism presents itself in several various Shapes — military Despot — ex. Despot — Is there no such Thing as a leg. Despot — The Leg. Authority ought to be restrained —

The Restraints upon the Legr. must be such as will operate within itself — No Check in a single Branch — Should have distinct and independant Branches — reciprocal Controul.

A single Executive — Triumvirate of Rome — 2 Triumvirate — Augustus rose superior — Sparta — Rome —

Pinckney[18a] — If Jersey can have an equal Representn. she will come into the Plan from Virginia —

Views — to amend the Confedn. if not amendable, then to propose a new Governmt. —

Solely recommendatory — Powers sufficient. Division of Territory; not seriously proposed — The due Settlemt. of the Importance of the States necessary — this done at present with Respect to Contribution.

England.

1 Congress unfortunately fixed on equal Representn. — they had not the Means of determining the Quota — If each State must have a Vote, each State must contribute equally —

Elsworth.[18a]

Randolph [18a] 1. Whether the Articles of the Confedn. can be so reformed as to answer the Purposes of a national Governmt. —

No Usurpation of Power in this Convention. The Spirit of the People in Favour of the Plan from Virginia —

[18a] In margin opposite words following.

Powers pursued; if Powers wanting, we should do what is right.

Our Debts remain unpaid while the federal Govt. remains as it is —

Delaware. [18a] The 13th Article — provides for the alteration of the Articles, then of course for the Alteration of the 5th. Article.

Annapolis [18a] Powers in a deliberate Assembly — ridiculous — We are only to compare Sentiments — Disdain Danger, and do what is necessary to our political Salvation — We must avail ourselves of the present Moment.

His Constituents will applaud, when he has done every Thing in his Power to relieve America —

No Provision agt. foreign Powers or Invasions. no Mony nor Men — Militia not sufficient —

No Provision agt. internal Insurrections. nor for the Maintenance of Treaties —

Coercion two Ways — 1. as to Trade — 2. as to an Army —

Legislation affecting Individuals the only Remedy. This Power too great to lodge in one Body —

Congress possess both Legislation and Execution —

The Variety of Interests [19] in the several States require a national Legislation; or else there may be a Combination of States —

The mode of electing Congress an Objn. — the Delegates will be under the Influence of its particular States.

Cabal and Intrigue of which such a Body as Congress may be capable. They are too numerous for an Executive.

No Provision under the Confedn. for supporting the Harmony of the States — their commercial Interests different.

No provision for Congress to settle Disputes —

No Provision made or Power in Congress for the Suppression of Rebellion — no Troops can be raised — Congress ought not to have the Power of raising Troops.

A Navigation Act may be necessary — Give Power to whom — not to Congress — capable of Intrigue and Cabal;

---

[19] A hand drawn on the margin points to this, as if indicating its importance.

Inadequacy of Representation; Want of Confidence in Congress —

Divide leg. and ex. Branches and then Doors may be open [19a]—Congress fallen considerably in their Reputation.

Doors not open in Congress.

This the last Moment ever will be offered —

[Paterson]

1. Because it accords with our Powers. Suppose an Attorney. Who can vote agt. it — If Confedn. cannot be amended, say so — The Experimt. has not been made.

2. Because it accords with the Sentiments of the People.

   1. Coms.

   2. News-papers — Political Barometer. Jersey never would have sent Delegates under the first Plan —

Not to sport Opinions of my own. Wt. can be done. A little practicable Virtue preferrable to Theory —

1. As States — independant of any Treaty or Confedn.

Each State is sovereign, free, and independant — Sovereignty includes Equality. We come here as States and as Equals — Why vote by States in Convention — We will not give up the Right —

Mr. Wilson — A Principle given up in the first Confedn.

2. As under the existing Articles of the Confedn.

5th. Article — unanimously entered into.

Back Lands — Jersey — Maryland —

A Contract. The Nature of a Contract. Solemnly entered into — Why break it — why not the new or present one be broke in the same Manner —

Convenience.

The last Clause in the Confedn. —

Some of the States will not consent —

Self-Destruction.

Abolition of the lesser States [19a] — Hitherto argued upon Principle — as States — as subsisting Treaties — The Danger to the lesser States — The Natural Progress of Power — Com-

---

[19a] In margin opposite words following.

bination of Parts — Orders — States — Proportion of Votes — State-Politicks and Attachments — Great Britain and America

Objns. The larger States contribute most, and therefore Representn. ought to be in Proportion —

No — they have more to protect.

A rich State and poor State in same Relation as a rich individual and a poor one.[19a] 2. For the Sake of preserving the Liberty of the others —

3. Wealth will have its Influence —

Objn. — Mr. Wilson — first Principles — All Authority derived from the People — The People entitled to exercise Authority in Person. One free Citizen ought to be of equal Importance with another — true — One free State of equal Importance with another — Both true when properly applied. The Beauty of all Knowledge consists in the Application —

A large County and a small County [19a] — One free Citizen ought to be of equal Importance with another — they are Members of the Society, and therefore true — England and Switzerland. Pennsylva. and Jersey — they have the same Privileges, partake in the same common Stock, for Instance, in back and unlocated Lands. The Genn. soon found out the Diffe. between a Pennsylva. and a Jersey-Man when we talked of Consolidn. then the Pennsyla. gave up $\frac{1}{3}$ — No; no — A Nation, when it is necessary to go by Majority of Votes, a State, when it is necessary to divide the common Stock —

Equalize the States — No Harm — no Hurt. No authority for that Purpose — and then it is impracticable —

Authority — Why talk of the first set of Propositions —

Impracticable — how does that appear — Make the Experiment — Propose the Measure to the Consideration of the States —

Objn. — There must be a national Governmt. to operate individually upon the People in the first Instance, and not upon the States — and therefore a Representation from the People at Large and not from the States —

1. Will the Operation and Force of the Govt. depend upon the mode of Representn. — No — it will depend upon the Quantum of Power lodged in the leg. ex. and judy. Depart-

ments — it will operate individually in the one Case as well as in the other —

2. Congress are empowered to act individually or to carry the Reqt. into Execn. in the same Manner as is set forth in the first Plan —

3. If not, it may be modified to answer the Purpose.

4. If it cannot be done, better than to have some States devoured by others —

Objn. — Congress not sufficient — there must be two Branches — a House of Delegates and a Senate; why, they will be a Check — This not applicable to the supreme Council of the States — The Representatives from the several States are Checks upon each other.

In a single State Party Heat and Spirit may pervade the whole, and a single Branch may of a sudden do a very improper Act — A second Branch gives Time for Reflexion; the Season of Calmness will return, etc. Is this likely to be the Case among the Representatives of 13 States —

What is the Fact — Congress has hitherto conducted with great Prudence and Sagacity — the People have been satisfied — Give Congress the same Powers, that you intend to give the two Branches, and I apprehend they will act with as much Propriety and more Energy than the latter.

The Chance for Wisdom greater — Refinement — Secretion —

The Expence will be enormous —

Congress the Sun of our political World.

WILSON

[A — 1] [20]

Propositions

from Virginia	from New Jersey
1. A Legislature consisting of two or three branches	1. A single Legislature.

---

[20] This document was found among the Wilson papers in the Library of the Historical Society of Pennsylvania. It is evidently an outline of Wilson's speech of this

2. On the original Authority of the People	2. On the derivative Authority of the Legislatures of the States
3. Representation of Citizens according to Numbers and Importance	3. Representation of States without Regard to Numbers and Importance
4. A single Executive Magistrate.	4. More than one Executive Magistrate.
5. A Majority empowered to act	5. A small Minority able to control
6. The national Legislature to legislate in all Cases to which the State Legislatures are incompetent, or in which the Harmony of the Union may be interrupted.	6. The United States in Congress vested with additional Powers only in a few inadequate Instances.
7. To negative Laws contrary to the Union or Treaties	7. To call forth the Powers of the confederated States in order [21] to compel Obedience.
8. Executive removeable on Impeachment and Conviction.	8. —— by Congress on Application by a Majority of the Executives of the States.
9. The Executive to have a qualified Negative	9. —— to have none.

day. There is also a preliminary draft which differs from this document mainly in the order of arrangement of the various items.

In the preliminary draft there was a sort of headline:

"I Proper Powers — A Body in which they may be safely lodged". And the first three items were in the order — 2, 3, 1.

[21] Crossed out in the preliminary draft: "To punish Opposition by calling".

10. Provision made for in-   10 ———— None
ferior national Tribunals

11. The Jurisdiction of the   11 ———— Only by Appeal in
national Tribunal to ex-   the dernier Resort.
tend to Cases of national
Revenue.

12. ———— to Questions that   12 ———— Only limited and
may involve the national   appellate Jurisdiction.
Peace

13. The national Govern-   13. The Alterations in the
ment to be ratified under   Confederation must be
the authority of the Peo-   confirmed by the "Legis-
ple by Delegates expressly   latures of every State"
appointed for that Pur-
pose.

[A — 2] [22]

Consider the different Points
in Question — 1. on Principle
— 2. on the declared Sense of
the Committee — 3. By some
striking Instances, which may
happen, if the Plan from New-
Jersey be adopted.

Uncertain what the Sense
of the People is on several
Points —

Reasons why it should be in
Favour of national Government — 1. from Interest — 2.
from Honour.

Distinction between Citizens
and State-Officers.

---

[22] The original document is written on the first three pages of a single folded
sheet. A–2 is written on the first inside page opposite A–3.

Uncertain how long the present Opinion of the People may continue unaltered.

But we mean that our Plan of national Government shall stand or fall by their Opinion.

In forming a Government for the United States two great Objects demand our Attention — 1. That proper Powers be given — 2. That the different Departments of Government be so instituted and arranged that proper Powers may, with Safety, be lodged in them.

The Plan from New-Jersey is liable to three general Objections

[A — 3] [22]

No. 1. 4. 5.)

1. The Government is instituted in an improper Manner —

To secure the Constitution the Legislature must be restrained: It can be restrained only in its Operations: That can be accomplished only by dividing it into distinct and independent Branches.

— legislative Authority single

— executive divided

2. It flows from an illegitimate Sources, the Legislative and Executive Powers of the States, and not

No. 2. 3. 13.)

the People at large.

Inequality of Representa-
tion —
— Great Britain —
Experience of the United
States.
— Solomon.

No. 6. 7. 8. 9. 10. 11. 12.)   3. It provides not sufficiently
for the true Ends of Gov-
ernment.

The legislative and exec-
utive Powers are too feeble
and dependent ——

They and the judicial
Power are too confined.

II. What

MONDAY, JUNE 18, 1787.

JOURNAL
Monday June 18. 1787.

The Order of the day being read.

The House resolved itself into a Committee of the whole House to consider of the State of the American Union

Mr President left the Chair

Mr Gorham took the Chair of the Committee

Mr President resumed the Chair.

Mr Gorham reported from the Committee that the Committee had made a further progress in the matter to them referred: and had directed him to move that they may have leave to sit again

Resolved that this House will to-morrow again resolve itself into a Committee of the whole House to consider of the state of the american Union.

and then the House adjourned till to-morrow at 11 oClock A. M.

In a Committee of the whole House
Monday June 18. 1787
Mr Gorham in the Chair.

It was moved by Mr Dickinson seconded by   to postpone the consideration of the first resolution submitted by Mr Paterson namely. in order to introduce the following.

"Resolved that the articles of confederation ought to be "revised and amended, so as to render the government of "the United States adequate to the Exigencies, the preserva- "tion, and the prosperity of the Union."

And on the question to agree to the same

it passed in the affirmative [Ayes — 10; noes — 0; divided — 1.][1]

---

[1] Vote 64, Detail of Ayes and Noes.

It was then moved and seconded that the Committee do now
rise, report a further progress, and request leave to sit again
The Committee then rose.

DETAIL OF AYES AND NOES

[Beginning of third loose sheet]

New Hampshire	Massachusetts	Rhode Island	Connecticut	New York	New Jersey	Pennsylvania	Delaware	Maryland	Virginia	North Carolina	South Carolina	Georgia	Questions	Ayes	Noes	Divided
[64]	aye		aye	aye	aye	dd	aye	aye	aye	aye	aye	aye	To postpone the first resolution offered by Mr Patterson in order to take up Mr. Dickinson's motion	10		1

MADISON

Monday June 18. in Committee of the whole. on the
propositions of Mr. Patterson & Mr. Randolph.

⟨On motion of Mr. Dickinson to postpone the 1st. Resolution in Mr. Patterson's plan, in order to take up the following.
viz: "that the articles of confederation ought to be revised
and amended so as to render the Government of the U. S.
adequate to the exigencies, the preservation and the prosperity of the union." the postponement was agreed to by 10
States, Pen: divided.⟩[2]

Mr. Hamilton, had been hitherto silent on the business
before the Convention, partly from respect to others whose
superior abilities age & experience rendered him unwilling to
bring forward ideas dissimilar to theirs, and partly from his
delicate situation with respect to his own State, to whose sentiments as expressed by his Colleagues, he could by no means
accede. The crisis however which now marked our affairs,
was too serious to permit any scruples whatever to prevail

---

[2] Taken from *Journal.*

over the duty imposed on every man to contribute his efforts
for the public safety & happiness. He was obliged therefore
to declare himself unfriendly to both plans. He was particularly opposed to that from N. Jersey, being fully convinced,
that no amendment of the confederation, leaving the States
in possession of their sovereignty could possibly answer the
purpose. On the other hand he confessed he was much discouraged by the amazing extent of Country in expecting the
desired blessings from any general sovereignty that could be
substituted. — As to the powers of the Convention, he thought
the doubts started on that subject had arisen from distinctions
& reasonings too subtle.[3] A *federal* Govt. he conceived to
mean an association of independent Communities into one.
Different Confederacies have different powers, and exercise
them in different ways. In some instances the powers are
exercised over collective bodies; in others over individuals. as
in the German Diet — & among ourselves in cases of piracy.
Great latitude therefore must be given to the signification of
the term. The plan last proposed departs itself from the
federal idea, as understood by some, since it is to operate
eventually on individuals. He agreed moreover with the
Honble. gentleman from Va. (Mr. R.) that we owed it to our
Country, to do on this emergency whatever we should deem
essential to its happiness. The States sent us here to provide
for the exigences of the Union. To rely on & propose any plan
not adequate to these exigences, merely because it was not
clearly within our powers, would be to sacrifice the means to
the end. It may be said that the *States* can not *ratify* a
plan not within the purview of the article of Confederation
providing for alterations & amendments. But may not the
States themselves in which no constitutional authority equal
to this purpose exists in the Legislatures, have had in view a
reference to the people at large. In the Senate of N. York,
a proviso was moved, that no act of the Convention should be
binding untill it should be referred to the people & ratified;
and the motion was lost by a single voice only, the reason

---

[3] See above June 16, note 2.

assigned agst. it, being that it ⟨might possibly⟩ be found an inconvenient shackle.

The great question is what provision shall we make for the happiness of our Country? He would first make a comparative examination of the two plans — prove that there were essential defects in both — and point out such changes as might render a *national one*, efficacious. — The great & essential principles necessary for the support of Government. are 1. an active & constant interest in supporting it. This principle does not exist in the States in favor of the federal Govt. They have evidently in a high degree, the esprit de corps. They constantly pursue internal interests adverse to those of the whole. They have their particular debts — their partcular plans of finance &c. all these when opposed to, invariably prevail over the requisitions & plans of Congress. 2. the love of power, Men love power. The same remarks are applicable to this principle. The States have constantly shewn a disposition rather to regain the powers delegated by them than to part with more, or to give effect to what they had parted with. The ambition of their demagogues is known to hate the controul of the Genl. Government. It may be remarked too that the Citizens have not that anxiety [4] to prevent a dissolution of the Genl. Govt as of the particular Govts. A dissolution of the latter would be fatal: of the former would still leave the purposes of Govt. attainable to a considerable degree. Consider what such a State as Virga. will be in a few years, a few compared with the life of nations. How strongly will it feel its importance & self-sufficiency? 3. an habitual attachment of the people. The whole force of this tie is on the side of the State Govt. Its sovereignty is immediately before the eyes of the people: its protection is immediately enjoyed by them. From its hand distributive justice, and all those acts which familiarize & endear Govt. to a people, are dispensed to them. 4. *Force* by which may be understood a *coertion of laws* or *coertion of arms.* Congs. have not the former except in few cases. In particular States, this coercion

---

[4] Crossed out "interest".

is nearly sufficient; tho' he held it in most cases, not entirely
so. A certain portion of military force is absolutely necessary
in large communities. Massts. is now feeling this necessity
& making provision for it. But how can this force be exerted
on the States collectively. It is impossible. It amounts to
a war between the parties. Foreign powers also will not be
idle spectators. They will interpose, the confusion will increase, and a dissolution of the Union ensue. 5. *influence.*
he did not ⟨mean⟩ corruption, but a dispensation of those
regular honors & emoluments, which produce an attachment
to the Govt. almost all the weight of these is on the side of
the States; and must continue so as long as the States continue
to exist. All the passions then we see, of avarice, ambition,
interest, which govern most individuals, and all public bodies,
fall into the current of the States, and do not flow in the stream
of the Genl. Govt. the former therefore will generally be an
overmatch for the Genl. Govt. and render any confederacy, in
its very nature precarious. Theory is in this case fully confirmed
by experience. The Amphyctionic Council had it would seem
ample powers for general purposes. It had in particular the
power of fining and using force agst. delinquent members.
What was the consequence. Their decrees were mere signals
of war. The Phocian war is a striking example of it. Philip
at length taking advantage of their disunion, and insinuating
himself into their Councils, made himself master of their
fortunes. The German Confederacy affords another lesson.
The authority of Charlemagne seemed to be as great as could
be necessary. The great feudal chiefs however, exercising
their local sovereignties, soon felt the spirit & found the means
of, encroachments, which reduced the imperial authority to
a nominal sovereignty. The Diet has succeeded, which tho'
aided by a Prince at its head, of great authority independently
of his imperial attributes, is a striking illustration of the weakness of Confederated Governments. Other examples instruct
us in the same truth. The Swiss cantons have scarce any
Union at all, and ⟨have been more than once at⟩ [5] war with

---

[5] Crossed out "are frequently at".

one another — How then are all these evils to be avoided? only by such a compleat sovereignty in the general Govermt. as will turn all the strong principles & passions above mentioned on its side. Does the scheme of N. Jersey produce this effect? does it afford any substantial remedy whatever? On the contrary it labors under great defects, and the defect of some of its provisions will destroy the efficacy of others. It gives a direct revenue to Congs. but this will not be sufficient. The balance can only be supplied by requisitions; which experience proves can not be relied on. If States are to deliberate on the mode, they will also deliberate on the object of the supplies, and will grant or not grant as they approve or disapprove of it. The delinquency of one will invite and countenance it in others. Quotas too must in the nature of things be so unequal as to produce the same evil. To what standard will you resort? Land is a fallacious one. Compare Holland with Russia: France or Engd. with other countries of Europe. Pena. with N. Carolia. will the relative pecuniary abilities in those instances, correspond with the relative value of land. Take numbers of inhabitants for the rule and make like comparison of different countries, and you will find it to be equally unjust. The different degrees of industry and improvement in different Countries render the first object a precarious measure of wealth. Much depends too on *situation.* Cont. N. Jersey & N. Carolina, not being commercial States & contributing to the wealth of the commercial ones, can never bear quotas assessed by the ordinary rules of proportion. They will & must fail ⟨in their duty.⟩ their example will be followed, and the Union itself be dissolved. Whence then is the national revenue to be drawn? from Commerce, even ⟨from⟩ exports which notwithstanding the common opinion are fit objects of moderate taxation, ⟨from⟩ excise, &c &c. These tho' not equal, are less unequal than quotas. Another destructive ingredient in the plan, is that equality of suffrage which is so much desired by the small States. It is not in human nature that Va. & the large States should consent to it, or if they did that they shd. long abide by it. It shocks too much the ideas of Justice, and every human feeling. Bad.

principles in a Govt. tho slow are sure in their operation, and will gradually destroy it. A doubt has been raised whether Congs. at present have a right to keep Ships or troops in time of peace. He leans to the negative. Mr. P.s plan provides no remedy. — If the powers proposed were adequate, the organization of Congs. is such that they could never be properly & effectually exercised. The members of Congs. being chosen by the States & subject to recall, represent all the local prejudices. Should the powers be found effectual, they will from time to time be heaped on them, till a tyrannic sway shall be established. The general power whatever be its form if it preserves itself, must swallow up the State powers. otherwise it will be swallowed up by them. It is agst. all the principles of a good Government to vest the requisite powers in such a body as Congs. Two Sovereignties can not co-exist within the same limits. Giving powers to Congs. must eventuate in a bad Govt. or in no Govt. The plan of N. Jersey therefore will not do. What then is to be done? Here he was embarrassed. The extent of the Country to be governed, discouraged him. The expence of a general Govt. was also formidable; unless there were such a diminution of expence on the side of the State Govts. as the case would admit. If they were extinguished, he was persuaded that great œconomy might be obtained by substituting a general Govt. He did not mean however to shock the public opinion by proposing such a measure. On the other ⟨hand⟩ he saw no *other* necessity for declining it. They are not necessary for any of the great purposes of commerce, revenue, or agriculture. Subordinate authorities he was aware would be necessary. There must be district tribunals: corporations for local purposes. But cui bono, the vast & expensive apparatus now appertaining to the States. The only difficulty of a serious nature which occurred to him, was that of drawing representatives from the extremes to the center of the Community. What inducements can be offered that will suffice? The moderate wages for the 1st. branch, would only be a bait to little demagogues. Three dollars or thereabouts he supposed would be the Utmost. The Senate he feared from a similar cause, would be filled by

certain undertakers who wish for particular offices under the
Govt. This view of the subject almost led him to despair
that a Republican Govt. could be established over so great an
extent. He was sensible at the same time that it would be
unwise to propose one of any other form. In his private
opinion he had no scruple in declaring, supported as he was
by the opinions of so many of the wise & good, that the British
Govt. was the best in the world: and that he doubted much
whether any thing short of it would do in America.[6] He hoped
Gentlemen of different opinions would bear with him in this, and
begged them to recollect the change of opinion on this subject
which had taken place and was still going on. It was once
thought that the power of Congs was amply sufficient to secure
the end of their institution. The error was now seen by every
one. The members most tenacious of republicanism, he observed, were as loud as any in declaiming agst. the vices of
democracy. This progress of the public mind led him to
anticipate the time, when others as well as himself would
join in the praise bestowed by Mr. Neckar on the British
Constitution, namely, that it is the only Govt. in the world
"which unites public strength with individual security." —
In every community where industry is encouraged, there will
be a division of it into the few & the many. Hence separate
interests will arise There will be debtors & Creditors &c.
Give all power to the many, they will oppress the few. Give
all power to the few they will oppress the many. Both therefore ought to have power, that each may defend itself agst.
the other. To the want of this check we owe our paper money
— instalment laws &c To the proper adjustment of it the
British owe the excellence of their Constitution. Their house
of Lords is a most noble institution. Having nothing to hope
for by a change, and a sufficient interest by means of their
property, in being faithful to the National interest, they form
a permanent barrier agst. every pernicious innovation, whether

---

[6] This is doubtless the basis of the charge that in the Convention Hamilton
favored the establishment of a monarchy. See Appendix A, CCXXXIII, CCLXXI,
CCXCII, CCXCIV, CCXCV, CCCIX, CCCXI, CCCXII, CCCXXIV, CCCXXVIII,
CCCLIV, CCCLXVII, CCCLXXX, CCCXCVII.

attempted on the part of the Crown or of the Commons. No temporary Senate will have firmness en'o' to answer the purpose. The Senate ⟨(of Maryland)⟩ which seems to be so much appealed to, has not yet been sufficiently tried. Had the people been unanimous & eager, in the late appeal to them on the subject of a paper emission they would would have yielded to the torrent. Their acquiescing in such an appeal is a proof of it. — Gentlemen differ in their opinions concerning the necessary checks, from the different estimates they form of the human passions. They suppose Seven years a sufficient period to give the Senate an adequate firmness, from not duly considering the amazing violence & turbulence of the democratic spirit. When a great object of Govt. is pursued, which seizes the popular passions, they spread like wild fire, and become irresistable. He appealed to the gentlemen from the N. England States whether experience had not there verified the remark. As to the Executive, it seemed to be admitted that no good one could be established on Republican principles. Was not this giving up the merits of the question; for can there be a good Govt. without a good Executive. The English model was the only good one on this subject. The Hereditary interest of the King was so interwoven with that of the Nation, and his personal emoluments so great, that he was placed above the danger of being corrupted from abroad — and at the same time was both sufficiently independent and sufficiently controuled, to answer the purpose of the institution at home. one of the weak sides of Republics was their being liable to foreign influence & corruption. Men of little character, acquiring great power become easily the tools of intermedling neibours. Sweeden was a striking instance. The French & English had each their parties during the late Revolution which was effected by the predominant influence of the former. What is the inference from all these observations? That we ought to go as far in order to attain stability and permanency, as republican principles will admit. Let one branch of the Legislature hold their places for life or at least during good-behaviour. Let the Executive also be for life. He appealed to the feelings of the members present whether a term of seven years, would induce the sacrifices of private affairs which an acceptance of public trust would require, so so as to ensure the services of the best Citizens. On this plan we should have in the Senate a permanent will, a weighty interest, which would answer essential purposes. But is this a Republican Govt. it will be asked? Yes, if all the Magistrates are appointed, and vacancies are filled, by the people, or a process of election originating with the people. He was sensible that an Executive constituted as he proposed would have in fact but little of the power and independence that might be necessary. On the other plan of appointing him for 7 years, he thought the Executive ought to have but little power. He would be ambitious, with the means of making creatures; and as the object of his ambition wd. be to *prolong* his power, it is probable that in case of a war, he would avail himself of the emergence, to evade or refuse a degradation from his place. An Executive for life has not this motive for forgetting his fidelity, and will therefore be a safer depositary of power. It will be objected probably, that such an Executive will be an *elective Monarch*, and will give birth to the tumults which characterise that form of Govt. He wd. reply that *Monarch* is an indefinite term. It marks not either the degree or duration of power. If this Executive Magistrate wd. be a monarch for life — the other propd. by the Report from the Committee of the whole, wd. be a monarch for seven years. The circumstance of being elective was also applicable to both. It had been observed by judicious writers that elective monarchies wd. be the best if they could be guarded agst. the *tumults* excited by the ambition and intrigues of competitors. He was not sure that tumults were an inseparable evil. He rather thought this character of Elective Monarchies had been taken rather from particular cases than from general principles. The election of Roman Emperors was made by the *Army*. In *Poland* the election is made by great rival *princes* with independent power, and ample means, of raising commotions. In the German Empire, The appointment is made by the Electors & Princes, who have equal motives & means, for exciting cabals & parties. Might ⟨not⟩ such a mode of election be devised among ourselves as will defend the community agst. these effects in any dangerous degree? Having made these observations he would read to the Committee a sketch of a plan which he shd. prefer to either of those under consideration. He was aware that it went beyond the ideas of most members. But will such a plan be adopted out of doors? In return ⟨he would ask⟩ will the people adopt the other plan? At present they will adopt neither. But ⟨he⟩ sees the Union dissolving or already dissolved — he sees evils operating in the States which must soon cure the people of their fondness for democracies — he sees that a great progress has been already made & is still going on in the public mind. He thinks therefore that the people will in time be unshackled from their prejudices; and whenever that happens, they will themselves not be satisfied at stopping where the plan of Mr. R. wd. place them, but be ready to go as far at least as he proposes. He did not mean to offer the paper he had sketched as a proposition to the Committee. It was meant only to give a more correct view of his ideas, and to suggest the amendments which he should probably propose to the plan of Mr. R. in the proper stages of its future discussion. He read his sketch in the words following:[7] towit

I "The Supreme Legislative power of the United States of America to be vested in two different bodies of men; the one to be called the Assembly, the other the Senate who together shall form the Legislature of the United States with power to pass all laws whatsoever subject to the Negative hereafter mentioned.

II The Assembly to consist of persons elected by the people to serve for three years.

III. The Senate to consist of persons elected to serve during good behaviour; their election to be made by electors chosen for that purpose by the people: in order to this the States to be divided into election districts. On the death, removal or resignation of any Senator his place to be filled out of the district from which he came.

---

[7] Several different texts of this document are in existence. For a discussion of these and of Hamilton's more detailed plan given to Madison at the close of the Convention, see Appendix F. See also further references in note 9, below.

IV. The supreme Executive authority of the United States to be vested in a Governour to be elected to serve during good behaviour — the election to be made by Electors chosen by the people in the Election Districts aforesaid —   The authorities & functions of the Executive to be as follows: to have a negative on all laws about to be passed, and the execution of all laws passed, to have the direction of war when authorized or begun; to have with the advice and approbation of the Senate the power of making all treaties; to have the sole appointment of the heads or chief officers of the departments of Finance, War and Foreign Affairs; to have the nomination of all other officers (Ambassadors to foreign Nations included) subject to the approbation or rejection of the Senate; to have the power of pardoning all offences except Treason; which he shall not pardon without the approbation of the Senate.

V. On the death resignation or removal of the Governour his authorities to be exercised by the President of the Senate till a Successor be appointed.

VI The Senate to have the sole power of declaring war, the power of advising and approving all Treaties, the power of approving or rejecting all appointments of officers except the heads or chiefs of the departments of Finance War and foreign affairs.

VII. The Supreme Judicial authority to be vested in Judges to hold their offices during good behaviour with adequate and permanent salaries. This Court to have original jurisdiction in all causes of capture, and an appellative jurisdiction in all causes in which the revenues of the general Government or the citizens of foreign nations are concerned.

VIII. The Legislature of the United States to have power to institute Courts in each State for the determination of all matters of general concern.

IX. The Governour Senators and all officers of the United States to be liable to impeachment for mal — and corrupt conduct; and upon conviction to be removed from office, & disqualified for holding any place of trust or profit — all impeachments to be tried by a Court to consist of the Chief or Judge of the Superior Court of Law of each State, provided such Judge shall hold his place during good behavior, and have a permanent salary.

X All laws of the particular States contrary to the Constitution or laws of the United States to be utterly void; and the better to prevent such laws being passed, the Governour or president of each state shall be appointed by the General Government[8] and shall have a negative upon the laws about to be passed in the State of which he is Governour or President

XI No State to have any forces land or Naval; and the Militia of all the States to be under the sole and exclusive direction of the United States, the officers of which to be appointed and commissioned by them

⟨On these several articles he entered into explanatory observations corresponding with the principles of his introductory reasoning [9]

Comittee rose & the House adjourned.⟩

---

[8] See Appendix A, CCXCVI.

[9] J. C. Hamilton (*History of the Republic of the United States*, III, 283–4), in giving a brief of this speech, states that it "occupied in the delivery between five and six hours, and was pronounced by a competent judge, (Gouverneur Morris), the most able and impressive he had ever heard."

Madison states that Hamilton "happened to call on me when putting the last hand" to the report of this speech. He "acknowledged its fidelity, without suggesting more than a few verbal alterations which were made." See Appendix A, CCCXCV and CCCCI, also CCCXXV, CCCXXIX, CCCXCI.

Gilpin (*Papers of Madison* II, 892–893) prints the following note, which seems to have been inspired if not written by Madison:

"The speech introducing the plan, as above taken down and written out, was seen by Mr. Hamilton, who approved its correctness with one or two verbal changes, which were made as he suggested. The explanatory observations which did not immediately follow, were to have been furnished by Mr. H. who did not find leisure at the time to write them out, and they were not obtained. Judge Yates, in his notes, appears to have consolidated the explanatory with the introductory observations of Mr. Hamilton (under date of June 19th, a typographical error). It was in the former, Mr. Madison observed, that Mr. Hamilton, in speaking of popular governments, however modified, made the remark attributed to him by Judge Yates, that they were '*but pork still, with a little change of sauce.*'"

Hunt makes no reference to this in his *Writings of James Madison*, and the present editor has not found it among the Madison papers.

YATES

MONDAY, JUNE 19th,[10] 1787.

Met pursuant to adjournment.   Present 11 states.

Mr. Hamilton. — To deliver my sentiments on so important a subject, when the first characters in the union have gone before me, inspires me with the greatest diffidence, especially when my own ideas are so materially dissimilar to the plans now before the committee — My situation is disagreeable, but it would be criminal not to come forward on a question of such magnitude.   I have well considered the subject, and am convinced that no amendment of the confederation can answer the purpose of a good government, so long as state sovereignties do, in any shape, exist; and I have great doubts whether a national government on the Virginia plan can be made effectual.   What is federal?   An association of several independent states into one.   How or in what manner this association is formed, is not so clearly distinguishable.   We find the diet of Germany has in some instances the power of legislation on individuals.   We find the United States of America have it in an extensive degree in the cases of piracies.

Let us now review the powers with which we are invested. We are appointed for the *sole* and *express* purpose of revising the confederation, and to *alter* or *amend* it, so as to render it effectual for the purposes of a good government.   Those who suppose it must be federal, lay great stress on the terms *sole* and *express*, as if these words intended a confinement to a federal government; when the manifest import is no more than that the institution of a good government must be the *sole* and *express* object of your deliberations.   Nor can we suppose an annihilation of our powers by forming a national government, as many of the states have made in their constitutions no provision for any alteration; and thus much I can say for the state I have the honor to represent, that when

---

[10] Evidently a mistake for June 18.

our credentials were under consideration in the senate, some members were for inserting a restriction in the powers, to prevent an encroachment on the constitution: it was answered by others, and thereupon the resolve carried on the credentials, that it might abridge some of the constitutional powers of the state, and that possibly in the formation of a new union it would be found necessary. This appears reasonable, and therefore leaves us at liberty to form such a national government as we think best adapted for the good of the whole. I have therefore no difficulty as to the extent of our powers, nor do I feel myself restrained in the exercise of my judgment under them. We can only propose and recommend — the power of ratifying or rejecting is still in the states. But on this great question I am still greatly embarrassed. I have before observed my apprehension of the inefficacy of either plan, and I have great doubts whether a more energetic government can pervade this wide and extensive country. I shall now show that both plans are materially defective.

1. A good government ought to be constant, and ought to contain an active principle.

2. Utility and necessity.

3. An habitual sense of obligation.

4. Force.

5. Influence.

I hold it, that different societies have all different views and interests to pursue, and always prefer local to general concerns. For example: New-York legislature made an external compliance lately to a requisition of congress; but do they not at the same time counteract their compliance by gratifying the local objects of the state so as to defeat their consession? And this will ever be the case. Men always love power, and states will prefer their particular concerns to the general welfare; and as the states become large and important, will they not be less attentive to the general government? What in process of time will Virginia be? She contains now half a million of inhabitants — in twenty-five years she will double the number. Feeling her own weight and importance, must she not become indifferent to the concerns of the union?

And where, in such a situation, will be found national attachment to the general government?

By *force*, I mean the *coercion* of law and the coercion of arms. Will this remark apply to the power intended to be vested in the government to be instituted by their plan? A delinquent must be compelled to obedience by force of arms. How is this to be done? If you are unsuccessful, a dissolution of your government must be the consequence; and in that case the individual legislatures will reassume their powers; nay, will not the interest of the states be thrown into the state governments?

By *influence*, I mean the regular weight and support it will receive from those who will find it their interest to support a government intended to preserve the peace and happiness of the community of the whole. The state governments, by either plan, will exert the means to counteract it. They have their state judges and militia all combined to support their state interests; and these will be influenced to oppose a national government. Either plan is therefore precarious. The national government cannot long exist when opposed by such a weighty rival. The experience of ancient and modern confederacies evince this point, and throw considerable light on the subject. The amphyctionic council of Greece had a right to require of its members troops, money and the force of the country. Were they obeyed in the exercise of those powers? Could they preserve the peace of the greater states and republics? or where were they obeyed? History shows that their decrees were disregarded, and that the stronger states, regardless of their power, gave law to the lesser.

Let us examine the federal institution of Germany. It was instituted upon the laudable principle of securing the independency of the several states of which it was composed, and to protect them against foreign invasion. Has it answered these good intentions? Do we not see that their councils are weak and distracted, and that it cannot prevent the wars and confusions which the respective electors carry on against each other? The Swiss cantons, or the Helvetic union, are equally inefficient.

Such are the lessons which the experience of others affords us, and from whence results the evident conclusion that all federal governments are weak and distracted. To avoid the evils deducible from these observations, we must establish a general and national government, completely sovereign, and annihilate the state distinctions and state operations; and unless we do this, no good purpose can be answered. What does the Jersey plan propose? It surely has not this for its object. By this we grant the regulation of trade and a more effectual collection of the revenue, and some partial duties. These, at five or ten per cent, would only perhaps amount to a fund to discharge the debt of the corporation.

Let us take a review of the variety of important objects, which must necessarily engage the attention of a national government. You have to protect your rights against Canada on the north, Spain on the south, and your western frontier against the savages. You have to adopt necessary plans for the settlement of your frontiers, and to institute the mode in which settlements and good government are to be made.

How is the expense of supporting and regulating these important matters to be defrayed? By requisition on the states, according to the Jersey plan? Will this do it? We have already found it ineffectual. Let one state prove delinquent, and it will encourage others to follow the example; and thus the whole will fail. And what is the standard to quota among the states their respective proportions? Can lands be the standard? How would that apply between Russia and Holland? Compare Pennsylvania with North-Carolina, or Connecticut with New-York. Does not commerce or industry in the one or other make a great disparity between these different countries, and may not the comparative value of the states from these circumstances, make an unequal disproportion when the data is numbers? I therefore conclude that either system would ultimately destroy the confederation, or any other government which is established on such fallacious principles. Perhaps imposts, taxes on specific articles, would produce a more equal system of drawing a revenue.

Another objection against the Jersey plan is, the unequal

representation. Can the great states consent to this? If they did it would eventually work its own destruction. How are forces to be raised by the Jersey plan? By quotas? Will the states comply with the requisition? As much as they will with the taxes.

Examine the present confederation, and it is evident they can raise no troops nor equip vessels before war is actually declared. They cannot therefore take any preparatory measure before an enemy is at your door. How unwise and inadequate their powers! and this must ever be the case when you attempt to define powers. — Something will always be wanting. Congress, by being annually elected, and subject to recall, will ever come with the prejudices of their states rather than the good of the union. Add therefore additional powers to a body thus organized, and you establish a *sovereignty* of the worst kind, consisting of a single body. Where are the checks? None. They must either prevail over the state governments, or the prevalence of the state governments must end in their dissolution. This is a conclusive objection to the Jersey plan.

Such are the insuperable objections to both plans: and what is to be done on this occasion? I confess I am at a loss. I foresee the difficulty on a consolidated plan of drawing a representation from so extensive a continent to one place. What can be the inducements for gentlemen to come 600 miles to a national legislature? The expense would at least amount to £100,000. This however can be no conclusive objection if it eventuates in an extinction of state governments. The burthen of the latter would be saved, and the expense then would not be great. State distinctions would be found unnecessary, and yet I confess, to carry government to the extremities, the state governments reduced to corporations, and with very limited powers, might be necessary, and the expense of the national government become less burthensome.

Yet, I confess, I see great difficulty of drawing forth a good representation. What, for example, will be the inducements for gentlemen of fortune and abilities to leave their houses and business to attend annually and long? It cannot be the wages; for these, I presume, must be small. Will not the power, therefore, be thrown into the hands of the demagogue or middling politician, who, for the sake of a small stipend and the hopes of advancement, will offer himself as a candidate, and the real men of weight and influence, by remaining at home, add strength to the state governments? I am at a loss to know what must be done — I despair that a republican form of government can remove the difficulties. Whatever may be my opinion, I would hold it however unwise to change that form of government. I believe the British government forms the best model the world ever produced, and such has been its progress in the minds of the many, that this truth gradually gains ground. This government has for its object *public strength* and *individual security*. It is said with us to be unattainable. If it was once formed it would maintain itself. All communities divide themselves into the few and the many. The first are the rich and well born, the other the mass of the people. The voice of the people has been said to be the voice of God; and however generally this maxim has been quoted and believed, it is not true in fact. The people are turbulent and changing; they seldom judge or determine right. Give therefore to the first class a distinct, permanent share in the government. They will check the unsteadiness of the second, and as they cannot receive any advantage by a change, they therefore will ever maintain good government. Can a democratic assembly, who annually revolve in the mass of the people, be supposed steadily to pursue the public good? Nothing but a permanent body can check the imprudence of democracy. Their turbulent and uncontrouling disposition requires checks. The senate of New-York, although chosen for four years, we have found to be inefficient. Will, on the Virginia plan, a continuance of seven years do it? It is admitted that you cannot have a good executive upon a democratic plan. See the excellency of the British executive — He is placed above temptation — He can have no distinct interests from the public welfare. Nothing short of such an executive can be efficient. The weak side of a republican government is the danger of foreign influence. This is unavoidable, unless it is so constructed as to bring forward its first characters in its support. I am therefore for a general government, yet would wish to go the full length of republican principles.

Let one body of the legislature be constituted during good behaviour or life.

Let one executive be appointed who dares execute his powers.

It may be asked is this a republican system? It is strictly so, as long as they remain elective.

And let me observe, that an executive is less dangerous to the liberties of the people when in office during life, than for seven years.

It may be said this constitutes an elective monarchy? Pray what is a monarchy? May not the governors of the respective states be considered in that light? But by making the executive subject to impeachment, the term monarchy cannot apply. These elective monarchs have produced tumults in Rome, and are equally dangerous to peace in Poland; but this cannot apply to the mode in which I would propose the election. Let electors be appointed in each of the states to elect the executive — (*Here Mr. H. produced his plan, a copy whereof is hereunto annexed*)[11] to consist of two branches — and I would give them the unlimited power of passing *all laws* without exception. The assembly to be elected for three years by the people in districts — the senate to be elected by electors to be chosen for that purpose by the people, and to remain in office during life. The executive to have the power of negativing all laws — to make war or peace, with the advice of the senate — to make treaties with their advice, but to have the sole direction of all military operations, and to send ambassadors and appoint all military officers, and to pardon all offenders, treason excepted, unless by advice of the senate. On his death or removal, the president of the senate to officiate, with the same powers, until another is elected. Supreme

---

[11] Not found, see *Records*, July 5, note 18.

judicial officers to be appointed by the executive and the senate. The legislature to appoint courts in each state, so as to make the state governments unnecessary to it.

All state laws to be absolutely void which contravene the general laws. An officer to be appointed in each state to have a negative on all state laws. All the militia and the appointment of officers to be under the national government.

I confess that this plan and that from Virginia are very remote from the idea of the people. Perhaps the Jersey plan is nearest their expectation. But the people are gradually ripening in their opinions of government — they begin to be tired of an excess of democracy — and what even is the Virginia plan, but *pork still, with a little change of the sauce.*[12]

Then adjourned to to-morrow.

KING [13]

Federal is an association of distinct Govts: into one — these fed. Govts. in some instances legislate on collective bodies, in others on individuals. The Confederation partakes of both — Piracies are cognizable by the Congress — &c.

Our powers have this object — the Freedom & Happiness of our Country — we must go all lengths to accomplish this Object — if the Legislatures have no powers to ratify because thereby they diminish their own Sovereignty the people may come in on revolution Principles —

We have power,

Upon the plan of the separation & indipendence of the States, you incourage those Habits, and opinions, that Esprit de Corps which is peculiar to the State and to every individual. These habits prefer their own State to those of the Genl. or fed. Govt. — this has been the case, State Debts, State Crs. have always stood before the fedl. Debr or Cr. —

---

[12] See Appendix A, CCCIII, CCCXCV. *Cf.* Genet's version of this speech in Appendix A, CCCX.

[13] Although there is no indication in the MS., these notes by King so evidently refer to Hamilton's speech of this date that they are inserted here without hesitation.

Man loves power — State Magistrates will desire to increase yr. own power at the Expense of the Genl. or fed. Govt.

One great objt. of Govt. is personal protection and the security of Property — if you establish a federal Govt. men will not be interested in the protection or preservation of the Genl. Govt. but they will in the existence of the State Govts. if the latter is dissolved and the former remains their persons & fortune will be safe — Besides the large States will be indisposed to remain connected —

Habits of obedience

Men will see their fortunes secured, their persons protected, offenders punished by State laws and State magistrates — they will love the Govt. that is thus immediate —

Force

The Force of law or the strength of Arms — The former is inefficient unless the people have the habits of Obedience — in this case you must have Arms — if this doctrine is applied to States — the system is utopian — you could not coerce Virgina — a fedl. Govt: is impracticable — you must call in foreign powers to aid the Genl. Govt. agt. the individual States — this will desolve the Union and destroy your Freedom

Influence

No govt. will be good without Influence. that is unless Men of Merit or the Pillars of Govt. are rewarded with Offices of Honor & Profit — the State Govts. have this influence — the fed. Govt. will be without it — this being true the Genl. Govt. will fail — as long as the States are rivals of the Genl. Govt. so long the Genl. will be subordinate —

How does History illustrate this point

The amphictions — had power to levy money men &c on the States — it was peculiarly federal — when a State failed the Amphictions fined — this was the case of the Phocians when Philip interposed —

Germany

their Diets are as weak as the amphictions, although the Emperor is bound to carry their Decrees into Execution — they put an Electorate under the Ban, & the Electorate puts the Diet & the Emperor at Defiance —

Switzerland

Their Diet is divided, their union is destroyed — part are in alliance wh France and the other part wh the U Netherlands

The Result is that all the passions of avarice, pride, ambition &c. shd. depend on the Genl. & not the State Govts. — you must make the national Sovereignty transcendent & entire —

The plan of N. Jersey

It proposes Requisitions on the States for such monies as the Impost does not yield — States will not comply — they have not — you have no standard to Quote

Numbers or Lands will not be a just Standard — an equal Difficulty arises in the Quotas of men — the States find men only in proportion to their Zeal — this was the Case in the late war — they cannot now obtain an honest adjustment of yr. Expence — for this gave large pecuniary bounties —

The Hic labor the hoc Opus is
the *Genl. Government*

The Extent of Territory, the Variety of Opinions, & numerous considerations, seem to prevent a General Govt: The expence of the Genl. Govt. is important — not less yn. 100,000£ an y

How will you induce Genl. to come into the Genl. Govt. — what will be yr. inducement: you can give them perhaps 3 Dols. pr. Diem. Men of first consequence will not come forward — it will be managed by undertakers & not by the most able hands — I fear Republicanism will not answr. and yet we cannot go beyond it — I think the British Govt. is the only proper one for such an extensive Country — this govt. unites the highest public strength with the most perfect individual security — we are not in a situation to receive it

— perhaps if it was established it wd. maintain itself — I am however sensible that it can't be established by consent, and we ought not to think of other means — We may attempt a general & not a federal Govt: let the senate hold yr. office for life or during good behavior; so of the Executive — This is republican if the people elect and also fill vacancies

HAMILTON[14]

Introduction

I Importance of the occasion

II — Solid *plan* without regard to *temporary opinion.*

III — If an ineffectual plan be again proposed it will beget despair & no government will grow out of consent

I [15] — Objections to the present confederation

I Entrusts the great interests of the nation to hands incapable of managing them —

All matters in which foreigners are concerned —

The care of the public peace: Debts

Power of treaty without power of execution

Common defence without power to raise troops have a fleet — raise money

— Power to contract debts without the power to pay —

— These great interests of the state must be well managed or the public prosperity must be the victim —

Legislates upon communities —

Where the legislatures are to act they will deliberate —

No sanction — { To ask money not to collect — & by an unjust measure

IV There seem to be but three lines of conduct.

I A league offensive and defensive, treaty of commerce, & apportionment of the public debt.

II An amendment of the present confederation by

---

[14] J. C. Hamilton (*Life of Hamilton*, II, 481–489) gives a similar outline. The important differences between that and the one in the text are noted.

[15] The matter here printed between III and IV is on the left-hand page opposite a brace, which appears intended to effect this sequence.

adding such powers as the public mind seems nearest being matured to grant.

III — The forming a new government to pervade the whole with decisive powers in short with complete sovereignty.

B — Last seems to be the prevailing sentiment —

I Its practicability to be examined —

    Immense extent unfavourable to representation —

    Vast expence —

    double setts of officers —

    Difficulty of judging of local circumstances —

☞   Distance has a physical effect upon mens minds —

    Difficulty of drawing proper characters from home —

    — Execution of laws feeble at a distance from government — particularly in the collection of revenue —

    Sentiment of Obedience ⎤
    Opinion   ⎦

C[16] — Amendment of Confederation according to present Ideas

    1 — Difficult because not agreed upon any thing

        Ex — *Impost*

            Commerce different *Theories* —

    — To ascertain the practicability of this let us examine the principles of civil obedience —

    Supports of Government —

    I — Interest to support it

    II — Opinion of Utility & necessity

    III Habitual sense of obligation

    IV — Force

    V — Influence.

I C   I   Interest

        Particular & general *interests*

        Esprit de Corps —

        — *Vox* populi *vox Dei*

---

[16] J. C. Hamilton inserts here the extract included above between III and IV.

II	II — Opinion of Utility & necessity
	1 — First will decrease with the growth of the *states*.
III [17]	III *Necessity*
	This does not apply to Fœderal Government —
	This may dissolve & yet the order of the community continue —
	Anarchy not a necessary consequence
IV	Habitual sense of obligation.
	This results from administration of private justice —
	Demand of service or money odious —
V	Force of two kinds.
	Coertion of laws *Coertion* of arms.
	First does *not exist* — & the last *useless* —
	Attempt to *use it* a war between the states —
	Foreign aid —
	Delinquency not confined to one.
VI —	Influence
	1 " from municipal Jurisdiction
	2 " appointment of Officers —
	4 [18] Military Jurisdiction
	5 Fiscal Jurisdiction

D   All these now reside in particular states

— Their governments are the chief sources of honor and emolument.

— *Ambition* Avarice.

To effect any thing Passions must be turned towards general government —?

Present Confederation cannot be amended unless the most important powers be given to Congress constituted as they are —

This would be liable to all objections against any form

---

[17] J. C. Hamilton drops out "III" before "Necessity" and inserts it where "IV" stands in the text, and changes the other numbers "IV" and "V" so as to make them correspond to the subjects and numbers in the summary which precedes.

[18] "Fiscal Jurisdiction" was originally placed between "2" and "4" and numbered "3". It was then struck out, and the original numbering left unchanged. J. C. Hamilton revised the numbering.

of general government with the addition of the want
of *Checks* —

E Perpetual effort in each member
  Influence of Individuals in office employed to excite
  jealousy & clamour
 State leaders
    Experience corresponds
    Grecian Republics
    Demosthenes says
      Athens 73 years
      Lacedaemon 27 —
      Thebans after battle of Leuctra —
      Phocians consecrated ground
      Philip &c

F Germanic *Empire*
  Charlemagne & his successors
  Diet Recesses —
  Electors now 7 excluding other

G Swiss Cantons
 Two diets —
 opposite *alliances* —
 Berne Lucerne
 To strengthen the Foerderal government powers too great
  must be given to a single branch

H Leage Offensive & Defensive &c
  particular Govs. might exert themselves &c
  But liable to usual Vicissi —
  — Internal Peace affected —
  Proximity of situation — natural enemies —
  Partial confederacies from unequal extent
  Power inspires ambition —
  Weakness begets jealousy
  Western territory —

Obj: Genius of republics pacific —

Answer — Jealousy of commerce as well as jealousy of power
    begets war —
      Sparta Athens Thebes Rome Carthage Venice
      Hanseatic Leage

England as many
Popular as Royal Wars
Lewis the 14h *Austria Bourbon* William & Anne —

Wars depend on triffling circumstances everywhere
        Dutchess of Malboroughs Glove
Foreign Conquest —
Dismemberment — Poland —
Foreign Influence —
Distractions set afloat Vicious humour
Standing armies by dissensions
Domestic Factions —
Montesquieu —
Monarchy in Southern States —

☞ Foederal Rights *Fisheries* —
        Wars destructive

I   Loss of advantages —
— Foreign Nations would not respect our rights nor grant
        us reciprocity —
Would reduce us to a passive Commerce
— Fisheries Navigation of the lakes, of the Mississippi
Fleet

The [19] general government must, in this case, not only have a strong soul, but *strong organs* by which that soul is to operate.

Here I shall give my sentiments of the best form of government — not as a thing attainable by us, but as a model which we ought to approach as near as possible.

British constitution best form.

Aristotle — Cicero — Montesquieu — Neckar.

Society naturally divides itself into two political divisions — the *few* and the *many*, who have distinct interests.

If government in the hands of the *few*, they will tyrannize over the many.

If [in] the hands of the many, they will tyrannize over the few.   It ought to be in the hands of both; and they should be separated.

---

[19] The remainder of this outline is taken from J. C. Hamilton's *Life of Hamilton.* It does not seem to be among the Hamilton MSS. in the Library of Congress.

This separation must be permanent.

Representation alone will not do.

Demagogues will generally prevail.

And if separated, they will need a mutual check.

This check is a monarch.

Each principle ought to exist in full force, or it will not answer its end.

The democracy must be derived immediately from the people.

The aristocracy ought to be entirely separated; their power should be permanent, and they should have the *caritas liberorum.*

They should be so circumstanced that they can have no interest in a change — as to have an effectual weight in the constitution.

Their duration should be the earnest of wisdom and stability.

'Tis essential there should be a permanent will in a community.

Vox populi, vox Dei.

Source of government — the unreasonableness of the people — separate interests — debtors and creditors, &c.

There ought to be a principle in government capable of resisting the popular current.

No periodical duration will come up to this.

This will always imply hopes and fears.

Creature and Creator.

Popular assemblies governed by a few individuals.

These individuals seeing their dissolution approach, will sacrifice.

The principle of representation will influence.

The most popular branch will acquire an influence over the other.

The other may check in ordinary cases, in which there is no strong public passion; but it will not in cases where there is — the cases in which such a principle is most necessary.

☞   Suppose duration seven years, and rotation.

One-seventh will have only one year to serve.

One-seventh—————————————two years.
One-seventh—————————————three years.
One-seventh—————————————four years.

A majority will look to a dissolution in four years by instalments.

The monarch must have proportional strength. He ought to be hereditary, and to have so much power, that it will not be his interest to risk much to acquire more.

The advantage of a monarch is this — he is above corruption — he must always intend, in respect to foreign nations, the true interest and glory of the people.

Republics liable to foreign corruption and intrigue — Holland — Athens.

Effect of the British government.

> A vigorous execution of the laws — and a vigorous defence of the people, will result.

> Better chance for a good administration.

> It is said a republican government does not admit a vigorous execution.

> It is therefore bad; for the goodness of a government consists in a vigorous execution.

The principle chiefly intended to be established is this — that there must be a permanent *will*.

Gentlemen say we need to be rescued from the democracy. But what the means proposed?

A democratic assembly is to be checked by a democratic senate, and both these by a democratic chief magistrate.

The end will not be answered — the means will not be equal to the object.

It will, therefore, be feeble and inefficient.

RECAPITULATION

I. Impossible to secure the union by any modification of foederal government.

II. League, offensive, and defensive, full of certain evils and greater dangers.

III. General government, very difficult, if not impracticable, liable to various objections.

What is to be done?

Answer. Balance inconveniences and dangers, and choose that which seems to have the fewest objections.

Expense admits of this answer. The expense of the state governments will be proportionably diminished.

Interference of officers not so great, because the objects of the general government and the particular ones will not be the same—Finance—Administration of private justice Energy will not be wanting in essential points, because the administration of private justice will be carried home to men's doors by the particular governments.

And the revenues may be collected from imposts, excises &c. If necessary to go further, the general government may make use of the particular governments.

The attendance of members near the seat of government may be had in the lower branch.

And the upper branch may be so constructed as to induce the attendance of members from any part.

But this proves that the government must be so constituted as to offer strong motives.

In short, to interest all the *passions* of individuals.

And turn them into that channel.

TUESDAY, JUNE 19, 1787.

Tuesday June 19. 1787.

The Order of the day being read

The House resolved itself into a Committee of the whole House to consider of the state of the American Union.

Mr President left the Chair

Mr Gorham took the Chair of the Committee

Mr President resumed the Chair.

Mr Gorham reported from the Committee that the Committee, having spent some time in the consideration of the propositions submitted to the House by the honorable Mr Paterson — and of the resolutions heretofore reported from a Committee of the whole House, both of which had been to them referred, were prepared to report thereon — and had directed him to report to the House that the Committee do not agree to the propositions offered by the honorable Mr Paterson — and that they again submit the resolutions, formerly reported, to the consideration of the House.

It was then moved and seconded to postpone the consideration of the first resolution, reported from the Committee till to-morrow.

and on the question to postpone
it passed in the affirmative

And then the House adjourned till to-morrow at 11 o'Clock A. M.

In a Committee of the whole House

Tuesday June 19. 1787

Mr Gorham in the Chair

On a question to adopt Mr Dickinson's motion — moved yesterday —

it passed in the negative   [Ayes — 4; noes — 6; divided — 1.]
It was then moved and seconded to postpone the consideration of the first proposition offered by Mr Paterson.
            passed in the affirmative   [Ayes — 9; noes — 2.]
It was then moved and seconded that the Committee do now
rise — and report to the House that they do not agree to the
propositions offered by the honorable Mr Paterson — and that
they report the resolutions offered by the honorable Mr Randolph, heretofore reported from a Committee of the whole
House
passed in the affirmative   [Ayes — 7; noes — 3; divided — 1.]
    The Committee then rose.

DETAIL OF AYES AND NOES

New Hampshire	Massachusetts	Rhode Island	Connecticut	New York	New Jersey	Pennsylvania	Delaware	Maryland	Virginia	North Carolina	South Carolina	Georgia	Questions	Ayes	Noes	Divided
[65]	no		aye	aye	aye	no	aye	dd	no	no	no	no	To adopt Mr Dickinson's motion offered as a substitute for Mr Paterson's	4	6	1
[66]	aye		aye	no	no	aye	aye	aye	aye	aye	aye	aye	To postpone the first proposition offered by Mr Paterson	9	2	
[67]	aye		aye	no	no	aye	no	dd	aye	aye	aye	aye	not to agree to the Jersey propositions but to report those offered by Mr Randolph	7	3	1

MADISON

Teusday June 19th. in Committee of whole. on the propositions
of Mr. Patterson.

⟨The Substitute offered yesterday by Mr. Dickenson being
rejected by a vote now taken on it; Con. N. Y. N. J. Del.
ay. Mas. Pa. V. N. C. S. C. Geo. no Mayd. divided Mr. Patterson's plan was again at large before the Committee ⟩[1]

---

[1] Taken from *Journal.*

Mr. M⟨adison⟩.   Much stress had been laid by some gentlemen on the want of power in the Convention to propose any
other than a *federal* plan.[2] To what had been answered by
others, he would only add, that neither of the characteristics
attached to a *federal* plan would support this objection.   One
characteristic, was that in a *federal* Government, the power was
exercised not on the people individually; but on the people
collectively, on the *States*.   Yet in some instances as in piracies, captures &c. the existing Confederacy, and in many
instances, the amendments to it ⟨proposed by Mr. Patterson⟩
must operate immediately on individuals.   The other characteristic was, that a *federal* Govt. derived its appointments not
immediately from the people, but from the States which they
respectively composed.   Here too were facts on the other side.
In two of the States, Connect. and Rh. Island, the delegates to
Congs. were chosen, not by the Legislatures, but by the people
at large; and the plan of Mr. P. intended no change in this
particular.

It had been alledged (by Mr. Patterson) that the Confederation having been formed by unanimous consent, could be
dissolved by unanimous Consent only   Does this doctrine
result from the nature of compacts? does it arise from any
particular stipulation in the articles of Confederation? If we
consider the federal union as analagous to the fundamental
compact by which individuals compose one Society, and which
must in its theoretic origin at least, have been the unanimous
act of the component members, it cannot be said that no dissolution of the compact can be effected without unanimous
consent.   a breach of the fundamental principles of the compact by a part of the Society would certainly absolve the other
part from their obligations to it.[3] If the breach of *any* article
by *any* of the parties, does not set the others at liberty, it is
because, the contrary is *implied* in the compact itself, and
particularly by that law of it, which gives an indefinite author-

---

[2] See above June 16, note 2.
[3] Crossed out as the next sentence: "Again a fundamental base of Civil Society
the social compact is that a majority in preserving the objects of the compact, the
majority shall in all cases   But to be satisfied".

ity to the majority to bind the whole in all cases.   This latter circumstance shews that we are not to consider the federal Union as analogous to the social compact of individuals: for if it were so, a Majority would have a right to bind the rest, and even to form a new Constitution for the whole, which the Gentn: from N. Jersey would be among the last to admit. If we consider the federal union as analogous not to the ⟨social⟩ compacts among individual men: but to the conventions among individual States.   What is the doctrine resulting from these conventions? [4]   Clearly, according to the Expositors of the law of Nations, that a breach of any one article, by any one party, leaves all the other parties at liberty, to consider the whole convention as dissolved, unless they choose rather to compel the delinquent party to repair the breach.   In some treaties indeed it is expressly stipulated that a violation of particular articles shall not have this consequence, and even that particular articles shall remain in force during war, which in general is understood to dissolve all susbsisting Treaties. But are there any exceptions of this sort to the Articles of confederation?   So far from it that there is not even an express stipulation that force shall be used to compell an offending member of the Union to discharge its duty.   He observed that the violations of the federal articles had been numerous & notorious.   Among the most notorious was an Act of N. Jersey herself; by which she *expressly refused* to comply with a constitutional requisition of Congs. — and yielded no farther to the expostulations of their deputies, than barely to rescind her vote of refusal without passing any positive act of compliance.   He did not wish to draw any rigid inferences from these observations.   He thought it proper however that the true nature of the existing confederacy should be investigated, and he was not anxious to strengthen the foundations on which it now stands

Proceeding to the consideration of Mr. Patterson's plan, he stated the object of a proper plan to be twofold.   1. to preserve the Union.   2. to provide a Governmt. that will remedy [5]

---

[4] Crossed out: "is that the intention of the parties?"   [5] Crossed out "all".

the evils felt by the States[6] both in their united and individual capacities. Examine Mr. P.s plan, & say whether it promises satisfaction in these respects.

1. Will it prevent those violations of the law of nations & of Treaties which if not prevented must involve us in the calamities of foreign wars? The tendency of the States to these violations has been manifested in sundry instances. The files of Congs. contain complaints already, from almost every nation with which treaties have been formed. Hitherto indulgence has been shewn to us. This cannot be the permanent disposition of foreign nations. A rupture with other powers is among the greatest of national calamities. It ought therefore to be effectually provided that no part of a nation shall have it in its power to bring them on the whole. The existing confederacy does ⟨not⟩ sufficiently provide against this evil. The proposed amendment to it does not supply the omission. It leaves the will of the States as uncontrouled as ever.

2. Will it prevent encroachments on the federal authority? A tendency to such encroachments has been sufficiently exemplified among ourselves, as well in every other confederated republic antient and Modern. By the federal articles, transactions with the Indians appertain to Congs. Yet in several instances, the States[7] have entered into treaties & wars with them. In like manner no two or more States can form among themselves any treaties &c without the consent of Congs. yet Virga & Maryd in one instance — Pena. & N. Jersey in another, have entered into compacts, without previous application or subsequent apology. No State again can of right raise troops in time of peace without the like consent [8] Of all cases of the league, this seems to require the most scrupulous observance. Has not Massts, notwithstanding, the most powerful member of the Union, already raised a body of troops? Is she not now augmenting them, without having even deigned to apprise Congs. of Her intention? In fine Have we not seen the public

---

[6] Crossed out "U. S."   [7] Crossed out "in question Georgia".

[8] Madison originally had written but struck out as the beginning of the sentence after "consent": "If any usurpation in the federal authority be worthy attention".

land dealt out to Cont. to bribe her acquiescence in the decree constitutionally awarded agst. her claim on the territory of Pena. —? for no other possible motive can account for the policy of Congs. in that measure? — if we recur to the examples of other confederacies, we shall find in all of them the same tendency of the parts to encroach on the authority of the whole. He then reviewed the Amphyctrionic & Achæan confederacies among the antients, and the Helvetic, Germanic & Belgic among the moderns, tracing their analogy to the U. States [9] — in the constitution and extent of their federal authorities — in the tendency of the particular members to usurp on these authorities; and [10] to bring confusion & ruin on the whole. — He observed that the plan of Mr. Pat—son besides omitting a controul over the States as a general defence of the federal prerogatives was particularly defective in two of its provisions. 1. Its ratification was not to be by the people at large, but by the *Legislatures*. It could not therefore render the acts of Congs. in pursuance of their powers even legally *paramount* to the Acts of the States. 2. It gave ⟨to the federal tribunal⟩ an appellate jurisdiction only — even in the criminal cases enumerated, The necessity of any such provision supposed a danger of undue acquittals in the State tribunals. Of what avail wd. an appellate tribunal be, after an acquttal? Besides in most if not all of the States, the Executives have by their respective *Constitutions* the right of pardg. How could this be taken from them by a *legislative ratification* only?

3. Will it prevent trespasses of the States on each other? Of these enough has been already seen. He instanced Acts of Virga. & Maryland which give a preference to their own citizens in cases where the Citizens ⟨of other states⟩ [11] are entitled to equality of privileges by the Articles of Confederation. He considered the emissions of paper money ⟨& other kindred measures⟩[11] as also aggressions. The States relatively to one an other being each of them either Debtor or Creditor;

---

[9] Crossed out "vesting their federal authorities both".
[10] Crossed out "in the obstinacy which".
[11] Probably but not certainly a later insertion.

The Creditor States must suffer unjustly from every emission by the debtor States. We have seen retaliating acts on this subject which threatened danger not to the harmony only, but the tranquillity of the Union. The plan of Mr. Paterson, not giving even a negative on the Acts of the States, left them as much at liberty as ever to execute their unrighteous projects agst. each other.

4. Will it secure [12] the internal tranquillity of the States themselves? The insurrections in Massts. admonished all the States of the danger to which they were exposed. Yet the plan of Mr. P. contained no provisions for supplying the defect of the Confederation on this point. According to the Republican theory indeed, Right & power being both vested in the majority, are held to be synonimous. According to fact & experience, a minority may in an appeal to force be an overmatch for the majority. 1. If the minority happen to include all such as possess the skill & habits of military life, with such as possess the great pecuniary resources, one third [13] may conquer the remaining two thirds. 2. one third of those who participate in the choice of rulers may be rendered a majority by the accession of those whose poverty disqualifies them from a suffrage, & who for obvious reasons may be more ready to join the standard of sedition than that of the established Government. 3. Where slavery exists, the Republican Theory becomes still more fallacious.

5. Will it secure a good internal legislation & administration to the particular States? In developing the evils which vitiate the political system of the U. S. it is proper to take into view those which prevail within the States individually as well as those which affect them collectively: Since the former indirectly affect the whole; and there is great reason to believe that the pressure of them had a full share in the motives which produced the present Convention. Under this head he enumerated and animadverted on 1. the multiplicity of the laws passed by the several States. 2. the mutability of their laws. 3. the injustice of them. 4. the impotence of

---

[12] Crossed out "a good internal Legis".   [13] Crossed out "or less".

them: observing that Mr. Patterson's plan contained no remedy for this dreadful class of evils, and could not therefore be received as an adequate provision for the exigencies of the Community.

6. Will it secure the Union agst. the influence of foreign powers over its members. He pretended not to say that any such influence had yet been tried: but it naturally to be expected that occasions would produce it. As lessons which claimed particular attention, he cited the intrigues practiced among the Amphictionic Confederates first by the Kings of Persia, and afterwards fatally by Philip of Macedon: Among the Achæans, first by Macedon & afterwards no less fatally by Rome: Among the Swiss by Austria, France & the lesser neighbouring Powers; among the members of the Germanic ⟨Body⟩ by France, England,[14] Spain & Russia —: and in the Belgic Republic, by all the great neighbouring powers. The plan of Mr. Patterson, not giving to the general Councils any negative on the will of the particular States, left the door open for the [15] like pernicious machinations among ourselves.

7. He begged the smaller States which were most attached to Mr. Pattersons plan to consider the situation in which it would leave them. In the first place they would continue to bear the whole expense of maintaining their Delegates in Congress. It ought not to be said that if they were willing to bear this burden, no others had a right to complain. As far as it led the small States to forbear keeping up a representation, by which the public business was delayed, it was evidently a matter of common concern. An examination of the minutes of Congress would satisfy every one that the public business had been frequently delayed by this cause; and that the States most frequently unrepresented in Congs. were not the larger States. He reminded the convention of another consequence of leaving on a small State the burden of Maintaining a Representation in Congs. During a considerable period of the War, one of the Representatives of Delaware, in whom alone before the signing of the Confederation the entire

---

[14] Crossed out "Prussia".   [15] Crossed out "same invidious policy from same".

vote of that State and after that event one half of its vote, frequently resided, was a Citizen & Resident of Pena. and held an office in his own State incompatible with an appointment from it to Congs.   During another period, the same State was represented by three delegates two of whom were citizens of Penna. — and the third a Citizen of New Jersey.[16]   These expedients must have been intended to avoid the burden of supporting delegates from their own State.   But whatever might have been ye. cause, was not in effect the vote of one State doubled, and the influence of another increased by it? ⟨In the 2d. place⟩ The coercion, on which the efficacy of the plan depends, can never be exerted but on themselves.   The larger States will be impregnable, the smaller only can feel the vengeance of it.   He illustrated the position by the history of the Amphyctionic Confederates: and the ban of the German Empire,   It was the cobweb wch. could entangle the weak, but would be the sport of the strong.

8. He begged them to consider the situation in which they would remain in case their pertinacious adherence to an inadmissable plan, should prevent the adoption of any plan.   The contemplation of such an event was painful; but it would be prudent to submit to the task of examining it at a distance, that the means of escaping it might be the more readily embraced.   Let the union of the States be dissolved and one of two consequences must happen.   Either the States must remain individually independent & sovereign; or two or more Confederacies must be formed among them.   In the first event would the small States be more secure agst. the ambition & power of their larger neighbours, than they would be under a general Government pervading with equal energy every part of the Empire, and having an equal interest in protecting every part agst. every other part?   In the second, can the

---

[16] "Thomas McKean represented the State of Delaware in the Congress of the Confederation from 1774 to 1783, and was Chief Justice of Pennsylvania from 1777 to 1799.

"On the 2d February, 1782, Thomas McKean and Samuel Wharton, citizens of Pennsylvania, and Philemon Dickinson, a citizen of New Jersey, were elected delegates to Congress for the State of Delaware." (Gilpin, *Papers of James Madison*, Vol. III, Appendix, p. lx, note 215.)

smaller expect that their larger neighbours would confederate with them on the principle of the present confederacy, which gives to each member, an equal suffrage; or that they would exact less severe concessions from the smaller States, than are proposed in the scheme of Mr. Randolph?

The great difficulty lies in the affair of Representation; and if this could be adjusted, all others would be surmountable. It was admitted by both the gentlemen from N. Jersey, (Mr. Brearly and Mr. Patterson) that it would not be *just to allow Virga.* which was 16 times as large as Delaware an equal vote only. Their language was that it would not be *safe for Delaware* to allow Virga. 16 times as many votes. The expedient proposed by them was that all the States should be thrown into one mass and a new partition be made into 13 equal parts. Would such a scheme be practicable? [17] The dissimelarities existing in the rules of property, as well as in the manners, habits and prejudices of the different States, amounted to a prohibition of the attempt. It had been found impossible for the power of one of the most absolute princes in Europe (K. of France) directed by the wisdom of one of the most enlightened and patriotic Ministers (Mr. Neckar) that any age has produced, to equalize in some points only the different usages & regulations of the different provinces. But admitting a general amalgamation and repartition of the States, to be practicable, and the danger apprehended by the smaller States from a proportional representation to be real; would not a particular and voluntary coalition of these with their neighbours, be less inconvenient to the whole community, and equally effectual for their own safety. If N. Jersey or Delaware conceive that an advantage would accrue to them from an equalization of the States, in which case they would necessaryly form a junction with their neighbors, why might not this end be attained by leaving them at liberty by the Constitution to form such a junction whenever they pleased? and why should they wish to obtrude a like arrangement on all the States, when it was, to say the least, extremely difficult, would

---

[17] Crossed out: "He thought not".

be obnoxious to many of the States, and when neither the inconveniency, nor the benefit of the expedient to themselves, would be lessened, by confining it to themselves. — The prospect of many new States to the Westward was another consideration of importance. If they should come into the Union at all, they would come when they contained but but few inhabitants. If they shd. be entitled to vote according to their proportions of inhabitants, all would be right & safe. Let them have an equal vote, and a more objectionable minority than ever might give law to the whole.

⟨On a question for postponing generally the 1st. proposition of Mr. Patterson's plan, it was agreed to: N. Y. &. N. J. only being no —⟩[18]

On the question ⟨moved by Mr. King⟩[19] whether the Committee should rise & Mr. Randolphs propositions be re-reported without alteration, which was in fact a question whether Mr. R's should be adhered to as preferable to those of Mr. Patterson; [20]

Massts. ay. Cont. ay. N. Y. no. N. J. no. Pa. ay. Del. no. Md. divd. Va. ay. N. C. ay. S. C. ay. Geo. ay. [Ayes — 7; noes — 3; divided — 1.]

⟨insert here from Printed Journal p. 13[4]. Copy of the Resoln. of Mr. R. as altered in the Come: and reported to the House⟩

The 1. propos (of Mr. Randolph's plan as reported from the Committee): "that Natl. Govt. ought to be established consisting &c". ⟨being⟩ taken up in ⟨the House.⟩

Mr. Wilson observed that by a Natl. Govt. he did not mean one that would swallow up the State Govts. as seemed to be wished by some gentlemen.[21] He was tenacious of the idea of preserving the latter. He thought, contrary to the opinion of (Col. Hamilton) that they might ⟨not⟩ only subsist but subsist on friendly terms with the former.[22] They were abso-

---

[18] Taken from *Journal*.   See also Appendix A, CLVIII (35).

[19] Taken from Yates.   [20] See Appendix A, CLVIII (12–15).

[21] See Appendix A, CXLVI.

[22] See Hamilton's statement following and debate of June 21, also Appendix A, CCXXI.

lutely necessary for certain purposes which the former could not reach. All large Governments must be subdivided into lesser jurisdictions. as Examples he mentioned Persia, Rome, and particularly the divisions & subdivisions of ⟨England by⟩ Alfred.

Col. Hamilton coincided with the proposition ⟨as it stood in the Report⟩. He had not been understood yesterday. By an abolition of the States, he meant that no boundary could be drawn between the National & State Legislatures; that the former must therefore have indefinite authority. If it were limited at all, the rivalship of the States would gradually subvert it. Even as Corporations the extent of some of them as Va. Massts. &c. would be formidable. *As States*, he thought they ought to be abolished. But he admitted the necessity of leaving in them, subordinate jurisdictions. The examples of Persia & the Roman Empire, cited by (Mr Wilson) were, he thought in favor of his doctrine: the great powers delegated to the Satraps & proconsuls, having frequently produced revolts, and schemes of independence.

Mr. King, wished as everything depended on this proposition, that no objections might be improperly indulged agst. the phraseology of it. He conceived that the import of the terms "States" "Sovereignty" "*national*" "federal," had been often used & applied in the discussion inaccurately & delusively. The States were not "sovereigns" in the sense contended for by some. They did not possess the peculiar features of sovereignty. They could not make war, nor peace, nor alliances, nor treaties. Considering them as political Beings, they were dumb, for they could not speak to any forign Sovereign whatever. They were deaf, for they could not hear any propositions from such Sovereign. They had not even the organs or faculties of defence or offence, for they could not of themselves raise troops, or equip vessels, for war. On the other side, if the Union of the States comprises the idea of a confederation, it comprises that also of consolidation. A Union of the States is a union of the men composing them, from whence a *national* character results to the whole. Congs. can act alone without the States — they can act & their acts will be binding agst. the Instructions of the States.   If they declare war, war is de jure declared, captures made in pursuance of it are lawful.   No acts of the States can vary the situation, or prevent the judicial consequences.   If the States therefore retained some portion of their sovereignty, they had certainly divested themselves of essential portions of it.   If they formed a confederacy in some respects — they formed a Nation in others.   The Convention could clearly deliberate on & propose any alterations that Congs. could have done under ye. federal articles. and could not Congs. propose by virtue of the last article, a change in any article whatever: And as well that relating to the equality of suffrage, as any other.   He made these remarks to obviate some scruples which had been expressed.   He doubted much the practicability of annihilating the States; but thought that much of their power ought to be taken from them.

Mr. Martin, said he considered that the separation from G. B. placed the 13 States in a state of nature towards each other; that they would have remained in that state till this time, but for the confederation; that they entered into the confederation on the footing of equality; that they met now to to amend it on the same footing, and that he could never accede to a plan that would introduce an inequality and lay 10 States at the mercy of Va. Massts. and Penna.

Mr. Wilson, could not admit the doctrine that when the Colonies became independent of G. Britain, they became independent also of each other.   He read the declaration of Independence, observing thereon that the *United Colonies* were declared to be free & independent States; and inferring that they were independent, not *Individually* but *Unitedly* and that they were confederated as they were independent, States.[23]

Col. Hamilton, assented to the doctrine of Mr. Wilson.   He denied the doctrine that the States were thrown into a State of nature   He was not yet prepared to admit the doctrine that the Confederacy, could be dissolved by partial infractions of

---

[23] Crossed out "In support of this exposition, he remarked that the Constitutions of all the States except that of So Ca were subsequent to the ".

it. He admitted that the States met now on an equal footing but could see no inference from that against concerting a change of the system in this particular. He took this occasion of observing for the ⟨purpose of⟩ appeesing the fears of the ⟨small ⟩[24] States, that two circumstances would render them secure under a national Govt. in which they might lose the equality of rank they now hold: one was the local situation of the 3 largest States Virga. Masts. & Pa. They were separated from each other by distance of place, and equally so by all the peculiarities which distinguish the interests of one State from those of another. No combination therefore could be dreaded. In the second place, as there was a gradation in the States from Va. the largest down to Delaware the smallest, it would always happen that ambitious combinations among a few States might & wd. be counteracted by defensive combinations of greater extent among the rest. No combination has been seen among large Counties merely as such, agst. lesser Counties. The more close the Union of the States, and the more compleat the authority of the whole; the less opportunity will be allowed the stronger States to injure the weaker.

Adjd.

YATES

TUESDAY, JUNE 19th, 1787.

Met pursuant to adjournment. Present 11 states.

On the consideration of the first resolve of the Jersey plan.

Mr. Madison. — This is an important question — Many persons scruple the powers of the convention. If this remark had any weight, it is equally applicable to the adoption of either plan. The difference of drawing the powers in the one from the people and in the other from the states, does not affect the powers. There are two states in the union where the members of congress are chosen by the people. A new government must be made. Our all is depending on it; and

---

[24] Probably but not certainly a later insertion.

if we have but a clause that the people will adopt, there is then a chance for our preservation. Although all the states have assented to the confederation, an infraction of any one article by one of the states is a dissolution of the whole. This is the doctrine of the civil law on treaties.[25]

Jersey pointedly refused complying with a requisition of congress, and was guilty of this infraction, although she afterwards rescinded her non-complying resolve. What is the object of a confederation? It is two-fold — 1st, to maintain the union; 2dly, good government. Will the Jersey plan secure these points? No; it is still in the power of the confederated states to violate treaties — Has not Georgia, in direct violation of the confederation made war with the Indians, and concluded treaties? Have not Virginia and Maryland entered into a partial compact? Have not Pennsylvania and Jersey regulated the bounds of the Delaware? Has not the state of Massachusetts, at this time, a considerable body of troops in pay? Has not congress been obliged to pass a conciliatory act in support of a decision of their federal court, between Connecticut and Pennsylvania, instead of having the power of carrying into effect the judgment of their own court? Nor does the Jersey plan provide for a ratification by the respective states of the powers intended to be vested. It is also defective in the establishment of the judiciary, granting only an appellate jurisdiction, without providing for a second trial; and in case the executive of a state should pardon an offender, how will it effect the definitive judgment on appeal? It is evident, if we do not *radically* depart from a federal plan, we shall share the fate of ancient and modern confederacies. The amphyctionic council, like the American congress, had the power of judging in the *last resort* in war and peace — call out forces — send ambassadors. What was its fate or continuance? Philip of Macedon, with little difficulty, destroyed every appearance of it. The Athenian had nearly the same fate — The Helvetic confederacy is rather a league — In the German confederacy the parts are too strong for the

---

[25] For Genet's interpretation of this speech, see Appendix A, CCCX.

whole — The Dutch are in a most wretched situation — weak in all its parts, and only supported by surrounding contending powers.

The rights of individuals are infringed by many of the state laws — such as issuing paper money, and instituting a mode to discharge debts differing from the form of the contract. Has the Jersey plan any checks to prevent the mischief? Does it in any instance secure internal tranquility? Right and force, in a system like this, are synonymous terms. When force is employed to support the system, and men obtain military habits, is there no danger they may turn their arms against their employers? Will the Jersey plan prevent foreign influence? Did not Persia and Macedon distract the councils of Greece by acts of corruption? And is not Jersey and Holland at this day subject to the same distractions? Will not the plan be burthensome to the smaller states, if they have an equal representation? But how is military coercion to enforce government? True, a smaller state may be brought to obedience, or crushed; but what if one of the larger states should prove disobedient, are you sure you can by force effect a submission? Suppose we cannot agree on any plan, what will be the condition of the smaller states? Will Delaware and Jersey be safe against Pennsylvania, or Rhode-Island against Massachusetts? And how will the smaller states be situated in case of partial confederacies? Will they not be obliged to make larger concessions to the greater states? The point of representation is the great point of difference, and which the greater states cannot give up; and although there was an equalization of states, state distinctions would still exist. But this is totally impracticable; and what would be the effect of the Jersey plan if ten or twelve new states were added?

Mr. King moved that the committee rise, and report that the Jersey plan is not admissible, and report the first plan.

Mr. Dickinson supposed that there were good regulations in both. Let us therefore contrast the one with the other, and consolidate such parts of them as the committee approve.

Mr. King's motion was then put — For it 7 states — 3 against — one divided. New-York in the minority.

The committee rose and reported again the first plan, and the inadmissibility of the Jersey plan.

The convention then proceeded to take the first plan into consideration.

The first resolve was read.

Mr. Wilson. I am (to borrow a sea-phrase) for taking a new departure, and I wish to consider in what direction we sail, and what may be the end of our voyage. I am for a national government, though the idea of federal is, in my view, the same. With me it is not a desirable object to annihilate the state governnents, and here I differ from the honorable gentleman from New-York. In all extensive empires a subdivision of power is necessary. Persia, Turkey and Rome, under its emperors, are examples in point. These, although despots, found it necessary. A general government, over a great extent of territory, must in a few years make subordinate jurisdictions. — Alfred the great, that wise legislator, made this gradation, and the last division on his plan amounted only to ten territories. With this explanation, I shall be for the first resolve.

Mr. Hamilton. I agree to the proposition. I did not intend yesterday a total extinguishment of state governments; but my meaning was, that a national government ought to be able to support itself without the aid or interference of the state governments, and that therefore it was necessary to have full sovereignty. Even with corporate rights the states will be dangerous to the national government, and ought to be extinguished, new modified, or reduced to a smaller scale.

Mr. King. None of the states are now sovereign or independent — Many of these essential rights are vested in congress. Congress, by the confederation, possesses the rights of the United States. This is a union of the men of those states. None of the states, individually or collectively, but in congress, have the rights of _peace_ or _war_. The magistracy in congress possesses the sovereignty — To certain points we are now a united people. Consolidation is already established. The confederation contains an article to make alterations — Congress have the right to propose such altera-

tions.   The 8th article respecting the quotas of the states, has
been altered, and eleven states have agreed to it.   Can it not
be altered in other instances?   It can, excepting the guarantee
of the states.

Mr. Martin.   When the states threw off their allegiance
on Great Britain, they became independent of her and each
other.   They united and confederated for mutual defence,
and this was done on principles of perfect reciprocity — They
will now again meet on the same ground.   But when a dissolution takes place, our original rights and sovereignties are
resumed. — Our accession to the union has been by states.
If any other principle is adopted by this convention, he will
give it every opposition.

Mr. Wilson.   The declaration of independence preceded
the state constitutions.   What does this declare?   In the name
of the people of these states, we are declared to be free and
independent.   The power of war, peace, alliances and trade,
are declared to be vested in congress.

Mr. Hamilton.   I agree to Mr. Wilson's remark. —
Establish a weak government and you must at times overleap the bounds.   Rome was obliged to create dictators.
Cannot you make propositions to the people because we before
confederated on other principles? — The people can yield to
them, if they will.   The three great objects of government,
agriculture, commerce and revenue, can only be secured by a
general government.

Adjourned to to-morrow morning.

KING

_18_ [_19_] _June_

Madison

Confedn. unanimously adopted can be dissolved only by
unanimous consent — this Position is not true — A contract
entered into by men or societies may be dissolved by the breach
of a single Articles — this is the case in Treaties — sometimes
however provision is made that the Breach of a single Article
shall not dissolve the Contn. or Treaty

Georgia has declared & prosecuted a war agt. the Indians — they have treated with them — N Jersey has expressly refused a constutitional Requisition — Virginia & Maryland have formed a Contract relative to the Potomack — Pennsylvania & NYk have agreed about their boundary — Massachussets has raised an Army, & are now about to augment that Establishment —

Will a federal Govt. answer —

Amphictions — to decide between the members — to mulct offenders — command the forces, sent Embass. chose the Comr. in Chief, and used the Genl. Forces agt. the deficient —

Athenian confed. similar to the Amphictions — their fate terminated by the strength of the members

Helvetic Confed. loose & weak and not like our situation —

Germanic Confedy.
    Loose & weak, the strength of individual Members exceed that of the whole —

The Netherlands — weak — no powers —

Wilson
    I dont agree that the Genl. Govt. will swallow up the states or yr. Government — I think they must be preserved they must be continued — they may live in harmony with the Genl. Government — our Country is too extensive for a single Govt. no Despot ever did govern a country so extensive — Persia is divided into 20 subordinate Govts. Rome governed by her Proconsuls — Alfred adopted the plan and formed societies of 10, to those of 100ds towns counties, &c — [26]

_____

[26] [Endorsed] June 19 | Confederation unanimously | formed, may be dissolved | without unanimity

Objections to a general or national Govt.[27]

This convention does not possess authority to propose any reform which is not purely federal —

2. If they proposed such power it wd be inexpedient to exercise it, because the small States wd. loose their State influence or equality, and because the Genius of the people is of that sort that such a Reform wd. be rejected —

Answer — The States under the confed. are not sovereign States — they can do no act but such as are of a subordinate nature or such as terminate in themselves — and even then in some instances they are restrained — Coinage. P. Office &c they are wholly incompentent to the exercise of any of the Gt. & distinguishing acts of Sovereignty — They can neither make nor receive to or from any other sovereign they have not the powers of injuring another, or of defending themselves from an Injury offered from another — they are deaf, dumb, and impotent — these Faculties are yielded up and the US in C. assd. hold and possess them, and they alone can exercise them — they are so far out of the controul of the separate States, yt. if every State in the Union was to instruct yr. Deleg. and those Delegates within ye powers of the Arts. of Union shd. do an act in violation of their Instructions it wd. nevertheless be valid

If they declare a war, any giving aid & comfort to the enemy wd. be Treason; if peace any capture on the high Seas wd. be piracy.

This remark proves yt. the States are now subordinate corporations or Societies and not Sovereigns — these imperfect States are the confederates, and they are the Electors of the Magistrates who exercise the national Sovereignty — The articles of Confedn. are perpetual union, — are partly federal & partly of the nature of a constitution or form of Govt. arising from & applying to the Citizens of the US. & not from the individual States —

The only criterion of determing what is federal and what is national is this, those acts which are for the government of

[27] Although not indicated in the MS. this is so evidently an outline of King's speech of this date that it is inserted here without hesitation.

the states only are purely federal, those which are for the Government of the Citizens of the individual States are national & not federal

If then the articles of Confedn. & perpetl. union have this twofold capacity, and if they provide for an alteration in a certain mode, why may not they be so altered as that the federal article may be changed to a national one and the national to a federal? I see no argument that can be objected to the authority — the 5. art. regulates the influence of the several States and makes them equal — does not the confed. authorise this alteration that instead of this Equality, that one State may have double the Influence of another — I conceive it does — and so of every Article except that wh destroys the Idea of a confedy. I think it may be proved that every article may be totally altered provided you have one guarantying to each State the right of regulating its private & internal affairs in the manner of a subordinate corporation —

But admiting that the Arts. of Confed. & Perpet. Union, or the powers of the Legis. did not extend to the proposed Reform; yet the public Expectations, & the public Danger requires it — the System proposed to be adopted is no scheme of a day, calculated to postpone the hour of Danger, & then leave it to fall with double ruin on our successors — It is no crude and undigested plan, the Child of narrow and unextensive views, brought forward und[er] the auspices of Cowardice & Irresolution. it is a measure of Decision, it is the foundation of Freedom & of national Glory — it will draw on itself, and be able to support the severest scrutiny & Examination — It is no idle Experiment, no romantic Speculation — the measure forces itself upon wise men, and if they have not firmness to look it in the face and protect it — Farwel to the Freedom of our Government — our military Glory will be tarnished, and our boasts of Freedom will be the scorn of the Enemies of Liberty [28]

---

[28] [Endorsed] K | Remarks in favour of a | Genl Govt instead of the old | Plan of the Confederation | Question of Powers

HAMILTON

Maddison — Breach of compact in one article releases the whole —

Treaties may still be violated by the states under the Jersey plan —

Appellate jurisdiction not sufficient because second trial cannot be had under it —

Attempt made by one of the greatest monarchs of Europe to equalize the local peculiarities of their separate provinces — in which the Agent fell a victim

WEDNESDAY, JUNE 20, 1787.

JOURNAL

Wednesday June 20. 1787.

The honorable William Blount Esquire a Deputy from the State of North Carolina attended and took his seat.

The following credentials were then produced and read.

(here insert Mr Blount's credentials) [1]

It was moved by Mr Ellsworth seconded by Mr Gorham to amend the first resolution reported from the Committee of the whole House so as to read as follows — namely,

Resolved that the government of the United States ought to consist of

a Supreme Legislative, Judiciary, and Executive.

On the question to agree to the amendment

it passed unanimously in the affirmative

It was then moved by Mr Lansing, seconded by Mr Sherman to postpone the consideration of the second resolution reported from the Committee, in order to take up the following, namely.

Resolved that the powers of legislation be vested in the United States in Congress.

and on the question to postpone

it passed in the negative. [Ayes — 4; noes — 6; divided — 1.]

It was then moved and seconded to adjourn

which passed in the negative [Ayes — 4; noes — 7.]

On motion of the Deputies of the State of Delaware the determination of the House on the second resolution reported from the Committee was postponed until to-morrow.

and then the House adjourned till to-morrow at 11 o'clock A. M.

---

[1] See Appendix B.

DETAIL OF AYES AND NOES

	New Hampshire	Massachusetts	Rhode Island	Connecticut	New York	New Jersey	Pennsylvania	Delaware	Maryland	Virginia	North Carolina	South Carolina	Georgia	Questions	Ayes	Noes	Divided
[68]	no			aye	aye	aye	no	aye	dd	no	no	no	no	to postpone the 2 resolution reported to take up the one offered by Mr Lansing	4	6	1
[69]	no			no	aye	aye	no	aye	aye	no	no	no	no	to adjourn	4	7	

MADISON

Wednesday June 20. ⟨1787. In Convention⟩

⟨Mr. William Blount from N. Carolina took his seat.[2]
1st. propos: of the Report of Come. of the whole before the House⟩

Mr. Elseworth ⟨2ded. by Mr. Gorham⟩[2] moves to alter it so as to run "that the Government of the United States ought to consist of a supreme legislative, Executive and Judiciary". This alteration he said would drop the word *national,* and retain the proper title "the United States." [3] He could not admit the doctrine that a breach of ⟨any of⟩ [4] the federal articles could dissolve the whole. It would be highly dangerous not to consider the Confederation as still subsisting. He wished also the plan of the Convention to go forth as an amendment to the articles of Confederation, since under this idea the authority of the Legislatures could ratify it. If they are unwilling, the people will be so too. If the plan goes forth to the people for ratification several succeeding Conventions within the States would be unavoidable. He did not like these conventions. They were better fitted to pull down than to build up Constitutions.

---

[2] Taken from *Journal.*

[3] On dropping the term "national," see Appendix A, CLVIII (35), CCCLVII, CCCLXXXVIII, also CCCLVI, and CCCXCII.

[4] Probably but not certainly a later insertion.

Mr. Randolph did not object to the change of expression, but apprised the gentleman who wished for it that he did not admit it for the reasons assigned; particularly that of getting rid of a reference to the people for ratification. The motion of Mr. Elsewth was acquiesed in. nem: con:

The 2d. Resoln. "that the national Legislature ought to consist of two branches". taken up.[5] the word "national" struck out as of course.

Mr. Lansing, observed that the true queston here was, whether the Convention would adhere to or depart from the foundation of the present Confederacy; and moved instead of ⟨the 2d⟩ Resolution "that the powers of Legislation be vested ⟨in the U. States⟩ in Congress"..[6] He had already assigned two reasons agst. such an innovation as was proposed. 1. the want of competent powers ⟨in the Convention⟩ — 2. the ⟨state⟩[7] of the public mind. It had been observed by ⟨Mr. M⟨adison⟩⟩ in discussing the first point, that in two States the Delegates to Congs. were chosen by the people. Notwithstanding the first appearance of this remark, it had in fact no weight, as the Delegates however chosen, did not represent the people merely as so many individuals; but as forming a sovereign State. ⟨Mr Randolph⟩ put it, he said, on its true footing namely that the public safety superseded the scruple arising from the review of our powers. But in order to feel the force of this consideration, the same impression must be had of the public danger. He had not himself the same impression, and could not therefore dismiss his scruple. ⟨Mr Wilson⟩ contended that as the Convention were only to recommend, they might recommend what they pleased. He differed much from him. any act whatever of so respectable a body must have a great effect, and if it does not succeed, will be a source of great dissentions. He admitted that there was no certain criterion of the public mind on the subject. He therefore recurred to the evidence of it given by the opposition in the States to the scheme of an Impost. It could

---

[5] On the debate over this resolution, see Appendix A, XXXIV, CLVIII (29–34), CXCVII, CCXXV, CCXLIX.

[6] Revised from *Journal*.   [7] Crossed out "immaturity".

not be expected that those possessing Sovereignty could ever voluntarily part with it. It was not to be expected from any one State, much less from thirteen. He proceeded to make some observations on the plan itself and the argumts. urged in support of it. The point of Representation could receive no elucidation from the case of England. The corruption of the boroughs did not proceed from their comparative smallness: but from the actual fewness of the inhabitants, some of them not having more than one or two. a great inequality existed in the Counties of England. Yet the like complaint of peculiar corruption in the small ones had not been made. It had been said that Congress represent the State Prejudices: will not any other body whether chosen by the Legislatures or people of the States, also represent their prejudices? It had been asserted by his Colleague (Col. Hamilton) [8] that there was no coincidence of interests among the large States that ought to excite fears of oppression in the smaller. If it were true that such a uniformity of interests existed among the States, there was equal safety for all of them, whether the representation remained as heretofore, or were proportioned as now proposed. It is proposed that the genl. Legislature shall have a negative on the laws of the States. Is it conceivable that there will be leisure for such a task? there will on the most moderate calculation, be as many Acts sent up from the States as there are days in the year. Will the members of the general Legislature be competent Judges? Will a gentleman from Georgia be a Judge of the expediency of a law which is to operate in N. Hamshire. Such a Negative would be more injurious than that of Great Britain heretofore was. It is said that the National Govt. must have the influence arising from the grant of offices and honors. In order to render ⟨such a Government⟩ effectual he believed such an influence to be necessary. But if the States will not agree to it, it is in vain, worse than in vain to make the proposition. If this influence is to be attained, the States must be entirely abolished. Will any one

---

[8] Crossed out: "the greatest objection agst. whose ideas in general was perhaps the repugnance of the people to them."

say this would ever be agreed to? He doubted whether any Genl Government equally beneficial to all can be attained. That now under consideration he is sure, must be utterly unattainable. He had another objection. The system was too novel & complex. No man could foresee what its operation will be either with respect to the Genl. Govt. or the State Govts. One or other it has been surmised must absorb the whole.

Col. Mason. did not expect this point would have been reagitated. The essential differences between the two plans, had been clearly stated. The principal objections agst. that of Mr. R. were the *want of power* & the *want of practicability*. There can be no weight in the first as the fiat is not to be *here*, but in the people. He thought with his colleague Mr. R. that there were besides certain crisises, in which all the ordinary cautions yielded to public necessity. He gave as an example, the eventual Treaty with G. B. in forming which the Commsrs of the U. S. had boldly disregarded the improvident shackles of Congs. had given to their Country an honorable & happy peace, and instead of being censured for the transgression of their powers, had raised to themselves a monument more durable than brass. The *impracticability* of gaining the public concurrence he thought was still more groundless. (Mr. Lansing) had cited the attempts of Congress to gain an enlargment of their powers, and had inferred from the miscarrige of these attempts, the hopelessness of the plan which he (Mr. L) opposed. He thought a very different inference ought to have been drawn; viz. that the plan which (Mr. L.) espoused, and which proposed to augument the powers of Congress, never could be expected to succeed. He meant not to throw any reflections on Congs. as a body, much less on any particular members of it. He meant however to speak his sentiments without reserve on this subject; it was a privilege of Age, and perhaps the only compensation which nature had given for, the privation of so many other enjoyments; and he should not scruple to exercise it freely. Is it to be thought that the people of America, so watchful over their interests; so jealous of their liberties, will give up their all, will surrender both the sword and the purse, to the same body, and that too not chosen immediately by themselves? They never will. They never ought. Will they trust such a body, with the regulation of their trade, with the regulation of their taxes; with all the other great powers, which are in contemplation? Will they give unbounded confidence to a secret Journal — to the intrigues — to the factions which in the nature of things appertain to such an Assembly? If any man doubts the existence of these characters of Congress, let him consult their Journals for the years, 78, 79, & 80 — It will be said, that if the people are averse to parting with power, why is it hoped that they will part with it to a National Legislature. The proper answer is that in this case they do not part with power: they only transfer it from one sett of immediate Representatives to another sett. Much has been said of the unsettled state of the mind of the people. he believed the mind of the people of America, as elsewhere, was unsettled as to some points; but settled as to others. In two points he was sure it was well settled. 1. in an attachment to Republican Government. 2. in an attachment to more than one branch in the Legislature. Their constitutions accord so generally in both these circumstances, that they seem almost to have been preconcerted. This must either have been a miracle, or have resulted from the genius of the people. The only exceptions to the establishmt. of two branches in the Legislatures are the State of Pa. & Congs. and the latter the only single one not chosen by the people themselves. What has been the consequence? The people have been constantly averse to giving that Body further powers — It was acknowledged by (Mr. Patterson) that his plan could not be enforced without military coertion. Does he consider the force of this concession. The most jarring elements of nature; fire & water themselves are not more incompatible that such a mixture of civil liberty and military execution. Will the militia march from one State to another, in order to collect the arrears of taxes from the delinquent members of the Republic? Will they maintain an army for this purpose? Will not the citizens of the invaded State assist one another till they rise as one

Man, and shake off the Union altogether. Rebellion is the only case in which ⟨the military force of the State can be properly⟩ [9] exerted agst. its Citizens. In one point of view he was struck with horror at the prospect of recurring to this expedient. To punish the non-payment of taxes with death, was a severity not yet adopted by depotism itself: yet this unexampled cruelty would be mercy compared to a military collection of revenue, in which the bayonet could make no discrimination between the innocent and the guilty. He took this occasion to repeat. that notwithstanding his solicitude to establish a national Government, he never would agree to abolish the State Govts. or render them absolutely insignificant. They were as necessary as the Genl. Govt. and he would be equally careful to preserve them. He was aware of the difficulty of drawing the line between them, but hoped it was not insurmountable. The Convention, tho' comprising so many distinguished characters, could not be expected to make a faultless Govt. And he would prefer trusting to posterity the amendment of its defects, rather than push the experiment too far.

Mr. Luther Martin agreed with ⟨Col Mason⟩ as to the importance of the State Govts. he would support them at the expense of the Genl. Govt. which was instituted for the purpose of that support. He saw no necessity for two branches, and if it existed Congress might be organized into two. He considered Congs as representing the people, being chosen by the Legislatures who were chosen by the people. At any rate, Congress represented the Legislatures; and it was the Legislatures not the people who refused to enlarge their powers. Nor could the rule of voting have been the ground of objection, otherwise ten of the States must always have been ready, to place further confidence in Congs. The causes of repugnance must therefore be looked for elsewhere. — At the separation from the British Empire, the people of America preferred the Establishment of themselves into thirteen separate sovereignties instead of incorporating themselves into one: to these

---

[9] Probably but not certainly a later correction. Madison first wrote "the public force can be". Yates uses the term "military force".

they look up for the security of their lives, liberties & properties: to these they must look up — The federal Govt. they formed, to defend the whole agst. foreign nations, in case of war, and to defend the lesser States agst. the ambition of the larger: they are afraid of granting powers unnecessarily, lest they should defeat the original end of the Union; lest the powers should prove dangerous to the sovereignties of the particular States which the Union was meant to support; and expose the lesser to being swallowed up by the larger. He conceived also that the people of the States having already vested their powers in their respective Legislatures, could not resume them without a dissolution of their Governments. He was agst. Conventions in the States: was not agst. assisting States agst. rebellious subjects; thought the *federal* plan of Mr. Patterson did not require coercion more than the *national one*, as the latter must depend for the deficiency of its revenues on requisitions & quotas, and that a national Judiciary extended into the States would be ineffectual, and would be viewed with a jealousy inconsistent with its usefulness.[10]

Mr. Sherman 2ded & supported Mr. Lansing's motion. He admitted two branches to be necessary in the State Legislatures, but saw no necessity for them in a Confederacy of States. The Examples were all, of a single Council. Congs. carried us thro' the war, and perhaps as well as any Govt. could have done. The complaints at present are not that the views of Congs. are unwise or unfaithful, but that that their powers are insufficient for the execution of their views. The national debt & the want of power somewhere to draw forth the National resources, are the great matters that press. All the States were sensible of the defect of power in Congs. He thought much might be said in apology for the failure of the State Legislatures to comply with the confederation. They were afraid of bearing too hard on the people, by accumulating taxes; no *constitutional* rule had been or could be observed in the quotas, — the accounts also were unsettled &

---

[10] Madison ended his report of this speech, but later crossed out: — "This was the substance of a very long speech".

every State supposed itself in advance, rather than in arrears. For want of a general system taxes to a due amount had not been drawn from trade which was the most convenient resource. As almost all the States had agreed to the recommendation of Congs. on the subject of an impost, it appeared clearly that they were willing to trust Congs. with ⟨power to draw a revenue from Trade.⟩ [11] There is no weight therefore in the argument drawn from a distrust of Congs. for money matters being the most important of all, if the people will trust them with power as to them, they will trust them with any other necessary powers. Congs. indeed by the confederation have in fact the right of saying how much the people shall pay, and to what purpose it shall be applied: and this right was granted to them in the expectation that it would in all cases have its effect. If another branch were to be added to Congs. to be chosen by the people, it would serve to embarrass. The people would not much interest themselves in the elections, a few designing men in the large districts would carry their points, and the people would have no more confidence in their new representatives than in Congs. He saw no reason why the State Legislatures should be unfriendly as had been suggested, to Congs. If they appoint Congs. and approve of their measures, they would be rather favorable and partial to them. The disparity of the States in point of size he perceived was the main difficulty. But the large States had not yet suffered from the equality of votes enjoyed by the small ones. In all great and general points, the interests of all the States were the same. The State of Virga. notwithstanding the equality of votes, ratified the Confederation without, or even proposing, any alteration. Massts. also ratified without any material difficulty &c. In none of the ratifications is the want of two branches noticed or complained of. To consolidate the States as some had proposed would dissolve our Treaties with foreign nations, which had been formed with us, as *Confederated* States. He did not however suppose that the creation of two branches in the Legislature would have such

---

[11] Probably but not certainly a later revision.   Madison first wrote "more power".

an effect. If the difficulty on the subject of representation can not be otherwise got over, he would agree to have two branches, and a proportional representation in one of them, provided each State had an equal voice in the other. This was necessary to secure the rights of the lesser States; otherwise three or four of the large States would rule the others as they please. Each State like each individual had its peculiar habits usages and manners, which constituted its happiness.[12] It would not therefore give to others a power over this happiness, any more than an individual would do, when he could avoid it.

Mr. Wilson, urged the necessity of two branches; observed that if a proper model was not to be found in other Confederacies it was not to be wondered at. The number of them was ⟨small⟩ & the duration of some at least short. The Amphyctionic & Achæan were formed in the infancy of political Science; and appear by their History & fate, to have contained radical defects, The Swiss & Belgic Confederacies were held together not by any vital principle of energy but by the incumbent pressure of formidable neighbouring nations: The German owed its continuance to the influence of the H. of Austria. He appealed to our own experience for the defects of our Confederacy. He had been 6 years in the 12 since the commencement of the Revolution, a member of Congress and had felt all its weaknesses. He appealed to the recollection of others whether on many important occasions, the public interest had not been obstructed by the small members of the Union. The success of the Revolution was owing to other causes, than the Constitution of Congress. In many instances it went on even agst. the difficulties arising from Congs. themselves — He admitted that the large States did accede as had been stated, to the Confederation in its present form. But it was the effect of necessity not of choice. There are other instances of their yielding from the same motive to the unreasonable measures of the small States. The situation of things is now a little altered. He insisted that a jealousy

---

[12] Crossed out: "of the people. As the individual who enters into Society retains the right of seeking his own happiness ".

would exist between the State Legislatures & the General Legislature: observing that the members of the former would have views & feelings very distinct in this respect from their constituents. A private citizen of a State is indifferent whether power be exercised by the Genl. or State Legislatures, provided it be exercised most for his happiness. His representative has an interest in its being exercised by the body to which he belongs. He will therefore view the National Legisl: with the eye of a jealous rival. He observed that the addresses of Congs. to the people at large, had always been better received & produced greater effect, than those made to the Legislatures.

On the question for postponing in order to take up Mr. Lansings proposition "to vest the powers of Legislation in Congs."

Masst. no. Cont. ay. N. Y. ay.[13] N. J. ay. Pa. no. Del. ay Md. divd. Va. no. N. C. no. S. C. no. Geo. no [Ayes — 4; noes — 6; divided — 1.]

On motion of the Deputies from Delaware, the question on the 2d. Resolution in the Report from the Committee of the whole was postponed till tomorrow.

adjd.

YATES

WEDNESDAY, JUNE 20th, 1787.

Met pursuant to adjournment. Present 11 states.

Judge Elsworth. I propose, and therefore move, to expunge the word *national*, in the first resolve, and to place in the room of it, *government of the United States*—which was agreed to, *nem. con.*

Mr. Lansing then moved, that the first resolve be postponed, in order to take into consideration the following: *That the powers of legislation ought to be vested in the United States in congress.*

---

[13] "N. Y. ay". was written in the MS. after the rest of the vote was recorded and may be a later insertion. *Journal* and Yates both include New York in the affirmative.

I am clearly of opinion that I am not authorized to accede to a system which will annihilate the state governments, and the Virginia plan is declarative of such extinction. It has been asserted that the public mind is not known. To some points it may be true, but we may collect from the fate of the requisition of the impost, what it may be on the principles of a national government. — When many of the states were so tenacious of their rights on this point, can we expect that *thirteen* states will surrender their governments up to a national plan? Rhode-Island pointedly refused granting it. Certainly she had a federal right so to do; and I hold it as an undoubted truth, as long as state distinctions remain, let the national government be modified as you please, both branches of your legislature will be impressed with local and state attachments. The Virginia plan proposes a negative on the state laws where, *in the opinion* of the national legislature, they contravene the national government: and no state laws can pass unless approved by them. — They will have more than a law in a day to revise; and are they competent to judge of the wants and necessities of remote states?

This national government will, from their power, have great influence in the state governments; and the existence of the latter are only saved in appearance. And has it not been asserted that they expect their extinction? If this be the object, let us say so, and extinguish them at once. But remember, if we devise a system of government which will not meet the approbation of our constituents, we are dissolving the union — but if we act within the limits of our power, it will be approved of; and should it upon experiment prove defective, the people will entrust a future convention again to amend it. Fond as many are of a general government, do any of you believe it can pervade the whole continent so effectually as to secure the peace, harmony and happiness of the whole? The excellence of the British model of government has been much insisted on; but we are endeavoring to complicate it with state governments, on principles which will gradually destroy the one or the other. You are sowing the seeds of rivalship, which must at last end in ruin.

Mr. Mason. The material difference between the two plans has already been clearly pointed out. The objection to that of Virginia arises from the want of power to institute it, and the want of practicability to carry it into effect. Will the first objection apply to a power merely recommendatory? In certain seasons of public danger it is commendable to exceed power. The treaty of peace, under which we now enjoy the blessings of freedom, was made by persons who exceeded their powers. It met the approbation of the public, and thus deserved the praises of those who sent them. The impracticability of the plan is still less groundless. These measures are supported by one who, at his time of life, has little to hope or expect from any government. Let me ask, will the people entrust their dearest rights and liberties to the determination of one body of men, and those not chosen by them, and who are invested both with the *sword* and *purse?* They never will —they never can—to a conclave, transacting their business secret from the eye of the public. Do we not discover by their public journals of the years 1778-9, and 1780, that factions and party spirit had guided many of their acts? The people of America, like all other people, are unsettled in their minds, and their principles fixed to no object, except that a republican government is the best, and that the legislature ought to consist of two branches. The constitutions of the respective states, made and approved of by them, evince this principle. Congress, however, from other causes, received a different organization. What, would you use military force to compel the observance of a social compact? It is destructive to the rights of the people. Do you expect the militia will do it, or do you mean a standing army? The first will never, on such an occasion, exert any power; and the latter may turn its arms against the government which employs them. I never will consent to destroy state governments, and will ever be as careful to preserve the one as the other. If we should, in the formation of the latter, have omitted some necessary regulation, I will trust my posterity to amend it. That the one government will be productive of disputes and jealousies against the other, I believe; but it will produce mutual safety. I shall close with observing, that though some gentlemen have expressed much warmth on this and former occasions, I can excuse it, as the result of sudden passion; and hope that although we may differ in some particular points, if we mean the good of the whole, that our good sense upon reflection, will prevent us from spreading our discontent further.

Mr. Martin. I know that government must be supported; and if the one was incompatible with the other, I would support the state government at the expense of the union — for I consider the present system as a system of slavery. Impressed with this idea, I made use, on a former occasion, of expressions perhaps rather harsh. If gentlemen conceive that the legislative branch is dangerous, divide them into two. They are as much the representatives of the states, as the state assemblies are the representatives of the people. Are not the powers which we here exercise given by the legislatures? (After giving a detail of the revolution and of state governments, Mr. M. continued.) I confess when the confederation was made, congress ought to have been invested with more extensive powers; but when the states saw that congress indirectly aimed at sovereignty, they were jealous, and therefore refused any farther concessions. The time is now come that we can constitutionally grant them not only new powers, but to modify their government, so that the state governments are not endangered. But whatever we have now in our power to grant, the grant is a state grant, and therefore it must be so organized that the state governments are interested in supporting the union. Thus systematized, there can be no danger if a small force is maintained.

Mr. Sherman. We have found during the war that though congress consisted of but one branch, it was that body which carried us through the whole war, and we were crowned with success. We closed the war, performing all the functions of a good government, by making a beneficial peace. But the great difficulty now is, how we shall pay the public debt incurred during that war. The unwillingness of the states to comply with the requisitions of congress, has embarrassed us greatly. — But to amend these defects in government I am not fond of speculation. I would rather proceed on experimental ground. We can so modify the powers of congress, that we will all be mutual supporters of one another. The disparity of the states can be no difficulty. We know this by experience — Virginia and Massachusetts were the first who unanimously ratified the old confederation. They then had no claim to more votes in congress than one. Foreign states have made treaties with us as confederated states, not as a national government. Suppose we put an end to that government under which those treaties were made, will not these treaties be void?

Mr. Wilson. The question before us may admit of the three following considerations:

1. Whether the legislature shall consist of one or two branches.

2. Whether they are to be elected by the state governments or by the people.

3. Whether in proportion to state importance, or states individually.

Confederations are usually of a short date. The amphyctionic council was instituted in the infancy of the Grecian republics — as those grew in strength, the council lost its weight and power. The Achæan league met the same fate — Switzerland and Holland are supported in their confederation, not by its intrinsic merit, but the incumbent pressure of surrounding bodies. Germany is kept together by the house of Austria. True, congress carried us through the war even against its own weakness. That powers were wanting, you Mr. President, must have felt. To other causes, not to congress, must the success be ascribed. That the great states acceded to the confederation, and that they in the hour of danger, made a sacrifice of their interest to the lesser states is true. Like the wisdom of Solomon in adjudging the child to its true mother, from tenderness to it, the greater states well knew that the loss of a limb was fatal to the confederation — they too, through tenderness sacrificed their dearest rights to preserve the whole. But the time is come, when justice will be done to their claims — Situations are altered.

Congress have frequently made their appeal to the people.

I wish they had always done it — the national government would have been sooner extricated.

Question then put on Mr. Lansing's motion and lost. — 6 states against 4 — one divided. New-York in the minority.

Adjourned till to-morrow morning.

KING

19 [20] June

Mason

The powers are ample; if they were not we shd. imitate the commissrs of the US who formed the Treaty of peace, who proceeded without power —

The System proposed is not impracticable — the public Mind is not agt. it — the reason why the Impost was opposed was because congress was a single Br. with Extive. Jud. & Legislative authority — they ought not to be trusted. the people ought not to rest satisfied with the secret Journals of a Conclave —

The people are unanimous in these points — 1st Republicanism —

— 2d Two Br. of the Legislature

The two Brs. being so unanimously adopted must have been the Effect of miracle or a proof of a fixed character or opinion among America —

The Genl. from N. Jersey proposed a military force to carry Requisitions into Execution — This never can be accomplished — you can no more execute civil Regulations by Military Force than you can unite opposite Elements, than you can mingle Fire with Water — military coercion wd. punish the innocent with the Guilty — therefore unjust —

But I never will consent to the Abolition of the State Govts. there never can be a Genl. Govt. that will perform their Offices — I will go a proper length in favor of the Genl. Government but I will take equal care of the State Govts — we cannot form a perfect System — there will be faults — we can trust our successors with farther amendments —

Martin. Maryld. I think the Confederation was formed for

the protection & safety of the particular States & not for those of the US.   I will not support the Genl. Govt. at the Expense of the particular States, but I will contend for the safety & happiness of the particular States at the Expense of the US —

One Br. or two Br — Sherman one is sufficient for confederated States — No precedent can be given of two Br. in the Govt. of confederated States — I am for an increase of the powers of Congress, & wish to preserve the State Governments, and am agt. a consolidation or Union — I think our Treaties wd. be void if we change the nature of our Confederacy — they are all formed with the US of NH. M. &c —

Wilson The question is whether the Legislat. shall consist of one or two Brs —
1 whether the Legis. of a single body

2 Whether it shall be elected by States or individuals —
3 & whether the states shall stand equal or the representation be proportionate to the Importance of the States —
 The antient confedes. were formed in the infancy of politicks — they soon fell victims to the inefficacy of yr. organization — because they had but one Br. there is no reason to adopt their Example —
The Dutch & Swiss confederacys are presirved by external balances — the Germanic Confed: is preserved by the power & Dominion of the House of Austria — our equality of votes was an occasional Compact — the Great States conducted like the true mother in the controversy of the Harlots, they like her in the claim of her child gave their sovereignty to the small States rather than it shd. be destroyed by the British King —

HAMILTON

Mr. Lansing—Resolved that the powers of legislation ought to be vested in the United States in Congress —
 — If our plan be not adopted it will produce those mischiefs which we are sent to obviate —
Principles of System —

— Equality of Representation —

Dependence of members of Congress on States —

So long as state distinctions exist state prejudices
will operate whether election be by *states* or
people —

— If no interest to *oppress* no need of *apportionment* —

— Virginia 16 — Delaware 1 —

— Will General Government have liesure to
examine state laws —?

— Will G Government have the necessary information?

— Will states agree to surrender?

— Let us meet public opinion & hope the progress
of sentiment will make future arrangements —

— Would like my system if it could be established —

System without example —

Mr. Mason — Objection to granting power to Congress arose
from their constitution.

Sword and *purse* in one body —

Two principles in which *America* are unanimous

1 attachment to Republican government

2 ——————— to two branches of legislature—

— Military *force* & *liberty* incompatible —

— Will people maintain a standing army?

— Will endeavour to preserve state governments & draw lines — trusting to posterity to
amend —

Mr Martin — General Government originally formed for the
preservation of state governments —

Objection to giving power to Congress has
originated with the legislatures — — —

10 of the states interested in an equal voice —

Real motive was an opinion that there ought to
be distinct governments & not a general
government —

If we should form a general government twould break to pieces — — —

— For common safety instituted a General government —

Jealousy of power the motive —

People have delegated all their authority to state government —

Coertion necessary to both systems —

Requisitions necessary upon one system as upon another —

In their *system* made requisitions necessary in the first instance but left Congress in the second instance — to assess themselves —

Judicial tribunals in the different states would become odious — — —

If we always to make a change shall be always in a state of infancy —

    ☞ States will not be disposed hereafter to strengthen the general government.

Mr. Sherman — Confederacy carried us through the war —

Non compliances of States owing to various embarrassment

Why should state legislatures be unfriendly?

State governments will always have the confidence & government of the people: if they cannot be conciliated no efficacious government can be established.

Sense of all states that one *branch is sufficient.*

If consolidated all treaties will be void.

State governments more fit for local legislation customs habits etc

THURSDAY, JUNE 21, 1787.

JOURNAL

June 21. 1787.

The honorable Jonathan Dayton Esquire, a Deputy of the State of New Jersey, attended and took his seat

The following credentials were produced and read. (here insert Mr Dayton's credentials).[1]

It was moved and seconded to agree to the second resolution reported from the Committee, namely,

Resolved that the Legislature consist of Two Branches.

which passed in the affirmative. [Ayes — 7; noes — 3; divided — 1.]

It was moved and seconded to amend the first clause of the 3rd resolution reported from the Committee so as to read

Resolved that the Members of the first branch of the Legislature ought to be appointed in such manner as the Legislature of each State shall direct

On the question to agree to the amendment it passed in the negative [Ayes — 4; noes — 6; divided —1.]

It was then moved and seconded to agree to the first clause of the third resolution as reported from the Committee, namely,

Resolved that the Members of the first branch of the Legislature ought to be elected by the People of the several States.[2] which passed in the affirmative [Ayes — 9; noes — 1; divided — 1.]

---

[1] See Appendix B.

[2] There seems to have been no formal action to strike out the word "National" in the 3d Resolution. In Wilson's copy of the Resolutions of the Convention used by the committee of Detail (see *Records*, July 27 — August 4), the 3d Resolution has "of the United States" inserted after "Legislature" and above the line.

It was moved and seconded to erase the word
"three" from the second clause of the third resolution, reported from the Committee
which passed in the affirmative [Ayes — 7; noes — 3; divided — 1.]

It was moved and seconded to insert the word
"Two" in the second clause of the third resolution reported from the Committee.
    which passed unanimously in the affirmative
and then the House adjourned till to-morrow at 11 o'Clock. A. M.

DETAIL OF AYES AND NOES

	New Hampshire	Massachusetts	Rhode Island	Connecticut	New York	New Jersey	Pennsylvania	Delaware	Maryland	Virginia	North Carolina	South Carolina	Georgia	Questions	Ayes	Noes	Divided
[70]	aye		aye	no	no	aye	no	dd	aye	aye	aye	aye		That the Legislature consist of Two Branches.	7	3	1
[71]	no		aye	no	aye	no	aye	dd	no	no	aye	no		To agree to Genl Pinckney's amendmt that the first branch be elected as the State Legislatures shall direct	4	6	1
[72]	aye		aye	aye	no	aye	aye	dd	aye	aye	aye	aye		That the first branch of the Legislature be elected by the People of the several States	9	1	1
[73]	aye		aye	no	dd	aye	no	no	aye	aye	aye	aye		To strike out the word three in the 2nd clause of the 4 resolution	7	3	1

MADISON

Thursday June 21.* in Convention

Mr. Jonathan Dayton from N. Jersey took his seat.
Doctr. Johnson. On a comparison of the two plans which

*(From June 21 to July 18 inclusive not copied by Mr. Eppes.)³

³ Madison's notes were loaned to Jefferson, whose son-in-law, John W. Eppes, evidently copied portions of them. See Appendix A, CCLXXV, CCLXXXIV, CCCXI, CCCXII, CCCXVI.

had been proposed from Virginia & N. Jersey, it appeared that the peculiarity which characterized the latter was its being calculated to preserve the individuality of the States. The plan from Va. did not profess to destroy this individuality altogether, but was charged with such a tendency. One Gentleman alone (Col. Hamilton) in his animadversions on the plan of N. Jersey, boldly and decisively contended for an abolition of the State Govts. Mr. Wilson & the gentleman from Virga. who also were adversaries of the plan of N. Jersey held a different language. They wished to leave the States in possession of a considerable, tho' a subordinate jurisdiction. They had not yet however shewn how this cd. consist with, or be secured agst. the general sovereignty & jurisdiction, which they proposed to give to the national Government. If this could be shewn in such a manner as to satisfy the patrons of the N. Jersey propositions, that the individuality of the States would not be endangered, many of their objections would no doubt be removed. If this could not be shewn their objections would have their full force. He wished it therefore to be well considered whether in case the States, as was proposed, shd. retain some portion of sovereignty at least, this portion could be preserved, without allowing them to participate effectually in the Genl. Govt., without giving them each a distinct and equal vote for the purpose of defending themselves in the general Councils.

Mr. Wilson's respect for Dr. Johnson, added to the importance of the subject led him to attempt, unprepared as he was, to solve the difficulty which had been started. It was asked how the genl. Govt. and individuality of the particular States could be reconciled to each other; and how the latter could be secured agst. the former? Might it not, on the other side be asked how the former was to be secured agst. the latter? It was generally admitted that a jealousy & rivalship would be felt between the Genl. & particular Govts. As the plan now stood, tho' indeed contrary to his opinion, one branch of the Genl. — Govt. (the Senate or second branch) was to be appointed by the State Legislatures. The State Legislatures, therefore, by this participation in the Genl. Govt. would have an opportunity of defending their rights. Ought not a recip-rocal opportunity to be given to the Genl. Govt. of defending itself by having an appointment of some one constituent branch of the State Govts. If a security be necessary on one side, it wd. seem reasonable to demand it on the other. But taking the matter in a more general view, he saw no danger to the States from the Genl. Govt. In case a combination should be made by the large ones it wd produce a general alarm among the rest; and the project wd. be frustrated. But there was no temptation to such a project. The States having in general a similar interest, in case of any proposition in the National Legislature to encroach on the State Legislatures, he conceived a general alarm wd. take place in the National Leg-islature itself, that it would communicate itself to the State Legislatures, and wd. finally spread among the people at large. The Genl. Govt. will be as ready to preserve the rights of the States as the latter are to preserve the rights of individuals; all the members of the former, having a common interest, as representatives of all the people of the latter, to leave the State Govts. in possession of what the people wish them to retain. He could not discover, therefore any danger what-ever on the side from which it had been apprehended. On the contrary, he conceived that in spite of every precaution the General Govt. would be in perpetual danger of encroach-ments from the State Govts.[4]

⟨Mr. Madison⟩ was of opinion that there was 1. less danger of encroachment from the Genl. Govt. than from the State Govts. 2. that the mischief from encroachments would be less fatal if made by the former, than if made by the latter. 1. All the examples of other confederacies prove the greater tendency in such systems to anarchy than to tyranny; to a disobedience of the members than to usurpations of the federal head. Our own experience had fully illustrated this tendency. — But it will be said that the proposed change in the prin-ciples & form of the Union will vary the tendency, that the Genl. Govt. will have real & greater powers, and will be

---

[4] See further Appendix A, CXLII.

derived in one branch at least from the people not from the Govts. of the States. To give full force to this objection, let it be supposed for a moment that indefinite power should be given to the Gen'l Legislature, and the States reduced to corporations dependent on the Genl. Legislature; why shd. it follow that the Gen'l Govt. wd. take from the States ⟨any⟩ [5] branch of their power as far as its operation was beneficial, and its continuance desirable to the people? In some of the States, particularly in Connecticut, all the Townships are incorporated, and have a certain limited jurisdiction. Have the Representatives of the people of the Townships in the Legislature of the State ever endeavored to despoil the Townships of any part of their local authority? As far as this local authority is convenient to the people they are attached to it; and their representatives chosen by & amenable to them ⟨naturally⟩ respect their attachment to this, as much as their attachment to any other right or interest: The relation of a Genl. Govt. to State Govts. is parallel. 2. Guards were more necessary agst. encroachments of the State Govts. — on the Genl. Govt. than of the latter on the former. The great objection made agst. an abolition of the State Govts. was that the Genl. Govt. could not extend its care to all the minute objects which fall under the cognizance of the local jurisdictions. The objection as stated lay not agst. the probable abuse of the general power, but agst. the imperfect use that could be made of it throughout so great an extent of country, and over so great a variety of objects. As far as its operation would be practicable it could not in this view be improper; as far as it would be impracticable, the conveniency of the Genl. Govt. itself would concur with that of the people in the maintenance of subordinate Governments. Were it practicable for the Genl. Govt. to extend its care to every requisite object without the cooperation of the State Govts. the people would not be less free as members of one great Republic than as members of thirteen small ones. A citizen of Delaware was not more free than a citizen of Virginia: nor would either

---

[5] Crossed out "one".

be more free than a citizen of America. Supposing therefore a tendency in the Genl. Government to absorb the State Govts. no fatal consequence could result. Taking the reverse of the supposition, that a tendency should be left in the State Govts. towards an independence on the General Govt. and the gloomy consequences need not be pointed out. The imagination of them, must have suggested to the States the experiment we are now making to prevent the calamity, and must have formed the chief motive with those present to undertake the arduous task.

On the question [6] for resolving "that the Legislature ought to consist of two Branches"

Mass ay. Cont. ay. N. Y. no. ⟨N. Jersey no⟩[7] Pa. ay. Del. no. Md. divd.[8] Va. ay. N. C. ay. S. C. ay. Geo. ay [Ayes — 7; noes — 3; divided — 1.]

The *third* resolution[9] of the Report taken into consideration.

Genl. Pinkney moved "that the 1st. branch, instead of being elected by the people, shd. be elected in such manner as the Legislature of each State should direct." He urged 1. that this liberty would give more satisfaction, as the Legislatures could then accomodate the mode to the conveniency & opinions of the people. 2. that it would avoid the undue influence of large Counties which would prevail if the elections were to be made in districts as must be the mode intended by the Report of the Committee. 3. that otherwise disputed elections must be referred to the General Legislature which would be attended with intolerable expence and trouble to the distant parts of the republic.

Mr. L. Martin seconded the Motion.[10]

Col. Hamilton considered the motion as intended manifestly to transfer the election from the people to the State Legislatures, which would essentially vitiate the plan. It would increase that State influence which could not be too

[6] See further Appendix A, CXXXVII, CLXVI, CCCXXXI.
[7] "N. Jersey no" taken from *Journal*, which is confirmed by Yates to this extent that he records three votes in the negative.
[8] Martin voted in the negative, see Appendix A, CLVIII (11, 37).
[9] On the composition of the lower house. [10] See Appendix A, CXCI.

watchfully guarded agst. All too must admit the possibility, in case the Genl. Govt. shd. maintain itself, that the State Govts. might gradually dwindle into nothing. The system therefore shd. not be engrafted on what might possibly fail.

Mr. Mason urged the necessity of retaining the election by the people. Whatever inconveniency may attend the democratic principle, it must actuate one part of the Govt. It is the only security for the rights of the people.

Mr. Sherman, would like an election by the Legislatures, best, but is content with plan as it stands.

Mr. Rutlidge could not admit the solidity of the distinction between a mediate & immediate election by the people. It was the same thing to act by oneself, and to act by another. An election by the Legislature would be more refined than an election immediately by the people: and would be more likely to correspond with the sense of the whole community. If this Convention had been chosen by the people in districts it is not to be supposed that such proper characters would have been preferred. The Delegates to Congs. he thought had also been fitter men than would have been appointed by the people at large.

Mr. Wilson considered the election of the 1st. branch by the people not only as the corner Stone, but as the foundation of the fabric: and that the difference between a mediate and immediate election was immense. The difference was particularly worthy of notice in this respect: that the Legislatures are actuated not merely by the sentiment of the people, but have an official sentiment opposed to that of the Genl: Govt. and perhaps to that of the people themselves.

Mr. King enlarged on the same distinction. He supposed the Legislatures wd. constantly choose men subservient to their own views as contrasted to the general interest; and that they might even devise modes of election that wd. be subversive of the end in view. He remarked several instances in which the views of a State might be at variance with those of the Gen'l. Govt. and mentioned particularly a competition between the National & State debts, for the most certain & productive funds.

Genl. Pinkney was for making the State Govts. a part of the General System. If they were to be abolished, or lose their agency, S. Carolina & other States would have but a small share of the benefits of Govt.

On the question for Genl. Pinkney motion to substitute election of 1st branch in such mode as the Legislatures should appoint, in stead of its being elected by the people

Masst. no. Cont. ay. N. Y. no. N. J. ay. Pa. no. Del. ay. Md. divd. Va. no. N. C. no. S. C. ay Geo. no. [Ayes — 4; noes — 6; divided — 1.]

Genl. Pinkney then moved that the 1st. branch be elected *by the people* in such mode as the Legislatures should direct; but waved it on its being hinted that such a provision might be more properly tried in the detail of the plan.

On the question for ye election of the 1st branch by the *people"*

Massts. ay. Cont. ay. N. Y. ay. N. J. no. Pa. ay. Del. ay. Md. divd. Va. ay. N. C. ay. S. C. ay Geo. ay. [Ayes — 9; noes — 1; divided — 1.]

Election of the 1st. branch "for the term of three years," considered [11]

Mr. Randolph moved to strike out, "three years" and insert "two years" — he was sensible that annual elections were a source of great mischiefs in the States, yet it was the want of such checks agst. the popular intemperance as were now proposed, that rendered them so mischievous. He would have preferred annual to biennial, but for the extent of the U. S. and the inconveniency which would result from them to the representatives of the extreme parts of the Empire. The people were attached to frequency of elections. All the Constitutions of the States except that of S. Carolina, had established annual elections.

Mr. Dickenson. The idea of annual elections was borrowed from the antient usage of England, a country much less extensive than ours. He supposed biennial would be inconvenient. He preferred triennial: and in order to prevent the incon-

---

[11] Upon this question see above June 12, and for the debate following, with the final determination of the question, see Appendix A, CLXVIII.

veniency of an entire change of the whole number at the same moment, suggested a rotation, by an annual election of one third.

Mr. Elseworth was opposed to three years. supposing that even one year was preferable to two years. The people were fond of frequent elections and might be safely indulged in one branch of the Legislature. He moved for 1 year.

Mr. Strong seconded & supported the motion.

Mr. Wilson being for making the 1st. branch an effectual representation of the people at large, preferred an annual election of it. This frequency was most familiar & pleasing to the people. It would be not more inconvenient to them, than triennial elections, as the people in all the States have annual meetings with which the election of the National representatives might be made to coin ——cide. He did not conceive that it would be necessary for the Natl. Legisl: to sit constantly; perhaps not half — perhaps not one fourth of the year.

Mr. M⟨adison⟩ was persuaded that annual elections would be extremely inconvenient and apprehensive that biennial would be too much so: he did not mean inconvenient to the electors; but to the representatives. They would have to travel seven or eight hundred miles from the distant parts of the Union; and would probably not be allowed even a reimbursement of their expences. Besides, none of those who wished to be re-elected would remain at the seat of Governmt. confiding that their absence would not affect them. The members of Congs. had done this with few instances of disappointment. But as the choice was here to be made by the people themselves who would be much less complaisant to individuals, and much more susceptible of impressions from the presence of a Rival candidate,[11a] it must be supposed that the members from the most distant States would travel backwards & forwards at least as often as the elections should be repeated. Much was to be said also on the time requisite for new members who would always form a large proportion, to acquire that knowledge of the affairs of the States in general without which their trust could not be usefully discharged.

[11a] Crossed out: "than the legislatures had been".

Mr. Sherman preferred annual elections, but would be content with biennial. He thought the representatives ought to return home and mix with the people. By remaining at the seat of Govt. they would acquire the habits of the place which might differ from those of their Constituents.

Col. Mason observed that the States being differently situated such a rule ought to be formed as would put them as nearly as possible on a level. If elections were annual the middle States would have a great advantage over the extreme ones. He wished them to be biennial; and the rather as in that case they would coincide with the periodical elections of S. Carolina as well as of the other States.

Coll. Hamilton urged the necessity of 3 years. there ought to be neither too much nor too little dependence, on the popular sentiments. The checks in the other branches of Governt. would be but feeble, and would need every auxiliary principle that could be interwoven. The British House of Commons were elected septennially, yet the democratic spirit of ye Constitution had not ceased. Frequency of elections tended to make the people listless to them; and to facilitate the success of little cabals. This evil was complained of in all the States. In Virga. it had been lately found necessary to force the attendance & voting of the people by severe regulations.

On the question for striking out "three years"

Massts. ay. Cont. ay. N. Y. no. N J. divd. Pa. ay. Del. no. Md. no. Va. ay. N. C. ay. S. C. ay. Geo. ay.   [Ayes — 7; noes — 3; divided — 1.]

The motion for "two years." was then inserted nem. con.

Adjd. [12]

YATES

THURSDAY, JUNE 21st, 1787.

Met pursuant to adjournment. Present 11 states.

Dr Johnson — It appears to me that the Jersey plan has for its principal object, the preservation of the state govern-

---

[12] See further Appendix A, XLVII.

ments. So far it is a departure from the plan of Virginia, which although it concentres in a distinct national government, it is not totally independent of that of the states. A gentleman from New-York, with boldness and decision, proposed a system totally different from both; and though he has been praised by every body, he has been supported by none. How can the state governments be secured on the Virginia plan? I could have wished, that the supporters of the Jersey system could have satisfied themselves with the principles of the Virginia plan and that the individuality of the states could be supported. It is agreed on all hands that a portion of government is to be left to the states. How can this be done? It can be done by joining the states in their legislative capacity with the right of appointing the second branch of the national legislature, to represent the states individually.

Mr. Wilson. If security is necessary to preserve the one, it is equally so to preserve the other. How can the national government be secured against the states? Some regulation is necessary. Suppose the national government had a component number in the state legislature? But where the one government clashed with the other, the state government ought to yield, as the preservation of the general interest must be preferred to a particular. But let us try to designate the powers of each, and then no danger can be apprehended nor can the general government be possessed of any ambitious views to encroach on the state rights.

Mr. Madison. I could have wished that the gentleman from Connecticut had more accurately marked his objections to the Virginia plan. I apprehended the greatest danger is from the encroachment of the states on the national government — This apprehension is justly founded on the experience of ancient confederacies, and our own is a proof of it.[13]

The right of negativing in certain instances the state laws, affords one security to the national government. But is the danger well founded? Have any state governments ever encroached on the corporate rights of cities? And if

---

[13] *Cf.* Genet's interpretation of this speech in Appendix A, CCCX.

it was the case that the national government usurped the state government, if such usurpation was for the good of the whole, no mischief could arise. — To draw the line between the two, is a difficult task. I believe it cannot be done, and therefore I am inclined for a general government.

If we cannot form a general government, and the states become totally independent of each other, it would afford a melancholy prospect.

The 2d resolve was then put and carried — 7 states for — 3 against — one divided. New-York in the minority.

The 3d resolve was then taken into consideration by the convention.

Mr. Pinkney. I move *that the members of the first branch be appointed in such manner as the several state legislatures shall direct*, instead of the mode reported. If this motion is not agreed to, the other will operate with great difficulty, if not injustice — If you make district elections and join, as I presume you must, many counties in one district, the largest county will carry the election as its united influence will give a decided majority in its favor.

Mr. Madison. I oppose the motion — there are difficulties, but they may be obviated in the details connected with the subject.

Mr. Hamilton. It is essential to the democratic rights of the community, that this branch be directly elected by the people. Let us look forward to probable events — There may be a time when state legislatures may cease, and such an event ought not to embarrass the national government.

Mr. Mason. I am for preserving inviolably the democratic branch of the government — True, we have found inconveniencies from pure democracies; but if we mean to preserve peace and real freedom, they must necessarily become a component part of a national government. Change this necessary principle, and if the government proceeds to taxation, the states will oppose your powers.

Mr. Sherman thought that an amendment to the proposed amendment is necessary.

Gov. Rutledge. It is said that an election by representatives is not an election by the people. This proposition is not correct. What is done by my order is done by myself. I am convinced that the mode of election by legislatures will be more refined, and better men will be sent.

Mr. Wilson. The legislature of the states by the proposed motion will have an uncontrolable sway over the general government. Election is the exercise of *original* sovereignty in the people — but if by representatives, it is only *relative* sovereignty.

Mr. King. The magistrates of the states will ever pursue schemes of their own, and this, on the proposed motion, will pervade the national government — and we know the state governments will be ever hostile to the general government.

Mr. Pinkney. All the reasoning of the gentlemen opposed to my motion has not convinced me of its impropriety. There is an *esprit de corps* which has made heretofore every *unfederal* member of congress, after his election, become strictly *federal*, and this I presume will ever be the case in whatever manner they may be elected.

Question put on Mr. Pinkney's motion and carried by 6 states against 4 — one divided.

Question then put on the resolve — 9 states for — 1 against — one divided.

Gov. Randolph. I move that in the resolve for the duration of the first branch of the general legislature, the word *three* be expunged, and the words *two years* be inserted.

Mr. Dickinson. I am against the amendment. I propose that the word *three* shall remain, but that they shall be removable annually in classes.

Mr. Sherman. I am for one year. Our people are accustomed to annual elections. Should the members have a longer duration of service, and remain at the seat of government, they may forget their constitutents, and perhaps imbibe the interest of the state in which they reside, or there may be danger of catching the *esprit de corps*.

Mr. Mason. I am for two years. One year is too short. — In extensive states four months may elapse before the returns can be known, Hence the danger of their remaining too long unrepresented.

Mr. Hamilton.   There is a medium in every thing.   I confess three years is not too long — A representative ought to
have full freedom of deliberation, and ought to exert an
opinion of his own.   I am convinced that the public mind will
adopt a solid plan — The government of New-York, although
higher toned than that of any other state, still we find great
listlessness and indifference in the electors; nor do they in
general bring forward the first characters to the legislature.
The public mind is perhaps not now ready to receive the best
plan of government, but certain circumstances are now pro-
gressing which will give a different complexion to it.

Two years duration agreed to.

Adjourned till to-morrow morning.

KING

20 [21] June

Johnson — The Gentleman from NYk is praised by every
gentleman, but supported by no gentleman — He goes directly
to ye abolition of the State Governts. and the erection of a
Genl. Govt. — All other Gentlemen agree that the national
or Genl. Govt. shd. be more powerful — & the State Govts.
less so.   Provision is made in the Virgina Project to secure
the Genl. Govt: but no provision is made for the security of
the State Government —   The plan from N Jersey provides
for the security of the State & Genl. Govt. —   If the advocates
for the Genl. Govt. agreeably to the Virgin. Plan can show
that the State Govts. will be secure from the Genl. Govt. we
may all agree —

Wilson — We have provided that the States or yr. Legislatures shall appt. a Brh. of the national Govt. let the Natl.
Govt. have a reciprocal power to elect or appoint one Br. of
each State Govt — I dont see how the State Govts will be
endangered — what power will the states possess, which the
Genl. Govt. will wish to possess? their powers if added wd.
not be of any considerable consequence — the attempt, how-

ever to acquire these powers wd. alarm the Citizens, who gave them to the States individually, and never intended them for the Genl. Govt. — The people wd. not suffer it —

Madison — The history of antient Confedys. proves that there never has existed a danger of the destruction of the State Govts. by encroachments of the Genl. Govts the converse of the proposition is true — I have therefore been assiduous to guard the Genl. from the power of the State Governments — the State Govts. regulate the conduct of their Citizens, they punish offenders — they cause Justice to be administered and do those arts wh endear the Govt. to its Citizens. The Citizens will not therefore suffer the Genl. Govt. to injure the State Govts —

The Convention agreed yt the Legislature shd. consist of two Brs —

The Delegates of So. Car. moved yt. the Election of the Members of the House shd. be agreeable to such mode as the several Legislatures shd. judge proper —

Wilson & Madison

Agt. the Election by the Legislatures and in favor of one by the People — the Election by the States will introduce a State Influence, their interest will oppose yt of the Genl. Govt: the Legislators will be not only Electors of the members of the House, — but they will manage the affairs of the States — The mode of Election may be essential to the Election, this may be different in the several States — if the Legislatures appt. they will instruct, and thereby embarrass the Delegate — not so if the Election is by the people — there will be no difficulty in yr. Election. the Returns may be made to the Legislatures of the several States — They may judge of contested Elections — On the Quest. 4 ay 1 divd. 6 no —

Question whether the Members of the House shd. hold yr. Office three or two years —

Dickerson — annual Elections are favorite ideas in America —

it suits Eng. they are a small Country — Annual or biennial or triennial are too short for America — I wd. agree on classing the house — let the Election be for 3 yrs and ⅓ go out & come in annually —

Elsworth & Strong — The fixed habit througout our country except So. Carolina is in favor of annual Elections —
Wilson — Agrees in annual Elections —
Mason — I dont see but that an annual Election will give an advantage to some States over the others — in Virginia & Georgia from the sparse and remote situation of the Inhabitants, we cd. not ascertain the persons elected under three years — The States wh are most compact will be first on the Floor and those of the extensive States will be absent — Remark let the election be previous three or 6 months to the time of meeting —
Hamilton — I prefer three years to a longer or shorter duration — three soon becomes two & two one — The Dependence is sufficient, & the independence is as little as it ought to be — [14]

HAMILTON [15]

Mr. Pinckney is of opinion that the first branch ought to be appointed in such manner as the legislatures shall direct
    Impracticable for general legislature to decide contested elections —

---

[14] [Endorsed] 20 June | 1 or 2 Branches? | Election of Reps by whom?
[15] This note is on the same sheet as the notes ascribed to June 19, but it probably refers to General Pinckney's remarks of this date.

FRIDAY, JUNE 22, 1787.

JOURNAL

Friday June 22.

[To strike out the 3 clause in ye 3 resolution — to substitute "their stipends to be ascertained by the Legislature to be paid out of the pub: treasury Ayes — 2; noes — 7; divided — 2.] [1]

It was moved and seconded to strike the following words out of the 4th clause in the 3rd resolution reported from the Committee namely

"To be paid out of the public treasury" [2]

On the question to strike out the words

it passed in the negative [Ayes — 4; noes — 5; divided — 2]

It was moved and seconded to strike the following words out of the 3rd resolution reported from the committee, namely

"to receive fixed stipends by which they may be compensated for the devotion of their time to public service" and to substitute the following clause, namely

"to receive an adequate compensation for their services"

On the question to agree to the amendment

it passed in the affirmative [Ayes — 11; noes — 0.]

It was then moved and seconded to take the vote of the House on the whole proposition namely

"To receive an adequate compensation for their services, to be paid out of the public Treasury."

An objection of order being taken to this motion — it was submitted to the House.

and on the question is the motion in order

it passed in the affirmative. [Ayes — 6; noes — 4; divided —1.] [3]

---

[1] Vote 74, Detail of Ayes and Noes.

[2] "National" is used instead of "public" in statement of question in Detail of Ayes and Noes, vote 75. See June 21 note 2.

[3] Vote 77, Detail of Ayes and Noes, where question is worded — "whether sep-

The determination of the House on the whole proposition was, on motion of the Deputies of the State of South Carolina, postponed till to-morrow.

It was moved and seconded to add the following clause to the 3rd resolution

> to be of the age of 25 years at least.
>
> which passed in the affirmative.   Ayes—7; noes—3; divided — 1.] -

It was moved and seconded to strike out the following words in the last clause of the 3rd resolution

"and under the national government for the space of One year after it's expiration"

> On the question to strike out the words
>
> it passed in the negative.   [Ayes — 4; noes — 4; divided — 3.]

and then the House adjourned till to-morrow at 11 o'Clock. A. M.

---

arate votes having been taken on diff: clauses of a proposition a question shall be taken on ye whole."

DETAIL OF AYES AND NOES

New Hampshire	Massachusetts	Rhode Island	Connecticut	New York	New Jersey	Pennsylvania	Delaware	Maryland	Virginia	North Carolina	South Carolina	Georgia	Questions	Ayes	Noes	Divided
[74]	no		no	dd	aye	aye	no	no	no	no	no	dd	To strike out the 3 clause in ye 3 resolution — to substitute "their stipends to be ascertained by the Legislature to be paid out of the pub: treasury	2	7	2
[75]	aye		aye	dd	no	no	no	no	no	aye	aye	dd	To strike out the words "to be paid out of the National Treasy"	4	5	2
[76]	aye		aye	aye	aye	aye	aye	aye	aye	aye	aye	aye	To receive an adequate compensation for their services	11		
[77]	dd		aye	no	aye	no	aye	aye	no	aye	aye	no	whether separate votes having been taken on diff: clauses of a proposition a question shall be taken on ye whole	6	4	1
[78]	no		aye	dd	aye	no	aye	aye	aye	aye	aye	no	To add the followg words to the clause of the 3 resolution to be of the age of 25 years at least	7	3	1
[79]	aye		no	dd	aye	dd	dd	no	no	aye	no	aye	To strike out the following words in the 3rd resolution namely and under the national govt for the space of One year after it's expiration	4	4	3

MADISON

Friday June 22. ⟨in Convention⟩

The clause ⟨in Resol. 3⟩ "to receive fixed stipends to be paid out of the Nationl. Treasury" considered.

Mr. Elseworth, moved to substitute payment by the States out of their own Treasurys: observing that the manners of different States were very different in the Stile of living and in the profits accruing from the exercise of like talents. What would be deemed therefore a reasonable compensation in some States, in others would be very unpopular, and might impede the system of which it made a part.

Mr. Williamson favored the idea. He reminded the House of the prospect of new States to the Westward. They would be poor — would pay little into the common Treasury — and would have a different interest from the old States. He did not think therefore that the latter ought to pay the expences of men who would be employed in thwarting their measures & interests.

Mr. Ghorum, wished not to refer the matter to the State Legislatures who were always paring down salaries in such a manner as to keep out of offices men most capable of executing the functions of them. He thought also it would be wrong to fix the compensations by the constitution, because we could not venture to make it as liberal as it ought to be without exciting an enmity agst. the whole plan. Let the Natl. Legisl: provide for their own wages from time to time; as the State Legislatures do. He had not seen this part of their power abused, nor did he apprehend an abuse of it.

Mr. Randolph feared we were going too far, in consulting popular prejudices. Whatever respect might be due to them, in lesser matters, or in cases where they formed the permanent character of the people, he thought it neither incumbent on nor honorable for the Convention, to sacrifice right & justice to that consideration. If the States were to pay the members of the Natl. Legislature, a dependence would be created that would vitiate the whole System. The whole nation has an interest in the attendance & services of the members. The Nationl. Treasury therefore is the proper fund for supporting them.

Mr. King, urged the danger of creating a dependence on the States by leavg. to them the payment of the members of the Natl. Legislature. He supposed it wd. be best to be explicit as to the compensation to be allowed. A reserve on that point, or a reference to the Natl. Legislature of the quantum, would excite greater opposition than any sum that would be actually necessary or proper.

Mr. Sherman contended for referring both the quantum and the payment of it to the State Legislatures.

Mr. Wilson was agst. *fixing* the compensation as circumstances would change and call for a change of the amount. He thought it of great moment that the members of the Natl. Govt. should be left as independent ⟨as possible⟩ of the State Govts. in all respects.

Mr. M⟨adison⟩ concurred in the necessity of preserving the compensations for the Natl. Govt. independent on the State Govts. but at the same time approved of *fixing* them by the constitution, which might be done by taking a standard which wd. not vary with circumstances.[4] He disliked particularly the policy suggested by Mr. Wiliamson of leaving the members from the poor States beyond the Mountains, to the precarious & parsimonious support of their constituents. If the Western States hereafter arising should be admitted into the Union, they ought to be considered as equals & as brethren. If their representatives were to be associated in the Common Councils, it was of common concern that such provisions should be made as would invite the most capable and respectable characters into the service.

Mr. Hamilton apprehended inconveniency from *fixing* the wages. He was strenuous agst. making the National Council dependent on the Legislative rewards of the States. Those who pay are the masters of those who are paid. Payment by the States would be unequal as the distant States would have to pay for the same term of attendance and more days in travelling to & from the seat of the Govt. He expatiated emphatically on the difference between the feelings & views of the *people* — & the *Governments* of the States arising from the personal interest & official inducements which must render the latter unfriendly to the Genl. Govt.

Mr. Wilson moved that the salaries of the 1st. branch "*be ascertained by the National Legislature*," and be paid out of the Natl. Treasury.

⟨Mr. Madison, thought the members of the Legisl. too much

---

[4] See Dickinson's statement on August 14 and Appendix A, CCX.

interested to ascertain their own compensation. It wd. be indecent to put their hands into the public purse for the sake of their own pockets.⟩⁵

On this question Mas. no. Con. no. N. Y. divd. N. J. ay. Pa. ay. Del. no. Md. no. Va. no. N. C. ⟨no⟩ S. C. ⟨no⟩ Geo. divd. [Ayes — 2; noes — 7; divided — 2.] ⁶

On the question for striking out "Natl. Treasury" ⟨as moved by Mr. Elseworth⟩ ⁷

⟨Mr. Hamilton renewed his opposition to it. He pressed the distinction between State Govts. & the people. The former wd. be the rivals of the Gen'l Govt. The State legislatures ought not therefore to be the pay masters of the latter.

Mr. Elesworth. If we are jealous of the State Govts. they will be so of us. If on going home I tell them we gave the Gen: Govt. such powers because we cd. not trust you. — will they adopt it. & witht. yr. approbation it is a nullity.⟩ ⁸

Masts. ay.* Cont. ay. N. Y. divd. N. J. no. Pena. no. Del. no. Md. no. Va. no, N. C. ay. S. C. ay. Geo. divd. [Ayes — 4; noes — 5; divided — 2.]

On a question for substituting "adequate compensation" in place of "fixt Stipends" it was agreed to nem. con. the friends of the latter being willing that the practicability of *fixing* the compensation should be considered hereafter in forming the details.

It was then moved by Mr. Butler that a question be taken on both points jointly; to wit "adequate compensation to be paid out of the Natl. Treasury." It was objected to as out of order, the parts having been separately decided on. The Presidt. referd. the question of order to the House, and it was

---

* It appeared that Massts. concurred, not because they thought the State Treasy. ought to be substituted; but because they thought nothing should be said on the subject, in which case it wd. silently devolve on the Natl. Treasury to support the National Legislature.

---

⁵ Taken from Yates.

⁶ Vote corrected from *Journal* and Yates; originally Madison recorded North Carolina and South Carolina in the affirmative.

⁷ Probably a mistake; Ellsworth's motion was not in this form; and Yates ascribes it to Rutledge. Madison evidently missed this part of the proceedings.

⁸ Taken from Yates.

determined to be in order. ⟨Con. N. J. Del. Md. N. C. S. C. — ay — N. Y. Pa. Va. Geo. no — Mass: divided.⟩[9] The question on the sentence was then postponed by S. Carolina in right of the State.[10]

Col. Mason moved to insert "twenty five years of age as a qualification for the members of the 1st. branch". He thought it absurd that a man to day should not be permitted by the law to make a bargain for himself, and tomorrow should be authorized to manage the affairs of a great nation. It was the more extraordinary as every man carried with him in his own experience a scale for measuring the deficiency of young politicians; since he would if interrogated be obliged to declare that his political opinions at the age of 21. were too crude & erroneous to merit an influence on public measures. It had been said that Congs. had proved a good school for our young men. It might be so for any thing he knew but if it were, he chose that they should bear the expence of their own education.

Mr. Wilson was agst. abridging the rights of election in any shape. It was the same thing whether this were done by disqualifying the objects of choice, or the persons chusing. The motion tended to damp the efforts of genius, and of laudable ambition. There was no more reason for incapacitating *youth* than *age*, when the requisite qualifications were found. Many instances might be mentioned of signal services rendered in high stations to the public before the age of 25: The present Mr. Pitt and Lord Bolingbroke were striking instances.

On the question for inserting "25 years of age"
Massts. no. Cont. ay. N. Y. divd. N. J. ay. Pa. no. Del. ay. Md. ay. Va. ay. N. C. ay. S. C. ay. Geo. no. [Ayes — 7; noes — 3; divided — 1.]

Mr. Ghorum moved to strike out the last member of 3 Resol: concerning ineligibility of members of 1st branch to offices, during the term of their membership & for one year after. He considered it as unnecessary & injurious.[11] ⟨It was true abuses had been displayed in G. B. but no one cd. say how

---

[9] Taken from *Journal.*   [10] See further August 14, note 7.
[11] See further, references under September 3, note 7.

far they might have contributed to preserve the due influence of the Gov't nor what might have ensued in case the contrary theory had been tried.⟩ [12]

Mr. Butler opposed it. this precaution agst. intrigue was necessary. ⟨He appealed to the example of G. B. where men got into Parlt. that they might get offices for themselves or their friends. This was the source of the corruption that ruined their Govt.⟩ [13]

Mr. King, thought we were refining too much. Such a restriction on the members would discourage merit. It would also give a pretext to the Executive for bad appointments, as he might always plead this as a bar to the choice he wished to have made.

Mr. Wilson was agst. fettering elections, and discouraging merit. He suggested also the fatal consequence in time of war, of rendering ⟨perhaps⟩ the best Commanders ineligible: appealing to our situation during the late ⟨war⟩, and indirectly leading to a recollection of the appointment of the Commander in Chief out of Congress.

Col. Mason was for shutting the door at all events agst. corruption. He enlarged on the venality and abuses in this particular in G. Britain: ⟨and alluded to the multiplicity of foreign Embassiess by Congs. The disqualification he regarded as a corner stone in the fabric.⟩ [13]

Col. Hamilton. There are inconveniences on both sides. We must take man as we find him, and if we expect him to serve the public must interest his passions in doing so. A reliance on pure patriotism had been the source of many of our errors. He thought the remark of Mr. Ghorum a just one. It was impossible to say what wd. be effect in G. B of such a reform as had been urged. It was known that ⟨one⟩ of the ablest politicians (Mr Hume) had pronounced all that influence on the side of the crown, which went under the name of corruption, an essential part of the weight which maintained the equilibrium of the Constitution.

---

[12] Substance of this taken from Yates, according to whom Gorham made remarks to this effect later in the debate, — in fact, they have no point until after the remarks of Butler and Mason.   [13] Taken from Yates.

On Mr. Ghorum's Motion for striking out "ineligibility".
Masts. ay. Cont. no. N. Y. divd. N. J. ay. Pa. divd. Del.
divd. Mard. no. Va. no. N. C. ay. S — C. no — Geo ay
[Ayes — 4; noes — 4; divided — 3.]
adjd.

YATES

FRIDAY, JUNE 22d, 1787.

Met pursuant to adjournment.

The clause of the 3d resolve, respecting the *stipends*, taken into consideration.

Judge Elsworth. I object to this clause. I think the state legislatures ought to provide for the members of the general legislature, and as each state will have a proportionate number, it will not be burthensome to the smaller states. I therefore move to strike out the clause.

Mr. Gorham. If we intend to fix the stipend, it may be an objection against the system, as the states would never adopt it. I join in sentiment to strike out the whole.

Gov. Randolph. I am against the motion. Are the members to be paid? Certainly — We have no sufficient fortunes to induce gentlemen to attend for nothing. If the state legislatures pay the members of the national council, they will controul the members, and compel them to pursue state measures. I confess the payment will not operate impartially, but the members must be paid, and be made easy in their circumstances. Will they attend the service of the public without being paid?

Mr. Sherman. The states ought to pay their members; and I judge of the approbation of the people on matters of government by what I suppose they will approve.

Mr. Wilson. — I am against going as far as the resolve. If, however, it is intended to throw the national legislature into the hand of the states, I shall be against it. It is possible the states may become unfederal, and they may then shake the national government. The members ought to be paid out of the national treasury.

Mr. Madison. Our attention is too much confined to the present moment, when our regulations are intended to be perpetual. Our national government must operate for the good of the whole, and the people must have a general interest in its support; but if you make its legislators subject to and at the mercy of the state governments, you ruin the fabric — and whatever new states may be added to the general government the expence will be equally borne.

Mr. Hamilton. I do not think the states ought to pay the members, nor am I for a fixed sum. It is a general remark, that he who pays is the master. If each state pays its own members, the burthen would be disproportionate, according to the distance of the states from the seat of government. If a national government can exist, members will make it a desirable object to attend, without accepting any stipend — and it ought to be so organized as to be efficient.

Mr. Wilson. I move *that the stipend be ascertained by the legislature and paid out of the national treasury.*

Mr. Madison. I oppose this motion. Members are too much interested in the question. Besides, it is indecent that the legislature should put their hands in the public purse to convey it into their own.

Question put on Mr. Wilson's motion and negatived — 7 states against — 2 for, and 2 divided.

Mr. Mason moved to change the phraseology of the resolve, that is to say, *to receive an adequate compensation for their services*, and to be paid out of the treasury. This motion was agreed to.

Mr. Rutledge. I move that the question be taken on these words, *to be paid out of the national treasury.*

Mr. Hamilton. It has been often asserted, that the interests of the general and of the state legislatures are precisely the same. This cannot be true. The views of the governed are often materially different from those who govern. The science of policy is the knowledge of human nature. A state government will ever be the rival power of the general government. It is therefore highly improper that the state legislatures should be the paymasters of the members of the national government. All political bodies love power, and it will often be improperly attained.

Judge Elsworth. If we are so exceedingly jealous of state legislatures, will they not have reason to be equally jealous of us. If I return to my state and tell them, we made such and such regulations for a general government, because we dared not trust you with any extensive powers, will they be satisfied? nay, will they adopt your government? and let it ever be remembered, that without their approbation your government is nothing more than a rope of sand.

Mr. Wilson. I am not for submitting the national government to the approbation of the state legislatures. I know that they and the state officers will oppose it. I am for carrying it to the people of each state.

Mr. Rutledge's motion was then put — 4 states for the clause — 5 against — 2 states divided. New-York divided.

The clause, to be ineligible to any office, &c. came next to be considered.

Mr. Mason moved that after the words, *two years*, be added, *and to be of the age of 25 years.*

Question put and agreed to — 7 ayes — 3 noes. New-York divided.

Mr. Gorham. I move that after the words, *and under the national government for one year after its expiration*, be struck out.

Mr. King for the motion. It is impossible to carry the system of exclusion so far; and in this instance we refine too much by going to *utopian* lengths. It is a mere cobweb.

Mr. Butler. We have no way of judging of mankind but by experience. Look at the history of the government of Great Britain, where there is a very flimsy exclusion — Does it not ruin their government? A man takes a seat in parliament to get an office for himself or friends, or both; and this is the great source from which flows its great venality and corruption.

Mr. Wilson. I am for striking out the words moved for. Strong reasons must induce me to disqualify a good man from office. If you do, you give an opportunity to the dependent or avaricious man to fill it up, for to them offices are objects of desire. If we admit there may be cabal and intrigue between the executive and legislative bodies, the exclusion of one year will not prevent the effects of it. But we ought to hold forth every honorable inducement for men of abilities to enter the service of the public. — This is truly a republican principle. Shall talents, which entit e a man to public reward, operate as a punishment? While a member of the legislature, he ought to be excluded from any other office, but no longer. Suppose a war breaks out and a number of your best military characters were members; must we lose the benefit of their services? Had this been the case in the beginning of the war, what would have been our situation? — and what has happened may happen again.

Mr. Madison. Some gentlemen give too much weight and others too little to this subject. If you have no exclusive clause, there may be danger of creating offices or augmenting the stipends of those already created, in order to gratify some members if they were not excluded. Such an instance has fallen within my own observation. I am therefore of opinion, that no office ought to be open to a member, which may be created or augmented while he is in the legislature.

Mr. Mason. It seems as if it was taken for granted, that all offices will be filled by the executive, while I think many will remain in the gift of the legislature. In either case, it is necessary to shut the door against corruption. If otherwise, they may make or multiply offices, in order to fill them. Are gentlemen in earnest when they suppose that this exclusion will prevent the first characters from coming forward? Are we not struck at seeing the luxury and venality which has already crept in among us? If not checked we shall have ambassadors to every petty state in Europe — the little republic of *St. Marino* not excepted. We must in the present system remove the temptation. I admire many parts of the British constitution and government, but I detest their corruption. — Why has the power of the crown so remarkably increased the last century? A stranger, by reading their laws, would suppose it considerably diminished; and yet, by the sole power of appointing the increased officers of government, corruption pervades every town and village in the kingdom. If such a restriction should abridge the right of election, it is still necessary, as it will prevent the people from ruining themselves; and will not the same causes here produce the same effects? I consider this clause as the corner-stone on which our liberties depend — and if we strike it out we are erecting a fabric for our destruction.

Mr. Gorham. The corruption of the English government cannot be applied to America. This evil exists there in the venality of their boroughs: but even this corruption has its advantage, as it gives stability to their government. We do not know what the effect would be if members of parliament were excluded from offices. The great bulwark of our liberty is the frequency of elections, and their great danger is the septennial parliaments.

Mr. Hamilton. In all general questions which become the subjects of discussion, there are always some truths mixed with falsehoods. I confess there is danger where men are capable of holding two offices. Take mankind in general, they are vicious — their passions may be operated upon. We have been taught to reprobate the danger of influence in the British government, without duly reflecting how far it was necessary to support a good government. We have taken up many ideas upon trust, and at last, pleased with our own opinions, establish them as undoubted truths. Hume's opinion of the British constitution confirms the remark, that there is always a body of firm patriots, who often shake a corrupt administration. Take mankind as they are, and what are they governed by? Their passions. There may be in every government a few choice spirits, who may act from more worthy motives. One great error is that we suppose mankind more honest than they are. Our prevailing passions are ambition and interest; and it will ever be the duty of a wise government to avail itself of those passions, in order to make them subservient to the public good — for these ever induce us to action. Perhaps a few men in a state, may, from patriotic motives, or to display their talents, or to reap the advantage of public applause, step forward; but if we adopt the clause we destroy the motive. I am therefore against all exclusions and refinements, except only in this case; that when a member takes his seat, he should vacate every other office. It is difficult to put any exclusive regulation into effect. We must in some degree submit to the inconvenience.

The question was then put for striking out — 4 ayes — 4 noes — 3 states divided. New-York of the number.

Adjourned till to-morrow morning.

SATURDAY, JUNE 23, 1787.

JOURNAL
Saturday June 23. 1787.

It was moved and seconded to agree to the proposition, which was postponed yesterday, on motion of the Deputies of the State of South Carolina, namely,

To receive an adequate compensation for their services, to be paid out of the Public Treasury.

On the question to agree to the proposition
it passed in the negative   [Ayes — 5; noes — 5; divided — 1.]

It was moved and seconded to strike out the following words in the third resolution reported from the Committee namely "by a particular State"

On the question to strike out the words
it passed in the affirmative   [Ayes — 8; noes — 3.]

It was moved and seconded to amend the third resolution by striking out the following words namely "or under the author-"ity of the United States during the term of service, and "under the national government for the space of one yea "after it's expiration" — and inserting the following clause, after the word "established" namely

"or the emoluments whereof shall have been augmented "by the Legislature of the United States during the time of "their being members thereof, and until they shall have "ceased to be Members for the space of one year"

On the question to agree to the amendment
it passed in the negative   [Ayes — 2; noes — 8; divided — 1.] [1]

It was moved and seconded to add after the words "ineligible to" the words

---

[1] Vote 82, Detail of Ayes and Noes, which notes that the motion was "Mr. Madison's".

"and incapable of holding"
which passed in the affirmative
It was moved and seconded to strike the words
"national government"
out of the third resolution
which passed in the affirmative
It was moved and seconded to strike the word "established"
out of the 3rd resolution
which passed in the affirmative
It was moved and seconded to add after the word "service"
in the third resolution, the words
"of the first branch"
which passed in the affirmative
[To agree to the last clause in the 3rd resolution as far as
the word service inclusive   Ayes—8; noes—2; divided—1.] [2]
It was then moved and seconded to agree to the words
"and for the space of one year after its expiration"
On the question to agree to these words
it passed in the negative [ayes — 4; noes — 6; divided — 1.]
And then the House adjourned till monday next at 11
o'clock, A. M.

[2] Vote 83, Detail of Ayes and Noes.

DETAIL OF AYES AND NOES

	New Hampshire	Massachusetts	Rhode Island	Connecticut	New York	New Jersey	Pennsylvania	Delaware	Maryland	Virginia	North Carolina	South Carolina	Georgia	Questions	Ayes	Noes	Divided
[80]	aye	no		no	aye	aye	no	aye	aye	no	no		dd	To agree to the following clause To receive an adequate compensation for their services — to be paid out of the pub: Treasy	5	5	1
[81]	no	aye		aye	aye	no	no	aye	aye	aye	aye		aye	To strike out these words in ye 3rd resolution "by a particular State"	8	3	
[82]	dd	aye		no	aye	no	no	no	no	no	no		no	To amend the 3rd resolution by strikg out these wds and inserting the follow words on Mr Madison's motion	2	8	1
[83]	dd	aye		aye	aye	no	aye	aye	aye	aye	aye		no	To agree to the last clause in the 3rd resolution as far as the word service inclusive.	8	2	1
[84]	no	no		aye	no	dd	aye	aye	no	no	aye		no	To agree to the following words "and for the space of one year after it's expiration"	4	6	1

MADISON

Saturday June 23. in Convention

⟨The 3. Resol: resumed.⟩

On Question yesterday postponed by S. Carol: for agreeing to the whole sentence "for allowing an adequate compensation to be paid out of the *Treasury of the U. States*"

Masts. ay. Cont. no. N. Y. no. N. J. ay. ⟨Pena. ay⟩ Del. no. Md. ⟨ay.⟩ Va. ay. N. C. no. S. C. no. Geo. divided. [Ayes — 5; noes — 5; divided — 1.] [3] So the question was lost, & the sentence not inserted.

---

[3] Madison inserted "Pena. ay" and changed Maryland's vote from "divd." to "ay". This was probably, but not certainly, done at a later date to conform to *Journal* and Yates.

Genl. Pinkney moves to strike out the ineligibility of members of the 1st. branch to offices established "by a particular State." [4]   He argued from the inconveniency to which such a restriction would expose both the members of the 1st. branch, and the States wishing for their services; from the [5] smallness of the object to be attained by the restriction.

⟨It wd. seem from the ideas of some that we are erecting a Kingdom to be divided agst. itself, he disapproved such a fetter on the Legislature.⟩[6]

Mr Sherman seconds the motion. ⟨It wd. seem that we are erecting a Kingdom at war with itself. The Legislature ought not to be fettered in such a case.⟩[6] on the question

Masts. no. Cont. ay. N. Y. ay. N. J. ay. Pa. no. Del. no. Md. ay. Va. ay. N. C. ay. S. C. ay. Geo. ay [Ayes — 8; noes — 3.]

Mr. M⟨adison⟩ renewed his motion yesterday made & waved [7] to render the members of the 1st. branch "ineligible during their term of service, & for one year after — to such offices only as should be established, or the emoluments thereof, augmented by the Legislature of the U. States during the time of their being members." He supposed that the unnecessary creation of offices, and increase of salaries, were the evils most experienced, & that if the door was shut agst. them, it might properly be left open for the appointt. of members to other offices as an encouragmt. to the Legislative service.

Mr. Alex: Martin seconded the motion.

⟨Mr. Butler. The amendt. does not go far eno' & wd. be easily evaded⟩ [8]

Mr. Rutlidge, was for preserving the Legislature as pure as possible, by shutting the door against appointments of its own members to offices, which was one source of its corruption.

---

[4] See further, references under September 3 note 7.

[5] Madison struck out " & the small additional addition which the removal of it would make to the dependence of this branch wch was meant to be dependant."

[6] These remarks ascribed to both Pinckney and Sherman were taken from Yates, who attributes them to Sherman. Madison doubtless first inserted them in the wrong place, and after recopying them in their proper place, he forgot to strike out his first insertion.

[7] See "Madison Memoranda" below, note 17.   [8] Taken from Yates.

Mr. Mason. The motion of ⟨my colleague⟩[9] is but a partial remedy for the evil. He appealed to ⟨him⟩[10] as a witness of the shameful partiality of the Legislature of Virginia to its own members. He enlarged on the abuses & corruption in the British Parliament, connected with the appointment of its members. He cd. not suppose that a sufficient number of Citizens could not be found who would be ready, without the inducement of eligibility to offices, to undertake the Legislative service. Genius & virtue it may be said, ought to be encouraged. Genius, for aught he knew, might, but that virtue should be encouraged by such a species of venality, was an idea, that at least had the merit of being new.

Mr. King remarked that we were refining too much in this business; and that the idea of preventing intrigue and solicitation of offices was chimerical. You say that no member shall himself be eligible to any office. Will this restrain him from availing himself of the same means which would gain appointments for himself, to gain them for his son, his brother, or any other object of his partiality. We were losing therefore the advantages on one side, without avoiding the evils on the other.

Mr. Wilson supported the motion. The proper cure he said for corruption in the Legislature was to take from it the power of appointing to offices. One branch of corruption would indeed remain, that of creating unnecessary offices, or granting unnecesary salaries, and for that the amendment would be a proper remedy. He animadverted on the impropriety of stigmatizing with the name of venality the laudable ambition of rising into the honorable offices of the Government; an ambition most likely to be felt in the early & most incorrupt period of life, & which all wise & free Govts. had deemed it sound policy, to cherish, not to check. The members of the Legislature have perhaps the hardest & least profitable task of any who engage in the service of the state. Ought this merit to be made a disqualification?

Mr. Sherman, observed that the motion did not go far enough. It might be evaded by the creation of a new office,

<hr>

[9] "My colleague" is Yates's phrase, Madison had originally written "Mr. Madison".   [10] Originally "Mr. M."

the translation to it of a person from another office, and the appointment of a member of the Legislature to the latter. A new Embassy might be established to a new court & an ambassador taken from another, in order to *create* a vacancy for a favorite member. He admitted that inconveniencies lay on both sides. He hoped there wd. be sufficient inducements to the public service without resorting to the prospect of desireable offices, and on the whole was rather agst. the motion of Mr. Madison.

Mr. Gerry thought there was great weight in the objection of Mr. Sherman. He added as another objection agst. admitting the eligibility of members in any case that it would produce intrigues of ambitious men for displacing proper officers, in order to create vacancies for themselves. In answer to Mr. King he observed that although members, if disqualified themselves might still intrigue & cabal for their sons, brothers &c, yet as their own interest would be dearer to them, than those of their nearest connections, it might be epected they would go greater lengths to promote it.

Mr. Madison had been led to this motion as a middle ground between an eligibility in all cases, and an absolute disqualification. He admitted the probable abuses of an eligibility of the members, to offices, particularly within the gift of the Legislature He had witnessed the partiality of such bodies to their own members, as had been remarked of the Virginia assembly by ⟨his colleague⟩[11] (Col. Mason). He appealed however to ⟨him⟩ [11] in turn to vouch another fact not less notorious in Virginia, that the backwardness of the best citizens to engage in the legislative service gave but too great success to unfit characters. The question was not to be viewed on one side only. The advantages & disadvantages on both ought to be fairly compared. The objects to be aimed at were to fill all offices with the fittest — characters, & to draw the wisest & most worthy citizens into the Legislative service. If on one hand, public bodies were partial to their own members; on the other they were as apt to be misled by taking char-

---

[11] See above notes 9 and 10.

acters on report, or the authority of patrons and dependents. All who had been concerned in the appointment of strangers on these recommendations must be sensible of this truth. Nor wd. the partialities of such Bodies be obviated by disqualifying their own members. Candidates for office would hover round the seat of Govt. or be found among the residents there, and practise all the means of courting the favor of the members. A great proportion of the appointments made by the States were evidently brought about in this way. In the general Govt. the evil must be still greater, the characters of distant states, being much less known ⟨throughout the U. States⟩ than those of the distant parts of the same State. The elections by Congress had generally turned on men living at the seat of ⟨the fedl⟩ Govt. or in its neighbourhood. — As to the next object, the impulse to the Legislative service, was evinced by experience to be in general too feeble with those best qualified for it. This inconveniency wd. also be more felt in the Natl. Govt. than in the State Govts as the sacrifices reqd. from the distant members wd. be much greater, and the pecuniary provisions, probably, more disproportiate. It wd. therefore be impolitic to add fresh objections to the ⟨Legislative⟩ service by an absolute disqualification of its members. The point in question was whether this would be an objection with the most capable citizens. Arguing from experience he concluded that it would. The Legislature of Virga would probably have been without many of its best members, if in that situation, they had been ineligible to Congs. to the Govt. & other honorable offices of the State.

⟨Mr. Butler thought Characters fit for office wd. never be unknown.⟩[12]

Col. Mason. If the members of the Legislature are disqualified, still the honors of the State will induce those who aspire to them, to enter that service, as the field in which they can best display & improve their talents, & lay the train for their subsequent advancement.

⟨Mr. Jenifer remarked that in Maryland, the Senators

---

[12] Taken from Yates.

chosen for five years, cd. hold no other office & that this circumstance gained them the greatest confidence of the people.⟩[13]

On the question for agreeing to the motion of Mr. Madison. Massts. divd. Ct. ay. N. Y. no. N. J. ay. Pa. no. Del. no. Md. no. Va. no. N. C. no. S. C. no. Geo. no.   [Ayes — 2; noes — 8; divided — 1.] [14]

Mr. Sherman movd. to insert the words "and incapable of holding" after the words "eligible to offices" wch. was agreed to without opposition.

The word "established" & the words "Natl. Govt." were struck out of Resolution 3d;

Mr. Spaight called for a division of the question, in consequence of which it was so put, as that it turned in the first member of it, "on the ineligibility of the members *during the term for which they were elected*" — whereon the States were, Massts. divd. Ct. ay. N. Y. ay. N. J. ay. Pa. no. Del. ay. Md. ay. Va. ay. N. C. ay. S. C. ay. Geo. no.

[Ayes — 8; noes — 2; divided — 1.]

On the 2d. member of the sentence extending ineligibility of members to one year after the term for which they were elected ⟨Col. Mason thought this essential to guard agst — evasions by resignations, and stipulations for office to be fulfilled at the expiration of the legislative term.   Mr. Gerry had known such a case.   Mr. Hamilton.   Evasions cd. not be prevented ÷ as by proxies — by friends holding for a year. and them opening the way &c.   Mr. Rutledge admitted the possibility of evasions but was for controuling them as possible.⟩ [13]   Mas. no. Ct. no. N. Y. ay. N. J. no. Pa. divd. Del. ay. ⟨Mard. ay.⟩[15] Va. ⟨no⟩[15] N. C. no. S. C. ay. Geo no

[Ayes — 4; noes — 6; divided — 1.]

Adjd.

─────────

Mem.[16] pa. 342.   Mr Ms motion renewed from preceding day — no allusion to it on that nor 3 preceding days.[17]

─────────

[13] Taken from Yates.   [14] See below "Madison Memoranda" and note 18.
    [15] Vote corrected from *Journal.*
    [16] Memoranda by Madison, see May 25, note 13.   These notes are undated but seem to refer to this day's records.
    [17] Yates reports speech of Madison to that effect, but without any formal motion.

pa. 350 quest. to agree to Mr Ms motion 2 ays 6 noes — still seems agreed to.[18]

YATES

SATURDAY, JUNE 23d, 1787.

Met pursuant to adjournment. Present 11 states.

Mr. Gorham. I move that the question which was yesterday proposed on the clause, *to be paid out of the national treasury,* be now put.

Question put — 5 ayes — 5 noes — one state divided. So the clause was lost.

Mr. Pinkney moved that that part of the clause which disqualifies a person from holding an office in the state, be expunged, because the first and best characters in a state may thereby be deprived of a seat in the national council.

Mr. Wilson. I perceive that some gentlemen are of opinion to give a bias in favor of state governments — This question ought to stand on the same footing.

Mr. Sherman. By the conduct of some gentlemen, we are erecting a kingdom to act against itself. The legislature ought to be free and unbiassed.

Question put to strike out the words moved for, and carried — 8 ayes, 3 noes.

Mr. Madison then moved, that after the word *established,* be added, *or the emoluments whereof shall have been augmented by the legislature of the United States, during the time they were members thereof, and for one year thereafter.*

Mr. Butler. The proposed amendment does not go far enough. How easily may this be evaded. What was the conduct of George the second to support the pragmatic sanction? To some of the opposers he gave pensions — others offices, and some, to put them out of the house of commons, he made lords. The great Montesquieu says, it is unwise to entrust persons with power, which by being abused operates to the advantage of those entrusted with it.

---

[18] It is not clear upon what grounds Madison states that this motion "still seems agreed to" in spite of the negative vote.

Governor Rutledge was against the proposed amendment. No person ought to come to the legislature with an eye to his own emolument in any shape.

Mr. Mason. I differ from my colleague in his proposed amendment. Let me state the practice in the state where we came from. There, all officers are appointed by the legislature. Need I add, that many of their appointments are most shameful. Nor will the check proposed by this amendment be sufficient. It will soon cease to be any check at all. It is asserted that it will be very difficult to find men sufficiently qualified as legislators without the inducement of emolument. I do believe that men of genius will be deterred unless possessed of great virtues. We may well dispense with the first characters when destitute of virtue — I should wish them never to come forward — But if we do not provide against corruption, our government will soon be at an end: nor would I wish to put a man of virtue in the way of temptation. Evasions, and caballing would evade the amendment. Nor would the danger be less, if the executive has the appointment of officers. The first three or four years we might go on well enough; but what would be the case afterwards? I will add, that such a government ought to be refused by the people — and it will be refused.

Mr. Madison. My wish is that the national legislature be as uncorrupt as possible. I believe all public bodies are inclined, from various motives, to support its members; but it is not always done from the base motives of venality. Friendship, and a knowledge of the abilities of those with whom they associate, may produce it. If you bar the door against such attachments, you deprive the government of its greatest strength and support. Can you always rely on the patriotism of the members? If this be the only inducement, you will find a great indifferency in filling your legislative body. If we expect to call forth useful characters, we must hold out allurements; nor can any great inconveniency arise from such inducements. The legislative body must be the road to public honor; and the advantage will be greater to adopt my motion, than any possible inconvenience.

Mr. King. The intimate association of offices will produce a vigorous support to your government. To check it would produce no good consequences. Suppose connections are formed? Do they not all tend to strengthen the government under which they are formed? Let therefore preferment be open to all men. We refine otherwise too much — nor is it possible we can eradicate the evil.

Mr. Wilson. I hope the amendment will be adopted. By the last vote it appears that the convention have no apprehension of danger of state appointments. It is equally imaginary to apprehend any from the national government. That such officers will have influence in the legislature, I readily admit; but I would not therefore exclude them. If any ill effects were to result from it, the bargain can as well be made with the legislature as with the executive. We ought not to shut the door of promotion against the great characters in the public councils, from being rewarded by being promoted. If otherwise, will not these gentlemen be put in the legislatures to prevent them from holding offices, by those who wish to enjoy them themselves?

Mr. Sherman. If we agree to this amendment, our good intentions may be prostrated by changing offices to avoid or evade the rule.

Mr. Gerry. This amendment is of great weight, and its consequences ought to be well considered. At the beginning of the war we possessed more than Roman virtue. It appears to me it is now the reverse. We have more land and stock-jobbers than any place on earth. It appears to me, that we have constantly endeavored to keep distinct the three great branches of government; but if we agree to this motion, it must be destroyed by admitting the legislators to share in the executive, or to be too much influenced by the executive, in looking up to him for offices.

Mr. Madison. This question is certainly of much moment. There are great advantages in appointing such persons as are known. The choice otherwise will be chance. How will it operate on the members themselves? Will it not be an objection to become members when they are to be excluded from office? For these reasons I am for the amendment.

Mr. Butler. These reasons have no force. Characters fit for offices will always be known.

Mr. Mason. It is said it is necessary to open the door to induce gentlemen to come into the legislature. This door is open, but not immediately. A seat in the house will be the field to exert talents, and when to a good purpose they will in due time be rewarded.

Mr. Jenifer. Our senators are appointed for 5 years and they can hold no other office. This circumstance gives them the greatest confidence of the people.

The question was put on Mr. Madison's amendment, and lost — 8 noes — 2 ayes — one state divided.

Question on the clause as amended before. Carried — 8 ayes — 2 noes — one state divided.

The question was next on the latter part of the clause.

Mr. Mason. We must retain this clause, otherwise evasions may be made. The legislature may admit of resignations and thus make members eligible — places may be promised at the close of their duration, and that a dependency may be made.

Mr. Gerry. And this actually has been the case in congress — a member resigned to obtain an appointment, and had it failed he would have resumed it.

Mr. Hamilton. The clause may be evaded many ways. Offices may be held by proxy — they may be procured by friends, &c.

Mr. Rutledge. I admit, in some cases, it may be evaded; but this is no argument against shutting the door as close as possible.

The question was then put on this clause, to wit: *and for the space of one year after its expiration* — and negatived.

Then adjourned to Monday morning.

MONDAY, JUNE 25, 1787.

JOURNAL

Monday June 25. 87.

It was moved and seconded to erase the word "national" and to substitute the words

"United States" (in the fourth resolution)

which passed in the affirmative.

It was moved and seconded to postpone the consideration of the first clause of the fourth resolution in order to take up the eighth resolution reported from the Committee.

On the question to postpone

it passed in the negative   [Ayes — 4;   noes — 7.]

It was moved and seconded to postpone the consideration of the fourth in order to take up the seventh resolution

On the question to postpone

it passed in the negative   [Ayes — 5;   noes — 6.] [1]

It was moved and seconded to agree to the first clause of the fourth resolution, namely

"Resolved that the Members of the second branch of the "Legislature of the United States ought to be chosen by the "individual Legislatures"

On the question to agree

it passed in the affirmative   [Ayes — 9;   noes — 2.]

It was moved and seconded to agree to the second clause of the fourth resolution, namely

"to be of the age of thirty years at least"

which passed unanimously in the affirmative

It was moved and seconded to erase the words

---

[1] Vote 86, Detail of Ayes and Noes, which is evidently mistaken in giving the summary of the vote.

"sufficient to ensure their independency" from the third
clause of the fourth resolution

 which passed in the affirmative [Ayes — 7; noes — 4.]
It was moved and seconded to add after the words "seven
years," in the fourth resolution, the words
 "to go out in fixed proportions"
It was moved and seconded to insert the word "six" instead
of "seven"
It was moved and seconded to amend the clause so as to
read
 "for four years, one fourth to go out annually"
No determination being taken on the three last motions
It was moved and seconded to erase the word "seven" from
the 3rd clause of the fourth resolution

  which passed in the affirmative [Ayes — 7; noes — 3;
    divided — 1.]
It was moved and seconded to fill up the blank in the 3rd
clause of the fourth resolution with the word "six"

  which passed in the negative [Ayes — 5; noes — 5;
    divided — 1.]
[To adjourn Ayes — 5; noes — 5; divided — 1.] [2]
It was moved and seconded to fill up the blank in the 3rd
clause of the fourth resolution with the word "five"

  which passed in the negative [Ayes — 5; noes — 5;
    divided — 1.]
[To adjourn Ayes — 7; noes — 4.] [3]
And then the House adjourned till to-morrow at 11 o'clock.
A. M.

---

 [2] Vote 91, Detail of Ayes and Noes.
 [3] Vote 93, Detail of Ayes and Noes. In the space for the question was originally
written, but then struck out: "to fill up the blank in ye 4 resolution with the words".
The secretary was evidently preparing to record the vote on "four years." See Yates,
below.

DETAIL OF AYES AND NOES

	New Hampshire	Massachusetts	Rhode Island	Connecticut	New York	New Jersey	Pennsylvania	Delaware	Maryland	Virginia	North Carolina	South Carolina	Georgia	Questions	Ayes	Noes	Divided
[85]		no		no	aye	no	no	no	no	aye	no	aye	aye	To postpone the 1st clause of the fourth resolution, to take up the eighth resolution	4	7	
[86]		no		no	no	no	no	no	no	no	aye	aye	aye	To postpone the 4th resolution to take up the seventh	3	8	
[87]		aye		aye	aye	aye	no	aye	aye	no	aye	aye	aye	That the second branch be elected by the State Legislatures	9	2	
[88]		no		aye	aye	aye	aye	aye	no	no	no	aye	aye	To strike out the words sufficient to secure their independency	7	4	
[89]		aye		aye	aye	aye	no	no	dd	no	aye	aye	aye	To strike the word "Seven" out of the 4th resolution	7	3	1
[90]		no		aye	no	no	aye	aye	dd	aye	aye	no	no	To fill up the blank in the 4 resolution wh the the word Six	5	5	1
[91]		no		aye	no	aye	aye	aye	dd	aye	no	no	no	To adjourn	5	5	1
[92]		no		aye	no	no	aye	aye	dd	aye	aye	no	no	To fill up the blank in the 4 resolution wh the word five	5	5	1
[93]		aye		aye	no	no	aye	aye	aye	aye	aye	no	no	To adjourn	7	4	

MADISON

Monday. June 25. in Convention.

Resolution 4.[4] ⟨being taken up.⟩

Mr. Pinckney ⟨spoke as follows⟩. — The efficacy of the System will depend on this article. In order to form a right judgmt. in the case it will be proper to examine the situation of this Country more accurately than it has yet been done.[5]

---

[4] Relating to the composition of the upper house.

[5] Crossed out: "It differed materially from that of Europe. We have no heredi-tary distinction of ranks, property is more equally divided. Few deserve the appellation of rich. The right of suffrage is more diffusive here, than in any other Country. This equality of property & rank is likely to be continued for ".

The people of the U. States are perhaps the most singular of any we are acquainted with. Among them there are fewer distinctions of fortune & less of rank, than among the inhabitants of any other nation. Every freeman has a right to the same protection & security; and a very moderate share of property entitles them to the possession of all the honors and privileges the public can bestow: hence arises a greater equality, than is to be found among the people of any other country, and an equality which is more likely to continue — I say this equality is likely to continue, because in a new Country, possessing immense tracts of uncultivated lands, where every temptation is offered to emigration & where industry must be rewarded with competency, there will be few poor, and few dependent — Every member of the Society almost, will enjoy an equal power of arriving at the supreme offices & consequently of directing the strength & sentiments of the whole Community. None will be excluded by birth, & few by fortune, from voting for proper persons to fill the offices of Government — the whole community will enjoy in the fullest sense that kind of political liberty which consists in the power the members of the State reserve to themselves, of arriving at the public offices, or at least, of having votes in the nomination of those who fill them.

If this State of things is true & the prospect of its continuing probable, it is perhaps not politic to endeavour too close an imitation of a Government calculated for a people whose situation is, & whose views ought to be extremely different

Much has been said of the Constitution of G. Britain. I will confess that I believe it to be the best constitution in existence; but at the same time I am confident it is one that will not or can not be introduced into this Country, for many centuries. — If it were proper to go here into a historical dissertation on the British Constitution, it might easily be shewn that the peculiar excellence, the distinguishing feature of that Governmt. can not possibly be introduced into our System — that its balance between the Crown & the people can not be made a part of our Constutition. — that we neither have or can have the members to compose it, nor the rights, privileges & properties of so distinct a class of Citizens to guard. — that the materials for forming this balance or check do not exist, nor is there a necessity for having so permanent a part of our Legislative, until the Executive power is so constituted as to have something fixed & dangerous in its principle — By this I mean a sole, hereditary, though limited Executive.

That we cannot have a proper body for forming a Legislative balance between the inordinate power of the Executive and the people, is evident from a review of the accidents & circumstances which give rise to the peerage of Great. Britain — I believe it is well ascertained that the parts which compose the British Constitution arose immediately from the forests of Germany; but the antiquity of the establishment of nobility is by no means clearly defined. Some authors are of opinion that the dignity denoted by the titles of dux et comes, was derived from the old Roman to the German Empire; while others are of opinion that they existed among the Germans long before the Romans were acquainted with them. The institution however of nobility is immemorial among the nations who may probably be termed the ancestors of Britain. — At the time they were summoned in England to become a part of the National Council, and the circumstances which have contributed to make them a constituent part of that constitution, must be well known to all gentlemen who have had industry & curiosity enough to investigate the subject — The nobles with their possessions & dependents composed a body permanent in their nature and formidable in point of power. They had a distinct interest both from the King and the people; an interest which could only be represented by themselves, and the guardianship could not be safely intrusted to others. — At the time they were originally called to form a part of the National Council, necessity perhaps as much as other cause, induced the Monarch to look up to them. It was necessary to demand the aid of his subjects in personal & pecuniary services. The power and possessions of the Nobility would not permit taxation from any assembly of which they were not a part: & the blending the deputies of the Commons with them, & thus forming what they called their parler-ment was perhaps as much the effect of chance as of any thing else. The Commons were at that time completely subordinate to the nobles, whose consequence & influence seem to have been the only reasons for their superiority; a superiority so degrading to the Commons that in the first Summons we find the peers are called upon to consult, the commons to consent. From this time the peers have composed a part of the British Legislature, and notwithstanding their power and influence have diminished & those of the Commons have increased, yet still they have always formed an excellent balance agst. either the encroachments of the crown or the people.

I have said that such a body cannot exist in this Country for ages, and that untill the situation of our people is exceedingly changed no necessity will exist for so permanent a part of the Legislature. To illustrate this I have remarked that the people of the United States are more equal in their circumstances than the people of any other Country — that they have very few rich men among them, — by rich men I mean those whose riches may have a dangerous influence, or such as are esteemed rich in Europe — perhaps there are not one hundred such on the Continent: that it is not probable this number will be greatly increased: that the genius of the people, their mediocrity of situation & the prospects which are afforded their industry in a country which must be a new one for centuries are unfavorable to the rapid distinction of ranks. The destruction of the right of primogeniture & the equal division of the property of Intestates will also have an effect to preserve this mediocrity: for laws invariably affect the manners of a people. On the other hand that vast extent of unpeopled territory which opens to the frugal & industrious a sure road to competency & independence will effectually prevent for a considerable time the increase of the poor or discontented, and be the means of preserving that equality of condition which so eminently distinguishes us.

If equality is as I contend the leading feature of the U.

States, where then are the riches & wealth whose representation & protection is the peculiar province of this permanent body. Are they in the hands of the few who may be called rich; in the possession of less than a hundred citizens? certainly not. They are in the great body of the people, among whom there are no men of wealth, and very few of real poverty. — Is it probable that a change will be created, and that a new order of men will arise? If under the British Government, for a century no such change was probable, I think it may be fairly concluded it will not take place while even the semblance of Republicanism remains. How is this change to be effected? Where are the sources from whence it is to flow? From the landed interest? No. That is too unproductive & too much divided in most of the States. From the Monied interest? If such exists at present, little is to be apprehended from that source. Is it to spring from commerce? I believe it would be the first instance in which a nobility sprang from merchants. Besides, Sir, I apprehend that on this point the policy of the U. States has been much mistakem. We have unwisely considered ourselves as the inhabitants of an old instead of a new country. We have adopted the maxims of a State full of people & manufactures & established in credit. We have deserted our true interest, and instead of applying closely to those improvements in domestic policy which would have ensured the future importance of our commerce, we have rashly & prematurely engaged in schemes as extensive as they are imprudent. This however is an error which daily corrects itself & I have no doubt that a few more severe trials will convince us, that very different commercial principles ought to govern the conduct of these States.

The people of this country are not only very different from the inhabitants of any State we are acquainted with in the modern world; but I assert that their situation is distinct from either the people of Greece or Rome, or of any State we are acquainted with among the antients. — Can the orders introduced by the institution of Solon, can they be found in the United States? Can the military habits & manners of Sparta be resembled to our habits & manners? Are the distinctions of Patrician & Plebeian known among us? Can the Helvetic or Belgic confederacies, or can the unwieldly, unmeaning body called the Germanic Empire, can they be said to possess either the same or a situation like ours? I apprehend not. — They are perfectly different, in their distinctions of rank, their Constitutions, their manners & their policy.

Our true situation appears to me to be this. — a new extensive Country containing within itself the materials for forming a Government capable of extending to its citizens all the blessings of civil & religious liberty — capable of making them happy at home. This is the great end of Republican Establishments. We mistake the object of our government, if we hope or wish that it is to make us respectable abroad. Conquest or superiority among other powers is not or ought not ever to be the object of republican systems. If they are sufficiently active & energetic to rescue us from contempt & preserve our domestic happiness & security, it is all we can expect from them, — it is more than almost any other Government ensures to its citizens.

I believe this observation will be found generally true: that no two people are so exactly alike in their situation or circumstances as to admit the exercise of the same Government with equal benefit: that a system must be suited to the habits & genius of the People it is to govern, and must grow out of them.

The people of the U. S. may be divided into three classes — *Professional men* who must from their particular pursuits always have a considerable weight in the Goverment while it remains popular — *Commercial men,* who may or may not have weight as a wise or injudicious commercial policy is pursued. — If that commercial policy is pursued which I conceive to be the true one, the merchants of this Country will not or ought not for a considerable time to have much weight in the political scale. — The third is the *landed interest,* the owners and cultivators of the soil, who are and ought ever to be the governing spring in the system. — These three classes, however distinct in their pursuits are individually equal in the political scale, and may be easily proved to have but one interest. The dependence of each on the other is mutual. The merchant depends on the planter. Both must in private as well as public affairs be connected with the professional men; who in their turn must in some measure depend on them. Hence it is clear from this manifest connection, & the equality which I before stated exists, & must for the reasons then assigned, continue, that after all there is one, but one great & equal body of citizens composing the inhabitants of this Country among whom there are no distinctions of rank, and very few or none of fortune.

For a people thus circumstanced are we then to form a Government & the question is what kind of Government is best suited to them.

Will it be the British Govt.? No. Why? Because G. Britain contains three orders of people distinct in their situation, their possessions & their principles. — These orders combined form the great body of the Nation, And as in national expences the wealth of the whole community must contribute, so ought each component part to be properly & duly represented. — No other combination of power could form this due representation, but the one that exists. — Neither the peers or the people could represent the royalty, nor could the Royalty & the people form a proper representation for the Peers. — Each therefore must of necessity be represented by itself, or the sign of itself; and this accidental mixture has certainly formed a Government admirably well balanced.

But the U. States contain but one order that can be assimilated to the British Nation. — this is the order of Commons. They will not surely then attempt to form a Government consisting of three branches, two of which shall have nothing to represent. They will not have an Executive & Senate (hereditary) because the King & Lords of England are so. The same reasons do not exist and therefore the same provisions are not necessary.

We must as has been observed suit our Governmt. to the people it is to direct. These are I believe as active, intelligent & susceptible of good Governmt. as any people in the world. The Confusion which has produced the present relaxed State is not owing to them. It is owing to the weakness & (defects) of a Govt. incapable of combining the various interests it is intended to unite, and destitute of energy. — All that we have to do then is to distribute the powers of Govt. in such a manner, and for such limited periods, as while it gives a proper degree of permanency to the Magistrate, will reserve to the people, the right of election they will not or ought not frequently to part with. — I am of opinion that this may be easily done; and that with some amendments the propositions before the Committee will fully answer this end.

No position appears to me more true than this; that the General Govt. can not effectually exist without reserving to the States the possession of their local rights. — They are the instruments upon which the Union must frequently depend for the support & execution of their powers, however immediately operating upon the people, and not upon the States.

Much has been said about the propriety of abolishing the distinction of State Governments, & having but one general System. Suffer me for a moment to examine this question.

(The residue of this speech was not ⟨furnished⟩[6]) ⟨like the above by Mr. Pinckeney.⟩ [7]

⟨The mode of constituting the 2d. branch being under consideration

The word "national" was struck out and "United States" inserted.⟩ [8]

Mr. Ghorum, inclined to a compromise as to the rule of proportion. He thought there was some weight in the objections of the small States. If Va. should have 16 votes & Delre. with several other States together 16. those from Virga. would be more likely to unite than the others, and would therefore have an undue influence. This remark was appli-

---

[6] Crossed out "obtained".

[7] This speech in Pinckney's own handwriting is among the Madison Papers. Madison has edited it slightly, and the order of the paragraphs is different, but Madison's order corresponds to Yates's report. The concluding paragraph in Yates, which Madison omits, is important. See also Appendix A, CCLXXIX.

[8] Taken from *Journal.*

cable not only to States, but to Counties or other districts of the same State. Accordingly the Constitution of Massts. had provided that the ⟨representatives of the⟩ [9] larger districts should not be in an exact ratio to their numbers. And experience he thought had shewn the provision to be expedient.

Mr. Read. The States have heretofore been in a sort of partnership. They ought to adjust their old affairs before they open a new account. He brought into view the appropriation of the common interest in the Western lands, to the use of particular States. Let justice be done on this head; let the fund be applied fairly & equally to the discharge of the general debt, and the smaller States who had been injured would listen then perhaps to those ideas of just representation which had been held out.

Mr. Ghorum. did not see how the Convention could interpose in the case. Errors he allowed had been committed on the Subject. But Congs. were now using their endeavors to rectify them. The best remedy would be such a Government as would have vigor enough to do justice throughout. This was certainly the best chance that could be afforded to the smaller States.

Mr. Wilson. the question is shall the members of the 2d. branch be chosen by the Legislatures of the States? When he considered the amazing extent of country — the immense population which is to fill it, the influence which the Govt. we are to form will have, not only on the present generation of our people & their multiplied posterity, but on the whole Globe, he was lost in the magnitude of the object. The project of Henry the 4th. & ⟨his Statesmen⟩ [10] was but the picture in miniature of the great portrait to be exhibited. He was opposed to an election by the State Legislatures. In explaining his reasons it was necessary to observe the twofold relation in which the people would stand. 1. as Citizens of the Gen'l Gov't. 2. as Citizens of their particular State. The Genl. Govt. was meant for them in the first capacity; the State Govts. in the second. Both Govts. were derived from the

---

[9] Probably but not certainly a later revision.   [10] Probably taken from Yates.

people — both meant for the people — both therefore ought to
be regulated on the same principles. The same train of ideas
which belonged to the relation of the Citizens to their State
Govts. were applicable to their relations to the Genl. Govt.
and in forming the latter, we ought to proceed, by abstracting
as much as possible from the idea of State Govts.[11] With
respect to the province & objects of the Gen'l Govt. they should
be considered as having no existence. The election of the 2d.
branch by the Legislatures, will introduce & cherish local
interests & local prejudices. The Genl. Govt. is not an assemblage of States, but of individuals for certain political purposes — it is not meant for the States, but for the individuals
composing them: the *individuals* therefore not the *States*,
ought to be represented in it: A proportion in this representation can be preserved in the 2d. as well as in the 1st.
branch; and the election can be made by electors chosen by
the people for that purpose. He moved an amendment to
that effect, which was not seconded.

  Mr. Elseworth saw no reason for departing from the mode
contained in the Report. Whoever chooses the member, he
will be a citizen of the State he is to represent & will feel the
same spirit and act the same part whether he be appointed
by the people or the Legislature. Every State has its particular views & prejudices, which will find their way into the
general councils, through whatever channel they may flow.
Wisdom was one of the characteristics which it was in contemplation to give the second branch. Would not more of it
issue from the Legislatures; than from an immediate election
by the people. He urged the necessity of maintaining the
existence & agency of the States. Without their co-operation
it would be impossible to support a Republican Govt. over
so great an extent of Country. An army could scarcely render
it practicable. The largest States are the Worst Governed.
Virga. is obliged to acknowledge her incapacity to extend her
Govt. to Kentucky. Masts can not keep the peace one hundred miles from her capitol and is now forming an army for

---

[11] Crossed out: "We ought to proceed as if no such govts. existed".

its support.   How long Pena. may be free from a like situation
can not be foreseen.   If the principles & materials of our Govt.
are not adequate to the extent of these single States; how can it
be imagined that they can support a single Govt. throughout
the U. States.   The only chance of supporting a Genl. Govt.
lies in engrafting it on that of the individual States.

⟨Docr. Johnson urged the necessity of preserving the State
Govts — which would be at the mercy of the Genl. Govt. on
Mr. Wilson's plan.

Mr. Madison thought it wd. obviate difficulty if the present resol: were postponed. & the 8th. taken up. which is to
fix the right of suffrage in the 2d. branch.⟩ [12]

Docr. Williamson professed himself a friend to such a system as would secure the existence of the State Govts.   The
happiness of the people depended on it.   He was at a loss to
give his vote, as to the Senate untill he knew the number of
its members.   In order to ascertain this, he moved to insert
these words after "2d. branch of Natl. Legislature" — "who
shall bear such proportion to the no. of the 1st. branch as 1
to   "   He was not seconded.

Mr. Mason.   It has been agreed on all hands that an efficient Govt. is necessary that to render it such it ought to have
the faculty of self-defence, that to render its different branches
effectual each of them ought to have the same power of self defence.   He did not wonder that such an agreement should have
prevailed in these points.   He only wondered that there should
be any disagreement about the necessity of allowing the State
Govts. the same self-defence.   If they are to be preserved as he
conceived to be essential, they certainly ought to have this
power, and the only mode left of giving it to them, was by
allowing them to appoint the 2d. branch of the Natl. Legislature.

Mr. Butler observing that we were put to difficulties at
every step by the uncertainty whether an equality or a ratio
of representation wd. prevail finally in the 2d. branch. moved
to postpone the 4th. Resol: & to proceed to the Resol: on that
point.   Mr. M⟨adison⟩ seconded him.

---

[12] Taken from Yates.

On the question

Massts. no. Cont. no. N. Y. ay. N. J. no. Pa. no. Del. no. Md. no. Va. ay. N C. no. S. C. ay. Geo. ay. [Ayes — 4; noes — 7.]

⟨On a question to postpone the 4 and take up the 7. Resol: Ays — Mard. Va. N. C. S. C. Geo. — Noes. Mas. Ct. N. Y. N. J. Pa. Del:⟩ [13]

On the question to agree "that the members of 2d. branch be chosen by the indivl. Legislatures"

Masts. ay. Cont. ay. N. Y. ay. N. J. ay. Pa. no. Del. ay. Md. ay. Va. no. N. C. ay. S. C. ay. Geo. ay.* [Ayes — 9; noes — 2.]

⟨On a question on the clause requiring the age of 30 years at least" — it was agreed to unanimously: [14]

On a question to strike out — the words "sufficient to ensure their independency" after the word "term" it was agreed to.[15]⟩

That the 2d. branch hold their offices for term of seven years", considered.

Mr. Ghorum suggests a term of "4 years", ⟨$\frac{1}{4}$ to be elected every year.⟩ [16]

Mr. Randolph. supported the idea of rotation, as favorable to the wisdom & stability of the Corps. ⟨which might possibly be always sitting, and aiding the executive.⟩ [18] And moves after "7 years" to add, "to go out in fixt proportion" [19] ⟨which was agreed to.⟩ [20]

---

* It must be kept in view that the largest States particularly Pennsylvania & Virginia always considered the choice of the 2d. Branch by the State Legislatures as opposed to a proportional Representation to which they were attached as a fundamental principle of just Government. The smaller States who had opposite views, were reenforced by the members from the large States most anxious to secure the importance of the State Governments.[17]

---

[13] Taken from *Journal*.   [14] Taken from *Journal* (confirmed by Yates).
[15] Taken from *Journal*.
[16] Taken from *Journal*, originally Madison had simply "a rotation".
[17] This note may be a later insertion.   [18] Taken from Yates.
[19] See Appendix A, CCXIX.
[20] Taken from Yates, but probably *Journal* (pp. 147–148) more correct that there was "no determination" on this point.
In the later revision of his notes, Madison at this point copied from Yates a sug-

Mr Williamson. suggests "6 years," as more convenient ⟨for Rotation than 7 years.⟩ [21]

Mr Sherman seconds him.

Mr Reed proposed that they sd. hold their offices "during good" behaviour. Mr. R. Morris seconds him.

Genl. Pinkney proposed "4 years". A longer term wd. fix them at the seat of Govt. They wd. acquire an interest there, perhaps transfer their property & lose sight of the States they represent. Under these circumstances the distant States wd. labour under great disadvantages.

Mr. Sherman moved to strike out "7 ⟨years" [22] in order⟩ to take questions on the several propositions. On the question to strike out "seven"

Masts. ay. Cont. ay. N. Y. ay. N. J. ay. Pa. no. Del. no. Md. divd. Va. no. N. C. ay. S. C. ay. Geo. ay. [Ayes — 7; noes — 3; divided — 1.]

On the question to insert "6 years, ⟨which failed 5 Sts. being ay. 5. no. & 1: divided.⟩

Masts. no. Cont. ay. N. Y. no. N. J. no. Pa. ay. Del. ay. Md. divd. Va. ay. N. C. ay. S. C. no. Geo. no.

⟨On a motion to adjourn, the votes were 5 for 5 agst. it & 1 divided. — Con. N. J. Pa. — Del. Va. — ay — Masts. N. Y. N. C. S. C. Geo: no. Maryd. divided.⟩ [23]

On the question for "5 years" it was lost

Masts. no. Cont. ay. N. Y. no. N. J. no. Pa. ay. Del. ay. Md. divd. Va. ay. N. C. ay. S. C. ⟨No.⟩ [24] Geo. No. [Ayes—5; noes — 5; divided — 1.]

Adjd. [25]

---

gestion by Read, but found that he had the same record a little farther on in his own notes, so crossed this out.

[21] Probably but not certainly a later insertion.

[22] Originally "states" instead of "years".

[23] Taken from *Journal*.

[24] Originally "S. C. ay" which made the total vote 6 ayes, 4 noes. Evidently a mistake, as Madison had recorded the motion "was lost." In later revision he made the vote conform to *Journal* and Yates.

[25] See further Appendix A, XLVIII.

YATES

MONDAY, JUNE 25th, 1787.

Met pursuant to adjournment. Present 11 states.

Mr. C. Pinkney. On the question upon the second branch
of the general legislature, as reported by the committee in
the fourth resolve, now under consideration, it will be necessary to enquire into the true situation of the people of this
country. Without this we can form no adequate idea what
kind of government will secure their rights and liberties.
There is more equality of rank and fortune in America than in
any other country under the sun; and this is likely to continue as long as the unappropriated western lands remain
unsettled. They are equal in rights, nor is extreme of poverty
to be seen in any part of the union. If we are thus singularly
situated, both as to fortune and rights, it evidently follows,
that we cannot draw any useful lessons from the examples of
any of the European states or kingdoms; much less can Great
Britain afford us any striking institution, which can be adapted
to our own situation — unless we indeed intend to establish an
hereditary executive, or one for life. Great Britain drew its
first rude institutions from the forests of Germany, and with
it that of its nobility. These having originally in their hands
the property of the state, the crown of Great Britian was
obliged to yield to the claims of power which those large possessions enabled them to assert. The commons were then too
contemptible to form part of the national councils. Many
parliaments were held, without their being represented, until
in process of time, under the protection of the crown, and forming distinct communities, they obtained some weight in the
British government. From such discordant materials brought
casually together, those admirable checks and balances, now
so much the boast of the British constitution, took their rise.
— But will we be able to copy from this original? I do not
suppose that in the confederation, there are one hundred
gentlemen of sufficient fortunes to establish a nobility; and
the equality of others as to rank would never admit of the

distinctions of nobility. I lay it therefore down as a settled principle, that equality of condition is a leading axiom in our government. It may be said we must necessarily establish checks, lest one rank of people should usurp the rights of another. Commerce can never interfere with the government, nor give a complexion to its councils. Can we copy from Greece or Rome? Have we their nobles or patricians? With them offices were open to few — The different ranks in the community formed opposite interests and produced unceasing struggles and disputes. Can this apply equally to the free yeomanry of America? We surely differ from the whole. Our situation is unexampled, and it is in our power, on different grounds, to secure civil and religious liberty; and when we secure these we secure every thing that is necessary to establish happiness. We cannot pretend to rival the European nations in their grandeur or power; nor is the situation of any two nations so exactly alike as that the one can adopt the regulations or government of the other. If we have any distinctions they may be divided into three classes.

1. Professional men.
2. Commercial men.
3. The landed interest.

The latter is the governing power of America, and the other two must ever be dependent on them — Will a national government suit them? No. The three orders have necessarily a mixed interest, and in that view, I repeat it again, the United States of America compose in fact but one order. The clergy and nobility of Great Britain can never be adopted by us. Our government must be made suitable to the people, and we are perhaps the only people in the world who ever had sense enough to appoint delegates to establish a general government. I believe that the propositions from Virginia, with some amendments, will satisfy the people. But a general government must not be made dependent on the state governments.

The United States include a territory of about 1500 miles in length, and in breadth about 400; the whole of which is divided into states and districts. While we were dependent on the crown of Great Britain, it was in contemplation to have formed the whole into one — but it was found impracticable. No legislature could make good laws for the whole, nor can it now be done. It would necessarily place the power in the hands of the few, nearest the seat of government. State governments must therefore remain, if you mean to prevent confusion. The general negative powers will support the general government. Upon these considerations I am led to form the second branch differently from the report. Their powers are important and the number not too large, upon the principle of proportion. I have considered the subject with great attention; and I propose this plan (reads it) and if no better plan is proposed, I will then move its adoption.

Mr. Randolph moved that the 4th resolve be divided, in the same manner as the 3d resolve.

Mr. Gorham moved the question on the first resolve. Sixteen members from one state will certainly have greater weight, than the same number of members from different states. We must therefore depart from this rule of apportionment in some shape or other — perhaps on the plan Mr. Pinkney has suggested.

Mr. Read. Some gentlemen argue, that the representation must be determined according to the weight of each state — That we have heretofore been partners in trade, in which we all put in our respective proportions of stock — That the articles of our co-partnership were drawn in forming the confederation — And that before we make a new co-partnership, we must first settle the old business. But to drop the allusion — we find that the great states have appropriated to themselves the common lands in their respective states — These lands having been forfeited as heretofore belonging to the king, ought to be applied to the discharge of our public debts. Let this still be done, and then if you please, proportion the representation, and we shall not be jealous of one another — A jealousy, in a great measure, owing to the public property appropriated by individual states — and which, as it has been gained by the united power of the confederation, ought to be appropriated to the discharge of the public debts.

Mr. Gorham. This motion has been agitated often in congress; and it was owing to the want of power, rather than inclination, that it was not justly settled. Great surrenders have been made by the great states, for the benefit of the confederation.

Mr. Wilson. The question now before us is, whether the second branch of the general legislature shall or shall not be appointed by the state legislatures. In every point of view it is an important question. The magnitude of the object is indeed embarrassing. The great system of Henry the IVth of France, aided by the greatest statesmen, is small when compared to the fabric we are now about to erect — In laying the stone amiss we may injure the superstructure; and what will be the consequence, if the corner-stone should be loosely placed? It is improper that the state legislatures should have the power contemplated to be given them. A citizen of America may be considered in two points of view — as a citizen of the general government, and as a citizen of the particular state, in which he may reside. We ought to consider in what character he acts in forming a general government. I am both a citizen of Pennsylvania and of the United States. I must therefore lay aside my state connections and act for the general good of the whole. We must forget our local habits and attachments. The general government should not depend on the state governments. This ought to be a leading distinction between the one and the other; nor ought the general government to be composed of an assemblage of different state governments — We have unanimously agreed to establish a general government — That the powers of peace, war, treaties, coinage and regulating of *commerce*, ought to reside in that government. And if we reason in this manner, we shall soon see the impropriety of admitting the interference of state governments into the general government. Equality of representation can not be established, if the second branch is elected by the state legislatures. When we are laying the foundation of a building, which is to last for ages, and in which millions are interested, it ought to be well laid. If the national government does not act upon state prejudices, state distinctions will be lost. I therefore move, *that the second branch of the legislature of the national government be elected by electors chosen by the people of the United States.*

Judge Elsworth. I think the second branch of the general legislature ought to be elected agreeable to the report. The other way, it is said, will be more the choice of the people — The one mode is as much so as the other. No doubt every citizen of every state is interested in the state governments; and elect him in whatever manner you please, whenever he takes a seat in the general government, it will prevail in some shape or other. The state legislatures are more competent to make a judicious choice, than the people at large. Instability pervades their choice. In the second branch of the general government we want wisdom and firmness. As to balances, where nothing can be balanced, it is a perfect *utopian* scheme. But still great advantages will result in having a second branch endowed with the qualifications I have mentioned. Their weight and wisdom may check the inconsiderate and hasty proceedings of the first branch.

I cannot see the force of the reasoning in attempting to detach the state governments from the general government. In that case, without a standing army, you cannot support the general government, but on the pillars of the state governments. Are the larger states now more energetic than the smaller? Massachusetts cannot support a government at the distance of one hundred miles from her capital, without an army; and how long Virginia and Pennsylvania will support their governments it is difficult to say. Shal we proceed like unskilful workmen, and make use of timber, which is too weak to build a first rate ship? We know that the people of the states are strongly attached to their own constitutions. If you hold up a system of general government, destructive of their constitutional rights, they will oppose it. Some are of opinion that if we cannot form a general government so as to destroy state governments, we ought at least to balance the one against the other. On the contrary, the only chance we have to support a general government is to graft it on the state governments. I want to proceed on this ground, as the safest, and I believe no other plan is practicable. In this way, and in this way only, can we rely on the confidence and support of the people.

Dr. Johnson. The state governments must be preserved: but this motion leaves them at the will and pleasure of the general government.

Mr. Madison. I find great differences of opinion in this convention on the clause now under consideration. Let us postpone it in order to take up the 8th resolve, that we may previously determine the mode of representation.

Mr. Mason. All agree that a more efficient government is necessary. It is equally necessary to preserve the state governments, as they ought to have the means of self-defence. On the motion of Mr. Wilson, the only means they ought to have would be destroyed.

The question was put for postponing, in order to take into consideration the 8th resolve, and lost — 7 noes — 4 ayes.

Question on the 1st clause in the 4th resolve — 9 states for — 2 against it.

The age of the senators (30 years) agreed to.

Mr. Gorham proposed that the senators be classed, and to remain 4 years in office; otherwise great inconveniences may arise if a dissolution should take place at once.

Gov. Randolph. This body must act with firmness. They may possibly always sit — perhaps to aid the executive. The state governments will always attempt to counteract the general government. They ought to go out in classes: therefore I move, *that they go out of office in fixed proportions of time,* instead of the words, *seven years.*

Mr. Read moved (though not seconded) that they ought to continue in office during good behaviour.

Mr. Williamson moved that they remain in office for six years.

Mr. Pinkney. I am for four years. Longer time would give them too great attachment to the states, where the general government may reside. They may be induced, from the proposed length of time, to sell their estates, and become inhabitants near the seat of government.

Mr. Madison. We are proceeding in the same manner that was done when the confederation was first formed — Its original draft was excellent, but in its progress and completion it became so insufficient as to give rise to the present convention. By the vote already taken, will not the temper of the state legislatures transfuse itself into the senate? Do we create a free government?

Question on Gov. Randolph's motion [26] — 7 ayes — 3 noes — one divided.

Motion to fix the term of service at six years — 5 ayes — 5 noes — one divided.

Do. for 5 years — 5 ayes — 5 noes — one divided.

The question for 4 years was not put; and the convention adjourned till to-morrow morning.

KING

25 June — Shall the Senate be elected by the State Legislatures?

Wilson — Every man will possess a double Character, that of a Citizen of the US. & yt. of a Citizen of an individl. State — The national Legis. will apply to ye. former Charactr — it ought then to be elected or appointed by the Citizens of the US, and not by the Legislatures of the individl States; Because they are characters peculiarly of a state feature & partaking of the State Citizenship rather yn. of that of the US — The State Legislrs. have no interest in the Genl. Govt. but the Citizens of every State have an important interest — this Distinction points out the Difference which shd. govern us in the appointment of the Natl. Govt. The natil. Govt. is one & yt. of the states another — Commerce, War, Peace, Treaties, &c are peculiar to the former — certain inferior and local Qualities are the province of the Latter — there is a line of separation; where ever the prerogatives lies on the side of the Genl. Govt. we are citizens of the nation or of the US — (although I think we shd. use a term in the singular Number), and so on the other side — We must not then refer our-

---

[26] The question was not on Randolph's motion, see Journal and Madison.

selves to the States or yr. Legislatures, but must proceed on the basis of the people; the Senate shd. be elected by Electors appointed by the people.

Elsworth — We must build our Genl. Govt. upon the vigour & strength of the State Govts — the Genl. Govt. could not proceed without them, or a large standing Army; Mass. cannot maintain her Republican Govt. without an Army — Pennsylvania will soon want it — Virginia can not & does not govern Kentucke — each of these States is too large for a Republican System — I am therefore for proceeding on the continuation of the States — let the 2d Br. or the Senate be elected by the State Legislatures —

Johnson — When the Question of State Security or State Individuality was presented — it was sd. by Mr. Wilson & Mr. Madison that the States were secured by the right of yr. Legislatures to appt. the members of the Senate or 2d. Br. of the Genl. Legislature. If Mr. Wilson's present plan of appointing the Senate obtains, the State individuality is insecure —

Mason — The Executive negatives both Brs of the Legislatr and each Br. has a negative on the other — and the Genl. Gov. have a neg. on the State Legislature — these regulations are necessary on the principles of self Defence — it is an instinctive principle in nature, and in a proper degree every being professes this power. If the State Legislatures are deprived of the Election of the 2d. or 1st Br. of the natil. Legislature the States are destitute of this principle of self protection — I wish them to continue & I shall not agree to deprive them of the power of a constitutional self Protection — [27]

[27] [Endorsed:] 25 June | Shall the Senators be elected | by the State Legislatures | Wilson no | Ellsworth aye | Mason aye

TUESDAY, JUNE 26, 1787.

JOURNAL
Tuesday June 26. 1787.

It was moved and seconded to amend the third clause of the fourth resolution reported from the Committee so as to read as follows, namely

"for nine years, one third to go out triennially"

which passed in the negative   [Ayes — 3; noes — 8.]

It was then moved and seconded to amend the third clause of the fourth resolution so as to read

"for six years, one third to go out biennially"

On the question to agree to the amendment

it passed in the affirmative [Ayes — 7; noes — 4.]

[to strike the following clause out of the 4 resolution "to receive fixed stipends by which they may be compensated for the devotion of their time to public service   Ayes — 5; noes — 6.] [1]

It was moved and seconded to amend the fourth clause of the fourth resolution so as to read

"to receive a compensation for the devotion of their time to the public service"

which passed in the affirmative [Ayes — 10; noes — 1.]

It was moved and seconded to erase the following words from the fourth resolution, namely

"out of the national Treasury,"

and to substitute the following namely

"by their respective States"

which passed in the negative [Ayes — 5; noes — 6.]

It was moved and seconded to agree to the following clause in the fourth resolution namely

"to be paid out of the public Treasury"

which passed in the negative [Ayes — 5; noes — 6.]

---

[1] Vote 96, Detail of Ayes and Noes.

It was moved and seconded to postpone the consideration of the last clause in the fourth resolution, as reported from the Committee, in order to take up the following proposition, offered as a substitute, namely

"to be ineligible to, and incapable of holding any office "under the authority of the United States (except those "peculiarly belonging to the functions of the second branch) "during the term for which they are elected"

On the question to postpone

it passed in the affirmative. [Ayes — 6; noes — 5.] [2]

It was then moved and seconded to add after the word "elected" the words

"and for One year thereafter"

which passed in the affirmative [Ayes — 7; noes — 4.]

It was then moved and seconded to agree to the proposition as amended namely

"to be ineligible to, and incapable of holding any office "under the authority of the United States (except those "peculiarly belonging to the functions of the second branch) "during the term for which they are elected, and for one "year thereafter"

which passed in the affirmative. [Ayes — 11; noes — 0.]

It was moved and seconded to add the following clause to the fourth resolution, namely

"and to be ineligible and incapable of holding any office "under a particular State"

which passed in the negative [Ayes — 3; noes — 8.]

It was moved and seconded to agree to the fifth resolution reported from the Committee namely.

"Resolved that each Branch ought to possess the right of originating acts"

which passed unanimously in the affirmative [Ayes — 11; noes — 0.]

and then the House adjourned till to-morrow at 11 o'clock A. M.

---

[2] Vote 100, Detail of Ayes and Noes, which notes that this motion was "Mr. Williamson's".

DETAIL OF AYES AND NOES

No.	Ayes	Noes	Divided	Questions	Georgia	South Carolina	North Carolina	Virginia	Maryland	Delaware	Pennsylvania	New Jersey	New York	Connecticut	Rhode Island	Massachusetts	New Hampshire
[94]	3	8		for nine years one third to go out triennially — second Branch	no	no	no	aye	no	aye	aye	no	no	no		no	
[95]	7	4		for six years, one third to go out biennially —	no	no	aye	aye	aye	aye	aye	no	no	aye		aye	
[96]	5	6		to strike the following clause out of the 4 resolution "to receive fixed stipends by which they may be compensated for the devotion of their time to public service	no	aye	no	no	aye	no	aye	no	no	aye		aye	
[97]	10	1		To agree to the follow'g clause in ye 4 resolution "To receive a compensation for the devotion of their time to the Public-Service."	aye	no	aye	aye	aye	aye	aye	aye	aye	aye		aye	
[98]	5	6		To strike out the the words "national Treasury and to substitute the words "by their respective States"	aye	aye	no	no	no	no	no	aye	aye	aye		no	
[99]	5	6		To agree to the following clause in the 4 resolution. "To be paid out of the public Treasury"	no	no	no	aye	aye	aye	aye	no	no	no		aye	
[100]	6	5		To postpone the last clause of the 4 resolution in order to take up Mr Williamson's motion	no	no	aye	aye	aye	aye	aye	no	no	aye		no	
[101]	7	4		to add the words and for One year thereafter	no	aye	aye	aye	aye	aye	no	no	aye	aye		no	
[102]	11			to be ineligible to & incapable of holding any office under ye authority of the U.S. (except &ca) during the term for wh they are elected, and for One year thereafter	aye	aye	aye	aye	aye	aye	aye	aye	aye	aye		aye	
[103]	3	8		and to be ineligible to & incapable of holding any office under a particular State	no	no	no	aye	no	no	aye	no	no	no		aye	
[104]	11			To agree to the 5th resolution reported from the Committee	aye	aye	aye	aye	aye	aye	aye	aye	aye	aye		aye	

[Beginning of fourth loose sheet]

MADISON

Tuesday. June 26. in Convention

The duration of the 2d. branch under consideration.

Mr. Ghorum moved to fill the blank with "six years". ⟨one third of the members to go out every second year.⟩ [3]

Mr Wilson 2ded. the motion.

Genl. Pinkney opposed six years in favor of four years. The States he said had different interests. Those of the Southern, and of S. Carolina in particular were different from the Northern. If the Senators should be appointed for a long term, they wd. settle in the State where they exercised their functions; and would in a little time be rather the representatives of that than of the State appoint'g them.

Mr. Read movd. that the term be nine years. This wd. admit of a very convenient rotation, one third going out triennially. He wd. still prefer "during good behaviour," but being little supported in that idea, he was willing to take the longest term that could be obtained.

Mr. Broome 2ded. the motion

Mr. Madison. In order to judge of the form to be given to this institution, it will be proper to take a view of the ends to be served by it. These were first to protect the people agst. their rulers: secondly to protect ⟨the people⟩ agst. the transient impressions into which they themselves might be led. A people deliberating in a temperate moment, and with the experience of other nations before them, on the plan of Govt. most likely to secure their happiness, would first be aware, that those chargd. with the public happiness, might betray their trust. An obvious precaution agst. this danger wd. be to divide the trust between different bodies of men, who might watch & check each other. In this they wd. be governed by the same prudence which has prevailed in organizing the subordinate departments of Govt. where all business liable to abuses is made to pass thro' separate hands, the one being a

---

[3] Taken from *Journal*, confirmed by Yates.

check on the other.   It wd. next occur to such a people, that
they themselves were liable to temporary errors, thro' want
of information as to their true interest, and that men chosen
for a short term, & employed but a small portion of that in
public affairs, might err from the same cause.   This reflection
wd. naturally suggest that the Govt. be so constituted, as that
one of its branches might have an oppy. of acquiring a competent knowledge of the public interests.   Another reflection
equally becoming a people on such an occasion, wd. be that
they themselves, as well as a numerous body of Representatives, were liable to err also, from fickleness and passion.   A
necessary fence agst. this danger would be to select a portion
of enlightened citizens, whose limited number, and firmness
might seasonably interpose agst. impetuous counsels.   It
ought finally to occur to a people deliberating on a Govt. for
themselves, that as different interests necessarily result from
the liberty meant to be secured, the major interest might under
sudden impulses be tempted to commit injustice on the minority.   In all civilized Countries the people fall into different
classes havg. a real or supposed difference of interests.   There
will be creditors & debtors, farmers, merchts. & manufacturers.
There will be particularly the distinction of rich & poor.   It
was true as had been observd. (by Mr Pinkney) we had not
among us those hereditary distinctions, of rank which were a
great source of the contests in the ancient Govts. as well as
the modern States of Europe, nor those extremes of wealth
or poverty which characterize the latter.   We cannot however be regarded even at this time, as one homogeneous mass,
in which every thing that affects a part will affect in the same
manner the whole.   In framing a system which we wish to
last for ages, we shd. not lose sight of the changes which ages
will produce.   An increase of population will of necessity
increase the proportion of those who will labour under all the
hardships of life, & secretly sigh for a more equal distribution
of its blessings.   These may in time outnumber those who are
placed above the feelings of indigence.   According to the equal
laws of suffrage, the power will slide into the hands of the
former.   No agrarian attempts have yet been made in this

Country, but symptoms of a leveling spirit, as we have understood, have sufficiently appeared in a certain quarters to give notice of the future danger. How is this danger to be guarded agst. on republican principles? How is the danger in all cases of interested co-alitions to oppress the minority to be guarded agst.? Among other means by the establishment of a body in the Govt. sufficiently respectable for its wisdom & virtue, to aid on such emergencies, the preponderance of justice by throwing its weight into that scale. Such being the objects of the second branch in the proposed Govt. he thought a considerable duration ought to be given to it. He did not conceive that the term of nine years could threaten any real danger; but in pursuing his particular ideas on the subject, he should require that the long term allowed to the 2d. branch should not commence till such a period of life as would render a perpetual disqualification to be re-elected little inconvenient either in a public or private view. He observed that as it was more than probable we were now digesting a plan which in its operation wd. decide forever the fate of Republican Govt we ought not only to provide every guard to liberty that its preservation cd. require, but be equally careful to supply the defects which our own experience had particularly pointed out.

Mr. Sherman. Govt. is instituted for those who live under it. It ought therefore to be so constituted as not to be dangerous to their liberties. The more permanency it has the worse if it be a bad Govt. Frequent elections are necessary to preserve the good behavior of rulers. They also tend to give permanency to the Government, by preserving that good behavior, because it ensures their re-election. In Connecticut elections have been very frequent, yet great stability & uniformity both as to persons & measures have been experienced from its original establishmt. to the present time; a period of more than 130 years. He wished to have provision made for steadiness & wisdom in the system to be adopted; but he thought six or ⟨four⟩ [4] years would be sufficient. He shd. be content with either.

---

[4] Corrected probably from Yates.

Mr. Read wished it to be considered by the small States that it was their interest that we should become one people as much as possible, that State attachments shd. be extinguished as much as possible, that the Senate shd. be so constituted as to have the feelings of citizens of the whole.

Mr. Hamilton. He did not mean to enter particularly into the subject. He concurred with Mr. Madison in thinking we were now to decide for ever the fate of Republican Government; and that if we did not give to that form due stability and wisdom, it would be disgraced & lost among ourselves, disgraced & lost to mankind for ever. He acknowledged himself not to think favorably of Republican Government; but addressed his remarks to those who did think favorably of it, in order to prevail on them to tone their Government as high as possible. He professed himself to be as zealous an advocate for liberty as any man whatever, and trusted he should be as willing a martyr to it though he differed as to the form in which it was most eligible. — He concurred also in the general observations of (Mr. Madison) on the subject, which might be supported by others if it were necessary. It was certainly true that nothing like an equality of property existed: that an inequality would exist as long as liberty existed, and that it would unavoidably result from that very liberty itself. This inequality of property constituted the great & fundamental distinction in Society. When the Tribunitial power had levelled the boundary between the *patricians* & *plebeians* what followed? The distinction between rich & poor was substituted. He meant not however to enlarge on the subject. He rose principally to remark that (Mr. Sherman) seemed not to recollect that one branch of the proposed Govt. was so formed, as to render it particularly the guardians of the poorer orders of citizens; nor to have adverted to the true causes of the stability which had been exemplified in Cont. Under the British system as well as the federal, many of the great powers appertaining to Govt. particularly all those relating to foreign Nations were not in the hands of the Govt. there. Their internal affairs also were extremely simple, owing to sundry causes many of which were peculiar to that

Country. Of late the Governmt. had entirely given way to the people, and had in fact suspended many of its ordinary functions in order to prevent those turbulent scenes which had appeared elsewhere. ⟨He asks Mr S. whether the State at this time, dare impose & collect a tax on ye people?⟩ [5] To those causes & not to the frequency of elections, the effect, as far as it existed ought to be chiefly ascribed.

Mr. Gerry. wished we could be united in our ideas concerning a permanent Govt. All aim at the same end, but there are great differences as to the means. One circumstance He thought should be carefully attended to. There were not $\frac{1}{1000}$ part of our fellow citizens who were not agst. every approach towards Monarchy. Will they ever agree to a plan which seems to make such an approach. The Convention ought to be extremely cautious in what they hold out to the people. Whatever plan may be proposed will be espoused with warmth by many out of respect to the quarter it proceeds from as well as from an approbation of the plan itself. And if the plan should be of such a nature as to rouse a violent opposition, it is easy to foresee that discord & confusion will ensue, and it is even possible that we may become a prey to foreign powers. He did not deny the position of Mr. — ⟨Madison.⟩ that the majority will generally violate justice when they have an interest in so doing; But did not think there was any such temptation in this Country. Our situation was different from that of G. Britain: and the great body of lands yet to be parcelled out & settled would very much prolong the difference. Notwithstanding the symtoms of injustice which had marked many of our public Councils, they had not proceeded so far as not to leave hopes, that there would be a sufficient sense of justice & virtue for the purpose of Govt. He admitted the evils arising from a frequency of elections: and would agree to give the Senate a duration of four or five years. [6] A longer term would defeat itself. It never would be adopted by the people.

Mr. Wilson did not mean to repeat what had fallen from

---

[5] Probably, but not certainly a later insertion taken from Yates.
[6] Crossed out: "To go further would bar the way."

others, but wd. add an observation or two which he believed had not yet been suggested. Every nation may be regarded in two relations 1 to its own citizens. 2 to foreign nations. It is therefore not only liable to anarchy & tyranny within but has wars to avoid & treaties to obtain from abroad. The Senate will probably be the depositary of the powers concerning the latter objects. It ought therefore to be made respectable in the eyes of foreign nations. The true reason why G. Britain has not yet listened to a commercial treaty with us has been, because she had no confidence in the stability or efficacy of our Government. 9 years with a rotation, will provide these desirable qualities; and give our Govt. an advantage in this respect over Monarchy itself. In a monarchy much must alway depend on the temper of the man. In such a body, the personal character will be lost in the political. He wd. add another observation. The popular objection agst. appointing any public body for a long term was that it might by gradual encroachments prolong itself first into a body for life, and finally become a hereditary one. It would be a satisfactory answer to this objection that as ⅓ would go out triennially, there would be always three divisions holding their places for unequal terms, and consequently acting under the influence of different views, and different impulses — On the question for 9 years. ⅓ to go out triennially [7]

Massts no. Cont. no. N. Y. no. N. J. no. Pa. ay. Del. ay. Md. no. Va. ay. N. C. no. S. C. no. Geo. no. [Ayes — 8; noes — 3.]

On the question for 6 years ⅓ to go out biennially [7]
Massts. ay. Cont. ay. N. Y. no. N. J. no. Pa. ay. Del. ay. Md. ay. Va. ay. N. C. ay. S. C. no. Geo. no. [Ayes — 7; noes — 4.]

"To receive fixt stipends by which they may be compensated for their services". considered

General Pinkney proposed "that no Salary should be allowed". As this ⟨(the Senatorial)⟩ branch was meant to represent the wealth of the Country, it ought to be composed of persons of wealth; and if no allowance was to be made the

---

[7] See further Appendix A, CXXXVII, CLVIII (33–34), CCXIX.

wealthy alone would undertake the service. ⟨He moved to strike out the Clause.⟩ [8]

Doctr: Franklin seconded the motion. He wished the Convention to stand fair with the people. There were in it a number of young men who would probably be of the Senate. If lucrative appointments should be recommended we might be chargeable with having carved out places for ourselves.

⟨On the question. —

Masts. Connecticut * Pa. Md. S. Carolina Ay.

N. Y. N. J. Del. Virga. N. C. Geo. no.⟩ [9]

Mr. Williamson moved to change the expression into these words towit. "to receive a compensation for the devotion of their time to the public Service". The motion was seconded by Mr. Elseworth. And was agreed to by all the States except S. Carola. It seemed to be meant only to get rid of the word "fixt" and leave greater room for modifying the provision on this point.

Mr. Elseworth moved to strike out "to be paid out of the natil. Treasury" and insert "to be paid by their respective States". If the Senate was meant to strengthen the Govt. it ought to have the confidence of the States. The States will have an interest in keeping up a representation and will make such provision for supporting the members as will ensure their attendance.

Mr. ⟨Madison⟩, considered this a departure from a fundamental principle, and subverting the end intended by allowing the Senate a duration of 6 years. They would if this motion should be agreed to, hold their places during pleasure; during the pleasure of the State Legislatures. One great end of the institution was, that being a firm, wise and impartial body, it might ⟨not⟩ only give stability to the Genl. Govt. in its operations on individuals, but hold an even balance among different

* ⟨Quer. whether Connecticut — should not be — No. & Delaware Ay.⟩

[8] Taken from *Journal* and Yates.
[9] Taken from *Journal*, but Madison first copied from the wrong page (p. 151 instead of 150) and made Delaware and Virginia affirmative with Connecticut and South Carolina negative; he then made the necessary correction and inserted the foot-note.

States. The motion would make the Senate like Congress, the mere Agents & Advocates of State interests & views, instead of being the impartial umpires & Guardians of justice and general Good. Congs. had lately by the establishment of a board with full powers to decide on the mutual claims be-between the U. States & the individual States, fairly acknowledged themselves to be unfit for discharging this part of the business referred to them by the Confederation.

Mr. Dayton considered the payment of the Senate by the States as fatal to their independence. he was decided for paying them out of the Natl Treasury.

On the question for payment of the Senate to be left to the States as moved by Mr. Elseworth

Massts. no. Cont. ay. N. Y. ay. N. J. ay. Pa. no. Del. no. Md. no. Va. no. N. C. no. S. C. ay. Geo. ay. [Ayes — 5; noes — 6.]

Col. Mason. He did not rise to make any motion, but to hint an idea which seemed to be proper for consideration. One important object in constituting the Senate was to secure the rights of property. To give them weight & firmness for this purpose, a considerable duration in office was thought necessary. But a longer term than 6 years, would be of no avail in this respect, if needy persons should be appointed. He suggested therefore the propriety of annexing to the office a qualification of property. He thought this would be very practicable; as the rules of taxation would supply a scale for measuring the degree of wealth possessed by every man.

A question was then taken whether the words "to be paid out of the public treasury." should stand"

Masts. ay. Cont no. N. Y. no. N. J. no. Pa. ay. Del. ay. Md. ay. Va. ay. N. C. no. S. C. no. Geo. no. [Ayes — 5; noes — 6.]

Mr. Butler moved to strike out the the ineligibility of Senators to *State offices*.[10]

Mr. Williamson seconded the motion.

Mr. Wilson remarked the additional dependence this wd.

---

[10] See further, references under September 3 note 7.

create in the Senators on the States. The longer the time he observed allotted to the officer, the more compleat will be the dependance, if it exists at all.

Genl. Pinkney was for making the States as much as could be conveniently done a part of the Genl. Gov't: If the Senate was to be appointed by the States, it ought in pursuance of the same idea to be paid by the States: and the States ought not to be barred from the opportunity of calling members of it into offices at home. Such a restriction would also discourage the ablest men from going into the Senate.

Mr. Wiliamson moved a resolution so penned as to admit of the two following questions. 1. whether the members of the Senate should be ineligible to & incapable of holding offices *under the U. States* [11]

2. whether &c. under the *particular States*.[11]

On the question to postpone in order to consider Williamson's Resoln: Masts. no. Cont. ay. N. Y. no. N. J. no. Pa. ay. Del. ay. Md. ay. Va. ay. N. C. ay. S. C. ay. Geo. ay. [Ayes—8; noes — 3.] [12]

Mr. Gerry & Mr. M⟨adison⟩ — move to add to Mr. Williamsons 1. quest: "and for 1 year thereafter." On this amendt.

Masts. no. Cont. ay N. Y. ay. N. J. no. P. no. Del. ay. Md. ay. Va. ay. N. C. ay. S. C. ay. Geo. no. [Ayes — 7; noes — 4.]

On Mr. Will—son's 1 Question as amended. vz. inelig: & incapable &c. &c. for 1 year &c. agd. unanimously.

On the 2. question as to ineligibility &c. to State offices.

Mas. ay. Ct. no. N. Y. no. N. J. no. P. ay. Del. no. Md. no. Va. ay. N. C. no. S. C. no. Geo. no. [Ayes — 3; noes — 8.]

⟨The 5 Resol: "that each branch have the right of originating acts" was agreed to nem: con:⟩ [13]

Adjd.

---

[11] The words in italics were underscored at a later date.

[12] Detail of Ayes and Noes, Vote 100, makes South Carolina and Georgia both negative.

[13] Taken from *Journal*, confirmed by Yates.

YATES

Tuesday, June 26th, 1787.

Met pursuant to adjournment. Present 11 states.

Mr. Gorham. My motion for 4 years' continuance, was not put yesterday. I am still of opinion that classes will be necessary, but I would alter the time. I therefore move that the senators be elected for 6 years, and that the rotation be triennial.

Mr. Pinkney. I oppose the time, because of too long a continuance. The members will by this means be too long separated from their constituents, and will imbibe attachments different from that of the state; nor is there any danger that members, by a shorter duration of office, will not support the interest of the union, or that the states will oppose the general interest. The state of South Carolina was never opposed in principle to congress, nor thwarted their views in any case, except in the requisition of money, and then only for want of power to comply — for it was found there was not money enough in the state to pay their requisition.

Mr. Read moved that the term of _nine years_ be inserted, in triennial rotation.

Mr Madison. We are now to determine whether the republican form shall be the basis of our government — I admit there is weight in the objection of the gentleman from South Carolina; but no plan can steer clear of objections. That great powers are to be given, there is no doubt; and that those powers may be abused is equally true. It is also probable that members may lose their attachments to the states which sent them — Yet the first branch will control them in many of their abuses. But we are now forming a body on whose wisdom we mean to rely, and their permanency in office secures a proper field in which they may exert their firmness and knowledge. Democratic communities may be unsteady, and be led to action by the impulse of the moment. — Like individuals they may be sensible of their own weakness, and may desire the counsels and checks of friends to guard them against the turbulency and weakness of unruly passions. Such are the various pursuits of this life, that in all civilized countries, the interest of a community will be divided. There will be debtors and creditors, and an unequal possession of property, and hence arises different views and different objects in government. This indeed is the ground-work of aristocracy; and we find it blended in every government, both ancient and modern. Even where titles have survived property, we discover the noble beggar haughty and assuming.

The man who is possessed of wealth, who lolls on his sofa or rolls in his carriage, cannot judge of the wants or feelings of the day laborer. The government we mean to erect is intended to last for ages. The landed interest, at present, is prevalent; but in process of time, when we approximate to the states and kingdoms of Europe; when the number of land-holders shall be comparatively small, through the various means of trade and manufactures, will not the landed interest be overbalanced in future elections, and unless wisely provided against, what will become of your government? In England, at this day, if elections were open to all classes of people, the property of the landed proprietors would be insecure. An agrarian law would soon take place. If these observations be just, our government ought to secure the permanent interests of the country against innovation. Landholders ought to have a share in the government, to support these invaluable interests and to balance and check the other. They ought to be so constituted as to protect the minority of the opulent against the majority. The senate, therefore, ought to be this body; and to answer these purposes, they ought to have permanency and stability. Various have been the propositions; but my opinion is, the longer they continue in office, the better will these views be answered.[14]

Mr. Sherman. The two objects of this body are permanency and safety to those who are to be governed. A bad government is the worse for being long. Frequent elections

---

[14] Compare Genet's interpretation of this, Appendix A, CCCX.

give security and even permanency. In Connecticut we have existed 132 years under an annual government; and as long as a man behaves himself well, he is never turned out of office. Four years to the senate is quite sufficient when you add to it the rotation proposed.

Mr. Hamilton. This question has already been considered in several points of view. We are now forming a republican government. Real liberty is neither found in despotism or the extremes of democracy, but in moderate governments.

Those who mean to form a solid republican government, ought to proceed to the confines of another government. As long as offices are open to all men, and no constitutional rank is established, it is pure republicanism. But if we incline too much to democracy, we shall soon shoot into a monarchy. The difference of property is already great amongst us. Commerce and industry will still increase the disparity. Your government must meet this state of things, or combinations will in process of time, undermine your system. What was the tribunitial power of Rome? It was instituted by the plebeans as a guard against the patricians. But was this a sufficient check? No — The only distinction which remained at Rome was, at last, between the rich and poor. The gentleman from Connecticut forgets that the democratic body is already secure in a representation. As to Connecticut, what were the little objects of their government before the revolution? Colonial concerns merely. They ought now to act on a more extended scale, and dare they do this? Dare they collect the taxes and requisitions of congress? Such a government may do well, if they do not tax, and this is precisely their situation.

Mr. Gerry. It appears to me that the American people have the greatest aversion to monarchy, and the nearer our government approaches to it, the less chance have we for their approbation. Can gentlemen suppose that the reported system can be approved of by them? Demagogues are the great pests of our government, and have occasioned most of our distresses. If four years are insufficient, a future convention may lengthen the time.

Mr. Wilson. The motion is now for nine years, and a

triennial rotation. Every nation attends to its foreign intercourse — to support its commerce — to prevent foreign contempt and to make war and peace. Our senate will be possessed of these powers, and therefore ought to be dignified and permanent. What is the reason that Great Britain does not enter into a commercial treaty with us? Because congress has not the power to enforce its observance. But give them those powers, and give them the stability proposed by the motion, and they will have more permanency than a monarchical government. The great objection of many is, that this duration would give birth to views inconsistent with the interests of the union. This can have no weight, if the triennial rotation is adopted; and this plan may possibly tend to conciliate the minds of the members of the convention on this subject, which have varied more than on any other question.

The question was then put on Mr. Read's motion, and lost, 8 noes — 3 ayes.

The question on 5 years, and a biennial rotation, was carried — 7 ayes — 4 noes. New-York in the minority.

Mr. Pinkney. I move that the clause for granting stipends be stricken out.

Question put — 5 ayes — 6 noes.

On the amendment to the question, *to receive a compensation* — 10 ayes — 1 no.

Judge Elsworth. I move that the words, *out of the national treasury*, be stricken out, and the words, *the respective state legislatures*, be inserted.

If you ask the states what is reasonable, they will comply — but if you ask of them more than is necessary to form a good government, they will grant you nothing.

Capt. Dayton. The members should be paid from the general treasury, to make them independent.

The question was put on the amendment and lost — 5 ayes — 6 noes.

Mr. Mason. I make no motion, but throw out for the consideration of the convention, whether a person in the second branch ought not to be qualified as to property?

The question was then put on the clause, and lost — 5 ayes — 6 noes.

It was moved to strike out the clause, *to be ineligible to any state office.*

Mr. Madison. Congress heretofore depended on state interests — we are now going to pursue the same plan.

Mr. Wilson. Congress has been ill managed, because particular states controlled the union. In this convention, if a proposal is made promising independency to the general government, before we have done with it, it is so modified and changed as to amount to nothing. In the present case, the states may say, although I appoint you for six years, yet if you are against the state, your table will be unprovided. Is this the way you are to erect an independent government?

Mr. Butler. This second branch I consider as the aristocratic part of our government; and they must be controlled by the states, or they will be too independent.

Mr. Pinkney. The states and general government must stand together. On this plan have I acted throughout the whole of this business. I am therefore for expunging the clause. Suppose a member of this house was qualified to be a state judge, must the state be prevented from making the appointment?

Question put for striking out — 8 ayes — 3 noes.

The 5th resolve, *that each house have the right of originating bills,* was taken into consideration, and agreed to.

Adjourned till to-morrow morning.

HAMILTON [15]

I Every government ought to have the means of self preservation

II — Combinations of a few large states might subvert

II — Could not be abused without a revolt

II   Different genius of the states and different composition of the body.

---

[15] It is impossible to assign these notes satisfactorily, but they probably belong to the proceedings of this day.

Note.   Senate could not desire [?] to promote such a class
III   Uniformity in the time of elections —

Objects of a Senate
To afford a double security against Faction in the house
of representatives
Duration of the Senate necessary to its Firmness
Information
sense of national character
Responsibility

M A S O N [16]

G. Mason begs the favor of Maj. Jackson to correct the
following Resolution, in the manner it hath been agreed to
by the Convention.

4. *Resolved,* That the members of the second branch of
the legislature of the United States ought to be chosen by the
individual legislatures, to be of the age of thirty years at least,
to hold their offices for the term of six years, one third to go
out biennially; to be ineligible to and incapable of holding any
office under the authority of the United States, except those
peculiarly belong to the functions of the second branch, during
the term for which they were chosen and for one year thereafter.

[16] This document found among the Mason papers is reprinted from K. M. Rowland, *Life of George Mason*, II, 118.   It seems to accord with the proceedings of this
day.

WEDNESDAY, JUNE 27, 1787.

JOURNAL
Wednesday June 27. 1787.

It was moved and seconded to postpone the consideration of the sixth resolution reported from the Committee in order to take up the seventh and eighth resolutions

On the question to postpone

it passed in the affirmative

It was moved and seconded to agree to the first clause of the seventh resolution namely

"Resolved that the right of suffrage in the first branch of "the national Legislature ought not to be according to the "rule established in the articles of confederation"

Before a determination was taken on the clause, the House adjourned till to-morrow at 11 o'Clock A. M.

MADISON
Wednesday June 27. in Convention

Mr. Rutlidge moved to postpone the 6th. ⟨Resolution, defining the powers of Congs.⟩: in order to take up the 7 & 8 which involved the most fundamental points; ⟨the rules of suffrage in the 2 branches⟩ which was agreed to nem. con.[1]

⟨A question being proposed on Resol: 7 declaring that the suffrage in the first branch sd. be according to an equitable ratio⟩[2]

---

[1] Madison had next recorded, but later struck out: "Mr. Lansing moved that the word 'not' be struck so that it might read 'that the right of suffrage in the first branch ought to be according to the rule established in the articles of Confederation'." Madison, Yates and *Journal* all record this motion on June 28.

[2] Here begins the important debate on proportional representation, which continued until the adoption of the Great Compromise on July 16. It had been discussed previously on May 30, June 9 and June 11. For a summary of the arguments for

Mr L. Martin [3] contended at great length and with great eagerness that the General Govt. was meant merely to preserve the State Governts: not to govern individuals: that its powers ought to be kept within narrow limits; that if too little power was given to it, more might be added; but that if too much, it could never be resumed: that individuals as such have little to do but with their own States; that the Genl. Govt. has no more to apprehend from the States composing ⟨the Union⟩ while it pursues proper measures, that a Govt. over individuals has to apprehend from its subjects: that to resort to the Citizens at large for their sanction to a new Governt. will be throwing them back into a State of Nature: that the dissolution of the State Govts. is involved in the nature of the process: that the people have no right to do this without the consent of those to whom they have delegated their power for State purposes; through their tongue only they can speak, through their ears, only, can hear: that the States have shewn a good disposition to comply with the Acts, of Congs. weak, contemptibly weak as that body has been; and have failed through inability alone to comply: that the heaviness of the private debts, and the waste of property during the war, were the chief causes of this inability; that he did not conceive the instances mentioned by Mr. M⟨adison⟩ of conpacts between Va. & Md. between Pa. & N. J. or of troops raised by Massts. for defence against the Rebels, to be violations of the articles of confederation — that an equal vote in each State was essential to the federal idea, and was founded in justice & freedom, not merely in policy: that tho' the States may give up this right of sovereignty, yet they had not, and ought not: that the States like individuals were in a State of nature equally sovereign & free.   In order to prove that individuals in a State of nature are equally free & independent he read passages from Locke, Vattel, Lord Summers — Priestly. To prove that the case is the same with States till they sur-

and against proportional representation, see Martin's *Genuine Information* in Appendix A, CLVIII (17–24), also further references on particular questions in the course of the debates June 27 to July 16.

[3] See June 28 note 2.

render their equal sovereignty, he read other passages in Locke & Vattel, and also Rutherford: that the States being equal cannot treat or confederate so as to give up an equality of votes without giving up their liberty: that the propositions on the table were a system of slavery for 10 States: that as Va. Masts. & Pa. have $\frac{42}{90}$ of the votes they can do as they please without a miraculous Union of the other ten: that they will have nothing to do, but to gain over one of the ten to make them compleat masters of the rest, that they can then appoint an Execute: & Judiciary & legislate for them as they please: that there was & would continue a natural predilection & partiality in men for their own States; that the States, particularly the smaller, would never allow a negative to be exercised over their laws: that no State in ratifying the Confederation had objected to the equality of votes; that the complaints at present run not agst. this equality but the want of power; that 16 members from Va. would be more likely to act in concert than a like number formed of members from different States; that instead of a junction of the small States as a remedy, he thought a division of the large States would be more eligible.—This was the substance of a speech ⟨which was continued⟩ more than three hours. He was too much exhausted he said to finish his remarks, and reminded the House that he should tomorrow, resume them.

Adjd.[4]

YATES

WEDNESDAY, JUNE 27th, 1787.

Met pursuant to adjournment. Present 11 states.

The 6th resolve was postponed, in order to take into consideration the 7th and 8th resolves. The first clause of the 7th was proposed for consideration, which respected the suffrage of each state in the first branch of the legislature.

(Mr. Martin, the attorney general from Maryland, spoke on this subject upwards of three hours. As his arguments

---

[4] See further, Appendix A, XLIX.

were too diffuse, and in many instances desultory, it was not possible to trace him through the whole, or to methodize his ideas into a systematic or argumentative arrangement. I shall therefore only note such points as I conceive merit most particular notice.)

The question is important, (said Mr. Martin,) and I have already expressed my sentiments on the subject. My opinion is, that the general government ought to protect and secure the state governments — others, however, are of a different sentiment, and reverse the principle.

The present reported system is a perfect medley of confederated and national government, without example and without precedent. Many who wish the general government to protect the state governments, are anxious to have the line of jurisdiction well drawn and defined, so that they may not clash. This suggests the necessity of having this line well detailed — possibly this may be done. If we do this, the people will be convinced that we meant well to the state governments; and should there be any defects, they will trust a future convention with the power of making further amendments.

A general government may operate on individuals in cases of general concern, and still be federal. This distinction is with the states, as states, represented by the people of those states. States will take care of their internal police and local concerns. The general government has no interest, but the protection of the whole. Every other government must fail. We are proceeding in forming this government as if there were no state governments at all. The states must approve, or you will have none at all. I have never heard of a confederacy having two legislative branches. Even the celebrated Mr. Adams, who talks so much of checks and balances, does not suppose it necessary in a confederacy. Public and domestic debts are our great distress. The treaty between Virginia and Maryland about the navigation of the Chesapeake and Potomac, is no infraction of the confederacy. The corner-stone of a federal government is *equality* of votes. States may surrender this right; but if they do, their liberties are lost.   If I err on this point, it is the error of the head, not of the heart.

The first principle of government is founded on the natural rights of individuals, and in perfect equality.   Locke, Vattel, Lord Somers, and Dr. Priestly, all confirm this principle. This principle of equality, when applied to individuals, is lost in some degree, when he becomes a member of a society, to which it is transferred; and this society, by the name of state or kingdom, is, with respect to others, again on a perfect footing of equality — a right to govern themselves as they please.   Nor can any other state, of right, deprive them of this equality.   If such a state confederates, it is intended for the good of the whole; and if it again confederate, those rights must be well guarded.   Nor can any state demand a surrender of any of those rights; if it can, equality is already destroyed.   We must treat as free states with each other, upon the same terms of equality that men originally formed themselves into societies.   Vattel, Rutherford and Locke, are united in support of the position, that states, as to each other, are in a state of nature.

Thus, says Mr. Martin, have I travelled with the most respectable authorities in support of principles, all tending to prove the equality of independent states.   This is equally applicable to the smallest as well as the largest states, on the true principles of reciprocity and political freedom.

Unequal confederacies can never produce good effects. Apply this to the Virginia plan.   Out of the number 90, Virginia has 16 votes, Massachusetts 14, Pennsylvania 12 — in all 42.   Add to this a state having four votes, and it gives a majority in the general legislature.   Consequently a combination of these states will govern the remaining nine or ten states.   Where is the safety and independency of those states?   Pursue this subject farther.   The executive is to be appointed by the legislature, and becomes the executive in consequence of this undue influence.   And hence flows the appointment of all your officers, civil, military and judicial. The executive is also to have a negative on all laws.   Suppose the possibility of a combination of ten states — he negatives a law — it is totally lost, because those states cannot form two thirds of the legislature. I am willing to give up private interest for the public good — but I must be satisfied first, that it is the public interest — and who can decide this point? A majority only of the union.

The Lacedemonians insisted, in the amphictionic council to exclude some of the smaller states from a right to vote, in order that they might tyrannize over them. If the plan now on the table be adopted three states in the union have the controul, and they may make use of their power when they please.

If there exists no separate interests, there is no danger of an equality of votes; and if there be danger, the smaller states cannot yield. If the foundation of the existing confederation is well laid, powers may be added — You may safely add a third story to a house where the foundation is good. Read then the votes and proceedings of congress on forming the confederation — Virginia only was opposed to the principle of equality — The smaller states yielded rights, not the large states — They gave up their claim to the unappropriated lands with the tenderness of the mother recorded by Solomon — they sacrificed affection to the preservation of others. — New-Jersey and Maryland rendered more essential services during the war than many of the larger states. The partial representation in congress is not the cause of its weakness, but the want of power. I would not trust a government organized upon the reported plan, for all the slaves of Carolina or the horses and oxen of Massachusetts. Price says, that laws made by one man or a set of men, and not by common consent, is slavery — And it is so when applied to states, if you give them an unequal representation. What are called human feelings in this instance are only the feelings of ambition and the lust of power.

Adjourned till to-morrow morning.

KING

Wednesday 27. June [5]

Martin I think that the proposed Reform of the confedn. must rest upon the State Govts: the reform ought to be for yr. safety and protection — whatever is of an external & merely general nature shall belong to the US. Whatever is internal and existing between the separate states & individuals shall belong to the particular States. if there shall be occasion for farther powers being given to the US. a future convention may propose ym. if you give more than enough, it never can be reclaimed — It is said if the Genl. Govt. legislates for individuals & not for States, the Govt. is not federal — but if the object of this Legislation is of an external nature, the Govt. is federal — Our Reform must be federal — The States are equal & must have equal Influence and equal votes — I will proceed on first principls. every man out of society is equal, in Freedom, & every other quality of man — Lock, Vattel, & others prove this position —

Martin —[6]

The States all agree to the equality of Votes except Virgin. & N. Car. the latter of wh. was divided — Remark. admit the Fact, yet the rule of Taxation was fixed — Congress could not raise a penny except agreeably to Rule of Taxation in the 8th Art — not even from the Post Office — But now we are to tax the people by any Rule the Legislat. may prefer — now then it is necessary to apportion the Representatives — 3 States will have 42 out of 90 votes. they will tyrannize — 10 States will be slaves.

Remark — The laws will be general and apply to the whole —

---

[5] King's notes are very confused in arrangement for June 27 and 28. It is impossible to determine the order satisfactorily. He has inserted one part, so that the date of June 27 comes twice and he has then endorsed the whole:

27 June | The States in the | Legislature 2 Br to | be equal —— | Martin aye | Madison no | Ch Pinkney aye

[6] This might be ascribed to June 28, but it is uncertain.

7. States may now combine — they are the lawful majority, and every one is bound —

The principles [7] are right but cannot be carried into effect.

P A T E R S O N [8]

June 27. 1787.

Have those who upon the present plan hold $\frac{1}{13}$ part of the Votes, a 13th part of the weight, — certainly not — upon this plan they sink to nothing

The Individual right of Citizens is given up in the State Govts. they cannot exercize it again in the Genl. Government.

It has never been complained of in Congress — the complaint there is the want of proper powers. [9]

---

[7] Place of this is uncertain, but probably belongs here.

[8] Found among the Paterson Papers, with Paterson's other notes of the Convention. These notes are in Brearley's handwriting.

[9] A hand drawn on the margin points to this argument as if indicating its importance.

THURSDAY, JUNE 28, 1787.

JOURNAL

Thursday June 28. 1787.

It was moved and seconded to amend the seventh resolution reported from the Committee so as to read as follows, namely

Resolved that the right of suffrage in the first branch of the Legislature of the United States ought to be in proportion to the whole number of white and other free citizens and inhabitants of every age, sex and condition including those bound to servitude for a term of years, and three fifths of all other persons not comprehended in the foregoing description, except Indians, not paying taxes in each State.

It was moved and seconded to erase the word "not" from the first clause of the seventh resolution so as to read

Resolved that the right of suffrage in the second branch of the Legislature of the United States ought to be according to the rule established in the articles of confederation

The determination of the House on the motion for erasing the word "not" from the first clause of the seventh resolution was postponed, at the request of the Deputies of the State of New-York till tomorrow,

And then the House adjourned till to-morrow at 11 o'Clock A. M

MADISON

Thursday June 28th. in Convention

Mr. L. Martin resumed his discourse, contending that the Genl. Govt. ought to be formed for the States, not for individuals: that if the States were to have votes in proportion to their numbers of people, it would be the same thing whether their ⟨representatives⟩ were chosen by the Legislatures or the

444

people; the smaller States would be equally enslaved; that if the large States have the same interest with the smaller as was urged, there could be no [1] danger in giving them an equal vote; they would not injure themselves, and they could not injure the large ones on that supposition without injuring themselves ⟨and if the interests were not the same the inequality of suffrage wd — be dangerous to the smaller States.⟩: that it will be in vain to propose any plan offensive to the rulers of the States, whose influence over the people will certainly prevent their adopting it: that the large States were weak at present in proportion to their extent: & could only be made formidable to the small ones, by the weight of their votes; that in case a dissolution of the Union should take place, the small States would have nothing to fear from their power; that if in such a case the three great States should league themselves together, the other ten could do so too: & that he had rather see partial Confederacies take place, than the plan on the table. This was the substance of the residue of his discourse which was delivered with much diffuseness & considerable vehemence.[2]

Mr. Lansing & Mr. Dayton moved to strike out "not." so that the 7 art: might read that the rights of suffrage in the 1st branch ought to be according to the rule established by the Confederation"

Mr. Dayton expressed great anxiety that the question might not be put till tomorrow; Governr. Livingston being kept away by indisposition, and the representation of N. Jersey thereby suspended.

Mr. Williamson. thought that if any political truth could be grounded on mathematical demonstration, it was that if the states were equally sovereign now, and parted with equal proportions of sovereignty, that they would remain equally sovereign. He could not comprehend how the smaller States would be injured in the case, and wished some gentleman would vouchsafe a solution of it. He observed that the small

[1] Crossed out "more".
[2] For interesting sidelights on this speech, see controversy between Ellsworth and Martin, Appendix A, CLXXXIX—CXCII, CXCIX.

States, if they had a plurality of votes would have an interest in throwing the burdens off their own shoulders on those of the large ones. He begged that the expected addition of new States from the Westward might be kept in view. They would be small States, they would be poor States,[3] they would be unable to pay in proportion to their numbers; their distance from market rendering the produce of their labour less valuable; they would consequently be ⟨tempted⟩ to combine for the purpose of laying burdens on commerce & consumption which would fall with greatest weight on the old States.

Mr. M⟨adison⟩ sd. he was much disposed to concur in any expedient not inconsistent with fundamental principles, that could remove the difficulty concerning the rule of representation. But he could neither be convinced that the rule contended for was just, nor necessary for the safety of the small States agst. the large States. That it was not just, had been conceded by Mr. Breerly & Mr. Patterson themselves. The expedient proposed by them was a new partition of the territory of the U. States. The fallacy of the reasoning drawn from the equality of Sovereign States in the formation of compacts, lay in confounding mere Treaties, in which were specified certain duties[4] to which the parties were to be bound, and certain rules by which their subjects were to be reciprocally governed in their intercourse, with a compact by which an authority was created paramount to the parties, & making laws for the government of them. If France, England & Spain were to enter into a Treaty for the regulation of commerce &c. with the Prince of Monacho & 4 or 5 other of the smallest sovereigns of Europe, they would not hesitate to treat as equals, and to make the regulations perfectly reciprocal. Wd. the case be the same if a Council were to be formed of deputies from each with authority and discretion, to raise money, levy troops, determine the value of coin &c? Would 30 or 40. million of people submit their fortunes into the hands, of a few thousands? If they did it would only prove that they expected more from the terror of their superior force, than they feared

---

[3] Crossed out "they would have different interests from the Altantic States; ".

[4] Crossed out "rules by ".

from the selfishness of their feeble ⟨associates⟩ Why are
Counties of the same States represented in proportion to their
numbers? Is it because the representatives are chosen by the
people themselves? so will be the representatives in the Nationl. Legislature. Is it because, the larger have more at
stake than the smaller? The case will be the same with the
larger & smaller States. Is it because the laws are to operate
immediately on their persons & properties? The same is the
case in some degree as the articles of confederation stand;
the same will be the case in ⟨a far greater degree⟩ [5] under the
plan proposed to be substituted. In the cases of captures,
of piracies, and of offenses in a federal army, the property &
persons of individuals depend on the laws of Congs. By the
plan ⟨proposed⟩ a compleat power of taxation, the highest
prerogative of supremacy is proposed to be vested in the
National Govt. Many other powers are added which assimilate it to the Govt. of individual States. The negative ⟨on
the State laws⟩ proposed, will make it an essential branch of
the State Legislatures & of course will require that it should
be exercised by a body established on like principles with the
other branches of those Legislatures.—That it is not necessary
to secure the small States agst. the large ones he conceived to
be equally obvious: Was a combination of the large ones
dreaded? this must arise either from some interest common
to Va. Masts. & Pa. & distinguishing them from the other
States ⟨or from the mere circumstance of similarity of size⟩ [6].
Did any such common interest exist? In point of situation
they could not have been more effectually separated from each
other by the most jealous citizen of the most jealous State.
In point of manners, Religion and the other circumstances,
which sometimes beget affection between different communities, they were not more assimilated than the other States. —
In point of the staple productions they were as dissimilar as
any three other States in the Union.

The Staple of Masts. was *fish*, of Pa. *flower*, of Va. *Tobo.*
Was a Combination to be apprehended from the mere circum-

[5] Crossed out "an essential manner"; probably but not certainly a later revision.
[6] Probably but not certainly a later revision.

stance of equality of size? Experience suggested no such danger. The journals of Congs. did not present any peculiar association of these States in the votes recorded. It had never been seen that different Counties in the same State, conformable in extent, but disagreeing in other circumstances, betrayed a propensity to such combinations. Experience rather taught a contrary lesson. Among individuals of superior eminence & weight in society, rivalships were much more frequent than coalitions. Among independent nations preeminent over their neighbours, the same remark was verified. Carthage & Rome tore one another to pieces instead of uniting their forces to devour the weaker nations of the Earth. The Houses of Austria & France were hostile as long as they remained the greatest powers of Europe. England & France have succeeded to the pre-eminence & to the enmity. To this principle we owe perhaps our liberty. A coalition between those powers would have been fatal to us. Among the principal members of antient & modern confederacies, we find the same effect from the same cause. The contintions, not the coalitions of Sparta, Athens & Thebes, proved fatal to the smaller members of the Amphyctionic Confederacy. The contentions, not the combinations of Prussia & Austria, have distracted & oppressed the Germanic empire. Were the large States formidable *singly* to their smaller neighbours? On this supposition the latter ought to wish for such a general Govt. as will operate with equal energy on the former as on themselves. The more lax the band, the more liberty the larger will have to avail themselves of their superior force. Here again Experience was an instructive monitor. What is ye situation of the weak compared with the strong in those stages of civilization in which the violence of individuals is least controuled by an efficient Government? The Heroic period of Antient Greece the feudal licentiousness of the middle ages of Europe, the existing condition of the American Savages, answer this question. What is the situation of the minor sovereigns in the great society of independent nations, in which the more powerful are under no controul but the nominal authority of the law of Nations? Is not the danger to the former exactly in proportion to their weakness. But there are cases still more in point. What was the condition of the weaker members of the Amphyctionic Confederacy. Plutarch (life of Themistocles) will inform us that it happened but too often that the strongest cities corrupted & awed the weaker, and that Judgment went in favor of the more powerful party. What is the condition of the lesser States in the German Confederacy? We all know that they are exceedingly trampled upon and that they owe their safety as far as they enjoy it, partly to their enlisting themselves, under the rival banners of the preeminent members, partly to alliances with neighbouring Princes which the Constitution of the Empire does not prohibit. What is the state of things in the lax system [7] of the Dutch Confederacy? Holland contains about $\frac{1}{3}$ the people, supplies about $\frac{1}{2}$ of the money, and by her influence, silently & indirectly governs the whole Republic. In a word; the two extremes before us are a perfect separation [8] & a perfect incorporation, of the 13 States. In the first case they would be independent nations subject to no law, but the law of nations. In the last, they would be mere counties of one entire republic, subject to one common law. In the first case the smaller states would have every thing to fear from the larger. In the last they would have nothing to fear. The true policy of the small States therefore lies in promoting those principles & that form of Govt. which will most approximate the States to the condition of Counties. Another consideration may be added. If the Genl. Govt. be feeble, the large States distrusting its continuance, and foreseeing that their importance & security may depend on their own size & strength, will never submit to a partition. Give to the Genl. Govt. sufficient energy & permanency, & you remove the objection. Gradual partitions of the large, & junctions of the small ⟨States⟩ will be facilitated, and time ⟨may⟩[9] effect that equalization, which is wished for by the small States, now, but can never be accomplished at once.

Mr. Wilson. The leading argument of those who contend

---

[7] Crossed out "more tranquil sessions ".
[8] Crossed out "independence ".   Crossed out "will ".

for equality of votes among the States is that the States as such being equal, and being represented not as districts of individuals, but in their political & corporate capacities, are entitled to an equality of suffrage. According to this mode of reasoning the representation of the burroughs in Engld which has been allowed on all hands to be the rotten part of the Constitution, is perfectly right & proper. They are like the States represented in their corporate capacity like the States therefore they are entitled to equal voices, old Sarum to as many as London. And instead of the injury supposed hitherto to be done to London, the true ground of complaint lies with old Sarum; for London instead of two which is her proper share, sends four representatives to Parliament.

Mr. Sherman. The question is not what rights naturally belong to men; but how they may be most equally & effectually[10] guarded in Society. And if some give up more than others in order to attain this end, there can be ⟨no⟩ room for complaint. To do otherwise, to require an equal concession from all, if it would create danger to the rights of some, would be sacrificing the end to the means. The rich man who enters into Society along with the poor man, gives up more than the poor man. yet with an equal vote he is equally safe. Were he to have more votes than the poor man in proportion to his superior stake, the rights of the poor man would immediately cease to be secure. This consideration prevailed when the articles of confederation were formed.

⟨The determination of the question from striking out the word "not" was put off till to morrow at the request of the Deputies of N. York.⟩[11]

[Dr. Franklin.] [12]

Mr. President

The small progress we have made after 4 or five weeks close

---

[10] Crossed out "best".   [11] Taken from *Journal.*

[12] Madison originally made an abstract of Franklin's speech in about 200 words. This was later stricken out — and this note made: "see opposite page & insert the speech of Doctr F in this place." On the opposite page under the heading "June 28, in convention" is the speech which is here given — but without Franklin's name.

Among the Franklin Papers in the Library of Congress is a copy of this speech differing hardly at all from the text except in more frequent use of capitals.

attendance & continual reasonings with each other — our different sentiments on almost every question, several of the last producing as many noes as ays, is methinks a melancholy proof of the imperfection of the Human Understanding. We indeed seem to feel[13] our own want of political wisdom, since we have been running about in search of it. We have gone back to ancient history for models of Government, and examined the different forms of those Republics which having been formed with the seeds of their own dissolution now no longer exist. And we have viewed Modern States all round Europe, but find none of their Constitutions suitable to our circumstances.

In this situation of this Assembly, groping as it were in the dark to find political truth, and scarce able to distinguish it when presented to us, how has it happened, Sir, that we have not hitherto once thought of humbly applying to the Father of lights to illuminate our understandings? In the beginning of the Contest with G. Britain, when we were sensible of danger we had daily prayer in this room for the divine protection. — Our prayers, Sir, were heard, and they were graciously answered. All of us who were engaged in the struggle must have observed frequent instances of a Superintending providence in our favor. To that kind providence we owe this happy opportunity of consulting in peace on the means of establishing our future national felicity. And have we now forgotten that powerful friend? or do we imagine that we no longer need his assistance? I have lived, Sir, a long time, and the longer I live, the more convincing proofs I see of this truth — *that God[14] governs in the affairs of men.* And if a sparrow cannot fall to the ground without his notice, is it probable that an empire can rise without his aid? We have been assured, Sir, in the sacred writings, that "except the Lord build the House they labour in vain that build it." I firmly believe this; and I also believe that without his concurring aid we shall succeed in this political building no better than the Builders of Babel: We shall be divided by our little

---

[13] "feei" is underscored in Franklin MS.
[14] "God" twice underscored in Franklin MS.

partial local interests; our projects will be confounded, and we ourselves shall become a reproach and bye word down to future ages. And what is worse, mankind may hereafter from this unfortunate instance, despair of establishing Governments by Human Wisdom and leave it to chance, war and conquest.

I therefore beg leave to move — that henceforth prayers imploring the assistance of Heaven, and its blessings on our deliberations, be held in this Assembly every morning before we proceed to business, and that one or more of the Clergy of this City be requested to officiate in that service ———

Mr. Sharman seconded the motion.

Mr. Hamilton & several others expressed their apprehensions that however proper such a resolution might have been at the beginning of the convention, it might at this late day, 1. bring on it some disagreeable animadversions. & 2. lead the public to believe that the embarrassments and dissentions within the convention, had suggested this measure. It was answered by Docr. F. Mr. Sherman & others, that the past omission of a duty could not justify a further omission — that the rejection of such a proposition would expose the Convention to more unpleasant animadversions than the adoption of it: and that the alarm out of doors that might be excited for the state of things within. would at least be as likely to do good as ill.

Mr. Williamson, observed that the true cause of the omission could not be mistaken. The Convention had no funds.

Mr. Randolph proposed in order to give a favorable aspect to ye. measure, that a sermon be preached at the request of the convention on 4th of July, the anniversary of Independence, — & thenceforward prayers be used in ye Convention every morning. Dr. Frankn. 2ded. this motion After several unsuccessful attempts for silently postponing the matter by adjourng. the adjournment was at length carried, without any vote on the motion.[15]

---

[15] In the Franklin MS. the following note is added: — "The Convention, except three or four persons, thought Prayers unnecessary." A distorted account of this incident is given in Appendix A, CCCLV; see also CXCV, CCCLXVII, CCCLXXIX and CCCXCIII.

YATES

THURSDAY, JUNE 28th, 1787.

Met pursuant to adjournment.

Mr. Martin in continuation.

On federal grounds, it is said, that a minority will govern a majority — but on the Virginia plan a minority would tax a majority. In a federal government, a majority of states must and ought to tax. In the local government of states, counties may be unequal — still numbers, not property, govern. What is the government now forming, over states or persons? As to the latter, their rights cannot be the object of a general government — These are already secured by their guardians, the state governments. The general government is therefore intended only to protect and guard the rights of the states as states.

This general government, I believe, is the first upon earth which gives checks against democracies or aristocracies. The only necessary check in a general government ought to be a restraint to prevent its absorbing the powers of the state governments. Representation on federal principles can only flow from state societies. Representation and taxation are ever inseperable — not according to the quantum of property, but the quantum of freedom.

Will the representatives of a state forget state interests? The mode of election cannot change it. These prejudices cannot be eradicated — Your general government cannot be just or equal upon the Virginia plan, unless you abolish state interests. If this cannot be done, you must go back to principles purely federal.

On this latter ground, the state legislatures and their constituents will have no interests to pursue different from the general government, and both will be interested to support each other. Under these ideas can it be expected that the people can approve the Virginia plan? But it is said, the people, not the state legislatures, will be called upon for approbation— with an evident design to separate the interest of the governors

from the governed.   What must be the consequence? Anarchy
and confusion.   We lose the idea of the powers with which
we are entrusted.   The legislatures must approve.   By them
it must, on your own plan, be laid before the people.   How
will such a government, over so many great states, operate?
Wherever new settlements have been formed in large states,
they immediately want to shake off their independency.
Why? Because the government is too remote for their good.
The people want it nearer home.

The basis of all ancient and modern confederacies is the
freedom and the independency of the states composing it.
The states forming the amphictionic council were equal,
though Lacedemon, one of the greatest states, attempted the
exclusion of three of the lesser states from this right.   The plan
reported, it is true, only intends to diminish those rights, not
to annihilate them — It was the ambition and power of the
great Grecian states which at last ruined this respectable
council.   The states as societies are ever respectful.   Has
Holland or Switzerland ever complained of the equality of
the states which compose their respective confederacies?
Bern and Zurich are larger than the remaining eleven cantons
— so of many of the states of Germany; and yet their governments are not complained of.   Bern alone might usurp the
whole power of the Helvetic confederacy, but she is contented
still with being equal.

The admission of the larger states into the confederation,
on the principles of equality, is dangerous— But on the Virginia system, it is ruinous and destructive.   Still it is the true
interest of all the states to confederate — It is their joint
efforts which must protect and secure us from foreign danger,
and give us peace and harmony at home.

(Here Mr. Martin entered into a detail of the comparative
powers of each state, and stated their probable weakness and
strength.)

At the beginning of our troubles with Great Britain, the
smaller states were attempted to be cajoled to submit to the
views of that nation, lest the larger states should usurp their
rights.   We then answered them — your present plan is

slavery, which, on the remote prospect of a distant evil, we will not submit to.

I would rather confederate with any single state, than submit to the Virginia plan. But we are already confederated, and no power on earth can dissolve it but by the consent of *all* the contracting powers — and four states, on this floor, have already declared their opposition to annihilate it. Is the old confederation dissolved, because some of the states wish a new confederation?

Mr. Lansing. I move that the word *not* be struck out of the resolve, and then the question will stand on its proper ground — and the resolution will read thus: *that the representation of the first branch be according to the articles of the confederation;* and the sense of the convention on this point will determine the question of a federal or national government.

Mr. Madison.[16] I am against the motion. I confess the necessity of harmonizing, and if it could be shown that the system is unjust or unsafe, I would be against it. There has been much fallacy in the arguments advanced by the gentleman from Maryland. He has, without adverting to many manifest distinctions, considered confederacies and treaties as standing on the same basis. In the one, the powers act collectively, in the other individually. Suppose, for example, that France, Spain and some of the smaller states in Europe, should treat on war or peace, or on any other general concern, it would be done on principles of equality; but if they were to form a plan of general government, would they give, or are the greater states obliged to give, to the lesser, the same and equal legislative powers? Surely not. They might differ on this point, but no one can say that the large states were wrong in refusing this concession. Nor can the gentleman's reasoning apply to the present powers of congress; for they may and do, in some cases, affect property, and in case of war, the lives of the citizens. Can any of the lesser states be endangered by an adequate representation? Where is the probability of a combination? What the inducements? Where is

---

[16] For Genet's interpretation of Madison's position see Appendix A, CCCX.

the similarity of customs, manners or religion? If there possibly can be a diversity of interest, it is the case of the three large states. Their situation is remote, their trade different. The staple of Massachusetts is fish, and the carrying trade — of Pennsylvania, wheat and flour — of Virginia, tobacco. Can states thus situated in trade, ever form such a combination? Do we find those combinations in the larger counties in the different state governments to produce rivalships? Does not the history of the nations of the earth verify it? Rome rivalled Carthage, and could not be satisfied before she was destroyed. The houses of Austria and Bourbon acted on the same view — and the wars of France and England have been waged through rivalship; and let me add, that we, in a great measure, owe our independency to those national contending passions, France, through this motive, joined us. She might, perhaps, with less expense, have induced England to divide America between them. In Greece the contention was ever between the larger states. Sparta against Athens — and these again, occasionally, against Thebes, were ready to devour each other. Germany presents the same prospect — Prussia against Austria. Do the greater provinces in Holland endanger the liberties of the lesser? And let me remark, that the weaker you make your confederation, the greater the danger to the lesser states. They can only be protected by a strong federal government. Those gentlemen who oppose the Virginia plan do not sufficiently analyze the subject. Their remarks, in general, are vague and inconclusive.

Captain Dayton. On the discussion of this question the fate of the state governments depend.

Mr. Williamson. If any argument will admit of demonstration, it is that which declares, that all men have an equal right in society. Against this position, I have heard, as yet, no argument, and I could wish to hear what could be said against it. What is tyranny? Representatives of representatives, if you give them the power of taxation. From equals take equals, and the remainder is equal. What process is to annihilate smaller states, I know not. But I know it must be tyranny, if the smaller states can tax the greater, in order to ease themselves. A general government cannot exercise direct taxation. Money must be raised by duties and imposts, &c. and this will operate equally. It is impossible to tax according to numbers. Can a man over the mountains, where produce is a drug, pay equal with one near the shore?

Mr. Wilson. I should be glad to hear the gentleman from Maryland explain himself upon the remark of Old Sarum, when compared with the city of London. This he has allowed to be an unjust proportion; as in the one place one man sends two members, and in the other one million are represented by four members. I would be glad to hear how he applies this to the larger and smaller states in America; and whether the borough, as a borough, is represented, or the people of the borough.

Mr. Martin rose to explain. Individuals, as composing a part of the whole of one consolidated government, are there represented.

The further consideration of the question was postponed.

Mr. Sherman. In society, the poor are equal to the rich in voting, although one pays more than the other. This arises from an equal distribution of liberty amongst all ranks; and it is, on the same grounds, secured to the states in the confederation — for this would not even trust the important powers to a majority of the states. Congress has too many checks, and their powers are too limited. A gentleman from New-York thinks a limited monarchy the best government, and no state distinctions. The plan now before us gives the power to four states to govern nine states. As they will have the purse, they may raise troops, and can also make a king when they please.

Mr. Madison. There is danger in the idea of the gentleman from Connecticut. Unjust representation will ever produce it. In the United Netherlands, Holland governs the whole, although she has only one vote. The counties in Virginia are exceedingly disproportionate, and yet the smaller has an equal vote with the greater, and no inconvenience arises.

Governor Franklin read some remarks, acknowledging the

difficulties of the present subject.   Neither ancient or modern
history, (said Gov. Franklin,) can give us light.   As a sparrow
does not fall without Divine permission, can we suppose that
governments can be erected without his will?   We shall, I
am afraid, be disgraced through little party views.   I move
that we have prayers every morning.

Adjourned till to-morrow morning.

KING

— 27 [28] June 1787 —

Madison — The Gentlemen who oppose the plan of a representation founded on Numbers, do not distinguish accurately —
they use general terms — speake of Tyranny — of the small
states being swallowed up by large ones. of combinations between Mass. Penn. & Virgin. no circumstance of Religion,
Habits, manners, mode of thinking, course of Business, manufactures, commerce, or natural productions establishes a common interest between them exclusive of all the other States —
If this was the case, there is no Fact in ye. History of man or
nations that authorities the Jealousy.   Engld. & France might
have divid America — The great States, of Athens & Sparta
members of the Amphictionic Council never combined to
oppress the other Cities — they were Rivals and fought each
other — The larger members of the Helvetic Union never
combined agt. the small states — Those of the Netherlands
never entered into such a combination — In Germany the
large Members have been at war wh. each other, but never
combined agt. the inferior members —

These Facts are founded in an inherent principle in the
Nature of man & Nations who are but an aggregate of men —
When Men or Nations are large, strong, and also nearly equal,
they immediately become Rivals — The Jealousy of each
other prevents their Union —

Pinckney.   Cs.

Remarks that the honors & Emoluments of the Union may
be the object of Combination.

Remark — The advocates for a confederation purely apply-ing to States — agree that the plan of Representation in pro-portion to Numbers will have the men free but the states will be degraded their sovereignty will be degraded —

PATERSON [17]

June 28th

Mr. Martin resumed his argument.

The Genl. Govt. is not to regulate the rights of Individuals, but that of States. The Genl. Govt. is to Govern Sover-eignties. then where the propriety of the several Branches — they cannot exist — there can be no such checks.

Amphictyonick Council of Greece represented by two from each town — who were notwithsg. the dispn. of the Towns equal — Rollins Ancient Hist. 4 Vol. pa. 79.

All the *Ancient* and *Modern* Confedns. and Leagues were as *equals* notwithstanding the *vast* disproportions in size and wealth.

If the large States, who have got a Majority, will adhere to their plan, we cannot help it, but we will publish to the world our plan and our principles, and leave it to judge.

Mr. Madison

Have we seen the Great Powers of Europe combining to oppress the small — [18]

Yes — the division of Poland.[19]

Mr. Williamson

They talk in vague Terms of the great States combining etc

Wants to know how it is possible that the large States can oppress the small [18]

The rule to tax the States according to their numbers would be cruel and unjust — it would Create a war.

Mr. Madison.

If you form the present Government, the States will be satisfied — and they will divide and sub-divide so as to become nearly equal —

---

[17] See June 27, note 8.   [19] Note by Paterson.

[18] A hand is drawn on the margin pointing to this, as if to indicate its importance.

FRIDAY, JUNE 29, 1787.

JOURNAL

Friday June 29. 1787.

It was moved and seconded to strike the word "not" out of the first clause of the seventh resolution reported from the Committee

On the question to strike out

it passed in the negative [Ayes—4; noes—6; divided—1.]

It was moved and seconded to agree to the first clause of the seventh resolution, as reported from the Committee namely.

Resolved that the right of suffrage in the first branch of the Legislature of the United States ought not to be according to the rule established in the articles of confederation but according to some equitable ratio of representation

On the question to agree

it passed in the affirmative [Ayes — 6; noes — 4; divided — 1.]

It was moved and seconded to postpone the farther consideration of the seventh in order to take up the eighth resolution

which passed in the affirmative [Ayes—9; noes — 2.]

It was moved and seconded to amend the eighth resolution reported from the Committee so as to read as follows namely

Resolved that in the second branch of the Legislature of the United States each State shall have an equal vote. —

Before the determination of the House was taken on the last motion, the House adjourned till to-morrow at 11 o'Clock A. M

DETAIL OF AYES AND NOES

New Hampshire	Massachusetts	Rhode Island	Connecticut	New York	New Jersey	Pennsylvania	Delaware	Maryland	Virginia	North Carolina	South Carolina	Georgia	Questions	Ayes	Noes	Divided
[105] no	aye	aye	aye	no	aye	dd	no	no	no	no			To strike the word "not" out of the first clause of the seventh resolution	4	6	1
[106] aye	no	no	no	aye	no	dd	aye	aye	aye	aye			To agree to the first clause of the seventh resolution as reported	6	4	1
[107] no	aye	aye	aye	aye	no	aye	aye	aye	aye	aye			To postpone the seventh in order to take up the eighth reso.	9	2	

MADISON

Friday June 29th in Convention

Doctr. Johnson. The controversy must be endless whilst Gentlemen differ in the grounds of their arguments; Those on one side considering the States as districts of people composing one political Society; those on the other considering them as so many political societies. The fact is that the States do exist as political Societies, and a Govt. is to be formed for them in their political capacity, as well as for the individuals composing them. Does it not seem to follow, that if the States as such are to exist they must be armed with some power of self-defence. This is the idea of (Col. Mason) who appears to have looked to the bottom of this matter. Besides the Aristocratic and other interests, which ought to have the means of defending themselves, the States have their interests as such, and are equally entitled to likes means. On the whole he thought that as in some respects the States are to be considered in their political capacity, and in others as districts of individual citizens, the two ideas embraced on different sides, instead of being opposed to each other, ought to be combined; that in *one* branch the *people*, ought to be represented; in the *other*, the *States*.

Mr. Ghorum.   The States as now confederated have no doubt a right to refuse to be consolidated, or to be formed into any new system.   But he wished the small States which seemed most ready to object, to consider which are to give up most, they or the larger ones.   He conceived that a rupture of the Union wd. be an event unhappy for all, but surely the large States would be least unable to take care of themselves, and to make connections with one another.   The weak therefore were most interested in establishing some general system for maintaining order.   If among individuals, composed partly of weak, and partly of strong, the former most ⟨need⟩ the protection of law & Government, the case is exactly the same with weak & powerful States.   What would be the situation of Delaware (for these things he found must be spoken out, & it might as well be done first as last) what wd. be the situation of Delaware in case of a separation of the States?   Would she not lie at the mercy of Pennsylvania?   would not her true interest lie in being consolidated with her, and ought she not now to wish for such a union with Pa. under one Govt. as will put it out of the power of Pena. to oppress her?   Nothing can be more ideal than the danger apprehended by the States, from their being formed into one nation.   Massts. was originally three colonies, viz old Massts. — Plymouth — & the province of Mayne.   These apprehensions existed then.   An incorporation took place; all parties were safe & satisfied; and every distinction is now forgotten.   The case was similar with Connecticut & Newhaven.   The dread of Union was reciprocal; the consequence of it equally salutary and satisfactory.   In like manner N. Jersey has been made one society out of two parts.   Should a separation of the States take place, the fate of N. Jersey wd. be worst of all.   She has no foreign commerce & can have but little.   Pa. & N. York will continue to levy taxes on her consumption.   If she consults her interest she wd. beg of all things to be annihilated.   The apprehensions of the small States ought to be appeased by another reflection.   Massts. will be divided.   The province of Maine is already considered as approaching the term of its annexation to it; and Pa. will probably not increase, considering the present state of her population, & other events that may happen. On the whole he considered a Union of the States as necessary to their happiness, & a firm Genl. Govt. as necessary to their Union. He shd. consider it as his duty if his colleagues viewed the matter in the same light he did to stay here as long as any other State would remain with them, in order to agree on some plan that could with propriety be recommended to the people.

⟨Mr. Elseworth, did not despair. He still trusted that some good plan of Govt. wd. be divised & adopted.⟩[1]

Mr. Read. He shd. have no objection to the system if it were truly national, but it has too much of a federal mixture in it. The little States he thought had not much to fear. He suspected that the large States felt their want of energy, & wished for a genl. Govt. to supply the defect. Massts. was evidently labouring under her weakness and he believed Delaware wd. not be in much danger if in her neighbourhood. Delaware had enjoyed tranquillity & he flattered himself wd. continue to do so. He was not however so selfish as not to wish for a good Genl. Govt. In order to obtain one the whole States must be incorporated. If the States remain, the representatives of the large ones will stick together, and carry every thing before them. The Executive also will be chosen under the influence of this partiality, and will betray it in his administration. These jealousies are inseparable from the scheme of leaving the States in Existence. They must be done away. The ungranted lands also which have been assumed by particular States must also be given up. He repeated his approbation of the plan of Mr. Hamilton, & wished it to be substituted in place of that on the table.

Mr. Madison agreed with Docr. Johnson, that the mixed nature of the Govt. ought to be kept in view; but thought too much stress was laid on the rank of the States as political societies. There was a gradation, he observed from the smallest corporation, with the most limited powers, to the largest

---

[1] Taken from Yates.

empire with the most perfect sovereignty. He pointed out
the limitations on the sovereignty of the States. as now confederated; ⟨their laws in relation to the paramount law of the
Confederacy were analogous to that of bye laws to the supreme
law, within a State.⟩[2] Under the proposed Govt. the ⟨powers
of the States⟩ will be much farther reduced. According to the
views of every member, the Genl. Govt. will have powers far
beyond those exercised by the British Parliament when the
States were part of the British Empire. It will in particular
have the power, without the consent of the State Legislatures,
to levy money directly on the people themselves; and therefore not to divest such *unequal* portions of the people as composed the several States, of an *equal* voice, would subject the
system to the reproaches & evils which have resulted from the
vicious representation in G. B.

He entreated the gentlemen representing the small States
to renounce a principle wch. was confessedly unjust, which
cd. never be admitted, & if admitted must infuse mortality
into a Constitution which we wished to last forever. He
prayed them to ponder well the consequences of suffering
the Confederacy to go to pieces. It had been sd. that the
want of energy in the large states wd. be a security to the
small. It was forgotten that this want of energy proceded
from the supposed security of the States agst. all external
danger. Let each State depend on itself for its security, &
let apprehensions arise of danger from distant powers or
from neighbouring States, & the languishing condition of all
the States, large as well as small, wd. soon be transformed
into vigorous & high toned Govts. His great fear was that
their Govts. wd. then have too much energy, that these might
not only be formidable in the large to the small States, but
fatal to the internal liberty of all. The same causes which
have rendered the old world the Theatre of incesssant wars,
& have banished liberty from the face of it, wd. soon produce
the same effects here. The weakness & jealousy of the small

---

[2] Substance taken from Yates. This is the very speech for the misrepresenting
of which Madison condemned Yates so severely. See Appendix A, CCCX,
CCCXXXIX–CCCXLI, CCCLVII, CCCLXV, CCCLXXXVIII, CCCXCI.

States wd. quickly introduce some regular military force agst. sudden danger from their powerful neighbours. The example wd. be followed by others, and wd. soon become universal. In time of actual war, great discretionary powers are constantly given to the Executive Magistrate. Constant apprehension of War, has the same tendency to render the head too large for the body. A standing military force, with an overgrown Executive will not long be safe companions to liberty. The means of defence agst. foreign danger, have been always the instruments of tyranny at home. Among the Romans it was a standing maxim to excite a war, whenever a revolt was apprehended. Throughout all Europe, the armies kept up under the pretext of defending, have enslaved the people. It is perhaps questionable, whether the best concerted system of absolute power in Europe cd. maintain itself, in a situation, where no alarms of external danger cd. tame the people to the domestic yoke. The insular situation of G. Britain was the principal cause of her being an exception to the general fate of Europe. It has rendered less defence necessary, and admitted a kind of defence wch. cd. not be used for the purpose of oppression. — These consequences he conceived ought to be apprehended whether the States should run into a total separation from each other, or shd. enter into partial confederacies. Either event wd. be truly deplorable; & those who might be accessary to either, could never be forgiven by their Country, nor by themselves.

* Mr. Hamilton observed that individuals forming political Societies modify their rights differently, with regard to suffrage. Examples of it are found in all the States. In all of them some individuals are deprived of the right altogether, not having the requisite qualification of property. In some of the States the right of suffrage is allowed in some cases and refused in others. To vote for a member in one branch, a certain quantum of property, to vote for a member in another branch of

* ⟨From this date he was absent till the   of   ⟩ ³

---

³ Crossed out: "This was the last day of his remaining with the Convention previous to   ". See further Appendix A, CCLXXI, CCCXIII.

the Legislature, a higher quantum of property is required. In like manner States may modify their right of suffrage differently, the larger exercising a larger, the smaller a smaller share of it.   But as States are a collection of individual men which ought we to respect most, the rights of the people composing them, or of the artificial beings resulting from the composition.   Nothing could be more preposterous or absurd than to sacrifice the former to the latter.   It has been sd. that if the smaller States renounce their *equality*, they renounce at the same time their *liberty*.   The truth is it is a contest for power, not for liberty.   Will the men composing the small States be less free than those composing the larger.   The State of Delaware having 40,000 souls will *lose power*, if she has $\frac{1}{10}$ only of the votes allowed to Pa. having 400,000: but will the people of Del: *be less free*, if each citizen has an equal vote with each citizen of Pa.   He admitted that common residence within the same State would produce a certain degree of attachment; and that this principle might have a certain influence in public affairs.   He thought however that this might by some precautions be in a great measure excluded: and that no material inconvenience could result from it, as there could not be any ground for combination among the States whose influence was most dreaded.   The only considerable distinction of interests, lay between the carrying & non-carrying States, which divide instead of uniting the largest States.   No considerable inconvenience had been found from the division of the State of N. York into different districts, of different sizes.

Some of the consequences of a dissolution of the Union, and the establishment of partial confederacies, had been pointed out.   He would add another of a most serious nature. Alliances will immediately be formed with different rival & hostile nations of Europes, who will foment disturbances among ourselves, and make us parties to all their own quarrels.   Foreign nations having American dominions are & must be jealous of us.   Their representatives betray the utmost anxiety for our fate, & for the result of this meeting, which must have an essential influence on it. — It had been said that respectability in the eyes of foreign Nations was not the object at which we aimed; that the proper object of republican Government was domestic tranquillity & happiness. This was an ideal distinction. No Governmt. could give us tranquillity & happiness at home, which did not possess sufficient stability and strength to make us respectable abroad. This was the critical moment for forming such a government. We should run every risk in trusting to future amendments. As yet we retain the habits of union. We are weak & sensible of our weakness. Henceforward the motives will become feebler, and the difficulties greater. It is a miracle that we were now here exercising our tranquil & free deliberations on the subject. It would be madness to trust to future miracles. A thousand causes must obstruct a reproduction of them.

⟨Mr. Peirce considered the equality of votes under the Confederation as the great source of the public difficulties. The members of Congs. were advocates for local advantages. State distinctions must be sacrificed as far as the general good required: but without destroying the States. Tho' from a small State he felt himself a Citizen of the U. S.⟩[4]

Mr. Gerry, urged that we never were independent States, were not such now, & never could be even on the principles of the Confederation. The States & the advocates for them were intoxicated with the idea of their *sovereignty*. He was a member of Congress at the time the federal articles were formed. The injustice of allowing each State an equal vote was long insisted on. He voted for it, but it was agst. his Judgment, and under the pressure of public danger, and the obstinacy of the lesser States. The present confederation he considered as dissolving. The fate of the Union will be decided by the Convention. If they do not agree on something, few delegates will probably be appointed to Congs. If they do Congs. will probably be kept up till the new System should be adopted — He lamented that instead of coming here like a band of brothers, belonging to the same family, we seemed to have brought with us the spirit of political negociators.

---

[4] Taken from Yates.

Mr. L. Martin. remarked that the language of the States being *Sovereign & independent*, was once familiar & understood; though it seemed now so strange & obscure. He read those passages in the articles of Confederation, which describe them in that language.

On the question as moved by Mr. Lansing. Shall the word "not" be struck out.

Massts. no. Cont. ay. N. Y. ay. N. J. ay. Pa. no. Del. ay. Md. divd. Va. no. N. C. no. S. C. no. Geo. no [Ayes — 4; noes — 6; divided — 1.]

On the ⟨motion to agree to the clause as reported. "that the rule of suffrage in the 1st. branch ought not to be according to that established by the Articles of Confederation.⟩ [5] Mass. ay. Cont. ⟨no⟩ N. Y. no. N. J. no. Pa. ay. Del. no. Md. divd. Va. ay. N. C. ay. S. C. ay. Geo. ay. [Ayes— 6; noes — 4; divided — 1.] [6]

Docr. Johnson & Mr. Elseworth moved to postpone the residue of the clause, and take up — ye 8 — Resol:
⟨On question⟩

Mass. no. Cont. ay. N. Y. ay. ⟨N. J. ay.⟩ Pa. ay. Del. no. Md. ay. Va. ay. N. C. ay. S. C. ay. Geo. ay. [Ayes — 9; noes — 2.] [7]

Mr. Elseworth moved that the rule of suffrage in the 2d. branch be the same with that established by the articles of confederation". He was not sorry on the whole he said that the vote just passed, had determined against this rule in the first branch. He hoped it would become a ground of compromise with regard to the 2d. branch. We were partly national; partly federal. The proportional representation in the first branch was conformable to the national principle & would secure the large States agst. the small. An equality of voices was conformable to the federal principle and was necessary to secure the Small States agst. the large. He trusted that on this middle ground a compromise would take place.

---

[5] Revised from *Journal*.

[6] Connecticut's vote corrected from *Journal* and Yates. On this vote see Appendix A, CLVIII (24).

[7] Vote corrected from *Journal* and Yates.

He did not see that it could on any other. And if no compromise should take place, our meeting would not only be in vain but worse than in vain. To the Eastward he was sure Massts. was the only State that would listen to a proposition for excluding the States as equal political Societies, from an equal voice in both branches. The others would risk every consequence rather than part with so dear a right. An attempt to deprive them of it, was at once cutting the body ⟨of America⟩ in two, and as he supposed would be the case, somewhere about this part of it. The large States he conceived would notwithstanding the equality of votes, have an influence that would maintain their superiority. Holland, as had been admitted (by Mr. ⟨Madison⟩) had, notwithstanding a like equality in the Dutch Confederacy, a prevailing influence in the public measures. The power of self-defence was essential to the small States. Nature had given it to the smallest insect of the creation. He could never admit that there was no danger of combinations among the large States. They will like individuals find out and avail themselves of the advantage to be gained by it. It was true the danger would be greater, if they were contiguous and had a more immediate common interest. A defensive combination of the small States was rendered more difficult by their greater number. He would mention another consideration of great weight. The existing confederation was founded on the equality of the States in the article of suffrage: was it meant to pay no regard to this antecedent plighted faith. Let a strong Executive, a Judiciary & Legislative power be created; but Let not too much be attempted; by which all may be lost. He was not in general a half-way man, yet he preferred doing half the good we could, rather than do nothing at all. The other half may be added, when the necessity shall be more fully experienced.

Mr. Baldwin would have wished that the powers of the General Legislature had been defined, before the mode of constituting it had been agitated. He should vote against the motion of Mr. Elseworth, tho' he did not like the Resolution as it stood in the Report of the Committee of the whole. He thought the second branch ought to be the representation of property, and that in forming it therefore some reference ought to be had to the relative wealth of their Constituents, and to the principles on which the Senate of Massts. was constituted. He concurred with those who thought it wd. be impossible for the Genl. Legislature to extend its cares to the local matters of the States.

Adjd.

YATES

FRIDAY, JUNE 29th, 1787.

Met pursuant to adjournment. Present 11 states.

Dr. Johnson. As the debates have hitherto been managed, they may be spun out to an endless length; and as gentlemen argue on different grounds, they are equally conclusive on the points they advance, but afford no demonstration either way. States are political societies. For whom are we to form a government? for the people of America, or for those societies? Undoubtedly for the latter. They must, therefore, have a voice in the second branch of the general government, if you mean to preserve their existence. The people already compose the first branch. This mixture is proper and necessary. For we cannot form a general government on any other ground.

Mr. Gorham. I perceive no difficulty in supposing a union of interest in the different states. Massachusetts formerly consisted of three distinct provinces — they have been united into one, and we do not find the least trace of party distinctions arising from their former separation. Thus it is that the interest of the smaller states will unite in a general government. It is thus they will be supported. Jersey, in particular, situated between Philadelphia and New-York, can never become a commercial state. It would be her interest to be divided, and part annexed to New-York and part to Pennsylvania — or otherwise the whole to the general government. Massachusetts cannot long remain a large state. The province of Maine must soon become independent of her. Pennsylvania can never become a dangerous state — her western country must at some period become separated from her, and consequently her power will be diminished. If some states will not confederate on a new plan, I will remain here, if only one state will consent to confederate with us.

Judge Elsworth. I do not despair but that we shall be so fortunate as to devise and adopt some good plan of government.

Judge Read. I would have no objection, if the government was more national — but the proposed plan is so great a mixture of both, that it is best to drop it altogether. A state government is incompatible with a general government. If it was more national, I would be for a representation proportionate to population. The plan of the gentleman from New-York is certainly the best — but the great evil is the unjust appropriation of the public lands. If there was but one national government, we would be all equally interested.

Mr. Madison.[8] Some gentlemen are afraid that the plan is not sufficiently national, while others apprehend that it is too much so. If this point of representation was once well fixed, we would come nearer to one another in sentiment. The necessity would then be discovered of circumscribing more effectually the state governments and enlarging the bounds of the general government. Some contend that states are sovereign, when in fact they are only political societies. There is a gradation of power in all societies, from the lowest corporation to the highest sovereign. The states never possessed the essential rights of sovereignty.[9] These were always vested in congress. Their voting, as states, in congress, is no evidence of sovereignty. The state of Maryland voted by counties — did this make the counties sovereign? The states, at present, are only great corporations, having the power of making by-laws, and these are effectual only if they are not contradictory to the general confederation. The states ought to be placed under the control of the general government — at least as much so as they formerly were under the king and British parliament.[9] The arguments, I observe, have taken a different turn, and I hope may tend to

---

[8] For Genet's interpretation of this speech, see Appendix A, CCCX.
[9] See Madison's explanation, Appendix A, CCCXCI, also CCCLXXXVIII.

convince all of the necessity of a strong energetic government, which would equally tend to give energy to, and protect the state governments. What was the origin of the military establishments of Europe? It was the jealousy which one state or kingdom entertained of another. This jealousy was ever productive of evil. In Rome the patricians were often obliged to excite a foreign war to divert the attention of the plebeians from encroaching on the senatorial rights. In England and France, perhaps, this jealousy may give energy to their governments, and contribute to their existence. But a state of danger is like a state of war, and it unites the various parts of the government to exertion. May not our distractions, however, invite danger from abroad? If the power is not immediately derived from the people, in proportion to their numbers, we may make a paper confederacy, but that will be all. We know the effects of the old confederation, and without a general government this will be like the former.

Mr. Hamilton. The course of my experience in human affairs might perhaps restrain me from saying much on this subject. I shall, however, give birth to some of the observations I have made during the course of this debate. The gentleman from Maryland has been at great pains to establish positions which are not denied. Many of them, as drawn from the best writers on government, are become almost self-evident principles. But I doubt the propriety of his application of those principles in the present discussion. He deduces from them the necessity that states entering into a confederacy must retain the equality of votes — this position cannot be correct — Facts plainly contradict it. The parliament of Great Britain asserted a supremacy over the whole empire, and the celebrated Judge Blackstone labors for the legality of it, although many parts were not represented. This parliamentary power we opposed as contrary to our colonial rights. With that exception, throughout that whole empire, it is submitted to. May not the smaller and greater states so modify their respective rights as to establish the general interest of the whole, without adhering to the right of equality? Strict representation is not observed in any of the state governments. The senate of New-York are chosen by persons of certain qualifications, to the exclusion of others. The question, after all is, is it our interest in modifying this general government to sacrifice individual rights to the preservation of the rights of an *artificial* being, called states? There can be no truer principle than this — that every individual of the community at large has an equal right to the protection of government. If therefore three states contain a majority of the inhabitants of America, ought they to be governed by a minority? Would the inhabitants of the great states ever submit to this? If the smaller states maintain this principle, through a love of power, will not the larger, from the same motives, be equally tenacious to preserve their power? They are to surrender their rights — for what? for the preservation of an artificial being. We propose a free government — Can it be so if partial distinctions are maintained? I agree with the gentleman from Delaware, that if the state governments are to act in the general government, it affords the strongest reason for exclusion. In the state of New-York, five counties form a majority of representatives, and yet the government is in no danger, because the laws have a general operation. The small states exaggerate their danger, and on this ground contend for an undue proportion of power. But their danger is increased, if the larger states will not submit to it. Where will they form new alliances for their support? Will they do this with foreign powers? Foreigners are jealous of our encreasing greatness, and would rejoice in our distractions. Those who have had opportunities of conversing with foreigners respecting sovereigns in Europe, have discovered in them an anxiety for the preservation of our democratic governments, probably for no other reason, but to keep us weak. Unless your government is respectable, foreigners will invade your rights; and to maintain tranquility it must be respectable — even to observe neutrality you must have a strong government. — I confess our present situation is critical. We have just finished a war which has established our independency, and loaded us with a heavy debt. We have still every motive to unite for our common defence — Our people are disposed to have a good government, but this disposition may not always prevail. It is difficult to amend confederations — it has been attempted in vain, and it is perhaps a miracle that we are now met — We must therefore improve the opportunity, and render the present system as perfect as possible. Their good sense, and above all, the necessity of their affairs, will induce the people to adopt it.

Mr. Pierce. The great difficulty in congress arose from the mode of voting. Members spoke on the floor as state advocates, and were biassed by local advantages. — What is federal? No more than a compact between states; and the one heretofore formed is insufficient. We are now met to remedy its defects, and our difficulties are great, but not, I hope, insurmountable. State distinctions must be sacrificed so far as the general government shall render it necessary — without, however, destroying them altogether. Although I am here as a representative from a small state, I consider myself as a citizen of the United States, whose general interest I will always support.

Mr. Gerry. It appears to me that the states never were independent — they had only corporate rights. Confederations are a mongrel kind of government, and the world does not afford a precedent to go by. Aristocracy is the worst kind of government, and I would sooner submit to a monarchy. We must have a system that will execute itself.

The question was then put on Mr. Lansing's motion, and lost — 4 ayes — 6 noes — one state divided.

Question on the clause — 6 ayes — 4 noes — and one state divided.

Judge Elsworth. I move that the consideration of the 8th resolve be postponed. Carried — 9 ayes — 2 noes.

I now move the following amendment to the resolve— *that in the second branch each state have an equal vote.* I confess that the effect of this motion is, to make the general government *partly federal and partly national.* This will secure tranquility, and still make it efficient; and it will meet the objections of the larger states. In taxes they will have a proportional weight in the first branch of the general legislature —

If the great states refuse this plan, we will be for ever separated. Even in the executive the larger states have ever had great influence. — The provinces of Holland ever had it. If all the states are to exist they must necessarily have an equal vote in the general government. Small communities when associating with greater, can only be supported by an equality of votes. I have always found in my reading and experience, that in all societies the governors are ever gradually rising into power.

The large states, although they may not have a common interest for combination, yet they may be partially attached to each other for mutual support and advancement. This can be more easily effected than the union of the remaining small states to check it; and ought we not to regard antecedent plighted faith to the confederation already entered into, and by the terms of it declared to be perpetual? And it is not yet obvious to me that the states will depart from this ground. When in the hour of common danger we united as equals, shall it now be urged by some that we must depart from this principle when the danger is over? Will the world say that this is just? We then associated as free and independent states, and were well satisfied — To perpetuate that independence, I wish to establish a national legislature, executive and judiciary, for under these we shall I doubt not preserve peace and harmony — nor should I be surprised (although we made the general government the most perfect in our opinion,) that it should hereafter require amendment — But at present this is as far as I possibly can go — If this convention only chalk out lines of a good government we shall do well.

Mr. Baldwin. It appears to be agreed that the government we should adopt ought to be energetic and formidable, yet I would guard against the danger of becoming too formidable. The second branch ought not to be elected as the first. Suppose we take the example of the constitution of Massachusetts, as it is commended for its goodness: There the first branch represents the people, and the second its property.

Mr. Madison. I would always exclude inconsistent principles in framing a system of government. The difficulty of getting its defects amended are great and sometimes insurmountable. The Virginia state government was the first which was made, and though its defects are evident to every person, we cannot get it amended. The Dutch have made four several attempts to amend their system without success. The few alterations made in it were by tumult and faction, and for the worse. If there was real danger, I would give the smaller states the defensive weapons—But there is none from that quarter. The great danger to our general government *is the great southern and northern interests of the continent, being opposed to each other. Look to the votes in congress, and most of them stand divided by the geography of the country, not according to the size of the states.*

Suppose the first branch granted money, may not the second branch, from state views, counteract the first? In congress, the single state of Delaware prevented an embargo, at the time that all the other states thought it absolutely necessary for the support of the army. Other powers, and those very essential, besides the legislative, will be given to the second branch — such as the negativing all state laws. I would compromise on this question, if I could do it on correct principles, but otherwise not — if the old fabric of the confederation must be the ground-work of the new, we must fail.

Adjourned till to-morrow morning.

KING

Friday — 29. June —

Question of Representation —

Johnson — The two sides of the house reason in such a manner that we can never meet — Those who contend for an equality of Votes among the States, define a State to be a mere association of men & then say these Associations are equal — on the other hand those who contend for a Representation in proportion to numbers, Define a State to be a District of

Country with a certain Number of Inhabitants, like a parish or County, and then say, these districts shd. have an influence in proportion to their Number of Inhabitants — both reason justly from yr. premises — we must then compromise — let both parties be gratified — let one House or Branch be formed by one Rule & & the other by another

Madison — We are vague in our Expressions — we speak of the sovereignty of the States — they are not sovereign — there is a regular gradation from the lowest Corporation, such as the incorporation of mechanicks to the most perft. Sovereignty — The last is the true and only Sovereignty — the states are not in that high degree Sovereign — they are Corporations with power of Bye Laws —

Hamilton

Men are naturally equal — societies or Nations are equal when independent — it is as reasonable that States shd. inter into a League departing from the Equality of States, as that men shd. inter into the Social Compact and agree to depart from the natural Equality of man — This is done in every Society — property goes into the Confederation, age, & minority are admitted — A man shall not be Elector or Elected, unless he is of a given Age, & possesses the adventitious circumstance of property — We propose that the people shd. be reprented in proportion to yr. numbers, the people then will be free — the avenues to every Office are equally open to every man; and the Laws are to be formed by a majority of the People — yet it is said the States will be destroyed & therefore the people will be slaves — The consequence is not true. The people are free, at the expense of a mere ideal & artificial being —

On the Question shall the rule of Confederation be departed with for a more equitable Ratio of Representation —

Cont. NYk. : N Jersey: & Delaware No

Maryland Divd.

Mass. Penn. Virgin. NC. SC. & Georg. Ay

Elsworth — moves that in the second Br, or ye Senate, each State shd. have one vote & no more —

The first Br. or the Democratic Br. will represent the people, the 2d. that of the States — the people will be secured, and the States will be protected —

if we don't agree in this measure, we have met in vain — None of the Eastern States except Mass. will ever agree to adopt the plan wh. abolishes the States — If the Southern States contend for this plan of a popular instead of State Representation we shall separate; the political body must be cut asunder at the Delaware — This mode of forming the Senate will secure the small states, and as the members of the large states although they can give but one vote will have more Influence than those of the small ones, they will not be injured — Holland has one voice only in the States General, yet her Influence is more than any two of the States — there is danger from the combination of the larger overpowering the small States — The Danger is not so great since the large States are separated, but yet there is danger — they will have the power to do it — if they have the power there is Danger — three or four States can more easily combine, than Nine or Ten States —

Madison — The Gentleman from Connecticut has proposed doing as much at this Time as is prudent, and leavg. future amendments to posterity — this a dangerous Doctrine — the Defects of the Amphictionick League were acknowledged, but they never cd. be reformed. The U Netherlands have attempted four several Times to amend their Confederation, but have failed in each Attempt — The fear of Innovation, and the Hue & Cry in favor of the Liberty of the people will prevent the necessary Reforms — If the States have equal, influence, and votes in the Senate, we are in the utmost Danger — Delaware during the War opposed and defeated an Embargo agreed to by 12. States; and continued to supply the Enemy with provisions during the war.[10]

---

[10] [Endorsed:] 29 June | Shall Representatives be equal | numbers from each State? or | founded on a census | N Y. N J Del — No | N Y N J Del — Equal betw States | Mar divided | M. Pen. Virg. N. & S. Car & Geor — census

PATERSON[11]

June 29th.

Doct. Johnson

If the States are represented as States — they must be represented as Individuals.

Mr. Gorham —

New-Jersey ought not to oppose the plan, as she at present pays the Taxes of Penn. and N. York, from which she would be relieved.

Mr. Madison

Will have the States considered as so many great Corporations, and not otherwise.

Col. Hamilton

That States have equal rights to vote, is not true It is estabd. by the Law of Nations that they have equal votes — but does it follow that they can not contract upon a different footing —

That the Genl. Governmt. will act, not only, upon the States, but upon Individuals.

As long as the State influence is kept up there will be danger — but the influence will not be as great as is apprehended.

The small States have had a lesson of State Honesty [11a]

It is a contest for power in the weaker States.[12]

Mr. Pierce

Gentlemen of Congress when they vote always connect with them the State views and politicks — and therefore —

Mr. Gerry.

That upon Tryal it has been found that the Articles of Confn. are not adequate —

That the small States have abused their power, and instanced Rho. Island.

---

[11] See June 27, note 8.

[11a] A marginal note opposite the line following.

[12] A hand drawn on the margin points to this as if to indicate its importance.

SATURDAY, JUNE 30, 1787.

JOURNAL

Saturday, June 30. 1787.

The following resolution was moved and seconded namely
   "Resolved that the President be requested to write to
"the supreme Executive of the State of New Hampshire and
"inform him that the business before the Convention is of
"such a nature as to require the immediate attendance of the
"Gentlemen appointed by that State to this Convention."
   On the question to agree to the resolution
it passed in the negative. [Ayes — 2; noes — 5; divided — 1.]
It was then moved and seconded to take up the resolution sub-
mitted to the consideration of the House yesterday. namely.
   Resolved that in the second Branch of the Legislature
of the United States each State shall have an equal vote.
   After some time passed in debate.
   [To adjourn   Ayes — 11; noes — o.] [1]
The House adjourned till Monday next at 11 oClock a. m.

DETAIL OF AYES AND NOES

	New Hampshire	Massachusetts	Rhode Island	Connecticut	New York	New Jersey	Pennsylvania	Delaware	Maryland	Virginia	North Carolina	South Carolina	Georgia	Questions	Ayes	Noes	Divided
[108]	no		no	aye	aye				dd	no	no	no		That the Presidt be requested to write to the President of New Hampshire to direct the attendance of the Deputies of that State	2	5	1
[109]	aye		aye	aye	aye	aye	aye	aye	aye	aye	aye	aye	aye	To adjourn	11		

[1] Vote 109, Detail of Ayes and Noes.

MADISON

Saturday June 30. 1787. in Convention

Mr. Brearly moved that the Presidt. write to the Executive of N. Hamshire, informing it that the business depending before the Convention was of such a nature as to require the immediate attendance of the deputies of that State. In support of his motion he observed that the difficulties of the subject and the diversity of opinions called for all the assistance we could possibly obtain. (it was well understood that the object was to add N. Hamshire to the no. of States opposed to the doctrine of proportional representation, which it was presumed from her relative size she must be adverse to).

Mr. Patterson seconded the motion

Mr. Rutlidge could see neither the necessity nor propriety of such a measure. They are not unapprized of the meeting, and can attend if they choose. Rho. Island might as well be urged to appoint & send deputies. Are we to suspend the business until the deputies arrive? if we proceed he hoped all the great points would be adjusted before the letter could produce its effect.

Mr. King. said he had written more than once as a private correspondent, & the answers gave him every reason to expect that State would be represented very shortly, if it shd. be so at all. Circumstances of a personal nature had hitherto prevented it. A letter cd. have no effect.

Mr. Wilson wished to know whether it would be consistent with the rule or reason of secrecy, to communicate to N. Hamshire [2] that the business was of such a nature as the motion described. It wd. spread a great alarm. Besides he doubted the propriety of soliciting any State on the subject; the meeting being merely voluntary — on the motion of Mr Brearly

Massts. no. Cont. no. N. Y. ay. N. J. ay. Pa. not on ye. floor. Del not on floor. Md. divd. Va. no. N. C. no. S. C.

---

[2] Crossed out "& not to other States".

no. Geo. not on floor. [Ayes — 2; noes — 5; divided — 1; absent — 3.]

The motion of Mr. Elseworth resumed for allowing each State an equal vote in ye 2d branch

Mr. Wilson did not expect such a motion after the establishment of ye. contrary principle in the 1st. branch; and considering the reasons which would oppose it, even if an equal vote had been allowed in the 1st. branch. The Gentleman from Connecticut (Mr. Elseworth) had pronounced that if the motion should not be acceded to, of all the States North of Pena. one only would agree to any Genl. Government. He entertained more favorable hopes of Connt. and of the other Northern States. He hoped the alarms exceeded their cause, and that they would not abandon a Country to which they were bound by so many strong and endearing ties. But should the deplored event happen, it would neither stagger his sentiments nor his duty. If the minority of the people of America refuse to coalesce with the majority on just and proper principles, if a separation must take place, it could never happen on better grounds. The votes of yesterday agst. the just principle of representation, were as 22 to 90 of the people of America. Taking the opinions to be the same on this point, and he was sure if there was any room for change it could not be on the side of the majority, the question will be shall less than $\frac{1}{4}$ of the U. States withdraw themselves from the Union, or shall more than $\frac{3}{4}$ renounce the inherent, indisputable, and unalienable rights of men, in favor of the artificial systems of States. If issue must be joined, it was on this point he would chuse to join it, The gentleman from Connecticut in supposing that the preponderancy secured to the majority in the 1st. branch had removed the objections to an equality of votes in the 2d. branch for the security of the minority narrowed the case extremely. Such an equality will enable the minority to controul in all cases whatsoever, the sentiments and interests of the majority. Seven States will controul six: seven States according to the estimates that had been used, composed $\frac{24}{90}$. of the whole people. It would be in the power then of less than $\frac{1}{3}$ to overrule $\frac{2}{3}$ whenever a question should happen to divide the States in that manner. Can we forget for whom we are forming a Government? Is it for *men*, or for the imaginary beings called *States*? Will our honest Constituents be satisfied with metaphysical distinctions? Will they, ought they to be satisfied with being told that the one third, compose the greater number of States. The rule of suffrage ought on every principle to be the same in the 2d. as in the 1st. branch. If the Government be not laid on this foundation, it can be neither solid nor lasting, any other principle will be local, confined & temporary. This will expand with the expansion, and grow with the growth of the U. States. — Much has been said of an imaginary combination of three States. Sometimes a danger of monarchy, sometimes of aristocracy has been charged on it. No explanation however of the danger has been vouchsafed. It would be easy to prove both from reason & history that rivalships would be more probable than coalitions; and that there are no coinciding interests that could produce the latter. No answer has yet been given to the observations of (Mr. ⟨Madison⟩)—on this subject. Should the Executive Magistrate be taken from one of the large States would not the other two be thereby thrown into the scale with the other States? Whence then the danger of monarchy? Are the people of the three large States more aristocratic than those of the small ones? Whence then the danger of aristocracy from their influence? It is all a mere illusion of names. We talk of States, till we forget what they are composed of. Is a real & fair majority, the natural hot-bed of aristocracy? It is a part of the definition of this species of Govt. or rather of tyranny, that the smaller number governs the greater. It is true that a majority [3] of States in the 2d. branch can not carry a law agst. a majority of the people in the 1st. But this removes half only of the objection. Bad Governts. are of two sorts. 1. that which does too little. 2. that which does too much: that which fails thro' weakness; and that which destroys [4] thro' oppression. Under which of these evils do the U. States at present groan? under the weakness

---

[3] Crossed out "seven".   [4] Crossed out "rules".

and inefficiency of its Govert. To remedy this weakness we
have been sent to this Convention. If the motion should be
agreed to, we shall leave the U. S. fettered precisely as heretofore; with the additional mortification of seeing the good
purposes of ye fair representation of the people in the 1st.
branch, defeated in 2d. Twenty four will still controul
sixty six. He lamented that such a disagreement should
prevail on the point of representation, as he did not foresee
that it would happen on the other point most contested, the
boundary between the Genl. & the local authorities. He
thought the States necessary & valuable parts of a good
system.

    Mr. Elseworth. The capital objection of Mr. Wilson
"that the minority will rule the majority" is not true. The
power is given to the few to save them from being destroyed
by the many. If an equality of votes had been given to them
in both branches, the objection might have had weight. Is
it a novel thing that the few should have a check on the many?
Is it not the case in the British Constitution the wisdom of
which so many gentlemen have united in applauding? Have
not the House of Lords, who form so small a proportion of
the nation a negative on the laws, as a necessary defence of
their peculiar rights agst the encroachmts of the Commons.
No instance ⟨of a Confederacy⟩ [5] has existed in which an
equality of voices has not been exercised by the members of
it. We are running from one extreme to another. We are
razing the foundations of the building. When we need only
repair the roof. No salutary measure has been lost for want
of *a majority of the States*, to favor it. If security be all that
the great States wish for the 1st. branch secures them. The
danger of combinations among them is not imaginary. Altho'
no particular abuses could be foreseen by him, the possibility
of them would be sufficient to alarm him. But he could
easily conceive cases in which they might result from such
combinations. Suppose that in pursuance of some commercial
treaty or arrangement, three or four free ports & no more

[5] Taken from Yates.

were to be established would not combinations be formed in favor of Boston, Philada. & & some port in Chesapeak? A like concert might be formed in the appointment of the great officers. He appealed again to the obligations of the federal pact which was still in force, and which had been entered into with so much solemnity, persuading himself that some regard would still be paid to the plighted faith under which each State small as well as great, held an equal right of suffrage in the general Councils. ⟨His remarks were not the result of partial or local views. The State he represented (Connecticut) held a middle rank.⟩[6]

Mr. M⟨adison. did justice to the able and close reasoning of Mr. E. but must observe that it did not always accord with itself.⟩[7] On another occasion, the large States were described ⟨by him⟩ as the Aristocratic States, ready to oppress the small. Now the small are the House of Lords requiring a negative to defend them agst the more numerous Commons. Mr. E. had also erred in saying that no instance had existed in which confederated States had not retained to themselves a perfect equality of suffrage. Passing over the German system in which the K. of Prussia has nine voices, he reminded Mr. E. of the Lycian confederacy, in which the component members had votes proportioned to their importance, and which Montesquieu recommends as the fittest model for that form of Government. Had the fact been as stated by Mr. E. it would have been of little avail to him, or rather would have strengthened the arguments agst. him; The History & fate of the several Confederacies modern as well as Antient, demonstrating some radical vice in their structure. In reply to the appeal of Mr. E. to the faith plighted in the existing federal compact, he remarked that the party claiming from others an adherence to a common engagement ought at least to be guiltless itself of a violation. Of all the States however Connecticut was perhaps least able to urge this plea. Besides the various

---

[6] Taken from Yates.

[7] Originally Madison had written "observed that the reasoning of Mr. E. at different times did not well accord." This was combined with a statement from Yates to produce the sentence in the text.

omissions to perform the stipulated acts from which no State was free, the Legislature of that State had by a pretty recent vote *positively refused* to pass a law for complying with the Requisitions of Congs. and had transmitted a copy of the vote to Congs. It was urged, he said, continually that an equality of votes in the 2d. branch was not only necessary to secure the small, but would be perfectly safe to the large ones whose majority in the 1st. branch was an effectual bulwark. But notwithstanding this apparent defence, the Majority of States might still injure the majority of people. 1. they could *obstruct* the wishes and interests of the majority. 2. they could *extort* measures, repugnant to the wishes & interest of the majority. 3. They could *impose* measures adverse thereto; as the 2d branch will probly exercise some great powers, in which the 1st will not participate. He admitted that every peculiar interest whether in any class of citizens, or any description of States, ought to be secured as far as possible. Wherever there is danger of attack there ought be given a constitutional power of defence. But he contended that the States were divided into different interests not by their difference of size, but by other circumstances; the most material of which resulted partly from climate, but principally from ⟨the effects of⟩ their having or not having slaves. These two causes concurred in forming the great division of interests in the U. States. It did not lie between the large & small States: it lay between the Northern & Southern. and if any defensive power were necessary, it ought to be mutually given to these two interests.[8] He was so strongly impressed with this important truth that he had been casting about in his mind for some expedient that would answer the purpose. The one which had occurred was that instead of proportioning the votes of the States in both branches, to their respective numbers of inhabitants computing the slaves in the ratio of 5 to 3. they should be represented in one branch according to the number of free inhabitants only; and in the other according to the whole no. counting the slaves as ⟨if⟩ free. By this

---

[8] Crossed out "as a security agst. the encroachments of each other."

arrangement the Southern Scale would have the advantage in one House, and the Northern in the other. He had been restrained from proposing this expedient by two considerations; one was his unwillingness to urge any diversity of interests on an occasion when it is but too apt to arise of itself — the other was the inequality of powers that must be vested in the two branches, and which wd. destroy the equilibrium of interests.

Mr. Elseworth assured the House that whatever might be thought of the Representatives of Connecticut the State was entirely federal in her disposition. ⟨He appealed to her great exertions during the War, in supplying both men & money. The muster rolls would show she had more troops in the field than Virga. If she had been delinquent, it had been from inability, and not more so than other States.⟩[9]

Mr. Sherman. Mr. M.⟨adison⟩ had animadverted on the delinquency of the States, when his object required him to prove that the Constitution of Congs. was faulty. Congs. is not to blame for the faults of the States. Their measures have been right, and the only thing wanting has been, a further power in Congs. to render them effectual.

Mr. Davy was much embarrassed and wished for explanations. The Report of the Committee allowing the Legislatures to choose the Senate, and establishing a proportional representation in it, seemed to be impracticable. There will according to this rule be ninety members in the outset, and the number will increase as new States are added. It was impossible that so numerous a body could possess the activity and other qualities required in it. Were he to vote on the comparative merits of the report as it stood, and the amendment, he should be constrained to prefer the latter. The appointment of the Senate by electors chosen by the people for that purpose was he conceived liable to an insuperable difficulty. The larger Counties or districts thrown into a general district, would certainly prevail over the smaller Counties or districts, and merit in the latter would be excluded altogether. The report therefore seemed to be right in referring the appointment to the Legislatures, whose agency in the general System did not appear to him objectionable as it did to some others. The fact was that the local prejudices & interests which could not be denied to exist, would find their way into the national Councils whether the Representatives should be chosen by the Legislatures or by the people themselves. On the other hand, if a proportional representation was attended with insuperable difficulties, the making the Senate the Representative of the States, looked like bringing us back to Congs. again, and shutting out all the advantages expected from it. Under this view of the subject he could not vote for any plan for the Senate yet proposed. He thought that in general there were extremes on both sides. We were partly federal, partly national in our Union. And he did not see why the Govt. might ⟨not⟩ in some respects operate on the States, in others on the people.

Mr Wilson admitted the question concerning the number of Senators, to be embarrassing. If the smallest States be allowed one, and the others in proportion, the Senate will certainly be too numerous. He looked forward to the time when the smallest States will contain 100,000 souls at least. Let there be then one Senator in each for every 100,000 souls, and let the States not having that no. of inhabitants be allowed one. He was willing himself to submit to this temporary concession to the small States: and threw out the idea as a ground of compromise.

Docr. Franklin The diversity of opinions turns on two points. If a proportional representation takes place, the small States contend that their liberties will be in danger. If an equality of votes is to be put in its place, the large States say their money will be in danger. When a broad table is to be made, and the edges ⟨of planks do not fit⟩ the artist takes a little from both, and makes a good joint. In like manner here both sides must part with some of their demands, in order that they may join in some accomodating proposition. He had prepared one which he would read, that it might lie on the table for consideration. The proposition was in the words following" [10]

---

[10] Franklin's draft of this proposal is given below.

"That the Legislatures of the several States shall choose & send an equal number of Delegates, namely   who are to compose the 2d. branch of the General Legislature —

That in all cases or questions wherein the Sovereignty of individual States may be affected, or whereby their authority over their own Citizens may be diminished, or the authority of the General Government within the several States augmented, each State shall have equal suffrage.

That in the appointment of all Civil Officers of ye. Genl. Govt. in the election of whom the 2d. branch may by the Constitution have part, each State shall have equal suffrage.

That in fixing the salaries of such officers, and in all allowances for public services, and generally in all appropriations & dispositions of money to be drawn out of the General Treasury; and in all laws for supplying that Treasury, the Delegates of the several States shall have suffrage in proportion to the Sums which their respective States do actually contribute to the treasury ("Where a ship had many owners this was the rule of deciding on her expedition. He had been one of the ministers from this Country to France during the joint war and wd. have been very glad if allowed a vote in distributing the money to carry it on.)[11]

Mr. King observed that the simple question was whether each State should have an equal vote in the 2d. branch; that it must be apparent to those gentlemen who liked neither the motion for this equality, nor the report as it stood, that the report was as susceptible of melioration as the motion; that a reform would be nugatory & nominal only if we should make another Congress of the proposed Senate: that if the adherence to an equality of votes was fixed & unalterable, there could not be less obstinacy on the other side, & that we were in fact cut insunder already, and it was in vain to shut our eyes against it: that he was however filled with astonishment that if we were convinced that every *man* in America was secured in all his rights, we should be ready to sacrifice this substantial good to the phantom of *State* sovereignty: that his feelings

---

[11] Taken from Yates.

were more harrowed & his fears more agitated for his Country than he could express, that he conceived this to be the last opportunity of providing for its liberty & happiness: that he could not therefore but repeat his amazement that when a just Governt. founded on a fair representation of the *people* of America was within our reach, we should renounce the blessing, from an attachment to the ideal freedom & importance of *States:* that should this wonderful illusion continue to prevail, his mind was prepared for every event, rather than sit down under a Govt. founded in a vicious principle of representation and which must be as shortlived as it would be unjust. He might prevail on himself to accede to some such expedient as had been hinted by Mr. Wilson: but he never could listen to an equality of votes as proposed in the motion.

Mr. Dayton. When assertion is given for proof, and terror substituted for argument, he presumed they would have no effect however eloquently spoken. It should have been shewn that the evils we have experienced have proceeded from the equality now objected to: and that the seeds of dissolution for the State Governments are not sown in the Genl. Government. He considered the system on the table as a novelty, an amphibious monster; and was persuaded that it never would be recd. by the people.

⟨Mr. Martin wd. never confederate if it could not be done on just principles⟩[12]

Mr ⟨Madison⟩ would acquiesce in the concession hinted by Mr. Wilson, on condition that a due independence should be given to the Senate. The plan in its present shape makes the Senate absolutely dependent on the States. The Senate therefore is only another edition of Congs. ⟨He knew the faults of that Body & had used a bold language agst. it. Still he wd. preserve the State rights, as carefully as the trials by jury.⟩[13]

Mr. Bedford, contended that there was no middle. way between a perfect consolidation and a mere confederacy of the States. The first is out of the question, and in the latter

---

[12] Taken from Yates.

[13] Crossed out: "with very few amendments. Make it properly and state which" with further illegible words. What was substituted was taken from Yates.

they must continue if not perfectly, yet equally soverign. If political Societies possess ambition avarice, and all the other passions which render them formidable to each other, ought we not to view them in this light here? Will not the same motives operate in America as elsewhere? If any gentleman doubts it let him look at the votes. Have they not been dictated by interest, by ambition? Are not the large States evidently seeking to aggrandize themselves at the expense of the small? They think no doubt that they have right on their side, but interest had blinded their eyes. Look at Georgia. Though a small State at present, she is actuated by the prospect of soon being a great one. S. Carolina is actuated both by present interest & future prospects. She hopes too to see the other States cut down to her own dimensions. N. Carolina has the same motives of present & future interest. Virga. follows. Maryd. is not on that side of the Question. Pena. has a direct and future interest. Massts. has a decided and palpable interest in the part she takes. Can it be expected that the small States will act from pure disinterestedness. Look at G. Britain. Is the Representation there less unequal? But we shall be told again that that is the rotten part of the Constitution. Have not the boroughs however held fast their constitutional rights? and are we to act with greater purity than the rest of mankind. An exact proportion in the Representation is not preserved in any one of the States. Will it be said that an inequality of power will not result from an inequality of votes. Give the opportunity, and ambition will not fail to abuse it. The whole history of mankind proves it. The three large States have a common interest to bind them together in commerce. But whether a combination as we suppose, or a competition as others suppose, shall take place among them, in either case, the smaller States must be ruined. We must like Solon make such a Governt. as the people will approve. Will the smaller States ever agree to the proposed degradation of them. It is not true that the people will not agree to enlarge the powers of the present Congs. The Language of the people has been that Congs. ought to have the power of collecting an impost, and of coercing the States when it may be necessary. On The first point they have been explicit & in a manner, unanimous in their declarations. And must they not agree to this & similar measures if they ever mean to discharge their engagements. The little States are willing to observe their engagements, but will meet the large ones on no ground but that of the Confederation. We have been told ⟨with a dictatorial air⟩ [14] that this is the last moment for a fair trial in favor of a good Governmt. It will be the last indeed if the propositions reported from the Committee go forth to the people. He was under no apprehensions. The Large States dare not dissolve the confederation. If they do the small ones will find some foreign ally of more honor and good faith, who will take them by the hand and do them justice. He did not mean by this to intimidate or alarm. It was a natural consequence; ⟨which ought to be avoided by Enlarging the federal powers not annihilating the federal system. This is what the people expect. All agree in the necessity of a more efficient Govt. and why not make such an one; as they desire.⟩ [15]

Mr. Elseworth,. Under a National Govt. he should participate in the National Security, ⟨as remarked by (Mr. King)⟩ [15] but that was all. What he wanted was domestic happiness. The Natl. Govt. could not descend to the local objects on which this depended. It could only embrace objects of a general nature. He turned his eyes therefore for the preservation of his rights [16] to the State Govts. From these alone he could derive the greatest happiness he expects in this life. ⟨His happiness depends on their existence, as much as a newborn infant on its mother for nourishment⟩. [15] If this reasoning was not satisfactory, he had nothing to add that could be so.

Mr. King was for preserving the States in a subordinate degree, and as far as they could be necessary for the purposes stated by Mr. Elsewth. He did not think a full answer had been given to those who apprehended a dangerous encroach-

---

[14] Probably but not certainly a later revision.
[15] Taken from Yates.   [16] Crossed out "happiness".

ment on their jurisdictions. Expedients might be devised as he conceived that would give them all the security the nature of things would admit of. In the establishment of Societies the Constitution was to the Legislature what the laws were to individuals. As the fundamental rights of individuals are secured by express provisions in the State Constitutions; why may not a like security be provided for the Rights of States in the National Constitution. The articles of Union between Engld. & Scotland furnish an example of such a provision in favor of sundry rights of Scotland. When that Union was in agitation, the same language of apprehension which has been heard from the smaller States, was in the mouths of the Scotch patriots. The articles however have not been violated and the Scotch have found an increase of prosperity & happiness. He was aware that this will be called a mere *paper security*. He thought it a sufficient answer to say that if fundamental articles of compact, are no sufficient defence against physical power, neither will there be any safety agst. it if there be no compact. He could not sit down, without taking some notice of the language of the honorable gentleman from Delaware (Mr Bedford). It was not he that had uttered a dictatorial language. This intemperance had marked the honorable gentleman himself. It was not he who with a vehemence unprecedented in that House, had declared himself ready to turn his hopes from our common Country, and court the protection of some foreign hand — This too was the language of the Honbl member, himself. He was grieved that such a thought had entered into his heart. He was more grieved that such an expression had dropped from his lips. ⟨The gentleman cd. only excuse it to himself on the score of passion. For himself whatever might be his distress, he wd. never court relief from a foreign power.⟩ [17]

Adjourned [18]

---

[17] Taken from Yates.   [18] See further, Appendix A, L–LII.

YATES

SATURDAY, JUNE 30th, 1787.

Met pursuant to adjournment. Present 11 states.

Judge Brearsley moved that the president be directed to write to the executive of New-Hampshire, requesting the attendance of its delegates.

Negatived — 2 ayes — 5 noes — one state divided.

The discussion of yesterday resumed.

Mr. Wilson. The question now before us is of so much consequence, that I cannot give it a silent vote — Gentlemen have said, that if this amendment is not agreed to, a separation to the north of Pennsylvania may be the consequence. — This neither staggers me in my sentiments or my duty. If a minority should refuse their assent to the new plan of a general government, and if they will have their own will, and without it, separate the union, let it be done; but we shall stand supported by stronger and better principles. The opposition to this plan is as 22 is to 90, in the general scale — not quite a fourth part of the union — Shall three fourths of the union surrender their rights for the support of that artificial being, called state interest? If we must join issue I am willing. I cannot consent that one fourth shall controul the power of three fourths.

If the motion is adopted, seven states will controul the whole, and the lesser seven compose 24 out of 90. One third must controul two thirds — 24 overrule 66. For whom do we form a constitution, for men, or for *imaginary beings* called states, a mere metaphysical distinction? Will a regard to *state* rights justify the sacrifice of the rights of *men*? If we proceed on any other foundation than the last, our building will neither be solid nor lasting. *Weight and numbers* is the only true principle — every other is local, confined or imaginary. Much has been said of the danger of the three larger states combining together to give rise to monarchy, or an aristocracy. Let the probability of this combination be explained, and it will be found that a rivalship rather than a confederacy will exist among them. Is there a single point in which this interest coincides? Supposing that the executive should be selected from one of the larger states, can the other two be gratified? Will not this be a source of jealousy amongst them, and will they not separately court the interest of the *smaller states*, to counteract the views of a favorite rival? How can an aristocracy arise from this combination more than amongst the smaller states? On the contrary, the present claims of the smaller states lead directly to the establishment of an aristocracy, which is the government of the few over the many, and the Connecticut proposal, removes only a small part of the objection. There are only two kinds of bad governments — the one which does *too much*, and therefore oppressive, and the other which does *too little*, and therefore weak. — Congress partakes of the latter, and the motion will leave us in the same situation and as much fettered as ever we were. The people see its weakness, and would be mortified in seeing our inability to correct it.

The gentleman from Georgia has his doubts how to vote on this question, and wishes some qualification of it to be made, — I admit there ought to be some difference as to the numbers in the second branch; and perhaps there are other distinctions which could, with propriety, be introduced — such for example as the qualifications of the elected, &c. However, if there are leading principles in the system which we adopt, much may be done in the detail. We all aim at giving the general government more energy. The state governments are necessary and valuable — No liberty can be obtained without them. On this question depends the essential rights of the general government and of the people.

Judge Elsworth. I have the greatest respect for the gentleman who spoke last. I respect his abilities, although I differ from him on many points — He asserts that the general government must depend on the equal suffrage of the people. But will not this put it in the power of few states to controul the rest? It is a novel thing in politics that the few controul the many. In the British government, the few, as a guard, have an equal share in the government. The house of lords, although few in number, and sitting in their own right, have an equal share in their legislature. They cannot give away the property of the community, but they can prevent the commons from being too lavish in their gifts. Where is or was a confederation ever formed, where equality of voices was not a fundamental principle? Mankind are apt to go from one extreme to another, and because we have found defects in the confederation, must we therefore pull down the whole fabric, foundation and all, in order to erect a new building totally different from it, without retaining any of its materials? What are its defects? It is said equality of votes has embarrassed us; but how? Would the real evils of our situation have been cured, had not this been the case? Would the proposed amendment in the Virginia plan, as to representation, have relieved us? I fancy not. Rhode-Island has been often quoted as a small state, and by its refusal once defeated the grant of the impost. Whether she was right in so doing is not the question; but was it a federal requisition? And if it was not, she did not, in this instance, defeat a federal measure.

If the larger states seek security, they have it fully in the first branch of the general government. But can we turn the tables and say that the lesser states are equally secure? In *commercial regulations* they will unite. If policy should require free ports, they would be found at Boston, Philadelphia and Alexandria. In the disposition of *lucrative offices* they would unite. But I ask no surrender of any of the rights of the great states, nor do I plead *duress* in the makers of the old confederation, nor suppose they soothed the danger, in order to resume their rights when the danger was over. No; small states must possess the power of self-defence or be ruined. Will any one say there is no diversity of interests in the states? And if there is, should not those interests be guarded and secured? But if there is none, then the large states have nothing to apprehend from an equality of rights. And let it be remembered, that these remarks are not the result of partial or local views. The state I represent is respectable, and in importance holds a middle rank.

Mr. Madison. Notwithstanding the admirable and close

reasoning of the gentleman who spoke last, I am not yet convinced that my former remarks are not well founded. I apprehend he is mistaken as to the fact on which he builds one of his arguments. He supposes that equality of votes is the principle on which all confederacies are formed — that of Lycia, so justly applauded by the celebrated Montesquieu, was different. He also appeals to our good faith for the observance of the confederacy. We know we have found one inadequate to the purposes for which it was made — Why then adhere to a system which is proved to be so remarkably defective? I have impeached a number of states for the infraction of the confederation, and I have not even spared my own state, nor can I justly spare his. Did not Connecticut refuse her compliance to a federal requisition? Has she paid, for the two last years, any money into the continental treasury? And does this look like government, or the observance of a solemn compact? Experience shows that the confederation is radically defective, and we must in a new national government, guard against those defects. Although the large states in the first branch have a weight proportionate to their population, yet as the smaller states have an equal vote in the second branch, they will be able to controul and leave the larger without any essential benefit. As peculiar powers are intended to be granted to the second branch, such as the negativing state laws, &c. unless the larger states have a proportionate weight in the representation, they cannot be more secure.

Judge Elsworth. My state has always been strictly federal, and I can with confidence appeal to your excellency (the president) for the truth of it, during the war. The muster-rolls will show that she had more troops in the field than even the state of Virginia. We strained every nerve to raise them; and we neither spared money or exertions to complete our quotas. This extraordinary exertion has greatly distressed and impoverished us, and it has accumulated our state debts — We feel the effects of it even to this day. But we defy any gentleman to shew that we ever refused a federal requisition. We are constantly exerting ourselves to draw money from the pockets of our citizens, as fast as it comes in; and it is the ardent wish of the state to strengthen the federal government. If she has proved delinquent through inability only, it is not more than others have been, without the same excuse.

Mr. Sherman. I acknowledge there have been failures in complying with the federal requisition. Many states have been defective, and the object of our convention is to amend these defects.

Col. Davie. I have great objection to the Virginia plan as to the manner the second branch is to be formed. It is impracticable. The number may, in time, amount to two or three hundred. This body is too large for the purposes for which we intend to constitute it. I shall vote for the amendment. Some intend a compromise. — This has been hinted by a member from Pennsylvania, but it still has its difficulties. The members will have their local prejudices. The preservation of the state societies must be the object of the general government. It has been asserted that we were *one* in war, and *one* in peace. Such we were as states; but every treaty must be the law of the land as it affects individuals. The formation of the second branch, as it is intended by the motion, is also objectionable. We are going the same round with the old confederation — No plan yet presents sufficient checks to a tumultuary assembly, and there is none therefore which yet satisfies me.

Mr. Wilson. On the present motion it was not proper to propose another plan. I think the second branch ought not to be numerous. I will propose an expedient — Let there be one member for every 100,000 souls, and the smallest states not less than one member each. This would give about twenty-six members. I make this proposal not because I belong to a large state, but in order to pull down a rotten house, and lay a foundation for a new building. To give *additional* weight to an old building is to hasten its ruin.

Governor Franklin. The smaller states, by this motion, would have the power of giving away the money of the greater states. There ought to be some difference between the first and second branches. Many expedients have been proposed, and I am sorry to remark, without effect. A joiner, when he wants to fit two boards, takes off with his plane the uneven parts from each side, and thus they fit. Let us do the same — we are all met to do something.

I shall propose an expedient: Let the senate be elected by the states equally — in all acts of sovereignty and authority, let the votes be equally taken — the same in the appointment of all officers, and salaries; but in passing of laws, each state shall have a right of suffrage in proportion to the sums they respectively contribute. Amongst merchants, where a ship has many owners, her destination is determined in that proportion. I have been one of the ministers to France from this country during the war, and we should have been very glad, if they would have permitted us a vote in the distribution of the money to carry on the war.

Mr. Martin. Mr. Wilson's motion or plan would amount to nearly the same kind of inequality.

Mr. King. The Connecticut motion contains all the vices of the old confederation. It supposes an imaginary evil — the slavery of state governments. And should this convention adopt the motion, our business here is at an end.

Capt. Dayton. Declamation has been substituted for argument. Have gentlemen shewn, or must we believe it, because it is said, that one of the evils of the old confederation was unequal representation? We, as distinct societies, entered into the compact. Will you now undermine the thirteen pillars that support it?

Mr. Martin. If we cannot confederate on just principles, I will never confederate in any other manner.

Mr. Madison.[19] I will not answer for supporting chimerical objects — but has experience evinced any good in the old confederation? I know it never can answer, and I have therefore made use of bold language against it. I do assert, that a national senate, elected and paid by the people, will have no more efficiency than congress; for the states will usurp the general government. I mean, however to preserve the state

---

[19] For Genet's interpretation of this speech see Appendix A, CCCX.

rights with the same care, as I would trials by jury; and I am willing to go as far as my honorable colleague.

Mr. Bedford. That all the states at present are equally sovereign and independent, has been asserted from every quarter of this house. Our deliberations here are a confirmation of the position; and I may add to it, that each of them act from interested, and many from ambitious motives. Look at the votes which have been given on the floor of this house, and it will be found that their numbers, wealth and local views, have actuated their determinations; and that the larger states proceed as if our eyes were already perfectly blinded. Impartiality, with them, is already out of the question — the reported plan is their political creed, and they support it, right or wrong. Even the diminutive state of Georgia has an eye to her future wealth and greatness — South Carolina, puffed up with the possession of her wealth and negroes, and North Carolina, are all, from different views, united with the great states. And these latter, although it is said they can never, from interested views, form a coalition, we find closely united in one scheme of interest and ambition, notwithstanding they endeavor to amuse us with the purity of their principles and the rectitude of their intentions, in asserting that the general government must be drawn from an equal representation of the people. Pretences to support ambition are never wanting. Their cry is, where is the danger? and they insist that altho' the powers of the general government will be increased, yet it will be for the good of the whole; and although the three great states form nearly a majority of the people of America, they never will hurt or injure the lesser states. *I do not, gentlemen, trust you.* If you possess the power, the abuse of it could not be checked; and what then would prevent you from exercising it to our destruction? You gravely alledge that there is no danger of combination, and triumphantly ask, how could combinations be effected? "The larger states," you say, "all "differ in productions and commerce; and experience shows "that instead of combinations, they would be rivals, and coun- "teract the views of one another." This, I repeat, is language calculated only to amuse us. Yes, sir, the larger states will be rivals, but not against each other — they will be rivals against the *rest of the states*. But it is urged that such a government would suit the people, and that its principles are equitable and just. How often has this argument been refuted, when applied to a *federal* government. The small states never can agree to the Virginia plan; and why then is it still urged? But it is said that it is not expected that the state governments will approve the proposed system, and that this house must directly carry it to THE PEOPLE for their approbation! Is it come to this, then, that *the sword* must decide this controversy, and that the horrors of war must be added to the rest of our misfortunes? But what have the people already said? "We "find the confederation defective — go, and give additional "powers to the confederation — give to it the imposts, regu- "lation of trade, power to collect the taxes, and the means to "discharge our foreign and domestic debts." Can we not then, as their delegates, agree upon these points? As their ambassadors, can we not clearly grant those powers? Why then, when we are met, must entire, distinct, and new grounds be taken, and a government, of which the people had no idea, be instituted? And are we to be told, if we wont agree to it, it is the last moment of our deliberations? I say, it is indeed the last moment, if we do agree to this assumption of power. The states will never again be entrapped into a measure like this. The people will say the *small* states would confederate, and grant further powers to congress; but you, the *large* states, would not. Then the fault will be yours, and all the nations of the earth will justify us. But what is to become of our public debts if we dissolve the union? Where is your plighted faith? Will you crush the smaller states, or must they be left unmolested? Sooner than be ruined, there are *foreign powers who will take us by the hand.* I say not this to threaten or intimidate, but that we should reflect seriously before we act. If we once leave this floor, and solemnly renounce your new project, what will be the consequence? You will annihilate your federal government, and ruin must stare you in the face. Let us then do what is in our power — *amend and enlarge the confederation, but not alter the federal system.* The people expect this, and no more. We all agree in the necessity of a more efficient government — and cannot this be done? Although my state is small, I know and respect its rights, as much, at least, as those who have the honor to represent any of the larger states.

Judge Elsworth   I am asked by my honorable friend from Massachusetts, whether by entering into a national government, I will not equally participate in national security? I confess I should; but I want domestic happiness, as well as general security. A general government will never grant me this, as it cannot know my wants or relieve my distress. My state is only as one out of thirteen. Can they, the general government, gratify my wishes? My happiness depends as much on the existence of my state government, as a new-born infant depends upon its mother for nourishment. If this is not an answer, I have no other to give.

Mr. King. I am in sentiment with those who wish the preservation of state governments; but the general government may be so constituted as to effect it. Let the constitution we are about forming be considered as a *commission* under which the general government shall act, and as such it will be the guardian of the state rights. The rights of Scotland are secure from all danger and encroachments, although in the parliament she has a small representation. May not this be done in our general government? Since I am up, I am concerned for what fell from the gentleman from Delaware — "*Take a foreign power by the hand*"! I am sorry he mentioned it, and I hope he is able to excuse it to himself on the score of passion. Whatever may be my distress, I never will court a foreign power to assist in relieving myself from it.

Adjourned till Monday next.

KING

Saturday 30 June

Question how shall the senate be formed, on the plan of an equal vote among the States or on that of a Representation of the people.

Wilson — The vote for the representation in the first Br. according to Numbers was opposed by abt. 22 out of 90 taking that number to represent the whole people of the US. The motion for an equality of Votes among the States will authorise a minority to controul the majority — Seven of the States united make but $\frac{24}{90}$th of the whole — this minority will govern or controul $\frac{66}{90}$ths — this wd. prove a fundamental Defect in the constitution

The Gentm. from Cont. (Elswth) says if the Senate is founded on the principles of a Representation of Numbers, we shall introduce a Monarchy or an Aristocracy — the three or four larger states will combine for Monarchy — if not this, yet for an aristocracy — 4 States will Govn. 9 States — But the Danger of a combination is not greater nor so great in the large States as in the small — The 7. States are only $\frac{24}{90}$, if they govern as is proposed An aristocracy govern because 24. govern or control 66 — [20]

P A T E R S O N [21]

Wilson.[21a] Did not expect this Question at this Stage of the Business.

Member of Connecticut said, not more than one State to Eastward would accede.

Sense of Duty.

This as to Contribn.[21a] 22 out of 90 — not $\frac{1}{4}$ —

Artificial Systems of States —

Easy to correct it.[21a] The voice of the Minority will vote away the Property of the Majority —

A Solecism.

7 States can control the 6.

States imaginary Beings abstracted from Men —

No other Foundation will be solid —

The 3 large States combined. Wt. He wants the Principles of the Combn. — they will be Rivals.

[20] [Endorsed:] June 30 | Numbs & choice of Senator | Wilson.
[21] From *American Historical Review*, IX, 336–338.
[21a] In margin, opposite words following.

Their Interests are different.

24 out of 90 carry more of an Aristocracy.

Why wish for an Union of the lesser States —[21a] 2 Kinds of bad Govt. — 1. That Govt. which does not do enough — and 2. that which does too much — Be as we were before we met.

Yes — but then the 2 Systems oppose each other.[21a] The System of Virginia and the System of Jersey agree as to the Powers —

Govt. by the States necessary. There can be no Difficulty as to this Point.

Mr. Elsworth.[21a] Objn. A Minority will govern a Majority. You put it in the Power of a few to prevent the Oppression of the many.

Political Societies are to govern —

In the Br. Constn. the few has a Check upon the many; and one upon both —

The House must be demolished — but it only wants a Shingle —

If Congress had voted by a Majority, all Evils would have been cured —

Rhode-Island — The Power not in Congress.

Are not the large States safe now —

Suppose the large States should agree that 4 free Ports should be established.

Suppose lucrative Offices —

Self-Preservation.

No Unity of Interests —

Mr. Maddison.[21a] The Confedn. inadequate to its Purposes.

Resoln. of Cont. refusing to comply with a federal Reqn.

Lycia. Germanick Body.[21a] Reported Violations in every State.

The Rule of Confdn. obtained by the Necessity of the Times —

The large States will not be secure by the lower Branch.

2d. Branch may possess a Negative over the Laws of the State-Legs.

Mr. Elsworth.[21a] Cont. has furnished more thn. her Quota as to Men —

Mr. Sherman.[21a]   Mr. Wilson asks, why the Interests of the lesser States cannot be as safe in the Hands of the larger States as in their own —

Mr. Davie — [21a]   The Resoln. as reported by the Comee. is impracticable — is too large —

The 2d. Branch being executive must sit constantly.

Mr. Wilson — [21a]   Not necessary to sit constantly —

Each State should have one Senator — 1 Member in the second for every 100,000 People; and 1 for the smallest State.

This a Compromise on the Part of the large States.

He will not insist upon small Matters — if the great Principles can be established —

Govt. placed upon a false Basis.

Doctr. Franklin.[21a]   The lesser States afraid of their Liberties; the larger States afraid of their Money.

Treaty between France and the U. S.   the latter had no Disposition over the Treasury of the former.

Mr. King.[21a]   Equality is the Vice of the present System.

Captn. Dayton.[21a]

Mr. Maddison.[21a]   The Amt. is Congress in a new Form; servile to the States.

No Disposn. in Cl. Rep. or Corporations to swallow up the Rest.

Mr. Bedford — [21a] Purity of Principle —

Mr. King.[21a]   Magna Charta of England.   Certain constl. Principles to be observed.

This a Consolidn.[21a]   Union of England and Scotland.

The King Bribed.[21a]   Power in the Magy. to prevent a Violation of fundamental Principles.

France — Ireland.[21a]   Govt. a *progressive Force.*

[Notes, probably for a speech not delivered.] [22]

1. The Equality of the States — Sovereignty and Equality

[21a] In margin, opposite words following.

[22] It is impossible to assign these notes satisfactorily.   They are all one document, and internal evidence points to some parts of the debate of June 30.

are convertible Terms.   Pennsylva. a distinct political Being. —

2. As under the existing Articles of the Confedn.   A Contract solemnly entered into.

3. The Danger to the lesser States.

4. The Impracticability of the present System.

5. Its Expence —

It must be admitted, that before a Treaty can be binding, each State must consent.

Objns. —

The larger States contribute most — and therefore Representn. ought to be in Proportn.

1. Ansr.   They have more to protect.   A rich State and a poor State in same Relation as a rich Individual and a poor one.

2. For the Sake of preserving the Liberty of the others — Compromise — Their System.

3. Wealth will have its Influence.

Objn.   Mr. Wilson — The Minority will vote away the Property of the Majority.

Ansr.   This secured by the first Branch —

The Majority will vote away the Liberties of the Minority — Wt. is Wealth when put in Competition with Freedom —

Madn.   Coercion never can be used agt. a large State.[22a] The lesser States will destroy the larger — Lamb and Lyon —

Objn.   Mr. Maddison — The Confedn. inadequate to its Purposes.   Repeated Violations in every State — Each Violation renders the Confedn. a Nullity —

1 No.   The same Power to rescind as to make.   It would be in the Power of one Party always to abrogate a Compact.

Objn.   Mr. Maddison — The Confedn. obtained by the Necessity of the Times.

Is the Plea of Compulsion set up.   Look at the Confedn. unanimously assented to — Mr. Wilson given up — Not complained of — We come here under that Confedn.

Objn.   Mr. King — Equality is the Vice of the present System.   How does it appear —

[22a] In margin, opposite words following.

Objectn. — Mr. King — The great Charter of England — Certain constitutional Principles to be observed — Power in the Magy. to prevent a Violation of fundamental Principles — Union of England and Scotland.

1. A Union or Consolidation — this a Confederacy.
2. It was to be sure agreed to — Bribery made use of —
3. A King.
4. The Vicinity of France —

The last Time of Meeting —

FRANKLIN[23]

PROPOSAL for Consideration.

That the Legislatures of the several States shall choose and send an equal Number of Delegates, namely   , who are to compose the second Branch of the general Legislature.

That in all Cases or Questions wherein the Sovereigntys of the Individual States may be affected, or whereby their Authority over their own Citizens may be diminished, or the Authority of the General Government within the several States augmented, each State shall have *equal* Suffrage.

That in the Appointment of all civil Officers of the *General Government*, in the Election of whom the Second Branch may by the Constitution have part, each State shall have *equal* Suffrage

That in fixing the Salaries of such Officers, & in all Allowances for public Services; & generally in all Appropriations and Dispositions of Money to be drawn out of the General Treasury, and in all Laws for supplying the Treasury, the Delegates of the several States shall have Suffrage *in proportion to the Sums their respective States do actually contributed to that Treasury, from their Taxes or internal Excises.*

That in Case general Duties should be laid by Impost on Goods imported, a liberal Estimation shall be made of the

---

[23] From the Franklin Papers, Vol. VIII, p. 1799.

Amount [24] of such Impost paid in the Price of the Commodities
by those States that import but little, and a proportionate
Addition shall be allowed of Suffrage to such States, ———
and an equal Diminution of the Suffrage of the States
importing

---

[24] Crossed out "Consumption".

MONDAY, JULY 2, 1787.

JOURNAL

Monday July 2. 1787.

It was moved and seconded to agree to the following resolution: namely.

Resolved that in the second Branch of the Legislature of the United States each State shall have an equal vote.

which passed in the negative [Ayes — 5; noes — 5; divided — 1.]

It was moved and seconded to appoint a Committee consisting of a Deputy from each State to whom the eighth resolution, and so much of the seventh resolution, reported from the Committee of the whole House, as has not been decided upon should be referred

On the question to agree to this motion

it passed in the affirmative [1]

and a Committee by ballot was appointed of

Mr Gerry, Mr Ellsworth, Mr Yates, Mr Paterson, Mr Franklin, Mr Bedford, Mr L Martin, Mr Mason, Mr Davie, Mr Rutledge and Mr Baldwin.

And then the House adjourned till Thursday next at 11 o'Clock A. M

---

[1] This question was divided: —

"To appoint a Committee", Ayes — 9; noes — 2; (Vote 111, Detail of Ayes and Noes.)

"The Committee to consist of a member from each State", Ayes — 10; noes — 1; (Vote 112, Detail of Ayes and Noes.)

DETAIL OF AYES AND NOES

	New Hampshire	Massachusetts	Rhode Island	Connecticut	New York	New Jersey	Pennsylvania	Delaware	Maryland	Virginia	North Carolina	South Carolina	Georgia	Questions	Ayes	Noes	Divided
[110]	no			aye	aye	aye	no	aye	aye	no	no	no	dd	That each State shall have an equal vote in ye second branch of the Legislature of the U. S.	5	5	1
[111]	aye			aye	aye	no	aye	no	aye	aye	aye	aye	aye	To appoint a Committee on the seventh and eighth resolutions	9	2	
[112]	aye			aye	aye	aye	no	aye	aye	aye	aye	aye	aye	The Committee to consist of a Member from each State	10	1	

MADISON

Monday July 2d. in Convention

On the question for allowing each State one vote in the Second branch as moved by Mr. Elseworth,

Massts. no. Cont. ay. N. Y. ay. N. J. ay. Pa. no. Del. ay. Md. ay. Mr. Jenifer being not present Mr. Martin alone voted Va. no. N. C. no. S. C. no. Geo. divd. Mr. Houston no Mr Baldwin ay [Ayes — 5; noes — 5; divided — 1.] [2]

Mr. Pinkney thought an equality of votes in the 2d. branch inadmissable. At the same time candor obliged him to admit that the large States would feel a partiality for their own Citizens & give them a preference, in appointments: that they might also find some common points in their commercial interests, and promote treaties favorable to them. ⟨There is a real distinction the Northern & Southn. interests.⟩ [3] N. Carola. S. Carol: & Geo. in their Rice & Indigo had a peculiar interest which might be sacrificed. How then shall the larger States be prevented from administering the Genl. Govt. as

---

[2] Upon this vote, especially the votes of Maryland and Georgia, see Appendix A, CLVIII (24).   [3] Taken from Yates.

they please, without being themselves unduly subjected to the will of the smaller? By allowing them some but not a full proportion. He was extremely anxious that something should be done, considering this as the last appeal to a regular experiment. Congs. have failed in almost every effort for an amendment of the federal System. Nothing has prevented a dissolution of it, but the appointmt. of this Convention; & he could not express his alarms for the consequences of such an event. He read his motion ⟨to form the States into classes, with an apportionment of Senators among them, (see art. 4 of his plan.)⟩[4]

General Pinkney. ⟨was willing the motion⟩[5] might be considered. He did not entirely approve it. He liked better the motion of Dr. Franklin (which see Saturday June 30). Some compromise seemed to be necessary: the States being exactly divided on the question for an equality of votes in the 2d. branch. He proposed that a Committee consisting of a member from each State should be appointed to devise & report some compromise.

Mr: L. Martin had no objection to a Commitment, but no modifications whatever could reconcile the Smaller States to the least diminution of their equal Sovereignty.

Mr. Sharman. We are now at a full stop, and nobody he supposed meant that we shd. break up without doing something. A Committee he thought most likely to hit on some expedient.

* Mr. Govr. Morris.[6] thought a Come. advisable as the Convention had been equally divided. He had a stronger reason also. The mode of appointing the 2d. branch tended

---

* He had just returned from N. Y. havg. left ye. Convention a few days after it commenced business.[7]

---

[4] Madison originally wrote "see it Monday June 25", but substituted "see art. 4 of his plan", referring to the spurious plan in the *Journal*.

[5] Madison originally wrote that Gen. Pinckney "seconded the motion in order that it might be considered", but changed it for the phrasing in the text.

[6] That Madison's report of this speech was approved by Morris, see Appendix A, CCCXCV, CCCCI, also CCCXIII, CCCXVII.

[7] See Appendix A, CCCLXXVIII and CCCLXXXIX.

he was sure to defeat the object of it. What is this object? to check the precipitation, changeableness, and excesses of the first branch. Every man of observation had seen in the democratic branches of the State Legislatures, precipitation — in Congress changeableness. in every department excesses agst. personal liberty private property & personal safety. What qualities are necessary to constitute a check in this case? *Abilities* and *virtue,* are equally necessary in both branches. Something more then is wanted. 1. the Checking branch must have a personal interest in checking the other branch. one interest must be opposed to another interest. Vices as they exist, must be turned agst. each other. 2. It must have great personal property, it must have the aristocratic spirit; it must love to lord it thro' pride, pride is indeed the great principle that actuates both the poor & the rich. It is this principle which in the former resists, in the latter abuses authority. 3. It should be independent. In Religion the Creature is apt to forget its Creator. That it is otherwise in political affairs. The late debates here are an unhappy proof. The aristocratic body, should be as independent & as firm as the democratic. If the members of it are to revert to a dependence on the democratic choice. The democratic scale will preponderate. All the guards contrived by America have not restrained the Senatorial branches of the Legislatures from a servile complaisance to the democratic. If the 2d. branch is to be dependent we are better without it. To make it independent, it should be for life.[8] It will then do wrong, it will be said. He believed so: He hoped so. The Rich will strive to establish their dominion & enslave the rest. They always did. They always will. The proper security agst them is to form them into a separate interest. The two forces will then controul each other. Let the rich mix with the poor and in a Commercial Country, they will establish an Oligarchy. Take away commerce, and the democracy will triumph. Thus it has been all the world over. So it will be among us. Reason tells us we are but men: and we are not

---

[8] See Appendix A, CCCLXXIX.

to expect any particular interference of Heaven in our favor.
By thus combining & setting apart, the aristocratic interest,
the popular interest will be combined agst. it. There will be
a mutual check and mutual security. 4. An independence
for life, involves the necessary permanency. If we change our
measures no body will trust us: and how avoid a change of
measures, but by avoiding a change of men. Ask any man if
he confides in Congs. if he confides in ⟨the State of⟩[9] Pena. if
he will lend his money or enter into contract? He will tell
you no. He sees no stability. He can repose no confidence.
If G. B. were to explain her refusal to treat with us, the same
reasoning would be employed.—He disliked the exclusion of
the 2d. branch from holding offices. It is dangerous. It is
like the imprudent exclusion of the military officers during
the war, from civil appointments. It deprives the Executive
of the principal source of influence. If danger be apprehended
from the Executive what a lift-handed way is this of obviating
it? If the son, the brother or the friend can be appointed, the
danger may be even increased, as the disqualified father &c.
can then boast of a disinterestedness which he does not possess. Besides shall the best, the most able, the most virtuous
citizens not be permitted to hold offices? Who then are to
hold them? He was also agst. paying the Senators. They
will pay themselves if they can. If they can not they will
be rich and can do without it. of such the 2d. branch ought
to consist; and none but such can compose it if they are not
to be paid — He contended that the Executive should appoint
the Senate & fill up vacancies. This gets rid of the difficulty
in the present question. You may begin with any ratio you
please; it will come to the same thing. The members being
independt. & for life, may be taken as well from one place as
from another.—It should be considered too how the scheme
could be carried through the States. He hoped there was
strength of mind eno' in this House to look truth in the face.
He did not hesitate therefore to say that loaves & fishes must
bribe the Demagogues. They must be made to expect higher

---

[9] Taken from Yates.

offices under the general than the State Govts. A Senate for life will be a noble bait. Without such captivating prospects, the popular leaders will oppose & defeat the plan. He perceived that the 1st. branch was to be chosen by the people of the States: the 2d. by those chosen by the people. Is not here a Govt. by the States. A Governt. by Compact between Virga. in the 1st. & 2d. branch; Massts. in the 1st & 2d. branch &c. This is going back to mere treaty. It is no Govt. at all. It is altogether dependent— on the States, and will act over again the part which Congs. has acted. A firm Governt. alone can protect our liberties. He fears the influence of the rich. They will have the same effect here as elsewhere if we do not by such a Govt. keep them within their proper sphere. We should remember that the people never act from reason alone. The rich will take advantage of their passions and make these the instruments for oppressing them. The Result of the Contest will be a violent aristocracy, or a more violent despotism. The schemes of the Rich will be favored by the extent of the Country. The people in such distant parts can not communicate & act in concert. They will be the dupes of those who have more Knowledge & intercourse. The only security agst. encroachments will be a select & sagacious body of men, instituted to watch agst. them on all sides. He meant only to hint these observations, without grounding any motion on them

Mr. Randolph favored the commitment though he did not expect much benefit from the expedient. He animadverted on the warm & rash language of Mr. Bedford on Saturday; reminded the small States that if the large States should combine some danger of which he did not deny there would be a check in the revisionary power of the Executive, and intimated that in order to render this still more effectual, he would agree that in the choice of the Executive each State should have an equal vote. He was persuaded that two such opposite bodies as Mr. Morris had planned could never long co-exist. Dissentions would arise as has been seen even between the Senate and H. of Delegates in Maryland, appeals would be made to the people; and in a little time commotions would be the result — He was far from thinking the large States could subsist of themselves any more than the small; an avulsion would involve the whole in ruin, and he was determined to pursue such a scheme of Government as would secure us agst. such a calamity.

Mr. Strong was for the Commitment; and hoped the mode of constituting both branches would be referred. If they should be established on different principles, contentions would prevail and there would never be a concurrence in necessary measures.

Docr. Williamson. If we do not concede on both sides, our business must soon be at an end. He approved of the commitment, supposing that as the Come. wd. be a smaller body, a compromise would be pursued with more coolness

Mr. Wilson objected to the Committee, because it would decide according to that very rule of voting which was opposed on one side. Experience in Congs. had also proved the inutility of Committees consisting of members from each State

⟨Mr. Lansing wd. not oppose the Commitment, though expecting little advantage from it.⟩[10]

Mr. M⟨adison⟩ opposed the commitment. He had rarely seen any other effect than delay from *such* Committees in Congs. Any scheme of compromise that could be proposed in the Committee might as easily be proposed in the House; and the report of the Committee when it contained merely the *opinion* of the Come. would neither shorten the discussion, nor influence the decision of the House.

Mr. Gerry was for the commitmt. Something must be done, or we shall disappoint not only America, but the whole world. He suggested a consideration of the State we should be thrown into by the failure of the Union. We should be without an Umpire to decide controversies and must be at the mercy of events. What too is to become of our treaties — what of our foreign debts, what of our domestic? We must make concessions on both sides. Without these the constitutions of the several States would never have been formed.

---

[10] Taken from Yates.

On the question "for commiting" ⟨generally⟩[11]

Massts. ay. Cont. ay. N. Y. ay. N. J. no. P. ay. Del. no. Md. ay. Va. ay. N. C. ay. S. C. ay. Geo. ay. [Ayes — 9; noes — 2.]

On the question for commiting "to a member from each State"

Massts. ay. Cont. ay. N. Y. ay. N. J. ay. Pa. no. Del. ay. Md. ay. Va. ay. N. C. ay. S. C. ay. Geo — ay. [Ayes — 10; noes — 1.]

The Committee elected by ballot, were Mr. Gerry, Mr. Elseworth, Mr. Yates, Mr. Patterson. Dr. Franklin, Mr. Bedford, Mr. Martin,[12] Mr. Mason, Mr. Davy. Mr. Rutledge, Mr. Baldwin.

That time might be given to the Committee, and to such as chose to attend to the celebrations on the anniversary of Independence, the Convention adjourned till Thursday.[13]

YATES

Monday, July 2d, 1787.

Met pursuant to adjournment. Present 11 states.

The question was then put on Mr. Elsworth's motion. 5 ayes — 5 noes — one state divided. So the question, as to the amendment, was lost.

Mr. Pinkney. As a professional man, I might say, that there is no weight in the argument adduced in favor of the motion on which we were divided; but candor obliges me to own, that equality of suffrage in the states is wrong. Prejudices will prevail, and they have an equal weight in the larger as in the smaller states. There is a solid distinction as to interest between the southern and northern states — To destroy the ill effects thereof, I renew the motion which I

---

[11] On the situation in the Convention that led to the referring of this question to a committee, see Appendix A, CLVIII(24), CLXXXI, CCXVIII, CCC, CCCXXXVI, CCCLV, also the references on the conclusion of the compromise in *Records*, July 16, note 4.

[12] See Appendix A, CLXXXIX.   [13] See further, Appendix A, LIII–LV.

made in the early stage of this business. (*See the plan of it before mentioned.*)

Gen. Pinkney moved for a select committee, to take into consideration both branches of the legislature.

Mr. Martin. It is again attempted to compromise. — You must give each state an equal suffrage, or our business is at an end.

Mr. Sherman. It seems we have got to a point, that we cannot move one way or the other. Such a committee is necessary to set us right.

Mr. Morris. The two branches, so equally poised, cannot have their due weight. It is confessed, on all hands, that the second branch ought to be a check on the first — for without its having this effect it is perfectly useless. — The first branch, originating from the people, will ever be subject to *precipitancy, changeability,* and *excess.* Experience evinces the truth of this remark without having recourse to reading. This can only be checked by *ability* and *virtue* in the second branch. On your present system, can you suppose that one branch will possess it more than the others? The second branch ought to be composed of men of great and established property — *an aristocracy.* Men, who from pride will support consistency and permanency; and to make them completely independent they must be chosen *for life,* or they will be a useless body. Such an aristocratic body will keep down the turbulency of democracy. But if you elect them for a shorter period, they will be only a name, and we had better be without them. Thus constituted, I hope they will shew us the weight of aristocracy.

History proves, I admit, that the men of large property will uniformly endeavor to establish tyranny. How then shall we ward off this evil? Give them the second branch, and you secure their weight for the *public good.* They become responsible for their conduct, and this lust of power will ever be checked by the democratic branch, and thus form a stability in your government. But if we continue changing our measures by the breath of democracy, who will confide in our engagements? Who will trust us? Ask any person whether he reposes any confidence in the government of congress, or that of the state of Pennsylvania — he will readily answer you, no. Ask him the reason, and he will tell you, it is because he has no confidence in their stability.

You intend also that the second branch shall be incapable of holding any office in the general government. — It is a dangerous expedient. They ought to have every inducement to be interested in your government. Deprive them of this right, and they will become inattentive to your welfare. The wealthy will ever exist; and you never can be safe unless you gratify them as a body, in the pursuit of honor and profit. Prevent them by positive institutions, and they will proceed in some left-handed way. A son may want a place—you mean to prevent him from promotion — They are not to be paid for their services — they will in some way pay themselves; nor is it in your power to prevent it. It is good policy that men of property be collected in one body, to give them one common influence in your government. Let vacancies be filled up as they happen, by the executive. Besides it is of little consequence, on this plan, whether the states are equally represented or not. If the state governments have the division of many of the loaves and fishes, and the general government few, it cannot exist. This senate would be one of the *baubles* of the general government. If you choose them for *seven* years, whether chosen by the people or the states; whether by equal suffrage or in any other proportion, how will they be a check? They will still have local and state prejudices. — A government by compact is no government at all. You may as well go back to your congressional federal government, where, in the character of ambassadors, they may form treaties for each state.

I avow myself the advocate of a strong government, still I admit that the influence of the rich must be guarded; and a pure democracy is equally oppressive to the lower orders of the community. This remark is founded on the experience of history. We are a commercial people, and as such will be obliged to engage in European politics. Local government cannot apply to the general government. These latter remarks I throw out only for the consideration of the committee who are to be appointed.

Gov. Randolph. I am in favor of appointing a committee; but considering the warmth exhibited in debate on Saturday, I have, I confess, no great hopes that any good will arise from it. Cannot a remedy be devised? If there is danger to the lesser states, from an unequal representation in the second branch, may not a check be found in the appointment of one executive, by electing him, by an equality of state votes? He must have the right of interposing between the two branches, and this might give a reasonable security to the smaller states. — Not one of the lesser states can exist by itself; and a dissolution of the confederation, I confess, would produce conventions, as well in the larger as in the smaller states. The principle of self-preservation induces me to seek for a government that will be stable and secure.

Mr. Strong moved to refer the 7th resolve to the same committee.

Mr. Wilson. I do not approve of the motion for a committee. I also object to the mode of its appointment — a small committee is the best.

Mr. Lansing. I shall not oppose the appointment, but I expect no good from it.

Mr. Madison. I have observed that committees only delay business; and if you appoint one from each state, we shall have in it the whole force of state prejudices. The great difficulty is to conquer former opinions. The motion of the gentleman from South Carolina can be as well decided here as in committee.[14]

Mr. Gerry. The world at large expect something from us. If we do nothing, it appears to me we must have war and confusion—for the old confederation would be at an end. Let us see if no concession can be made. Accommodation is absolutely necessary, and defects may be amended by a future convention.

The motion was then put to appoint a committee on the

---

[14] For Genet's interpretation of Madison's attitude, see Appendix A, CCCX.

8th resolve, and so much of the 7th as was not agreed to. Carried — 9 states against 2.

And, *by ballot*, the following members were appointed:

Massachusetts,	Mr. Gerry.
Connecticut,	Mr. Elsworth.
New-York,	Mr. Yates.
New-Jersey,	Mr. Patterson.
Pennsylvania,	Mr. Franklin.
Delaware,	Mr. Bedford.
Maryland,	Mr. Martin.
Virginia,	Mr. Mason.
North Carolina,	Mr. Davie.
South Carolina,	Mr. Rutledge.
Georgia,	Mr. Baldwin.

The convention then adjourned to Thursday, the 5th of July.

W I L S O N [15]

Resolved

That the second Branch of the national [16] Legislature shall be elected in the following manner — that the States be divided into   [17] Districts; the first to comprehend the States of   the second to comprehend the States of   the third to comprehend the States of   the fourth to comprehend the States of   and &c.
——— that the Members shall be elected by the said Districts in the Proportion following, in the first District

Resolved

That the Members of the second Branch be elected for   Years, and that immediately after the first Election they be divided by Lot into   Classes; that the Seats of the

---

[15] Found among the Wilson papers in the Library of the Historical Society of Pennsylvania. It is in Wilson's handwriting but would seem to be a copy of Pinckney's proposal renewed on this day.

[16] Crossed out "federal".   [17] Crossed out "four great".

Members of the first Class shall be vacated at the Expiration of the first Year, that the second the second Year, and so on continually; to the End that the   Part of the second Branch, as nearly as possible may be annually chosen

Resolved

That it shall be in the Power of the national[18] Legislature, for the Convenience and Advantage of the good People of the United States, to divide them into such further and other Districts for the Purposes aforesaid,[19] as to the said Legislature shall appear necessary

---

[18] Crossed out "federal".

[19] Crossed out "of electing the Members of the said second Branch".

TUESDAY, JULY 3, 1787.

YATES

TUESDAY, JULY 3d, 1787.[1]

The *grand committee* met. Mr. Gerry was chosen chairman. The committee proceeded to consider in what manner they should discharge the business with which they were entrusted. By the proceedings in the convention they were so equally divided on the important question of *representation in the two branches*, that the idea of a concilatory adjustment must have been in contemplation of the house in the appointment of this committee. But still how to effect this salutary purpose was the question. Many of the members, impressed with the utility of a general government, connected with it the indispensible necessity of a representation from the states *according to their numbers and wealth;* while others, equally tenacious of the rights of the states, would admit of no other representation but such *as was strictly federal,* or in other words, *equality of suffrage.* This brought on a discussion of the principles on which the house had divided, and a lengthy recapitulation of the arguments advanced in the house in support of these opposite propositions. As I had not openly explained my sentiments on any former occasion on this question, but constantly in giving my vote, *showed my attachment to the national government on federal principles, I took this occasion to explain my motives* — (*See a copy of my speech hereunto annexed.*)*

* It is matter of regret that this document cannot be found: the principles it contained are perhaps embodied in the letter from Mr. Yates and Mr. Lansing to Gov. George Clinton, on their retiring from the convention.

---

[1] See Martin's account of the discussions in the committee, Appendix A, CLVIII (24–26), and Gerry's account in CLXXXI. See also Madison's note below, July 5.

That committee sessions were not secret, see Appendix A, CXC.

These remarks gave rise to a motion of Dr. Franklin, which after some modification was agreed to, and made the basis of the following report of the committee.

The committee to whom was referred the eighth resolution, reported from the committee of the whole house, and so much of the seventh as had not been decided on, submit the following report:

That the subsequent propositions be recommended to the convention, on condition that both shall be generally adopted.

That in the first branch of the legislature, each of the states now in the union, be allowed one member for every 40,000 inhabitants, of the description reported in the seventh resolution of the committee of the whole house — That each state, not containing that number, shall be allowed one member.

That all bills for raising or apportioning money, and for fixing salaries of the officers of government of the United States, shall originate in the first branch of the legislature, and shall not be altered or amended by the second branch; and that no money shall be drawn from the public treasury, but in pursuance of appropriations to be originated in the first branch.

That in the second branch of the legislature, *each state shall have an equal vote.*

THURSDAY, JULY 5, 1787.

JOURNAL
Thursday July 5. 1787.

The honorable Mr Gerry reported from the Committee, to whom were referred the eighth resolution and such part of the seventh resolution as had not already been decided on by the House, that the Committee had directed him to submit the following report to the consideration of the House, — and the same being delivered in at the Secretary's table was read once throughout, and then by paragraphs and is as follows. namely.

The Committee to whom were referred the eighth resolution reported from the Committee of the whole House, and so much of the seventh as hath not been decided on submit the following report.

"That the subsequent propositions be recommended to the Convention, on condition that both shall be generally adopted.

1st That in the first branch of the Legislature each of the States now in the Union be allowed one Member for every forty thousand inhabitants of the description reported in the seventh resolution of the Committee of the whole House. That each State not containing that number shall be allowed one Member — That all Bills for raising or appropriating money and for fixing the salaries of the Officers of the Government of the United States, shall originate in the first Branch of the Legislature, and shall not be altered or amended by the second Branch — and that no money shall be drawn from the public Treasury but in pursuance of appropriations to be originated by the first Branch.

2ndly That in the second Branch of the Legislature each State shall have an equal Vote.[1]

---

[1] A copy of this report is among the Brearley Papers. In the margin opposite the 2d proposition is written — "Agreed 6 ay. 3 no. 2 divided." See July 7, Vote 120.

It was moved and seconded to postpone the consideration of the first proposition contained in the report, in order to take up the second.

On the question to postpone

it passed in the negative [Ayes — 2; noes — 8.]

It was then moved and seconded to postpone the first clause of the report in order to take up the following namely.

That the suffrages of the several States be regulated and proportioned according to the sums to be paid towards the General Revenue by the inhabitants of each State respectively — That an apportionment of suffrages, according to the ratio aforesaid, shall be made and regulated at the end of years from the first Meeting of the Legislature of the United-States — and so from time to time at the end of every years thereafter — but that for the present, and until the period first above mentioned shall have one suffrage &ca

and on the question to postpone

it passed in the negative [Ayes — 1; noes — 8.][2]

and then the House adjourned till to-morrow at 11 o'Clock A. M.

DETAIL OF AYES AND NOES

	New Hampshire	Massachusetts	Rhode Island	Connecticut	New York	New Jersey	Pennsylvania	Delaware	Maryland	Virginia	North Carolina	South Carolina	Georgia	Questions	Ayes	Noes	Divided
[113]	no		no	aye		no	no	no	no	no		aye	no	To postpone the first proposition reported from the grand Committee, in order to take up the second.	2	8	
[114]	no		no	no		no	no	no	no	no		aye		To postpone the first clause of the report to take up Mr Rutledge's motion	1	8	

[2] Vote 114, Detail of Ayes and Noes, which states that the motion was "Mr. Rutledge's".

MADISON

Thursday July 5th. in Convention

Mr. Gerry delivered in from the Committee appointed on Monday last the following Report.[3]

"The Committee to whom was referred the 8th Resol. of the Report from the Committee of the whole House, and so much of the 7th. as has not been decided on submit the following Report: That the subsequent propositions be recommended to the Convention on condition that both shall be generally adopted. 1. that in the 1st. branch of the Legislature each of the States now in the Union shall be allowed 1 member for every 40,000 inhabitants of the description reported in the 7th Resolution of the Come. of the whole House: that each State not containing that number shall be allowed 1 member: that all bills for raising or appropriating money, and for fixing the Salaries of the Officers of the Governt. of the U. States shall originate in the 1st branch of the Legislature, and shall not be altered or amended by the 2d branch: and that no money shall be drawn from the public Treasury, but in pursuance of appropriations to be originated in the 1st branch" II. that in the 2d branch each State shall have an equal vote" *

Mr. Ghorum observed that as the report consisted of propositions mutually conditional he wished to hear some explana-

---

* This report was founded on a motion in the Committe made by Dr. Franklin. It was barely acquiesced in by the members from the States opposed to an equality of votes in the 2d. branch and was evidently considered by the members on the other side, as a gaining of their point. A motion was made by Mr. Sherman† in the Committee to the following effect "that each State should have an equal vote in the 2d branch; provided that no decision therein should prevail unless the majority of States concurring should also comprize a majority of the inhabitants of the U. States". This motion was not much deliberated on nor approved in the Committee. A similar proviso had been proposed in the debates on the articles of Confederation in 1777. to the articles giving certain powers to "nine States." See Journals of Congs. for 1777. p. 462.

† He acted in place of Mr. Elseworth who was kept away by indisposition.

---

[3] Madison's report is identical with that of the Journal and Yates except for a very few verbal differences too slight to be worth noticing, — *e. g.*, "was" for "were", "has" for "hath", etc.

tions touching the grounds on which the conditions were estimated.

Mr. Gerry. The Committee were of different opinions as well as the Deputations from which the Come. were taken, and agreed to the Report merely in order that some ground of accommodation might be proposed. Those opposed to the equality of votes have only assented conditionally; and if the other side do not generally agree will not be under any obligation to support the Report.

⟨Mr. Wilson. thought the Committee had exceeded their powers.

Mr. Martin was for taking the question on the whole report.

Mr. Wilson was for a division of the question: otherwise it wd. be a leap in the dark.⟩[4]

Mr- ⟨Madison.⟩ could not regard the exclusive privilege of originating money bills as any concession on the side of the small States. Experience proved that it had no effect. If seven States in the upper branch wished a bill to be originated, they might surely find some member from some of the same States in the lower branch who would originate it. The restriction as to amendments was of as little consequence. Amendments could be handed privately by the Senate to members in the other house. Bills could be negatived that they might be sent up in the desired shape. If the Senate should yield to the obstinacy of the 1st. branch the use of that body as a check would be lost. If the 1st. branch should yield to that of the Senate, the privilege would be nugatory. Experience had also shewn both in G. B. and the States having a similar regulation that it was a source of frequent & obstinate altercations. These considerations had produced a rejection of a like motion on a former occasion when judged by its own merits. It could not therefore be deemed any concession on the present, and left in force all the objections which had prevailed agst. allowing each State an equal voice. He conceived that the Convention was reduced to the alternative [5] of either departing from justice in order to conciliate

---

[4] Taken from Yates.   [5] Crossed out "delusion".

the smaller States, and the minority of the people of the U. S. or of displeasing these by justly gratifying the larger States and the majority of the people. He could not himself hesitate as to the option he ought to make. The Convention with justice & the majority of the people on their side, had nothing to fear. With injustice and the minority on their side they had every thing to fear. It was in vain to purchase concord in the Convention on terms which would perpetuate discord among their Constituents. The Convention ought to pursue a plan which would bear the test of examination, which would be espoused & supported by the enlightened and impartial part of America, & which they could themselves vindicate & urge. It should be considered that altho' at first many may judge of the system recommended, by their opinion of the Convention, yet finally all will judge of the Convention by the system. The merits of the system alone can finally & effectually obtain the public suffrage. He was not apprehensive that the people of the small States would obstinately refuse to accede to a Govt. founded on just principles, and promising them substantial protection.[6] He could not suspect that Delaware would brave the consequences of seeking her fortunes apart from the other States, rather than submit to such a Govt: much less could he suspect that she would pursue the rash policy of courting foreign support, which the warmth of one of her representatives (Mr. Bedford) had suggested, or if she shd. that any foreign nation wd. be so rash as to hearken to the overture. As little could he suspect that the people of N. Jersey notwithstanding the decided tone of the gentlemen from that State, would choose rather to stand on their own legs, and bid defiance to events,[7] than to acquiesce under an establishment founded on principles the justice of which they could not dispute, and[8] absolutely necessary to redeem them from the exactions levied on them by the commerce of the neighbouring States. A review of other States would prove that there was as little reason to apprehend an inflexible opposition elsewhere. Harmony in the Convention was no

---

[6] Crossed out "justice".
[7] Crossed out "all consequen".
[8] Crossed out "calculated to".

doubt much to be desired. Satisfaction to all the States, in the first instance still more so. But if the principal States comprehending a majority of the people of the U. S. should concur in a just & judicious plan, he had the firmest hopes that all the other States would by degrees accede to it.[9]

Mr. Butler said he could not let down his idea of the people. of America so far as to believe they, would from mere respect to the Convention adopt a plan evidently unjust. He did not consider the privilege concerning money bills as of any consequence. He urged that the 2d. branch ought to represent the States according to their property.

Mr. Govr. Morris. thought the form as well as the matter of the Report objectionable. It seemed in the first place to render amendments impracticable.[10] In the next place, it seemed to involve a pledge to agree to the 2d. part if the 1st. shd. be agreed to. He conceived the whole aspect of it to be wrong. He came here as a Representative of America; he flattered himself he came here in some degree as a Representative of the whole human race; for the whole human race will be affected by the proceedings of this Convention. He wished gentlemen to extend their views beyond the present moment of time; beyond the narrow limits of place from which they derive their political origin. If he were to believe some things which he had heard, he should suppose that we were assembled to truck and bargain for our particular States. He can—not descend to think that any gentlemen are really actuated by these views. We must look forward to the effects of what we do. These alone ought to guide us. Much has been said of the sentiments of the people. They were unknown. They could not be known. All that we can infer is that if the plan we recommend be reasonable & right; all who have reasonable minds and sound intentions will embrace it,[11]

---

[9] Crossed out: "These observations wd. show that he was not only fixed in his opposition to the Report of the Comme. but was prepared for any want that might follow a negative of its".

[10] Crossed out "and to require an adoption or negation in the lump".

[11] Crossed out: "He did not like the desponding language   But we should **never** agree, that the States will, unite in".

notwithstanding what had been said by some Gentlemen. Let us suppose that the larger States shall agree; and that the smaller refuse: and let us trace the consequences. The opponents of the system in the smaller States will no doubt make a party, and a noise for a time, but the ties of interest, of kindred & of common habits which connect them with the other States will be too strong to be easily broken. In N. Jersey particularly he was sure a great many would follow the sentiments of Pena. & N. York. This Country must be united. If persuasion does not unite it, the sword will. He begged that this consideration might have its due weight. The scenes of horror attending civil commotion can not be described, and the conclusion of them will be worse than the term of their continuance. The stronger party will then make traytors of the weaker; and the Gallows & Halter will finish the work of the sword. How far foreign powers would be ready to take part in the confusions he would not say. Threats that they will be invited have it seems been thrown out. He drew the melancholy picture of foreign intrusions as exhibited in the History of Germany, and urged it as a standing lesson to other nations. He trusted that the Gentlemen who may have hazarded such expressions, did not entertain them till they reached their own lips. But returning to the Report he could not think it in any respect calculated for the public good. As the 2d. branch is now constituted, there will be constant disputes & appeals to the States which will undermine the Genl. Government & controul & annihilate the 1st branch. Suppose that the Delegates from Massts. & Rho I. in the upper House disagree, and that the former are outvoted. What Results? they will immediately declare that their State will not abide by the decision, and make such representations as will produce that effect — The same may happen as to Virga. & other States. Of what avail then will be what is on paper. State attachments, and State importance have been the bane of this Country. We cannot annihilate; [12] but we may perhaps take out the teeth of the serpents. He

---

[12] Crossed out "the States".

wished our ideas to be enlarged to the true interest of man, instead of being circumscribed within the narrow compass of a particular Spot. And after all how little can be the motive yielded by selfishness for such a policy. Who can say whether he himself, much less whether his children, will the next year be an inhabitant of this or that State.

Mr. Bedford. He found that what he had said as to the small States being taken by the hand, had been misunderstood; and he rose to explain. He did not mean that the small States would court the aid & interposition of foreign powers. He meant that they would not consider the federal compact as dissolved untill it should be so by the acts of the large States. In this case the consequence of the breach of faith on their part, and the readiness of the small States to fulfill their engagements, would be that foreign nations having demands on this Country would find it their interest to take the small States by the hand, in order to do themselves justice. This was what he meant. But no man can foresee to what extremities the small States may be driven by oppression. He observed also in apology that some allowance ought to be made for the habits of his profession in which warmth was natural & sometimes necessary. But is there not an apology in what was said by (Mr. Govr. Morris) that the sword is to unite: by Mr. Ghorum that Delaware must be annexed to Penna. and N. Jersey divided between Pena. and N. York. To hear such language without emotion, would be to renounce the feelings of a man and the duty of a citizen — As to the propositions of the Committee, the lesser States have thought it necessary to have a security somewhere. This has been thought necessary for the Executive Magistrate of the proposed Govt. who has a sort of negative on the laws; and is it not of more importance that the States should be protected, than that the Executive branch of the Govt. shd. be protected. In order to obtain this, the smaller ⟨States⟩ have conceded as to the ⟨constitution of the⟩ first branch, and as to money bills. If they be not gratified by correspondent concessions as to the 2d. branch is it to be supposed they will ever accede to the plan; and what will be the consequence if nothing should

be done! The condition of the U. States requires that something should be immediately done. It will be better that a
defective plan should be adopted, than that none should be
recommended. He saw no reason why defects might not be
supplied by meetings 10, 15 or 20 years hence.

Mr. Elseworth said he had not attended the proceedings of
the Committee, but was ready to accede to the compromise
they had reported. Some compromise was necessary; and
he saw none ⟨more⟩ convenient or reasonable.

Mr. Williamson hoped that the expressions of individuals
would not be taken for the sense of their colleagues, much
less of their States which was not & could not be known. He
hoped also that the meaning of those expressions would not be
misconstrued or exaggerated. He did not conceive that (Mr.
Govr. Morris) meant that the sword ought to be drawn agst. the
smaller States. He only pointed out the probable consequences of anarchy in the U. S. A similar exposition ought to be
given of the expressions (of Mr. Ghorum). He was ready to
hear the Report discussed; but thought the propositions contained in it, the most objectionable of any he had yet heard.

Mr. Patterson said that he had when the Report was agreed
to in the Come. reserved to himself the right of freely discussing
it. He acknowledged that the warmth complained of was improper; but he thought the Sword & the Gallows as little calculated to produce conviction. He complained of the manner in
which Mr. M— & Mr. Govr. Morris had treated the small States.

Mr. Gerry. Tho' he had assented to the Report in the Committee, he had very material objections to it. We were however
in a peculiar situation. We were neither the same Nation nor
different Nations. We ought not therefore to pursue the one
or the other of these ideas too closely. If no compromise should
take place what will be the consequence. A secession he foresaw would take place; for some gentlemen seem decided on it;
two different plans will be proposed, and the result no man
could foresee. If we do not come to some agreement among
ourselves some foreign sword will probably do the work for us.

Mr. Mason. The Report was meant not as specific propositions to be adopted, but merely as a general ground of ac-

comodation. There must be some accomodation on this point, or we shall make little further progress in the work. Accomodation was the object of the House in the appointment of the Committee; and of the Committee in the Report they had made. And however liable the Report might be to objections, he though it preferable to an appeal to the world by the different sides, as had been talked of by some Gentlemen. It could not be more inconvenient to any gentleman to remain absent from his private affairs, than it was for him: but he would bury his bones in this city rather than expose his Country to the Consequences of a dissolution of the Convention without any thing being done.

The 1st. proposition in the Report for fixing the representation in the 1st. branch, one member for every 40,000 inhabitants, being taken up.

Mr. Govr. Morris objected to that scale of apportionment. He thought property ought to be taken into the estimate as well as the number of inhabitants. Life and liberty were generally said to be of more value, than property. An accurate view of the matter would nevertheless prove that property was the main object of Society. The savage State was more favorable to liberty than the Civilized; and sufficiently so to life. It was preferred by all men who had not acquired a taste for property; it was only renounced for the sake of property which could only be secured by the restraints of regular Government. These ideas might appear to some new, but they were nevertheless just. If property then was the main object of Govt. certainly it ought to be one measure of the influence due to those who were to be affected by the Governmt. He looked forward also to that range of New States which wd. soon be formed in the west. He thought the rule of representation ought to be so fixed as to secure to the Atlantic States a prevalence in the National Councils. The new States will know less of the public interest than these, will have an interest in many respects different, in particular will be little scrupulous of involving the Community in wars the burdens & operations of which would fall chiefly on the maritime States. Provision ought therefore to be made to prevent the maritime States from being hereafter outvoted by them. He thought this might be easily done by irrevocably fixing the number of representatives which the Atlantic States should respectively have, and the number which each new State will have. This wd. not be unjust, as the western settlers wd. previously know the conditions on which they were to possess their lands. It would be politic as it would recommend the plan to the present as well as future interest of the States which must decide the fate of it.

Mr. Rutlidge. The gentleman last up had spoken some of his sentiments precisely. Property was certainly the principal object of Society. If numbers should be made the ⟨rule of representation, the Atlantic States will be subjected to the Western. He moved [x] that the first proposition in the report be postponed in order to take up the following viz. "that the suffrages of the several States be regulated and proportioned according to the sums to be paid towards the general revenue by the inhabitants of each State respectively; that an apportionment of suffrages, according to the ratio aforesaid shall be made and regulated at the end of   years from the 1st. meeting of the Legislature of the U. S. and at the end of every   years but that for the present, and until the period above mentioned, the suffrages shall be for N. Hampshire   Massachts.   &c — [13]

Col. Mason said the case of new States was not unnoticed in the Committee; but it was thought and he was himself decidedly of opinion that if they made a part of the Union, they ought to be subject to no unfavorable discriminations. Obvious considerations required it.

Mr. Radolph concurred with Col. Mason.

On question on Mr. Rutlidges motion.[x]

Masts. no. Cont. no. N. Y. no. N. J. no. Pa. no. Del. no. Maryd. no. Va. no. N. C. no. S. C. ay. Geo. not on floor [Ayes — 1; noes — 9; absent — 1.][14]

adjd.[15]

---

[13] Taken from *Journal*, Madison had originally recorded only the substance of the motion.   [14] Detail of Ayes and Noes, Vote 114, omits New Jersey.

[15] See further, Appendix A, LVI.

YATES

THURSDAY, JULY 5th, 1787.

Met pursuant to adjournment.

The report of the committee was read.

Mr. Gorham. I call for an explanation of the principles on which it is grounded.

Mr. Gerry, the chairman, explained the principles.

Mr. Martin. The one representation is proposed as an expedient for the adoption of the other.

Mr. Wilson. The committee has exceeded their powers.

Mr. Martin proposed to take the question on the whole of the report.

Mr. Wilson. I do not chuse to take a leap in the dark. I have a right to call for a division of the question on each distinct proposition.

Mr. Madison. I restrain myself from animadverting on the report, from the respect I bear to the members of the committee. But I must confess I see nothing of concession in it.

The originating money bills is no concession on the part of the smaller states, for if seven states in the second branch should want such a bill, their interest in the first branch will prevail to bring it forward — it is nothing more than a nominal privilege.

The second branch, small in number, and well connected, will ever prevail. The power of regulating trade, imposts, treaties, &c. are more essential to the community than raising money, and no provision is made for those in the report— We are driven to an unhappy dilemma. Two thirds of the inhabitants of the union are to please the remaining one third by sacrificing their essential rights.

When we satisfy the majority of the people in securing their rights, we have *nothing* to fear; in any other way, *every thing*. The smaller states, I hope will at last see their true and real interest. — And I hope that the warmth of the gentleman from Delaware will never induce him to yield to his own suggestion of seeking for foreign aid.

(At this period Messrs. YATES and LANSING left the convention,[16] and the remainder of the session was employed to
complete the constitution on the principles already adopted.
See the revised draft of the constitution and the constitution
of the United States, with all the ratified amendments as at
present existing, in the appendix.)

☞ The preceding Notes of the late Chief Justice YATES,
contained in two hundred and forty-five pages,* of two volumes,
were copied by me, literally, from the original manuscript
in his hand writing. — The several papers referred to did not
accompany his notes.[17]

JOHN LANSING. Jun.

* The number of pages in the manuscript.

K I N G

5. July 87.

Gr. Morris. On a question reported by a Grand Comee.
that in the popular Br. every 40,000 Inhabitants shd. be
entitled to send one Member — Observed that Numbers ought
not to be the rule — admit that they now are, yet when the
Western Country is settled it may not be so — We must take
care that we don't establish a Rule wh. will enable the poor
but numerous Inhabs. of the western Country to destroy the
Atlantic States — Men don't unite for liberty or Life, they
possess both in the savage state in the highest perfection they
unite for the _protection of property_

Govr. Rutledge — I agree with Mr. Morris Property is the
object of Society, I propose that the representation shd. be

---

[16] New York's vote continued to be recorded, however, through July 10.

On Yates and Lansing leaving the Convention, and on their general attitude,
see Appendix A, CLVIII (27), CLXVII, CLXXXV, CCXVII, CCLXIX, CCCX,
CCCXXXIX, CCCLXXVII, CCCLXXXVIII, CCCXCI, CCXCII, CCCXCVII.

[17] The various documents printed in the appendix to Yates were evidently copied
from the _Journal_ (1819).

in proportion to the Taxes paid in a given District — I wish the property to be represented — I do not think numbers are a proper Index of Wealth now, it will be much less so hereafter —

Randolph[18]

PATERSON

Maddison.

The Interest of the smaller States to come into the Measure — Delaware — foreign Power — New-Jersey.   Single and unconnected.

Butler.

The People will not agree to it.

G. Morris.

Suppose the larger States agree — the smaller States must come in.

Jersey would follow the Opinions of New York and Pennsylva.

The Sword must decide —

The strongest Party will make the weaker Traitors and hang them — foreign Power.

Should be open to Conviction —

— The larger States must prevail — they must decide; they are most powerful.

Not Members of a Synod, or Conventicle —

---

[18] [Endorsed:] July 5 | Gov. Mor. M Rutledge | not Numbers but Property the | Principle of Repn.

FRIDAY, JULY 6, 1787.

JOURNAL
Friday July 6. 1787.

It was moved and seconded to refer the first clause of the first proposition reported from the grand Committee to a special Committee

which passed in the affirmative [Ayes — 7; noes — 3; divided — 1.]

It was moved and seconded that the Committee consist of five members.

which was unanimously agreed to — and a Committee was appointed by ballot of

Mr G. Morris, Mr Gorham Mr Randolph, Mr Rutledge, and Mr King.

It was moved and seconded to postpone the remainder of the first proposition in order to take up the second.

which passed in the affirmative [Ayes — 8; noes — 3.]

It was moved and seconded to postpone the consideration of the second proposition

which passed in the affirmative [Ayes — 6; noes — 3; divided — 2.]

It was moved and seconded to resume the consideration of the second clause of the first proposition, which had been postponed in order to take up the second proposition

which passed in the affirmative

On the question shall the following clause stand as part of the report, namely.

3 "That all Bills for raising or appropriating money, and "for fixing the salaries of the Officers of the Government of "the United States, shall originate in the first branch of the "Legislature, and shall not be altered or amended by the second "Branch — and that no money shall be drawn from the Public

"Treasury but in pursuance of appropriations to be originated "by the first Branch."

it passed in the affirmative [Ayes — 5; noes — 3; divided — 3.][1]

and then the House adjourned till to-morrow at 11 o'Clock

DETAIL OF AYES AND NOES

	New Hampshire	Massachusetts	Rhode Island	Connecticut	New York	New Jersey	Pennsylvania	Delaware	Maryland	Virginia	North Carolina	South Carolina	Georgia	Questions	Ayes	Noes	Divided
[115]	aye		aye	no	no	aye	no	dd	aye	aye	aye	aye		To commit the 1st clause of the propositions reported from the grand Committee.	7	3	1
[116]	no		no	aye	aye	aye	aye	aye	aye	no	aye	aye		To postpone the remainder of the first to take up the second proposn	8	3	
[117]	dd		aye	dd	aye	no	aye	aye	aye	no	no	aye		To postpone the consideration of the second Proposition reported from the grand Committee	6	3	2
[118]	dd		aye	dd	aye	no	aye	aye	no	aye	no	dd		To agree to the second clause of the first proposition reported from the grand Committee	5	3	
[119]	aye		aye	no	aye	aye	aye	aye	no	aye	aye	aye		Whether the last vote was determined in the affirmative	9	2	

[1] Vote 118, Detail of Ayes and Noes.

The printed *Journal* (p. 161) inserted after this a question and vote from Detail of Ayes and Noes (Vote 119), "whether the vote so standing was determined in the affirmative" — Ayes, 9; noes, 2. There is nothing in the Detail of Ayes and Noes to indicate that this vote belongs here rather than on July 7. Madison originally recorded it on the latter date and he was probably right. See below note 5, and July 7, note 4.

MADISON

Friday July 6th. in Convention

Mr. Govr. Morris moved to commit so much of the Report as relates to "1 member for every 40,000 inhabitants" His view was that they might absolutely fix the number for each State in the first instance; leaving the Legislature at liberty to provide for changes in the relative importance of the States, and for the case of new States.[2]

Mr. Wilson 2ded. the motion; but with a view of leaving the Committee under no implied shackles.

Mr. Ghorum apprehended great inconveniency from fixing directly the number of Representatives to be allowed to each State. He thought the number of Inhabitants the true guide; tho' perhaps some departure might be expedient from the full proportion. The States also would vary in their relative extent, by separations of parts of the largest States. A part of Virga. is now on the point of a separation. In the province of Mayne a Convention is at this time deliberating on a separation from Masts. In such events, the number of representatives ought certainly to be reduced. He hoped to see all the States made small by proper divisions, instead of their becoming formidable as was apprehended, to the Small States. He conceived that let the Genl. Government be modified as it might, there would be a constant tendency in the State Governmts. to encroach upon it: it was of importance therefore that the extent of the States shd. be reduced as much & as fast as possible. The stronger the Govt. shall be made in the first instance the more easily will these divisions be effected; as it will be of less consequence in the opinion of the States whether they be of great or small extent.

Mr. Gerry did not think with his Colleague that the large States ought to be cut up. This policy has been inculcated by the middling and smaller States, ungenerously & contrary to the spirit of the Confederation. Ambitious men will be

---

[2] See Appendix A, CLXXXI.

apt to solicit needless divisions, till the States be reduced to the size of Counties. If this policy should still actuate the small States, the large ones cou'd not confederate safely with them; but would be obliged to consult their safety by confederating only with one another. He favored the Commitment and thought that Representation ought to be in the Combined ratio of numbers of Inhabitants and of wealth, and not of either singly.

Mr. King wished the clause to be committed chiefly in order to detach it from the Report with which it had no connection. He thought also that the Ratio of Representation proposed could not be safely fixed, since in a century & a half our computed increase of population would carry the number of representatives to an enormous excess; that ye. number of inhabitants was not the proper index of ability & wealth; that property was the primary object of Society; and that in fixing a ratio this ought not to be excluded from the estimate. With regard to New States, he observed that there was something peculiar in the business which had not been noticed. The U. S. were now admitted to be proprietors of the Country, N. West of the Ohio. Congs. by one of their ordinances have impoliticly laid it out into ten States, and have made it a fundamental article of compact with those who may become settlers, that as soon as the number in any one State shall equal that of the smallest of the 13 original States, it may claim admission into the Union. Delaware does not contain it is computed more than 35,000 souls, and for obvious reasons will not increase much for a considerable time. It is possible then that if this plan be persisted in by Congs. 10 new votes may be added, without a greater addition of inhabitants than are represented by the single vote of Pena. The plan as it respects one of the new States is already irrevocable, the sale of the lands having commenced, and the purchasers & settlers will immediately become entitled to all the privileges of the compact.

Mr. Butler agreed to the Commitment if the Committee were to be left at liberty. He was persuaded that the more the subject was examined, the less it would appear that the number of inhabitants would be a proper rule of proportion. If there were no other objection the changeableness of the standard would be sufficient. He concurred with those who thought some balance was necessary between the old & New States. He contended strenuously that property was the only just measure of representation. This was the great object of Governt: the great cause of war, the great means of carrying it on.

Mr. Pinkney saw no good reason for committing. The value of land had been found on full investigation to be an impracticable rule. The contributions of revenue including imports & exports, must be too changeable in their amount; too difficult to be adjusted; and too injurious to the non-commercial States. The number of inhabitants appeared to. him the only just & practicable rule. He thought the blacks ought to stand on an equality with whites: But wd. — agree to the ratio settled by Congs. He contended that Congs. had no right under the articles of Confederation to authorize the admission of new States; no such case having been provided for.

Mr. Davy, was for committing the clause in order to get at the merits of the question arising on the Report. He seemed to think that wealth or property ought to be represented in the 2d. branch; and numbers in the 1st. branch.

On the motion for committing as made by Mr. Govr. Morris.

Masts. ay — Cont. ay. N. Y. no. N. J. no. Pa ay. Del. no. Md. divd. Va. ay. N. C. ay. S. C. ay. Geo. ay. [Ayes — 7; noes — 3; divided — 1.]

The members appd. by Ballot were Mr. Govr. Morris, ⟨Mr. Gorham.⟩[3] Mr. Randolph. Mr. Rutlidge. Mr. King.

Mr. Wilson signified that his view in agreeing to the Commitmt. was that the Come might consider the propriety of adopting a scale similar to that established by the Constitution of Masts. which wd give an advantage to ye. small States without substantially departing from a rule of proportion.

Mr. Wilson & Mr. Mason moved to postpone the clause

---

[3] Madison originally recorded "Mr. Ghorum" before Morris, but later revised it as given here, *i. e.*, in accordance with *Journal*.

relating to money bills in order to take up the clause relating to an equality of votes in the second branch.

On the question Masts. no. Cont. no. N. Y. ay. N. J. ay. Pa. ay. Del. ay. Md. ay. Va. ay. N. C no. S. C. ay. Geo. ay. [Ayes — 8; noes — 3.]

The clause relating to equality of votes being under consideration,

Docr. Franklin observed that this question could not be properly put by itself, the Committee having reported several propositions as mutual conditions of each other. He could not vote for it if separately taken, but should vote for the whole together.

Col. Mason perceived the difficulty & suggested a reference of the rest of the Report to ye Committee just appointed, that the whole might be brought into one view.

Mr. Randolph disliked ye. reference to that Committee, as it consisted of members from States opposed to the wishes of the smaller States, and could not therefore be acceptable to the latter.

Mr. Martin & Mr. Jenifer moved to postpone the clause till the Come. last appointed should report.

Mr. M⟨adison⟩ observed that if the uncommitted part of the Report was connected with the part just committed, it ought also, to be committed; if not connected, it need not be postponed till report should be made.

On the question ⟨for postponing moved by Mr. Martin & Mr. Jennifer

    Cont. N. J. Del. Md. Va. Geo., ay.

    Pa. N. C. S. C. . . . . no

    Mas. N. Y. . . . . divided⟩[4]

The 1st. clause relating to the originating of money bills was then resumed.

Mr. Governr. Morris was opposed to a restriction of this right in either branch, considered merely in itself and as unconnected with the point of representation in the 2d. branch. It will disable the 2d. branch from proposing its own money

---

[4] Taken from *Journal.*

plans, and giving the people an opportunity of judging by comparison of the merits of those proposed by the 1st. branch.

Mr. Wilson could see nothing like a concession here on the part of the smaller States. If both branches were to say yes or no, it was of little consequence which should say yes or no first, which last. If either was indiscriminately to have the right of originating, the reverse of the Report. would he thought be most proper; since it was a maxim that the least numerous body was the fittest for deliberation; the most numerous for decision. He observed that this discrimination had been transcribed from the British into several American constitutions. But he was persuaded that on examination of the American experiment, it would be found to be a trifle light as air. Nor could he ever discover the advantage of it in the parliamentary history of G. Britain. He hoped if there was any advantage in the privilege, that it would be pointed out.

Mr. Williamson thought that if the privilege were not common to both branches it ought rather to be confined to the 2d. as the bills in that case would be more narrowly watched, than if they originated with the branch having most of the popular confidence.

Mr. Mason. The consideration which weighed with the Committee was that the 1st. branch would be the immediate representatives of the people, the 2d. would not. Should the latter have the power of giving away the peoples money, they might soon forget the Source from whence they received it. We might soon have an aristocracy. He had been much concerned at the principles which had been advanced by some gentlemen, but had the satisfaction to find they did not generally prevail. He was a friend to proportional representation in both branches; but supposed that some points must be yielded for the sake of accomodation.

Mr. Wilson. If he had proposed that the 2d. branch should have an independent disposal of public money, the observations of (Col. Mason) would have been a satisfactory answer. But nothing could be farther from what he had said. His question was how is the power of the 1st. branch increased or that of the 2d. diminished by giving the proposed privilege to the former? Where is the difference, in which branch it begins if both must concur, in the end?

Mr. Gerry would not say that the concession was a sufficient one on the part of the small States. But he could not but regard it in the light of a concession. It wd. make it a constitutional principle that the 2d. branch were not possessed of the Confidence of the people in money matters, which wd. lessen their weight & influence. In the next place if the 2d. branch were dispossessed of the privilege, they wd. be deprived of the opportunity which their continuance in office 3 times as long as the 1st. branch would give them of make'g three successive essays in favor of a particular point.

Mr. Pinkney thought it evident that the Concession was wholly on one side, ⟨that of the large States, the privilege of originating money bills being of no account.⟩

Mr. Govr. Morris had waited to hear the good effects of the restriction. As to the alarm sounded, of an aristocracy, his creed was that there never was, nor ever will be a civilized Society without an Aristocracy. His endeavor was to keep it as much as possible from doing mischief. The restriction if it has any real operation will deprive us of the services of the 2d. branch in digesting and proposing money bills of which it will be more capable than the 1st. branch, It will take away the responsibility of the 2d branch, the great security for good behavior. It will always leave a plea as to an obnoxious money bill that it was disliked, but could not be constitutionally amended; nor safely rejected. It will be a dangerous source of disputes between the two Houses. We should either take the British Constitution altogether or make one for ourselves. The Executive there has dissolved two Houses as the only cure for such disputes. Will our Executive be able to apply such a remedy? Every law directly or indirectly takes money out of the pockets of the people. Again what use may be made of such a privilege in case of great emergency? Suppose an enemy at the door, and money instantly & absolutely necessary for repelling him, may not the popular branch avail itself of this duress, to extort concessions from the Senate destructive of the Constitution itself. He illustrated this danger by the example of the Long Parliament's expedts. for subverting the H. of Lords: concluding on the whole that the restriction would be either useless or pernicious.

Docr. Franklin did not mean to go into a justification of the Report; but as it had been asked what would be the use of restraining the 2d. branch from medling with money bills, he could not but remark that it was always of importance that the people should know who had disposed of their money, & how it had been disposed of. It was a maxim that those who feel, can best judge. This end would, he thought, be best attained, if money affairs were to be confined to the immediate representatives of the people. This was his inducement to concur in the report. As to the danger or difficulty that might arise from a negative in the 2d. where the people wd. not be proportionally represented, it might easily be got over by declaring that there should be no such Negative: or if that will not do, by declaring that there shall be no such branch at all.

Mr. Martin said that it was understood in the Committee that the difficulties and disputes which had been apprehended, should be guarded agst. in the detailing of the plan.

Mr. Wilson. The difficulties & disputes will increase with the attempts to define & obviate them. Queen Anne was obliged to dissolve her Parliamt. in order to terminate one of these obstinate disputes between the two Houses. Had it not been for the mediation of the Crown, no one can say what the result would have been. The point is still sub judice in England. He approved of the principles laid down by the Honble President ⟨(Docr. Franklin)⟩ his Colleague, as to the expediency of keeping the people informed of their money affairs. But thought they would know as much, and be as well satisfied, in one way as in the other.

Genl. Pinkney was astonished that this point should have been considered as a concession. He remarked that the restriction to money bills had been rejected on the merits singly considered, by 8 States agst. 3. and that the very States which now called it a concession, were then agst. it as nugatory or improper in itself.

On the question whether the clause ⟨relating to money bills⟩ in the Report of the Come. consisting of a member from each State, shd. stand as part of the Report —

Massts. dividd. Cont. ay. N. Y. divd. N. J. ay. Pa. no. Del. ay. Md. ay. Va. no. N. C. ay. S. C. no. Geo. divd. [Ayes—5; noes — 3; divided — 3.]

A question was then raised whether the question was carried in the affirmative: there being but 5 ays out of 11 States present. The words of the rule are" (see May 28)

⟨On the question: Mas. Cont. N. J. Pa. Del. Md. N. C.

S. C. Geo. . . . . ay

N. Y. Va. . . . . no⟩[5]

(In several preceding instances like votes had sub silentio been entered as decided in the affirmative.)

Adjourned

---

[5] Vote taken from *Journal*, which is probably mistaken in assigning the vote to this day's records. See above note 1, and July 7, note. 4.

SATURDAY, JULY 7, 1787.

JOURNAL
Saturday July 7. 1787.

A letter from W. Rawle, Secretary to the Library company of Philadelphia, addressed to His Excellency the President of the Convention, enclosing a resolve of that company granting the use of their books to the Members of the Convention, being read.[1]

On motion

Resolved that the Secretary, by letter, present the thanks of the Convention to the Directors of the Library Company for their polite attention.

[Whether the last vote was determined in the affirmative

Ayes — 9; noes — 2.][2]

It was moved and seconded that the second proposition

---

[1] Sir.

I have the honor to transmit to you as President of the Convention, a resolve of the directors of the Library Company in this City.

I am Sir with perfect respect

your most humble servant

W: RAWLE.

Third Street

6th July 1787.

[Endorsed:] Wm. Rawle July 6. 1787. with a resolve of the Library Company of Philadelphia. ———

At a meeting of the directors of the Library company of Philadelphia on Thursday the 5th July 1787

Resolved That the librarian furnish the gentlemen who compose the Convention now sitting with such books as they may desire during their continuance at Philadelphia, taking receipts for same.

By order of the directors,

W: RAWLE *Secretary.*

[2] Vote 119, Detail of Ayes and Noes. This refers to the last vote of July 6 and probably belongs here. See July 6, note 1, note 5, and below note 4.

reported from the grand Committee stand part of the report namely

"That in the second Branch of the Legislature each State shall have an equal vote"

which passed in the affirmative [Ayes — 6; noes — 3; divided — 2.][3]

It was then moved and seconded to postpone the consideration of the report from the grand Committee until the special Committee report.

which passed in the affirmative [Ayes — 6; noes — 5.]

And then the House adjourned till Monday next at 11 o'Clock A. M.

DETAIL OF AYES AND NOES

	New Hampshire	Massachusetts	Rhode Island	Connecticut	New York	New Jersey	Pennsylvania	Delaware	Maryland	Virginia	North Carolina	South Carolina	Georgia	Questions	Ayes	Noes	Divided
[119]	aye	aye		no	aye	aye	aye	aye	no	aye	aye	aye		Whether the last vote was determined in the affirmative	9	2	
[120]	dd			aye	aye	aye	no	aye	aye	no	aye	no	dd	whether the second proposition reported from the grand Committee shall stand part of the report.	6	3	2
[121]	aye	aye		no	aye	aye	aye	aye	no	no	no	no		To postpone the consideration of the report from the grand Comme until the special Comme report	6	5	

MADISON

Saturday, July 7. in Convention [4]

"Shall the clause allowing each State one vote in the 2d. branch. stand as part of the Report"? ⟨being taken up —⟩

---

[3] Vote 120, Detail of Ayes and Noes; see July 5, note 1.

[4] Madison originally had recorded at the beginning of this day's notes:

"On the question whether the question depending yesterday at the time of ad-

Mr. Gerry. This is the critical question. He had rather agree to it than have no accomodation. A Governt. short of a proper national plan if generally acceptable, would be preferable to a proper one which if it could be carried at all, would operate on discontented States. He thought it would be best to suspend the question till the Comme. yesterday appointed, should make report.

Mr. Sherman Supposed that it was the wish of every one that some Genl. Govt. should be established. An equal vote in the 2d. branch would, he thought, be most likely to give it the necessary vigor. The small States have more vigor in their Govts. than the large ones, the more influence therefore the large ones have, the weaker will be the Govt. In the large States it will be most difficult to collect the real & fair sense of the people. Fallacy & undue influence will be practiced with most success: and improper men will most easily get into office. If they vote by States in the 2d. branch, and each State has an equal vote, there must be always a majority of States as well as a majority of the people on the side of public measures, & the Govt. will have decision and efficacy. If this be not the case in the 2d. branch there may be a majority of the States agst. public measures, and the difficulty of compelling them to abide by the public determination, will render the Government feebler than it has ever yet been.

Mr. Wilson was not deficient in a conciliating temper, but firmness was sometimes a duty of higher obligation. Conciliation was also misapplied in this instance. It was pursued here rather among the Representatives, than among the Constituents; and it wd. be of little consequence, if not established among the latter; and there could be little hope of its being established among them if the foundation should not be laid in justice and right.

On Question shall the words stand as part of the Report?

---

journment shd. be entered in the affirmative, Masts. ay. Cont. ay. N. Y. no. N. J. ay. Pa. ay. Del. ay. Md. ay. Va. no. N. C. ay. S. C. ay. Geo. ay." [Ayes, 9; noes, 2.]

Journal recorded this question and vote under July 6. Accordingly Madison inserted this vote in his records of July 6 and struck out the above note. Madison's original record was probably correct. See July 6, note 1, and note 5.

Massts. divd. Cont. ay. N. Y. ay. N. J. ay. Pa. no. Del. ay. Md. ay. Va. no. N. C. ay. S. C. no. Geo. divd. [Ayes — 6; noes — 3: divided — 2.]

(Note. several votes were given here in the affirmative or were divd. because another final question was to be taken on the whole report.)

Mr. Gerry thought it would be proper to proceed to enumerate & define the powers to be vested in the Genl. Govt. before a question on the report should be taken as to the rule of representation in the 2d. branch.

Mr. ⟨Madison,⟩ observed that it wd. be impossible to say what powers could be safely & properly vested in the Govt. before it was known, in what manner the States were to be represented in it. He was apprehensive that if a just representation were not the basis of the Govt. it would happen, as it did when the articles of Confederation were depending, that every effectual prerogative would be withdrawn or withheld, and the New Govt. wd. be rendered as impotent and as short lived as the old.

Mr. Patterson would not decide whether the privilege concerning money bills were a valuable consideration[5] or not: But he considered the mode & rule of representation in the 1st. branch as fully so, and that after the establishment of that point, the small States would never be able to defend themselves without an equality of votes in the 2d. branch. There was no other ground of accommodation. His resolution was fixt. He would meet the large States on that Ground and no other. For himself he should vote agst. the Report, because it yielded too much.

Mr. Govr. Morris. He had no resolution unalterably fixed except to do what should finally appear to him right. He was agst. the Report because it maintained the improper Constitution of the 2d. branch. It made it another Congress, a mere whisp of straw. It had been sd. (by Mr. Gerry) that the new Governt. would be partly national, partly federal; that it ought in the first quality to protect individuals; in

---

[5] Crossed out "concession".

the second, the States.   But in what quality was it to protect the aggregate interest of the whole.   Among the many provisions which had been urged, he had seen none for supporting the dignity and splendor of the American Empire.   It had been one of our greatest misfortunes that the great objects of the nation had been sacrificed constantly to local views; in like manner as the general interests of States had been sacrificed to those of the Counties.   What is to be the check in the Senate? none; unless it be to keep the majority of the people from injuring particular States.   But particular States ought to be injured for the sake of a majority of the people, in case their conduct should deserve it.   Suppose they should insist on claims evidently unjust, and pursue them in a manner detrimental to the whole body.   Suppose they should give themselves up to foreign influence.   Ought they to be protected in such cases.   They were originally nothing more than colonial corporations.   On the declaration of Independence, a Governnt. was to be formed.   The small States aware of the necessity of preventing anarchy, and taking advantage of the moment, extorted from the large ones an equality of votes. Standing now on that ground, they demand under the new system greater rights as men, than their fellow Citizens of the large States.   The proper answer to them is that the same necessity of which they formerly took advantage does not now exist, and that the large States are at liberty now to consider what is right, rather than what may be expedient We must have an efficient Govt. and if there be an efficiency in the local Govts. the former is impossible.   Germany alone proves it.   Notwithstanding their common diet, notwithstanding the great prerogatives of the Emperor as head of the Empire, and his vast resources as sovereign of his particular dominions, no union is maintained: foreign influence disturbs every internal operation, & there is no energy whatever in the general Governmt.   Whence does this proceed? From the energy of the local authorities; from its being considered of more consequence to support the Prince of Hesse, than the Happiness of the people of Germany.   Do Gentlemen wish this to be ye case here.   Good God, Sir, is it possible they can so delude themselves. What if all the Charters & Constitutions of the States were thrown into the fire, and all their demagogues into the ocean. What would it be to the happiness of America. And will not this be the case here if we pursue the train in wch. the business lies. We shall establish an Aulic Council without an Emperor to execute its decrees. The same circumstances which unite the people here, unite them in Germany. They have there a common language, a common law, common usages and manners — and a common interest in being united; yet their local jurisdictions destroy every tie. The case was the same in the Grecian States. The United Netherlands are at this time torr. in factions. With these examples before our eyes shall we fcrm establishments which must necessarily produce the same effects. It is of no consequence from what districts the 2d. branch shall be drawn, if it be so constituted as to yield an asylum agst. these evils. As it is now constituted he must be agst. its being drawn from the States in equal portions. But shall he was ready to join in devising such an amendment of the plan, as will be most likely to secure our liberty & happiness.

Mr. Sherman & Mr. Elseworth moved to postpone the Question ⟨on the Report from the Committee of a member from each State, in order to wait for the Report from the come. of 5 last appointed.⟩[6] —

Masts. ay. Cont. ay. N. Y. no. N. J. ay Pa. ay. Del. ay. Maryland ay Va. no. N. C. no. S. C—no. Geo. no. [Ayes — 6; noes — 5.]

Adjd.[7]

KING

Saturday 7. July —

Question shall the States have an equal vote in the 2d Br. or Senate —

Gerry — I am in favor of the measure provided that the 1st

Br. shall originate money Bills & appropriate Monies — we must consult the prejudices & Interest of the States — 2 or 3 thousd. Men are in Office in the several States — their Influence will be in favor of the Equality of Votes among the States.

Wilson —

Madison An Equality of votes in ye. Senate will enable _a minority_ to hold the Majority — they will compel the majority to submit to their particular Interest or they will withhold their Assent to essential & necessary measures — I have known one man where his State was represented by only two & were divided oppose Six States in Cong. on an import. occasion for 3 days, and finally compelled ym. to gratify his Caprice in order to obtain his suffrage — the Senate will possess certain exclusive powers, such as the appointment to Offices &c — If the States have equal votes — a minority of the people or an Aristocracy will appt. the Gt. Officers. Besides ye. small States will be near the Seat of Govt. a Quorum of the first Br. may be easily assembled they may carry a measure in yt. Br. agt. the sense of the Majority if present, & the Senate may confirm it — Virgin. has objected to every addition of powers to those of Congress, because they made but $\frac{1}{13}$ of the Legislature when they ought to have $\frac{1}{6}$ —

Patterson — I hope the Question will be taken. If we do not agree that the Senate be composed of Delegates from the several States, each state having an equal Vote, the smaller States agreeing that Money Bills & money appropriations shall originate in the first Br. to be composed on the principles of a Repn. of the People — If we cannot agree in this, the small states will never agree on any other Terms — we had better divide & lose no longer Time —

I think I shall vote agt. the Report because I think the exclusive origination of money Bills & ye appropn of Money being vested in the 1. Br. is giving up too much on ye part of the small States

Gov Morris — Let us examine what the small States call the

consideration wh. they give for the privilege of an equal Vote in the 2. Br. or Senate — How did it happen originally that the Votes were equal—when G. Britain pressed us, the small states said go on in your opposition without us, or give us an equal Vote — they obtained it — they now say there is a sacred Compact — But we are proposing new & farther powers — the Gt. states may now say the present Confed. is defective our Convention proves it — we will not now agree to strengthen the Union unless you let us in in proportion our Interest —

Unless we can form a vigourous general Govt. we must expect vigourous State Govts: & a weak general Govt. Although Germany has an Emperor & a powerful one a common language, Religion, Customs, Interest, and Habits, yet the Glory of her princes, and of free Cities are preferred to that of a peaceful & powerful whole and the Imperial Honors are less regarded than those of the subordinate princes. · In this plan we shall have an aulic Council without An Emperor to execute their Decrees.[8]

PATERSON

Gerry.

About 2,000 Men in the smaller States, who compose the Executives, Legislatives, and Judiciaries; all interested in opposing the present Plan, because it tends to annihilate the State-Governments.

Sherman —

If a Majority of the lesser states be agt. the Laws of the national Governmt.; those Laws cannot be executed — There must then be a Branch immediately from the States.

Wilson —

An Agreemt. elsewhere cannot be expected unless the Representation be fair —

Madison.

1. The Upper Branch may put a Veto upon the Acts of the lower Branch.

---

[8] [Endorsed:] 7 July | States equal in the Senate | Gerry — aye | Madison no | G Morris no | Patterson aye

2. May extort a Concurrence. The smaller States near the Centre; they may compose a Majority of the Quorum.

Gerry —

The larger States will have more Influence; they have in Congress; this from the Nature of Things.

G. Morris —

Great Care will be taken to lessen the Powers of the 2d. Branch —

Corporations to be protected.

Separate colonial Existances —

Corporations — The small States — go on and fight out the Revn. or give us an equal Vote.

The small States say, that they will have greater Rights as Citizens —

Must have such a Govt. as will give Safety —

State-Policy not a proper Object for a vigorous Governmt.

In Proportion to the Vigour and Strength of the State Governmts. will be the Febleness of the general Governmt. —

We must have it in View eventually to lessen and destroy the State Limits and Authorities —

The Germanick Constn. — The Emperor has never been able to collect them — the separate Parts were too independant —

JOURNAL

Monday July 9. 1787.

The honorable Daniel Carrol Esquire One of the Deputies from the State of Maryland attended and took his seat.

The honorable Mr G. Morris, from the Committee to whom was referred the first clause of the first proposition reported from the grand Committee, informed the House that the Committee were prepared to report — He then read the report in his place, and the same being delivered in at the Secretary's table was read once throughout, and then by paragraphs — and is as follows, namely.

The Committee to whom was referred the first clause of the first proposition reported from the grand Committee beg leave to report

That in the first meeting of the Legislature of the United States the first branch thereof consist of fifty six Members, of which number

New Hampshire shall have ....Two.
Massachusetts ....Seven
Rhode Island ....One
Connecticut ....Four
New-York ....Five
New-Jersey ....Three
Pennsylvania ....Eight
Delaware ....One
Maryland ....Four
Virginia ....Nine
North Carolina ....Five
South Carolina ....Five
Georgia ....Two.

2 But as the present situation of the States may probably alter

as well in point of wealth as in the number of their inhabitants
that the Legislature be authorised from time to time to augment the number of representatives: and in case any of the
States shall hereafter be divided, or any two or more States
united, or any new State created within the limits of the United
States the Legislature shall possess authority to regulate the
number of representatives in any of the foregoing cases upon
the principles of their wealth and number of inhabitants.

It was moved and seconded to postpone the consideration of
the first paragraph of the report in order to take up the second.

which passed in the affirmative

On the question to agree to the second paragraph of the report

it passed in the affirmative   [Ayes — 9; noes — 2.]

It was moved and seconded to refer the first paragraph of the
report to a Committee of One member from each State,

which passed in the affirmative [Ayes — 9; noes — 2.]

and a Committee was appointed by ballot of.

The honorable Mr King, Mr Sherman, Mr Yates, Mr Brearely,
Mr G. Morris, Mr Read, Mr Carrol, Mr Madison, Mr Williamson,
Mr Rutledge, and Mr Houston.

and then the House adjourned until to-morrow at 11
o'clock A. M.

DETAIL OF AYES AND NOES

New Hampshire	Massachusetts	Rhode Island	Connecticut	New York	New Jersey	Pennsylvania	Delaware	Maryland	Virginia	North Carolina	South Carolina	Georgia	Questions	Ayes	Noes	Divided
[122] aye	aye		no	no	aye	aye	aye	aye	aye	aye	aye	aye	To agree to the second clause of the report of the Committee to whom was referred the first clause of ye 1st propo: reported from ye gr: Committee	9	2	
[123] aye	aye		no	aye	aye	aye	aye	aye	aye	aye	no	aye	To refer the first paragraph of the report to a Committee of One Member from each State.	9	2	

MADISON

Monday July 9th. in Convention

⟨Mr. Daniel Carroll from Maryland took his Seat.⟩[1]

Mr. Govr. Morris ⟨delivered a⟩ report from the Come. of 5 members to whom was committed the clause in the Report of the Come. consisting of a member from each State, stating the proper ratio of Representatives in the 1st. branch, to be as 1 to every 40,000 inhabitants, as follows viz

" The Committee to whom was referred the 1st. clause of the 1st. proposition reported from the grand Committee, beg leave to report I.¶ that in the 1st. meeting of the Legislature the 1st. branch thereof consist of 56. members of which Number N. Hamshire shall have 2. Massts. 7. R.Id.1. Cont. 4. N. Y. 5. N. J. 3. Pa. 8. Del. 1. Md. 4. Va. 9. N. C. 5, S. C. 5. Geo. 2. II¶ —. But as the present situation of the States may probably alter as well in point of wealth as in the number of their inhabitants, that the Legislature be authorized from time to time to augment ye. number of Representatives. And in case any of the States shall hereafter be divided, or any two or more States united, or any new States created within the limits of the United States, the Legislature shall possess authority to regulate the number of Representatives in any of the foregoing cases, upon the principles of their wealth and number of inhabitants."

Mr. Sherman wished to know on what principles or calculations the Report was founded. It did not appear to correspond with any rule of numbers, or of any requisition hitherto adopted by Congs.

Mr. Gorham. Some provision of this sort was necessary in the outset. The number of blacks & whites with some regard to supposed wealth was the general guide Fractions could not be observed. The Legislre. is to make alterations from time to time as justice & propriety may require, Two objections prevailed agst. the rate of 1 member for every

---

[1] Taken from *Journal.*

40,000. inhts. The 1st. was that the Representation would soon be too numerous: the 2d. that the Westn. States who may have a different interest, might if admitted on that principal by degrees, out-vote the Atlantic. Both these objections are removed. The number will be small in the first instance and may be continued so, and the Atlantic States having ye. Govt. in their own hands, may take care of their own interest, by dealing out the right of Representation in safe proportions to the Western States. These were the views of the Committee.

Mr. L Martin wished to know whether the Come. were guided in the ratio, by the wealth or number of inhabitants of the States, or by both; noting its variations from former apportionments by Congs.

Mr. Govr. Morris & Mr. Rutlidge moved to postpone the 1st. paragraph relating to the number of members to be allowed each State in the first instance, and to take up the 2d. paragraph authorizing the Legislre to alter the number from time to time according to wealth & inhabitants.[2] The motion was agreed to nem. con.

On Question on the 2d. paragh. taken without any debate

Masts. ay. Cont. ay. N. Y. no. N. J. no. Pa. ay. Del. ay. Md. ay. Va. ay. N. C. ay. S. C. ay. Geo. ay. [Ayes — 9; noes — 2.]

Mr. Sherman moved to refer the 1st. part apportioning the Representatives to a Comme. of a member from each State.

Mr. Govr. Morris seconded the motion; observing that this was the only case in which such Committees were useful.

Mr. Williamson. thought it would be necessary to return to the rule of numbers. but that the Western States stood on different footing. If their property shall be rated as high as that of the Atlantic States, then their representation ought to hold a like proportion. Otherwise if their property was not to be equally rated.

Mr Govr. Morris. The Report is little more than a guess. Wealth was not altogether disregarded by the Come.[2] Where

---

[2] See Appendix A, CCCLXXIX.

it was apparently in favor of one State whose nos. were superior to the numbers of another, by a fraction only, a member extraordinary was allowed to the former: and so vice versa. The Committee meant little more than to bring the matter to a point for the consideration of the House.

Mr. Reed asked why Georgia was allowed 2 members, when her number of inhabitants had stood below that of Delaware.

Mr. Govr. Morris.   Such is the rapidity of the population of that State, that before the plan takes effect, it will probably be entitled to 2 Representatives

Mr. Randolph disliked the report of the Come. but had been unwilling to object to it.   He was apprehensive that as the number was not to be changed till the Natl. Legislature should please, a pretext would never be wanting to postpone alterations, and keep the power in the hands of those possessed of it. He was in favor of the commitmt. to a member from each State

Mr. Patterson considered the proposed estimate for the future according to the Combined rule of numbers and wealth, as too vague.   For this reason N. Jersey was agst. it.   He could regard negroes slaves in no light but as property.   They are no free agents, have no personal liberty, no faculty of acquiring property, but on the contrary are themselves property, & like other property entirely at the will of the Master. Has a man in Virga. a number of votes in proportion to the number of his slaves? and if Negroes are not represented in the States to which they belong, why should they be represented in the Genl. Govt.   What is the true principle of Representation?   It is an expedient by which an assembly of certain individls. chosen by the people is substituted in place of the inconvenient meeting of the people themselves.   If such a meeting of the people was actually to take place, would the slaves vote? they would not.   Why then shd. they be represented.   He was also agst. such an indirect encouragemt. of the slave trade; observing that Congs. in their act relating to the change of the 8 art: of Confedn. had been ashamed to use the term "Slaves" & had substituted a description.[3]

---

[3] For further discussion of question here raised, see debates July 11–13, and note 5, July 11.

Mr. ⟨Madison,⟩ reminded Mr. Patterson that his doctrine of Representation which was in its principle the genuine one, must for ever silence the pretensions of the small States to an equality of votes with the large ones. They ought to vote in the same proportion in which their citizens would do, if the people of all the States were collectively met. He suggested as a proper ground of compromise, that in the first branch the States should be represented according to their number of free inhabitants; And in the 2d. which had for one of its primary objects the guardianship of property, according to the whole number, including slaves.

Mr. Butler urged warmly the justice & necessity of regarding wealth in the apportionment of Representation.

Mr. King had always expected that as the Southern States are the richest, they would not league themselves with the Northn. unless some respect were paid to their superior wealth. If the latter expect those preferential distinctions in Commerce & other advantages which they will derive from the connection they must not expect to receive them without allowing some advantages in return. Eleven out of 13 of the States had agreed to consider Slaves in the apportionment of taxation; and taxation and Representation ought to go together.

On the question for committing the first paragraph of the Report to a member from each State.
Masts. ay. Cont. ay. N. Y. no. N. J. ay. Pa. ay. Del. ay. Md ay. Va. ay. N. C. ay. S. C. no. Geo. ay.   [Ayes — 9; noes — 2.]

The Come. appointed were.   Mr King. Mr. Sherman, Mr. Yates, Mr. Brearly, Mr. Govr. Morris, Mr. Reed, Mr. Carrol, Mr. Madison, Mr. Williamson, Mr. Rutlidge, Mr. Houston.
Adjd.

PATERSON

Monday 9th. July, 87.

Gorham.
Report of Comee.

Necessary, that the Atlantic States should take Care of themselves; the Western States will soon be very numerous.

TUESDAY, JULY 10, 1787.

JOURNAL
Tuesday July 10. 1787.

1 The honorable Mr King from the grand Committee to whom was referred the first paragraph of the report of a Comnittee consisting of Mr G. Morris, Mr Gorham, Mr Randolph, Mr Rutledge, and Mr King, informed the House that the Committee were prepared to report — He then read the report in his place, and the same being delivered in at the Secretary's table was again read, and is as follows, namely.

That in the original formation of the Legislature of the United States, the first Branch thereof shall consist of sixty five members,

of which number

New Hampshire shall send	Three.
Massachusetts	Eight
Rhode Island	One.
Connecticut	Five
New York	Six
New-Jersey	Four.
Pennsylvania	Eight
Delaware	One
Maryland	Six
Virginia	Ten
North Carolina	Five
South Carolina	Five
Georgia	Three.

It was moved and seconded to amend the report by striking out the word "Three" in the apportionment of representation to New Hampshire, and inserting the word "Two"

which passed in the negative. [Ayes — 2; noes — 9.]
It was moved and seconded to amend the report by striking out the word "five" in the apportionment of representation to North Carolina, and inserting the word "six"

which passed in the negative. [Ayes — 3; noes — 8.] It was moved and seconded to amend the report by striking out the word "five" in the apportionment of representation to South Carolina and inserting the word "six"

which passed in the negative. [Ayes — 4; noes — 7.] It was moved and seconded to amend the report by striking out the word "Three" in the apportionment of representation to Georgia and inserting the word "four"

which passed in the negative. [Ayes — 4; noes — 7.] It was moved and seconded to double the number of representatives, in the first branch of the Legislature of the United States, apportioned by the report of the grand Committee to each State.

which passed in the negative. [Ayes — 2; noes — 9.] On the question to agree to the report of the grand Committee.

it passed in the affirmative [Ayes — 9; noes — 2.] It was moved and seconded to add the following amendment after the second paragraph of the report from the Committee consisting of Mr Morris, Mr Gorham, Mr Randolph, Mr Rutledge and Mr King. —

"That in order to ascertain alterations in the population "and wealth of the States the Legislature of the United States "be required to cause a proper census and estimate to be "taken once in every term of   years."

It was moved and seconded to postpone the consideration of the last motion in order to take up the following. namely

"That the Committee of eleven, to whom was referred "the report of the Committee of five on the subject of repre- "sentation, be requested to furnish the Convention with the "principles on which they grounded the report."

which passed in the negative. [Ayes — 1; noes — 10.]

[To adjourn   Ayes — 10; noes — 1.][1]

And then the House adjourned till to-morrow at 11 o'clock A. M.

---

[1] Vote 131, Detail of Ayes and Noes. This doubtless belongs here, partly because of its position between Votes 130 and 132, and because it is the last time New York's vote is recorded.

DETAIL OF AYES AND NOES

	[131]	[130]	[129]	[128]	[127]	[126]	[125]	[124]
			[Beginning of fifth loose sheet]					
New Hampshire								
Massachusetts	aye	no	aye	no	no	no	no	no
Rhode Island								
Connecticut	no	no	aye	no	no	no	no	no
New York	no	aye	no	no	no	no	no	no
New Jersey	no	no	aye	aye	no	no	no	no
Pennsylvania	no	no	aye	aye	no	no	no	no
Delaware	no	no	aye	aye	no	aye	no	no
Maryland	no	no	aye	no	no	no	no	no
Virginia	no	no	aye	aye	aye	no	no	no
North Carolina	no	no	aye	no	aye	aye	aye	no
South Carolina	aye	no	aye	no	aye	aye	aye	aye
Georgia	no	aye	no	no	aye	aye	aye	aye
Ayes	1	2	9	4	4	4	3	2
Noes	10	9	2	7	7	7	8	9
Divided								

Questions

[124] To strike out the word "three" in the apportionment of representation to New Hampshire, and insert the word "Two."

[125] To strike out the word "five" in the representation of North Carolina, nd insert the word "six"

[126] To strike out the word "five" in the representation of South Carolina and insert "six"

[127] To strike out the word "three" in the representation of Georgia and insert the word "four"

[128] To double the representation reported from the Committee.

[129] To agree to the report of the grand Committee. Mr. King Chairman

[130] To postpone the motion for ascertaining the future representation

[131] To adjourn

MADISON

Teusday. July 10.   In Convention

Mr. King reported from the Come. yesterday appointed that the States at the 1st. meeting of the General Legislature, should be represented by 65 members in the following proportions, to wit.   N. Hamshire by 3, Masts. 8. R. Isd. 1. Cont. 5. N. Y. 6. N. J. 4. Pa. 8. Del. 1. Md. 6. Va. 10. N: C. 5. S. C. 5, Georgia 3.[2]

Mr. Rutlidge moved that N. Hampshire be reduced from 3 to 2. members.   Her numbers did not entitle her to 3 and it was a poor State.

Genl. Pinkney seconds the motion.

Mr. King.   N. Hamshire has probably more than 120,000 Inhabts. and has an extensive country of tolerable fertility. Its inhabts therefore may be expected to increase fast.   He remarked that the four Eastern States having 800,000 souls, have ⅓ fewer representatives than the four Southern States, having not more than 700,000 souls rating the blacks, as 5 for 3.   The Eastern people will advert to these circumstances, and be dissatisfied.   He believed them to be very desirous of uniting with their Southern brethren but did not think it prudent to rely so far on that disposition as to subject them to any gross inequality.   He was fully convinced that the question concerning a difference of interests did not lie where it had hitherto been discussed, between the great & small States; but between the Southern & Eastern.   For this reason he had been ready to yield something in the proportion of representatives for the security of the Southern.   No principle would justify the giving them a majority.   They were brought as near an equality as was possible.   He was not averse to giving them a still greater security, but did not see how it could be done.

Genl. Pinkney.   The Report before it was committed was

---

[2] For the basis of the determination of these numbers, see below, and Appendix **A,** CXV, CXXIII, CLVIII (38), CLXXVI–CLXXX, CCXXV.

more favorable to the S. States than as it now stands. If they are to form so considerable a minority, and the regulation of trade is to be given to the Genl. Government, they will be nothing more than overseers for the Northern States. He did not expect the S. States to be raised to a majority of representatives, but wished them to have something like an equality. At present by the alterations of the Come. in favor of the N. States they are removed farther from it than they were before. One member had indeed been added to Virga. which he was glad of as he considered her as a Southern State. He was glad also that the members of Georgia were increased.

Mr. Williamson was not for reducing N. Hamshire from 3 to 2. but for reducing some others. The Southn. Interest must be extremely endangered by the present arrangement. The Northn. States are to have a majority in the first instance and the means of perpetuating it.

Mr. Dayton observed that the line between the Northn. & Southern interest had been improperly drawn: that Pa. was the dividing State, there being six on each side of her.

Genl. Pinkney urged the reduction, dwelt on the superior wealth of the Southern States, and insisted on its having its due weight in the Government.

Mr. Govr. Morris regretted the turn of the debate. The States he found had many Representatives on the floor. Few he fears were to be deemed the Representatives of America. He thought the Southern States have by the report more than their share of representation. Property ought to have its weight; but but not all the weight. If ⟨the Southn. States are to⟩ supply money. The Northn. States are to spill their blood. Besides, the probable Revenue to be expected from the S. States has been greatly overated. He was agst. reducing N. Hamshire.

Mr. Randolph was opposed to a reduction of N. Hamshire, not because she had a full title to three members: but because it was in his contemplation 1. to make it the duty instead of leaving it in the discretion of the Legislature to regulate the representation by a periodical census. 2. to require more than a bare majority of votes in the Legislature in certain cases, & particularly in commercial cases.[3]

On the question for reducing N. Hamshire from 3 to 2 Represents. ⟨it passed in the negative⟩

Masts. no. Cont. no. N. J. no. Pa. no. Del. no. Md. no. Va. no. N. C. ay.* S. C. ay. Geo. no.*   [Ayes — 2; noes — 8.][4]

Genl. Pinkney & Mr. Alexr. Martin moved that 6 Reps. instead of 5 be allowed to N. Carolina

On the question, ⟨it passed in the negative⟩

Masts. no. Cont. no. N. J. no. Pa. no. Del. no. Md. no. Va. no. N. C. ay. S. C. ay Geo. ay.   [Ayes — 3; noes — 7.][4]

Genl. Pinkney & Mr. Butler made the same motion in favor of S. Carolina

On the Question ⟨it passed in the negative⟩

Masts. no. Cont. no. ⟨N. Y. no.⟩[5] N. J. no. Pa. no. Del. ay. Md. no. Va. no. N. C. ay. S. C. ay. Geo. ay   [Ayes — 4; noes — 7.]

Genl. Pinkney & Mr. Houston moved that Georgia be allowed 4 instead of 3 Reps. urging the unexampled celerity of its population. On the Question, ⟨it passed in the Negative⟩

Masts. no. Cont. no. ⟨N. Y. no⟩[5] N. J. no. Pa. no. Del. no. Md. no. Va. ay. N: C. ay. S. C. ay. Geo. ay.   [Ayes — 4; noes — 7.]

Mr. M⟨adison⟩ moved that the number allowed to each State be doubled.[6] A *majority* of a *Quorum* of 65 members, was too small a number to represent the whole inhabitants of the U. States; They would not possess enough of the confidence of the people, and wd. be too sparsely taken from the people, to bring with them all the local information which would be frequently wanted. Double the number will not be too great even with the future additions from New States.

---

* ⟨In the printed Journal, N. C. no. Geo. ay.⟩

---

[3] For "an accommodating proposition to small States" suggested by Randolph, see Appendix A, LVIII, and *Records* of July 16.

[4] New York is included in Detail of Ayes and Noes.

[5] New York's vote is taken from *Journal*.

[6] On this motion, see Appendix A, CLXXXI.

The additional expence was too inconsiderable to be regarded in so important a case. And as far as the augmentation might be unpopular on that score, the objection was over-balanced by its effect on the hopes of a greater number of the popular Candidates.

Mr. Elseworth urged the objection of expence,[7] & that the greater the number, the more slowly would the business proceed; and the less probably be decided as it ought, at last — He thought the number of Representatives too great in most of the State Legislatures: and that a large number was less necessary in the Genl. Legislature than in those of the States, as its business would relate to a few great, national Objects only.

Mr. Sherman would have preferred 50 to 65. The great distance they will have to travel will render their attendance precarious and will make it difficult to prevail on a sufficient number of fit men to undertake the service. He observed that the expected increase from New States also deserved consideration.

Mr. Gerry was for increasing the number beyond 65. The larger the number the less the danger of their being corrupted. The people are accustomed to & fond of a numerous representation, and will consider their rights as better secured by it. The danger of excess in the number may be guarded agst. by fixing a point within which the number shall always be kept.

Col. Mason admitted that the objection drawn from the consideration of expence, had weight both in itself, and as the people might be affected by it. But he thought it outweighed by the objections agst. the smallness of the number. 38, will he supposes, as being a majority of 65, form a quorum. 20 will be a majority of 38. This was certainly too small a number to make laws for America. They would neither bring with them all the necessary information relative to various local interests nor possess the necessary confidence of the people. After doubling the number, the laws might still be made by so few as almost to be objectionable on that account.

---

[7] See Appendix A, CCXVIII.

Mr. Read was in favor of the motion. Two of the States (Del. & R. I.) would have but a single member if the aggregate number should remain at 65. and in case of accident to either of these one State wd. have no representative present to give explanations or informations of its interests or wishes. The people would not place their confidence in so small a number. He hoped the objects of the Genl. Govt. would be much more numerous than seemed to be expected by some gentlemen, and that they would become more & more so. As to New States the highest number of Reps. for the whole might be limited, and all danger of excess thereby prevented.

Mr. Rutlidge opposed the motion. The Representatives were too numerous in all the States. The full number allotted to the States may be expected to attend ⟨& the lowest possible quorum shd. not therefore be considered —⟩. The interests of their Constituents will urge their attendance too strongly for it to be omitted: and he supposed the Genl. Legislature would not sit more than 6 or 8 weeks in the year.

On the question for doubling the number, ⟨it passed in the negative.⟩

Masts. no. Cont. no. N. Y. no. N. J. no. Pa. no. Del ay. Md. no. Va. ay. N. C. no. S. C. no. Geo. no. [Ayes — 2; noes — 9.]

On the question for agreeing to the apportionment of Reps. as amended ⟨by the last committee it passed in the affirmative⟩,

Mas. ay. Cont. ay. N. Y. ay. N. J. ay. Pa. ay. Del ay. Md. ay. Va. ay. N. C. ay. S. C. no. Geo. no. [Ayes — 9; noes — 2.]

Mr. Broom gave notice to the House that he had concurred with a reserve to himself of an intention to claim for his State an equal voice in the 2d. branch: which he thought could not be denied after this concession of the small States as to the first branch.

Mr. Randolph moved ⟨as an amendment to the report of the Comme. of five⟩ "that in order to ascertain the alterations in the population & wealth of the several States the Legislature should be required to cause a census, and estimate to be taken within one year after its first meeting; and every   years thereafter — and that the Legislre. arrange the Representation accordingly." [8]

Mr Govr. Morris opposed it as fettering the Legislature too much. Advantage may be taken of it in time of war or the apprehension of it, by new States to extort particular favors. If the mode was to be fixed for taking a census, it might certainly be extremely inconvenient; if unfixt the Legislature may use such a mode as will defeat the object: and perpetuate the inequality. He was always agst. such Shackles on the Legislre. They had been found very pernicious in most of the State Constitutions. He dwelt much on the danger of throwing such a preponderancy into the Western Scale, suggesting that in time the Western people wd. outnumber the Atlantic States. He wished therefore to put it in the power of the latter to keep a majority of votes in their own hands. It was objected he said that if the Legislre. are left at liberty, they will never readjust the Representation. He admitted that this was possible, but he did not think it probable unless the reasons agst. a revision of it were very urgent & in this case, it ought not to be done.

It was moved to postpone the proposition of Mr. Randolph in order to take up the following, viz. "that the Committee of Eleven, to whom was referred the report of the Committee of five on the subject of Representation, be requested to furnish the Convention with the principles on which they grounded the Report," which was disagreed to: ⟨S. C. only voting in the affirmative.⟩ [9]

Adjourned. [10]

---

[8] See Appendix A, CLXXVI.

[9] Taken from *Journal*. It is probable but not certain that all of this last paragraph is a later insertion taken from *Journal*.

[10] See further Appendix A, LIX, LX.

P A T E R S O N [11]

Number of Inhabitants.

New Hampshire in 1774 . . . . .100,000.
Massachusetts in 1774 . . . . .400,000.
Rhode-Island by a Return to the Legislature in Feby.
   1783.
     48.538 Whites. ⎱
      3.331 Blacks. ⎰   51.869.
Connecticut in 1774 . . . .
    Whites   192.000. ⎱
    Blacks (nearly) 6.000. ⎰ . . . . .198.000.
        in 1782 nearly . . . . .220.0.0.
New York in 1756.   96.775.
        in 1771. 168.000.
        in 1786. Whites 219.996. ⎱ . .238.885.
                    Blacks 18.889 ⎰
New Jersey in 1783.   139.000.
    about 10,000 Blacks included —
Pennsylvania —
Delaware —
Maryland in 1774 estimated at.   350.000.
    Blacks $\frac{3}{7}$ . . . .   150.000.
Virginia in 1774 . . . .   650.000.
    Blacks as 10 to 11 . . . . . .   300.000.
In the lower States the accts. are not to be depended
    on —

The Proportion of Blacks.

In Connecticut as 1. to 33.
The same Ratio will answer for Massachusetts —
In Rhode-Island as 1 to $15\frac{1}{2}$.
In New York as 1 to 12 nearly.
In New Jersey as 1 to 13 nearly.

Virginia _____ 9.   10
Massts. _____ 7.   8

[11] Reprinted from *American Historical Review*, IX, 328–330.

Pennsylva.	8.	8
Maryland	4.	6.
Connecticut	4.	5.
New York	5.	6.
N. Carolina	5.	5.
S. Carolina	5.	5.
N. Jersey	3.	4.
New Hampshire	2.	3.
Rh. Island	1.	1
Del.	1.	1
Georgia	2.	3.
	56.	65

4 Eastn. States	17.
5 Middle States	25.
4 Southn. States	23.
	65

BREARLEY [12]

States	N. of Whites	N. of Blacks
New-Hampshire	82,000 — 102,000	
Massachusetts Bay...	352,000	
Rhode Island	58,000	
Connecticut	202,000	
New-York	238,000	
New-Jersey	138,000 — 145,000	
Pennsylvania	341,	
Delaware	37,000	
Maryland	174,000	80,000
Virginia suppd.......	300,000	300,000
North Carolina	181,000	
South Carolina	93,000	
Georgia	27,000	

[Endorsed:] Return of the Numbers in the several States

---

[12] Among the papers of Brearley relating to the Federal Convention, and turned over by his executor, General Bloomfield, to John Quincy Adams, is this document — on both sides of a single sheet. A somewhat different estimate of the population of the several states will be found in Appendix A, CLXXI. A similar statement of "Quota of Tax" and "Delegates" is given under June 9.

	Quota of Tax	Delegates
Virginia	512,974	16
Massachusetts	448,854	14
Pennsylvania	410,378	$12\frac{3}{4}$
Maryland	283,034	$8\frac{3}{4}$
Connecticut	264,182	8
New York	256,486	8
North Carolina	218,012	$6\frac{3}{4}$
South Carol na	192,366	6
New-Jersey	166,716	5
New-Hampse	105,416	$3\frac{1}{4}$
Rhode Island	64,636	2
Delaware	44,886	$1\frac{1}{4}$
Georgia	32,060	1
	3,000,000	90

Sepr 27th 1785.

[Endorsed:] hon. D. Brearly Esq

WEDNESDAY, JULY 11, 1787.

JOURNAL
Wednesday July 11. 1787.

The amendment offered to the second paragraph of the report from the Committee, consisting of Mr G. Morris, Mr Gorham, Mr Randolph Mr Rutledge and Mr King, being withdrawn — It was moved[1] and seconded to substitute the following resolution, namely.

"Resolved That in order to ascertain the alterations that may
"happen in the population and wealth of the several States
"a census shall be taken of the free inhabitants of each State,
"and three fifths of the inhabitants of other description on
"the first year after this form of Government shall have been
"adopted — and afterwards on every term of   years;
"and the Legislature shall alter or augment the representa-
"tion accordingly"

It was moved and seconded to strike out the words
        "three fifths of"
which passed in the negative. [Ayes — 3; noes — 7.]

It was moved and seconded to postpone the consideration of the resolution proposed in order to take up the following[2] namely.

Resolved That at the end of   years from the meeting of the Legislature of the United-States and at the expiration of every   years thereafter the Legislature of the United States be required to apportion the representation of the several States according to the principles of their wealth and population.

On the question to postpone, it passed in the negative
                                    [Ayes — 5; noes — 5.]

---

1 "Offered by Mr. W'mson", Vote 133, Detail of Ayes and Noes.
2 "Offered by Mr. Rutledge", Vote 133, Detail of Ayes and Noes.

It was moved and seconded to agree to the first clause of the resolution, namely.

"That in order to ascertain the alterations that may hap-
"pen in the population and wealth of the several States a
"Census shall be taken of the free inhabitants of each State"
    which passed in the affirmative [Ayes — 6; noes — 4.]
    [To adjourn. Ayes — 1; noes — 9.] [3]
It was moved and seconded to agree to the following clause
of the resolution, namely

"and three fifths of the inhabitants of other description"
    which passed in the negative. [Ayes — 4; noes — 6.]
It was moved and seconded to agree to the following clause
of the resolution, namely

"On the first year after this form of government shall
"have been adopted"
    which passed in the affirmative [Ayes — 7; noes — 3.]
It was moved and seconded to fill up the blank with the word
"fifteen"
which passed unanimously in the affirmative [Ayes — 10;
    noes — 0.]
It was moved and seconded to add after the words fifteen
years the words "at least"
    which passed in the negative [Ayes — 5; noes — 5.]
It was moved and seconded to agree to the following clause
of the resolution namely

"and the Legislature shall alter or augment the representation accordingly"
which passed unanimously in the affirmative [Ayes — 10;
    noes — 0.]
On the question to agree to the resolution as amended
it passed unanimously in the negative. [Ayes — 0; noes
    — 10.]
and then the House adjourned till to-morrow at 11 o'clock
A. M.

---

[3] Vote 135, Detail of Ayes and Noes.

DETAIL OF AYES AND NOES

Question	NH	Mass.	RI	Conn.	NY	NJ	Penn.	Del.	Md.	Va.	NC	SC	Ga.	Ayes	Noes	Divided
[132] To strike out the words "Three fifths of"		no		no		no	no	aye	no	no	no	aye	aye	3	7	
[133] To postpone ye resolution offered by Mr W'mson in order to take up another offered by Mr Rutledge — respecting the census.		aye		no		no	aye	no	no	no	aye	aye	aye	5	5	
[134] To agree to the first clause of the resolution offered by Mr Williamson to ascertain alterations of wealth & population		aye		aye		no	aye	aye	no	aye	aye	no	no	6	4	
[135] To adjourn.		no		no		no	no	no	no	no	no	no	aye	1	9	
[136] To agree to the words "and three-fifths of the inhabitants of other description."		no		aye		no	no	no	no	aye	aye	aye	aye	4	6	
[137] To agree to the words On the first year		aye		no		no	aye	aye	no	aye	aye	aye	aye	7	3	
[138] To fill up the blank with the word "fifteen"		aye		aye		aye	aye	aye	aye	aye	aye	aye	aye	10		
[139] To add the words "at least"		aye		no		aye	aye	no	no	aye	aye	aye	aye	5	5	
[140] On the last Clause of the resolution		aye		aye		no	aye	aye	aye	aye	aye	aye	aye	10	5	
[141] To agree to the resolution as amended		no		no		no	no	no	no	no	no	no	no	10	10	

States recorded (column headers): New Hampshire, Massachusetts, Rhode Island, Connecticut, New York, New Jersey, Pennsylvania, Delaware, Maryland, Virginia, North Carolina, South Carolina, Georgia.

MADISON

Wednesday July 11. in Convention

Mr. Randolph's motion requiring the Legislre. to take a periodical census for the purpose of redressing inequalities in the Representation was resumed.

Mr. Sherman was agst. Shackling the Legislature too much. We ought to choose wise & good men, and then confide in them.

Mr. Mason. The greater the difficulty we find in fixing a proper rule of Representation, the more unwilling ought we to be, to throw the task from ourselves, on the Genl. Legislre. He did not object to the conjectural ratio which was to prevail in the outset; but considered a Revision from time to time according to some permanent & precise standard as essential to ye. fair representation required in the 1st. branch. According to the present population of America, the Northn. part of it had a right to preponderate, and he could not deny it. But he wished it not to preponderate hereafter when the reason no longer continued. From the nature of man we may be sure, that those who have power in their hands will not give it up while they can retain it. On the Contrary we know they will always when they can rather increase it. If the S. States therefore should have $\frac{3}{4}$ of the people of America within their limits, the Northern will hold fast the majority of Representatives. $\frac{1}{4}$ will govern the $\frac{3}{4}$. The S. States will complain: but they may complain from generation to generation without redress. Unless some principle therefore which will do justice to them hereafter shall be inserted in the Constitution, disagreable as the declaration was to him, he must declare he could neither vote for the system here nor support it, in his State. Strong objections had been drawn from the danger to the Atlantic interests from new Western States. Ought we to sacrifice what we know to be right in itself, lest it should prove favorable to States which are not yet in existence. If the Western States are to be admitted into the Union as they arise, they must, he wd. repeat, be treated as equals, and subjected to no degrading discriminations. They will have the same pride & other passions which we have, and will either not unite with or will speedily revolt from the Union, if they are not in all respects placed on an equal footing with their brethren. It has been said they will be poor, and unable to make equal contributions to the general Treasury. He did not know but that in time they would be both more numerous & more wealthy than their Atlantic brethren.[4] The extent & fertility of their soil, made this probable; and though Spain might for a time deprive them of the natural outlet for their productions, yet she will, because she must, finally yield to their demands. He urged that numbers of inhabitants; though not always a precise standard of wealth was sufficiently so for every substantial purpose.

Mr. Williamson was for making it the duty of the Legislature to do what was right & not leaving it at liberty to do or not do it. He moved that Mr. Randolph's proposition be postpond. in order to consider the following "that in order to ascertain the alterations that may happen in the population & wealth of the several States, a census shall be taken of the free white inhabitants and $\frac{3}{5}$ths of those of other descriptions on the 1st year ⟨after this Government shall have been adopted⟩ and every   year thereafter; and that the Representation be regulated accordingly."

Mr. Randolph agreed that Mr. Williamson's propositon should stand in the place of his. He observed that the ratio fixt for the 1st. meeting was a mere conjecture, that it placed the power in the hands of that part of America, which could not always be entitled to it, that this power would not be voluntarily renounced; and that it was consequently the duty of the Convention to secure its renunciation when justice might so require; by some constitutional provisions. If equality between great & small States be inadmissible, because in that case unequal numbers of Constituents wd. be represented by equal number of votes; was it not equally inadmissible that a larger & more populous district of America should

---

[4] Crossed out, "tho' perhaps not before they might choose to become a separate people".

hereafter have less representation, than a smaller & less populous district.   If a fair representation of the people be not
secured, the injustice of the Govt. will shake it to its foundations.   What relates to suffrage is justly stated by the celebrated Montesquieu, as a fundamental article in Republican
Govts.   If the danger suggested by Mr. Govr. Morris be real,
of advantage being taken of the Legislature in pressing moments, it was an additional reason, for tying their hands in
such a manner that they could not sacrifice their trust to
momentary considerations.   Congs. have pledged the public
faith to New States, that they shall be admitted on equal
terms.   They never would nor ought to accede on any other.
The census must be taken under the direction of the General
Legislature.   The States will be too much interested to take
an impartial one for themselves.

Mr. Butler & Genl. Pinkney [5] insisted that blacks be
included in the rule of Representation, *equally* with the Whites:
⟨and for that purpose moved that the words "three fifths" be
struck out.⟩

Mr Gerry thought that $\frac{3}{5}$ of them was to say the least the
full proportion that could be admitted.

Mr. Ghorum.   This ratio was fixed by Congs. as a rule of
taxation.   Then it was urged by the Delegates representing
the States having slaves that the blacks were still more inferior
to freemen.   At present when the ratio of representation is to
be established, we are assured that they are equal to freemen.
The arguments on ye. former occasion had convinced him
that $\frac{3}{5}$ was pretty near the just proportion and he should vote
according to the same opinion now.

Mr. Butler insisted that the labour of a slave in S. Carola.
was as productive & valuable as that of a freeman in Massts.,
that as wealth was the great means of defence and utility to
the Nation they were equally valuable to it with freemen; and
that consequently an equal representation ought to be allowed

---

[5] This begins the debate on the "three-fifths rule" which was finally adopted on
July 13.   The question had previously been broached on June 11 and July 9.   See
also Appendix A, CLVIII (38–39), CLXXI, CLXXII, CCXVI, CCXXV, CCXCVIII,
CCCXXVII, CCCXXXVI.

for them in a Government which was instituted principally for the protection of property, and was itself to be supported by property.

Mr. Mason. could not agree to the motion, notwithstanding it was favorable to Virga. because he thought it unjust. It was certain that the slaves were valuable, as they raised the value of land, increased the exports & imports, and of course the revenue, would supply the means of feeding & supporting an army, and might in cases of emergency become themselves soldiers. As in these important respects they were useful to the community at large, they ought not to be excluded from the estimate of Representation. He could not however regard them as equal to freemen and could not vote for them as such. He added as worthy of remark, that the Southern States have this peculiar species of property, over & above the other species of property common to all the States.

Mr. Williamson reminded Mr. Ghorum that if the Southn. States contended for the inferiority of blacks to whites when taxation was in view, the Eastern States on the same occasion contended for their equality. He did ⟨not⟩ however either then or now, concur in either extreme, but approved of the ratio of $\frac{3}{5}$.

On Mr. Butlers motion for considering blacks as equal to Whites in the apportionmt. of Representation

Massts. no. Cont. no. (N. Y. not on floor.) N. J. no. Pa. no. Del. ay. Md. no. ⟨Va no⟩[6] N. C. no. S. C. ay. Geo. ay. [Ayes — 3; noes — 7.]

Mr. Govr. Morris said he had several objections to the proposition of Mr. Williamson. 1. It fettered the Legislature too much. 2. it would exclude some States altogether who would not have a sufficient number to entitle them to a single Representative. 3. it will not consist with the Resolution passed on Saturday last authorizing the Legislature to adjust the Representation from time to time on the principles of population & wealth or with the principles of equity. If slaves were to be considered as inhabitants, not as wealth, then the sd. Resolution would not be pursued: If as wealth,

---

[6] Taken from *Journal.*

then why is no other wealth but slaves included? These objections may perhaps be removed by amendments. His great objection was that the number of inhabitants was not a proper standard of wealth. The amazing difference between the comparative numbers & wealth of different Countries, rendered all reasoning superfluous on the subject. Numbers might with greater propriety be deemed a measure of stregth, than of wealth, yet the late defence made by G. Britain agst. her numerous enemies proved in the clearest manner, that it is entirely fallacious even in this respect.

Mr. King thought there was great force in the objections of Mr. Govr. Morris: he would however accede to the proposition for the sake of doing something.

Mr. Rutlidge contended for the admission of wealth in the estimate by which Representation should be regulated. The Western States will not be able to contribute in proportion to their numbers, they shd. not therefore be represented in that proportion. The Atlantic States will not concur in such a plan. He moved that "at the end of   years after the 1st. meeting of the Legislature, and of every   years thereafter, the Legislature shall proportion the Representation according to the principles of wealth & population"

Mr. Sherman thought the number of people alone the best rule for measuring wealth as well as representation; and that if the Legislature were to be governed by wealth, they would be obliged to estimate it by numbers. He was at first for leaving the matter wholly to the discretion of the Legislature; but he had been convinced by the observations of (Mr. Randolph & Mr. Mason) that the _periods_ & the _rule_ of revising the Representation ought to be fixt by the Constitution

Mr. Reid thought the Legislature ought not to be too much shackled. It would make the Constitution like Religious Creeds, embarrassing to those bound to conform to them & more likely to produce dissatisfaction and Scism, than harmony and union.

Mr. Mason objected to Mr. Rutlidge motion, as requiring of the Legislature something too indefinite & impracticable, and leaving them a pretext for doing nothing.

Mr. Wilson had himself no objection to leaving the Legislature entirely at liberty. But considered wealth as an impracticable rule.

Mr. Ghorum. If the Convention who are comparatively so little biassed by local views are so much perplexed, How can it be expected that the Legislature hereafter under the full biass of those views, will be able to settle a standard. He was convinced by the arguments of others & his own reflections, that the Convention ought to fix some standard or other.

Mr. Govr. Morris. The argts. of others & his own reflections had led him to a very different conclusion. If we can't agree on a rule that will be just at this time, how can we expect to find one that will be just in all times to come. Surely those who come after us will judge better of things present, than we can of things future. He could not persuade himself that numbers would be a just rule at any time. The remarks of (Mr Mason) relative to the Western Country had not changed his opinion on that head. Among other objections it must be apparent they would not be able to furnish men equally enlightened, to share in the administration of our common interests. The Busy haunts of men not the remote wilderness, was the proper School of political Talents. If the Western people get the power into their hands they will ruin the Atlantic interests. The Back members are always most averse to the best measures He mentioned the case of Pena. formerly. The lower part of the State had ye. power in the first instance. They kept it in yr. own hands. & the country was ye. better for it. Another objection with him agst admitting the blacks into the census, was that the people of Pena. would revolt at the idea of being put on a footing with slaves. They would reject any plan that was to have such an effect. Two objections had been raised agst. leaving the adjustment of the Representation from time to time, to the discretion of the Legislature. The 1. was they would be unwilling to revise it at all. The 2 that by referring to *wealth* they would be bound by a rule which if willing, they would be unable to execute. The 1st. objn. distrusts their fidelity. But if their duty, their honor & their oaths will not bind them, let us not put into their hands our liberty, and all our other great interests. let us have no Govt. at all. 2. If these ties will bind them. we need not distrust the practicability of the rule. It was followed in part by the Come. in the apportionment of Representatives yesterday reported to the House. The best course that could be taken would be to leave the interests of the people to the Representatives of the people.

Mr. ⟨*Madison*⟩ was not a little surprised to hear this implicit confidence urged by a member who on all occasions, had inculcated So strongly, the political depravity of men, and the necessity of checking one vice and interest by opposing to them another vice & interest. If the Representatives of the people would be bound by the ties he had mentioned, what need was there of a Senate? What of a Revisionary power? But his reasoning was not only inconsistent with his former reasoning, but with itself. at the same time that he recommended this implicit confidence to the Southern States in the Northern Majority, he was still more zealous in exhorting all to a jealousy of a Western majority. To reconcile the gentln. with himself it must be imagined that he determined the human character by the points of the compass. The truth was that all men having power ought to be distrusted[7] to a certain degree. The case of Pena. had been mentioned where it was admitted that those who were possessed of the power in the original settlement, never admitted the new settlmts. to a due share of it. England was a still more striking example. The power there had long been in the hands of the boroughs, of the minority; who had opposed & defeated every reform which had been attempted. Virga. was in a lesser degree another example. With regard to the Western States, he was clear & firm in opinion that no unfavorable distinctions were admissible either in point of justice or policy. He thought also that the hope of contributions to the Treasy. from them

---

[7] Crossed out: "both distrusted & confided in to a certain degree, that if there was any difference in men it did not depend in different situations it must [illegible word] that if any real difference lay between them in the different situations mentioned ".

had been much underrated.   Future contributions it seemed
to be understood on all hands would be principally levied on
imports and exports.   The extent & fertility of the Western
Soil would for a long time give to agriculture a preference
over manufactures.   Trials would be repeated till some articles
could be raised from it that would bear a transportation to
places where they could be exchanged for imported manufactures.   Whenever the Mississpi should be opened to them, which
would of necessity be ye. case as soon as their ᵗheir population would subject them to any considerable share of the public
burdin, imposts on their trade could be collected with less
expense & greater certainty, than on that of the Atlantic
States.   In the meantime, as their supplies must pass thro'
the *Atlantic States* their contributions would be levied in the
same manner with those of the Atlantic States. — He could
not agree that any substantial objection lay agst. fixig numbers
for the perpetual standard of Representation.   It was said
that Representation & taxation were to go together; that
taxation & wealth ought to go together, that population and
wealth were not measures of each other.   He admitted that
in different climates, under different forms of Govt. and in
different stages of civilization the inference was perfectly just.
He would admit that in no situation numbers of inhabitants
were an accurate measure of wealth.   He contended however
that in the U. States it was sufficiently so for the object in
contemplation.   Altho' their climate varied considerably, yet
as the Govts. the laws, and the manners of all were nearly the
same, and the intercourse between different parts perfectly
free, population, industry, arts, and the value of labour, would
constantly tend to equalize themselves.   The value of labour,
might be considered as the principal criterion of wealth and
ability to support taxes; and this would find its level in different places where the intercourse should be easy & free, with as
much certainty as the value of money or any other thing.
Wherever labour would yield most, people would resort, till
the competition should destroy the inequality.   Hence it is
that the people are constantly swarming from the more to
the less populous places — from Europe to Ama from the

Northn. & middle parts of the U. S. to the Southern & Western. They go where land is cheaper, because there labour is dearer. If it be true that the same quantity of produce raised on the banks of the Ohio is of less value than on the Delaware, it is also true that the same labor will raise twice or thrice, the quantity in the former, that it will raise in the latter situation.

Col. Mason, Agreed with Mr. Govr. Morris that we ought to leave the interests of the people to the Representatives of the people: but the objection was that the Legislature would cease to be the Representatives of the people. It would continue so no longer than the States now containing a majority of the people should retain that majority. As soon as the Southern & Western population should predominate, which must happen in a few years, the power wd be in the hands of the minority, and would never be yielded to the majority, unless provided for by the Constitution

On the question for postponing Mr. Williamson's motion, in order to consider that of Mr. Rutlidge ⟨it passed in the negative⟩. Massts. ay. Cont. no. N. J. no. Pa. ay. Del. ay. Md. no. Va. no. N. C. no. S. C. ay. Geo — ay. [Ayes — 5; noes — 5.]

On the question on the first clause ⟨of Mr. Williamson's motion⟩ as to taking a census of the *free* inhabitants. ⟨it passed in the affirmative⟩ Masts. ay. Cont. ay. N. J. ay. Pa. ay. Del. no. Md. no. Va. ay. N. C. ay. S. C. no. Geo. no. [Ayes — 6; noes — 4.]

the next clause as to $\frac{3}{5}$ of the negroes considered

Mr. King. being much opposed to fixing numbers as the rule of representation, was particularly so on account of the blacks. He thought the admission of them along with Whites at all, would excite great discontents among the States having no slaves. He had never said as to any particular point that he would in no event acquiesce in & support it; but he wd. say that if in any case such a declaration was to be made by him, it would be in this. He remarked that in the ⟨temporary⟩ allotment of Representatives made by the Committee, the Southern States had received more than the number of their white & three fifths of their black inhabitants entitled them to.

Mr. Sherman. S. Carola. had not more beyond her proportion than N. York & N. Hampshire, nor either of them more than was necessary in order to avoid fractions or reducing them below their proportion. Georgia had more; but the rapid growth of that State seemed to justify it. In general the allotment might not be just, but considering all circumstances, he was satisfied with it.

Mr. Ghorum. supported the propriety of establishing numbers as the rule. He said that in Massts. estimates had been taken in the different towns, and that persons had been curious enough to compare these estimates with the respective numbers of people; and it had been found even including Boston, that the most exact proportion prevailed between numbers & property. He was aware that there might be some weight in what had fallen from his colleague, as to the umbrage which might be taken by the people of the Eastern States. But he recollected that when the proposition of Congs for changing the 8th. art: of Confedn. was before the Legislature of Massts. the only difficulty then was to satisfy them that the negroes ought not to have been counted equally with whites instead of being counted in the ratio of three fifths only.*

Mr. Wilson did not well see on what principle the admission of blacks in the proportion of three fifths could be explained. Are they admitted as Citizens? Then why are they not admitted on an equality with White Citizens? Are they admitted as property? then why is not other property admitted into the computation? These were difficulties however which he thought must be overruled by the necessity of compromise. He had some apprehensions also from the tendency of the blending of the blacks with the whites, to give disgust to the people of Pena. as had been intimated by his colleague (Mr Govr. Morris). But he differed from him in thinking numbers of inhabts. so incorrect a measure of wealth. He had seen the Western settlemts. of Pa. and on a comparison of them with the City of Philada. could discover little other difference, than that property was more unequally divided among individuals

---

* ⟨They were then to have been a rule of taxation only.⟩[8]

---

[8] Probably but not certainly a later insertion.

here than there.   Taking the same number in the aggregate in the two situations he believed there would be little difference in their wealth and ability to contribute to the public wants.

Mr. Govr. Morris was compelled to declare himself reduced to the dilemma of doing injustice to the Southern States or to human nature, and he must therefore do it to the former.   For he could never agree to give such encouragement to the slave trade as would be given by allowing them a representation for their negroes, and he did not believe those States would ever confederate on terms that would deprive them of that trade.

On Question for agreeing to include ⅗ of the blacks

Masts. no. Cont. ay N. J. no. Pa. no. Del. no. Mard.* no. Va. ay. N. C. ay. S. C. no. Geo. ay [Ayes — 4; noes —6.]

On the question as to taking census "the first year after meeting of the Legislature"

Masts. ay. Cont. no. N. J. ay. Pa. ay. Del. ay. Md. no. Va. ay. N. C. ay. S. ay. Geo. no. [Ayes — 7; noes — 3.]

On filling the blank for the periodical census with 15 years". agreed to nem. con.

Mr. ⟨Madison⟩ moved to add after "15 years," the words "at least" that the Legislature might anticipate when circumstances ⟨were likely to⟩ render a particular year inconvenient.

On this motion for adding "at least", ⟨it passed in the negative the States being equally divided.⟩

Mas..ay. Cont. no. N. J. no. Pa. no. Del. no. Md. no. Va. ay. N. C. ay. S. C. ay. Geo. ay. [Ayes — 5; noes — 5.]

A change of the phraseology ⟨of the other clause⟩ so as to read; "and the Legislature ⟨shall alter or augment the representation accordingly" was⟩ agreed to nem. con.

On the question on the whole ⟨resolution of Mr. Williamson as amended.⟩

Mas. no. Cont. no. N. J. no. Del. no. Md. no. Va. no. N. C. no. S. C. no—Geo—no [Ayes — 0; noes — 9.][9]

---

* ⟨Mr. Carrol sd. in explanation of the vote of Md. that he wished the phraseology to be so altered as to obviate if possible the danger which had been expressed of giving umbrage to the Eastern & Middle States.⟩

---

[9] Pennsylvania is included in the negative in Vote 141, Detail of Ayes and Noes.

THURSDAY, JULY 12, 1787.

JOURNAL

Thursday July 12. 1787.

It was moved and seconded to add the following clause to the last resolution agreed to by the House, respecting the representation in the first branch of the Legislature of the U. S. — namely.

"Provided always that direct Taxation ought to be pro-"portioned according to representation"
    which passed unanimously in the affirmative.

It was moved and seconded to postpone the consideration of the first clause in the report from the first grand Committee
    which passed in the affirmative

It was moved and seconded to add the following amendment to the last clause adopted by the House namely

"and that the rule of contribution by direct taxation for the support of the government of the United States shall be the number of white inhabitants, and three fifths of every other description in the several States, until some other rule that shall more accurately ascertain the wealth of the several States can be devised and adopted by the Legislature

The last amendment being withdrawn — it was moved and seconded to substitute the following, namely.

"And in order to ascertain the alteration in the representation which may be required from time to time by the changes in the relative circumstances of the States — Resolved that a Census be taken within two years from the first meeting of the Legislature of the United States, and once within the term of every   years afterwards of all the inhabitants of the United States in the manner, and according to the ratio recommended by Congress in their resolution of.   and that the Legislature of the United States shall arrange the representation accordingly.

It was moved and seconded so to alter the last clause adopted by the House that together with the amendment proposed the whole should read as follows namely

"Provided always that representation ought to be propor-
"tioned according to direct Taxation, and in order to ascer-
"tain the alteration in the direct Taxation which may be
"required from time to time by the changes in the relative
"circumstances of the States — Resolved that a Census be
"taken within two years from the first meeting of the Legis-
"lature of the United States, and once within the term of
"every   years afterwards of all the inhabitants of the
"United States in the manner and according to the ratio
"recommended by Congress in their resolution of April 18.
"1783 — and that the Legislature of the United States shall
"proportion the direct Taxation accordingly"

It was moved and seconded to strike out the word "Two" and insert the word "Six"

which passed in the affirmative [Ayes — 5; noes — 4; divided — 1.]

[To fill up the blank with the number "Twenty" in taking the Census. Ayes — 3; noes — 7.] [1]

It was moved and seconded to fill up the blank with the word "Ten"

which passed in the affirmative [Ayes — 8; noes — 2.]

It was moved and seconded to strike out the words "in the manner and according to the ratio recommended by Congress in their recommendation of April 18. 1783 — and to substitute the following namely "of every description and condition"

which passed in the negative. [Ayes — 2; noes — 8.]

The question being about to be put upon the clause as amended — The previous question was called for,

and passed in the negative. [Ayes — 1; noes — 8; divided — 1.]

On the question to agree to the clause, as amended, namely

"Provided always that representation ought to be prop-tioned according to direct Taxation and in order to ascertain

---

[1] Vote 143, Detail of Ayes and Noes.

the alteration in the direct Taxation which may be required from time to time by the changes in the relative circumstances of the States — Resolved that a Census be taken within six years from the first meeting of the Legislature of the United States and once within the term of every Ten years afterwards of all the inhabitants of the United States in the manner and according to the ratio recommended by Congress in their resolution of April 18. 1783 — and that the Legislature of the U. S. shall proportion the direct Taxation accordingly

[Ayes — 6; noes — 2; divided — 2.]

And then the House adjourned until to-morrow at 11 o'Clock. A. M.

DETAIL OF AYES AND NOES

	N. Hampshire	Massachusetts	Rhode Island	Connecticut	New York	New Jersey	Pennsylvania	Delaware	Maryland	Virginia	North Carolina	South Carolina	Georgia	Questions	Ayes	Noes	Divided
[142]	no	aye		aye	aye	dd	aye	no		no	aye	no		To strike out the word "two" and insert the word "six" in taking the first census	5	4	1
[143]	no	aye		aye	aye	no	no	no	no	no	no			To fill up the blank with the number "Twenty" in taking the Census.	3	7	
[144]	aye	no		no	aye	aye	aye	aye	aye	aye	aye			To fill up the blank with the number "Ten"	8	2	
[145]	no	no		no	no	no	no	no	no			aye	aye	To insert the words "of every description and condition"	2	8	
[146]	no	no		aye	no	dd	no	no	no	no	no			for the previous question	1	8	1
[147]	dd	aye		no	aye	no	aye	aye	aye	dd	aye			To agree to the resolution which regulates the Census &c	6	2	2

MADISON

Thursday. July 12.   In Convention

Mr. Govr. Morris moved to add to the clause empowering the Legislature to vary the Representation according to the principles of wealth & number of inhabts. a "proviso that taxation shall be in proportion to Representation".

Mr Butler contended again that Representation sd. be according to the full number of inhabts. including all the blacks; admitting the justice of Mr. Govr. Morris's motion.

Mr. Mason also admitted the justice of the principle, but was afraid embarrassments might be occasioned to the Legislature by it. It might drive the Legislature to the plan of Requisitions.

Mr. Govr. Morris, admitted that some objections lay agst. his motion, but supposed they would be removed by restraining the rule to *direct* taxation. With regard to indirect taxes on *exports* & imports & on consumption, the rule would be inapplicable. Notwithstanding what had been said to the contrary he was persuaded that the imports & consumption were pretty nearly equal throughout the Union.

General Pinkney liked the idea. He thought it so just that it could not be objected to. But foresaw that if the revision of the census was left to the discretion of the Legislature, it would never be carried into execution. The rule must be fixed, and the execution of it enforced by the Constitution. He was alarmed at what was said yesterday,[x] concerning the Negroes. He was now again alarmed at what had been thrown out concerning the taxing of exports. S. Carola. has in one year exported to the amount of £600,000 Sterling all which was the fruit of the labor of her blacks. Will she be represented in proportion to this amount? She will not. Neither ought she then to be subject to a tax on it. He hoped a clause would be inserted in the system restraining the Legislature from a taxing Exports.

Mr. Wilson approved the principle, but could not see how it could be carried into execution; unless restrained to direct taxation.

Mr. Govr. Morris having so varied his motion by inserting the word "direct". It passd. ⟨nem. con. as follows — 'pro-

[x] By Mr Govr Morris.[2]

[2] Possibly a later insertion.

vided always that direct taxation ought to be proportioned to representation".)[3]

Mr. Davie, said it was high time now to speak out. He saw that it was meant by some gentlemen to deprive the Southern States of any share of Representation for their blacks. He was sure that N. Carola. would never confederate on any terms that did not rate them at least as $\frac{3}{5}$. If the Eastern States meant therefore to exclude them altogether the business was at an end.

Dr. Johnson, thought that wealth and population were the true, equitable rule of representation; but he conceived that these two principles resolved themselves into one; population being the best measure of wealth. He concluded therefore that ye. number of people ought to be established as the rule, and that all descriptions including blacks *equally* with the whites, ought to fall within the computation. As various opinions had been expressed on the subject, he would move that a Committee might be appointed to take them into consideration and report thereon.

Mr. Govr. Morris. It has been said that it is high time to speak out. As one member, he would candidly do so. He came here to form a compact for the good of America. He was ready to do so with all the States: He hoped & believed that all would enter into such a Compact. If they would not he was ready to join with any States that would. But as the Compact was to be voluntary, it is in vain for the Eastern States to insist on what the Southn States will never agree to. It is equally vain for the latter to require what the other States can never admit; and he verily belived the people of Pena. will never agree to a representation of Negroes. What can be desired by these States more than has been already proposed; that the Legislature shall from time to time regulate Representation according to population & wealth.

Gen. Pinkney desired that the rule of wealth should be ascertained and not left to the pleasure of the Legislature;

[3] Taken from *Journal*. There seem to be at least two later and one contemporary series of corrections in Madison's notes of this day, and it is not possible always to distinguish positively between them.

and that property in slaves should not be exposed to danger under a Govt. instituted for the protection of property.

⟨The first clause in the Report of the first Grand Committee was postponed⟩[4]

Mr. Elseworth. In order to carry into effect the principle established, moved ⟨to add to the last clause adopted by the House the words following "and that the rule of contribution by direct taxation for the support of the Government of the U. States shall be the number of white inhabitants, and three fifths of every other description in the several States, until some other rule that shall more accurately ascertain the wealth of the several States can be devised and adopted by the Legislature"⟩ [4]

Mr. Butler seconded the motion in order that it might be committed.

Mr. Randolph was not satisfied with the motion. The danger will be revived that the ingenuity of the Legislature may evade ⟨or pervert the rule so as to⟩ perpetuate the power where it shall be lodged in the first instance. He proposed in lieu of Mr. Elseworth's motion, "that in order to ascertain the alterations ⟨in Representation⟩ that may be required from time to time by changes in the relative circumstances of the States, a census shall be taken within two years ⟨from⟩ the 1st. meeting of the Genl. Legislature ⟨of the U. S.⟩, and once within ⟨the term of⟩ every   year afterwards, of ⟨all⟩ the inhabitants ⟨in the manner &⟩ according to the ⟨ratio recommended by Congress in their resolution⟩ of the ⟨18th⟩ day of ⟨Apl. 1783; (rating the blacks at ⅗ of their number)⟩ and that the Legislature of the U. S. shall arrange the Representation accordingly."[5]—He urged strenuously that express security ought to be provided for including slaves in the ratio of Representation. He lamented that such a species of property existed. But as it did exist the holders of it would require this security. It was perceived that the design was entertained by some of excluding slaves altogether; the Legislature therefore ought not to be left at liberty.

---

[4] Taken from _Journal._   [5] Revised from _Journal._

Mr. Elseworth withdraws his motion & seconds that of Mr. Randolph.

Mr. Wilson observed that less umbrage would perhaps be taken agst. an admission of the slaves into the Rule of representation, if it should be so expressed as to make them indirectly only an ingredient in the rule, by saying that they should enter into the rule of taxation: and as representation was to be according to taxation, the end would be equally attained. He accordingly ⟨moved & was 2ded so to alter the last clause adopted by the House, that together with the amendment proposed the whole should read as follows — provided always that the representation ought to be proportioned according to direct taxation, and in order to ascertain the alterations in the direct taxation which may be required from time to time by the changes in the relative circumstances of the States. Resolved that a census be taken within two years from the first meeting of the Legislature of the U. States, and once within the term of every   years afterwards of all the inhabitants of the U. S. in the manner and according to the ratio recommended by Congress in their Resolution of April 18 1783; and that the Legislature of the U. S. shall proportion the direct taxation accordingly"⟩[6]

Mr. King. Altho' this amendment varies the aspect somewhat, he had still two powerful objections agst. tying down the Legislature to the rule of numbers. 1. they were at this time an uncertain index of the relative wealth of the States. 2. if they were a just index at this time it can not be supposed always to continue so. He was far from wishing to retain any unjust advantage whatever in one part of the Republic. If justice was not the basis of the connection it could not be of long duration. He must be short sighted indeed who does not foresee that whenever the Southern States shall be more numerous than the Northern, they can & will hold a language that will awe them into justice. If they threaten to separate now in case injury shall be done them, will their threats be less urgent or effectual, when force shall

---

[6] Taken from *Journal.*

back their demands. Even in the intervening period there will no point of time at which they will not be able to say, do us justice or we will separate. He urged the necessity of placing confidence to a certain degree in every Govt. and did not conceive that the proposed confidence as to a periodical readjustment of the representation exceeded that degree.[7]

Mr. Pinkney moved to amend Mr. Randolph's motion so as to make "blacks equal to the whites in the ratio of representation". This he urged was nothing more than justice. The blacks are the labourers, the peasants of the Southern States: they are as productive of pecuniary resources as those of the Northern States. They add equally to the wealth, and considering money as the sinew of war, to the strength of the nation. It will also be politic with regard to the Northern States as taxation is to keep pace with Representation.

Genl. Pinkney moves to insert 6 years instead of two, as the period ⟨computing from 1st meeting of ye Legis —⟩ within which the first census should be taken. On this question for ⟨inserting six instead of two" in the proposition of Mr. Wilson, it passed in the affirmative⟩

Masts. no. Ct. ay. N. J. ay. Pa. ay. Del. divd. Mayd. ay. Va. no. N. C. no. S. C. ay. Geo. no. [Ayes — 5; noes — 4; divided — 1.]

On a question for filling the blank for ye. periodical census with 20 years, ⟨it passed in the negative⟩

Masts. no. Ct. ay. N. J. ay. P. ay. Del. no. Md. no. Va. no. N. C. no. S. C. no. Geo. no. [Ayes — 3; noes — 7.]

On a question for 10 years, ⟨it passed in the affirmative.⟩

Mas. ay. Cont. no. N. J. no. P. ay. Del. ay. Md. ay. Va. ay. N. C. ay. S. C. ay. Geo. ay. [Ayes — 8; noes — 2.]

On Mr. Pinkney's motion for rating blacks as equal to whites instead of as $\frac{3}{5}$.

Mas. no. Cont. no. (Dr Johnson ay) N. J. no. Pa. no. (3 agst. 2) Del. no. Md. no. Va. no. N. C. no. S. C. ay. Geo — ay. [Ayes — 2; noes — 8.]

---

[7] See King's own note below.

Mr. Randolph's proposition ⟨as varied by Mr. Wilson being⟩ read for question on the whole.

Mr. Gerry, urged that the principle of it could not be carried into execution as the States were not to be taxed as States. With regard to taxes in imports, he conceived they would be more productive — Where there were no slaves than where there were; the consumption being greater —

Mr. Elseworth. In case of a poll tax there wd. be no difficulty. But there wd. probably be none. The sum allotted to a State may be levied without difficulty according to the plan used by the State in raising its own supplies.[8] On the question on ye. whole proposition; ⟨as proportioning representation to direct taxation & both to the white & $\frac{3}{5}$ of black inhabitants, & requiring a census within six years — & within every ten years afterwards.⟩ [9]

Mas. divd. Cont. ay. N. J. no. Pa. ay. Del. no. Md. ay. Va. ay. N. C. ay. S. C. divd. Geo. ay. [Ayes — 6; noes — 2; divided — 2.] [10]

K I N G [11]

But if after the taking of the   Census, experience shall evince that the foregoing Rule of Taxation is not in a just proportion to the relative Wealth and population of the several States, that the Legislature be authorised to devise & adopt such other Rule or Ratio, as may bear a more direct proportion to the relative Wealth & population of the States in Union — [12]

---

[8] The Journal records here that the "previous question" was called for and defeated.

[9] On the adoption of this resolution, see Appendix A, CXV, CLXXII, CCXII, CCLXI, CCLXV, CCXCVIII, CCCXXVII, CCCXXXVI.

[10] See further, Appendix A, LXI.

[11] Found among the King papers, and only ascribed to this day's records because it corresponds to a speech by King.

[12] [Endorsed:] Proposal in case the Census shd. not represent the wealth of the Country

FRIDAY, JULY 13, 1787.

JOURNAL
Friday July 13. 1787.

It was moved and seconded to postpone the consideration of that clause in the report of the grand Committee, which respects the originating of money bills in the first Branch — in order to take up the following, namely

"That in the second branch of the Legislature of the United-States each State shall have an equal vote"

It was moved and seconded to add the following amendment to the last clause agreed to by the House, namely

"That from the first meeting of the Legislature of the United States until a Census shall be taken, all monies to be raised for supplying the public Treasury by direct Taxation shall be assessed on the inhabitants of the several States according to the number of their representatives respectively in the first Branch

It was moved and seconded to postpone the consideration of the amendment

which passed in the negative   [Ayes — 4; noes — 6.]

On the question to agree to the amendment

it passed in the negative   [Ayes — 5; noes — 5.]

It was moved and seconded to agree to the following amendment namely

That from the first meeting of the Legislature of the United States until a Census shall be taken, all monies for supplying the public Treasury by direct Taxation shall be raised from the several States according to the number of their representatives respectively in the first Branch

which passed in the affirmative[1] [Ayes—5; noes—4; divided — 1.]

---

[1] This amendment is not included in the compromise adopted on July 16 (see *Records* of that date) but it is among the Resolutions referred to the Committee of Detail.

It was moved and seconded to reconsider the second clause
of the report from the Committee of five — entered on the
Journal of the 9th inst
    which was unanimously agreed to.
It was moved and seconded to alter the second clause reported
from the Committee of five, entered on the Journal of the 9th
instant, so as to read as follows namely
    "But as the present situation of the States may probably
alter in the number of their inhabitants that the Legislature
of the United States be authorised from time to time to apportion the number of representatives: and in case any of the
States shall hereafter be divided, or any two or more States
united, or any new States created within the limits of the
United States, the Legislature of the U. S. shall possess authority to regulate the number of representatives in any of the
foregoing cases upon the principle of their number of inhabitants, according to the provisions hereafter mentioned —
    On the question to agree to the clause as amended
        it passed in the affirmative [Ayes — 9; noes — 0;
divided — 1.]²
It was moved and seconded to add after the word "divided"
the following words, namely
    "or enlarged by addition of territory"
    which passed unanimously in the affirmative [Ayes — 10;
noes — 0.]
    [To adjourn   Ayes — 6; noes — 4.]³
and then the House adjourned until to-morrow at 11 o'Clock
A M.

---

² Vote 151, Detail of Ayes and Noes, which notes that the amendment was "proposed by Mr. Randolph".
³ Vote 153, Detail of Ayes and Noes.

DETAIL OF AYES AND NOES

New Hampshire	Massachusetts	Rhode Island	Connecticut	New York	New Jersey	Pennsylvania	Delaware	Maryland	Virginia	North Carolina	South Carolina	Georgia	Questions	Ayes	Noes	Divided
[148]		no		aye		aye	no	aye	aye	no	no	no	no	To postpone the motion "That all monies shall be assessed until the Census be taken conformably to the number of repres: in ye first branch.	4	6	
[149]	aye		no		no	aye	no	no	no	aye	aye	aye	To agree to the last Motion	5	5	
[150]	aye		no		no	dd	no	no	aye	aye	aye	aye	To agree to a modification of the last motion	5	4	1
[151]	aye		aye		aye	aye	dd	aye	aye	aye	aye	aye	To agree to the amendment proposed by Mr Randolph to ye second clause of ye report entered on ye journals of the 9 inst	9		1
[152]	aye		aye		aye	aye	aye	aye	aye	aye	aye	aye	To add after the word "divided" the words "or enlarged by addition of territory"	10		
[153]	aye		aye		no	no	aye	aye	no	aye	aye	no	To adjourn	6	4	

MADISON

Friday. July 13. In Convention

⟨It being moved to postpone the clause in the Report of the Committee of Eleven as to the originating of money bills in *the first* branch, in order to take up the following — "that in the 2d branch each State shall have an equal voice."⟩[4]

Mr. Gerry, moved ⟨to add as an amendment to the last clause agreed to by the House⟩[4] "That from the first meeting of the Legislature ⟨of the U. S⟩ till a census shall be taken all monies to be raised ⟨for supplying the public Treasury⟩ by direct taxation, shall be assessed on the inhabitants of the

[4] Taken from *Journal*.

⟨several⟩ States, according to the ⟨number of their⟩ Representatives ⟨respectively⟩ in the 1st. branch." [5] He said this would be as just before as after the Census: according to the general principle that taxation & Representation ought to go together.

Mr. Williamson feared that N. Hamshire will have reason to complain. 3 members were allotted to her as a liberal allowance for this reason among others, that she might not suppose any advantage to have been taken of her absence. As she was still absent, and had no opportunity of deciding whether she would chuse to retain the number on the condition, of her being taxed in proportion to it, he thought the number ought to be reduced from three to two, before the question on Mr. G's motion

Mr. Read could not approve of the proposition. He had observed he said in the Committee a backwardness in some of the members from the large States, to take their full proportion of Representatives.[x] He did not then see the motive. He now suspects it was to avoid their due share of taxation. He had no objection to a just & accurate adjustment of Representation & taxation to each other.

Mr. Govr. Morris & Mr. M.⟨adison⟩ answered that the charge itself involved an acquittal, since notwithstanding the augmentation of the number of members allotted to Masts. & Va. the motion for proportioning the burdens thereto was made by a member from the former State & was approved by Mr. M from the latter who was on the Come. Mr. Govr. Morris said that he thought Pa. had her ⟨due⟩ share in 8 members; and he could not in candor ask for more. Mr. M. said that having always conceived that the difference of interest in the U. States lay not between the large & small, but the N. & Southn. States, and finding that the number of

[x] He alluded to the satisfaction expressed by Mr Govr. Morris at the number of 8 first allotted to Pena. and the desire expressed by Mr. Madison, that instead of augmenting the no of Va. N. Carol. & S. Carol. might receive an augmentation. The augmentation of the *no* of Masts. from 7 to 8 was made in ye. Come. at the instance of Mr. King, tho' Mr. Read seemed to have supposed the contrary.[6]

[5] Revised from *Journal.*   [6] This note was later struck out by Madison.

members allotted to the N. States was greatly superior, he should have preferred, an addition of two members to the S. States, to wit one to N & 1 to S. Carla. rather than of one member to Virga. He liked the present motion, because it tended to moderate the views both of the opponents & advocates for rating very high, the negroes.[7]

Mr. Elseworth hoped the proposition would be withdrawn. It entered too much into detail. The general principle was already sufficiently settled. As fractions can not be regarded in apportioning the ⟨no. of⟩ *representatives*, the rule will be unjust until an actual census shall be made. after that taxation may be precisely proportioned according to the principle established, to the *number of inhabitants*.

Mr. Wilson hoped the motion would not be withdrawn. If it shd. it will be made from another quarter. The rule will be as reasonable & just before, as after a Census. As to fractional numbers, the Census will not destroy, but ascertain them. And they will have the same effect after as before the Census: for as he understands the rule, it is to be adjusted not to the number of *inhabitants*, but of *Representatives*.

Mr. Sherman opposed the motion. He thought the Legislature ought to be left at liberty: in which case they would probably conform to the principles observed by Congs.

Mr. Mason did not know that Virga. would be a loser by the proposed regulation, but had some scruple as to the justice of it. He doubted much whether the conjectural rule which was to precede the census, would be as just, as it would be rendered by an actual census.

Mr. Elseworth & Mr. Sherman moved to postpone the motion ⟨of Mr. Gerry⟩, on ye. question, it passed in the negative

Mas. no. Cont. ay. N. J. ay. Pa. no. Del. ay. Md. ay. Va. no. N. C. no. S. C. no. Geo. no. [Ayes — 4; noes — 6.]

Question on Mr. Gerry's motion, ⟨it passed in the negative, the States being equally divided.⟩

---

[7] Madison struck out his original ending to this sentence: "as they are to augment the proportion of representatives for the States possessing them."

Mas. ay. Cont. no. N. J. no. *Pa. ay.* Del. no. Md. no. *Va. no.* N. C. ay. S. C. ay. Geo. ay. [Ayes — 5; noes — 5.]

Mr. Gerry finding that the loss of the question had proceeded from an objection with some, to the proposed assessment of direct taxes on the *inhabitants* of the States, which might restrain the legislature to a poll tax, moved his proposition again, but so varied as to authorize the assessment on the States, which wd. leave the mode to the Legislature ⟨viz "that from the 1st meeting of the Legislature of the U. S. untill a census shall be taken, all monies for supplying the public Treasury by direct taxation shall be raised from the several States according to the number of their representatives respectively in the 1st. branch"⟩ [8]

⟨On this varied question it passed in the affirmative⟩

Mas. ay. Cont. no. N. J. no. *Pa. divd.* Del. no. Md. no. *Va. ay.* N. C. ay. S. C. ay. Geo. ay. [Ayes — 5; noes — 4; divided — 1.]

On the motion of Mr. Randolph, the vote of saturday last authorizing the Legislre. to adjust from time to time, the representation upon the principles of *wealth* & numbers of inhabitants was ⟨reconsidered by common consent in order to strike out "Wealth" and adjust the resolution to that requiring periodical revisions according to the number of whites & three fifths of the blacks: the motion was in the words following — "But as the present situation of the States may probably alter in the number of their inhabitants, that the Legislature of the U. S. be authorized from time to time to apportion the number of representatives: and in case any of the States shall hereafter be divided or any two or more States united or new States created within the limits of the U. S. the Legislature of U. S. shall possess authority to regulate the number of Representatives in any of the foregoing cases, upon the principle of their number of inhabitants; according to the provisions hereafter mentioned."⟩ [9]

Mr. Govr. Morris opposed the alteration as leaving still

---

[8] Taken from *Journal.*

[9] Madison originally had recorded the substance of this but crossed it out, and copied the resolution from *Journal.*

an incoherence. If Negroes were to be viewed as inhabitants, and the revision was to proceed on the principle of numbers of inhabts. they ought to be added in their entire number, and not in the proportion of ⅗. If as property, the word wealth was right, and striking it out would. produce the very inconsistency which it was meant to get rid of. — The train of business & the late turn which it had taken, had led him he said, into deep meditation on it, and He wd. candidly state the result. A distinction had been set up & urged, between the Nn. & Southn. States. He had hitherto considered this doctrine as heretical. He still thought the distinction groundless. He sees however that it is persisted in; and that the Southn. Gentleman will not be satisfied unless they see the way open to their gaining a majority in the public Councils. The consequence of such a transfer of power from the maritime to the interior & landed interest will he foresees be such an oppression of commerce, that he shall be obliged to vote for ye. vicious principle of equality in the 2d. branch in order to provide some defence for the N. States agst. it. But to come now more to the point, either this distinction is fictitious or real: if fictitious let it be dismissed & let us proceed with due confidence. If it be real, instead of attempting to blend incompatible things, let us at once take a friendly leave of each other. There can be no end of demands for security if every particular interest is to be entitled to it. The Eastern States may claim it for their fishery, and for other objects, as the Southn. States claim it for their peculiar objects. In this struggle between the two ends of the Union, what part ought the Middle States in point of policy to take: to join their Eastern brethren according to his ideas. If the Southn. States get the power into their hands, and be joined as they will be with the interior Country they will inevitably bring on a war with Spain for the Mississippi. This language is already held. The interior Country having no property nor interest exposed on the sea, will be little affected by such a war. He wished to know what security the Northn. & middle States will have agst. this danger. It has been said that N. C. S. C. and Georgia only will in a little time have a majority of the people of America. They must in that case include the great interior Country, and every thing was to be apprehended from their getting the power into their hands.

Mr. Butler. The security the Southn. States want is that their negroes may not be taken from them which some gentlemen within or without doors, have a very good mind to do. It was not supposed that N. C. S. C & Geo. would have more people than all the other States, but many more relatively to the other States than they now have. The people & strength of America are evidently bearing Southwardly & S. westwdly.

Mr. Wilson. If a general declaration would satisfy any gentleman he had no indisposition to declare his sentiments. Conceiving that all men wherever placed have equal rights and are equally entitled to confidence, he viewed without apprehension the period when a few States should contain the superior number of people. The majority of people wherever found ought in all questions to govern the minority. If the interior Country should acquire this majority they will not only have the right, but will avail themselves of it whether we will or no. This jealousy misled the policy of G. Britain with regard to America. The fatal maxims espoused by her were that the Colonies were growing too fast, and that their growth must be stinted in time. What were the consequences? first. enmity on our part, then actual separation. Like consequences will result on the part of the interior settlements, if like jealousy & policy be pursued on ours. Further. if numbers be not a proper rule, why is not some better rule pointed out. No one has yet ventured to attempt it. Congs. have never been able to discover a better. No State as far as he had heard, has suggested any other. In 1783, after elaborate discussion of a measure of wealth all were satisfied then as they are now that the rule of numbers, does not differ much from the combined rule of numbers & wealth. Again he could not agree that property was the sole or the primary object of Govert. & Society. The cultivation & improvement of the human mind was the most noble object. With respect to this object, as well as to other *personal* rights, numbers were surely the natural & precise measure of Representation. And with respect to property, they could not vary much from the precise measure.   In no point of view however could the establishmt. of numbers as the rule of representation in the 1st. branch vary his opinion as to the impropriety of letting a vicious principle into the 2d. branch. — On the question to strike out *wealth* & to make the change as moved by Mr. Randolph, ⟨it passed in the affirmative —⟩

Mas. ay. Cont. ay. N. J. ay. Pa. ay. Del. divd. Md. ay. Va. ay. N. C. ay. S. C. ay. Geo. ay.   [Ayes — 9; noes — 0; divided — 1.]

Mr Reed moved to insert after the word — "divided," "or enlarged by addition of territory" which was agreed to nem. con. (his object probably was to provide for such cases as an enlargmt. of Delaware by annexing to it the Peninsula on the East Side of Chesapeak)

Adjourned [10]

---

[10] Manasseh Cutler records a visit on July 13 to Franklin, who showed him "a snake with two heads, preserved in a large vial. . . . He was then going to mention a humorous matter that had that day taken place in Convention, in consequence of his comparing the snake to America, . . . but the secrecy of Convention matters was suggested to him, which stopped him, and deprived me of the story."   See Appendix A, LXII.